Roy Porter (1946–2002) was one of the most versatile and brilliant historians of his generation. The only child of a working-class family from south London, he studied history at Christ's College, Cambridge, and obtained fellowships both there and at Churchill College, Cambridge. In 1979 he moved to the Wellcome Institute for the History of Medicine, London. His broad interests and work encompassed the history of geology, British social history, and many facets of the history of medicine, where he pioneered the investigation of the history of the patient. His many books include *Enlightenment: Britain and the Creation of the Modern World*, *London: a Social History* and his seminal history of psychiatry, *Mind Forg'd Manacales* (1987) which won the American Historical Association's Leo Gershoy Prize. He was also a talented communicator to a wider public, through radio and television. He was elected a fellow of the British Academy, and to honorary fellowships in the Royal College of Physicians and the Royal College of Psychiatrists. His characteristic energy, zest and wide erudition are wonderfully displayed in *The Faber Book of Madness*.

The Faber Book of
MADNESS

Edited by Roy Porter

ff

faber and faber

For Dorothy

First published in 1991
by Faber and Faber Limited
3 Queen Square London WC1N 3AU
This paperback edition first published in 2003

Printed in England by Clays Ltd, St Ives plc

A CIP record for this book is
available from the British Library

ISBN 0-571-14388-1

6 8 10 9 7 5

Contents

Illustrations

Editor's Note

The first refuge of the anthologist is to rifle the minds and files of his friends. I am no exception. I am particularly grateful to the following who have so eagerly, promptly, and generously responded to my appeal for ideas, extracts, and a little sanity: Jonathan Andrews, Michael Barfoot, Peter Bartlett, Sandra Billington, Peter Burke, Michael Clark, Margaret Evans, John Forrester, Ruth Harris, Renate Hauser, Nicholas Hervey, Sue Limb, Michael Neve, Danny Pick, Trevor Turner and James Twiggs.

Janice Wilson and Caroline Prentice have been superb research assistants throughout, and, as ever, Andy Foley has xeroxed with enthusiasm and accuracy. David Brady, Anne Darlington and William Schupbach have all proved helpful well beyond the call of duty with the illustrations.

My thanks to everyone at Faber, especially to Will Sulkin who set the project off; to Roger Osborne, who saw it through; to Helen Dore for her superb copy-editing; and to Kate Chapman for her fine index.

Introduction

'Some student of human society has observed that one half of mankind does not know how the other half lives', opens the auto-biography of a mental patient who signed himself 'Warmark'. The rich may not understand the poor, men may be abysmally ignorant about women, and atheists may lack all feel for faith; but the experience perhaps most profoundly closed to most of us is that of madness.*

Of course, we all endorse the truth of the old saw that 'all the world's mad except thee and me, and even thee's a little cracked'; and don't we all sometimes feel that Life will one day drive even our own ultra-sane selves round the twist? Even so, the torments and tangles of true alienation of mind – beset by other-worldly voices and visions, controlled by irresistible powers, losing its sense of identity, undergoing extremes of exhilaration or despair – retain their mysteries, perennially fearful, darkly fascinating.

This anthology aims to offer some *entrée* and guide to that unknown world, from which by no means all travellers return.

What is madness? In *Hamlet* the old pedant Polonius hints at the problem, only to conclude that to try to 'define true madness, what is it but to be nothing else but mad?'. Possibly: though, as the extracts in this anthology will show, that has never stopped people

---

*Throughout this book, I shall use the term 'madness' as an umbrella term. Psychiatrists today often object to such a usage, suggesting that it is unscientific and somehow demeaning. Surely, however, it is the right term, because it conveys the richest resonances in everyday parlance. For it is widely applied to many people besides the clinically certifiable, and includes all manner of abnormalities and extremes of thought and emotion (I can be mad over you, mad at you, madly in love with you). No synonym or euphemism is half so evocative.

trying to divine its true identity. The following pages will not settle the issue; but I have endeavoured to present a rich miscellany of the experience of madness from the viewpoints of numerous parties: psychiatrists, whose job it has been to establish the nature and origin of the condition; nurses, friends, family and others who have lived with and cared for the disturbed; writers and artists, theologians and philosophers even, who have claimed, rightly or wrongly, to be able to enter imaginatively, empathetically or rationally, into the state. But, above all, I have given pride of place to the writings of the 'mad' themselves – by which I mean all those who have been judged by themselves or by society to be intellectually, emotionally or behaviourally disturbed, from 'mere' depressives or neurotics to the full-blown 'lunatics' of old, or those who would nowadays be deemed schizophrenics or psychotics.

The stereotype of the mad author – and the paradox he presents: genius, or compulsive scribbler? – is familiar enough. It may come as a slight surprise, however, that over the centuries so many mad people have not only written down their experiences, but have had them preserved and published. It would not be hard to list several hundred autobiographical books in the English language alone, written by those whom society has certified mad at some time or another in their lives, to say nothing of the oceans of testimony of the disturbed frozen in the records of law courts and asylums, and, more recently, in the annals of psychoanalysis. Readers may well be more familiar with certain fictional mad people – the hero of Gogol's *Diary of a Madman*, or, for that matter, Ophelia – than with any authentic sufferer. If so, I hope this volume may convince readers that many mad people have left works well worth reading, and in their own right, rather than merely to satisfy any ghoulish desires.

This partly explains the bias of what follows. Earlier anthologies – and nearly all of them have been North American in origin and emphasis – have given greatest prominence to the progress of psychiatric theories: a case in point is John Paul Brady's *Classics of American Psychiatry*. I have chosen, instead, to concentrate on more personal, autobiographical writings. I have also tried to avoid exclusive concentration upon horror stories from the asylum. No one can deny that when, from the late eighteenth century onwards, mental patients wrote down their experiences, what most sought to convey was the evils of the psychiatric hospital and of their own treatment inside. In view of the laudable campaigns from the 1950s to reform, or close down, such 'bins' and 'bughouses', it is no surprise that anthologists of madness – for instance, Thomas Szasz in *The Age of Madness*, and Dale Peterson in *A Mad People's History of Madness* – have concentrated upon exposing such 'museums of madness'.

That campaign has been conducted; I have tried to stand back a bit further. I have included a larger number of accounts of madness in the centuries before the rise of the empire of the asylum. And I have included a fuller spectrum of the experiences about which the disoriented have chosen, or felt driven, to write. I have included sections surveying their attempts to reconstruct what led to breakdown in the first place, and their desire to document the process of mental disintegration itself: is it a vertigo of the senses, an atomization of language, a breakdown of the capacity to discriminate between reality and illusion, the literal and the figurative; is it the irruption of other consciousnesses from Below (the Unconscious, the Satanic) or from Above – or what? And I have included madness in some of its wider associations, including its relations with genius and with sexuality.

The delicious danger facing the anthologist of madness lies in not knowing where to stop. No doubt about what must be included: the writings of the mad, and those describing mad people both documentary and fictional. But how much further and in what directions? Should substantial quantities of psychiatric texts be included? – not, I hasten to add, because psychiatry itself should be viewed as insane (though there may be occasional doubts on that score) but because psychiatry takes madness for its subject. I have steered clear of tracing the history of psychiatry; this has already been magnificently done in such works as Richard Hunter and Ida Macalpine's *Three Hundred Years of Psychiatry: 1535–1860*. In general, where I have extracted the writings of psychiatrists, it has not been for their theoretical innovations, but for what they have been saying something insightful about patients, or about themselves.

And then what of those on the borderlands of madness – the ecstatic visionary, the religious prophet, the melancholy churchyard

sonneteer, the *distrait* eccentric? Following Dryden's perception
that 'thin partitions' alone divide madness from inspiration, I have
followed no hard-and-fast rule, and have relied upon my own
judgement (which others may judge eccentric). To keep the book
within bounds, however, I have, as a general rule, omitted topics
which abut on madness but which deserve (and, in some cases, have
received) fuller treatment elsewhere: dreams, drugs and diabolism,
for example. I have also excluded the literatures of fantasy and
mysticism.

In making selections, I have often gone back into earlier ages. I
see no sign that our era boasts more interesting lunatics than earlier
ones, or monopolizes insight into psychopathological processes. I
have given space to writings from earlier centuries, because many of
them are hard to come by. And rather than fill this volume with
readily-to-hand passages from Freud and *One Flew Over the
Cuckoo's Nest* (although I do in fact quote from both), I have
brought forward unfamiliar figures, such as George Trosse or
Alexander Cruden (still honoured as the compiler of the standard
Concordance to the Bible, if almost unknown as a litigious, amorous madman in the Malvolio mould).

The passages which follow express a range of views, sometimes
forcibly. The distinguished American physician and signatory to the
Declaration of Independence, Benjamin Rush, argues that insanity
lies in the blood; various lunatics claim to have suffered severe
psychiatric abuse. I am not concerned with the *truth* of any such
assertions; rather, I have included what I find interesting or moving.
Neither has my aim been to achieve 'balance'. Anthologies, surely,
are allowed the licence of being more thought-provoking than fair.

What does strike me, however, is the insight shown by sufferers –
insight into the psychopathological traumas which have troubled
them, insight into their own encounters with those who have
judged them, or cared for them: insights into psychodynamics not
always reciprocated.

To say this is not to disparage psychiatry. Through advances in
neurophysiology, biochemistry and genetics, modern psychiatry is
immeasurably improving our understanding of mental abnormality. And over the dark ages of scientific ignorance, psychiatry
was constantly saddled with the invidious responsibility of having

to handle those whom society was only too happy to cast out: out of mind, out of sight. But the writings of these outcasts, the so-called mad or ex-mad people to be found in the following pages, cannot simply be written off as delusional. They contain astonishing insights into their own disturbances and into the wider questions of normality and abnormality, imagination and judgement, authenticity and personality, power and oppression, the divided self.

Further Reading

There are other anthologies in this area. The best are:

John Paul Brady (ed.), *Classics of American Psychiatry: 1810–1934* (St Louis, Missouri: Warren H. Green, Inc., 1975)

Michael Glenn (ed.), *Voices from the Asylum* (New York: Harper and Row, 1974)

Charles E. Goshen, *Documentary History of Psychiatry: A Source Book on Historical Principles* (London: Vision, 1967)

Richard A. Hunter and Ida Macalpine, *Three Hundred Years of Psychiatry: 1535–1860* (London: Oxford University Press, 1963)

Bert Kaplan, *The Inner World of Mental Illness* (New York: Harper and Row, 1964)

D. Peterson (ed.), *A Mad People's History of Madness* (Pittsburgh: University of Pittsburgh Press, 1982)

V. Skultans, *Madness and Morals: Ideas on Insanity in the Nineteenth Century* (London and Boston: Routledge & Kegan Paul, 1975)

Thomas S. Szasz, *The Age of Madness. The History of Involuntary Mental Hospitalization Presented in Selected Texts* (London: Routledge & Kegan Paul, 1975)

For the history of madness and the rise of psychiatry, see:

Franz G. Alexander and Sheldon T. Selesnick, *The History of Psychiatry: An Evaluation of Psychiatric Thought and Practice from Prehistoric Times to the Present* (London: George Allen and Unwin, 1967)

Though somewhat dated, still the fullest general history of psychiatry.

L. Feder, *Madness in Literature* (Princeton: Princeton University Press, 1980)
A lively survey of the representation of madness in fiction.

Michel Foucault, *La Folie et la Déraison: Histoire de la Folie à l'Age Classique* (Paris: Librairie Plon, 1961); abridged as *Madness and Civilization: A History of Insanity in the Age of Reason*, trans. Richard Howard (New York: Random House, 1965)
The most searching analysis of the symbiotic histories of reason and unreason.

Sander L. Gilman, *Seeing the Insane* (New York: Brunner, Mazel, 1982)
A richly illustrated survey of cultural images of madness.

Roy Porter, *A Social History of Madness: Stories of the Insane* (London: Weidenfeld and Nicolson, 1987)
Attempts to examine madness from the viewpoint of the insane.

Andrew Scull, *Museums of Madness: The Social Organization of Insanity in Nineteenth-Century England* (London: Allen Lane; New York: St Martin's Press, 1979)
– *Decarceration: Community Treatment and the Deviant – A Radical View* (2nd edn, Oxford: Polity Press; New Brunswick, New Jersey: Rutgers University Press, 1984)
A provocative pair of books explaining the rise and fall of the asylum.

Thomas S. Szasz, *The Manufacture of Madness* (New York: Dell, 1970; London: Paladin, 1972)
– *The Myth of Mental Illness: Foundations of a Theory of Personal Conduct* (London: Granada, 1972; rev. edn, New York: Harper and Row, 1974)
Szasz interprets the rise of institutional psychiatry as a new witch-hunt.

Elliot S. Valenstein, *Great and Desperate Cures: The Rise and Decline of Psychosurgery and Other Radical Treatments for Mental Illness* (New York: Basic Books, 1986)
An introduction to modern psychotherapeutics.

Useful works of reference are:

John Howells (ed.), *World History of Psychiatry* (New York: Brunner, Mazel, 1968)

John G. Howells and M. Livia Osborn, *A Reference Companion to the History of Abnormal Psychology* (Westport, Conn.: Greenwood Press, 1984)

[1]

Reason and Madness

What is reason? What is madness? Where lie the dividing lines? And who can discern and police them? Regarding his committal to Bethlem,* the Restoration playwright Nathaniel Lee reputedly said, 'They called me mad, and I called them mad, and damn them, they outvoted me.' It's a problem that can be posed in more philosophical terms, but it won't go away, and it has been a key concern of any number of thinkers, inside and outside the psychiatric profession, sane and insane.

Many moralists, like Erasmus or Robert Burton, have chosen to dub all the world crazy, or at least to hint that all of us live in jeopardy of the shipwreck of reason or the poisonous intoxication of the passions. Others have argued – a line much endorsed by modern feminists – that madness is but a label pinned by the respectable on those they cannot tolerate; or, worse, that normal society is, in actuality, so pressurizing or alienating that it drives the most vulnerable souls to distraction before, in the guise of help, further persecuting them with punitive psychotherapeutics. Might it be true that civilization itself, far from being a safe stronghold against unreason and emotional instability, is truly their precipitant?

---

*Bethlem – or Bedlam in popular parlance – started as a religious house in the thirteenth century, roughly on the site of what is today London's Liverpool Street railway station. By the fifteenth century it was beginning to be famous for caring for lunatics. Escaping dissolution at the Reformation, it was rebuilt on a palatial scale at Moorfields, then the northern outskirts of London, in the 1670s; but the grandeur of the building did not prevent an unenviable, if perhaps unjustified, reputation for cruelty and corruption within, which lasted until a series of reforms in the nineteenth century, following a further move to Lambeth, south of the river – to the building now used to house the Imperial War Museum. The work of Bethlem Hospital continues today in Beckenham, Kent. *See Plates 2 and 3.*

And all too often, in any case, as might be concluded from some of the more bizarre therapies documented below, the palaver of treating the mentally disordered appears to have been so illogical as to call into question the supposed divide between Reason's guardians and those who allegedly endanger it. The early nineteenth-century British psychiatrist John Haslam argued early in his career that reason and madness were as distinct as black and white, straight and crooked; in old age, however, he confessed that he knew no one who was in his right mind, save only the Almighty.

So what do we mean by madness? Is it the absence of reason? (Or isn't that what we call idiocy?) Or is it, rather, the antithesis of right reason – *wrong* reason, drawing consistent deductions from false premises? Or is it, as in the craziness of *amour fou* or the *crime passionel*, the self whirled up in a tornado of passion?

Is madness something more sinister altogether, a perversion of the will, a warping of the personality, as in the psychopath? Or is it all these things together, in some amalgam that defies analysis? Despite all the philosophers, theologians, psychiatrists and jurists, the questions: 'What is sanity?' 'What is madness?', and the ensuing paradoxes: 'Can reason itself be unreasonable?' 'Is there a method in madness, a truth in folly?', though endlessly debated in the corridors of psychiatry and in the verbal gymnastics of witty fools, preserve their mysteries still.

―――――――

A riddle of reason. The American poet Emily Dickinson gradually withdrew herself physically from the world, confining herself to her own room, and, as her verse reveals, withdrew mentally and psychologically as well. Her intense need to protect herself from threats of control were widely seen as a form of illness.

> Much Madness is divinest Sense –
> To a discerning Eye –
> Much Sense – the starkest Madness –
> 'Tis the Majority
> In this, as All, prevail –
> Assent – and you are sane –

Demur – you're straightway dangerous –
And handled with a Chain –
Emily Dickinson, 'Much Madness is divinest Sense' (c. 1862)

=

The madness of the world, as seen by the vegetarian and Baptist,
Thomas Tryon

To Speak Truth, the World is but a great *Bedlam*, where those that
are *more mad*, lock up those that are *less*; the *first* presumptuously,
and knowingly, committing Evils both against God their Neighbours and themselves; but the *last*, not knowing what they do, are
as it were next door to *innocency*, especially when the Evil
Properties were not awakened, nor predominant in the Complexion
in the time of their Senses: Tell me I pray? Are not all these
Intemperances, Violence, Oppression, Murder and savage Evils,
and Superfluities deservedly to be accounted the worst Effects of
Madness? As also, Lying, Swearing, vain Imaginations, and living
in and under the power of evil Spirits, more to be dreaded than the
condition of those that want the use of Senses and Reason; and
therefore are esteemed Mad?
Thomas Tryon, *A Discourse of the Causes, Natures and Cure of Phrensie,*
Madness or Distraction (1689)

=

When I was a little boy
    I had but little wit;
'Tis a long time ago,
    And I have no more yet;
Nor ever, ever shall,
    Until that I die,
For the longer I live
    The more fool am I.

'Lack Wit', anon.

=

The Evangelical reformer Lord Shaftesbury was Chairman of the Lunacy Commission for half a century. He made the following diary entry after a routine asylum visit.

Visited Peckham Asylum (a private madhouse) on Saturday last. Long affair – six hours. What a lesson! How small the interval – a hair's breadth – between reason and madness. A sight, too, to stir apprehension in one's own mind. I am visiting in authority today. I may be visited by authority tomorrow. God be praised that there are any visitations at all; time was when such care was unknown. What an awful condition that of a lunatic! His words are generally disbelieved, and his most innocent peculiarities perverted; it is natural that it should be so; we know him to be insane; at least, we are told that he is so; and we place ourselves on guard – that is, we give to every word, look, gesture a value and meaning which oftentimes it cannot bear, and which it would never bear in ordinary life. Thus we too readily get him in, and too sluggishly get him out, and yet what a destiny!

Shaftesbury Diaries (18 November 1844)

=

An island, intire of itself?

Madness is not only acute frustration, but a chasm without a bridge; despite which, together with the fact that I have said that an unbridgable gulf separates you from us lunatics, this gulf or abyss is more apparent than real; for the actual line is very slender.

The mad are innocent, and can therefore do no wrong; for madness is as death, in that one is transferred to another life, and, like death, one passes over to it without knowing that one has crossed the border. The mad are exclusive; for each madman is self-contained, and lives in a little world of his own. Hence, they who would pass to him cannot, neither can he pass to them. It is a novel escape from reality – from reality which may at times be far worse than any madness – as I know to my cost. To escape reality we can only die, or become insane – which is the same.

Reality to the lunatic is your equivalent to insanity. To you, insanity is a sad state, to be deplored. To the insane, reality is not only a state to be deplored, but to be avoided at all costs; for on the occasions when the lunatic relapses into sanity, he at once observes it to be a most disagreeable and impractical state; for insanity is far more practical than any phase of real life ever can be. In actual life, reality is the recipient of many knocks and buffetings, and the victim of all the storms that blow. Whereas, insanity encounters no such tempests; for one lives in a world of make-believe where, despite the raging of the storm, one's illusions remain unshaken. These illusions are immovable; so that when one pursues the subject, one quickly agrees that the thought is the deed – that an insane belief is an insane act, and *vice versa*.

H. G. Woodley, *Certified* (1947)

=

The anti-psychiatry movement of the 1960s, of which David Cooper was one of the most articulate spokesmen, repudiated the medical notion that madness was a clinical disease. Cooper saw it as process and relationship, inseparable from the wider webs of society and culture.

The madness about which I'm writing is the madness that is more or less present in each one of us and not only the madness that gets the psychiatric baptism by diagnosis of 'schizophrenia' or some other label invented by the specialized psycho-police agents of final phase capitalist society. So when I use the word 'madman' here I'm not referring to a special race of people, but the madman in me is addressing the madman in you in the hope that the former madman speaks clearly or loudly enough for the latter to hear.

The 'language of madness' means the way that this universal madness is expressed not only in uttered, audible words, but in a type of action, running across experience, that is 'mad dis-course'.

David Cooper, *The Language of Madness* (1978)

=

Speaking through the mouthpiece of an unreliable narrator, Jonathan Swift (see also page 42) offers a typically ironical panegyric to the madness of 'modernism' in politics, religion and intellectual affairs.

Nor shall it any ways detract from the just Reputation of this famous
Sect, that its Rise and Institution are owing to such an Author as I
have described *Jack* to be; A Person whose Intellectuals were over-
turned, and his Brain shaken out of its Natural Position; which we
commonly suppose to be a Distemper, and call by the Name of
Madness or *Phrenzy*. For, if we take a Survey of the greatest Actions
that have been performed in the World, under the Influence of Single
Men; which are, *The Establishment of New Empires by Conquest:
The Advance and Progress of New Schemes in Philosophy; and the
contriving, as well as the propagating of New Religions*: We shall
find the Authors of them all, to have been Persons, whose natural
Reason hath admitted great Revolutions from their Dyet, their
Education, the Prevalency of some certain Temper, together with the
particular Influence of Air and Climate. Besides, there is something
Individual in human Minds, that easily kindles at the accidental
Approach and Collision of certain Circumstances, which tho' of
paltry and mean Appearance, do often flame out into the greatest
Emergencies of Life. For great Turns are not always given by strong
Hands, but by lucky Adaption, and at proper Seasons; and it is of no
import, where the Fire was kindled, if the Vapor has once got up into
the Brain. For the *upper Region* of Man, is furnished like the *middle
Region* of the Air; The Materials are formed from Causes of the
widest Difference, yet produce at last the same Substance and Effect.
Mists arise from the Earth, Steams from Dunghils, Exhalations from
the Sea, and Smoak from Fire; yet all Clouds are the same in
Composition, as well as Consequences: and the Fumes issuing from a
Jakes, will furnish as comely and useful a Vapor, as Incense from an
Altar. Thus far, I suppose, will easily be granted me; and then it will
follow, that as the Face of Nature never produces Rain, but when it is
overcast and disturbed, so Human Understanding, seated in the
Brain, must be troubled and overspread by Vapours, ascending from
the lower Faculties, to water the Invention, and render it fruitful.
Now, altho' these Vapours (as it hath been already said) are of as
various Original, as those of the Skies, yet the Crop they produce,
differs both in Kind and Degree, meerly according to the Soil.

                              Jonathan Swift, *A Tale of a Tub* (1704)

Method in it

POLONIUS: What do you read, my lord?
HAMLET: Words, words, words.
POLONIUS: What is the matter, my lord?
HAMLET: Between who?
POLONIUS: I mean, the matter that you read, my lord.
HAMLET: Slanders, sir; for the satirical rogue says here that old
   men have grey beards; that their faces are wrinkled; their eyes
   purging thick amber and plum-tree gum; and that they have a
   plentiful lack of wit, together with most weak hams – all which,
   sir, though I most powerfully and potently believe, yet I hold it
   not honesty to have it thus set down; for you yourself, sir, shall
   grow old as I am, if, like a crab, you could go backward.
POLONIUS: (*Aside*) Though this be madness, yet there is method
   in't.

William Shakespeare, *Hamlet* (1604)

===

*Samuel Johnson suffered from depression and compulsive
behaviour, and entertained a dread of going mad. In his philosophical novel* Rasselas, *the sage Imlac warns of the dire consequences of giving free rein to imagination and appetite.*

THE DANGEROUS PREVALENCE OF IMAGINATION

'Disorders of intellect', answered Imlac, 'happen much more often
than superficial observers will easily believe. Perhaps, if we speak
with rigorous exactness, no human mind is in its right state. There
is no man whose imagination does not sometimes predominate
over his reason, who can regulate his attention wholly by his will,
and whose ideas will come and go at his command. No man will
be found in whose mind airy notions do not sometimes tyrannize,
and force him to hope or fear beyond the limits of sober probability. All power of fancy over reason is a degree of insanity;
but while this power is such as we can control and repress it is not
visible to others, nor considered as any depravation of the mental
faculties: it is not pronounced madness but when it comes

ungovernable, and apparently influences speech or action.

'To indulge the power of fiction, and send imagination out upon the wing, is often the sport of those who delight too much in silent speculation. When we are alone we are not always busy; the labour of excogitation is too violent to last long; the ardour of enquiry will sometimes give way to idleness or satiety. He who has nothing external that can divert him must find pleasure in his own thoughts, and must conceive himself what he is not; for who is pleased with what he is? He then expatiates in boundless futurity, and calls from all imaginable conditions that which for the present moment he should most desire, amuses his desires with impossible enjoyments, and confers upon his pride unattainable dominion. The mind dances from scene to scene, unites all pleasures in all combinations, and riots in delights which nature and fortune, with their bounty, cannot bestow.

'In time some particular train of ideas fixes the attention; all other intellectual gratifications are rejected; the mind, in weariness or leisure, recurs constantly to the favourite conception, and feasts on the luscious falsehood whenever she is offended with the bitterness of truth. By degrees the reign of fancy is confirmed; she grows first imperious, and in time despotic. Then fictions begin to operate as realities, false opinions fasten upon the mind, and life passes in dreams of rapture or of anguish.

'This, Sir, is one of the dangers of solitude, which the hermit has confessed not always to promote goodness and the astronomer's misery has proved to be not always propitious to wisdom.'

Samuel Johnson, *The History of Rasselas, Prince of Abyssinia* (1759)

===

Is civilization the triumph of reason over chaos? Or do the pressures of progress cause distraction and despair? 'Civilization and its discontents' was a burning issue long before Freud: here its cause is pleaded by the nineteenth-century humanitarian Dorothea Lynde Dix, who did much to reform attitudes towards insanity and the treatment of the insane in the United States.

There are, in proportion to numbers, more insane in cities than in large towns, and more insane in villages than among the same number of inhabitants dwelling in scattered settlements.

Wherever the intellect is most excited, and health lowest, there is an increase of insanity. This malady prevails most widely, and illustrates its presence most commonly in mania, in those countries whose citizens possess the largest civil and religious liberty; where, in effect, every individual, however obscure, is free to enter upon the race for the highest honors and most exalted stations; where the arena of competition is accessible to all who seek the distinctions which acquisition and possession of wealth assures, and the respect accorded to high literary and scholastic attainments. Statesmen, politicians, and merchants, are peculiarly liable to insanity. In the United States, therefore, we behold an illustration of my assertion. The kingdoms of Western Europe, excepting Portugal, Spain, and the lesser islands dependent on Great Britain, rank next to this country in the rapid development of insanity. Sir Andrew Halliday, in a letter to Lord Seymour, states that the number of the insane in England has become more than tripled in the last twenty years. Russia in Europe, Turkey, and Hungary, together with most of the Asiatic and African countries exhibit but little insanity. The same is remarked by travellers, especially by Humboldt, of a large part of South America. Those tracts of North America inhabited by Indians, and the sections chiefly occupied by the negro race, produce comparatively very few examples. The colored population is more liable to attacks of insanity than the negro.

This terrible malady, the source of indescribable miseries, does increase, and must continue fearfully to increase, in this country, whose free, civil, and religious institutions create constantly various and multiplying sources of mental excitement. Comparatively but little care is given in cultivating the moral affections in proportion with the intellectual development of the people. Here, as in other countries, forcible examples may be cited to show the mischiefs which result alike from religious, social, civil, and revolutionary excitements. The Millerite delusions prepared large numbers for our hospitals; so also the great conflagrations in New York, the Irish riots and firemen's mobs in Philadelphia; and the last presidential elections throughout the country levied heavily on the mental health of its citizens.

[Dorothea Dix], *Memorial D. L. Dix, Praying a Grant of Land for the Relief and Support of the Indigent and Incurable Insane in the United States, June 23, 1848*

Others felt less sure, among them George Man Burrows, whose treatise on insanity was acknowledged as the most authoritative of its time. The author drew on his first-hand experience with the two London asylums he founded – one in Chelsea, and a larger one, The Retreat, in Clapham.

As the multiplication of moral causes is co-relative with the degree and progress of civilization, it might be inferred, that savage nations are exempt from insanity – the curse of polished life. Rush asserts, that it is unknown among the North American Indians, and the infrequency of it has been noticed among those of South America. But the more remote and savage, the less likely are the natural habits to be ascertained: and hence I suspect some fallacy in this conclusion.

The passions of barbarians are always strong, and sometimes furious; and most evince that their affections are violent. Their organization is the same as the more civilized; and when such people become contaminated by association, they contract the same diseases. Why, therefore, should it be imagined savages never go mad?

The natives of the Indian peninsula, who are far more temperate in diet, and have their passions much more under control, are yet very prone to insanity; and several asylums are now established in the different presidencies for their reception. It is true, they are more civilized than the American aborigines; but if civilization bring not with it the wants, and vices, and consequent diseases, of Europeans, the exciting causes of mental derangement among the Peninsular Indians appear to be inadequate to produce this physical effect. As they are, indubitably, a very ancient race, hereditary predisposition probably exercises a considerable influence upon them.

Moral philosophers love to theorize on the passive virtues of unsophisticated aborigines, and fancy them as void of vice as the fabulous race who adorned the golden age.

> – 'When man, yet new,
> No rule but uncorrupted reason knew.'

Viewing man, however, as he really is, wherever he inhabits, I judge him to be always so much the slave of his passions, as to be liable, among other ills, to insanity.

George Man Burrows, *Commentaries on the Causes, Forms, Symptoms and Treatment, Moral and Medical, of Insanity* (1828)

=

Entering the 'madness and civilization' discussion, the French philosopher Michel Foucault in his Histoire de la folie à l'age classique: folie et déraison, *argued that the history of madness could not be traced in isolation: it had to be seen in symbiosis with its opposite, and enemy, reason. Here Franco Basaglia, in 'conversation' with R. D. Laing about understanding the treatment of the insane (see also page 264), summarizes Foucault's view.*

No history of madness exists that is not also a history of reason. Foucault's attempt to trace the itinerary of the madman's silence and speech throughout the centuries is the search for an interpretation of what is ultimately 'the monologue of reason about madness'. But implied in such a monologue is an act that will prove to be essential to the evolution of madness, by inscribing it on the language of those who listen and judge, and by confining its expression within the framework of an alien logic. The history of madness is that of the gradual evolution of values, rules, beliefs and systems of power; the latter constitute judgments upon which the social group is based and which bear the imprint of all phenomena that affect the process of organizing social life.

Over the centuries, the rational and the irrational come to coexist, while remaining separate. Yet they are drawn closer once reason is in a position to neutralize madness by recognizing it as a part of itself, as well as by defining a separate space for its existence. Such a process does not merely represent the evolution of science and knowledge. Nor does it only signify the transition of madness from tragic experience in the world to sin, guilt, scandal, condemnation, and objectification of unreason – elements which, in our critical view, are still fused and present in madness. Nor does it simply represent the signs of an animality that surfaces or flares up as long as reason is able to view it critically, differentiate it, sort it out. Nor is it merely a measure of the extent to which people's fears and miseries are obliterated by torture, repression, authority, science, and power.

Nancy Scheper-Hughes and Anne M. Lovell (eds), *Psychiatry Inside Out: Selected Writings of Franco Basaglia* (1987)

=

Madness viewed as the negation of everything that elevates humanity above the beasts. The eminent French physician Philippe Pinel was celebrated for the reforms he achieved in the treatment of the insane in France – particularly at the notorious Bicêtre and La Salpêtrière hospitals. He wrote a number of distinguished books, including the Traité médico-philosophique sur l'aliénation ou la manie.

Of all the afflictions to which human nature is subject, the loss of reason is at once the most calamitous and interesting. Deprived of this faculty, by which man is principally distinguished from the beasts that perish, the human form is frequently the most remarkable attribute that he retains of his proud distinction. His character, as an individual of the species, is always perverted; sometimes annihilated. His thoughts and actions are diverted from their usual and natural course. The chain which connected his ideas in just series and mutual subserviency, is dissevered. His feelings for himself and others are new and uncommon. His attachments are converted into aversions, and his love into hatred. His consciousness even is not unfrequently alienated; insomuch, that with equal probability he may fancy himself a deity, an emperor, or a mass of inanimate matter. Once the ornament and life of society, he is now become a stranger to its pleasures or a disturber of its tranquillity. Impatient of restraint, and disposed to expend the unusual effervescence of his spirits in roving and turbulence, coercion of the mildest kind adds fury to his delirium, and colours with jealousy or suspicion every effort of friendly or professional interest in his fate. His personal liberty is at length taken from him; and taken from him perhaps by his nearest relative or dearest friend. Retaining his original sensibility, or rendered more acutely sensible by opposition to his will and deprivation of his usual gratifications, co-operating with a morbid excitement of his nervous functions, he gives himself up to all the extravagances of maniacal fury, or sinks inexpressibly miserable into the lowest depths of despondence and melancholy. If the former, he resembles in ferocity the tyger, and meditates destruction and revenge. If the latter, he withdraws from society, shuns the plots and inveiglements which he imagines to surround him, and fancies himself an object of human persecution and treachery, or a victim of divine vengeance and reprobation. To this melancholy train of symptoms, if not early and judiciously treated, ideotism, or a state of the most abject degradation, in most instances, sooner or later succeeds. The figure of the human species is now all that remains to him, 'and like the ruins of a once magnificent edifice, it only serves to remind us of its former dignity and grandeur,' and to awaken our gloomiest reflections – our tenderest regret for the departure of the real and respectable man.

Philippe Pinel, *A Treatise on Insanity* (1806)

=

As the antithesis of civilized man, madness stands as his fiercest critic, holding up the mirror to hypocrisy.

The world is all but madness
Then why are we confined
To live by law, and lie in straw
With hungar almost pined . . .

Take my locks take my bolts off,
Wee'le be as free as they be,
Who keep such state, that none dare prate
Yet are as mad as may be.

Thomas Jordan, writing as a Bedlamite (1642)

=

In his magisterial Anatomy of Melancholy, *Robert Burton portrayed madness as the mock and self-inflicted scourge of mankind. His best-selling and enormously influential work (a favourite of Dr Johnson) covers the causes, symptoms and cure of melancholy, with particular attention to the melancholy of love and religion. Every point is illustrated by a wealth of wide-ranging quotation from writers of all ages and nations. See Plate 1.*

Of the necessity and generality of this which I have said, if any man doubt, I shall desire him to make a brief survey of the world, as Cyprian advised Donatus, *supposing himself to be transported to the top of some high mountain, and thence to behold the tumults and chances of this wavering world, he can't choose but either laugh at, or pity it.* S. Hierom, out of a strong imagination, being in the wilderness, conceived with himself that he then saw them dancing in Rome; and if thou shalt either conceive, or climb to see, thou shalt soon perceive that all the world is mad, that it is melancholy, dotes: that it is (which Epichthonius Cosmopolites expressed not many years since in a map) made like a fool's head (with that Motto, A head requiring hellebore), a crazed head, a fool's Paradise, or, as Apollonius, a common prison of gulls, cheaters, flatterers, &c., and needs to be reformed. Strabo, in the Ninth Book of his Geography, compares Greece to the picture of a man, which comparison of his Nicholas Gerbelius, in his exposition of Sophianus' map, approves; the breast lies open from those Acroceraunian hills in Epirus to the Sunian promontory in Attica; Pagæ & Megara are the two shoulders; that Isthmus of Corinth the neck; and Peloponnesus the head. If this allusion hold, 'tis sure a mad head, Morea may be *Moria* [Folly]; and to speak what I think, the inhabitants of modern Greece swerve as much from reason & true religion at this day, as that Morea doth from the picture of a man. Examine the rest in like sort, and you shall find that Kingdoms and Provinces are melancholy, cities and families, all creatures, vegetal, sensible, and rational, that all sorts, sects, ages, conditions, are out of tune, as in Cebes' Table, before they come into the world, they are intoxicated by error's cup, from the highest to the lowest have need of physick, and those particular actions in Seneca, where father & son prove one another mad, may be general; Porcius Latro shall plead against us all. For indeed who is not a fool, melancholy, mad? – Who attempts nothing foolish, who is not brain-sick? Folly, melancholy, madness, are but one disease, *delirium* is a common name to all.

Robert Burton, *The Anatomy of Melancholy* (1621)

=

Is reason a universal standard? Or does rationality, like beauty, lie in the eye of the beholder? Psychiatry claims to be the acme of reason, but it has not always seemed so to its patients.

There was one short period in hospital when I saw people in authority as larger than normal. This was reinforced by the fact that the psychiatrist sat in a high chair at his desk, while the chair for the patient was more comfortable but very low. I had this changed-relative-size delusion while talking to Dr Zimmer one day and I became aware of its nature and burst out laughing. I was reminded of the Thurber cartoon where the psychiatrist asks the patient, 'What do you mean by saying that all the people you see look like rabbits?' In the picture the psychiatrist is seen with a rabbit's head and long ears. In one area of my mind the critical faculty was sufficiently alert to remind me that delusions of appearance are not really true. The distortion of size was a way of expressing the fact that Dr Zimmer was powerful and I was helpless. I knew it and my incorrigible self could laugh at Dr Zimmer to his face, and in a later interview explain why. But I was still at that time totally deluded about the unseen world, and did not yet know if I was in a normal hospital.

Morag Coate, *Beyond All Reason* (1964)

=

HAMLET: I am but mad north-north-west: when the wind is southerly I know a hawk from a hand-saw.

William Shakespeare, *Hamlet* (1604)

=

The paradoxes of psychiatry

A favorite thesis among us, when we were out of humor or fed up, was that psychiatry smells of baloney, that all psychiatrists are nuts. They often seemed so.

Paschall, for instance, assured me now that I was doing much better, improving, because I felt awful! Since I loathed the dump, was sore again at everybody, had the blues and was convinced the three months' treatment had done me no good at all, he was sure I was getting better!

He had a hard time convincing me of this, and an even harder time convincing Marjorie, who went to him a couple of successive afternoons in tears and had lost her nerve again about this being a wholesome place for me.

Paschall insisted that the paradox was true – that it would have been unwholesome if I had remained in love with it. The hospital already had a queer little group of 'trusties,' less than half a dozen, who could get their discharge papers and walk out free any day they liked, but who probably would never go. They were happy here, no longer 'mentally disturbed,' but they had lost the courage, or the wish, to face the world outside.

William Seabrook, Asylum (1935)

=

Madness moves in a mysterious way.

Insanity is no respecter of persons, but lighteth where it listeth, on rich and poor, on king and peasant, on hovel and palace; thus, instead of being confined with the common or garden madman, I am confined here with artists, musicians, teachers and doctors; and it was when I encountered doctors as certified lunatics that the hopelessness of present-day psychiatry in dealing with the psychoses struck me with such force. Alas! Physician heal thyself! But no, he cannot, nor can any other now do so; for mental disease is never of mushroom growth, but is either predisposed or caused by injury or disease – disease which could have been staved off in its infancy, but not in its prime; for although it is true that emotional disturbances, such as grief, fear, worry, anxiety over business and financial matters, love affairs and family disagreements, may give rise to mental disorder, and that such disorders may give rise to an attack of insanity, it really ought to be borne in mind that in such an event there is some previous weakness, or predisposition.

H. G. Woodley, Certified (1947)

=

A philosopher of the Age of Reason defines madness.

FOLIE: MADNESS

We call madness that disease of the organs of the brain which inevitably prevents a man from thinking and acting like others. Unable to administer his property he is declared incapable; unable to have ideas suitable for society, he is excluded from it; if he is dangerous he is locked up; if he is violent he is tied up. Sometimes he is cured by baths, blood-letting and diet.

What is important to notice is that this man is by no means without ideas. He has them like all other men when he is awake, and often when he is asleep. It may be asked how his spiritual, immortal soul, lodged in his brain, receiving all ideas very clearly and distinctly through the senses, nevertheless never judges sanely. It sees objects as the souls of Aristotle and Plato, Locke and Newton saw them. How then, receiving the perceptions experienced by the wisest, does it make of them an extravagant combination, without being able to help itself?

If this simple and eternal substance has the same instruments of action as have the souls of the wisest brain, it must reason like them. Who could prevent it from so doing? I most readily understand that if my madman saw red and the wise men blue; if, when the wise men hear music, my madman hears the braying of a donkey; if, when they listen to a sermon, my madman thinks that he is at the theatre; if, when they hear yes, he hears no; then his soul must think in a different manner from others. But my madman has the same perceptions as they; there is no apparent reason why his soul, having received all its tools from the senses, cannot use them. It is pure, they say; in itself it is not subject to any infirmity; it is thus provided with all necessary aid; whatever happens in its body, nothing can change its essence; nevertheless it is conducted to Colney Hatch in its bodily garment.

This reflection may arouse the suspicion that the faculty of thinking, given by God to man, is subject to derangement like the senses. A lunatic is a sick man whose brain is in bad health, just as the man who has gout is a sick man who has pains in his feet and hands. He thought with his brain as he walked with his feet, without knowing anything about his incomprehensible ability to walk nor of his no less incomprehensible ability to think. People have gout in the brain as in the feet. In short, after a thousand arguments perhaps only faith can convince us that a simple and immaterial substance can be ill.

Learned men or doctors will say to the madman: 'My friend, although you have lost your common sense, your soul is as spiritual as pure, as immortal as ours. But our souls are well housed, and yours badly, the windows of its house are blocked up, it lacks air, it suffocates.' The madman would reply in his lucid moments: 'My friends, as usual you take for granted the matter at issue. My windows are as open as yours since I see the same objects and hear the same words: it must therefore follow that my soul makes bad use of my senses, or that my soul is itself only a vitiated sense, a depraved quality. In a word, either my soul is mad in itself or I have no soul.'

One of the doctors might reply: 'My dear colleague, god has perhaps created mad souls, as he has created wise souls.' The madman would reply: 'If I believed what you tell me I'd be even madder than I am. For pity's sake, you who know so much about it, tell me why I'm mad.'

If the doctors still have a little sense they would reply: 'We don't know.' They will never understand why a brain has incoherent ideas; they will understand no better why another brain has regulated and consistent ideas. They will believe themselves to be wise, and they will be as mad as the lunatic.

Voltaire, *Philosophical Dictionary* (1764)

=

Echoing Chekhov's Ward 6, *Valeriy Tarsis's novel uses the mad-house as a metaphor for Soviet tyranny.*

'What the West and the whole free world is trying to prevent is *man* being turned back into a communized anthropomorphic ape. It took thousands of years for the individual to emerge from the herd. Now the atavistic instinct has revived – significantly, among the "proletarians," the spiritually destitute who, naturally, are led by blinkered fanatics. All great thinkers have been aristocrats of the spirit, and not one of them, from Heraclitus to Nietzsche, could have fathered the wretched doctrine of that bearded German philistine Marx – nor does anyone follow him except our blockheaded talmudists and the demagogues who make up our ruling junta. But I firmly believe that man will triumph and not the ape. I believe that Russia will enter the new century liberated and renewed in spirit and that by then communism will only be a nursery bogy to frighten our grandchildren. This is why I take no stock in all these pious doctrines of modesty, self-sacrifice, peaceful co-existence, the reduction of all human gifts and potentialities to a single operation on the conveyor belt and of all mental and material needs to a pauper's ration. They are nothing but hypocritical puritanism masquerading as revolution, a new scholasticism more dead than the medieval, a new captivity more terrifying than Babylon. . . .'

'Aren't you overstating your case?' said Golin in his sleepy voice; even his eyelids drooped whenever he argued for longer than a minute.

'What difference does it make if I do? Don't you see that the so-called facts about our way of life are soap bubbles – a bunch of nursery balloons strung on a thin thread? Don't you think that if it weren't for the millions of policemen to guard them, the people would have cut the thread long ago and let these pretty bubbles of illusion be blown away, together with their makers and distributors? How can you over- or under-estimate the qualities of a soap bubble? They depend on what your imagination makes of them. To face the truth, your imagination has to be very rich and daring – unfortunately yours, Vasily Vasilyevich, keeps you trailing after old-fashioned ghosts. You float in the air, completely cut off from reality, and you can't come down to earth. You are as naïve as Don Quixote and none of your efforts can get you further than the madhouse. God! the number of useless victims there are! The crowds of Isaacs climbing on to altars of their own free will – not even on their fathers' initiative – and lying down like lambs under the sacrificial knife – instead of snatching it up and sticking it into the fat priests!'

After breakfast it was time for aminodin.

Valeriy Tarsis, *Ward 7: An Autobiographical Novel* (1965)

'Mad' is a stigma. A feminist shows it can simply be a negative label for female behaviour of which men don't approve.

'Crazy' is when a woman doesn't want to live with her husband any more. 'Sane' is when she decides to wear a skirt and apply for a job at Bell Telephone. You don't agree? You must not be a judge or a psychiatrist, then. (Of course, there aren't many female judges or psychiatrists.) In Pennsylvania, the criterion for a court's decision to involuntarily commit a person is if she or he is 'mentally disabled and in need of care or treatment.' But such a vague standard is naturally interpreted according to white, male, middle-class, conventional values.

Beginning with the college date who tries to convince you that you must be crazy because you won't sleep with him, a woman has to deal with the likelihood that she will be labeled mentally ill or disturbed when she refuses to conform to standard roles. Lesbians are sick, women who are depressed after the birth of a child are ill, old maids must have something wrong up there. Unfortunately, there are more sanctions attached to female nonconformity than mere name-calling. Women can be committed involuntarily to psychiatric institutions for these manifestations of insanity. Here are some examples of real women who at one time during the past few years were imprisoned at Haverford State Hospital, Haverford, Pa. Names have been changed.

Madeline is in her late thirties. The first time she was hospitalized her husband had her committed because she was neglecting her appearance and refused to have sexual relations with him. Of course, she had been seriously depressed following the birth of each of her three children and didn't want to become pregnant again.

Susan Dworking Levering, 'She Must be Some Kind of Nut' (1972)

=

Can you be mad, and know it, at the same time?

Directly after this, the patients in front of me seemed to change, and each assumed the form of some semi-human animal, according to whatever animal characteristics were predominant in his face and gait. They looked, in truth, far more like hideous animals on two

legs than like men. I then heard from the air behind me my Christian name called twice, in a very sad and warning manner, by my
mother's voice. I turned round and angrily accused one of the
patients of having done this by ventriloquism. Then all the patients
seemed to me to be harnessed by invisible ropes to some invisible
plough, which I had to guide in the sight of the whole of heaven and
of all the beings that were therein; while at the same time, all round
me, scarlet and purple confetti came whirling in wheels out of my
body, and fell, not like small pieces of paper, but with the dull,
heavy, swishing rattle of leaden hail into the imaginary furrow I
was ploughing. The only thing that kept me from dashing myself
against a wall or tree, or something, was the thought of the verse:
'Though thy sins be as scarlet, yet shall they be white as snow'. I
also thought of Jason overcoming the fiery bulls and sowing the
serpent's teeth that sprang up as enemies against him, and I saw
that it was but a parable. He had to overcome strong passions,
repent for his sins, and then fight and overcome their consequences
on his mind; and the reward was restoration to a kingdom – his
father's kingdom. The fact that I was able to think like this at the
time shews me that though my body was in pain, my sight distorted, and reason on the brink, I still had the powers of human
understanding.

    D. Davidson, *Remembrances of a Religio-Maniac: An Autobiography*
                                                            (1912)

                            =

A bus driver left a trail of death and destruction when he went
berserk in April, killing one woman and seriously injuring five
others.

Mr Eddie Brown, of Waldgrave Road, Broadgreen, Liverpool,
was dragged from his cab screaming: 'We are all going to die. You
are dead, I am taking you with me. I am God. I am the Devil,'
Liverpool Crown Court was told yesterday.

Mr Brown pleaded not guilty to the murder of Mrs Kathleen
Savage, aged 36, of Alness Drive, Rainhill.

His plea of guilty to manslaughter due to diminished responsibility was accepted by the court. He was ordered to be detained in a
high-security hospital.

Mr Michael Maguire, QC, prosecuting, told the court that Mr Brown said in a statement to police: 'I had a terrible experience the night before. I rang my father and told him I was going mad. He said if I could ring him about it I was responsible enough and I was not mad.'

Guardian (3 October 1980)

=

Daniel Schreber writes to his old asylum superintendent, explaining why he has written the memoirs of his confinement.

OPEN LETTER TO PROFESSOR FLECHSIG

Dear Professor,

I take the liberty of enclosing a copy of 'Memoirs of a Patient Suffering from a Nervous Illness', which I have written, and beg you to examine it in a kindly spirit.

You will find your name mentioned frequently ... partly in connection with circumstances which might be painful to you ... My aim is solely to further knowledge of truth in a vital field, that of religion.

I am absolutely certain that in this regard I command experiences which – when generally acknowledged as valid – will act fruitfully to the highest possible degree among the rest of mankind. Equally I have no doubt that your name plays an essential role in the genetic development of the circumstances in question, in that certain nerves taken from your nervous system became 'tested souls' in the sense described in Chapter 1 of the 'Memoirs', and in this capacity achieved supernatural power by means of which they have for years exerted a damaging influence on me and still do to this day. You like other people may be inclined at first to see nothing but a pathological offspring of my imagination in this; but I have an almost overwhelming amount of proof of its correctness, details of which you will find in the content of my 'Memoirs'. I still feel daily and hourly the damaging influence of the miracles of those 'tested souls'; the voices that speak to me even now shout your name again and again at me hundreds of

times every day in this context, in particular as the instigator of
those injuries; and this despite the fact that the personal relations
which existed between us for some time have long since receded
into the background for me; I could hardly therefore have any
reason to keep on thinking of you, especially with any sense of
grievance.

Daniel Paul Schreber, *Memoirs of My Nervous Illness* (1903)

=

John Perceval, son of the only British Prime Minister to be assassin-
ated, Spencer Perceval, became religiously insane, and was confined
in two of the most prestigious English asylums, Ticehurst House
and Brislington House, for a total period of about eighteen months,
during the 1830s. On his release he wrote a two-volume work,
appearing in 1838 and 1840, exposing the counter-productivity of
the psychiatric regimes to which he had been subjected. The book
reveals unrivalled insight into the mental processes and emotional
turmoil of the insane.

To be silent and incommunicative is a singularity; but that singularity becomes reasonable, when a man is denied liberty of expression and action, and confined with perfect strangers, amidst those
whose interest it is to suspect and pervert his ways; aware of that
which you, enthroned in the conceit of a more sound understanding, are daily forgetting, that the weakness of his mind renders it
peculiarly improper for him to open the secrets of his heart to men
with whom he has even no acquaintance. To halloo, to bawl, to
romp, to play the fool, are in ordinary life, signs of irregularity, but
they become necessary to men placed in our position, to disguise or
drown feelings for which we have no relief; too great for expression, too sacred for the prying eye of impertinent, impudent, and
malevolent curiosity. I will be bound to say that the greatest part of
the violence that occurs in lunatic asylums is to be attributed to the
conduct of those who are dealing with the disease, not to the
disease itself; and that that behaviour which is usually pointed out
by the doctor to the visitors as the symptoms of the complaint for
which the patient is confined, is generally more or less a reasonable,

and certainly a natural result, of that confinement, and its particular refinements in cruelty; for all have their select and exquisite moral and mental, if not bodily, tortures.

John T. Perceval, *A Narrative of the Treatment Received by a Gentleman, During a State of Mental Derangement* (1838/40)

=

Philosophers long acknowledged two different sorts of defective reason, that of lunatics and that of idiots. John Locke explains the differing defects in their understanding.

The defect in *Naturals*, seems to proceed from want of quickness, activity, and motion, in the intellectual Faculties, whereby they are deprived of Reason: whereas *mad Men*, on the other side, seem to suffer by the other Extream. For they do not appear to me to have lost the Faculty of Reasoning: but having joined together some *Ideas* very wrongly, they mistake them for Truths; and they err, as Men do, that argue right from wrong Principles. For by the violence of their Imaginations, having taken their Fansies for Realities, they make right deduction from them. Thus you shall find a distracted Man phansying himself a King, with a right inference, requires suitable Attendance, Respect and Obedience: Others who have thought themselves made of glass, have used the caution necessary to preserve such brittle Bodies. Hence it comes to pass, that a Man, who is very sober, and of a right Understanding in all other things, may in one particular, be as frantick as any in *Bedlam*; if either by any sudden very strong impression, or long fixing his Fancy upon one sort of Thoughts, incoherent *Ideas* have been cemented together so powerfully, as to remain united. But there are degrees of Madness, as of Folly; the disorderly jumbling Ideas together, is in some more, and some less. In short, herein seems to lie the difference between Idiots and mad Men, That mad Men put wrong Ideas together, and so make wrong Propositions, but argue and reason right from them: But Idiots make very few or no Propositions, but argue and reason scarce at all.

John Locke, *An Essay Concerning Human Understanding*
(4th edn, 1700)

=

Along similar lines, Clifford Beers, who became a leading American campaigner on behalf of the insane, explains that, during his own mental crisis, he suffered not a loss of reason, but reasoning from wrong premises.

During the entire period of my depression, every publication seemed to have been written and printed for me, and me alone. Books, magazines, and newspapers seemed to be special editions. The fact that I well knew how inordinate would be the cost of such a procedure in no way shook my belief in it. Indeed, that I was costing my persecutors fabulous amounts of money was a source of secret satisfaction. My belief in special editions of newspapers was strengthened by items which seemed too trivial to warrant publication in any except editions issued for a special purpose. I recall a seemingly absurd advertisement, in which the phrase, 'Green Bluefish,' appeared. At the time I did not know that 'green' was a term used to denote 'fresh' or 'unsalted.'

During the earliest stages of my illness I had lost count of time, and the calendar did not right itself until the day when I largely regained my reason. Meanwhile, the date on each newspaper was, according to my reckoning, two weeks out of the way. This confirmed my belief in the special editions as a part of the Third Degree.

Most sane people think that no insane person can reason logically. But this is not so. Upon unreasonable premises I made most reasonable deductions, and that at the time when my mind was in its most disturbed condition. Had the newspapers which I read on the day which I supposed to be February 1st borne a January date, I might not then, for so long a time, have believed in special editions. Probably I should have inferred that the regular editions had been held back. But the newspapers I had were dated about two weeks *ahead*. Now if a sane person on February 1st receives a newspaper dated February 14th, he will be fully justified in thinking something wrong, either with the publication or with himself. But the shifted calendar which had planted itself in my mind meant as much to me as the true calendar does to any sane business man. During the seven hundred and ninety-eight days of depression I drew countless incorrect deductions. But, such as they were, they were deductions, and essentially the mental process was not other than that which takes place in a well-ordered mind.

Clifford Beers, *A Mind that Found Itself: An Autobiography* (1923)

=

Madness may be misunderstanding: but is madness itself misunderstood by reason?

This may appear an extraordinary digression, but I introduce it to show, that many persons confined as lunatics are only so because they are not understood, and continue so because they do not understand themselves. Acknowledging their affections, and palavered over to obey their affections, they yield themselves up wholly to them; not discriminating, not listening to the inward monitor, which commands them to recollect what is due to their own rights, and to their own independence, and to their own honour. By this means their conduct is inconsistent; and when they are admitted into the presence of the relations who have neglected them, they become deranged and disordered through contending feelings. My case was different from this: the doctors would fain have made me, or have found me such a simpleton as one of these. But I knew my rights; and I did not know how to lie. There was no danger to be apprehended to my understanding from my meeting my relations. I understood my position too well: but knowing that position, and my correct feelings in consequence, knowing also that my family were blind to their real position in respect of me, and could not make allowance for these feelings; whilst I was not afraid to meet them, I expressed my reluctance and my indifference to do so, previous to their having made me any apology. This I felt due to myself, on account of the embarrassing position in which I knew I should find myself, if they came to see me, full of their wonted cordiality, unable, through irreflection, to believe that I could really be offended with them, and finding me stern as a rock, and cold to their addresses. I felt this also due to them, to prevent any indecorous language on my part, to which I might be provoked by the cruelties and the difficulties of my situation, and give way through the weakness of my health of body and of mind. For I knew my strength, and did not wish to try it beyond its power; and though, willing if necessary, to meet my relations (and to embrace them if they admitted their error), I could not do so, so long as they disrespected my complaints... And I declare to God that I was of sound mind in this respect, for no man is fit to correspond with persons he is offended with, upon the topics of complaint, but through a third person, particularly not one so cruelly confined as I had been and still was. It was unhandsome and unjust in my family not to attend to these remonstrances. Of Dr Newington's conduct I cannot speak with becoming dignity. He knew that he was sowing the seeds of discord between son and parent, brother and sister, and brother and brother, and yet he continued to degrade himself to accept office as the restorer of peace between us, on grounds incompatible with my religion, my honesty, and my honour, or to be as my gaoler for life if I did not accept them. Surely there is no villany greater than that of these men. Yet, 'who hath believed our report?' to whom is the iniquity of this system revealed?

> John T. Perceval, *A Narrative of the Treatment Received by a Gentleman, During a State of Mental Derangement* (1838/40)

=

'I am not mad.'

Just before leaving for the train, I stated very clearly that I lodged a solemn protest, which would be heard later on, against my being imprisoned this time as a lunatic, though I could do nothing now, and must not resist, but obey the fifth Commandment; and I added, with emphasis, the usual statement that madmen make: 'I am not mad; the whole world is mad, and full of insanity in its greedy race for wealth and power, lust and pleasure; yet I am not mad.' My father said that he had thought of every other possible thing, and whether there was any other way, but there was nothing else he could do; and I know now that he was perfectly right. Before I left, I said, with great emphasis, that there was no need to bother about me now, but that my brother would certainly be attacked by the devil, and I requested them to watch him carefully. I then went up to my room to put on my boots, and, feeling the blow too great, could only fall down on my knees and say, 'Lord, Thou knowest!' Instantly I felt He did know every little in and out of the whole

affair, and, opening a Bible and asking for certain guidance this
once as to what was going to happen to me, I read a short passage
ending in the words: 'And they said unto him, thou shalt go, and
there thou shalt be tried before thy elders.' I do not remember the
place, and it is not in the Bible; and yet I saw those words on the
page in front of me, and went off with the words, 'to be tried before
thy elders', in my mind, and thought somehow that it meant to be
cross-examined before some doctors of theology as to my knowledge of the Scriptures and their practical application. I then went
downstairs, and quite cheerfully started off under escort for an
asylum.

D. Davidson, *Remembrances of a Religio-Maniac: An Autobiography*
(1912)

=

Delusions of librarianship

Mr Alfred Tennyson presents his compliments to the Governor of
Witley Hospital for Convalescent Lunatics, and requests him to be
so kind as to take precautions, that his patients should not pay
visits to Aldworth, as two did yesterday (one describing himself as
assistant librarian of the British Museum).

Mr Tennyson is very glad if they in any way enjoyed themselves
here, and hopes that they did not suffer from their long walk.

Alfred Tennyson, letter to the Governor of Witley Hospital for
Convalescent Lunatics (21 October 1877)

=

*A favourite literary conceit features the 'witty fool', cannier than
the sane society surrounding him. The journalist Ned Ward, con-
tributing to a satirical magazine of London impressions, published
at the turn of the eighteenth century, claimed to find one in Bethlem
Hospital (see page 1).*

... holding forth with much vehemence against Kingly government.
I told him he deserv'd to be hang'd for talking of treason. 'Now,'
says he, 'you're a fool, for we madmen have as much privilege of
speaking our minds as an ignorant dictator when he spews out his

nonsense to a whole parish ... you may talk what you will, and
nobody will call you in question for it. Truth is persecuted everywhere abroad, and flies hither for sanctuary, where she sits as safe
as a knave in a church, or a whore in a nunnery. I can use her as I
please and that's more than you dare to.'

Edward Ward, The London Spy (1703)

=

Live out the ideals to which the world pays lip-service, and you are
martyred as a madman.

I always dreamed of Utopia and I was not content merely to dream.
Therefore my story.

You are one person; I am another. I have thought long and hard
about this world we live in; I have dreamed wild dreams – crazy
dreams, if you will – in the hope of being able to make this life a
better thing for us all. And that is why all windows are barred, all
doors are locked, all exits are guarded.

I would save the world; therefore I am locked up to save the
world from me. Such, at least, is the superficial viewpoint. Fortunately, I am able to see through mere surface appearances to the
subtle maneuverings behind the scenes; I can know that the State
Hospital – the 'insane asylum' – is but my temporary prison, and
will prove to be my steppingstone to the fulfillment of all my
dreams.

I remember back to January 1953, when two men knocked at the
door and said, 'The doctor at the State Hospital wants to see you.'

'I have an appointment to see someone about an hour from now.'

'You can see the doctor, then keep your appointment.'

That sounded reasonable enough, so, like the meek lamb before
the slaughter, I went along, I made no objection when each stood
on one side of me, when they sat between me and the doors of the
hospital limousine, when they ushered me into the hospital building
to answer a few simple, routine questions put to me by the doctor.

William L. Moore, The Mind in Chains:
The Autobiography of a Schizophrenic (1955)

=

Wise words in the mouth of a professional fool

FOOL: Mark it, nuncle:
  Have more than thou showest,
  Speak less than thou knowest,
  Lend less than thou owest,
  Ride more than thou goest,
  Learn more than thou trowest,
  Set less than thou throwest;
  Leave thy drink and thy whore,
  And keep in-a-door,
  And thou shalt have more
  Than two tens to a score.
KENT: This is nothing, fool.

William Shakespeare, King Lear (1608)

=

Catch-22

It was a horrible joke, but Doc Daneeka didn't laugh until Yossarian came to him one mission later and pleaded again, without any real expectation of success, to be grounded. Doc Daneeka snickered once and was soon immersed in problems of his own, which included Chief White Halfoat, who had been challenging him all that morning to Indian wrestle, and Yossarian, who decided right then and there to go crazy.

'You're wasting your time,' Doc Daneeka was forced to tell him.

'Can't you ground someone who's crazy?'

'Oh, sure. I have to. There's a rule saying I have to ground anyone who's crazy.'

'Then why don't you ground me? I'm crazy. Ask Clevinger.'

'Clevinger? Where *is* Clevinger? You find Clevinger and I'll ask him.'

'Then ask any of the others. They'll tell you how crazy I am.'

'They're crazy.'

'Then why don't you ground them?'

'Why don't they ask me to ground them?'

'Because they're crazy, that's why.'

'Of course they're crazy,' Doc Daneeka replied. 'I just told you they're crazy, didn't I? And you can't let crazy people decide whether you're crazy or not, can you?'

Yossarian looked at him soberly and tried another approach. 'Is Orr crazy?'

'He sure is,' Doc Daneeka said.

'Can you ground him?'

'I sure can. But first he has to ask me to. That's part of the rule.'

'Then why doesn't he ask you to?'

'Because he's crazy,' Doc Daneeka said. 'He has to be crazy to keep flying combat missions after all the close calls he's had. Sure, I can ground Orr. But first he has to ask me to.'

'That's all he has to do to be grounded?'

'That's all. Let him ask me.'

'And then you can ground him?' Yossarian asked.

'No. Then I can't ground him.'

'You mean there's a catch?'

'Sure there's a catch,' Dòc Daneeka replied. 'Catch-22. Anyone who wants to get out of combat duty isn't really crazy.'

There was only one catch and that was Catch-22, which specified that a concern for one's own safety in the face of dangers that were real and immediate was the process of a rational mind. Orr was crazy and could be grounded. All he had to do was ask; and as soon as he did, he would no longer be crazy and would have to fly more missions. Orr would be crazy to fly more missions and sane if he didn't, but if he was sane he had to fly them. If he flew them he was crazy and didn't have to; but if he didn't want to he was sane and had to. Yossarian was moved very deeply by the absolute simplicity of this clause of Catch-22 and let out a respectful whistle.

'That's some catch, that Catch-22,' he observed.

'It's the best there is,' Doc Daneeka agreed.

Joseph Heller, *Catch-22* (1961)

=

Utter nonsense

> Hey diddle diddle,
> The cat and the fiddle,
> The cow jumped over the moon;
> The little dog laughed
> To see such sport,
> And the dish ran away with the spoon.

Probably the best-known nonsense verse in the language, a considerable amount of nonsense has been written about it. One of the few statements which can be authenticated is that it appeared in print *c.* 1765. A quotation which may possibly refer to it is in *A lamentable tragedy mixed ful of pleasant mirth, conteyning the life of Cambises King of Percia*, by Thomas Preston, printed 1569,

> They be at hand Sir with stick and fidle;
> They can play a new dance called hey-didle-didle.

Another is in *The Cherry and the Slae* by Alexander Montgomerie, 1597,

> But since ye think't an easy thing
> To mount above the moon,
> Of your own fidle take a spring
> And dance when ye have done.

Earlier in the poem a cow had been mentioned. There seems little foundation for JOH's oft quoted deduction that the unmeaning *Hey diddle diddle* is a corruption of ʾ Ἀδ'ἄδηλα, δῆλα δ'ᾁδε. Probably he knew he was being hoaxed when he was presented with a parallel verse in 'ancient' Greek. He omits the statement in his 1853 edition. Some other of the 'origin' theories which may safely be discounted are (i) that it is connected with Hathor worship; (ii) that it refers to various constellations ('Taurus, Canis minor, &c.); (iii) that it describes the flight from the rising of the waters in Egypt (little dog, the Dog Star, or 'Sohet'; fiddler, beetle, hence scarab; cow jumping over the moon, symbol of sky, &c.); (iv) that it portrays Elizabeth, Lady Katherine Grey, and the Earls of Hertford and Leicester; (v) that it tells of Papist priests urging the labouring class to work harder; (vi) that the expression 'Cat and the fiddle' comes (*a*) from Katherine of Aragon (Katherine la Fidèle), (*b*) from Catherine, wife of Peter the Great, and (*c*) from Caton, a supposed Governor of Calais (Caton le fidèle). There are grounds, albeit slight, for believing the expression comes from the game of cat (trap-ball) and the fiddle (i.e. music) provided by some old-time inns. The sanest observation on this rhyme seems to have been made by Sir Henry Reid, 'I prefer to think', he says, 'that it commemorates the athletic lunacy to which the strange conspiracy of the cat and the fiddle incited the cow.'

Iona and Peter Opie (eds), *The Oxford Dictionary of Nursery Rhymes*
(1951)

The Sources of Disorder

Ever since the Ancient Greeks, insanity has been deemed a disease and claimed by medicine. But it has remained shrouded in mystery. Whereas complaints such as measles involve clearly delineated physical symptoms, the manifestations of madness, by contrast, though often flamboyant and bizarre, can be quite fleeting and fantastically labile – cries and gestures, moods and movements that commonly produce no lasting perceptible physical change, nothing discernible even in a post-mortem. Worse, madness often displays symptoms that mimic and mock other disorders. Describing and diagnosing mental disorders remain enigmatic in principle and difficult in practice.

And, of course, this protean quality applies particularly to the question of origins. Madness affects both mind and body: but does it initiate from the body, or from the mind, or from both, or either, or neither? Might the deliriousness of a wandering mind, for instance, be the very essence of insanity? Or is delirium just the secondary effect upon the consciousness of some micro-organic pathogen or biochemical disturbance?

Down the centuries, speculations have endlessly proliferated as to the aetiology of insanity (and, in their turn, some of the wilder attempts to fix the name and nature of mental disorder have themselves been denounced as mental aberrations). Many eminent medical men have tried to identify the somatic seat of insanity. The guts long had their champions as the prime site of lunacy, perhaps because of the powerful associations between digestive disorders and hypochondria, gluttony and nightmares, narcotics and hallucinations. Others have favoured the heart or the blood (thinking perhaps of broken hearts and boiling blood); the eighteenth century grew fascinated by 'nervous' symptoms and suggested that the nervous system held the secret. And, as the pathways between the nerves and the cortex grew better understood (though scientific research into the electrical circuitry of the brain and its localized functions made slow authentic progress before about a century ago), so insanity was increasingly regarded as something wrong in the head (hence 'nut cases', or 'head cases' with 'screws loose').

Yet, down the centuries, dissections of madmen's brains often proved disappointingly negative. In any case, disorders such as hysteria seemed to flit around the body with such caprice as to mock all hope of nailing down the organ or system responsible, to say nothing of casting doubt on the capacity of the medical profession to distinguish the truly afflicted from mere malingerers and *malades imaginaires*.

The problems of pinning down madness in the body point to one of the attractions of regarding it only incidentally as a physical affliction, but primarily as psychogenic, all in the mind. Surely it must be a malady of the mind, or of the understanding or imagination, or of the passions or propensities, the will or spirit, the soul or psyche. But therein, once again, lies the rub. In our culture supersaturated with the concepts of Christian theology and the Cartesian *cogito*, it is easy to verbalize about such non-material faculties or functions, but are they real or merely words? And, if real, where are they to be found? The topography of consciousness has always been a dark continent, its territory deeply disputed. Is it a self-evident fact about *homo sapiens* that we are material beings capped by some central, immaterial, quintessential *res cogitans*, or a comparable *je ne sais quoi*? Or is such a notion – the notorious 'ghost in the machine' – nothing but a religious vestige, tenable only by a high-jump of faith, a *credo quia impossibile*?

And things get even more murky when the Unconscious is further invoked as the well-spring of mental disturbance. For even if it truly exists (*uncogito, ergo sum*?), the Unconscious is, definitionally, the Unknown, beyond our ken, its ancient history as near lost in early infancy as makes no difference, provoking the hoary accusation that the Freudian Unconscious is no better than the devil in disguise.

The quest for the source of madness in the body, or in the mind, evidently sparks insoluble problems. It is therefore not surprising that people have looked elsewhere. The fault, dear Brutus ... Lifestyles and habits, and their accompanying social pressures, have often been blamed. It's bourgeois morality that drives you crazy; or capitalism; or communism; or the system, any system. External forces such as Satan or the Almighty were once standardly invoked as visiting madness upon poor sinners, diabolical or divine. And if not society, why *not* the stars, being 'born under Saturn'? Over the centuries, almost every known evil has been held responsible for causing madness: drink, lust, pride, the family – and even tea.

============

What is madness?

Madness is a distemper of such a nature, that very little of real use can be said concerning it; the immediate causes will for ever disappoint our search, and the cure of that disorder depends on *management* as much as *medicine*.

> John Monro (see page 279), *Remarks on Dr Battie's Treatise on Madness* (1758)

==

A mystery. William Pargeter (1760–1810) was a physician and a naval chaplain. His own preferred treatment of lunatics involved a kind of 'Mesmeric' fixing of the patient with his eye.

The *original* or *primary* cause of Madness is a mystery, and utterly inexplicable by human reason. Thus far, however, has been discovered, that there is a fluid continually secreted by the cerebrum and cerebellum, and propelled into the nervous tubuli, from whence it is called a nervous fluid, &c. This fluid (or electric aura, as some style it) is capable of manifold variations – either in its quantity, it may become too much or too little – or it may admit of many alterations in its quality, and may become thicker and thinner in its consistence than it ought to be – it may likewise, from causes to us unknown, assume other and different qualities. A certain morbid or *irritating* principle or quality of that fluid acting upon

the brain is the *primary* cause of Insanity, with all the unaccountable phenomena which attend it; but what the *specific* nature of
that morbid quality or principle is, it is impossible to conceive, and
it will, no doubt, for ever remain a secret.

> – Nec meus audet
> Rem tentare pudor, quam vires ferre recusent

Here our researches must stop, and we must declare, that
'wonderful are the works of the Lord, and his ways past finding
out'.

William Pargeter, *Observations on Maniacal Disorders* (1792)

=

*And the mystery of madness followed from the paradox of man.
Western traditions in philosophy and theology – Platonism,
Christianity, Cartesianism – have envisaged the human being as 'a
great amphibium', divided into mind (or spirit or soul) and body.
The connections between psyche and soma have baffled under-
standing.*

The operations of the mind on the body and *é contra*, is also a
mystery, and does not come under a mechanical mode of reasoning;
it being impossible to decypher and trace out the several steps and
ways of procedure of those agents, which can by no means be
brought under the cognizance of our senses. In inquiries therefore
of this kind, there must be allowed some further *data* than need be,
in such as are merely *physical*. *Baron Haller*, in his first lines of
Physiology, observes, that 'they have behaved modestly, who con-
fessing themselves ignorant, as to the manner in which the body
and mind are united, have contented themselves with proceeding no
farther than the known laws, which the Creator himself has prescribed; without inventing and supplying us with conjectures not
supported by experience.'

William Pargeter, *Observations on Maniacal Disorders* (1792)

=

Just some of the things that drive people crazy

11thly. Domestic disturbances and quarrels have made more husbands, wives, and daughters nervous, than the sword has slain; and ought, on this ground, to be most religiously guarded against.

12thly. Disappointed love has ruined the constitutions, broken down the mental powers, and inflicted more intense misery on a greater number of females, than LOVE ever made happy. The number which become nervous from this cause, is greater than from most others.

13thly. Onanism. To this baneful practice, the deterioration of early beauty, the loss of brilliancy in the eye, and a smooth surface of the forehead; the appearance of premature age; fidgetiness, eccentricity, *unevenness of temper*, unnatural quickness, or great dullness and stupidity; incompetency, impotency, idiocy, wretchedness, and aberration of mind, are to be frequently ascribed. It is true, that it is not always, but very often, to *this cause*, in both sexes, these symptoms can be traced.

14thly. The excessive desire of children.

15thly. Extreme hunger, continued some days.

16thly. Love of admiration.

17thly. Self-esteem.

18thly. Great fear.

19thly. Mistaken perceptions of real religion and of Christian doctrines, and the grounds of acceptance both of our prayers, duties, and persons with God.

20thly. Hard, intense, and *long-continued studies*.

21stly. Blows on the head.

22ndly. Mal-formation of the *cranium*.

23rdly. Lightning.

24thly. Gambling.

25thly. Jealousy.

26thly. The sudden death of persons in our presence.

27thly. The horrors of a storm at sea.

28thly. The fearful associations of being awoke from sound sleep while the house is on fire.

29thly. The sight of a public execution.

30thly. Sudden and unexpected changes of fortune.

31stly. And INFLUENZA – are but a few of the exciting causes of nervous disease that have come under our notice. But we have not leisure to select more, nor time to offer any remarks on these, or give any more cases of illustration.

William Willis Moseley, *Eleven Chapters on Nervous and Mental Conditions* (1838)

=

Where does insanity lie? The great late eighteenth-century American physician, Benjamin Rush (see page xiv), believed that mania, like almost all other fevers and diseases, had its origin in the inflammatory properties of the blood. He was a merciless bleeder.

1 The most ancient opinion of the proximate cause of intellectual derangement, or what has been called madness, is that it is derived from a morbid state of the liver, and that it discovers itself in a vitiated state of the bile. Hippocrates laid the foundation of this error by his encomium upon Democritus, whom he found employed in examining the liver of a dumb animal in order to discover the cause of madness.

2 Madness has been said to be the effect of a disease in the spleen. This viscus is supposed to be affected in a peculiar manner in that grade of madness which has been called hypochondriasis. For many years it was known in England by no other name than the spleen, and even to this day, persons who are affected with it are said to be spleeny, in some parts of the New England states.

3 A late French writer, Dr Prost, in an ingenious work entitled 'Médecine Eclairée par Observation et l'Overture des Corps', has taken pains to prove that madness is the effect of a disease in the intestines, and particularly of their peritoneal coat. The marks of inflammation which appear in the bowels in persons who have died of madness, have no doubt favoured this opinion; but these morbid appearances, as well as all those which are often met with in the liver, spleen, and occasionally in the stomach, in persons who have died of madness, are the effects and not the causes of the disease. They are induced either, 1, by the violent or protracted exercises of the mind attracting or absorbing the excitement of those viscera, and thereby leaving them in that debilitated state which naturally

disposes them to inflammation and obstruction. Thus diseases in the stomach induce torpor and costiveness in the alimentary canal. Thus too local inflammation often induces coldness and insensibility in contiguous parts of the body. Or, 2, they are induced by the re-action of the mind from the impressions which produce madness, being of such nature as to throw its morbid excitement upon those viscera with so much force as to produce inflammation and obstruction in them. That they are induced by one, or by both these causes, I infer from the increased secretion and even discharge of bile which succeed a paroxysm of anger; from the pain in the left side, or spleen, which succeeds a paroxysm of malice or revenge; and from the pain, and other signs of disease in the bowels and stomach which follow the chronic operations of fear and grief. That the disease and disorders of all the viscera that have been mentioned, are the effects, and not the causes of madness, I infer further from their existing for weeks, months and years in countries subject to intermitting fevers, without producing madness, or even the least alienation of mind.

4 Madness, it has been said, is the effect of a disease in the nerves. Of this, dissections afford us no proofs; on the contrary, they generally exhibit the nerves after death from madness in a sound state. I object further, to this opinion, that hysteria, which is universally admitted to be seated chiefly in the nerves and muscles, often continues for years, and sometimes during a long life, without inducing madness, or if the mind be alienated for a few minutes in one of its paroxysms, it is only from its bringing the vascular system into sympathy, in which I shall say presently the cause of madness is primarily seated. The reaction of the mind from the impressions which produce hysteria, discovers itself in the bowels, in the kidneys, and in most of the muscular parts of the body.

5 and lastly. Madness has been placed exclusively in the mind. I object to this opinion, 1, because the mind is incapable of any operations independently of impressions communicated to it through the medium of the body. 2, Because there are but two instances upon record of the brain being found free from morbid appearances in persons who have died of madness. One of these instances is related by Dr Stark, the other by Dr De Haen. They probably arose from the brain being diseased beyond that grade in

which inflammation and its usual consequences take place. Did cases of madness reside exclusively in the mind, a sound state of the brain ought to occur after nearly every death from that disease.

I object to it, 3, because there are no instances of primary affections of the mind, such as grief, love, anger, or despair, producing madness until they had induced some obvious changes in the body, such as wakefulness, a full or frequent pulse, costiveness, a dry skin, and other symptoms of bodily indisposition.

I know it has been said in favour of madness being an ideal disease, or being seated primarily in the mind, that sudden impressions from fear, terror, and even ridicule have sometimes cured it. This is true, but they produce their effects only by the healthy actions they induce in the brain. We see several other diseases, particularly hiccup, head-ache, and even fits of epilepsy, which are evidently affections of the body, cured in the same way by impressions of fear and terror upon the mind.

Having rejected the abdominal viscera, the nerves, and the mind, as the primary seats of madness, I shall now deliver an opinion, which I have long believed and taught in my lectures, and that is, that the cause of madness is seated primarily in the blood-vessels of the brain, and that it depends upon the same kind of morbid and irregular actions that constitute other arterial diseases. There is nothing specific in these actions. They are part of the unity of disease, particularly of fever; of which madness is a chronic form, affecting that part of the brain which is the seat of the mind.

Benjamin Rush, *Medical Inquiries and Observations upon the Diseases of the Mind* (1812)

=

Is mental disorder in the mind, or in the body? Patients have generally preferred to think they have an organic disorder, and diplomatic doctors have usually avoided such bleak words as lunacy, preferring euphemisms like 'nervous complaint'. Sylvia Plath's autobiographical novel The Bell Jar, *with its illuminating account of mental disturbance, was first published in January 1963, under the pseudonym 'Victoria Lucas', a month before its author's suicide.*

'Don't you want to get up today?'

'No.' I huddled down more deeply in the bed and pulled the sheet up over my head. Then I lifted a corner of the sheet and peered out. The nurse was shaking down the thermometer she had just removed from my mouth.

'You *see*, it's normal.' I had looked at the thermometer before she came to collect it, the way I always did. 'You *see*, it's normal, what do you keep taking it for?'

I wanted to tell her that if only something were wrong with my body it would be fine, I would rather have anything wrong with my body than something wrong with my head, but the idea seemed so involved and wearisome that I didn't say anything. I only burrowed down further in the bed.

Sylvia Plath, *The Bell Jar* (1963)

=

Proposing a bodily source is an effective means of robbing insanity of any glamour.

The Practitioners of this famous Art, proceed in general upon the following Fundamental; That, *the Corruption of the Senses is the Generation of the Spirit*: Because the *Senses* in Men are so many Avenues to the Fort of *Reason*, which in this Operation is wholly block'd up. All Endeavours must be therefore used, either to divert, bind up, stupify, fluster, and amuse the *Senses*, or else to justle them out of their Stations; and while they are either absent, or otherwise employ'd or engaged in a Civil War against each other, the *Spirit* enters and performs its Part.

Jonathan Swift, *A Tale of a Tub* (1704)

=

From within psychiatry, Freud suggested that the psyche comprised different drives which, when in conflict, produced psychoneurotic conditions. Such ideas, however, had had a long pedigree in the idiom of religion, as this extract from the seventeenth-century puritan Richard Sibbes shows.

We see, that the soule hath disquiets proper to it selfe, besides those griefes of Sympathy that arise from the body; for here the soule complains of the soule it selfe, as when it is out of the body it hath torments and joyes of its owne. And if these troubles of the soule bee not well cured, then by way of fellowship and redundance they will affect the outward man, and so the whole man shall be inwrapt in miserie ... If there were no enemie in the world, nor Devill in hell, we carry that within us, that if it be let loose will trouble us more then all the world besides ... Therefore we must conceive in a godly man, a double selfe, one which must be denied, the other which must denie; one that breeds all the disquiet, and another that stilleth what the other hath raised ...

That which most troubles a good man in all troubles, is himselfe, so farre as he is unsubdued; he is more disquieted with himselfe, than with all troubles out of himselfe; when hee hath gotten the better once of himselfe, whatsoever falls from without, is light; where the spirit is enlarged, it cares not much for outward bondage; where the spirit is lightsome, it cares not much for outward darkenesse; where the spirit is setled, it cares not much for outward changes; where the spirit is one with it selfe, it can beare outward breaches; where the spirit is sound, it can beare outward sicknesse. Nothing can bee very ill with us, when all is well within. This is the comfort of a holy man, that though hee bee troubled with himselfe, yet by reason of the spirit in him which is his better selfe, hee workes out by degrees, what ever is contrary ... Hee that is at peace in himselfe, will be peaceable to others, peaceable in his family, peaceable in the Church, peaceable in the State; The soule of a wicked man is in perpetuall sedition; being alwayes troubled in it selfe, it is no wonder if it be troublesome to others. Unity in our selves is before unity with others ...

Richard Sibbes, The Soules Conflict with It Selfe (1635)

=

If madness has a physical source, what is it? An old tradition sees the belly as the organ determining the health of the spirits.

As for the *Original Seed*, or Spring of Phrensies or Madness in the Body, it must be noted, besides what hath been already said, that there is in the Pipe of the Artery of the *Stomach*, a vital Faculty of the Soul, for the inbeaming of Rayes of Light into the *Heart*, so long as it is in a good state, but when through Passions and Disorders it behaveth it self rashly, or amiss, then presently Heart-burning, Fainting, Giddiness of the Head, Appoplexes, Epilexsies, Drousie-Evils, Watchings, Madnesses, Head-akes, Convultions, &c. by the means we have herein before described are sturred up.

Thomas Tryon (see page 3), *A Discourse of the Causes, Natures and Cure of Phrensie, Madness or Distraction* (1689)

═

Beware lobster, Dorothea Lieven warns her lover.

It is less than three weeks since he came to call on me. I was alone with him. He told me that he was sometimes seized by fits of madness, during which he was not responsible for his actions. At this alarming information, I went up to the bell-cord and stood sentinel until the Duke of York came in and rescued me from our tête-à-tête. Afterward, I told my husband that I thought Harden-brot was talking very incoherently. He made enquiries and was told that he was in excellent health and had never shown any sign of madness. Two days later, he went off his head. He was put in charge of two doctors from Bedlam and died yesterday in a violent fit of madness ... Don't ever think of eating lobster after dinner: that is what the poor lunatic used to do.

Princess Lieven, letter to Prince Metternich (27 January 1821)

═

It has long been recognized that women can become delirious after childbirth (see, for example, the case of Anne Sexton, page 86), though the cause of this 'post-partum psychosis' – in septicaemia – has been understood only during the last century. Margery Kempe was born in King's Lynn, around 1373. Her 'book', which she dictated, being illiterate, comprises perhaps the earliest auto-biography in the English language. In it she describes how she went out of her mind after giving birth.

And when she was at any time sick or troubled, the devil said in her mind that she should be damned, for she was not shriven of that fault. Therefore, after her child was born, and not believing she would live, she sent for her confessor, as said before, fully wishing to be shriven of her whole lifetime, as near as she could. And when she came to the point of saying that thing which she had so long concealed, her confessor was a little too hasty and began sharply to reprove her before she had fully said what she meant, and so she would say no more in spite of anything he might do. And soon after, because of the dread she had of damnation on the one hand, and his sharp reproving of her on the other, this creature went out of her mind and was amazingly disturbed and tormented with spirits for half a year, eight weeks and odd days.

And in this time she saw, as she thought, devils opening their mouths all alight with burning flames of fire, as if they would have swallowed her in, sometimes pawing at her, sometimes threatening her, sometimes pulling her and hauling her about both night and day during the said time. And also the devils called out to her with great threats, and bade her that she should forsake her Christian faith and belief, and deny her God, his mother, and all the saints in heaven, her good works and all good virtues, her father, her mother, and all her friends. And so she did. She slandered her husband, her friends, and her own self. She spoke many sharp and reproving words: she recognized no virtue nor goodness; she desired all wickedness; just as the spirits tempted her to say and do, so she said and did. She would have killed herself many a time as they stirred her to, and would have been damned with them in hell, and in witness of this she bit her own hand so violently that the mark could be seen for the rest of her life. And also she pitilessly tore the skin on her body near her heart with her nails, for she had no other implement, and she would have done something worse, except that she was tied up and forcibly restrained both day and night so that she could not do as she wanted.

And when she had long been troubled by these and many other temptations, so that people thought she should never have escaped from them alive, then one time as she lay by herself and her keepers were not with her, our merciful Lord Christ Jesus – ever to be trusted, worshipped be his name, never forsaking his servant in time of need – appeared to his creature who had forsaken him, in the likeness of a man, the most seemly, most beauteous, and most amiable that ever might be seen with man's eye, clad in a mantle of purple silk, sitting upon her bedside, looking upon her with so blessed a countenance that she was strengthened in all her spirits, and he said to her these words: 'Daughter, why have you forsaken me, and I never forsook you?'

Margery Kempe, *The Book of Margery Kempe* (c. 1420)

=

Negative emotions, vices and sins – or simply too much of any kind of passion – have been blamed as the cause of insanity.

The truth is, *Pride* may justly be said to be the chief *Procatarick*, or remote original cause of *Madness*; for an abusive Self flattering Perswasion, Credulity, or Esteem of Falshood, do at first Seduce a person into *Presumption*, and a despising of others, or into an Indignation of *Self-Love, Anger, Hatred*, or Wrathfulness, towards his Neighbour; from whence proceeds *Irreligion, Unbelief, Superstition, impenitent Arrogance, drunken Disparation*, and *sottish Carelessness*. For as *Faith* is the Gate unto *Humility*, which is the Truth of the Intelector Understanding, so a credulous esteem or judgment of Falshood is the entrance of Presumption and Arrogancy, and the *first madness of the Soul*. But other Disturbances, as *Love, Desire, Sorrow, Fear, Terror*, &c. are especially stirred up by extrinsical occasion, and therefore they do produce their effects, not only in the Soul, but in the Body. For all passions do in their beginning take away *sleep*, weaken the Appetite and Digestive Faculties, and impress *dark Ideas* upon the Spirits, and at length through a long immoderate, strong, or sudden inordinacy, those Idæas do infatuate the *Archeus*, subvert the *Judgment*, and the Soul is, as it were, shaken out of its place.

Thomas Tryon (see page 3), *A Discourse of the Causes, Natures and Cure of Phrensie, Madness or Distraction* (1689)

=

Lust

This appetite, which was implanted in our natures for the purpose of propagating our species, when excessive, becomes a disease both of the body and mind. When restrained, it produces tremors, a flushing of the face, sighing, nocturnal pollutions, hysteria, hypochondriasis, and in women the furor uterinus. When indulged in an undue or a promiscuous intercourse with the female sex, or in onanism, it produces seminal weakness, impotence, dysury, tabes dorsalis, pulmonary consumption, dyspepsia, dimness of sight, vertigo, epilepsy, hypochondriasis, loss of memory, manalgia, fatuity, and death. From a number of letters addressed to me, for advice, I shall select but three, in which many of those symptoms are mentioned, and deplored in the most pathetic terms. The first is from a physician in Massachusetts, dated September 4th, 1793.

'The gentleman whose case is now submitted to you is about twenty-five years of age, meagre, gloomy, and restless, has a bad countenance, and a lax state of bowels. He imputes his indisposition to his excessive devotedness to Venus, which he thinks has been induced by a morbid state of his body. He has been married three years, had no connection with the sex before he married, and, although he feels disgusted with his strong venereal propensities, he cannot resist them. I advised him to separate himself from his wife by travelling, which he did, but without experiencing any relief from his disease. He has earnestly requested me to render him impotent, if I could not give him the command of himself in any other way. I have tried several remedies in his case; nothing has done him any good except the sugar of lead, which I was soon obliged to lay aside, from its producing a severe nervous cholic. Wishing to know whether his disease was not seated in his imagination only, I asked whether the gratification of his appetite was equal to his desires. Dixit, per annos tres, quinque vices se coitum fecisse in horis viginti quatuor, et semper semine ejecto [He told me that during the three years of his marriage he had regularly made love to his wife five times a day, achieving orgasm on each occasion].'

Benjamin Rush (see page xiv), *Medical Inquiries and Observations upon the Diseases of the Mind* (1812)

—

Mad with love, the theme of Hazlitt's autobiographical account of his obsessional love for Sarah Walker, a tailor's daughter

A THOUGHT.

I am not mad, but my heart is so; and raves within me, fierce and untameable, like a panther in its den, and tries to get loose to its lost mate, and fawn on her hand, and bend lowly at her feet.

ANOTHER.

Oh! thou dumb heart, lonely, sad, shut up in the prison-house of this rude form, that hast never found a fellow but for an instant, and in very mockery of thy misery, speak, find bleeding words to express thy thoughts, break thy dungeon-gloom, or die pronouncing thy Infelice's name!

ANOTHER.

Within my heart is lurking suspicion, and base fear, and shame and hate; but above all, tyrannous love sits throned, crowned with her graces, silent and in tears.

William Hazlitt, *Liber Amoris: or The New Pygmalion* (1823)

=

Fear, however, is perhaps the most commonly recorded emotional source of mental collapse.

It was New Year's when I first experienced what I called *Fear*. It literally fell on me, how I know not. It was afternoon, the wind was stronger than ever and more mournful. I was in the mood to listen to it, my whole being attuned to it, palpitating, awaiting I know not what. Suddenly Fear, agonizing, boundless Fear, overcame me, not the usual uneasiness of unreality, but real fear, such as one knows at the approach of danger, of calamity. And the wind, as if to add to the turmoil, soughed its interminable protests, echoing the muffled groans of the forest.

Fear made me ill; just the same I ran out to visit a friend who was staying at a nearby sanatorium. To get there, a way led through the woods, short and well-marked. Becoming lost in the thick fog, I circled round and round the sanatorium without seeing it, my fear augmenting all the while. By and by I realized that the wind inspired this fear; the trees too, large and black in the mist, but particularly the wind. At length I grasped the meaning of its message: the frozen wind from the North Pole wanted to crush the earth, to destroy it. Or perhaps it was an omen, a sign that the earth was about to be laid waste.

Marguerite Sechehaye, *Reality Lost and Regained: Autobiography of a Schizophrenic Girl, with Analytic Interpretation* (1951)

=

Bad habits are often identified as a leading cause of mental disorder. Overwork was often blamed, leading to the disease, widely diagnosed early in this century, of 'brain-fag'.

Our philosophical transactions and the physiological parts of many foreign literary Emphemerides furnish us with numerous examples of the morbid or fatal effects of *excessive study*. As the humours are more abundantly derived to any part which is in action, there must be a greater accumulation in the brain of the studious, which increasing the tone and motion of vessels, produces many fatal distempers – The *remote* causes already enumerated, are such as act upon the mind.

William Pargeter (see page 36), *Observations on Maniacal Disorders* (1792)

=

Madness has often been attributed to hard drinking and habitual intoxication. Trotter's treatise is important for reversing the arrow of influence, and arguing that particular mental dispositions trigger uncontrollable drinking in the first place.

Drunkenness itself, is a temporary madness. But in constitutions where there is a predisposition to insanity and idiotism, these diseases are apt to succeed the paroxysm, and will often last weeks and months after it. Wounds and contusions of the brain and cranium, with other organic lesions, have a similar effect. I have known numberless instances of these kinds of *Mania* and *Amentia*. In courts of justice we often hear of men, who are convicted of improper conduct, pleading for mitigation of punishment, from acting under temporary insanity. A small quantity of liquor is apt to derange these people: in such subjects the blood would appear to be over accumulated in the head, or circulates unequally there, and thus causes delirium. Seamen, who are so much exposed to blows and wounds of the head, from the nature of their duty, are very liable to affections of this kind.

Thomas Trotter, *An Essay on Drunkenness* (1804)

===

Opium was freely available in England in earlier centuries, and widely used for recreational as well as medicinal purposes. Jones was one of the earliest to draw attention to its dangers.

Wine and Opium, in a due quantity, (but Opium, in a far less quantity, as was said) cause a pleasant, gay, and good Humour, Courage, Bravery, Magnanimity, Promptitude in Business, Expediteness in Management, Serenity, Euphory, or easy under-going of Labour, Journeys, Fatigues, &c. Both take away Sadness, Grief, Melancholy, Fear, Depression of Spirits, &c. Both cause Promptitude to Venery (*Sine Cerere & Baccho friget Venus:*) So Wine and Opium prevent and cure Cold, open the Pores, promote Perspiration and Sweat, especially the following Mornings, as Sir Theodore Mayern, my self, and others, have observ'd of Opium, and is notorious as to Wine. Both cause Sleep, and take away the Sense of Pain, and require a greater Dose than ordinary in Propor-tion to the Pain; both take off Shiverings from Fear, Cold, or Ague Fits, and cause Mirth, Contentation, and Acquiescence, Driness of the Mouth, Thirst, a Sense of Heat within us, a Dreaming Condi-tion, pleasant Dreams . . . Nocturnal Pollution, and in some Consti-tutions both cause Vigilancy; but Wine and Opium cause that more rarely than Sleep: Both stop, and cause Vomiting if they stay too long at Stomach; Both moderate Hunger . . . and are good in a canine Appetite; Both cause Swimming in the Head, &c. So *Both in an Excessive Dose*, do cause, at first, Mirth, and afterwards a kind of Drunken Sopor in some, in others Fury, or Madness, Sardonick Laughter, and Weight at Stomach, Vomitings, Hiccoughs, great Heat at Stomach, Debility, and laxity of all Parts, Faltring of the

Tongue, Scotomies and Darkness of the Eyes, Vertigo's, Laxity of the Cornea of the Eye, Dilatation of the Pupilla, Deadness of the Eyes to the View, Loss of Memory, Venereal Fury, a high Colour, profuse Sweats, Purging sometimes, Alienation of the Mind, Loss of Memory; and lastly, greater or lesser Effects according to the Dose, Constitution, &c. *So A long and lavish Use of both*, Causes a dull and moapish Disposition, Dropsies, Fall of humours upon Weaken'd Parts, a Sleepy Disposition, Want of Appetite, Weakness of Digestion, Aptitude to Sterility, and Abortion, early Decrepiteness, Stooping in the Back, Trembling of the Hands, Weakness of Memory, Shortness of Life, Difficulty and Danger in suddenly leaving them off, Revive such as sink for Want of either, and supply the Want of each other.

John Jones, The Mysteries of Opium Reveal'd (1700)

=

Odd though it may seem, tea-drinking was the centre of stormy controversy in the eighteenth century, many authorities being convinced that the habit, already becoming part of the British way of life, inevitably led to physical and mental crisis.

But besides this degeneracy, which we thus derive from our progenitors, we may add, that by the frequent and immoderate use of tea – long fasting – inflammatory food – turning day into night, and night into day, the order of nature is most shamefully inverted – our time, which was given us for far more valuable purposes, is vilely prostituted – every active instrument of health is mutilated and maimed – our bodies become enervated – our intellectual faculties impaired, and the date of life abridged; at length we sink into the arms of everlasting rest, with a *fashionable* death, the natural consequence of a *fashionable* life. With what additional force must the practice and pursuit of the foregoing evils operate on female constitutions, whose frame and contexture are so delicate and tender; and it is seriously to be remarked, that in this age, it is easier to meet with a *mad*, than an *healthy* woman of *fashion*. A descant on the present mode of living, as it respects diet – the non-naturals – the baneful effects of the public education of females, &c. would be in this place a digression, but may probably be considered at

some future period. For the present, I shall only observe, that the
grievances above stated are incontestible, and experience furnishes
us with numerous and enormous instances, of the pernicious consequences of luxurious indulgence to the morals and constitutions
of mankind.

William Pargeter (see page 36), *Observations on Maniacal Disorders*
(1792)

=

*Not least, external disasters have always been seen as prime causes
of inner collapse. The French Revolution produced a heavy crop of
maniacs.*

A gentleman, the father of a respectable family, lost his property by
the revolution, and with it all his resources. His calamities soon
reduced him to a state of insanity. He was treated by the usual
routine of baths, blood-letting and coercion. The symptoms, far
from yielding to this treatment, gained ground, and he was sent to
Bicêtre as an incurable maniac. The governor, without attending to
the unfavourable report which was given of him upon his admission, left him a little to himself, in order to make the requisite
observations upon the nature of his hallucination. Never did a
maniac give greater scope to his extravagance. His pride was
incompressible and his pomposity most laughably ridiculous. To
strut about in the character of the prophet Mahomet, whom he
believed himself to be, was his great delight. He attacked and struck
at every body that he met with in his walks, and commanded their
instant prostration and homage. He spent the best part of the day in
pronouncing sentences of proscription and death upon different
persons, especially the servants and keepers who waited upon him.
He even despised the authority of the governor. One day his wife,
bathed in tears, came to see him. He was violently enraged against
her, and would probably have murdered her, had timely assistance
not gone to her relief. What could mildness and remonstrance do
for a maniac, who regarded other men as particles of dust? He was
desired to be peaceable and quiet. Upon his disobedience, he was
ordered to be put into the strait-waistcoat, and to be confined in his
cell for an hour, in order to make him feel his dependence. Soon

after his detention, the governor paid him a visit, spoke to him in a friendly tone, mildly reproved him for his disobedience, and expressed his regret that he had been compelled to treat him with any degree of severity. His maniacal violence returned again the next day. The same means of coercion were repeated. He promised to conduct himself more peaceably; but he relapsed again a third time. He was then confined for a whole day together. On the day following he was remarkably calm and moderate. But another explosion of his proud and turbulent disposition made the governor feel the necessity of impressing this maniac with a deep and durable conviction of his dependence. For that purpose he ordered him to immediate confinement, which he declared should likewise be perpetual, pronounced this ultimate determination with great emphasis, and solemnly assured him, that, for the future, he would be inexorable. Two days after, as the governor was going his round, our prisoner very submissively petitioned for his release. His repeated and earnest solicitations were treated with levity and derision. But in consequence of a concerted plan between the governor and his lady, he again obtained his liberty on the third day after his confinement. It was granted him on his expressly engaging to the governess, who was the ostensible means of his enlargement, to restrain his passions and by that means to skreen her from the displeasure of her husband for an act of unseasonable kindness. After this, our lunatic was calm for several days, and in his moments of excitement, when he could with difficulty suppress his maniacal propensities, a single look from the governess was sufficient to bring him to his recollection. When thus informed of impropriety in his language or conduct, he hastened to his own apartment to reinforce his resolution, lest he might draw upon his benefactress the displeasure of the governor, and incur, for himself, the punishment from which he had just escaped. These internal struggles between the influence of his maniacal propensities and the dread of perpetual confinement, habituated him to subdue his passions, and to regulate his conduct by foresight and reflection. He was not insensible to the obligations which he owed to the worthy managers of the institution, and he was soon disposed to treat the governor, whose authority he had so lately derided, with profound esteem and attachment. His insane propensities and recollections gradually, and at length, entirely disappeared. In six months he was completely restored. This very respectable gentleman is now indefatigably engaged in the recovery of his injured fortune.

Philippe Pinel (see page 12), *A Treatise on Insanity* (1806)

=

Disasters can of course be self-inflicted: a lesson always central to Stoicism.

Hannibal, a conqueror all his life, met with his match, and was subdued at last. One is brought in triumph, as Cæsar into Rome, Alcibiades into Athens, crowned, honoured, admired; by-and-by his statues demolished, he hissed out, massacred, &c. Magnus Gonsalvo, that famous Spaniard, was of the Prince and people at first honoured, approved; forthwith confined & banished; 'tis Polybius his observation, grievous enmities, and bitter calumnies, commonly follow renowned actions. One is born rich, dies a beggar: sound to-day, sick to-morrow: now in most flourishing estate, fortunate and happy, by-and-by deprived of his goods by foreign enemies, robbed by thieves, spoiled, captivated, impoverished, as they of Rabbah, *put under iron saws, and under iron harrows, and under axes of iron, and cast into the tile-kiln.*

> Why, friends, so often did you call me happy?
> He that has fallen never was secure. (BOETHIUS)

... And which is worse, as if discontents and miseries would not come fast enough upon us, man is a devil to his fellow man; we maul, persecute, and study how to sting, gall, and vex one another with mutual hatred, abuses, injuries; preying upon, and devouring, as so many ravenous birds; and, as jugglers, pandars, bawds, cozening one another; or raging as wolves, tigers, and devils, we take a delight to torment one another; men are evil, wicked, malicious, treacherous, and naught, not loving one another, or loving themselves, not hospitable, charitable, nor sociable, as they ought to be, but counterfeit, dissemblers, ambidexters, all for their own ends, hard-hearted, merciless, pitiless, and, to benefit themselves, they care not what mischief they procure to others.

Robert Burton (see page 13), *The Anatomy of Melancholy* (1621)

Independently of Freud, whenever people have reflected, 'Why did I undergo turmoil of mind?', they have instinctively looked back to their early lives, as in this retrospective memoir by a patient in Broadmoor, Britain's first asylum for the criminally insane.

As I look back upon my early years, I cannot doubt that the circumstances of my upbringing prepared the way for the disaster which was to ruin my career.

I was the eldest son of a country parson whose income from all sources seldom exceeded £250 per annum. My brothers and myself were therefore schooled from the first to realize that our education, if any, would depend mainly on our own efforts.

There was musical talent on both sides of the family, and my parents early discovered that I had inherited a voice of more than average quality. I was accordingly sent at the age of ten to compete for admission to one of the best-known choir schools in the country. I proved successful, and thus began in a sense to earn my livelihood at a time when most children are barely out of the nursery.

The fees for boys enrolled as choristers in this school were purely nominal, keep and education being provided in return for services rendered. The education, both musical and general, was excellent, but the regime exacting and the food scanty. Cathedral services, with long hours of rehearsal, made inroads upon the working day, and in consequence the time devoted to general education was comparatively short. But lack of time was balanced by intensity of study.

The headmaster, a pronounced neurotic, had a wonderful record of success with his pupils. But his methods were frankly those of a slave-driver, and his ideas of discipline stern to the point of brutality. In these enlightened days they would assuredly have involved him in police-court proceedings. The cane, no doubt, is at times a necessary instrument for the control of youthful spirits. But this ill-balanced pedagogue went further. It was an uneventful day when one or other of us did not go to bed with knuckles bruised by pencil-raps and ears sore from repeated pulling.

Such petty physical inflictions were varied by a sort of solitary confinement during which the offender was cut off from all association with his schoolfellows. All participation in conversation, games and recreations, and even in class-work was forbidden to such 'disgusting little cads'. At times I myself spent day after day standing in a corner during school hours or pacing an unfrequented section of the playing-field when games were in progress.

This inhuman regime, in addition to overwork and underfeeding, frequently proved too great a strain for growing children. My own constitution was none too robust, and at the end of my third year in the school my heart and nervous system were found to be severely strained. On medical advice I was removed by my parents and given six months' holiday.

'Warmark', 'Guilty but Insane': A Broadmoor Autobiography (1931)

=

Freud's hysterical female patients sometimes complained of child-hood sexual abuse by a male relative, usually their father. Freud regarded these tales as wish-fulfilling fantasies on the part of the patients and discounted them. More recently psychiatrists have been listening with a more sympathetic ear.

'Did you ever discuss with anyone in the family what your father had done?'

'My father always denied the whole thing. He would say I'd dreamed it up. When I was grown up I asked Mallory, my older sister, if daddy ever tried to fool with her. She said no. I told her about the rape. She believed me.

'I've wondered why he'd chosen me to attack rather than Mallory. At the time of the rape she was fifteen, well-developed, and beautiful; she'd won beauty contests at school. Maybe it was because I was weaker and easier to overcome. I know now I'd done nothing to make him act that way, and there was no way I could have prevented what happened. But still it hurts. I felt singled out; I don't like that.'

'He never tried anything later on with your sister who was born that day?'

'He did. Mallory told me that once, when Jane was about twelve – he was drunk – he threw her down on the sofa and asked her to give him a little. She ran away to Mallory's house. He ran after her, but he couldn't get her.'

Her tale was now raising several issues in my mind that I would continue to consider after the end of the session. Could I be certain that the father's attack upon Ruth had really occurred? I wanted to know if she could tell the difference between something actually seen, heard, or felt and something imagined or dreamed.

I felt sure that such events as she had described do happen; besides having read about them I had been told about them in my office by mothers and fathers, as well as by daughters. Ruth's father's later attempt at sexual relations with Jane was compatible with his sexual attack upon Ruth. I recalled Sigmund Freud's views about his patients' stories of having been sexually seduced and assaulted in childhood. He had become convinced that his patients' stories were fantasies, and that the seductions and assaults had never actually happened; he believed his patients had invented stories of others' sexual interest in themselves to fend off memories of their own childhood erotic feelings. A problem with Freud's position, I recognized, is that although he had ascribed an interesting motive to his patients for inventing their stories, he had furnished no evidence that the stories were actually inventions. I also reasoned that even if one supposed Freud to be correct about his own patients' stories, one could not thereby assume such stories from other patients to be fantasies. There are many reported experiences that one cannot be certain correspond to actual events. People can lie and can also deceive themselves. It is helpful to have access to an independent source of evidence such as either a written record dating from near the time of the declared happening, or someone else's testimony. In Ruth's case there was nothing in writing, and the only avowed witness to the event besides her was the father, who had had no reason to corroborate her narrative and much reason to deny it. I trusted Ruth's story, since I felt no reason not to. Had she made up her tale, I thought, she would have to have also concocted the bleeding, the pain, the bruises, and her mother having seen the bruises, and her father having acknowledged them.

Morton Schatzman, *The Story of Ruth:
One Woman's Haunting Psychiatric Odyssey* (1980)

Otherworldly forces – God or the Devil – have seen stout service as the sources of mental derangement. Here John Perceval (see page 23) explains to his brother, Spencer, the Providential cause of his insanity.

The cause of my madness, Spencer, is this: That all things about me do appear to me so beautiful and so lovely, through the Holy Spirit, which is upon me and in me, and through me unto them, and in them or upon them and through them unto me, that I do not know how to behave myself to any thing about me as I should do, in a reasonable manner: and I have an inward tormentor and an outward tormentor, harassing and tormenting, reproving me for (being a hypocrite) hypocritizing before them; for loving them too much, and not reproving them in spirit, or in word, or in demeanour; and at the same time accusing me, and taunting me, and ridiculing me, and agonizing me in a worse manner, for being uncharitable in all my attempts to reason in any way so as to come to any conclusion whatever, with regard to their real worth, merit, or actual spiritual state. Moreover, in attempting to do a duty of any kind, I am immediately assailed with doubts and fears and scruples, and anxiety of heart and mind, and body too at times; so that my nature, or a hypocritical fear upon me, makes me find that my nature shrinks from doing it. At the same time I feel it right, and that it must be done; and I can have no peace of mind, or heart, or conscience, unless it is done; at the same time, in doing it, I load my heart and conscience with agonies of mind and spirit. Even as I was writing to you my eyeballs seemed seared, and knives to be in my eyes. I will explain to you the reason of this. Spencer, you might have saved me from much of my agony on board-ship, and on my miserable, melancholy, horrible, agonizing bed, in Dublin and Bristol. You do not know what insanity is; but you are a spiritual man; and you should have weighed every thought, every word, every motion, every feature, and expression of my features, in Dublin. All I remember of you is, that your conduct was most affectionate towards me; but you could have done more for me; for you believed the miraculous power of God Almighty to preserve his elect.

John T. Perceval, *A Narrative of the Treatment Received by a Gentleman, During a State of Mental Derangement* (1838/40)

Moon-mad. In many cultures, the moon has been seen to be associ-
ated with madness, and the full moon to induce 'lunacy'. Such
astrological notions had largely been dismissed in elite circles by the
eighteenth century, but continued to have a popular circulation.

Dr Forbes Winslow, in his attractive work on 'Light: its Influence
on Life and Health,' quotes several old writers who maintain, and
some of the facts that may have given a colour of truth to, the
long-accepted theory that insane persons were directly affected by
the lunar beam, and 'liable to periods of lucidity or mental repose,
caused by the various phases of the moon'. Towards the conclusion
of his argument, Dr Winslow observes: 'It is impossible altogether
to ignore the evidence of such men as Pinel, Daquin, Guislain, and
others, yet the experience of modern psychological physicians is to
a great degree opposed to the deductions of these eminent men. Is it
not probable that there is some degree of truth on both sides of the
question: in other words, that the alleged changes observed among
the insane at certain phases of the moon may arise, not from the
direct, but the indirect influence of the planet? It is well known that
certain important and easily recognizable meteorological phenomena result from the varied positions of the moon; that the rarity of
the air, the electric conditions of the atmosphere, the degree of heat,
dryness, moisture, and amount of wind prevailing, are all more or
less modified by the state of the moon. In the generality of bodily
diseases, what obvious changes are observed to accompany the
meterological conditions referred to? Surely those suffering from
diseases of the brain and nervous system affecting the mind cannot,
with any show of reason, be considered as exempt from the operation of agencies that are universally admitted to affect patients
afflicted with other maladies. That the insane do appear to a degree
unusually agitated at the full of the moon, particularly if its bright
light is permitted uninterruptedly to enter the room where they
sleep, there cannot be a doubt. This phenomena may, I think, be
accounted for apart altogether from the hypothesis of there being
anything specific in the composition of the lunar ray.' Dr Winslow
adds, in a note, 'An intelligent lady, who occupied for about five
years the position of matron in my establishment for insane ladies,
has remarked that she invariably observed a great agitation among

the patients when the moon was at its full.' 'Such,' he adds, 'has been the prevalence of this opinion that when patients were brought in former times to Bethlem Hospital, especially from the country, their friends have generally stated them to be worse at some particular change in the moon, and of the necessity they were under, at those times, of having recourse to coercion. Some of these patients, after recovering, have stated that the overseer or master of the workhouse himself has frequently been so much under the dominion of this planet, that, without waiting for any display of increased turbulence on the part of the lunatics, he has barbarously bound, chained, flogged, and deprived them of food, according as he discovered the moon's age by the almanac.'

John Timbs, *Doctors and Patients* (1876)

prudent

[3]

The Black Dog

Disorders such as schizophrenia and mania may excite greater terror, but no terms have been of wider significance in close encounters with mental afflictions than 'melancholy' and its modern brood, like neurosis and anxiety. The reasons are plain. While few go in daily dread of suffering a first-order psychosis, many of us can expect at some time in our lives to be crushed by what used to be called 'lowness of spirits' or the 'vapours' – conditions whose current analogues might range from being 'blue' or 'down', to authentic clinical depression or the classic 'nervous breakdown'.

Such conditions carry rather ambiguous implications. Depression can be a burden almost impossible to bear, jeopardizing our personal sense of worth and standing in the community. It's often on the slippery slope to suicide.

Yet there may be another side, something bitter-sweet to be savoured in a wistful, contemplative sorrow. Given man's mortality and the mutability of things, given the dog-eats-dog ferocity of Machiavellian politics – so argued Robert Burton in his positively obsessional anatomizing of melancholy – one would have to be a great oaf not to meet life's changes and chances with sober sadness. In the guise of a 'melancholy fool', Jaques in *As You Like It* could philosophically forearm himself against outrageous fortune.

Thus fortified, the melancholic liked to think of himself as a rather superior being. In the theorizings of Aristotle, 'melancholy' was the temperament of the artist or poet (see Section 18, below): it accounted for his being so 'difficult' – restless, touchy, a loner – but also for his creative genius, his individual register. Moreover, from the Renaissance courtier onwards, a certain distance or disdain – eccentricity, even – was regarded as the escutcheon of gentility and good breeding. Still later, in the age of sensibility, top people were expected to betray, or even cultivate, some delicate nervous traits, or to be a bit 'hippish' – high society made one highly strung. And on both sides of the Atlantic, eminent Victorians positively revelled in hypochondria (mainly a male condition), hysteria (strictly for the ladies), and the 'blue devils' (a form of dyspepsia, validating invalidism). By 1900, it was fashionable to be 'neurasthenic'. Today, in very superior modern circles, especially in Manhattan, one risks losing caste without an eligible shrink, with whom one should preferably be engaged in 'analysis interminable'.

Over the centuries, depression has provided a language for interpreting and responding to life's problems: to isolation, or the intolerable pressures of business; to nonentity, or fame; to poverty, or the embarrassment of riches; to illness, or intimations of mortality. James Boswell, who penned a newspaper column under the pen-name 'The Hypochondriack', suggested that it was the done thing amongst the *beau monde* to develop depression, because its sufferings were hallmarks of a beautiful soul, proofs of superior sensibility. (Samuel Johnson, far more vulnerable to genuine depression – 'the black dog' was his own phrase for the mood which frequently overwhelmed him – called Boswell a silly ass for flirting with such dangerous nonsense.)

Delicately poised between normalcy and severe mental illness, the neurotic or depressive has been regaled with a rich repertoire of treatments, ranging from commonsensical attempts to instil gaiety – with music, philosophy, company, and activity ('Be not solitary, be not idle', was Burton's parting advice) – to the elaborate rituals of the most lavish and long-running remedy ever devised for a mental malady, Freudian psychoanalysis. Neurotics, the cynic might say, have been accorded such attention because they are, in all senses, a uniquely rewarding group of patients.

No, no, go not to Lethe, neither twist
  Wolf's-bane, tight-rooted, for its poisonous wine;
Nor suffer thy pale forehead to be kissed
  By nightshade, ruby grape of Proserpine;

Make not your rosary of yew-berries,
　　Nor let the beetle, nor the death-moth be
　　　Your mournful Psyche, nor the downy owl
A partner in your sorrow's mysteries;
　　For shade to shade will come too drowsily,
　　　And drown the wakeful anguish of the soul.

But when the melancholy fit shall fall
　　Sudden from heaven like a weeping cloud,
That fosters the droop-headed flowers all,
　　And hides the green hill in an April shroud;
Then glut thy sorrow on a morning rose,
　　Or on the rainbow of the salt sand-wave,
　　　Or on the wealth of globèd peonies;
Or if thy mistress some rich anger shows,
　　Imprison her soft hand, and let her rave,
　　　And feed deep, deep upon her peerless eyes.

She dwells with beauty – Beauty that must die;
　　And Joy, whose hand is ever at his lips
Bidding adieu; and aching Pleasure nigh,
　　Turning to poison while the bee-mouth sips.
Aye, in the very temple of Delight
　　Veiled Melancholy has her sovran shrine,
　　　Though seen of none save him whose strenuous tongue
　　Can burst Joy's grape against his palate fine;
His soul shall taste the sadness of her might,
　　And be among her cloudy trophies hung.
　　　　　　　　John Keats, 'Ode on Melancholy' (1819)

=

The teachings of Ancient Greek medicine, which retained their hold through the Middle Ages and the Renaissance, saw depression as due to a superfluity of the humour 'black bile', thus accounting for the black looks and black moods of the sufferer.

Melancholy is a humour, boystous & thycke, and is bredde of troubled drastes of blode: & hath his name of melon – that is black, & colim, that is humor: wherupon it is called melancolia, as it

were a black humor: & so phisiciens cal it colera nigra coler black:
For the colour therof declineth toward blackness. Some melancoli is
kindly & som unkindly . . .

Of this humour havying maistry in any body, these ben the
sygnes and tokens. Fyrste the colour of the skynne chaungeth into
blacke or bloo: Soure savour, sharpe – and erthy is felte in the
mouth. By the qualite of the humour the pacient is feynte – and
fereful in hert without cause. And so all, that have this passion, are
ferefull without cause, & oft sory. And that is through the melancoli humor that constreineth & closeth the herte. And so if we aske
of suche hevy folkes – what they fere, or wherfore they ben sory –
they have none answere. Some wene that they shoulde dey anone
unreasonably: Some drede enmyte of some man: Some love and
desyre dethe. Wherfore in libro Passionum Galen sayth It is no
wondre, though they that suffer coleram nigram be very sorye, and
have suspeccion of dethe. For no thynge is more dredeful outwarde
in the bodye than derkenesse. And so when any derke thyng heeleth
the brayne – as melancoly flewme – the pacyent muste nedes drede.
For he bearethe with hym the cause why he shulde drede. And
therfore he dreameth dreadefull darke dreames – and verye yll to
see – and of stynkynge savour and smelle. Of which is bredde
passio melancolia.

Bartholomaeus Anglicus, *De Proprietatibus Rerum* (1535)

=

Burton's Anatomy of Melancholy *(see page 13) carried a Frontispiece keyed into an accompanying versified Argument, illustrating
the modalities of melancholy – the hypochondriac, the lover, the
religious enthusiast, and so forth – with the self-preoccupied author
at the centre.*

THE ARGUMENT OF THE FRONTISPIECE

TEN distinct Squares here seen apart.
Are joined in one by Cutter's art.

I

Old *Democritus* under a tree,
Sits on a stone with book on knee;
About him hang there many features,
Of Cats, Dogs, and such like creatures,
Of which he makes Anatomy,
The seat of Black Choler to see.
Over his head appears the sky,
And Saturn, Lord of Melancholy.

II

To th' left a landscape of *Jealousy*,
Presents itself unto thine eye.
A Kingfisher, a Swan, an Hern,
Two fighting-Cocks you may discern;
Two roaring Bulls each other hie,
To assault concerning Venery.
Symbols are these; I say no more,
Conceive the rest by that's afore.

III

The next of *Solitariness*
A portraiture doth well express,
By sleeping Dog, Cat: Buck and Doe,
Hares, Conies in the desart go:
Bats, Owls the shady bowers over,
In melancholy darkness hover.
Mark well: If't be not as't should be,
Blame the bad Cutter, and not me.

IV

I' th' under Column there doth stand
Inamorato with folded hand;
Down hangs his head, terse and polite,
Some ditty sure he doth indite.
His lute and books about him lie,
As symptoms of his vanity.
If this do not enough disclose,
To paint him, take thyself by th' nose.

V

Hypochondriacus leans on his arm,
Wind in his side doth him much harm,
And troubles him full sore, God knows,
Much pain he hath and many woes.
About him pots and glasses lie,
Newly brought from's Apothecary.
This Saturn's aspects signify,
You see them portray'd in the sky.

VI

Beneath them kneeling on his knee,
A *Superstitious* man you see:
He fasts, prays, on his Idol fixt,
Tormented hope and fear betwixt:
For hell perhaps he takes more pain,
Than thou dost heaven itself to gain.
Alas poor Soul, I pity thee,
What stars incline thee so to be?

VII

But see the *Madman* rage down right
With furious looks, a ghastly sight.
Naked in chains bound doth he lie,
And roars amain he knows not why!
Observe him; for as in a glass,
Thine angry portraiture it was.
His picture keeps still in thy presence;
'Twixt him and thee, there's no difference.

VIII–IX

Borage and *Hellebore* fill two scenes,
Sovereign plants to purge the veins
Of Melancholy, and cheer the heart,
Of those black fumes which make it smart;
To clear the Brain of misty fogs,
Which dull our senses, and Soul clogs.
The best medicine that e'er God made
For this malady, if well assay'd.

X

Now last of all to fill a place,
Presented is the *Author's* face;
And in that habit which he wears,
His image to the world appears.
His mind no art can well express,
That by his writings you may guess.
It was not pride, nor yet vain glory,
(Though others do it commonly,)
Made him do this: if you must know,
The Printer would needs have it so.

Then do not frown or scoff at it,
Deride not, or detract a whit.
For surely as thou dost by him,
He will do the same again.
Then look upon't, behold and see,
As thou like'st it, so it likes thee.
And I for it will stand in view,
Thine to command, Reader, Adieu!

> Robert Burton, *The Anatomy of Melancholy* (1621)

=

Debts, chronic physical illness, and domestic troubles led Scotland's national poet to address Alexander Cunningham with self-pitying Shakespearian echo.

Canst thou minister to a mind diseased? Canst thou speak peace and rest to a soul tost on a sea of troubles without one friendly star to guide her course, and dreading that the next surge may overwhelm her? Canst thou give to a frame, trembling alive as the tortures of suspense, the stability and hardihood of the rock that braves the blast? If thou canst not do the least of these, why wouldst thou disturb me in my miseries with thy inquiries after me?

*

For these two months I have not been able to lift a pen. My constitution and frame were, *ab origine*, blasted with a deep incurable taint of hypochondria, which poisons my existence. Of late a number of domestic vexations, and some pecuniary share in the ruin of these ***** times; losses which, though trifling, were yet what I could ill bear, have so irritated me, that my feelings at time could only be envied by a reprobate spirit listening to the sentence that dooms it to perdition.

Are you deep in the language of consolation? I have exhausted in reflection every topic of comfort. *A heart at ease* would have been charmed with my sentiments and reasonings; but as to myself, I was like Judas Iscariot preaching the gospel; he might melt and mould the hearts of those around him, but his own kept its native incorrigibility.

Still there are two great pillars that bear us up, amid the wreck of misfortune and misery. The ONE is composed of the different modifications of a certain noble, stubborn something in man, known by the names of courage, fortitude, magnanimity. The OTHER is made up of those feelings and sentiments, which, however the sceptic may deny them, or the enthusiastic disfigure them, are yet, I am convinced, original and component parts of the human soul; those *senses of the mind*, if I may be allowed the expression, which connect us with and link us to, those awful obscure realities – an all-powerful and equally beneficent God; and a world to come, beyond death and the grave. The first gives the nerve of combat, while a ray of hope beams on the field: – the last pours the balm of comfort into the wounds which time can never cure.

Robert Burns, letter to Alexander Cunningham (25 February 1794)

==

David Hume describes his nervous collapse in his late teens to Dr George Cheyne (see page 195). It is interesting to speculate how far the youthful nervous breakdown suffered by the great Scottish philosopher contributed to his later doctrines of philosophical and psychological scepticism and his doubts about the stability of individual identity.

You must know then that from my earliest Infancy, I found alwise a strong Inclination to Books & Letters. As our College Education in Scotland, extending little further than the Languages, ends commonly when we are about 14 or 15 Years of Age, I was after that

left to my own Choice in my Reading, & found it encline me almost
equally to Books of Reasoning & Philosophy, & to Poetry & the
polite Authors. Every one, who is acquainted either with the
Philosophers or Critics, knows that there is nothing yet establisht in
either of these two Sciences, & that they contain little more than
endless Disputes, even in the most fundamental Articles. Upon
Examination of these, I found a certain Boldness of Temper,
growing in me, which was not enclin'd to submit to any Authority
in these Subjects, but led me to seek out some new Medium, by
which Truth might be establisht. After much Study, & Reflection
on this, at last, when I was about 18 Years of Age, there seem'd to
be open'd up to me a new Scene of Thought, which transported me
beyond Measure, & made me, with an Ardor natural to young
men, throw up every other Pleasure or Business to apply entirely to
it. The Law, which was the Business I design'd to follow, appear'd
nauseous to me, & I cou'd think of no other way of pushing my
Fortune in the World, but that of a Scholar & Philosopher. I was
infinitely happy in this Course of Life for some Months; till at last,
about the beginning of Septr 1729, all my Ardor seem'd in a
moment to be extinguisht, & I cou'd no longer raise my Mind to
that pitch, which formerly gave me such excessive Pleasure. I felt no
Uneasyness or Want of Spirits, when I laid aside my Book; &
therefore never imagind there was any bodily Distemper in the
Case, but that my Coldness proceeded from a Laziness of Temper,
which must be overcome by redoubling my Application. In this
Condition I remain'd for nine Months, very uneasy to myself, as
you may well imagine, but without growing any worse, which was
a Miracle.

There was another particular, which contributed more than any
thing, to waste my Spirits & bring on me this Distemper, which
was, that having read many Books of Morality, such as Cicero,
Seneca & Plutarch, & being smit with their beautiful Represent-
ations of Virtue & Philosophy, I undertook the Improvement of my
Temper & Will, along with my Reason & Understanding. I was
continually fortifying myself with Reflections against Death, &
Poverty, & Shame, & Pain, & all the other Calamities of Life.
These no doubt are exceeding useful, when join'd with an active
Life; because the Occasion being presented along with the

Reflection, works it into the Soul, & makes it take a deep Impression, but in Solitude they serve to little other Purpose, than to waste the Spirits, the Force of the Mind meeting with no Resistance, but wasting itself in the Air, like our Arm when it misses its Aim. This however I did not learn but by Experience, & till I had already ruin'd my Health, tho' I was not sensible of it.

Some Scurvy Spots broke out on my Fingers, the first Winter I fell ill, about which I consulted a very knowing Physician, who gave me some Medicines, that remov'd these Symptoms, & at the same time gave me a Warning against the Vapors, which, tho I was laboring under at that time, I fancy'd myself so far remov'd from, & indeed from any other Disease, except a slight Scurvy, that I despis'd his Warning. At last about Aprile 1730, when I was 19 Years of Age, a Symptom, which I had notic'd a little from the beginning, encreas'd considerably, so that tho' it was no Uneasyness, the Novelty of it made me ask Advice. It was what they call a Ptyalism or Watryness in the mouth. Upon my mentioning it to my Physician, he laught at me, & told me I was now a Brother, for that I had fairly got the Disease of the Learned. Of this he found great Difficulty to perswade me, finding in myself nothing of that lowness of Spirit, which those, who labor under that Distemper so much complain of. However upon his Advice, I went under a Course of Bitters, & Anti-hysteric Pills. Drunk an English Pint of Claret Wine every Day, & rode 8 or 10 Scotch Miles. This I continu'd for about 7 Months after.

Tho I was sorry to find myself engag'd with so tedious a Distemper yet the Knowledge of it, set me very much at ease, by satisfying me that my former Coldness, proceeded not from any Defect of Temper or Genius, but from a Disease, to which any one may be subject. I now began to take some Indulgence to myself; studied moderately, & only when I found my Spirits at their highest Pitch, leaving off before I was weary, & trifling away the rest of my Time in the best manner I could. In this way, I liv'd with Satisfaction enough; and on my return to Town next Winter found my Spirits very much recruited, so that, tho they sunk under me in the higher Flights of Genius, yet I was able to make considerable Progress in my former Designs. I was very regular in my Diet & way of Life from the beginning, & all that Winter, made it a constant Rule to ride twice or thrice a week, & walk every day. For these Reasons, I expected when I return'd to the Countrey, & cou'd renew my Exercise with less Interruption, that I wou'd perfectly recover. But in this I was much mistaken. For next Summer, about May 1731 there grew upon [me] a very ravenous Appetite, & as quick a Digestion, which I at first took for a good Symptom, & was very much surpriz'd to find it bring back a Palpitation of Heart, which I had felt very little of before. This Appetite, however, had an Effect very unusual, which was to nourish me extremely; so that in 6 weeks time I past from the one extreme to the other, & being before tall, lean, & raw-bon'd became on a sudden, the most sturdy, robust, healthful-like Fellow you have seen, with a ruddy Complexion & a chearful Countenance. In excuse for my Riding, & care of my Health, I alwise said, that I was afraid of a Consumption; which was readily believ'd from my Looks; but now every Body congratulate me upon my thorow Recovery. This unnatural Appetite wore off by degrees, but left me as a Legacy, the same Palpitation of the heart in a small degree, & a good deal of Wind in my Stomach, which comes away easily, & without any bad Goût, as is ordinary. However, these Symptoms are little or no Uneasyness to me. I eat well; I sleep well. Have no lowness of Spirits; at least never more than what one of the best Health may feel, from too full a meal, from sitting too near a Fire, & even that degree I feel very seldom, & never almost in the Morning or Forenoon. Those who live in the same Family with me, & see me at all times, cannot observe the least Alteration in my Humor, & rather think me a better Companion than I was before, as choosing to pass more of my time with them. This gave me such Hopes, that I scarce ever mist a days riding, except in the Winter-time; & last Summer undertook a very laborious task, which was to travel 8 Miles every Morning & as many in the Forenoon, to & from a mineral Well of some Reputation. I renew'd the Bitters & Anti-hysteric Pills twice, along with Anti-scorbutic Juices last Spring, but without any considerable Effect, except abating the Symptoms for a little time.

Thus I have given you a full account of the Condition of my Body, & without staying to ask Pardon, as I ought to do, for so tedious a Story, shall explain to you how my Mind stood all this time, which on every Occasion, especially in this Distemper, have a very near Connexion together. Having now Time & Leizure to cool my inflam'd Imaginations, I began to consider seriously, how I shou'd proceed in my Philosophical Enquiries. I found that the moral Philosophy transmitted to us by Antiquity, labor'd under the same Inconvenience that has been found in their natural Philosophy, of being entirely Hypothetical, & depending more upon Invention than Experience. Every one consulted his Fancy in erecting Schemes of Virtue & of Happiness, without regarding human Nature, upon which every moral Conclusion must depend. This therefore I resolved to make my principal Study, & the Source from which I wou'd derive every Truth in Criticism as well as Morality. I believe 'tis a certain Fact that most of the Philosophers who have gone before us, have been overthrown by the Greatness of their Genius, & that little more is requir'd to make a man succeed in this Study than to throw off all Prejudices either for his own Opinions or for this of others. At least this is all I have to depend on for the Truth of my Reasonings, which I have multiply'd to such a degree, that within these Years, I find I have scribled many a Quire of Paper, in which there is nothing contain'd but my own Inventions. This with the Reading most of the celebrated Books in Latin, French & English, & acquiring the Italian, you may think a sufficient Business for one in perfect Health; & so it wou'd, had it been done to any Purpose: But my Disease was a cruel Incumbrance on me. I found that I was not able to follow out any Train of Thought, by one continued Stretch of View, but by repeated Interruptions, & by refreshing my Eye from Time to Time upon other Objects. Yet with this Inconvenience I have collected the rude Materials for many Volumes; but in reducing these to Words, when one must bring the Idea he comprehended in gross, nearer to him, so as to contemplate its minutest Parts, & keep it steddily in his Eye, so as to copy these Parts in Order, this I found impracticable for me, nor were my Spirits equal to so severe an Employment. Here lay my greatest Calamity. I had no Hopes of delivering my Opinions with such Elegance & Neatness, as to draw to me the Attention of the World, & I wou'd rather live & dye in Obscurity than produce them maim'd & imperfect.

Such a miserable Disappointment I scarce ever remember to have heard of. The small Distance betwixt me & perfect Health makes me the more uneasy in my present Situation. Tis a Weakness rather than a Lowness of Spirits which troubles me, & there seems to be as great a Difference betwixt my Distemper & common Vapors, as betwixt Vapors & Madness.

I have notic'd in the Writings of the French Mysticks, & in those of our Fanatics here, that, when they give a History of the Situation of their Souls, they mention a Coldness & Desertion of the Spirit, which frequently returns, & some of them, at the beginning, have been tormented with it many Years. As this kind of Devotion depends entirely on the Force of Passion, & consequently of the Animal Spirits, I have often thought that their Case & mine were pretty parralel, & that their rapturous Admirations might discompose the Fabric of the Nerves & Brain, as much as profound Reflections, & that warmth or Enthusiasm which is inseperable from them.

However this may be, I have not come out of the Cloud so well as they commonly tell us they have done, or rather began to despair of ever recovering. To keep myself from being Melancholy on so dismal a Prospect, my only Security was in peevish Reflections on the Vanity of the World & of all humane Glory; which, however just Sentiments they may be esteem'd, I have found can never be sincere, except in those who are possest of them. Being sensible that all my Philosophy wou'd never make me contented in my present Situation, I began to rouze up myself; & being encourag'd by Instances of Recovery from worse degrees of this Distemper, as well as by the Assurances of my Physicians, I began to think of something more effectual, than I had hitherto try'd. I found, that as there are two things very bad for this Distemper, Study & Idleness, so there are two things very good, Business & Diversion; & that my whole Time was spent betwixt the bad, with little or no Share of the Good. For this reason I resolved to seek out a more active Life, & tho' I cou'd not quit my Pretensions in Learning, but with my last Breath, to lay them aside for some time, in order the more effectually to resume them.

Upon Examination I found my Choice confin'd to two kinds of Life; that of a travelling Governor & that of a Merchant. The first, besides that it is in some respects an idle Life, was, I found, unfit for me; & that because from a sedentary & retir'd way of living, from a

bashful Temper, & from a narrow Fortune, I had been little accus-
tom'd to general Companies, & had not Confidence & Knowledge
enough of the World to push my Fortune or be serviceable in that
way. I therefore fixt my Choice upon a Merchant; & having got
Recommendation to a considerable Trader in Bristol. I am just now
hastening thither, with a Resolution to forget myself, & every thing
that is past, to engage myself, as far as is possible, in that Course of
Life, & to toss about the World, from the one Pole to the other, till I
leave this Distemper behind me.

As I am come to London in my way to Bristol, I have resolved, if
possible, to get your Advice, tho' I shou'd take this absurd Method
of procuring it. All the Physicians, I have consulted, tho' very able,
cou'd never enter into my Distemper; because not being Persons of
great Learning beyond their own Profession, they were unacquainted with these Motions of the Mind. Your Fame pointed you out as
the properest Person to resolve my Doubts, & I was determin'd to
have some bodies Opinion, which I cou'd rest upon in all the
Varieties of Fears & Hopes, incident to so lingering a Distemper. I
hope I have been particular enough in describing the Symptoms to
allow you to form a Judgement; or rather perhaps have been too
particular. But you know 'tis a Symptom of this Distemper to
delight in complaining & talking of itself.

The Questions I wou'd humbly propose to you are: Whether
among all these Scholars, you have been acquainted with, you have
ever known any affected in this manner? Whether I can ever hope
for a Recovery? Whether I must long wait for it? Whether my
Recovery will ever be perfect, & my Spirits regain their former
Spring & Vigor, so as to endure the Fatigue of deep & abstruse
thinking? Whether I have taken a right way to recover? I believe all
proper medicines have been us'd, & therefore I need mention
nothing of them.

David Hume, letter to Dr George Cheyne (1734)

Brought up in the early nineteenth century by his utilitarian father
in an ethic of strict rational calculation, John Stuart Mill suffers a
nervous breakdown the moment he allows his feelings to intrude.

It was in the autumn of 1826. I was in a dull state of nerves, such as
everybody is occasionally liable to; unsusceptible to enjoyment or
pleasurable excitement; one of those moods when what is pleasure
at other times, becomes insipid or indifferent; the state, I should
think, in which converts to Methodism usually are, when smitten
by their first 'conviction of sin'. In this frame of mind it occurred to
me to put the question directly to myself, 'Suppose that all your
objects in life were realized; that all the changes in institutions and
opinions which you are looking forward to, could be completely
effected at this very instant: would this be a great joy and happiness
to you?' And an irrepressible self-consciousness distinctly
answered, 'No!' At this my heart sank within me: the whole foundation on which my life was constructed fell down. All my happiness was to have been found in the continual pursuit of this end.
The end had ceased to charm, and how could there ever again be
any interest in the means? I seemed to have nothing left to live for.
    At first I hoped that the cloud would pass away of itself; but it
did not. A night's sleep, the sovereign remedy for the smaller
vexations of life, had no effect on it. I awoke to a renewed consciousness of the woful fact. I carried it with me into all companies,
into all occupations. Hardly anything had power to cause me even a
few minutes oblivion of it. For some months the cloud seemed to
grow thicker and thicker. The lines in Coleridge's 'Dejection' – I
was not then acquainted with them – exactly describe my case:

> A grief without a pang, void, dark and drear,
> A drowsy, stifled, unimpassioned grief,
> Which, finds no natural outlet or relief
> In word, or sigh, or tear.

In vain I sought relief from my favourite books; those memorials of
past nobleness and greatness, from which I had always hitherto
drawn strength and animation. I read them now without feeling, or
with the accustomed feeling *minus* all its charm; and I became
persuaded, that my love of mankind, and of excellence for its own

sake, had worn itself out. I sought no comfort by speaking to others of what I felt. If I had loved any one sufficiently to make confiding my griefs a necessity, I should not have been in the condition I was. I felt, too, that mine was not an interesting, or in any way respectable distress. There was nothing in it to attract sympathy. Advice, if I had known where to seek it, would have been most precious. The words of Macbeth to the physician often occurred to my thoughts.* But there was no one on whom I could build the faintest hope of such assistance. My father, to whom it would have been natural to me to have recourse in any practical difficulties, was the last person to whom, in such a case as this, I looked for help. Everything convinced me that he had no knowledge of any such mental state as I was suffering from, and that even if he could be made to understand it, he was not the physician who could heal it.

*MACBETH: Cure her of that,
   Canst thou not minister to a mind diseas'd,
   Pluck from the memory a rooted sorrow,
   Raze out the written troubles of the brain,
   And with some sweet oblivious antidote
   Cleanse the stuffed bosom of that perilous stuff
   Which weighs upon the heart?
DOCTOR: Therein the patient
   Must minister to himself.

John Stuart Mill, *Autobiography* (c.1853)

=

Depression is melancholy minus its charms.

Susan Sontag

=

The psychological costs of fast-lane living, as experienced by an American film-maker

What *are* you frightened of? What was it? I was going to a shrink once a week and still the anxiety increased. Why didn't Dr Allen help me? Dammit, I'd been seeing him religiously for ten years, ever since about the time I left my husband. It was a routine, like brushing my teeth, a normal part of my life, as it was for most of the people I knew. He gave me Valium and I was taking it by the handful. So why was the terror growing? I must talk to him, must get more pills, must do something.

Somehow the anxiety decreased when I reached Steve's editing room and saw him smiling at me. I was safe. He handed me the clip I would show at the luncheon.

'I hate this awards thing. It takes time away from us,' I said. 'But when I get back, we'll make magic for Mr O'Connor.'

'Don't pout, Barb. We're in good shape. You're just in a bitchy mood because you have to go out for lunch.' It had become a joke between us. Only a few people knew the reason I preferred Rocko's sandwiches to '21.'

'I know you,' he said as he hugged me goodbye. 'Now get out of here and be wonderful.'

I decided to walk to '21,' but I had taken only a few steps east on Fifty-seventh Street when the terror began again. My hands became drenched in perspiration. I held on to the sides of the buildings for support and struggled to catch my breath. My God, if anyone saw me, he would think I was drunk. I made it to Tenth Avenue and went into a grimy diner filled with the truckdrivers who claimed Fifty-seventh Street as their territory.

'Please,' I said to the harried waitress, 'I only want a glass of water.' I fumbled for the pills in my purse. 'I'll pay you. I won't take up your table at lunchtime. I'll pay you.' I closed my eyes and tried to catch my breath. How long have I been living like this?

The waitress set a glass of water on the table and I gulped it down with two Valium. I inhaled deeply as I waited for the anxiety to subside. In about ten minutes I felt better, or at least able to walk out of the diner. I hailed a cab and urged the driver to hurry. I was late. Be gracious, be cool. You're winning an award.

The private dining room at '21' was crammed with other winners, all beaming, all drinking white wine and chatting with animation. I tore into the room and began the social thing. And when it was time for my speech, I forgot my terror of just a few moments before. The pills, the wine, or maybe it was just being involved and not thinking about it.

Barbara Gordon, *I'm Dancing as Fast as I Can* (1981)

=

A sober sadness

> Hence, vain deluding joys,
> The brood of folly, without father bred,
> How little you bested,
> Or fill the fixed mind with all your toys!
> But hail, thou Goddess, sage and holy!
> Whose saintly visage is too bright,
> To hit the sense of human sight;
> Come, pensive Nun, devout and pure,
> Sober, stedfast, and demure,
> All in a robe of darkest grain,
> Flowing with majestic train,
> And sable stole of Cypruss lawn,
> Over thy decent shoulders drawn.
> Come, but keep thy wonted state,
> With even step and musing gait,
> And looks commercing with the skies,
> Thy rapt soul sitting in thine eyes;
> There held in holy passion still,
> Forget thyself to marble, till
> With a sad leaden downward cast,
> Thou fix them on the earth as fast.

John Milton, *Il Penseroso* (1632)

=

The magnificence of melancholy, imagined by Bryan Proctor, a leading Victorian Lunacy Commissioner and minor man of letters

> There is a mighty Spirit, known on earth
> By many names, tho' one alone becomes
> Its mystery, its beauty, and its power . . .
>
> But in the meditative mind it lives,
> Sheltered, caressed, and yields a great return;
> And in the deep silent communion
> Which it holds ever with the poet's soul,

Tempers, and doth befit him to obey
High inspiration ...

Grief may sublime itself, and pluck the sting
From out its breast, and muse until it seem
Etherial, starry. speculative, wise,
But then it is that Melancholy comes,
Out charming grief – (as the gray morning stills
The Tempest oft) and from its fretful fire
Draws a pale light, by which we see ourselves
The present, and the future, and the past.

Bryan Proctor, 'Melancholy', in *Dramatic Scenes and Other Poems*
(1857)

=

*Thomas Gray indulged a certain melancholy, seeing it as a kind of
negative capacity, conducive to poetic creativity.*

Mine, you are to know, is a white Melancholy, or rather *Leuco-choly* ... which though it seldom laughs or dances, nor ever
amounts to what one calls Joy or Pleasure, yet is a good easy sort of
a state, and *ça ne laisse que de s'amuser*. The only fault of it is
insipidity; which is apt now and then to give a sort of Ennui, which
makes one form certain little wishes that signify nothing. But there
is another sort, black indeed, which I have now and then felt, that
has something in it like Tertullian's rule of faith, *Credo quia
impossibile est*; for it believes, nay, is sure of everything that is
unlikely, so it be but frightful; and on the other hand excludes and
shuts its eyes to the most possible hopes, and everything that is
pleasurable; from this the Lord deliver us!

Thomas Gray, letter to Richard West (27 May 1742)

=

Here rests his head upon the lap of Earth
A Youth to Fortune and to Fame unknown.
Fair Science frown'd not on his humble birth,
And Melancholy mark'd him for her own.

Large was his bounty, and his soul sincere,
Heav'n did a recompence as largely send:
He gave to Mis'ry all he had, a tear,
He gain'd from Heav'n ('twas all he wish'd) a friend.

No farther seek his merits to disclose,
Or draw his frailties from their dread abode,
(There they alike in trembling hope repose,)
The bosom of his Father and his God.

Epitaph to Gray's 'Elegy Written in a Country Churchyard' (1750)

═

Gray's 'Elegy' was echoed by an asylum inmate paying tribute to his unsung fellow victims.

Beneath no rugged elms, no yew-tree's shade
Where heaves the turf in many a mouldering heap,
Each in his narrow cell for ever laid
The rude ones of the asylum sleep.

Oft did the harvest to their sickle yield;
Their furrow oft the stubborn glebe has broke;
How docile when they drove their team afield!
And bowed the woods beneath their sturdy stroke.

Perhaps in this neglected spot is laid
Some heart once pregnant with celestial fire;
Hands that the rod of empire might have sway'd,
Or waked to ecstasy the living lyre.

Even so, his bones from insult to protect,
No frail memorial is erected nigh,
No couth nor uncouth rhymes in sculpture decked,
Attract the notice of a passer-by.

On no one could this parting soul rely,
For pious drops as closing eyes require;
Ev'n from the tomb a voice 'Asylum' cries,
As now his body damps that cursed fire.

Worriedly, Mr X the maniac doth say:
'Oft did I see him at the peep of dawn
Rushing with short sharp steps a block away
To bring the coals across that darned old lawn.

'Why, there at the foot of yonder nodding beech
That wreathes its darned old twisted roots so high,
His ungainly length at siesta hour would stretch
Upon that seat the ruddy chief walks by.

'Hard by yon seat, and smiling as in scorn,
Muttering his wayward fancies, he would rove;
Now drooping, woeful-wan, like one forlorn,
Or crazed with hunger for the want of love.

'One day I missed him at his 'customed drill;
The block away, nor near his favourite tree;
Another came; nor yet with Paranoia Bill
Nor on his seat, nor at Male C. was he.'

And now, much under-due, they hurry away;
Quick through the backway path we see him borne;
Approach to read, you'll find there is no lay
Graved on a stone beneath an aged thorn.

THE EPITAPH

Here lies his head upon the lap of earth,
A man to fortune and to fame unknown;
'Cause psychiatry failed to prove its worth
Did melancholy keep him for her own.

Great was his madness, though his soul sincere;
Heaven did a recompense as largely send:
He spent on misery all he had – his tears,
But gained from Heaven all could he wish – a friend.

H. G. Woodley, *Certified* (1947)

=

Beset by self-fulfilling self-absorption, intellectuals often portrayed
themselves as particularly prey to vapours and black humours.

I own I had forgot it, tho' it is very *à propos*, and may serve likewise
to make us conceive more easily why the hypochondriack Passion
should be called the Disease of the Learned. But I'll proceed.

  Immoderate Grief, Cares, Troubles and Disappointments are
likewise often Concomitant Causes of this Disease; but most commonly in such, as either by Estate, Benefices, or Employments have
a sufficient Revenue to make themselves easie: Men that are already
provided for, or else have a Livelyhood by their Callings amply
secured, are never exempt from Sollicitudes, and the keeping not
only of Riches, but even moderate Possessions, is always attended
with Care.

B. Mandeville, *A Treatise of the Hypochondriack*
and Hysterick Diseases (1730)

==

Believing himself temperamentally ill-suited to the bustle of Town,
the poet William Cowper retired to the depths of the Buckingham-
shire countryside, only to be exposed to the taedium vitae *brought*
on by solitude.

> Look where he comes – in this embower'd alcove
> Stand close conceal'd, and see a statue move:
> Lips busy and eyes fixt, foot falling slow,
> Arms hanging idly down, hands clasp'd below,
> Interpret to the marking eye distress,
> Such as its symptoms can alone express.
> That tongue is silent now, that silent tongue
> Could argue once, could jest or join the song;
> Could give advice, could censure or commend,
> Or charm the sorrows of a drooping friend.
> Renounc'd alike its office and its sport,
> Its brisker and its graver strains fall short:
> Both fail beneath a fever's secret sway,
> And like a summer-brook are past away.
> This is a sight for pity to peruse,

Till she resemble faintly what she views;
Till sympathy contract a kindred pain
Pierc'd with the woes that she laments in vain.
This, of all the maladies that man infest,
Claims most compassion and receives the least. . . .
'Tis not, as heads that never ach suppose,
Forgery of fancy and a dream of woes:
Man is an harp, whose chords elude the sight,
Each yielding harmony dispos'd aright.
The screws revers'd (a task which if He please,
God in a moment executes with ease)
Ten thousand, thousand strings at once go loose,
Lost, till He tune them, all their power and use. . . .
No wounds like those a wounded spirit feels,
No cure for such, till God, who makes them, heals.

William Cowper, 'Retirement' (1782)

=

The superiority of hypochondria?

Why is it that all men who have excelled in philosophy, in politicks, in poetry, or in the arts, have been subject to melancholy?

Aristotle, whose profound investigation and variety of knowledge I always consider with wonder and reverence, appears to have admitted, the opinion that melancholy is the concomitant of distinguished genius; and indeed he illustrates the opinion with much philosophical ability, and many remarks upon real life, as it fell under his own observation, selecting at the same time renowned characters of antiquity, to whom melancholy was said to be constitutional.

We Hypochondriacks may be glad to accept of this compliment from so great a master of human nature, and to console ourselves in the hour of gloomy distress, by thinking that our sufferings mark our superiority. I may use the expression we Hypochondriacks, when addressing myself to my atrabilious brethren in general, and not be afraid of giving offence; though I should not chuse to do it to any particular person, as there might be some danger from irritable delicacy. Hypochondriacks themselves are not agreed that they have reason to be vain, or proud of their malady; and even if that were the case, it might not be quite safe to single one out.

James Boswell (see page 62), 'On Hypochondria' (1778)

=

The prophylactic hypochondria of one of Charles Darwin's Wedgwood nieces

She was always going to rest, in case she might be tired later on in the day, or even the next day . . . And when there were colds about she often wore a kind of gas-mask of her own invention. It was an ordinary wire kitchen strainer, stuffed with antiseptic cotton-wool, and tied on like a snout, with elastic over her ears. In this she would receive her visitors and discuss politics in a hollow voice out of her eucalyptus-scented seclusion.

B. and H. Wedgwood, *The Wedgwood Circle* (1980)

=

Around the turn of this century, a scare grew up about the so-called deterioration of the national stock, due to the growing numbers of so-called neurasthenics, neuropaths and other degenerates. Voluntary or compulsory eugenics was widely touted as the solution to the problem of the 'half-mads'. A doctor looks back.

Grievous as is the burden of insanity in these days, widespread as are the sorrow and anxiety attending it, I verily believe that the weight of the misery caused by the half-mads is heavier than that attributable to the genuine article. The out-and-out lunatic can be controlled and his injurious influence circumscribed, but the half-mad is practically unrestrained and free to go about broadcasting trouble and perplexity.

There is, I believe, scarcely a family in these days that does not include some psychopathic or neuropathic member, not certifiable, passing muster as a self-regulating human being, often as one who is injured and misunderstood, but who is more or less or from time to time abnormal, difficult, irritable, depressed, suspicious, capricious, eccentric, impulsive, unreasonable, cranky, deluded, and subject to all kinds of imaginary maladies and nervous agitations, thus diffusing discomfort and perturbation around.

The sound-minded members of the family come in time to realize the situation. They come to know that there is 'a twist' or 'a screw loose' as they phrase it, that it is not merely temper that is at fault, but some kind of cussedness associated with a constitutional taint or bad health.

But there is nothing to be done but to put up with it as best they may. The family doctor and ultimately a specialist is consulted, change of environment, of climate, of companionship are tried, rest in bed and rapid locomotion are alternated, and when bromides and aspirin and electricity and sunlight treatment have all failed, perhaps hypnotism or Christian science or psycho-analysis is invoked.

The nursing home is a refuge from time to time, and voluntary seclusion in a mental hospital, when they can be persuaded to adopt it, is a welcome relief. These half-mads are a public as well as a domestic nuisance, for fads and freaks have a special attraction for them, and I could name societies that derive a considerable support from people with judgments so ill-balanced as to be really mentally defective.

It must be a long wait, but Eugenism must do something toward the elimination of these half-mads.

Sir James Crichton-Browne, *The Doctor's Second Thoughts* (1931)

=

William Wordsworth's sister Dorothy began to suffer senile dementia in her fifties.

Dorothy seems to have recognized the onset of her own mental confusion some time in the year 1835. Though they cannot exactly be dated, three lines of verse in her last journal suggest her self-awareness:

> My tremulous prayers feeble hands
> Refuse to labour with the mind
> And *that* too oft is misty dark & blind.

The first clear sign of imbalance occurred on 17 February 1835; it took the form, common in early senility, of irritation with those nearest to her. For the first time, there is open criticism of William and Mary. Early in February they planned a long visit to London, to lobby the Prime Minister, Peel, to use his influence in finding a safe job for Willy. Peel, whose Government was threatened, had declared his inability to help on 3 February, only to receive a lengthy letter of appeal from William, written on the 5th. A fortnight later, William followed it by a visit with Mary to London, to plead his son's cause. He had evidently discussed this with Dorothy who, normally, would agree to anything which might help her nephew. Now, faced with what she felt desertion of herself and Dora – though Sara remained to care for them at Rydal – she burst out:

> Wm & Mary left us to go to London. Both in good spirits till the last parting came – when I was overcome. My spirits much depressed ... More than I have done I cannot do therefore shall only state my sorrow that our Friendship is so little prized & that they can so easily part from the helpless invalids.

Her distress continued in uncharacteristic, almost childish, entries. On 21 February, 'No letter from Wm & M. to me a great disappointment' and two days later, 'W. & M. too full of business'. Her writing deteriorates, and by the middle of March is nearly illegible, though she was still capable of following the news: on Friday, 10 April, 'All public affairs chearless!'

Robert Gittings and Jo Manton, *Dorothy Wordsworth* (1985)

=

The poetry of Anne Sexton, who committed suicide at the age of forty-six, is most powerfully coloured by her own experience of hospitalization as the result of a series of mental breakdowns, the first, in 1954 (coincidentally the year of publication of Antonia White's Beyond the Glass, *see page 234), being diagnosed as caused by post-partum depression (see page 44).*

> God went out of me
> as if the sea dried up like sandpaper,
> as if the sun became a latrine.

God went out of my fingers.
They became stone.
My body became a side of mutton
and despair roamed the slaughterhouse.

Someone brought me oranges in my despair
but I could not eat a one
for God was in that orange.
I could not touch what did not belong to me.
The priest came,
he said God was even in Hitler.
I did not believe him
for if God were in Hitler
then God would be in me.
I did not hear the bird sounds.
They had left.
I did not see the speechless clouds,
I saw only the little white dish of my faith
breaking in the crater.
I kept saying:
I've got to have something to hold on to.
People gave me Bibles, crucifixes,
a yellow daisy,
but I could not touch them,
I who was a house full of bowel movement,
I who was a defaced altar,
I who wanted to crawl toward God
could not move nor eat bread.

So I ate myself,
bite by bite,
and the tears washed me,
wave after cowardly wave,
swallowing canker after canker
and Jesus stood over me looking down
and He laughed to find me gone,
and put His mouth to mine
and gave me His air.

My kindred, my brother, I said
and gave the yellow daisy
to the crazy woman in the next bed.

Anne Sexton, 'The Sickness Unto Death', in
The Awful Roaring Toward God (1977)

=

The savage god

I was prompted to write a short piece for the op-ed page of the *Times*. The argument I put forth was fairly straightforward: the pain of severe depression is quite unimaginable to those who have not suffered it, and it kills in many instances because its anguish can no longer be borne. The prevention of many suicides will continue to be hindered until there is a general awareness of the nature of this pain. Through the healing process of time – and through medical intervention or hospitalization in many cases – most people survive depression, which may be its only blessing; but to the tragic legion who are compelled to destroy themselves there should be no more reproof attached than to the victims of terminal cancer. . . .

Depression afflicts millions directly, and many millions more who are relatives or friends of victims. As assertively democratic as a Norman Rockwell poster, it strikes indiscriminately at all ages, races, creeds, and classes, though women are at considerably higher risk than men. The occupational list (dressmakers, barge captains, sushi chefs, Cabinet members) of its patients is too long and tedious; it is enough to say that very few people escape being a potential victim of the disease, at least in its milder form. Despite depression's eclectic reach, it has been demonstrated with fair convincingness that artistic types (especially poets) are particularly vulnerable to the disorder – which in its graver, clinical manifestation takes upward of 20 percent of its victims by way of suicide. Just a few of these fallen artists, all modern, make up a sad but scintillant roll call: Hart Crane, Vincent Van Gogh, Virginia Woolf, Arshile Gorky, Cesare Pavese, Romain Gary, Sylvia Plath, Mark Rothko, John Berryman, Jack London, Ernest Hemingway, Diane Arbus, Tadeusz Borowski, Paul Celan, Anne Sexton, Sergei Esenin, Vladimir Mayakovsky – the list goes on. (The Russian poet

Mayakovsky was harshly critical of his great contemporary Esenin's suicide a few years before, which should stand as a caveat for all who are judgmental about self-destruction.) When one thinks of these doomed and splendidly creative men and women, one is drawn to contemplate their childhoods, where, to the best of anyone's knowledge, the seeds of the illness take strong root; could any of them have had a hint, then, of the psyche's perishability, its exquisite fragility? And why were they destroyed, while others – similarly stricken – struggled through?

William Styron, 'Darkness Visible' (1989)

=

What might today be called manic-depressive types were previously commonly seen as especially prey to suicide.

A young gentleman, twenty-four years of age, endowed with a most vivid imagination, came to Paris to study the law, and flattered himself with the belief that nature had destined him for a brilliant station at the bar. An enthusiast for his own convictions, he was an inflexible disciple of Pythagoras in his system of diet: he secluded himself from society, and pursued, with the utmost ardour and obstinacy, his literary projects. Some months after his arrival, he was seized with great depression of spirits, frequent bleeding at the nose, spasmodic oppression of the chest, wandering pains of the bowels, troublesome flatulence and morbidly increased sensibility. Sometimes he came to me in a very cheerful state of mind, when he used to say, 'How happy he was, and that he could scarcely express the supreme felicity which he experienced.' At other times, I found him plunged in the horrors of consternation and despair. Thus, most acutely miserable, he frequently, and with great earnestness, intreated me to put an end to his sufferings. The characters of the profoundest hypochondriasis were now become recognizable in his feelings and conduct. I saw the approaching danger, and I conjured him to change his manner of life. My advice was unequivocally rejected. The nervous symptoms of the head, chest and bowels continued to be progressively exasperated. His intervals of complacency and cheerfulness were succeeded by extreme depression and pusillanimity and terror, and inexpressible anguish.

Overpowered nearly by his apprehensions, he often and earnestly entreated me to rescue him from the arms of death. At those times I invited him to accompany me to the fields, and after walking for some time, and conversing together upon subjects likely to console or amuse him, he appeared to recover the enjoyment of his existence: but, upon returning to his chambers, his perplexities and terrors likewise returned. His despair was exasperated by the confusion of ideas to which he was constantly subject, and which interferred so much with his studies. But what appeared, altogether, to overwhelm him, was the distressing conviction that his pursuit of fame and professional distinction must be for ever abandoned. Complete lunacy, at length, established its melancholy empire. One night, he bethought himself that he would go to the play, to seek relief from his own too unhappy meditations. The piece which was presented, was the 'Philosopher without knowing it'. He was instantly seized with the most gloomy suspicions, and especially with a conviction, that the comedy was written on purpose and represented to ridicule himself. He accused me with having furnished materials for the writer of it, and the next morning he came to reproach me, which he did most angrily, for having betrayed the rights of friendship, and exposed him to public derision. His dilirium observed no bounds. Every monk and priest he met with in the public walks, he took for comedians in disguise, dispatched there for the purpose of studying his gestures, and of discovering the secret operations of his mind. In the dead of night he gave way to the most terrific apprehensions, – believed himself to be attacked sometimes by spies, and at others, by robbers and assassins. He once opened his window with great violence and cried out murder and assistance with all his might. His relations, at length, determined to have him put under a plan of treatment, similar to that which was adopted at the ci-de-vant Hôtel Dieu; and, with that view, sent him under the protection of a proper person, to a little village in the vicinity of the Pyrenees. Greatly debilitated both in mind and body, it was some time after agreed upon that he should return to his family residence, where, on account of his paroxysms of delirious extravagance, succeeded by fits of profound melancholy, he was insulated from society. Ennui and insurmountable disgust with life, absolute refusal of food, and dissatisfaction with every thing, and every body that came near him, were among the last ingredients of his bitter cup. To conclude our affecting history: he one day eluded the vigilance of his keeper; and, with no other garment on than his shirt, fled to a neighbouring wood, where he lost himself, and where, from weakness and inanition, he ended his miseries. Two days afterwards he was found a corpse. In his hand was found the celebrated work of Plato on the immortality of the soul.

Philippe Pinel (see page 12), *A Treatise on Insanity* (1806)

4

Lunatics at Large

One of the classic marks of the mad person is that he or she 'sees things' – things that are not there. Not surprisingly, therefore, it has been a matter of the deepest concern – of unconscious anxiety, perhaps – to society and the psychiatric profession that they should feel fully confident of their ability to know a lunatic when they see one. Much in our cultural heritage has bolstered such confidence. Ever since Antiquity, the theories of physiognomy, humours and complexions developed by Greek medicine fed the assumption that madness was as madness looked. Melancholics would be passive, listless, withdrawn, broadcasting the 'black looks' produced by black bile or the melancholic humour. Maniacs would resemble the brutes to whose bestial condition their inordinate vices had reduced them. They would be wearing scarce a stitch of clothing (maybe just the odd symbolic animal skin); they would sport leonine manes of hair, and would bare their teeth. When Edgar in *King Lear* wants to pass himself off as a wandering lunatic ('Poor Tom'), he knows exactly the appropriate occupational uniform. In the Renaissance world of emblematic representations, stereotypically crazy people (Ophelias, wild men, Bedlamite beggars, motley fools, melancholy malcontents) looked the part, rather like a shepherd with his smock and crook, or a king with his crown.

Over the years, as psychiatry strove to turn itself into a science, this key postulate was upheld: that a certain portraiture would describe, define and, to some degree, diagnose the insane. Hence the 'photofit' case histories drawn up by mad doctors lavished astonishing attention on bone structures and the musculature of expression, and highlighted the slightest abnormalities of mien and demeanour. The psychiatrist's skill proved remarkably akin to that other art of identification emergent in the nineteenth century, that of the detective.

Various dangers, of course, lurked for the unwary. For one thing, stereotyping – the philosophy of 'you know one when you see one' – is all too readily self-confirming. Psychiatry easily trapped itself in its own *idées fixes* concerning the ways madness walked and talked. On occasion, it even trained its patients to behave according to certain scripts. On show until the 1770s before the visiting public, the inmates of the human zoo of Bethlem (see page 1) clearly assumed antic dispositions for the tourists' benefit – and those who performed their parts well, according to the conventions, would be rewarded with showers of halfpence. In late nineteenth-century Paris, Jean-Martin Charcot, that Napoleon of hysteria, unwittingly 'trained' his sexy young female patients to give melodramatic hysterical performances in front of large and enthusiastic crowds of doctors and students, all male, almost as though they were a cabaret. The professor, it seems, was no less victim of this bizarre charade than his patients.

The passage below from Maudsley reveals a further risk. As the threat of insanity loomed ever larger, and the techniques for identifying abnormalities grew ever more sophisticated, the endeavour of psychiatry to gain recognition as a science became self-defeating – crazy, even – because of its disposition to treat *everything* as a potential psychopathological sign. Psychiatry felt the need to be on its guard: it mustn't miss a trick. The early nineteenth-century 'discovery' of monomaniacs – those who seemed normal enough, except when provoked upon one particular mental weak spot – showed how readily devious psychopaths might wise up and feign normality (pretending to be normal, psychiatrists concluded, was itself a psychological disorder). Hence the need for constant vigilance, an attitude paralleled by Freud's insistence that nothing is accidental and without significance, nothing should be taken at face value.

A case of paranoia? Who is to say how far doctors themselves began to see and hear things that were not there? In a classic experiment a generation ago, a group of students deliberately secured admission into an American psychiatric hospital, claiming to be suffering from schizophrenic symptoms. Thereafter they behaved totally normally, but (by virtue of being under psychiatric scrutiny) their behaviour – including their routine note-taking – was recorded as indicative of various psychopathologies.

The lunatic is classically the person who sees things that are not there. It is a definition which may, however, prove rather elastic.

A wise fool

In Gloucestershire dwelt one that cured frantic men in this manner: when their fit was on them, he would put them in a gutter of water – some to the knees, some to the middle, and some to the neck, as the disease was on them. So one that was well amended, standing at the gate by chance, a gentleman came riding by with his hawks and his hounds. The fellow called to him and said, 'Gentleman, whither go you?'

'On hunting,' quoth the gentleman.

'What do you with all those kites and dogs?'

'They be hawks and hounds,' quoth the gentleman.

'Wherefore keep you them?' quoth the other.

'Why,' quoth he, 'for my pleasure.'

'What do they cost you a year to keep them?'

'Forty pounds,' quoth the gentleman.

'And what do they profit you?' quoth he.

'Some ten pounds,' quoth the gentleman.

'Get thee quickly hence,' quoth the fellow, 'for if my master find thee here he will put thee into the gutter up to the throat.'

John Wardroper, _Jest Upon Jest_ (1970)

Late Victorian psychiatry was anxious about the growth of latent lunacy in the population, a predisposition to mental disease in apparently normal people, which one day would make itself felt. Henry Maudsley, the most influential psychiatric spokesman of his day, aimed to perfect an expert gaze to pick up all the hidden signs. Maudsley provided the funding for the setting up of the Maudsley Hospital, the first British institution for the insane largely devoted to scientific research.

What are the bodily and mental marks of the insane temperament? That there are such is most certain; for although the varieties of this temperament cannot yet be described with any precision, no one who accustoms himself to observe closely will fail to be able to say positively in many instances whether an insane person, and even a sane person in some instances, comes of an insane family or not. An irregular and unsymmetrical conformation of the head, a want of regularity and harmony of the features, and, as Morel holds, malformations of the external ear, are sometimes observed. Convulsions are apt to occur in early life; and there are tics, grimaces, or other spasmodic movements of muscles of face, eyelids, or lips afterwards. Stammering and defects of pronunciation are also sometimes signs of the neurosis. In other cases there are peculiarities of the eyes, which, though they may be full and prominent, have a vacillating movement, and a vacantly-abstracted, or half-fearful, half-suspicious, and distrustful look. There may, indeed, be something in the eye wonderfully suggestive of the look of an animal. The walk and manner are uncertain, and, though not easily described in words, may be distinctly peculiar. With these bodily traits are associated peculiarities of thought, feeling, and conduct. Without being insane, a person who has the insane neurosis strongly marked is thought to be strange, queer, and not like other persons. He is apt to see things under novel aspects, or to think about them under novel relations, which would not have occurred to an ordinary mortal. Punning on words is, I am inclined to think, sometimes an indication of the temperament, and so also that higher kind of wit which startles us with the use of an idea in a double sense; of both which aptitudes no better example can be given than that of Charles Lamb. His case, too, may show that the insane temperament is compatible with, and indeed it not seldom coexists with, considerable genius. Even those who have it in a more marked form often exhibit remarkable special talents and aptitudes, such as an extraordinary talent for music, or for calculation, or a prodigious memory for details, when they may be little better than imbecile in other things.

Henry Maudsley, *Body and Mind: An Inquiry into their Connection and Mutual Influence, Specially in Reference to Mental Diseases* (1873)

=

Mad with grief

Re-enter OPHELIA.

[LAERTES:] O, heat dry up my brain! tears seven times salt
   Burn out the sense and virtue of mine eye!
   By heaven, thy madness shall be paid with weight
   Till our scale turn the beam. O rose of May!
   Dear maid, kind sister, sweet Ophelia!
   O heavens! is't possible a young maid's wits
   Should be as mortal as an old man's life?
   Nature is fine in love; and where 'tis fine
   It sends some precious instance of itself
   After the thing it loves.
OPHELIA: (*Sings*) They bore him barefac'd on the bier;
    Hey non nonny, nonny, hey nonny;
    And in his grave rain'd many a tear –
   Fare you well, my dove!
LAERTES: Hadst thou thy wits, and didst persuade revenge,
   It could not move thus.
OPHELIA: You must sing 'A-down, a-down', an you call him
   a-down-a. O, how the wheel becomes it! It is the false steward,
   that stole his master's daughter.
LAERTES: This nothing's more than matter.
OPHELIA: There's rosemary, that's for remembrance; pray you,
   love, remember. And there is pansies, that's for thoughts.
LAERTES: A document in madness . . .

                 William Shakespeare, *Hamlet* (1604)

=

*Seen as victims of society, the mad offered the pre-Romantics
boundless opportunities for sentimentality. Henry Mackenzie's
lovelorn Bedlamite clearly owes more to Ophelia than to reality.*

The unfortunate young lady had till now seemed entranced in
thought, with her eyes fixed on a little garnet-ring she wore on her
finger: she turned them now upon Harley. 'My Billy is no more!'
said she, 'do you weep for my Billy? Blessings on your tears! I
would weep too, but my brain is dry; and it burns, it burns, it

burns!' – She drew nearer to Harley. – 'Be comforted, young Lady,' said he, 'your Billy is in heaven.' 'Is he, indeed? and shall we meet again? And shall that frightful man' (pointing to the keeper) 'not be there? – Alas! I am grown naughty of late; I have almost forgotten to think of heaven: yet I pray sometimes; when I can, I pray; and sometimes I sing; when I am saddest, I sing: – You shall hear me, hush!

> 'Light be the earth on Billy's breast,
> 'And green the sod that wraps his grave!'

There was a plaintive wildness in the air not to be withstood; and, except the keeper's, there was not an unmoistened eye around her.

'Do you weep again?' said she; 'I would not have you weep: you are like my Billy; you are, believe me; just so he looked when he gave me this ring; poor Billy! 'twas the last time ever we met! –

''Twas when the seas were roaring – I love you for resembling my Billy; but I shall never love any man like him.' – She stretched out her hand to Harley; he pressed it between both of his, and bathed it with his tears. – 'Nay, that is Billy's ring,' said she, 'you cannot have it, indeed; but here is another, look here, which I plaited to-day of some gold-thread from this bit of stuff; will you keep it for my sake? I am a strange girl; – but my heart is harmless: my poor heart! it will burst some day; feel how it beats.' – She press'd his hand to her bosom, then holding her head in the attitude of listening – 'Hark! one, two, three! be quiet, thou little trembler; my Billy's is cold! – but I had forgotten the ring.' – She put it on his finger. – 'Farewell! I must leave you now.' – She would have withdrawn her hand; Harley held it to his lips. – 'I dare not stay longer; my head throbs sadly: farewel!' – She walked with a hurried step to a little apartment at some distance. Harley stood fixed in astonishment and pity! his friend gave money to the keeper. – Harley looked on his ring. – He put a couple of guineas into the man's hand: 'Be kind to that unfortunate' – He burst into tears, and left them.

Henry Mackenzie, The Man of Feeling (1771)

*In earlier times, the lunatic was typically identified by his tendency
to be a wanderer. Though a humane man, Thomas More is in no
doubt that the proper recourse with lunatics is to beat the madness
out of them.*

Another was one, whyche after that he had fallen in to ye frantike
heresyes, fell soone after in to playne open fransye bysyde. And all
be it that he had therfore ben put uppe in bedelem, and afterwarde
by betynge and correccyon gathered hys remembraunce to hym,
and beganne to come agayne to hym selfe beynge theruppon set at
lyberty and walkynge about abrode, hys olde fansyes beganne to
fall agayne in his hed. And I was fro dyvers good holy places
advertised, that he used in his wanderynge aboute, to come into the
chyrche, & there make many madde toyes & tryfles, to the trouble
of good people in the dyvyne servyce and specially wold he be most
besy in the tyme of most sylence, whyle the preste was at the
secretes of the masse aboute ye levacyon. And yf he spyed any
woman knelynge at a forme yf her hed hynge any thynge low in her
medytacyons, than wolde he stele behynde her, & yf he were not
letted wolde laboure to lyfte up all her clothes & caste then quyte
over her hed, wheruppon I beyng advertysed of these pageauntes,
and beynge sent unto and requyred by very devout relygyouse
folke, to take some other order wyth hym caused him as he came
wanderyng by my dore, to be taken by the constables and bounden
to a tre in the strete byfore the whole towne, and there they stryped
hym with roddys therfore tyl he waxed wery and somwhat lenger.
And it appeared well that hys remembraunce was good inough,
save yt wente about in grasynge tyll it was beten home. For he could
than very well reherse hys fawtes hym selfe, and speke and trete
very well, and promyse to do afterwarde as well. And veryly god be
thanked I here none harme of hym now.

Thomas More, *The Apologye of Syr T. More, Knyght* (1533)

==

*To the eighteenth-century observer, the village idiot is seen as
half-wild, and is allowed, or expected, to fend for himself.*

We had in this village more than twenty years ago an idiot-boy, whom I well remember, who, from a child, showed a strong pro-pensity to bees; they were his food, his amusement, his sole object. And as people of this cast have seldom more than one point in view, so this lad exerted all his few faculties on this one pursuit. In the winter he dozed away his time, within his father's house, by the fireside, in a kind of torpid state, seldom departing from the chimney-corner; but in the summer he was all alert, and in quest of his game in the fields, and on sunny banks. Honey-bees, humble-bees, and wasps, were his prey whenever he found them: he had no apprehensions from their stings, but would seize them *nudis manibus*, and at once disarm them of their weapons, and suck their bodies for the sake of their honey-bags. Sometimes he would fill his bosom between his shirt and his skin with a number of these captives; and sometimes would confine them in bottles. He was a very *merops apiaster*, or bee-bird; and very injurious to men that kept bees; for he would slide into their bee-gardens, and, sitting down before the stools, would rap with his finger on the hives, and so take the bees as they came out. He has been known to overturn hives for the sake of honey, of which he was passionately fond. Where metheglin was making he would linger round the tubs and vessels, begging a draught of what he called bees' wine. As he ran about he used to make a humming noise with his lips, resembling the buzzing of bees. This lad was lean and sallow, and of a cadaver-ous complexion; and, except in his favourite pursuit, in which he was wonderfully adroit, discovered no manner of understanding. Has his capacity been better, and directed to the same object, he had perhaps abated much of our wonder at the feats of a more modern exhibitor of bees: and we may justly say of him now,

> 'Thou,
> Had thy presiding star propitious shone,
> Should'st Wildman be.'

When a tall youth he was removed from hence to a distant village, where he died, as I understand, before he arrived at manhood.

Gilbert White, *The Natural History and Antiquities of Selborne* (1789)

=

'The Frantic Lady'

I burn; my brain consumes to ashes!
Each eye-ball too like lightning flashes!
Within my breast there glows a solid fire,
Which in a thousand ages can't expire!

    Blow, blow, the winds' great ruler!
      Bring the Po and the Ganges hither;
      'Tis sultry weather;
      Pour them all on my soul,
      It will hiss like a coal,
    But be never the cooler.

    'Twas pride hot as hell,
    That first made me rebell,
From love's awful throne a curst angel I fell;
    And mourn now my fate,
    Which myself did create:
Fool, fool, that consider'd not when I was well!

    Adieu! ye vain transporting joys!
    Off, ye vain fantastic toys! –
That dress this face – this body – to allure!
    Bring me daggers, poison, fire!
    Since scorn is turn'd into desire.
All hell feels not the rage, which I, poor I, endure.

    In Thomas Percy, *Reliques of Ancient English Poetry* (1857)

=

*When is a madman not a madman? The Victorians felt themselves
on the horns of a dilemma. Their instinct towards liberty supported
the idea that eccentrics, such as the notorious rich Hitchin hermit,
'Mad Lucas', who boarded himself up for many years in his own
home, should be left alone. Their paternalistic and therapeutic
ethics urged them to 'help'. The issue is debated here by the leading
psychiatrist of the day, Daniel Hack Tuke, great-grandson of Samuel Tuke (see page 135), and author of* Insanity in Ancient and
Modern Life, with chapters on its prevention (1878) *and* Chapters
in the History of the Insane in the British Isles (1882).

The condition of the hermit . . . did really pass beyond the limit of eccentricity. His emotions were perverted by disease; but while his case was primarily one of Moral Insanity – a madness of action rather than of language – a state of degraded feeling rather than intellectual incapacity – his suspicions at times took the form of a definite delusion, which our legal friends, in search of their favourite test, ought to admit to possess some weight; and here I would add that it should be carefully borne in mind that his isolation and seclusion, and neglect of his residence and dress, did not arise from his diseased mental condition, and the solution of the problem of his life can be found by tracing back his history to the unfavourable circumstances of his childhood, acting upon his brain in all probability predisposed to mental disease . . .

I conclude this sketch by briefly referring to the question which must present itself in such cases as this, namely, whether a man who thus acts and lives ought or ought not to be interfered with? I am, of course, well aware that this could not be done merely on the ground of the neglect of his property or his mode of life, seeing that our law, unlike the Code Napoleon and that of ancient Rome, allows unthrifts and wasters of property to do as they like. But assuming that proofs of his insanity were conclusive, would it or would it not have been desirable to place him under care? He was not dangerous to others, nor was he dangerous to himself, except in a very general sense, but might he not have benefited, and really been more comfortable, if under medical treatment and control?

Richard Whitmore, Mad Lucas: The Strange Story of England's
Most Famous Hermit (1983)

=

In Charlotte Brontë's Jane Eyre, *the first Mrs Rochester's condition is portrayed as hereditary – her mother had also been certified as insane. The images used to describe the encounter here say much of the contemporary view of madness in Victorian England.*

In a room without a window, there burnt a fire, guarded by a high and strong fender, and a lamp suspended from the ceiling by a chain: Grace Poole bent over the fire, apparently cooking something in a saucepan. In the deep shade, at the further end of the room, a figure ran backwards and forwards. What it was, whether beast or human being, one could not, at first sight, tell: it grovelled, seemingly, on all fours; it snatched and growled like some strange wild animal: but it was covered with clothing; and a quantity of dark, grizzled hair, wild as a mane, hid its head and face.

'Good-morrow, Mrs Poole!' said Mr Rochester. 'How are you? and how is your charge today?'

'We're tolerable, sir, I thank you,' replied Grace, lifting the boiling mess carefully on to the hob: 'rather snappish, but not 'rageous.'

A fierce cry seemed to give the lie to her favourable report: the clothed hyena rose up, and stood tall on its hind feet.

'Ah, sir, she sees you!' exclaimed Grace: 'you'd better not stay.'

'Only a few moments, Grace: you must allow me a few moments.'

'Take care then, sir! – for God's sake, take care!'

The maniac bellowed: she parted her shaggy locks from her visage, and gazed wildly at her visitors.

Charlotte Brontë, *Jane Eyre* (1847)

===

While in Jean Rhys's version of Bertha Rochester's story, the heroine appears as a very different figure, anticipating her end with remarkable self-possession.

When I was out on the battlements it was cool and I could hardly hear them. I sat there quietly. I don't know how long I sat. Then I turned round and saw the sky. It was red and all my life was in it. I saw the grandfather clock and Aunt Cora's patchwork, all colours, I saw the orchids and the stephanotis and the jasmine and the tree of life in flames. I saw the chandelier and the red carpet downstairs and the bamboos and the tree ferns, the gold ferns and the silver, and the soft green velvet of the moss on the garden wall. I saw my doll's house and the books and the picture of the Miller's Daughter. I heard the parrot call as he did when he saw a stranger, *Qui est là? Qui est là?* and the man who hated me was calling too, Bertha! Bertha! The wind caught my hair and it streamed out like wings. It might bear me up, I thought, if I jumped to those hard stones. But when I looked over the edge I saw the pool at Coulibri. Tia was there. She beckoned to me and when I hesitated, she laughed. I heard her say, You frightened? And I heard the man's voice, Bertha! Bertha! All this I saw and heard in a fraction of a second. And the sky so red. Someone screamed and I thought, *Why did I scream?* I called 'Tia!' and jumped and woke.

Grace Poole was sitting at the table but she had heard the scream too, for she said, 'What was that?' She got up, came over and looked at me. I lay still, breathing evenly with my eyes shut. 'I must have been dreaming,' she said. Then she went back, not to the table but to her bed. I waited a long time after I heard her snore, then I got up, took the keys and unlocked the door. I was outside holding my candle. Now at last I know why I was brought here and what I have to do. There must have been a draught for the flame flickered and I thought it was out. But I shielded it with my hand and it burned up again to light me along the dark passage.

Jean Rhys, Wide Sargasso Sea (1966)

=

Nikolai Gogol's civil service post in St Petersburg gave him insight into the bureaucratic machine of Tsar Nicholas I's oppressive regime, against which Poprischkin, the 'Nobody' of the Diary, vainly struggles. Poprischkin believes he is the rightful heir to the Spanish throne; Gogol himself was overtaken by religious mania and despair towards the end of his life, believing he was under orders to destroy his work, and finally starving himself to death.

THE 25TH

Today the Grand Inquisitor came into the room, but as soon as I heard his footsteps I hid under the table. When he saw I wasn't there, he started calling out. First he shouted: 'Poprishchin! – I didn't say a word. Then: 'Axenty Ivanov! Titular Councillor! Nobleman! – still I didn't reply. 'Ferdinand the Eighth, King of Spain!' I was in half a mind to stick my head out, but thought better of it. 'No, my friend, you can't fool me! I know only too well you're going to pour cold water over my head.' He spotted me all the same and drove me out from under the table with his stick. The damned thing is terribly painful. But my next discovery that every cock has its Spain, tucked away under its feathers, made up for all these torments. The Grand Inquisitor left in a very bad mood however and threatened me with some sort of punishment. But I didn't care a rap about his helpless rage, as I knew full well he was functioning like a machine, a mere tool of the English.

DA 34 TE MTH EARY ЯƎᗺᴙUAЯ 349

No, I haven't the strength to endure it any longer! Good God, what are they doing to me? They're pouring cold water over my head! They won't listen to me or come and see me. What have I done to them! Why do they torture me so? What can they want from a miserable wretch like me? What can I offer them when I've nothing of my own? I can't stand this torture any more. My head is burning and everything is spinning round and round. Save me! Take me away! Give me a troika with horses swift as the whirlwind! Climb up, driver, and let the bells ring! Soar away, horses, and carry me from this world! Further, further, where nothing can be seen, nothing at all! Over there the sky whirls round. A little star shines in the distance; the forest rushes past with its dark trees and the moon shines above. A deep blue haze is spreading like a carpet; a guitar string twangs in the mist. On one side is the sea, on the other is Italy. And over there I can see Russian peasant huts. Is that my house looking dimly blue in the distance? And is that my mother sitting at the window? Mother, save your poor son! Shed a tear on his aching head! See how they're torturing him! Press a wretched orphan to your breast! There's no place for him in this world! They're persecuting him! Mother, have pity on your poor little child . . .

And did you know that the Dhey of Algiers* has a wart right under his nose?

*The reference is to Hussein Pasha, deposed by the French in 1830. (Trans.)

Nikolai Gogol, *Diary of a Madman* (1834)

*The wandering lunatic of Shakespeare's time – the Tom o' Bedlam –
was regarded as little higher than a beast on the Chain of Being. He
was frequently whipped from parish to parish.*

Enter EDGAR.
EDGAR: I heard myself proclaim'd
  And by the happy hollow of a tree
  Escap'd the hunt. No port is free; no place
  That guard and most unusual vigilance
  Does not attend my taking. Whiles I may scape
  I will preserve myself; and am bethought
  To take the basest and most poorest shape
  That ever penury in contempt of man
  Brought near to beast. My face I'll grime with filth.
  Blanket my loins, elf all my hairs in knots,
  And with presented nakedness outface
  The winds and persecutions of the sky.
  The country gives me proof and precedent
  Of Bedlam beggars, who, with roaring voices,
  Strike in their numb'd and mortified bare arms
  Pins, wooden pricks, nails, sprigs of rosemary;
  And with this horrible object, from low farms,
  Poor pelting villages, sheep-cotes, and mills
  Sometimes with lunatic bans, sometime with prayers,
  Enforce their charity. Poor Turlygod! poor Tom!
  That's something yet. Edgar I nothing am.
                    William Shakespeare, *King Lear* (1608)

═══

*Writers liked to use pen portraits of the insane as object lessons in
morality. This vignette was written only three years after George
III suffered his first severe bout of madness.*

Of *arrogant Insanity*, the ingenious *Dr Perfect* relates the following
astonishingly curious case: – Some years ago, a poor man, who
having studied the art of government and the balance of the European power with greater attention than his business, grew insane,
and fancied himself a king, and, in this situation, was admitted into

the workhouse of St Giles's in the Fields, where there happened to be an idiot of nearly his own age; this imaginary king appointed the idiot his prime minister, besides which post, he officiated as his barber and menial servant; he brought their common food, and stood behind his majesty whilst he dined, when he had permission to make his own repast. There would sit, the king upon an eminence, and his minister below him, for whole days, issuing their precepts to their imaginary subjects; in this manner they lived about six years, when, unfortunately, the minister, impelled by hunger, so far deviated from his line of allegiance, as to eat his breakfast before his sovereign appeared, which so exasperated the king, that he flew upon him, and would certainly have put a period to his existence, if he had not been prevented; when his anger was thought to have abated, the minister was again introduced to his quondam sovereign, but he seized him immediately, and could never after be prevailed on to see him. The degraded minister catched a fever in his exile, and when his majesty was beginning to relent, and almost prevailed upon to forgive him, he died; which had such an effect upon this fancied monarch, that, after living almost without sustenance, in a continued silence, a few weeks, he died of mere grief. Ill-fated monarch! thou couldest not, as can the illustrious monarch of the present day, if his minister were to 'pay his tribute into the treasury to which we must all be taxed', appoint another, who would guide the reins of empire with as much prudence and success as the present one hath done: throughout thy whole territory, there was not found one hardy enough to engage in the arduous task; and equally unable to support the weight of government alone, as to descend to the peaceable, but unhonoured, vale of retirement, thou didst quietly yield up thy life and sceptre together!

William Pargeter (see page 36), *Observations on Maniacal Disorders*
(1792)

=

Nebuchadnezzar was a powerful Old Testament symbol of the enemy of righteousness afflicted by God with madness and reduced to utter bestiality. See also page 179 and Plate 6.

While the word was in the king's mouth, there fell a voice from heaven, saying, O king Nebuchadnezzar, to thee it is spoken; The kingdom is departed from thee. And they shall drive thee from men, and thy dwelling shall be with the beasts of the field; they shall make thee to eat grass as oxen, and seven times shall pass over thee, until thou know that the most High ruleth in the kingdom of men, and giveth it to whomsoever he will. The same hour was the thing fulfilled upon Nebuchadnezzar: and he was driven from men, and did eat grass as oxen, and his body was wet with the dew of heaven, till his hairs were grown like eagles' feathers, and his nails like birds' claws.

Daniel 4: 31–3

=

The developing science of psychiatry dreaded mistaking the sane for the mad, and the mad for the sane. John Conolly, perhaps the most reflective of the early Victorian psychiatrists, pondered whether cases of duplicity could be exposed.

I was, a few years ago, requested to see a man, confined in gaol for the crime of cutting off his wife's head. This man had made no attempt to deny the deed, or to escape the consequences. For some time after he was taken to prison, his conduct was quiet, and on common subjects he would talk in a common way with his fellow-prisoners. When he was asked about the murder, and reminded that he would certainly be hanged for it, he always said he did not know that he had done any harm. After being confined five or six weeks, he occasionally showed a disposition to be violent; and, on one occasion, put a handkerchief round his neck as if he intended to hang himself. Subsequently, he became taciturn, and his demeanour changed to that of an imbecile person, which it was at the time of my seeing him. He wore a woollen cap, which he had taken from one of the other prisoners, and carried a piece of wood about with him, which he represented, by signs, to be his sword; for he would not speak, nor answer any questions; only breaking silence now and then by repeating the word 'cabbage', without any kind of meaning. He had buttons and other common trinkets tied round his wrist; and he had made a great many attempts to walk out of the hospital of the prison, in which he was lodged. When a watch or

any shining substance was shown to him, he would assume an
idiotic smile, and begin to dance.

Notwithstanding all these appearances, I could not help suspecting that the man was playing a part. The nature of his crime, and
his conduct after committing it, certainly went far to support the
idea of his insanity; and the insanity might have been coming on
some time before the murder; and although he might be cunning, he
might still be insane. Yet the mixed character of his mental disorder, and the rapid supervention of idiotcy on a quiet form of
insanity, in a man of thirty-five, seemed to me to be unusual
circumstances. There was nothing in his manner which *might* not
very easily have been the effect of imitation; and although he would
not answer questions, I observed that he both heard and understood them; at least, when I asked him, a little sharply and
unexpectedly, if he did not know me, he immediately looked up,
which he would not do at other times, and shook his head. I saw
too, that although he never looked directly at any one, except at
that particular moment, he was in reality very watchful of their
movements, even when they were distant from him: several proofs
of this occurred in a short time, and he always made a sudden run
towards the door when any body opened it to go out.

John Conolly, *An Inquiry Concerning the Indications of Insanity, with
Suggestions for the Better Protection and Care of the Insane* (1830)

=

Sometimes the 'normal' behave more strangely than the peculiar.

People who hold minority opinions, even though these may be
posthumously proved correct, are often called 'mad,' or at least
'eccentric' during their lifetime. But that they can hold either advanced or demoded views distasteful to the community as a whole,
shows them to be far less suggestible than their 'normal' contem-
poraries; and no patients can be so difficult to influence by suggestion as the chronic mentally ill. Ordinary persons also have
much greater powers of adaptation to circumstance than most
eccentrics or psychotics. During the London Blitz, ordinary
civilians became conditioned to the most bizarre and horrifying
situations; they would go calmly about their work though well

aware that neighbours had been buried alive in bombed houses around them. They realized that to worry about the victims when nothing more could be done to extricate them, would lead to their own nervous collapse. In fact, those who broke down during the London Blitz were for the most part abnormally anxious or abnormally fatigued persons who could no longer adapt themselves to the unusual horrors and stresses.

> William Sargant, *Battle for the Mind: A Physiology of Conversion and Brain-washing* (1957)

=

> Three wise men of Gotham
> Went to sea in a bowl;
> If the bowl had been stronger,
> My story would have been longer.
>
> > 'The Wise Men of Gotham', anon.

=

Himself the son of an assassinated prime minister (see page 23), John Perceval doubtless felt a bit miffed when a fellow lunatic, Mr N—, insisted, 'I am the Duke of Somerset': hence his own uncharacteristic muteness.

Mr N—, my spirits called Mr Fazakerley, and my spirit of delicacy and contrition. He was a short, thin, sharp featured man, with light grey eyes, a mouth always pursed with sardonic smiles, a head partly bald and partly grey. He carried his hands usually in his waistcoat or trouser pockets; walked with a nonchalant obstinate air, and with an awkward gait, halting on one leg. He was a man of pride. He sat usually in one chair by the fire-place, his elbow leaning on a table, and never spoke to any around him; once or twice only I heard him ask a question, and give directions to the servants, who treated him with decorum. Two or three times a day he rose from his chair and went into the yard, where he stood with his head raised up, his hands on his hips, his face wearing the appearance of choking, and cried aloud, 'I take my oath before God, &c. &c. &c., that I *am* the Duke of Somerset, and that I give and bequeath all my jewels, large possessions, &c. &c., to his

majesty and his heirs for ever. So help me God. Amen!' When I
went into the yard at liberty, the spirits desired me also to take his
position, and to cry out in like manner; 'I am the lost hope of a
noble family;' but after attempting it three or four times, I shrunk
from so exposing my feelings, and my situation.

   John T. Perceval, *A Narrative of the Treatment Received by a
   Gentleman, During a State of Mental Derangement* (1838/40)

==

*Writing figures large in our cameos of the insane. They have clearly
found it a matter of urgency to authenticate their own condition
and prove their mental powers, just as authorities have often been
suspicious of their charges' attempts to document and protest
against their treatment.*

During the latter part of that first week I wrote many letters, so
many, indeed, that I soon exhausted a liberal supply of stationery.
This had been placed at my disposal at the suggestion of my
conservator, who had wisely arranged that I should have whatever I
wanted, if expedient. It was now at my own suggestion that the
supervisor gave me large sheets of manila wrapping paper. These I
proceeded to cut into strips a foot wide. One such strip, four feet
long, would suffice for a mere *billet-doux*; but a real letter usually
required several such strips pasted together. More than once letters
twenty or thirty feet long were written; and on one occasion the
accumulation of two or three days of excessive productivity, when
spread upon the floor, reached from one end of the corridor to the
other – a distance of about one hundred feet. My hourly output was
something like twelve feet, with an average of one hundred and fifty
words to the foot. Under the pressure of elation one takes pride in
doing everything in record time. Despite my speed my letters were
not incoherent. They were simply digressive, which was to be
expected, as elation befogs one's 'goal idea'. Though these epi-
stolary monstrosities were launched, few reached those to whom
they were addressed; for my conservator had wisely ordered that
my literary output be sent in bulk to him. His action was exasper-
ating, but later I realized that he had done me a great favor when he
interposed his judgment between my red-hot mentality and the cool

minds of the workaday world. Yet this interference with what I deemed my rights proved to be the first step in the general overruling of them by tactless attendants and, in particular, by a certain assistant physician.

Clifford Beers (see page 25), *A Mind that Found Itself:*
An Autobiography (1923)

=

Hallucinations: real or unreal?

I asked, 'What do you mean by "crazy"?'

'Out of my mind, mad, nuts – you know, crazy.'

I considered her notion that she was going crazy understandable. Some psychiatrists might have agreed with her, though I did not. In a recent well-publicized study, eight sane individuals – three psychologists, a psychology graduate student, a psychiatrist, a pediatrician, a painter, and a housewife – sought admission as mental patients to twelve different American hospitals. At the hospital admission offices they complained of only one symptom, which they had invented for the purposes of the study: hearing voices. They said the voices were unclear, but as far as they could tell, the voices were saying 'empty,' 'hollow,' 'thud.' Besides saying they heard voices, and besides falsifying their names and (in some cases) their vocations and employments, they told the truth in all details about themselves, their life histories, and their circumstances.

All eight pseudopatients were admitted to psychiatric wards. From the time they were admitted, all behaved normally and stopped asserting they were hearing voices. Yet all eight were kept in the hospital for periods from seven to fifty-two days, the average stay being nineteen days.

The psychiatrists of these eight pseudopatients kept them in the hospital for one reason alone: the pseudopatients were hallucinating. In Ruth's idiom, they were hearing things that weren't there. Seven of the eight pseudopatients were labeled 'schizophrenic' on admission. This means that some psychiatrists consider the report of hallucinations alone, in the absence of any other evidence of insanity, as warranting the diagnosis 'schizophrenia' and requiring admission to a mental ward.

It was therefore reasonable for Ruth to fear that I might regard her as crazy, and I had to reassure her many times that I did not. The closest translation of 'crazy' in psychiatric language is 'psychotic.' Besides the psychoses that reflect known disorders of the body or the brain, from which she was not suffering, there are two major groups of psychoses: the schizophrenias and the depressions. Was she undergoing one of these? The American psychiatrists in the study just cited had been mistaken in labeling their pseudopatients schizophrenic. The pseudopatients had been displaying none of schizophrenia's standard manifestations. The same was true of Ruth. Hallucinations are not a primary or defining feature of schizophrenia. One can be considered schizophrenic without hallucinating and, more importantly, one can hallucinate without being regarded as schizophrenic.

Certainly Ruth was depressed, both in the lay sense of the term – feeling unhappy much of the time – and in the psychiatric sense, as she was suffering from diminished appetite, weight loss, disturbed sleep, feelings of swelling in the head, crying spells, feelings of shame and guilt, and suicidal thoughts. However, she was not depressed to a degree that would ordinarily be regarded as psychotic. For example, unlike people with a depressive psychosis, she was clear and logical in her thinking, and lively in her speech, facial expressions, and movements. She did not feel that the world was barren or that her future was hopeless.

Morton Schatzman, *The Story of Ruth: One Woman's Haunting Psychiatric Odyssey* (1980)

5

Going Through It

Samuel Johnson lived in fear of going mad, and, as a precautionary measure, apparently entrusted his great friend, Mrs Hester Thrale, with a chain and padlock, for emergency use. It was Johnson's way of resolving the existential conundrum that, in the event of losing one's mind, one would, definitionally, be unable to respond prudently. After all, if you could tell you were out of your mind, would not this prove that you had reason enough to be judged sane? Many mental patients have noted that recognition of their own *in*sanity was the first step on the road to recovery.

Sufferers have often felt impelled to record the experience of losing mental control and its accompanying vertiginous disorientations in consciousness. Some may have attempted this at the very moment they felt they were losing control, but in general the accounts we have are retrospective and, to that degree, 'literary' artefacts. Sometimes they are *ex post facto* rationalizations: to redeem their self-esteem, alleged lunatics have felt driven to explain to the world how it came about that they were ever mistaken for crazy, although, in reality, their behaviour (while possibly misinterpreted) was sweet reason itself. Quite often those who have been restored to reason have wanted to document, by way of an *apologia pro vita sua*, their own descent into hell, tracing how extraordinary concatenations of circumstances (intense religious devotions, financial or family worries, job pressures, or whatever) precipitated them over the brink.

And they have tried to make sense of their own *experience* of such events, charting loss of rapport with reality, or the onset of being commanded by irresistible external forces – what the stage Bedlamite in the song (page 116) calls 'angry furies'. Moving accounts trace this sensation of being reduced to a puppet or automaton, defenceless against merciless space-invaders of both mind and body.

What was it like to live through this nightmare, alienated from self and society, suspended between multiple planes of existence that wove in and out of each other, aware of disorientation but, initially at least, unable to rectify it?

Above all, such sufferers have sought to overcome misunderstanding: from *my* viewpoint at least, they often tell us, what I did seemed completely rational – indeed, was far more rational than the methods used by doctors or other authorities.

These generally retrospective accounts throw some light upon the consciousness of the mentally ill. Some sufferers regard their condition in essentially negative terms: pain, invasion, confusion, being paralysed with fear. Others see what they underwent as a healthy or, at least, a necessary process, an indirect exploration and resolution via 'absurdity' of problems long tormenting their being. For others still, madness is a divine visitation, an epiphany, the entry into a new and glorious realm of the spirit or imagination.

──────

Can the madman recognize his madness? Or is true self-knowledge a symptom of sanity? This old conundrum was put into personal terms by John Perceval (see page 23), reflecting upon his mistaken understanding in his early days in the asylum.

I was not now aware that I was lunatic, nor did I admit this idea until the end of the year. I knew that I was prevented from discharging my duties to my Creator and to mankind, by some misunderstanding on my part; for which, on the authority of my spiritual accusers, I considered that I was wilfully guilty; racking my mind at the same time to divine their meaning. I imagined now that I was placed in this new position as a place of trial, that it might be seen whether I would persist in my malignant, or cowardly, or sluggish disobedience to the last. I imagined at the same time, that I was placed here '*to be taught of the spirits*', that is, (for they all spoke in different keys, tones, and measures, imitating usually the voices of relations or friends), to learn what was the nature of each spirit that spoke to me, whether a spirit of fun, of humour, of sincerity, of honesty, of honour, of hypocrisy, of perfect obedience, or what not, and to acquire knowledge to answer to the suggestions or arguments of each, as they in turn addressed me, or to choose which I would obey.

John T. Perceval, *A Narrative of the Treatment Received by a Gentleman, During a State of Mental Derangement* (1838/40)

=

Another bite at the same cherry

However, I thought it over, and decided to interest myself in the study, so that when winter, with its dark nights and black-out, came upon me, I should make my hobby the writing of a book. I had little doubt that much had already been written about asylums; for much has been written about *everything*, although we are slow to realize it. I thought that possibly somebody had written the story of the 'sane' man in a lunatic asylum – the horrors of it all, and the perjury that had been resorted to to get him there.

Indeed, the one and only thing that is typical of *all* lunatics is their inability to comprehend that they are insane; anything else whatever they are at one time or another able to understand, but to tell them that they are insane is really wasting words; for they at once pity you in your great ignorance in thinking such a thing possible.

H. G. Woodley, *Certified* (1947)

=

Madness may or may not be a hidden world, but society incessantly creates its own stereotypes about the experience of madness. This Bedlam ballad typically imagines the lunatic suffering from a mental rambling that provides an inner analogue to his mundane fate.

> Forth from the dark and dismal cell,
> And from the deep abyss of hell,
> Mad Tom is come to the world again,
> To see if he can cure his distemper'd brain.

Fears and cares oppress my soul,
Hark! how the angry furies howl,
Pluto laughs, and Proserpine is glad,
To see poor naked Tom a Bedlam mad.

Through the world I wander night and day,
    To find my straggling senses,
In an angry mood old Time,
    With his Pentateuch of tenses.

With me he spyes, away he flies,
    For Time will stay for no man;
In vain with cries I rend the skies,
    For pity is not common.

Cold and comfortless I lie,
Help! oh help! or else I die;
Hark! I hear Apollo's team,
    The Carman 'gins to whistle,
Chaste Diana bends her bow,
    And the Boar begins to bristle.

Come Vulcan, with tooth and tackles,
And knock off my troublesome shackles;
Bid Charles make ready his wain,
To find my lost senses again.

Last night I heard the Dog-star bark,
Mars met Venus in the dark:
Limping Vulcan heat an iron bar,
And furiously ran at the God of War.

Mars with his weapon laid about,
Limping Vulcan had the gout,
For his broad horns hung so in his light,
That he could not see to aim aright.

Mercury, the nimble Post of Heaven,
    Stay'd to see the quarrel,
Bacchus giantly bestrid
    A strong beer barrel.

To me he drank, I did him thank,
  But I could drink no cyder;
He drank whole Butts till he burst his guts,
  But mine were ne'er the wider.

Poor Tom is very dry,
A little drink for charity:
Hark! I hear Acteon's hounds!
  The Huntsman whoops and hollows,
Ringwood, Rockwood, Jowler, Bowman,
  All the chase doth follow.

The man in the moon drinks claret,
Eats powder'd beef, turnip, and carrot,
But a cup of old Malaga sack,
Will fire the bush at his back.

'Tom 'a' Bedlam', in Thomas Percy, *Reliques of Ancient English Poetry*
(1857)

=

Becoming an angel

In the night I woke under the most dreadful impressions; I heard a voice addressing me, and I was made to imagine that my disobedience to the faith, in taking the medicine overnight, had not only offended the Lord, but had rendered the work of my salvation extremely difficult, by its effect upon my spirits and humours. I heard that I could only be saved now by being changed into a spiritual body; and that a great fight would take place in my mortal body between Satan and Jesus; the result of which would either be my perfection in a spiritual body, or my awaking in hell. I am not sure whether before or after this, I was not commanded to cry out aloud, for consenting to which I was immediately rebuked, as unmindful of the promise I had made to my friend. A spirit came upon me and prepared to guide me in my actions. I was lying on my back, and the spirit seemed to light on my pillow by my right ear, and to command my body. I was placed in a fatiguing attitude, resting on my feet, my knees drawn up and on my head, and made to swing my body from side to side without ceasing. In the meantime, I heard voices without and within me, and sounds as of the clanking of iron, and the breathing of great forge bellows, and the force of flames. I understood that I was only saved by the mercy of Jesus, from seeing, as well as hearing, hell around me; and that if I were not obedient to His spirit, I should inevitably awake in hell before the morning. After some time I had a little rest, and then, actuated by the same spirit, I took a like position on the floor, where I remained, until I understood that the work of the Lord was perfected, and that now my salvation was secured; at the same time the guidance of the spirit left me, and I became in doubt what next I was to do. I understood that this provoked the Lord, as if I was affecting ignorance when I knew what I was to do, and, after some hesitation, I heard the command, to *take your position on the floor again then*', but I had no guidance or no perfect guidance to do so, and could not resume it. I was told, however, that my salvation depended upon my maintaining that position as well as I could until the morning; and oh! great was my joy when I perceived the first brightness of the dawn, which I could scarcely believe had arrived so early. I then retired to bed. I had imagined during the night that the fire of hell was consuming my mortal body – that the Spirit of Jesus came down to me to endure the pain thereof for me, that he might perfect in me a spiritual body to His honour and glory. I imagined that the end of this work was, that I was already in the state of one raised from the dead; and that any sin or disobedience in this body was doubly horrible and loathsome, inasmuch as it was in a body actually regenerated and clothed upon with the Holy Ghost. I imagined also that the Holy Ghost had in a special manner descended, and worked with Jesus to save me. I considered it a proof of the truth of my imaginations, when on rising, being perplexed by two different guidings that came upon me, I looked down upon my limbs which were white and of a natural colour; and again I looked down on my limbs, when one half of my frame appeared in a state of scarlet inflammation. When I went to dress, this had again subsided.

Before I rose from my bed, I understood that I was now to proceed through the world *as an angel*, under the immediate guidance of the Lord, to proclaim the tidings of his second coming. With that came an uncertain impression that I was to do this in an extraordinary way, and by singing – and this idea haunted me throughout my changes of insanity. I had also an *uncertain* impression of a like nature, that I was to go and show myself before the lord lieutenant or the General of the Forces, that I was to breakfast there, and to meet, either at the lord lieutenant's, a prince of the blood royal; or at the General's, a duke, to whom I was to proclaim the near coming of the Lord.

My guidance not being sure, and my folly or my faith not being firm enough, I reflected on Mary Campbell's advice, and determined to be guided by what appeared the natural path of duty. And, at the risk of offending the Holy Spirit and the Lord, to prefer showing my gratitude to Captain H. who had shown me so many kind attentions, and to attend his humble table. I now conceived again that I was to speak to them in an unknown tongue, and to make confessions, and to show signs and wonders: my words and ideas were to be supplied to me. I did not, however, dare to attempt any thing, for I felt no guidance, and I shrank from the ridicule of beginning to speak, and having nothing to say. My whole conduct became confused, my language ambiguous and doubtful. After breakfast, I prayed to be left alone, which was accorded with some difficulty. When alone in the breakfast room, I expected to be guided to prayer; but a spirit guided me and placed me on a chair, in a constrained position, with my head turned to *look at the clock*, the hand of which I saw proceeding to the first quarter; I understood I was to leave the position when it came to the quarter; when, however, it came to the quarter, I was anxious to be on the safe side, and I waited till it was at least half a minute past. Having done this, I was not a whit the wiser; but on the contrary, I felt that I had again offended by my want of exact punctuality, proving my want of confidence. I was then directed to lie on the floor, with my face to the ground, in an attitude of supplication and humiliation. I heard a spirit *pray in me*, and *reason in me*, and *with me*, and ultimately, another spirit, desiring certain gifts of the Holy Spirit to be given me, amongst which prophecy, tongues, miracles, and discernment of spirits; soon after, I was overwhelmed with a sudden and mighty conviction of my utter worthlessness; and being asked how I could expect the Lord to take me, and on what conditions I craved his favour; another spirit cried out in me, and for me, '*Lord! take me as I am.*'

John T. Perceval, *A Narrative of the Treatment Received by a Gentleman, During a State of Mental Derangement* (1838/40)

=

Becoming a wolf: the richly deserved fate of Ferdinand, the Duchess of Malfi's villainous brother in Webster's play. In return for his attempts to drive his sister insane (by sending Bedlamite lunatics to attend her, among other methods), Ferdinand himself succumbs to raving madness – and it takes the form of lycanthropy (see page 398).

FERDINAND: Leave me.

MALATESTI: Why doth your lordship love this solitariness?

FERDINAND: Eagles commonly fly alone: they are crows, daws, and starlings that flock together. Look, what's that follows me?

MALATESTI: Nothing, my lord.

FERDINAND: Yes.

MALATESTI: 'Tis your shadow.

FERDINAND: Stay it; let it not haunt me.

MALATESTI: Impossible, if you move, and the sun shine.

FERDINAND: I will throttle it. (*Throws himself down on his shadow*)

MALATESTI: O, my lord, you are angry with nothing.

FERDINAND: You are a fool: how is't possible I should catch my shadow, unless I fall upon't? When I go to hell, I mean to carry a bribe; for, look you, good gifts evermore make way for the worst persons.

PESCARA: Rise, good my lord.

FERDINAND: I am studying the art of patience.

PESCARA: 'Tis a noble virtue.

FERDINAND: To drive six snails before me from this town to Moscow; neither use goad nor whip to them, but let them take their own time; – the patient'st man i'the world match me for an experiment; – and I'll crawl after like a sheep-biter.

CARDINAL: Force him up.

(*They raise him.*)

FERDINAND: Use me well, you were best. What I have done, I have done: I'll confess nothing.

DOCTOR: Now let me come to him. – Are you mad, my lord? are you out of your princely wits?

FERDINAND: What's he?

PESCARA: Your doctor.

FERDINAND: Let me have his beard sawed off, and his eye-brows filed more civil.

DOCTOR: I must do mad tricks with him, for that's the only way on't. – I have brought your grace a salamander's skin to keep you from sun-burning.

FERDINAND: I have cruel sore eyes.

DOCTOR: The white of a cockatrix's egg is present remedy.

FERDINAND: Let it be a new-laid one, you were best – Hide me from him: physicians are like kings – They brook no contradiction.

DOCTOR: Now he begins to fear me: now let me alone with him.

John Webster, The Duchess of Malfi (c. 1614)

=

I felt a Cleaving in my Mind –
As if my Brain had split –
I tried to match it – Seam by Seam –
But could not make them fit.

The thought behind, I strove to join
Unto the thought before –
But Sequence ravelled out of Sound
Like Balls – upon a Floor.

Emily Dickinson (see page 2), 'I felt a Cleaving in my Mind' (c. 1864)

=

Racked by religious guilt, a conviction of damnation, and a feeling of social inadequacy, the young William Cowper, a clergyman's son, embarks upon suicide, or rather, perhaps, suicide attempts.

In this manner the time passed till the day began to break. I heard the clock strike seven, and instantly it occurred to me that there was no time to be lost. The chambers would soon be opened, and my friend would call upon me to take me with him to Westminster. 'Now is the time,' thought I, – 'this is the crisis; – no more dallying with the love of life.' I arose, and, as I thought, bolted the inner door of my chambers, but was mistaken; my touch deceived me, and I left it as I found it. My preservation indeed, as it will appear, did not depend upon that incident; but I mention it, to show that the good providence of God watched over me to keep open every way of deliverance, that nothing might be left to hazard. Not one hesitating thought now remained; but I fell greedily to the execution of my purpose. My garter was made of a broad scarlet binding, with a sliding buckle being sewn together at the end: by the help of the buckle I made a noose, and fixed it around my neck, straining it so tight, that I hardly left a passage for my breath, or for the blood to circulate, the tongue of the buckle held it fast. At each corner of the bed, was placed a wreath of carved work, fastened by an iron pin, which passed up through the midst of it. The other part of the garter, which made a loop, I slipped over one of these, and hung by it some seconds, drawing my feet under me, that they might not touch the floor; but the iron bent, and the carved work slipped off, and the garter with it. I then fastened it to the frame of the tester, winding it round, and tying it in a strong knot. The frame broke short and let me down again. The third effort was more likely to succeed. I set the door open, which reached within a foot of the ceiling; and by the help of a chair I could command the top of it; and the loop being large enough to admit a large angle of the door, was easily fixed, so as not to slip off again. I pushed away the chair with my feet, and hung at my whole length. While I hung there, I distinctly heard a voice say three times, *"Tis over!"* Though I am sure of the fact and was so at the time, yet it did not at all alarm me, or affect my resolution. I hung so long, that I lost all sense, all consciousness of existence.

When I came to myself again, I thought myself in hell; the sound of my own dreadful groans was all that I heard; and a feeling like that produced by a flash of lightning, just beginning to seize upon me, passed over my whole body. In a few seconds I found myself fallen with my face to the floor. In about half a minute, I recovered my feet, and reeling, and staggering, stumbled into bed again. By the blessed providence of God, the garter which had held me till the bitterness of temporal death was past, broke, just before eternal death had taken place upon me. The stagnation of the blood under one eye, in a broad crimson spot, and a red circle about my neck, showed plainly that I had been on the brink of eternity. The latter, indeed, might have been occasioned by the pressure of the garter; but the former was certainly the effect of strangulation; for it was not attended with the sensation of a bruise, as it must have been, had I, in my fall, received one in so tender a part. And I rather think the circle round my neck was owing to the same cause; for the part was not excoriated, nor at all in pain.

Soon after I got into bed, I was surprised to hear a noise in the dining-room, where the laundress was lighting a fire. She had found the door unbolted, notwithstanding my design to fasten it, and must have passed the bed-chamber door while I was hanging on it, and yet never perceived me. She heard me fall, and presently came to ask if I were well; adding, she feared I had been in a fit.

William Cowper, *Memoir of the Early Life of William Cowper, Esq.*
(1816)

==

Consigned to Bethlem (see page 1) in 1796, James Tilly Matthews believed he was systematically being tortured by a gang of French spies operating a Mesmeric machine which controlled his mind and body in the following ways (and many other besides).

Fluid Locking – A locking or constriction of the fibres of the root of the tongue, laterally, by which the readiness of speech is impeded.

Cutting soul from sense – A spreading of the magnetic warp, chilled in its expansion, from the root of the nose, diffused under the basis of the brain, as if a veil were interposed; so that the sentiments of the heart can have no communication with the operations of the intellect.

Stone-making – The gang pretend they can at pleasure produce a precipitation in the bladder of any person impregnated, and form a calculus. They boast of having effected this in a very complete manner for the late Duke of Portland.

Thigh-talking – To effect this, they contrive so to direct their *voice-sayings* on the external part of the thigh, that the person assailed is conscious that his organ of hearing, with all its sensibility, is lodged in that situation. The sensation is distinctly felt in the thigh, and the subject understood in the brain.

Kiteing – This is a very singular and distressing mode of assailment, and much practised by the gang. As boys raise a kite in the air, so these wretches, by means of the air-loom and magnetic impregnations, contrive to lift into the brain some particular idea, which floats and undulates in the intellect for hours together; and how much soever the person assailed may wish to direct his mind to other objects, and banish the idea forced upon him, he finds himself unable; as the idea which they have kited keeps waving in his mind, and fixes his attention to the exclusion of other thoughts. He is, during the whole time, conscious that the kited idea is extraneous, and does not belong to the train of his own cogitations.

Sudden death-squeezing by them termed *Lobster-cracking* – This is an external pressure of the magnetic atmosphere surrounding the person assailed, so as to stagnate his circulation, impede his vital motions, and produce instant death.

In short, I do not know any better way for a person to comprehend the general nature of such lobster-cracking operation, than by supposing himself in a sufficiently large pair of nut-crackers or lobster-crackers, with teeth, which should pierce as well as press him through every particle within and without; he experiencing the whole stress, torture, driving, oppressing, and crush all together.

Stomach-skinning consists in rendering the stomach raw and sore, as if it had been scalded, and the internal coat stripped off.

Apoplexy-working with the nutmeg-grater consists in violently forcing the fluids into the head; and where such effort does not suddenly destroy the person, producing small pimples on the temples, which are raised, and rough like the holes in a nutmeg-grater: in a day or two they gradually die away.

Lengthening the brain – As the cylindrical mirror lengthens the countenance of the person who views himself in such glass, so the assailants have a method by which they contrive to elongate the brain. The effect produced by this process is a distortion of any idea in the mind, whereby that which had been considered as most serious becomes an object of ridicule. All thoughts are made to assume a grotesque interpretation; and the person assailed is surprised that his fixed and solemn opinions should take a form which compels him to distrust their identity, and forces him to laugh at the most important subjects. It can cause good sense to appear as insanity, and convert truth into a libel; distort the wisest institutions of civilized society into the practices of barbarians, and strain the Bible into a jest book.

Thought-making – While one of these villains is sucking at the brain of the person assailed, to extract his existing sentiments, another of the gang, in order to lead astray the sucker (for deception is practised among themselves as a part of their system; and there exists no honor, as amongst thieves, in the community of these rascals) will force into his mind a train of ideas very different from the real subject of his thoughts, and which is seized upon as the desired information by the person sucking; whilst he of the gang who has forced the thought on the person assailed, laughs in his sleeve at the imposition he has practised.

Laugh-making consists in forcing the magnetic fluid, rarified and subtilized, on the vitals, [*vital touching*] so that the muscles of the face become screwed into a laugh or grin.

John Haslam, *Illustrations of Madness* (1810)

=

Despairing of a Europe tearing itself apart in the First World War, the dancer Nijinsky offered Tolstoyan truths which were interpreted by his wife and doctors as proofs of mental instability.

I know that Mars is uninhabited because it is a frozen body. Mars was like the earth, but that was many billions of years ago. The earth will also be like Mars but in a few hundred years hence. The earth is suffocating, therefore I am asking everybody to abandon factories and listen to me. I know that this is necessary for the salvation of the earth.

My caretaker is stupid – he drinks, imagining that he is well, but he is killing himself. I am the Saviour. I am Nijinsky and not Christ. I love Christ, because He was like me. I love Tolstoy, because he was like me. I want to save the entire earth from suffocation. All the scientists must leave their books and come to me, and I will help everyone because I know so much. I am a man in God. I am not afraid of death. I beg people not to be afraid of me. I am a man with faults, like other people. I want to improve myself. I must not be killed because I love everyone equally.

I will go to Zurich and will see the town, which is a commercial town, and God will be with me.

I am not intelligence, but mind. Tolstoy spoke about the mind, Schopenhauer also. I too write about mind. My philosophy is truth and not invention. Nietzsche became insane because he realized at the end of his life that everything he had written was absurd. He became frightened of people and went mad. I will not be frightened if people throw themselves at me. I understand crowds. I can manage them, although I am not a commander. I like family life; I love all children, and I like to play with them. I understand them. I am a child, and I am a father. I am a married man. I love my wife and want to help her in life. I know why men run after girls. I know what a girl is. Man and woman are one; I prefer married people because they know life. Married people make mistakes but they live. *I am husband and wife in one.* I love my wife. I love my husband. I do not like a husband and wife to be debauched. I am a physical body but not physical love. I am love for mankind. I want the government to allow me to live where I like. My wife is a good woman, so is my child, and they shall not be hurt.

I will write a great deal because I want to explain to people the meaning of death and life. I cannot write quickly because my muscles are getting tired. I cannot any more. I am a martyr – I feel pain. I am fond of writing; I want to help people, but I cannot write because I am tired. I want to finish, but God does not let me. I write until God stops me.

Romola Nijinsky (ed.), The Diary of Vaslav Nijinsky (1937)

=

Autobiographers of insanity record the agonizing and obscene experience of falling under the irresistible command of alien powers.

After this, I heard some voices tell me to tell some of the attendants who were standing near the foot of the bed to kiss my great toe. I refused stoutly, and said I was not the Pope, and only a man like the attendants themselves.

'Never mind; do what we ask you,' came the voices.

I went on to state that St Paul and St Barnabas had rent their clothes and cast dust and ashes on their heads, sooner than allow anything in the nature of worship to be offered to them.

'Never mind; do what we ask you. We want to see whether they have any *faith* at all, for it is the only chance of salvation they have got.'

This upset all my calculations, for their salvation was more important to me than any horror and repulsion I might feel at doing a thing so much against my grain; so I put my foot out, and told them to do so 'for the sake of their salvation'.

I should never, and could never, have done a thing which I regarded as blasphemous, and altogether absurd, if I had not felt that it was my duty to obey these voices. I knew that it made me look a fool; and not only this, but I was afraid it might provoke the attendants to set on me. I never in all my life saw such a look of disgust as came over their faces, and I was thankful they did not shew it in any more active manner.

D. Davidson, *Remembrances of a Religio-Maniac: An Autobiography*
(1912)

===

James Hogg was one of the earliest to record the experience of dual personality.

Immediately after this I was seized with a strange distemper, which neither my friends nor physicians could comprehend, and it confined me to my chamber for many days; but I knew, myself, that I was bewitched, and suspected my father's reputed concubine of the deed. I told my fears to my reverend protector, who hesitated concerning them, but I knew by his words and looks that he was conscious I was right. I generally conceived myself to be two people. When I lay in bed, I deemed there were two of us in it; when I sat up, I always beheld another person, and always in the same position from the place where I sat or stood, which was about three paces off me towards my left side. It mattered not how many or how few were present: this my second self was sure to be present in his place; and this occasioned a confusion in all my words and ideas that utterly astounded my friends, who all declared, that instead of being deranged in my intellect, they have never heard my conversation manifest so much energy or sublimity of conception; but for all that, over the singular delusion that I was two persons, my reasoning faculties had no power. The most perverse part of it was, that I rarely conceived *myself* to be any of the two persons. I thought for the most part that my companion was one of them, and my brother the other; and I found, that to be obliged to speak and answer in the character of another man, was a most awkward business at the long run.

Who can doubt, from this statement, that I was bewitched, and that my relatives were at the ground of it?

James Hogg, *The Private Memoirs and Confessions of a Justified Sinner*
(1818)

=

The summer sun ray
shifts through a suspicious tree.
though I walk through the valley of the shadow
It sucks the air
and looks around for me.

The grass speaks.
I hear green chanting all day.
I will fear no evil, fear no evil
The blades extend
and reach my way.

The sky breaks.
It sags and breathes upon my face.
in the presence of mine enemies, mine enemies
The world is full of enemies.
There is no safe place.

Anne Sexton (see page 86), 'Noon Walk on the Asylum Lawn', in *To Bedlam and Part Way Back* (1960)

=

Looking back, John Perceval (see page 23) saw his madness as a state of irresolvable uncertainty, in which he became aware of the disorientation of his mind and senses but incapable of correcting them.

Let no man mock at the understanding that could so patiently or humbly submit to such seemingly absurd teachings; but rather let him fear and pray that the power of the Lord to confound the judgment and wisdom of man may not be put forth upon him.

My mind was not destroyed, without the ruin of my body. My delusions, though they often made me ridiculous, did not derange my understanding unaided by the poisonous medicines and unnatural treatment of my physicians. Then when I became insane, the knowledge of that fact appears to have given to every one who had to deal with me carte blanche to act towards me, as far as seemed good unto himself, in defiance of nature, of common sense, and of humanity. The wonder is, not that I fell, but that, having through my fall come into the net which is spread by the arts and malice of the lunatic doctors, I could endure their treatment, and, recovering from under it, exercise my own native sense of justice boldly in spite of their will, whilst still unsound in judgment, and ultimately ride triumphant over the waves of misfortune! My senses were all mocked at and deceived. In reading, my eyes saw words in the paper which when I looked again were not. The forms of those around me and their features changed, even as I looked on them. Nature appeared at times renewed, and in a beautiful medium that reminded me of the promises of the gospel and the prophecies concerning the times of refreshing and renewal; in a few minutes she again appeared trite and barren of virtue, as I had used to know her. I heard the voices of invisible agents, and notes so divine, so pure, so holy, that they alone perhaps might recompense me for my sufferings. My sense of feeling was not the same, my smell, my taste, gone or confounded.

Believing in miraculous agency, and the subject of miraculous sensations, I received these as the word and guidance of God, for their beauty and their apparent tendency to promote purity and benevolence. And if I doubted, my doubts were overwhelmed if not dissipated by compunction at attributing what was so kind, so lovely, so touching, to any but the divine nature, and by fear of committing the sin against the Holy Ghost. Whatever then appeared contradictory, or did not turn out as I expected, I attributed to my disobedience or want of understanding, not to want of truth in my mediator.

John T. Perceval, *A Narrative of the Treatment Received by a Gentleman, During a State of Mental Derangement* (1838/40)

6

Delusions

There is no more splendid cache of psychopathological material than the delusions recorded over the centuries by the insane. Psychiatrists and historians alike, however, have shown but desultory interest in them, and have paid little attention to the problems of teasing out their meaning. Of course, techniques have always existed for plucking meaning out of nonsense, and decoding the weirder products of the human consciousness. In Antiquity, Artemidorus systematized the methods of dream interpretation (including, in a manner premonitory of the Freudian 'no means yes' decoding device, exegesis by opposites), while medieval commentators developed highly elaborate hermeneutic arts for the elucidation of symbolic double meanings in holy writings.

Perhaps because of the rather dubious standing of these esoteric skills, the early psychological medicine stimulated by the Scientific Revolution preferred to promote methodologies deriving not from textual criticism but from the physical sciences, staking faith in facts, numbers and strict observation of patients. The pioneer psychiatrists of the Age of the Enlightenment showed little interest in the challenge of decoding the delusions of the mad. Their aim was primarily to establish the fact that the visions of visionaries were indeed void of truth, being the preposterous products of defective sense organs, faulty cognitive procedures or of 'vapours', wafting up from the stomach, that occluded the judgement. Asylum superintendents were wary of prying too deeply into their patients' delusional systems, lest this unwittingly gave them credibility, or fostered hysterical self-absorption.

Not until Freud did a school of psychiatry emerge, avowedly committed to the belief that what the patients said – at least, when properly translated – contained the key to the nature and source of their disorder, and should form base-point for its cure. It is no accident that Freud's earliest systematic treatise – and many would say, his finest book – is a manual of dream interpretation. Freud's conviction that nothing is accidental, irrelevant or meaningless, that everything, including 'Freudian slips', has its significance, finds parallels, also around the turn of the century, in the development of techniques of art therapy for the disturbed; and, somewhat later, in the use of Rorschach ink-blot tests in cognitive psychology. Even Freud, however, thought his semiotic approach had its therapeutic limits. It would work with neurotics, who retained some hold upon reality, albeit as through a glass darkly. The method was unlikely to succeed with psychotics.

Examining the delusions of the disturbed, we find, not surprisingly, the shadow of terrorism. Their nightmares and daydreams are haunted by predators and persecutors, sinister omnipotent invaders, invisible demons and shady operators. They bespeak conditions in which the subject is utterly incapable of protecting himself against fears and threats we commonly experience but usually find the resources – psychological and social – to manage, or to divert.

How can we trust the testimony of our senses, the reliability of the world-pictures conjured up by our imaginations? The worldling sees a black cloud, his fundamentalist friend spies the Devil. Is one right, and the other wrong? Do different sensory systems literally present different pictures to different people? Or should we be speaking of rival, relative readings of reality? In the end, when reality is at issue, it is usually one man's word against another, or rather the word of the common mass, or of common sense, or of scientific authority, against the lone individual (though, in cases of mass hysteria, the line becomes increasingly hard to draw). Are we here dealing with problems in the neurophysiology of the senses, or in the conventions of culture – an incapacity to discriminate between animate and inanimate, the figural and the literal? If I tell a friend he has welcomed me regally, he will only jump to the conclusion that he is a king if he is disordered in his senses, or, at least, if he does not understand the uses of metaphor.

John Perceval and Daniel Schreber, possibly the two most acute self-analysts of what happens when your mind becomes deranged, both attributed their own bouts of disorder to their inability to master the dislocations between things, concepts, names and words. Perceval also reports that he began to recover his mental grip when he recognized that his inner voices were, in truth, audible sounds, but ones traceable to the squeaking of door hinges or the hissing of gas jets.

Viktor Tausk, one of Freud's most creative, though tragic, followers, wrote a famous account of the phenomenon of the 'influencing-machine', the classic engine of oppression experienced by the paranoid. Themselves successors to the Devil and his minions, such imagined machines were, in former times, made of iron and driven by steam. Later, such primitive technology was replaced by electricity. Today, these phantom influencing-machines that torment the persecuted have taken on board the gadgets of science fiction or keep fully abreast with the latest computer designs; and the minds of their pathetic victims are infiltrated by ghostly software formatted with dastardly schemes for reprogramming the mind. Among the extracts that follow, the experiences of James Tilly Matthews, tortured by an 'Air Loom' machine, capture the fascination with textile machinery shown in the age of industrialization, and the allure of the Mesmeric *baquets* (see page 144 and Plate 10). It is time someone wrote the cultural history of delusions.

———

I could find no rest, for horrible images assailed me, so vivid that I experienced actual physical sensation. I cannot say that I really saw images; they did not represent anything. Rather I felt them. It seemed that my mouth was full of birds which I crunched between my teeth, and their feathers, their blood and broken bones were choking me. Or I saw people whom I had entombed in milk bottles, putrefying, and I was consuming their rotting cadavers. Or I was devouring the head of a cat which meanwhile gnawed at my vitals. It was ghastly, intolerable.

Marguerite Sechehaye, *Reality Lost and Regained: Autobiography of a Schizophrenic Girl, with Analytic Interpretation* (1951)

———

The folklore of lunacy rings the changes upon a standard repertoire of delusions supposedly experienced by depressives with over-vivid imaginations. Most famous, perhaps, is the man who believed he was made of glass. Another is this delusion of self-importance.

HISTORIES OF CERTAINE MELANCHOLIKE PERSONS, WHICH HAVE HAD STRANGE IMAGINATIONS

The pleasantest dotage that ever I read, was of one Sienois a Gentleman, who had resolved with himselfe not to pisse, but to dye rather, and that because he imagined, that when he first pissed, all his towne would be drowned. The Phisitions shewing him, that all his bodie, and ten thousand more such as his, were not able to containe so much as might drowne the least house in the towne, could not change his minde from this foolish imagination. In the end they seeing his obstinacie, and in what danger he put his life, found out a pleasant invention. They caused the next house to be set on fire, & all the bells in the town to ring, they perswaded diverse servants to crie, to the fire, to the fire, & therewithall send of those of the best account in the town, to crave helpe, and shew the Gentleman that there is but one way to save the towne, and that it was, that he should pisse quickelie and quench the fire. Then this sillie melancholike man which abstained from pissing for feare of loosing his towne, taking it for graunted, that it was now in great hazard, pissed and emptied his bladder of all that was in it, and was himselfe by that means preserved.

André du Laurens, *A Discourse of the Preservation of the Sight* (1599)

=

The patient who believed he was nobody

Some years ago, a patient much afflicted with melancholic and hypochondriacal symptoms, was admitted by his own request. He had walked from home, a distance of 200 miles, in company with a friend; and on his arrival, found much less inclination to converse on the absurd and melancholy views of his own state, than he had previously felt.*

*Though this patient was much less disposed to converse upon the subject, his hypochondriacal ideas remained, as the following description of himself, taken nearly verbatim from his own mouth, will prove: 'I have no soul; I have neither heart, liver, nor lungs; nor any thing at all in my body, nor a drop of blood in my veins. My bones are all burnt to a cinder: I have no brain; and my head is sometimes as hard as iron, and sometimes as soft as a pudding.' A fellow patient, also an hypochondriac, amused himself in versifying this affectingly ludicrous description in the following lines:

> A miracle, my friends, come view,
> A man, admit his own words true,
>   Who lives without a soul;
> Nor liver, lungs, nor heart has he,
> Yet, sometimes, can as cheerful be
>   As if he had the whole.
>
> His head (take his own words along)
> Now hard as iron, yet are long
>   Is soft as any jelly;
> All burnt his sinews, and his lungs;
> Of his complaints, not fifty tongues
>   Could find enough to tell ye.
>
> Yet he who paints his likeness here,
> Has just as much himself to fear,
>   He's wrong from top to toe;
> Ah friends! pray help us, if you can,
> And make us each again a man,
>   That we from hence may go.

Samuel Tuke, *Description of The Retreat, an Institution near York for Insane Persons of The Society of Friends, containing an account of its origin and progress, the modes of treatment, and a statement of cases*
(1813)

===

Disembodied voices often interact contrapuntally with the day-to-day world.

Deborah was standing in the small seclusion room forward of the hall. Her lunch tray had been brought by a nurse, who fumbled with the keys (her difference), and was pale, remembering perhaps the secret bedlam horror-nightmares of her own keeping. Those, at least, Deborah shared, believed, understood. She whispered her comfort and saw the nurse get hard in the face with fear, and turn, stumbling over her own feet to hang on the fraction of the edge of her balance.

Deborah put out a hand almost instinctively, since clumsiness had made them kin, and the hand got to the nurse's arm and held her for a second. Balance caught the young woman and swung her towards vertical again and she pulled her arm away, strong in her fear, and tottered out of the room.

Suffer, Deborah said to all the assembled ones in Yr, the Yri metaphor for greeting. *I am a conductor of lightnings and burnings. Passes through me from doctor, flows to nurse. Here I have been copper wire all the time and people had been mistaking me for brazen!*

Anterrabae laughed. *Be witty*, he said, shedding hair-sparks in his unending, unconsuming, fiery fall. *Outside this room, ward, hospital, such as that and that even, when her shift is through, laugh, walk, breathe, in an element that you will never understand or know. Their breath in and out, blood, bones, night and day are not of the same substance as yours. Your substance is fatal to them. If they are ever infected with your element they will die of it or go insane.*

'Like the Pit?'

Exactly so.

Deborah cried out in horror at her power to destroy. She fell on the floor, moaning softly. 'Too much power, too much hurt. Don't let anyone hurt like that – not like that! Not like that ... like that ...'

Then she was standing above herself, dressed in her Yri rank and name, kicking the herself that was on the floor, kicking her low in the stomach and in the tumourous place that gave like a rotten melon. When the ceremonial creak of leave-taking sounded, the sky was burdening itself with darkness outside the barred window. She looked out, finding herself erect and in front of the window and saying quietly, 'Let me die, all of you.' If they would all come together against her, she knew that she could not live. There was no joy or happiness or peace or freedom worth this suffering. 'End me, Anterrabae, Collect, all you others. Once and for all, crush me against the world!'

The light was put on from the outside and the key grated in the lock. 'Just checking,' the change-of-shift nurse said gaily, but when she saw Deborah's face, she turned back to the one behind her. 'Finish the ward check and get a pack set up.'

Deborah did not know what look she was carrying in front of what self, but she was greatly relieved. Help was coming by virtue of some of the misery which was apparently leaking through the mask. 'Out at the eyeholes, maybe ...' she murmured to the people who came after a while.

Hannah Green, *I Never Promised You a Rose Garden* (1964)

=

The voices threaten ECT (see page 280).

'We'll give her shock treatment tomorrow,' one said. 'A worse shock than she's ever had; and she can't escape. You've locked the door securely?'

'Yes,' replied the other. 'She's down for shock. It will put her in her place I tell you. She needs to be taught a lesson. No breakfast for her tomorrow.'

'No breakfast,' the other voice repeated. 'She's for shock.'

My heart beat fast so that I found it hard to breathe; I was overcome by such a feeling of panic that although it seemed like breaking and distorting the only image of sky that was left to me, I smashed the window with my fist, to get out or to get at the glass and destroy myself to prevent the coming of tomorrow and the dreaded EST.

For gone now were the old 'brave' days at Cliffhaven when I had preserved enough calm to queue for treatment and to watch the beds with the unconscious patients in them, being wheeled from the treatment room. Ever since the morning in Four-Five-and-One when they had surprised me by giving me two consecutive treatments, although I had been given no more, and although, as I learned, I had been transferred to Lawn Lodge because they could 'do nothing with me', I still lived in dread of the morning when the door would be unlocked and the nurse would greet me with, 'No breakfast for you this morning. Keep on your nightgown and your dressing gown. You're for treatment.'

Hearing the commotion of breaking glass the nurse hurried to the room and burst in, and I was put into the opposite room which was dark and shuttered, and I climbed shivering between the cold stiff sheets made colder by the mackintosh under them, and uncomfortable by the stalks of straw sticking through the mattress. I was given paraldehyde and slept.

The next morning my fear returned, yet I found out that I had been mistaken, that I was not 'for treatment.'

I could no longer control my fear; it persisted and grew stronger and day after day I made myself a nuisance by asking, asking, asking if they were planning to give me EST or to do anything terrible to me, to bury me alive in a tunnel in the earth so that no matter how long I called for help no one would hear me, to remove part of my brain and turn me into a strange animal who had to be led about with a leather collar and chain and wearing a striped dress.

And now whenever I saw the Matron and Sister Wolf talking together I suffered agonies of suspense. I knew they were talking about me; they were planning to murder me with electricity, to send me to Mount Eden Prison where I would be hanged at daybreak. Sometimes I screamed at Matron and Sister to stop their conversation; sometimes now I attacked the nurses because I knew they were hiding the truth from me, refusing to tell me the fearful plans they were making. And I had to know. I had to know. How else could I make arrangements to protect myself, to gather all the devices for use in extreme emergency and take things calmly so that I would know which to use? If only there had been someone to tell me!

I would have asked the assurance of the doctor but where was he? It was well known that Lawn Lodge patients were 'so far gone' that it was not much use the doctor devoting his valuable time to them, that it was wiser for him to be attending the others, the Ward Seven and the convalescent people who could be 'saved.' Only once I saw the doctor pass through the dayroom of Lawn Lodge. He limped quickly from door to door. On his face was an expression of horror and fear that changed to incredulity as if he were saying to himself, 'It is not so. I am a young enthusiastic doctor, only a few years out of medical school. I live with my wife and child across the road in the house provided for me. My God what means the hospitality of the soul?'

Janet Frame, *Faces in the Water* (1961)

*To our post-Freudian eyes, the delusions of former days may speak
loud and clear to us in languages apparently foreign to the ears of
earlier psychiatry.*

It is not long ago since a very learned and ingenious Gentleman, so
far started from his Reason, as to believe, that his Body was
metamorphos'd into a Hobby-Horse, and nothing would serve his
Turn, but that his Friend, who came to see him, must mount his
Back and ride. I must confess, that all the philosophy I was Master
of, could not dispossess him of this Conceit; 'till by application of
generous Medicines, I restor'd the disconcerted nerves to their
regular Motions, and, by that Means, gave him a Sight of his Error.

                    Nicholas Robinson, *A New System of the Spleen* (1729)

=

*Guillotined nightly: a lunatic in post-Revolutionary Paris. Jean-
Etienne-Dominique Esquirol was a favourite pupil of Philippe
Pinel (see page 12), who initiated him into his humane methods of
treating the insane. See Plate 14.*

We have at Charenton a monomaniac, thirty years of age, who is
persuaded that he is conducted every night into the vaults of the
opera. There, and even sometimes without leaving his chamber,
they pierce him with knives, plunge poniards into his back and
breast, and take off now an arm, now a thigh. They even cut off his
head. When it is remarked to this unfortunate man that his head is
upon his shoulders, that he preserves his members, and that his
body presents no wound nor cicatrix, he replies with animation:
*'These are the wretches, the magnetizers and freemasons, who have
the secret of readjusting the limbs, so that no evidence of their
amputations shall appear.'* If we insist: *'You have an understanding'*, he replies, *'with these monsters and brigands. Slay me, slay
me! I cannot resist the sufferings which they cause me to endure,
nor their cruelty.'* The father of this monomaniac, and his former
partner, are especially accused by him as the chiefs of all the villains
who nightly torture him.

              J.-E.-D. Esquirol, *Mental Maladies: A Treatise on Insanity* (1845)

=

Toes, Tartars and Turks

Ben Jonson, whose memory was remarkably tenacious, and whose imagination was sufficiently lively, appears now and then to have experienced these morbid or false sensations. He told Drummond, that he had spent a whole night in lying looking at his great toe, about which he had seen Tartars and Turks, Romans and Carthaginians, riding and fighting: but he knew that these were the effect of his heated fancy. The vision which he had whilst at Sir Robert Cotton's house in the country, of his son who was dying of the plague in London, had probably a similar origin.

John Conolly, (see page 107), *An Inquiry Concerning the Indications of Insanity, with Suggestions for the Better Protection and Care of the Insane* (1830)

=

Clockwork chimeras

A celebrated watchmaker, at Paris, was infatuated with the chimera of perpetual motion, and to effect this discovery, he set to work with indefatigable ardour. From unremitting attention to the object of his enthusiasm coinciding with the influence of revolutionary disturbances, his imagination was greatly heated, his sleep was interrupted, and, at length, a complete derangement of the understanding took place. His case was marked by a most whimsical illusion of the imagination. He fancied that he had lost his head on the scaffold; that it had been thrown promiscuously among the heads of many other victims; that the judges, having repented of their cruel sentence, had ordered those heads to be restored to their respective owners, and placed upon their respective shoulders; but that, in consequence of an unfortunate mistake, the gentlemen, who had the management of that business, had placed upon his shoulders the head of one of his unhappy companions. The idea of this whimsical exchange of his head, occupied his thoughts night and day; which determined his relations to send him to the Hôtel Dieu. Thence he was transferred to the Asylum de Bicêtre. Nothing could equal the extravagant overflowings of his heated brain. He sung, cried, or danced incessantly; and, as there

appeared no propensity in him to commit acts of violence or
disturbance, he was allowed to go about the hospital without
controul, in order to expend, by evaporation, the effervescent
excess of his spirits. 'Look at these teeth,' he constantly cried; –
'Mine were exceedingly handsome; – these are rotten and decayed.
My mouth was sound and healthy: this is foul and diseased. What
difference between this hair and that of my own head.' To this state
of delirious gaiety, however, succeeded that of furious madness. He
broke to pieces or otherwise destroyed whatever was within the
reach or power of his mischievous propensity. Close confinement
became indispensable. Towards the approach of winter his violence
abated; and, although he continued to be extravagant in his ideas,
he was never afterwards dangerous. He was, therefore, permitted,
when ever he felt disposed, to go to the inner court. The idea of the
perpetual motion frequently recurred to him in the midst of his
wanderings; and he chalked on all the walls and doors as he passed,
the various designs by which his wondrous piece of mechanism was
to be constructed. The method best calculated to cure so whimsical
an illusion, appeared to be that of encouraging his prosecution of it
to satiety. His friends were, accordingly, requested to send him his
tools, with materials to work upon, and other requisites, such as
plates of copper and steel, watch-wheels, &c. The governor permitted him to fix up a work-bench in his apartment. His zeal was
now redoubled. His whole attention was rivetted upon his favourite
pursuit. He forgot his meals to devote his whole time and attention
to his business. There still remained another maniacal impression to
be counteracted; – that of the imaginary exchange of his head,
which unceasingly recurred to him. A keen and an unanswerable
stroke of pleasantry seemed best adapted to correct this fantastic
whim. Another convalescent of a gay and facetious humour,
instructed in the part he should play in this comedy, adroitly turned
the conversation to the subject of the famous miracle of Saint
Denis. Our mechanician strongly maintained the possibility of the
fact, and sought to confirm it by an application of it to his own
case. The other set up a loud laugh, and replied with a tone of the
keenest ridicule: 'Madman as thou art, how could Saint Denis kiss
his own head? Was it with his heels?' This equally unexpected and
unanswerable retort, forcibly struck the maniac. He retired

confused amidst the peals of laughter, which were provoked at his
expense, and never afterwards mentioned the exchange of his head.
Close attention to his trade for some months, completed the restoration of his intellect. He was sent to his family in perfect health;
and has, now for more than five years, pursued his business without
a return of his complaint.

Philippe Pinel, (see page 12), *A Treatise on Insanity* (1806)

=

Delusions of persecution are commonly accompanied by the fallacy
of self-reference: the conviction that one is personally the fulcrum
and focus of all the (generally malign) activity of the world.

Delusions of persecution – which include 'delusions of self-
reference' – though a source of annoyance while I was in an inactive
state, annoyed and distressed me even more when I began to move
about and was obliged to associate with other patients. To my
mind, not only were the doctors and attendants detectives; each
patient was a detective and the whole institution was a part of the
Third Degree. Scarcely any remark was made in my presence that I
could not twist into a cleverly veiled reference to myself. In each
person I could see a resemblance to persons I had known, or to the
principals or victims of the crimes with which I imagined myself
charged. I refused to read; for to read veiled charges and fail to
assert my innocence was to incriminate both myself and others. But
I looked with longing glances upon all printed matter and, as my
curiosity was continually piqued, this enforced abstinence grew to
be well-nigh intolerable.

Clifford Beers, (see page 25), *A Mind that Found Itself:*
An Autobiography (1923)

=

Not all visions, however, are malign.

I had two unseen visitors that night in fairly quick succession. The
first was the spirit of a man. He made love to me tenderly but
briefly. His composition was of a different texture from mine and,

like a wisp of cloud pressing against a fine-meshed screen, he passed straight through me and was gone.

The second visitor was my companion of the afternoon. A man, yet more than a man. When he made love to me it was with a vigour that fired my whole being. His composition was also different from mine, but in the opposite direction. His passion, untempered and unhumanized by flesh, left me inwardly a little burnt. We sat together afterwards in comfortable companionship for a time, but this relaxation was no more than a brief preparation for the grave and strenuous work we had to do.

The task before us was no less than to lift Christ down from the cross. Not the lifeless body on a wooden cross outside Jerusalem. This concerned the living person who had been recrucified, and in a different way, through the influence of those on his own followers who, in imagery and worship, had concentrated their imagination of his physical sufferings and failed to grasp the mental and spiritual cost of the event. He had been lifted above life and immobilized in the posture in which so many of his worshippers wished to view him. What my companion had now to do, with my support, was very hard, but it was achieved. Afterwards there was a tremendous leap to be made across a gulf in which this earth was a stepping stone. Some great superhuman personage took part. He landed momentarily with one leg in the same place as one of mine, so that for a few seconds from mid-thigh downwards he shared my flesh. Then he was gone.

A few seconds later my right leg, which was the one that had been used, went into spasm. I thought quickly, and in the circumstances rather surprisingly, in terms of localized cerebral overstimulation; I lay down and called out, 'Send for a doctor.' I was confident of being heard by supernatural means. I lost consciousness and, when I came to, the spasm was relieved. Then it began again, even more severely, and this time there was no question of a neurological cause of the pain. I had been caught in the collision between two worlds, my leg was crushed between them and was being totally destroyed. For the first time in my life I screamed. I lost consciousness again, but just before doing so I saw as a kind of retinal after-image the shape of my severed leg in a phantasmagoric red colour; this image was being projected as a portent to other parts of the universe, where it caused much wonder and alarm.

Morag Coate, *Beyond All Reason* (1964)

=

Many mentally disturbed people have described persecuting engines. One of the earliest and fullest of such accounts was recorded by James Tilly Matthews around 1800 (see Plate 10).

The annexed figure of the air-loom, sketched by Mr Matthews, together with *his* explanations, will afford the necessary information concerning this curious and wonderful machine.

REFERENCES

a a The top of the apparatus, called by the assassins air-loom machine, pneumatic machine, &c. being as a large table.
b b The metals which the workers grasp to deaden the sympathy.
c The place where the pneumaticians sit to work the loom.
d Something like piano-forte keys, which open the tube valves within the air-loom, to spread or feed the warp of magnetic fluid.
e e Levers, by the management of which the assailed is wrenched, stagnated, and the sudden-death efforts made upon him, &c. The levers are placed at those points of elevation, *viz.* the one nearly down, at which I begin to let go my breath, taking care to make it a regular, not in any way a hurried breathing. The other, the highest, is where it begins to strain the warp, and by which time it becomes necessary to have taken full breath, to hold till the lever was so far down again. This invariably is the vital-straining. But in that dreadful operation by them termed lobster-cracking, I always found it necessary to open my mouth somewhat sooner than I began to take in breath: I found great relief by so doing, and always imagined, that as soon as the lever was at the lowest (by which time I had nearly let go my breath), the elasticity of the fluid about me made it recoil from the forcible suction of the loom, much in the manner as a wave recoils or shrinks back after it has been forced forward on the sands in the ebbing or flowing of the tide: and then remains solely upon its own gravity, till the general flux or stress again

forces it forward in form of a wave. Such appears to me the action of the fluid, which, from the time the lever being fully down, loses all suction-force upon it. I always thought that by so opening my mouth, which many strangers, and those familiar or about me, called sometimes singularity, at others affectation and pretext, and at others asthmatic, &c. instantly let in such momentarily eman-cipated fluid about me, and enabled me sooner, easier, and with more certainty, to fill my lungs without straining them, and this at every breathing.

f Things, apparently pedals, worked by the feet of the pneumaticians.

g Seemingly drawers, forming part of the apparatus as eudiometer, &c. &c.

h The cluster of upright open tubes or cylinders, and by the assass-ins termed their *musical glasses*, which I have so often mentioned, and perceived when they were endeavouring to burst my person, by exploding the interior of the cavity of the trunk. I now find an exact likeness in the Cyclopedia, which, being in electricity, is termed a battery.

i The apparatus mentioned as standing upon the air-loom, which the assassins were ever so watchful and active, by deadening the sympathy, to prevent my holding sight of; so that I could never ascertain what the bulky upper parts were, although the lower parts have appeared as distinct as the strength of the drawing shews. But I never had longer than the slow-glimpse-sight.

k l m The bulky upper parts, which, though always indistinct, appeared once or twice to be hid by an horizontal broad projection, and which has often made me query whether they rose through an aperture of the cellar ceiling into the room above, which the assass-ins' brain-sayings have frequently seemed to acknowledge.

n The windmill kind of sails I have so often mentioned, only seen by the glimpse of sympathy; and to prevent my judging of which, the assassins would dash with full strong sympathy or brain-saying, 'a whirligig', used by children for amusement. But such windmill ever appeared as standing on the table.

o The barrels, which I perceived so distinctly after such long watching, to catch the sight of the famous goose-neck-retorts, which, by the assassins, are asserted to be about their loom, for supplying it with the distilled gazes, as well poisoned as magnetic, but which did not expose the goose-necks, which are here given, to shew the kind the assassins have, during ten years, some thousand times asserted they had: for while I was dwelling upon retorts themselves, which I had expected to find of metal, as stills, but which appeared distinctly hooped barrels standing on end on the floor, they cut the sympathy, and have ever since at all my attempts dashed or splashed the inward nerves of vision to bully and baffle me out of it.

p q r That part of the brass apparatus, so often seen distinctly of bright brass, standing on a one step-high boarded floor, having a bright iron railing around it, the part not here shewn was never distinct.

s s The warp of magnetic-fluid, searching between the person impregnated with such fluid, and the air-loom magnets to which it is prepared; which being a multiplicity of fine wires of fluid, forms the sympathy, streams of attraction, repulsion, &c. as putting the different poles of the common magnet to objects operates; and by which sympathetic warp the assailed object is affected at pleasure: as by opening a vitriolic gaz valve he becomes tortured by the fluid within him; becoming agitated with the corrosion through all his frame, and so on in all their various modes of attacking the human body and mind, whether to actuate or render inactive; to make ideas or to steal others; to bewilder or to deceive; thence to the driving with rage to acts of desperation, or to the dropping dead with stagnation, &c. &c. &c. Though so distinct to me by sympathy I have never caught the inward vision thereof, not even by glimpse; but the assassins pretend, when heated, that it becomes luminous and visible to them for some yards from the loom, as a weakish rainbow, and shews the colours according to the nature of the gazes from which it is formed, or wherewith the object is impregnated: as green for the cooper-streams or threads, red for the iron, white for the spermatic animal-seminal, &c.

t Shews the situation of the repeaters, or active worriers, when such were employed during the active exertions so long made to worry me down.

u One of the assassins called by the rest Jack the Schoolmaster, who calls his exertions to prevent my writing or speaking correctly, *dictating*, he ever intruding his own style and endeavouring to force it upon me. He pretends to be the short-hand-writer, to register or record every thing which passes. He appears to have a seat with a desk some steps above the floor.

v The female of the gang called by the others Charlotte: she has always spoken French, even by her brain-sayings; but I yet doubt whether she be a French woman, though so much of that description of person, for frequently it is English–French: though this may be from *their* vocabulary being English and French combined.

w The one I call the common liar of the gang, by them termed Sir Archy, who often speaks in obscene language. There has never been any fire in the cellar where the machinery is placed.

x Suppose the assailed person at the greater distance of several hundred feet, the warp must be so much longer directly towards him, but the farther he goes from the pneumatic machine, the weaker becomes its hold of him, till I should think at one thousand feet he would be out of danger. I incline to think that at such distance or little more, the warp would break, and that the part nearest his person would withdraw into him, and that next the loom would shrink into whatever there held it.

y The middle man working the air-loom, and in the act of Lobster-cracking the person represented by the figure X.

The assassins say they are not five hundred feet from me; but from the uncommon force of all their operations, I think they are much nearer.

They have likewise related that many other gangs are stationed in different parts of the metropolis who work such instrument for the most detrimental purposes. Near every public office an air-loom is concealed, and if the police were sufficiently vigilant, they might detect a set of wretches at work near the Houses of Parliament, Admiralty, Treasury, &c. and there is a gang established near St Luke's Hospital. The force of assailment is in proportion to the proximity of the machine; and it appears that the interposition of walls causes but a trifling difference: perhaps at the distance of 1000 feet a person might be considered out of the range of its influence. Independently of the operation of this complex and powerful machine termed an Air-loom, which requires the person assailed to be previously saturated with magnetic fluid, a number of emissaries, who are termed *novices*, are sent about in different directions to prepare those who may hereafter be employed in the craft and mystery of event-working. This is termed *Hand-impregnation*, and is effected in the following manner: an inferior member of the gang (generally a novice), is employed in this business. He is furnished with a bottle containing the magnetic fluid which issues from a valve on pressure. If the object to be assailed be sitting in a coffee-house, the pneumatic practitioner hovers about him, perhaps enters into conversation, and during such discourse, by opening the valve, sets at liberty the volatile magnetic fluid which is respired by the person intended to be assailed.

John Haslam (see page 2), *Illustrations of Madness* (1810)

=

A patient in Ticehurst House private lunatic asylum

Henry Crofts Rutter, thirty-six, single, snuff manufacturer, Protestant: 'says that he is an extraordinarily strong man; that he has copulated 300 times with a woman in one night; and that if his parts fail him, it is his intention to get a little steam-engine and insert it up his anus to help him on'.

Ticehurst House records, vol. 26 (c. 1840)

=

One man's vision is another man's delusion.

I assert for My Self that I do not behold the outward Creation & that to me it is hindrance & not Action, it is as the Dirt upon my feet, No part of Me. 'What,' it will be Question'd , 'When the Sun rises, do you not see a round disk of fire somewhat like a Guinea?' O no, no, I see an Innumerable company of the Heavenly host crying, 'Holy, Holy, Holy is the Lord God Almighty.' I question not my Corporeal or Vegetative Eye any more than I would Question a Window concerning a Sight. I look thro' it & not with it.

William Blake, 'A Vision of the Last Judgment' (1810)

=

Hounded by father-in-law

M. P. at the age of thirty years, made the campaign of 1807 in Prussia, in the capacity of an officer of marine. He remained for a long period in a cantonment that was extremely humid, and in consequence was seized with intermittent fever, attended by delirium. At the age of thirty-one years, while on leave of absence on account of his health, he was married to a charming lady, and introduced to a family in which he was treated as a son. Shortly after, he is seized with delirium, and attempts to commit suicide. Committed to my care, he is restored in three months. On his return to his family, he is the happiest of men. He returns to the army, with the rank of Lieutenant of the marine guard, and makes the campaigns of 1810 and 1811. In July of the latter year, in consequence of an excitement resulting from an act of injustice, he suffers from a return of delirium, which terminates with the year. In the campaign of 1814, M. P. is named chief of the squadron of the marine guard. Soon after, a new attack is provoked by the abdication of Bonaparte. In 1815 he returns to duty during the hundred days, in opposition to the advice of the family of his wife. After the second abdication, M. P., seized anew, takes up a frightful aversion to his wife and her family, who were previously the objects of his strongest regard. Nothing removes this dislike. He deserts his adopted family, and makes the journey to Rome, afoot and alone, impelled by religious considerations. Scarcely has he set foot upon the soil of Italy, than, one day, overcome by fatigue, he sits down upon a rock, and experiences an extraordinary visitation. God appears to him, and he has a vision for the first time. From henceforth, he believes that he is followed by his father-in-law, who throws in his way every possible obstacle to the accomplishment of his journey. He sees, hears, and contends with him. Nevertheless, he reaches his place of destination. Having returned to France, he is placed in the hospital at Avignon, where he permits his beard to grow, neglects the most ordinary attentions which propriety requires, imposes fasts upon himself, engages in no occupation, and employs no means of diverting his mind.

J.-E.-D. Esquirol (see page 139), *Mental Maladies:*
A Treatise on Insanity (1845)

=

Persecuted by the system

Some time after I discovered that the Persecutor was none other than the electric machine, that is, it was the 'System' that was punishing me. I thought of it as some vast world-like entity encompassing all men. At the top were those who gave orders, who imposed punishment, who pronounced others guilty. But they were themselves guilty. Since every man was responsible for all other men, each of his acts had a repercussion on other beings. A formidable interdependence bound all men under the scourge of culpability. Everyone was part of the System. But only some were aware of being part.

They were the ones who were 'enlightened' ... as I was. And it was at the same time both an honor and a misfortune to have this awareness. Those who were not part of it – though actually, of course, they were – were unaware of the System. As a result, they felt not at all guilty, and I envied them intensely.

At this moment, the ring closed: the Land of Enlightenment was the same as the System. That is why to enter into it was to become insensible of everything except culpability, the supreme punishment, freely granted by the System. I was guilty, abominably, intolerably guilty, without cause and without motive. Any punishment, the very worst, could be imposed on me – it could never deliver me of the load. Because, as I have already said, the most dreadful punishment was to make me feel eternally, universally culpable.

It was only when I was near 'Mama,' my analyst, that I felt a little better. But even for this, nearly an hour had to go by. Indeed, it was only toward the end of the hour, and sometimes not until twenty minutes after it, that I made contact with 'Mama.' When I arrived, I was as if frozen. I saw the room, the furniture, 'Mama' herself, each thing separate, detached from the others, cold, implacable, inhuman, by dint of being without life. Then I began to relate what had happened since the last visit and relived it in the telling. But the sound of my voice and the meaning of my words seemed strange. Every now and then, an inner voice interrupted sneeringly, 'Ah, Ah!' and mockingly repeated what I had said.

Marguerite Sechehaye, *Reality Lost and Regained: Autobiography of a Schizophrenic Girl, with Analytic Interpretation* (1951)

=

Black Mick

I had not been long in the asylum before I felt certain that curious
and unearthly evil powers and influences were at work as well as
good ones. As God Himself had appeared in a visible, tangible, and
earthly form, I concluded that it was reasonable to suppose Satan
would appear also, and I prayed that he might be forced to manifest
himself, for I was certain he was hiding incognito somewhere in the
background. At the psychic moment in walked Black Mick,
apparently from nowhere, and without the slightest noise of the
opening and shutting of any doors. He was puffing his chest out,
and trying to make himself look as large and important as the
proverbial frog. I was not in the least alarmed, rather amused,
especially when he sat down in the chair usually occupied by my
guardian and began to talk in a very friendly way with poor,
ignorant, religious Johnnie. In a few minutes the latter grew red in
the face, and began to glow all over with a sort of religious ecstasy;
then he jumped up from his seat, threw himself on his knees, seized
Mick's hairy paw, and began to slobber all over it. I was disgusted,
got up, and ejaculating under my breath the fortieth article of my
faith, which ran shortly. 'To hell with the Pope,' I walked into the
other room, for it seemed to me that it did not matter in the least to
the poor patient whose hand he kissed.

I felt very suspicious, and went up to Mick afterwards and asked
him if he was a Roman Catholic. He said he was. I then asked him if
he was a Christian. With a great effort he said he was. I refused to
believe it, and told him he was an Anarchist. He laughed at this,
and seemed very pleased at being thought such an interesting
character. My suspicion was only momentary, and I never really
believed he was the devil, partly, I suppose, because I had considerably less faith in the existence of such a personality than I had
in the existence of God.

D. Davidson, *Remembrances of a Religio-Maniac: An Autobiography*
(1912)

Who are you? John Perceval (see page 23) explains the superim-
position of his delusions upon the staff and patients of the asylum,
thereby creating the illusion of multiple personality.

Now all these persons, and each person around me, wore a triple
character, according to each of which I was in turns to address
them. Samuel Hobbs, for example, was at times to be worshipped
in the character of *Jesus*, at times to be treated familiarly as *Her-*
minet Herbert, a spiritual body, at times to be dealt with as plain
Samuel Hobbs. The stout old patient was at times knelt to as the
Lord Jehovah; at times he was Mr *Waldony*, a spiritual body; at
times a gentleman. So with the rest: and these changes took place so
instantaneously, that I was completely puzzled as to my deportment
towards them. I saw individuals and members of the family of Dr F
— [Fox], approach me in great beauty, and in obedience to a voice,
my inclinations sprang forward to salute them, when in an instant,
their appearance changed, and another command made me hesitate
and draw back. In the same manner, when books, pencils, pens, or
any occupation was presented to me, I turned from one page and
one object, to another, and back again, usually ending in a fit of
exasperation and inward indignation, against the guidance that so
perplexed me.

   Besides the personages I have already taken notice of, there were
eleven patients in the room, to each of which my spirits gave a
name, and assigned a particular office towards me. There were
three I addressed as Mr Fitzherbert; a Captain P — Who was my
spirit of family pride; a Captain W — , who was my spirit of
joviality; a Mr — , a Quaker, who was my *spirit* of simplicity; a Mr
D — , who for a long time I imagined to be, and addressed as, Dr F
— [Fox?] and afterwards as one of my uncles; a Mr A — , who was
my fifth brother, and my spirit of contrition; the Rev. Mr J — , a
Devonshire curate, who was one of my first cousins, my spirit of
affection, and the representation of the apostle St. John; a Mr J —
who was my spirit of honesty, and my youngest brother; a Mr — ,
who thought himself the Duke of Somerset, and whom I addressed
as Mr Fazakerley, my spirit of delicacy and contrition; and Captain
— a dark man, who had lost his left leg, and the use of his left arm;
and who for six months stood up in one position, and for six

months sat down in one position – him my spirits called Patience; and told me he was my executioner, waiting for the decision of the jury upon me, to officiate on me, but still one of my best friends.

John T. Perceval, *A Narrative of a Treatment Received by a Gentleman, During a State of Mental Derangement* (1838/40)

7

Possession

It is possible to have a short way with all manner of religious 'visions'. Religion, one can argue, *all* religion, is delusional *per se*, or at least some kind of intellectual or cognitive error. In effect, this was Freud's position. God was an illusion, and religion, though all too real, was but a mental projection to meet neurotic needs, to be explained culturally in terms, for instance, of the sublimation skywards of suppressed physical sexual urges (and, in Freud's later writings, in respect of death wishes and so forth). In adopting this stance, which reduced religion to psychopathology, Freud was inheriting the mantle of the more brutal of the Enlightenment *philosophes*, who regarded religion as a morbid thought secretion of sick brains (thus explaining why people commonly turned pious only on their deathbed).

From a less *parti pris* viewpoint, it is not hard to see why the history of religion and the history of madness have been so closely interlinked in Western culture. Christianity set faith (or what Freud called 'wish-fulfilment') above reason, and so set extraordinary store by belief. Moreover, it promoted a world-view in which the population of earthlings was massively outnumbered by equally real (indeed, in a strict, theological sense, even more real), immaterial, invisible, incorporeal entities – the souls of the departed, in Heaven or Hell, or maybe in limbo or purgatory; angels, and Satan and all his emissaries (to say nothing of the wood-demons and ghosts omnipresent in folklore). Both God and Satan appeared to humans, and spoke to them, often in dreams. Both the Holy Ghost and the Devil could take possession of individuals, as part of a psychomachy, a struggle for the soul. In the light of such utterly orthodox convictions, it has always been perfectly acceptable for

Christians to regard transcendental religious experiences as integral to the structure of reality.

Yet, over the last 300 years at least, more so in theory than in fact. For, rather as the Churches accept, in principle, the reality of miracles, or the prospect of the Second Coming, but tend to discount claimed sightings of these, fearing that countenancing credulity damages the fabric of faith, so too with visions and spirit possession. These days, the Roman Catholic or Anglican who claims to be filled with the Holy Ghost, or the Devil, is something of an embarrassment, even to his fellow-believers. His priest will try to persuade him that he is speaking metaphorically; and, if he persists, he may be invited to see a doctor.

This suspicion towards claims of individual illumination has a long pedigree. In the studied moderation of their *via media*, seventeenth-century Anglican bishops played down supposed instances of demonic possession and visions, fearing that these offered substance to the pretensions of Papist and Puritan extremists: they tended to attribute them to fraud or the self-deluding fantasies of ignorant women. In a similar manner, the vaunted spiritual indwellings of Methodist converts in the eighteenth century, and other Evangelicals in later revivalist movements, were often put down by an unholy alliance of prelates and psychological doctors as having been provoked by some form of mental disorder, or as an expression of mass hysteria amongst the vulgar. The result has been that individuals who have personally claimed direct, special Revelation (or demonic possession) have seen themselves in no way as mad, but as walking the strict road of true biblical religion, from which the Churches have backslid.

Does intense exposure to religion often provoke mental disorder? Or does religion merely provide a ready-made language through which people can express otherwise rather intangible experiences? It is hard to tell. What is noteworthy is that, even today, florid delusions are still commonly expressed via the *dramatis personae* and stage-props of religion. Perhaps this marks an authentic and ingrained need in the human psyche to build bridges linking the tangible, everyday world with the Beyond.

Unclean spirits

And when he was come out of the ship, immediately there met him
out of the tombs a man with an unclean spirit, Who had his
dwelling among the tombs; and no man could bind him, no, not
with chains: Because that he had been often bound with fetters and
chains, and the chains had been plucked asunder by him, and the
fetters broken in pieces; neither could any man tame him. And
always, night and day, he was in the mountains, and in the tombs,
crying, and cutting himself with stones. But when he saw Jesus afar
off, he ran and worshipped him. And cried with a loud voice, and
said, What have I to do with thee, Jesus, thou Son of the most high
God. I adjure thee by God, that thou torment me not. For he said
unto him, Come out of the man, thou unclean spirit. And he asked
him, What is thy name? And he answered, saying, My name is
Legion: for we are many. And he besought him much that he would
not send them away out of the country. Now there was there nigh
unto the mountains a great herd of swine feeding. And all the devils
besought him, saying, Send us into the swine, that we may enter
into them. And forthwith Jesus gave them leave. And the unclean
spirits went out, and entered into the swine: and the herd ran
violently down a steep place into the sea, (they were about two
thousand;) and were choked in the sea. And they that fed the swine
fled, and told it in the city, and in the country. And they went out to
see what it was that was done. And they came to Jesus, and see him
that was possessed with the devil, and had the legion, sitting, and
clothed, and in his right mind: and they were afraid.

                                                    Mark 5:2–15

                              =

Whom the gods destroy, they first make mad.
(χOν θεός θὲλει ἀπόλεσαι, πρῶτ᾽ ἀπόφρεναι.)
                              Euripides, *Fragment* (5th century BC)

                              =

Demonic possession

Demoniacus or *Demoniaci* be the latin wordes. In greke it is named *Demonici*. In Englyshe it is named he or they the which be mad and possessed of the devyll or devyls, and theyr propertie is to hurt and kyll them selfe, or else to hurt and kyll any other thynge, therfore let every man beware of them, and kepe them in a sure custody.

The cause of this matter
This matter doth passe all maner of syckenesses and diseases, and is a feareful and a terryble thynge to se a devyl or devyls shoulde have so muche and so greate a power over man as it is specifyed of such persons dyvers tymes in the gospell, specially in the ix. Chapitre of Marke . . .

The fyrst tyme that I did dwell in Rome, there was a gentyl-woman of Germany the whiche was possessed of devyls, & was brought to Rome to be made whole. For within the precynct of S. Peters church without S. Peters chapel standeth a pyller of white marble grated rounde about with Yron, to the whiche our Lord Jesus Chryste dyd lye in hym selfe in Pylates hall, as the Romaynes doth say, to the which pyller al those that be possessed of the devyll, out of dyvers countres and nacions be brought thyther, and as they saye of Rome such persons be made there whole. Amonge al other this woman of Germany whiche is CCCC, myles and odde, frome Rome was brought to the pyller I then there beying present with great strength and vyolently with a xx. or mo men this woman was put into that pyller within the yron grate and after her dyd go in a Preest, and dyd examyne the woman under this maner in the Italyan tonge. Thou devyl or devyls I do abjure the by the potenciall power of the father and of the sonne our Lorde Jesus Chryste and by the vertue of the holy ghoste that thou do shew to me, for what cause that thou doest possesse this woman, what wordes was answered I wyll not wryte, for men wyll not beleve it but wolde say it were a foule and great lye, but I did heare that I was afrayd to tary any longer lest that the devyls shulde have come out of her and to have entred into me, remembrynge what is specified in the viii. Chapitre of S. Mathewe when that Jesus Christ had made ii. men whole the whiche was possessed of a legion of devyls. A legion is ix.

M.ix.C. nynety and nyne, the sayd devyls dyd desyre Jesus that when
they were expelled out of the aforesayd two men, that they myght
enter into a herde of hogges, and so they dyd, and the hogges dyd
runne into the sea and were drowned. I consyderynge this, and weke
of faith and afeard, crossed my selfe and durst not to heare and se
suche matters, for it was to stupendious and above all reason.

Andrew Boorde, The Breviary of Healthe (1547)

=

Prey to the foul fiend

Enter EDGAR, disguised as a madman.

EDGAR: Away! the foul fiend follows me.
    Through the sharp hawthorn blows the cold wind.
    Humh! go to thy cold bed and warm thee.
LEAR: Didst thou give all to thy daughters? And art thou come to this?
EDGAR: Who gives anything to poor Tom? whom the foul fiend hath
    led through fire and through flame, through ford and whirlpool,
    o'er bog and quagmire; that hath laid knives under his pillow and
    halters in his pew, set ratsbane by his porridge; made him proud of
    heart, to ride on a bay trotting-horse over four-inched bridges, to
    course his own shadow for a traitor. Bless thy five wits! Tom's
    a-cold. O, do de, do de, do de. Bless thee from whirlwinds,
    star-blasting, and taking! Do poor Tom some charity, whom the
    foul fiend vexes. There could I have him now – and there – and
    there again – and there.
    (*Storm still.*)
LEAR: What, has his daughters brought him to this pass?

William Shakespeare, King Lear (1608)

=

*Up until the eighteenth century, it was almost universally believed
that Satan and his minions had the power to inject themselves into
their victims, creating both mental and bodily sickness. A prime text,
spelling out such beliefs, and urging the prosecution of witches and
other emissaries of the Devil, was the* Malleus Maleficarum (The
Hammer of Those who Inflict Evil: *1486).*

CHAPTER X

Of the Method by which Devils through the Operations of Witches sometimes actually possess Men.

It has been shown in the previous chapter how devils can enter the heads and other parts of the body of men, and can move the inner mental images from place to place. But someone may doubt whether they are able at the instance of witches to obsess men entirely; or feel some uncertainty about their various methods of causing such obsession without the instance of witches. And to clear up these doubts we must undertake three explanations. First, as to the various methods of possession. Secondly, how at the instance of witches and with God's permission devils at times possess men in all those ways. Thirdly, we must substantiate our arguments with facts and examples.

With reference to the first, we must make an exception of that general method by which the devil inhabits a man in any mortal sin. S. Thomas, in Book 3, quest. 3, speaks of this method where he considers the doubt whether the devil always substantially possesses a man when he commits mortal sin; and the reason for the doubt is that the indwelling Holy Ghost always forms a man with grace, according to I. *Corinthians*, iii: Ye are the temple of God, and the spirit of God dwelleth in you. And, since guilt is opposed to grace, it would seem that there were opposing forces in the same place.

And there he proves that to possess a man can be understood in two ways: either with regard to the soul, or with regard to the body. And in the first way it is not possible for the devil to possess the soul, since God alone can enter that; therefore the devil is not in this way the cause of sin, which the Holy Spirit permits the soul itself to commit; so there is no similitude between the two.

But as to the body, we may say that the devil can possess a man in two ways, just as there are two classes of men: those who are in sin, and those who are in grace. In the first way, we may say that, since a man is by any mortal sin brought into the devil's service, in so far as the devil provides the outer suggestion of sin either to the senses or to the imagination, to that extent he is said to inhabit the

character of a man when he is moved by every stirring of temptation, like a ship in the sea without a rudder.

The devil can also essentially possess a man, as is clear in the case
of frantic men. But this rather belongs to the question of punishment than that of sin, as will be shown; and bodily punishments are
not always the consequence of sin, but are inflicted now upon
sinners and now upon the innocent. Therefore both those who are
and those who are not in a state of grace can, in the depth of the
incomprehensible judgement of God, be essentially possessed by
devils. And though this method of possession is not quite pertinent
to our inquiry, we have set it down lest it should seem impossible to
anyone that, with God's permission, men should at times be substantially inhabited by devils at the instance of witches.

We may say, therefore, that just as there are five ways in which
devils by themselves, without witches, can injure and possess man,
so they can also do so in all those ways at the instance of witches;
since then God is the more offended, and greater power of
molesting men is allowed to the devil through witches. And the
methods are briefly the following, excepting the fact that they
sometimes plague a man through his external possessions: sometimes they injure men only in their own bodies; sometimes in their
bodies and in their inner faculties; sometimes they only tempt them
inwardly and outwardly; others they at times deprive of the use of
their reason; others they change into the appearance of irrational
beasts. We shall speak of these methods singly.

But first we shall rehearse five reasons why God allows man to be
possessed, for the sake of preserving a due order in our matter. For
sometimes a man is possessed for his own greater advantage; sometimes for a slight sin of another; sometimes for his own venial sin;
sometimes for another's heavy sin; and sometimes for his own
heavy sin. For all these reasons let no one doubt that God allows
such things to be done by devils at the instance of witches; and it is
better to prove each of them by the Scriptures, rather than by recent
examples, since new things are always strengthened by old
examples.

H. Sprenger and J. Institoris, *Malleus Maleficarum* (1486)

Protestants such as Robert Burton (see page 13) upheld such beliefs
no less vigorously than Catholics. Burton ascribed most of the
melancholy in the world to the Devil's doings.

Thus the Devil reigns, and in a thousand several shapes, as a roaring
lion still seeks whom he may devour, by earth, sea, land, air, as yet
unconfined, though some will have his proper place the air, all that
space betwixt us & the Moon for them that transgressed least, &
Hell for the wickedest of them; here, as though in prison to the end of
the world, afterwards thrust into the place of doom, as Austin holds
in The City Of God. But be [he] where he will, he rageth while he may
to comfort himself, as Lactantius thinks, with other men's falls, he
labours all he can to bring them into the same pit of perdition with
him. For *men's miseries, calamities, and ruins, are the Devil's*
banqueting dishes. By many temptations, and several engines, he
seeks to captivate our souls. The Lord of lies, saith Austin, *as he was*
deceived himself, he seeks to deceive others, the ring-leader to all
naughtiness, as he did by Eve & Cain, Sodom and Gomorrah, so
would he do by all the world. Sometimes he tempts by covetousness,
drunkenness, pleasure, pride, &c., errs, dejects, saves, kills, protects,
and rides some men, as they do their horses. He studies our overthrow, and generally seeks our destruction; and although he pretend
many times human good, and vindicate himself for a God, by curing
of several diseases, by restoring health to the sick and sight to the
blind, as Austin declares, as Apollo, Æsculapius, Isis, of old have
done; divert plagues, assist them in wars, pretend their happiness, yet
nothing so impure, nothing so pernicious, as may well appear by
their tyrannical and bloody sacrifices of men to Saturn and Moloch,
which are still in use amongst those barbarous Indians, their several
deceits and cozenings to keep men in obedience, their false oracles,
sacrifices, their superstitious impositions of fasts, penury, &c., her-
esies, superstitious observations of meats, times, &c. by which they
crucify the souls of mortal men, as shall be shewed in our Treatise of
Religious Melancholy. As Bernard expresseth it, by God's permission he rageth a while, hereafter to be confined to hell and darkness,
which is prepared for him and his Angels.

Robert Burton, *The Anatomy of Melancholy* (1621)

=

A few registered dissent, and, like Reginald Scot, denied that Satan truly had the power to possess people's minds. In Scot's view, witches were in the grip not of His Satanic Majesty but of melancholy delusions.

How melancholie abuseth old women, and of the effects thereof by sundrie examples
If anie man advisedlie marke their words, actions, cogitations, and gestures, he shall perceive that melancholie abounding in their head, and occupieng their braine, hath deprived or rather depraved their judgements, and all their senses: I meane not of coosening witches, but of poore melancholike women, which are themselves deceived. For you shall understand, that the force which melancholie hath, and the effects that it worketh in the bodie of a man, or rather of a woman, are almost incredible. For as some of these melancholike persons imagine, they are witches and by witchcraft can worke woonders, and doo what they list: so doo other, troubled with this disease, imagine manie strange, incredible, and impossible things . . . But if they may imagine, that they can transforme their owne bodies, which neverthelesse remaineth in the former shape: how much more credible is it, that they may falselie suppose they can hurt and infeeble other mens bodies; or which is lesse, hinder the comming of butter?&c. But what is it that they will not imagine, and consequentlie confesse that they can doo; speciallie being so earnestlie persuaded thereunto, so sorelie tormented, so craftilie examined, with such promises of favour, as wherby they imagine, that they shall ever after live in great credit & welth?&c.

Reginald Scot, The Discoverie of Witchcraft (1584)

=

The physician Edward Jorden passionately argued, in early seventeenth-century England, that what was commonly taken to be demonic possession, was actually nothing other than routine, natural illness, in particular, 'the mother', or hysteria.

Amatus Lusitanus reporteth of one *Dina Clara*, a maide of 18. yeares of age, which had every day two or three such strange fits, as those that were about her, gave out that that she was haunted with an evill spirit.

In those fits every part of her body was distorted, she felt nothing, nor perceived any thing: but had all her sences benummed, her hart beating, her teeth close shut together: yet for an houres space or two she would have such strong motions, that shee would weary the strongest men that came at her. When she had beene three weekes in this case, her left arme began to be resolved with a palsie, &c. He being called unto her prescribed such remedies as are usuall in this case, and within few dayes recovered her, to the great admiration of the beholders.

Petrus Forrestus maketh mention of another maid of 22. yeares old, which dwelt with a Burgermaster of *Delft* in *Holland*, who falling in love with a yong man, fell also into these fits of the Mother: which held her many houres together with such violent horrible accidents, as hee never sawe the like: her whole body being pulled to and fro with convulsive motions, her belly sometimes lifted up, and sometimes depressed, a roaring noise heard within her, with crying and howling, a distortion of her armes and handes: insomuch as those about her thought her to be possessed with a divell, and out of all hope of recovery. He being called unto her in Ianuarie 1565. applied convenient remedies as there he setteth downe, and in a short time restored her to her health againe.

Many more such like examples might bee produced both out of authenticall writers in our profession and out of our own experiences, which yet do live (were it not that late examples would bee offensive to rehearse:) but these may suffice to show how easily men unexperienced in those extraordinarie kindes of diseases, may mistake the causes of them: when through admiration of the unwonted and grievous accidents they behold, they are caried unto Magicall and Metaphysicall speculations. But the learned Phisition who hath first beene trained up in the study of Philosophy, and afterwards confirmed by the practise and experience of all manner particular causes shall bee farther declared: and yet no such consent can bee shewed in them with any supernatural affect, as that they may any way cause or encrease it. Wherefore the rule of *Hyppocrates* must needes be true; that if these *Symptoms* do yeeld unto naturall remedies, they must also bee naturall themselves.

Edward Jorden, *A Briefe Discourse of a Disease Called
the Suffocation of the Mother* (1603)

=

LEAR: O! how this mother swells up toward my heart;
    Hysterica passio! down, thou climbing sorrow!
    Thy element's below. Where is this daughter?

                    William Shakespeare, *King Lear* (1608)

═

*Believing in the madness of the Cross, the divine wisdom of babes
and sucklings, and the raptures and illuminations of ecstatic mys-
tics, Christians also espoused a faith in holy folly. In his* Praise of
Folly, *Erasmus urged that Christian folly was true wisdom.*

The supreme reward for man is no other than a kind of madness.
First consider how Plato imagined something of this sort when he
wrote that the madness of lovers is the highest form of happiness.
For anyone who loves intensely lives not in himself but in the object
of his love, and the further he can move out of himself into his love,
the happier he is. Now, when the soul is planning to leave the body
and ceases to make proper use of its organs, it is thought to be mad,
and doubtless with good reason. This, surely, is what is meant by
the popular expressions 'he is beside himself', 'come to' and 'he is
himself again'. Moreover, the more perfect the love, the greater the
madness – and the happier. What, then, will life in heaven be like,
to which all pious minds so eagerly aspire? The spirit will be the
stronger, and will conquer and absorb the body, and this it will do
the more easily for having previously in life purged and weakened
the body in preparation for this transformation. Then the spirit will
itself be absorbed by the supreme Mind, which is more powerful
than its infinite parts. And so when the whole man will be outside
himself, and be happy for no reason except that he is so outside
himself, he will enjoy some ineffable share in the supreme good
which draws everything into itself. Although this perfect happiness
can only be experienced when the soul has recovered its former
body and been granted immortality, since the life of the pious is no
more than a contemplation and foreshadowing of that other life, at
times they are able to feel some foretaste and savour of the reward
to come. It is only the tiniest drop in comparison with the fount of
eternal bliss, yet it far exceeds all pleasures of the body, even if all
mortal delights were rolled into one, so much does the spiritual

surpass the physical, the invisible the visible. This is surely what the prophet promises: 'Eye has not seen nor ear heard, nor have there entered into the heart of man the things which God has prepared for those that love him.' And this is the good part of Folly which is not taken away by the transformation of life but is made perfect.

So those who are granted a foretaste of this – and very few have the good fortune – experience something which is very like madness. They speak incoherently and unnaturally, utter sound without sense, and their faces suddenly change expression. One moment they are excited, the next depressed, they weep and laugh and sigh by turns; in fact they truly are quite beside themselves. Then when they come to, they say they don't know where they have been, in the body or outside it, awake or asleep. They cannot remember what they have heard or seen or said or done, except in a mist, like a dream. All they know is that they were happiest when they were out of their senses in this way, and they lament their return to reason, for all they want is to be mad for ever with this kind of madness. And this is only the merest taste of the happiness to come.

But I've long been forgetting who I am, and I've 'overshot the mark'. If anything I've said seems rather impudent or garrulous, you must remember it's Folly and a woman who's been speaking. At the same time, don't forget the Greek proverb 'Often a fool speaks a word in season', though of course you may think this doesn't apply to women. I can see you're all waiting for a peroration, but it's silly of you to suppose I can remember what I've said when I've been spouting such a hotchpotch of words. There's an old saying, 'I hate a fellow-drinker with a memory', and here's a new one to put alongside it: 'I hate an audience which won't forget.'

And so I'll say Goodbye. Clap your hands, live and drink; distinguished initiates of FOLLY.

Desiderius Erasmus, The Praise of Folly (1511)

=

Though occasionally accused of being a heretic, Margery Kempe (see page 44) won a certain reputation as a holy woman, partly on account of preternatural behaviour such as continuous wailing and weeping and swooning at the name of Jesus.

Thus with all these things turning upside down, this creature, who for many years had gone astray and always been unstable, was perfectly drawn and stirred to enter the way of high perfection, of which perfect way Christ our Saviour in his own person was the example. Steadfastly he trod it and duly he went it once before.

Then this creature – of whom this treatise, through the mercy of Jesus, shall show in part the life – was touched by the hand of our Lord with great bodily sickness, through which she lost her reason for a long time, until our Lord by grace restored her again, as shall be shown more openly later. Her worldly goods, which were plentiful and abundant at that date, were a little while afterwards quite barren and bare. Then was pomp and pride cast down and laid aside. Those who before had respected her, afterwards most sharply rebuked her; her kin and those who had been friends were now her greatest enemies.

Then she, considering this astonishing change, and seeking succour beneath the wings of her spiritual mother, Holy Church, went and humbled herself to her confessor, accusing herself of her misdeeds, and afterwards did great bodily penance. And within a short time our merciful Lord visited this creature with abundant tears of contrition day by day, insomuch that some men said she could weep when she wanted to, and slandered the work of God.

She was so used to being slandered and reproved, to being chided and rebuked by the world for grace and virtue with which she was endued through the strength of the Holy Ghost, that it was to her a kind of solace and comfort when she suffered any distress for the love of God and for the grace that God wrought in her. For ever the more slander and reproof that she suffered, the more she increased in grace and in devotion of holy meditation, of high contemplation, and of wonderful speeches and conversation which our Lord spoke and conveyed to her soul, teaching her how she would be despised for his love, and how she should have patience, setting all her trust, all her love and all her affection on him alone.

She knew and understood many secret things which would happen afterwards, by inspiration of the Holy Ghost. And often, while she was kept with such holy speeches and conversation, she would so weep and sob that many men were greatly astonished, for they little knew how at home our Lord was in her soul. Nor could she herself ever tell of the grace that she felt, it was so heavenly, so high above her reason and her bodily wits; and her body so feeble at the time of the presence of grace that she could never express it with words as she felt it in her soul.

Then this creature had great dread of the delusions and deceptions of her spiritual enemies. She went by the bidding of the Holy Ghost to many worthy clerks, both archbishops and bishops, doctors of divinity, and bachelors as well. She also spoke with many anchorites, and told them of her manner of life and such grace as the Holy Ghost of his goodness wrought in her mind and in her soul, as far as her wit would serve her to express it. And those to whom she confided her secrets said she was much bound to love our Lord for the grace that he showed to her, and counselled her to follow her promptings and her stirrings, and trustingly believe they were of the Holy Ghost and of no evil spirit.

Some of these worthy clerics took it, on peril of their souls and as they would answer to God, that this creature was inspired with the Holy Ghost, and bade her that she should have a book written of her feelings and her revelations.

Margery Kempe, *The Book of Margery Kempe* (c. 1420)

=

Religious delusions? Or a parody of them? A patient in an Edinburgh asylum in the late nineteenth century, John Home, discusses religious politics.

Morningside Asylum 30 March 1889

Dear Sir

I have to thank you for your letter of yesterdate, and shall have the pleasure of paying you £10 the moment I am released from this charming suburban abode. I would willingly pay £100 instead of the smaller sum for having been so fortunate as to secure so charming a wife. She is the fairest of Erin's fair daughters and far outstrips any of our Scottish lassies.

I note what you say as to 'Assuming you to marry a lady born on 14th Decr 1864' my dear sir it is not a question of assumption at all as I am as thoroughly altho' as yet not so regularly married to my

Charmer as Henry is to his. Our marriage took place on the 10th Inst in presence of Witnesses which ceremony was followed by the signing of a written Declaration. My Wife is a Roman Catholic but as since coming here I have become as utter an unbeliever as my Ancestor David Hume all creeds are alike to me. Besides I have a strong impression that whenever Albert Edward ascends the throne vice Vic. resigned or deceased, Episcopacy will be restored and the Roman Catholic will will [sic] once more become the National Religion. This is not however the only great change about to occur as I have just received a heaven letter informing me that the Trinity are about to abdicate and that the Right Honble Ben Dizzy is to be crowned Lord of Heaven & Earth and to exchange the Coronet which a loving Earthly Queen gave him for a Golden Crown, and that W.E.G. is to look on at a distance from the place of torment & every now & then to extend that tongue which has wrought so much mischief imploringly to Dizzy with a request that he may be allowed to dip the tip of it for a moment in water which Dizzy will on all occasions refuse lest it should have the effect of reinvigorating him & stirring him up to introduce a bill for the Disestablishment of the Church of the Redeemed.

Things I am informed will go on very much as at present – for example you are to be appointed Collector of the Widows Fund of the Society of Fallen Angels and Harry is to be Sole Secretary of the Honble Co of Archers who will be furnished with bows and arrows, Harry being created a Duke, not merely a Knight. The Knight is to be appointed Bow Maker & is to be ordered to bank all the gold not in the City of Destruction Bank, but in the Bank of Grace of which the following are the officials – Manager Henry Inglis, Secretary W. C. Murray, Treasurer J. D. Wormald, Accountant Henry Callender, Teller James Renton. There is to be a clause inserted in the Bank Charter that in the event of the Bank's affairs becoming involved, in no event is George Auldis Padwick to be appointed Liquidator, but Donald Smith Peddie is to be appointed with the sole charge of the Fund for the benefit of the Widows of the Bank officials. Certain other appointments are also to be made – for example the Right Honble J. H. A. Serjeant Busfuz is to be Lord Advocate, and James Auldis Crown Agent – Da Duncan continuing as at present to do all the work and sign all the letters.

As Dizzy intends to suppress the Bible there will be no occasion for
an Agent for the Bible board & accordingly J.P. is to be created
Marquis of Shitman and J.H. who for many years did all the work
for him both legal and political is to have free access at all times to
the glorious creatures who inhabit the realms of bliss.

This is the way lunatics Write
Yours faithfully
John Home

> Letter from John Home to John Cooke Esq. (30 March 1889),
> John Home Letters, Medical Archives Centre MSS
> (Edinburgh University Library)

=

*By the Age of Enlightenment, the authenticity of extreme religious
transports was being impugned, and they were being relegated to
the domain of psychopathology. Erasmus Darwin, Charles Darwin's grandfather, viewed religious enthusiasm as a form of mental
illness.*

Spes religiosa. Superstitious hope. This maniacal hallucination in its
milder state produces, like sentimental love, an agreeable reverie;
but when joined with works of supererogation, it has occasioned
many enormities. In India devotees consign themselves by vows to
most painful and unceasing tortures ... While in our part of the
globe fasting and mortification, as flagellation, has been believed to
please a merciful deity! The serenity, with which many have suffered cruel martyrdoms, is to be ascribed to this powerful reverie.

Mr—, a clergyman, formerly of this neighbourhood, began to
bruise and wound himself for the sake of religious mortification,
and passed much time in prayer, and continued whole nights alone
in the church. As he had a wife and family of small children, I
believed the case to be incurable; as otherwise the affection and
employment in his family connections would have opposed the
beginning of this insanity. He was taken to a madhouse without
effect, and after he returned home, continued to beat and bruise
himself, and by this kind of mortification, and by sometimes long
fasting, he at length became emaciated and died. I once told him in

conversation, that 'God was a merciful being, and could not delight in cruelty, but that I supposed he worshipped the devil'. He was struck with this idea, and promised me not to beat himself for three days, and I believe kept his word for one day. If this idea had been frequently forced on his mind, it might probably have been of service. When works of supererogation have been of a public nature, what cruelties, murders, massacres, has not this insanity introduced into the world.

Erasmus Darwin, *Zoonomia: or The Laws of Organic Life* (1794)

==

Methodism was widely denounced as a form of mass hysteria. William Pargeter had stronger reasons than most for so characterizing it, for as well as being a healer of the sick at heart, he was also an Anglican clergyman.

Fanaticism is very common cause of Madness. Most of the Maniacal cases that ever came under my observation, proceeded from religious *enthusiasm*; and I have heard it remarked by an eminent physician, that almost all the insane patients, which occurred to him at one of the largest hospitals in the *metropolis*, had been deprived of their reason, by such strange infatuation. The *doctrines* of the *Methodists* have a greater tendency than those of any other sect, to produce the most deplorable effects on the human understanding. The brain is perplexed in the mazes of mystery, and the imagination overpowered by the tremendous description of future torments. – I shall subjoin a case or two, in which Insanity was manifestly the cause of *religious delusion*.

CASE I

I was sent for to a respectable farmer, in the country; I found him very low and melancholy – inconsistent in his conversation, and seemed to labour under great distress concerning his future state. His friends had been obliged some time before to place him in an house for the reception of lunatics. I could do him very little service, as I was unable to remove the cause. This man's misfortunes originated in a very curious fact: he was publicly reproved by a clergyman for sleeping during divine service, which gave him so much offence, that he seceded from the Church, and attached himself to the *Methodists*; these *deluded people* soon reduced him to the unhappy state in which I found him. I could not learn on strict enquiry, that previously to this circumstance, he had exhibited any symptoms of mental derangement; but was esteemed a lively, chearful, and pleasant companion.

William Pargeter (see page 36), *Observations on Maniacal Disorders*
(1792)

=

Methodism makes you mad.

Enthusiasm and insanity bear such close affinity, that the shades are often too indistinct to define which is one and which the other. Exuberance of zeal on any subject, in some constitutions, soon ripens into madness: but excess of religious enthusiasm, unless tempered by an habitual command over the affective passions, usually and readily degenerates into fanaticism; thence to superstition the transition is in sequence; and permanent delirium too often closes the scene. Enthusiasm and superstition, however, are not necessarily in sequence; for they are as opposite in character as, generally, in effect. The one is almost always the concomitant of genius or a vigorous mind, and may inspire the purest piety or benevolence, or emulate deeds of the highest glory: while the other seldom invades genius, except when extenuated by some corporeal disorder; but is commonly confined to the weak, the timid, and the uninformed; and in them produces either the blindest fury or the most gloomy despondency, and sometimes the wildest schemes for propitiating the offended DEITY.

George Man Burrows (see page 10), *Commentaries on the Causes, Forms, Symptoms and Treatment, Moral and Medical, of Insanity*
(1828)

=

By the early nineteenth century, demonic possession was routinely seen as a psychopathological phenomenon, except in the narrower circles of the religious lunatic fringe. Throughout the history of insanity, malfunctions of the womb have often been blamed for

*causing psychological disturbances in women (the term 'hysteria'
being derived from the Greek word for uterus). Such beliefs survive
today in the folklore of PMT (pre-menstrual tension).*

Though demonomania may be unusual at this day, it will not be
uninteresting to point out and determine its characters. If the possessed no longer exist, there are still some monomaniacs who
consider themselves in the power of the devil. I have collected
certain facts respecting demonomania, and have compared them
with what demonographers have related. Their resemblance has
satisfied me that the symptoms that I observed are the same, with
the signs of possession pointed out by authors, or contained in the
accounts of the trials of sorcerers and those possessed. After having
given a brief history of demonomania, we will pass on to an
analysis and comparison of the symptoms of this malady, with
those that attend other forms of melancholy.

A. D., a servant woman forty-six years of age, was of medium
size, had chestnut colored hair, small hazel eyes, a dark complexion, and an ordinary degree of fulness of habit. Endowed with
great susceptibility, she has much self-esteem, and was religiously
educated. Fourteen years of age. First menstruation, and since that
period the menses have been scanty and irregular. Thirty years. She
becomes attached to a young man, whom they will not permit to
marry her. She becomes sad and melancholic, believing herself
abandoned by every body. The menses cease, not to appear again.
She engages with extreme ardor in devotional exercises, makes a
vow of chastity, and devotes herself to Jesus Christ. Sometime after
this, she fails in her promises, and remorse seizes upon her. She
regards herself as condemned, given over to the evil one, and suffers
the torments of hell. Six years she passes in this state of delirium
and torments; after which, exercise, dissipation and the influence of
time, restore her to reason and her ordinary occupations. Forty
years of age. Forsaken by a new lover, D. renews her vows of
chastity, and passes her time in prayer. One day, while on her knees
reading the imitation of Jesus Christ, a young man enters her
chamber, says that he is Jesus Christ, that he has come to console
her, and that if she will but trust him, she will have no longer
occasion to fear the devil. She yields. For the second time she

considers herself in the power of the devil, and experiences all the torments of hell and despair. Sent to the Salpêtrière, she spends most of her time in bed, groaning night and day, eating little, continually complaining, and relating her misfortunes to all. Forty-six years of age, March 16th, 1813. This woman is transferred to the infirmary for the insane. Her emaciation is extreme, skin, earthy, face pale and convulsive, the eyes dull and fixed; the breath fetid, the tongue dry, rough, and interspersed with whitish points. She refuses nourishment, although she says that she is tormented by hunger and thirst. There is insomnia, together with a small and feeble pulse, head heavy, with a burning sensation internally, and a feeling as if bound with a cord externally. There is a painful constriction of the throat, and she is constantly rolling up the skin of her neck with her fingers, and crowding it behind the sternum; assuring us that the devil draws it, and that he strangles and prevents her from swallowing any thing. There is considerable tension of the muscles of the abdomen, attended by constipation; and upon the back of the right hand and left foot, are scrofulous tumors. The devil has extended a cord from the sternum to the pubes, which prevents the patient from standing up. He is in her body, burning and pinching it. He also gnaws her heart, and rends her entrails. She is surrounded by flames, and in the midst of the fires of hell, though we see them not. No one may credit it, but her ills are unprecedented, frightful, eternal. She is damned. Heaven can have no compassion upon her.

J.-E.-D. Esquirol (see page 139), *Mental Maladies:
A Treatise on Insanity* (1845)

=

The coming of psychodynamics in the twentieth century, especially as formulated by Jung, gave a new lease of life to religious techniques applied to mental disorders.

I went to a country rector who advertised himself as a psychologist. It is a curious feature of English law that, although any unqualified person is forbidden to practise even the simplest forms of surgery or medicine, anybody may describe himself as a psychologist or a mental healer. This country rector had a number of assistants and he assured me that I should reach complete adjustment with my wife if I took a course of psycho-analysis with one of his lady helpers. I agreed to do this although, when he mentioned the sum of money involved, I realized that even if I failed to benefit from the treatment another person would. This young woman called me by my Christian name and treated me like a child. A large part of the treatment consisted of what she called 'flexing', which meant that I had to relax and fall into her arms. If I had wished to become an acrobat this would have been a very useful accomplishment. No doubt if I had continued the treatment for fourteen or fifteen years I should have been well on the way towards a cure, and possibly by the end of my life the treatment would have terminated success-fully. Fortunately, financial considerations left me with no choice. I had to stop.

> John Vincent, *Inside the Asylum* (1948)

=

Christian teachings created the expectation that believers might be addressed by supernatural voices. George Trosse, a worldling Cavalier, was to discover, however, that it was not easy to distin-guish between the voice of the Lord and that of His Arch-enemy.

While I was thus walking up and down, hurried with these worldly disquieting Thoughts, I perceiv'd a *Voice*, (*I heard it plainly*) saying unto me, *Who art thou?* Which, knowing it could be the voice of *no Mortal*, I concluded was the *Voice of God*, and with Tears, as I remember, reply'd, *I am a very great Sinner, Lord!* Hereupon, I withdrew again into the *Inner-Room*, securing and barring the Door upon me, & betook my self to a *very proper and seasonable Duty*, namely, *Secret Prayer*; performing it with some kind of *Conscience* towards *God*, and with Hopes to receive some *Good* at his Hands, (which I *never* did all my Life-Time *before*). But it was an *impudent* and *proud Prayer*: For I *pray'd in my own Strength*, as tho' I was good enough to have *Communion* with an *Holy God*, and worthy enough to have Access to Him, and Success with him, as to all I pray'd for. I look'd not to the *Spirit* to *help* me in Prayer, nor to the *Lord Jesus* to render it *acceptable*. So that altho' I had liv'd a *Sinner* and a *Publican* all my Days, yet now I pray'd like a

Pharisee, with a *carnal Confidence*, which was an infinite Dis-
honour to God, and could not but be a *great Provocation*, as the
Event prov'd.

For while I was praying upon my Knees, I heard a Voice, as I
fancy'd, as it were just behind me, saying, *Yet more humble; Yet
more humble*; with some Continuance. And not knowing the
Meaning of the *Voice*, but undoubtedly concluding it came from
God, I endeavour'd to comply with it. Considering that I kneel'd
upon something, I remov'd it; and then I had some kind of Intimation given me, that that was what was requir'd. Thus I kneel'd
upon the Ground: But the *Voice* still continu'd, *Yet more humble;
Yet more humble*. In Compliance with it I proceeded to pluck down
my *Stockings*, and to kneel upon my *bare Knees*: But the same
awful Voice still sounding in mine Ears, I proceeded to pull off my
Stockings, and then my *Hose*, and my *Doublet*; and as I was thus
uncloathing my self, I had a strong internal Impression, that all was
well done, and a full Compliance with the Design of the *Voice*. In
Answer likewise to this *Call*, I would *bow* my Body as *low as
possibly I could*, with a great deal of Pain, & *this* I often repeated:
But *all* I could do was not *low enough*, nor *humble enough*. At last,
observing that there was an Hole in the Planking of the Room, I lay
my self down flat upon the Ground, and thrust in my Head there as
far as I could: but because I could not fully do it, I put my Hand
into the Hole, and took out *Earth* and *Dust*, and sprinkled it on my
Head; some *Scripture Expressions* at that Time offering themselves
to my Mind, I thought *this* was the *Lying down in Dust and Ashes*
thereby prescrib'd.

At length, standing up before the *Window*, I either *heard a Voice*,
which bid me, or *had a strong Impulse*, which excited me, to *cut off
my Hair*; to which I reply'd *I have no Scissors*. It was then hinted,
that a *Knife would do it*; but I answer'd, *I have none*. Had I had
one, I verily believe, this *Voice* would have gone from my *Hair* to
my *Throat*, and have commanded me to *cut it*: For I have all
Reason to conclude, that the *Voice* was the Voice of *Satan*, and that
his Design was, to *humble* me as *low as Hell*: But the Absence of a
proper Instrument prevented it.

Thus, pretending the *Worship of God*, I fell, in effect, to the
Worshipping of the Devil; and my Falling on my Knees before *God*

issu'd in a Prostration at the *proud Usurper*'s Feet. I am perswaded, that *many* of the Quakers formerly were deluded by *such Voices* and *Impulses* from the *Impure Spirit*, which they mistook for the *Holy Spirit of God*; many of them having been grosly ignorant, and so fitted to entertain such Delusions of the *Devil*, as I *then* was.

George Trosse, *The Life of the Reverend Mr George Trosse* (1714)

=

Under command

'Kneel down and pray,' said the voice.

'Where shall I kneel?'

'There, in the sunlight by the fireplace. Be sure to kneel in the sunlight.'

I deposited the brush on the mantelpiece, and knelt down as directed.

'Lean more forward into the sunlight,' ordered the voice.

I obeyed.

'Bend your head lower.'

Again I obeyed; and my hair, which was hanging loose, fell all over my face.

'Push back your hair from off your face,' the voice commanded.

'Oh, what *does* it matter where my hair is when I am praying?' I exclaimed impatiently, for these elaborate preparations were beginning to annoy me. However, I pushed back my hair as directed, but as my head remained in the bent position ordered, my hair immediately tumbled once more over my face, shutting out all view of everything except what was directly beneath my eyes. This happened to be a small black coal-scuttle.

Reflected in this shiny surface I saw quite distinctly a picture of a very well-known woman occultist. (She is unacquainted with me, but I am acquainted with her both through her books and her lectures.)

'Oh,' I thought, 'this is all right. She understands all about these things. Evidently this is part of some occult experiment, and when the fiend appears she means to tackle it.'

I did not feel in the least afraid, and was racking my brain to think what prayer would be suited to this most unusual occasion, when suddenly I experienced a violent, physical sensation inside my body. It did not in the least hurt me, but it was so violent and unaccountable it frightened me. I could not understand what was happening to me. (I neither saw nor heard anything.)

I thought to myself, 'Has this perhaps something to do with that fiend that they were warning me against?' And instantly the voices confirmed this fear, saying that the fiend had now got inside my body; that the explanation of this whole mysterious sensation was that I had been seduced by a fiend, and that I should therefore have a fiend-child.

[E. Thelmar], *The Maniac* (1909)

=

Driven crazy by his analyst and by the drugs prescribed by another psychiatrist, John Balt murdered his wife, Claire. He then heard the divine voice.

God spoke to me and told me about it. The second world war had been Armageddon. Hitler's Germany and militaristic Japan had been the forces of evil. Although they had almost won, the forces of good had finally prevailed and now the tree of life could flourish. History was this tree of life. Its roots reached into the fiery lava of creation. The history of mankind thus far was the trunk. Now with Armageddon past the trunk would produce billions of branches and leaves. From the earth, mankind would populate tens of thousands of universes. Already death was stopping around the world. Very soon it would cease altogether. The soul was in the brain, and the brain lived forever. Men would live forever. Life was eternal.

President Kennedy spoke to me on the telecommunicator. God had contacted him, for the United States was to be the seat of government for the new divinely ordered world, which would be proclaimed on a great holiday called Universals Day. On that day at eight o'clock in the morning, Washington time, President Kennedy would go on radio and television to announce the start of the earthly heaven and to make known God's will that death should end. At eleven o'clock, God would descend from Heaven; and I was vouchsafed a vision of this scene so inconceivably beautiful that it brought tears to my eyes. Magnificent colors resplendent in the new sunlight, gold everywhere. On one side of the stupendous Figure was Moses; on the other, Jesus. A dazzling city would spread out from the point where they would touch earth, wide-streeted and gold-domed.

I was to be the human symbol of the great holiday. God would receive me and I would become his great minister-writer-historian forever. President Kennedy wanted me to help him compose his speech for that great morning, and I telecommunicated the words that had come from above: 'The history of mankind is a tree of life whose roots go back to the fiery lava of creation and whose crown reaches upward into the stars.'

Claire contacted me on the telecommunicator. She was at our hillside home in the Valley. It had already become a shrine because it had become known to thousands of people by divine inspiration that from it the best view could be had of the Descent.

'I'm growing taller,' she said. 'And so are the children. Stand up, John, and see if you aren't growing taller too.'

I stood by the bars and saw that she was right. I measured at least seven feet.

'God has arranged it that way,' said Claire. 'An angel came last night and told me. You and I and the children are to be over ten feet tall. We're the first, but through us, mankind will know that it is to become a race of giants. Our hearts are changing too, John. If they were to examine you now they'd find that your heart had six chambers instead of four. It is a heart that is meant for all eternity. I'm so happy for everyone, John.'

'Why has God chosen us?'

'Because we've loved each other so much.'

John Balt, *By Reason of Insanity* (1972)

=

A religious zoo

On the way I asked him whether I was not right, and whether it was not the case that He was God Himself and not a man at all.

'I suppose I am,' was his reply.

I then asked: 'How can I possibly call you by an ordinary man's name?'

He told me simply to call him J— in that place, and I was as delighted as a child in the thought that the Eternal had actually taken a human form and come to look after me, and I continued so for some considerable time.

My guardian and I soon entered two large rooms opening into one another, in which the patients remained when indoors. A short passage across an old closed-up hall connected the two rooms, which at one time had been the dining-room and the drawing-room of an old-fashioned country house.

To say I was surprised is not the word, when, for the first time in my life, I saw a number of beings who, from their poor, mis-shapen bodies or distorted countenances, seemed hardly human. The first thing I thought was that I was in some sort of sacred precincts attached to some sort of idol-temple, where a number of old semi-petrified, but still living teraphim or images, representing some sort of worship, were kept alive and fed. Some of the types strangely reminded me, I know not why, of characters I had read about in the Bible. I had not opened the book for years, nor did I open one all the time I was in this asylum, or for twelve years afterwards; but as a child, a small knowledge of sacred history and some of the characters therein portrayed had been instilled into me, though the only picture on sacred subjects I remembered, or indeed have any vivid memory of now, was one out of a small book called 'Line upon Line'. It was Moses before Pharoah where the various serpents were moving about along the floor in the wrong way, making loops above the ground, instead of creeping sideways with the whole belly pressed against it. Indeed, it was an old clergyman's calling attention to this curious mistake in the picture that impressed it on my memory, and I told my guardian this one day when talking to him about pictures.

Here, now, in the flesh was to be seen Nebuchadnezzar, hairy and grey, with long nails, large elephantine ears, and a restless suspicious look in his wild eyes as he paced to and fro like some big baboon in a cage, and every now and then hurried off to admire himself in a looking-glass. When he got to the glass, he used to protrude his lips as far as he could and work violently, curling his moustache and pulling at his beard with both hands. Then he used to plaster down his hair, and dart off to the wash-room to wax the

ends of his moustache with soap. After this, he always went to a chair
and, with a satisfied little snigger, crossed himself reverently, and sat
in a peculiar attitude for some time, only to jump up again, pace
round in the same ridiculous manner, and eventually go through the
same decorative process. I never saw a human being so like an old
monkey in appearance and antics: but he thought himself a beautiful
thing, and for a short time he insisted on following me about. I was
told that old Van (so he was called, short for old Vanity) had been in
a crack regiment once, but had become insane and grown monstrous, as patients sometimes do. My guardian once gently pointed out
to me some of his peculiarities that reminded me of things unpleas-
antly near home. I had it in my mind that somewhere or other I had
seen something just like him before, but I could not remember where.
I told my guardian this, and very soon afterwards it crossed my mind
that it was the old rogue monkey who had been driven from his herd
and had taken such a fancy to me when I was an infant.

Here also, cooped up in the asylum, was dark, ponderous Herod,
whose bloated and voluptuous Semitic pride, curiously mixed with
obsequiousness, still showed itself through the hunted, restless, and
depressed look of a closely confined lunatic.

D. Davidson, *Remembrances of a Religio-Maniac: An Autobiography*
(1912)

=

Persecuted by God

> Hatred and vengeance, my eternal portion,
> Scarce can endure delay of execution:
> Wait with impatient readiness, to seize my
>   Soul in a moment.
>
> Damn'd below Judas; more abhorr'd than he was,
> Who, for a few pence, sold his holy master.
> Twice betray'd, Jesus me, the last delinquent,
>   Deems the profanest.
> Man disavows, and Deity disowns me.
> Hell might afford my miseries a shelter;
> Therefore hell keeps her everhungry mouths all
>   Bolted against me.

Hard lot! Encompass'd with a thousand dangers,
Weary, faint, trembling with a thousand terrors,
Fall'n, and if vanquish'd, to receive a sentence
    Worse than Abiram's:
Him, the vindictive rod of angry justice
Sent, quick and howling, to the centre headlong;
I, fed with judgments, in a fleshly tomb, am
    Buried above ground.
William Cowper, 'Hatred and Vengeance, My Eternal Portion' (1774)

8

Mad, Bad – or Themselves Victims?

There have always been individuals regarded as crazy, and these have been taken care of, or neglected, in a variety of ways. The question of what precisely constituted insanity, or idiocy, and of whether a particular individual met those criteria, might remain essentially academic. Until, that is, the person in question tangled with the law – perhaps because of making a will, or coming into an inheritance, perhaps because of being suspected of committing a crime. For it is a standard feature of the thinking underpinning legal systems, that legal agents must be capable of being held responsible for their actions.

Under what circumstances, then, might a will be set aside, or a supposed felon escape punishment, by reason of insanity? In certain nations, notably France, the notion of the *crime passionel* has enjoyed a considerable sway. Crimes committed under the driving force of 'irresistible passion' (for example, jealousy at seeing one's wife in the embraces of another) have been treated as instances of temporary insanity and have led to acquittal. 'Irresistible impulse' has never gone down well in phlegmatic Britain (perhaps because, as one Victorian judge pointed out, the Bench might retaliate by feeling an irresistible impulse to see the prisoner swing).

English common law, instead, has argued that the sorts of crime that may evade the full rigours of the law are those committed in the grip of cognitive delusions – for instance, if one strangles one's wife under the delusion that she is a python encoiling itself around one's body. The 'delusion defence' was eloquently pleaded by Thomas Erskine in the celebrated case of James Hadfield, who attempted to assassinate George III under the religious delusion that only by such an act could he save the world; and it was subsequently given stricter formulation in the M'Naghten Rules.

With the rise of the asylum, the law became further involved in the regulation of lunacy. Strict certification procedures became essential to prevent wrongful confinement. Again, the law was commonly invoked to judge precisely in what way, and to what extent, a person was to be deemed sufficiently crazy to warrant compulsory detention with temporary loss of civil rights. Where did wilfulness and eccentricity in the handling of one's affairs spill over into blatant incompetence and uncontrollable irresponsibility? At what point did society require to be protected from a lunatic? Was it justifiable to protect a lunatic from his own reckless actions?

These questions show that more than the law is at stake. There are moral and political decisions to be made. Since the Nazi purge of schizophrenics and the mentally deficient, and the Stalinist brain-washings, we have become highly conscious of the potential for the political abuse of psychiatry. A very different critique suggests, by contrast, that England is a land that has held liberty so dear as to be overrun with weirdos.

===

Pleading insane

As I walked up the steps that led into the dock, I was still conscious only of indifference and of my double personality. One verdict or another could make but little odds. In either case, my life was finished. '*La commedia è finita* – the comedy is ended,' whispered my old self from its hiding-place. 'Your conscience is clear of malice. If death is waiting for you, death is rest and oblivion, freedom at least from that intolerable prison life, this degradation in the public pillory. If you are doomed to live, no matter. You cannot help yourself. In any case you may not long survive the incarceration that awaits you. Hold up your head and brace your shoulders. Let them see that you are not afraid.' So it was with a firm step and head held high that I advanced to learn my fate.

The jury filed into the box. 'Do you find the prisoner guilty or not guilty?' came the question. The foreman fumbled with a slip of paper. 'We find the prisoner guilty but insane.' Only then did the judge's voice betray his feelings; the Law and Medicine are at daggers drawn in cases of this kind. 'Let the prisoner be detained until His Majesty's pleasure be known' came the sentence, and the red gown had vanished through the door at the back of the dais.

'Warmark', *'Guilty but Insane': A Broadmoor Autobiography* (1931)

=

A former soldier, James Hadfield, shot at George III in 1799. He was defended by the great lawyer Thomas Erskine who attempted to prove him the victim of an insane delusion. Hadfield apparently believed that, for the world to be saved, God demanded the sacrifice of his own life. He knew no more foolproof way to ensure his own death than to assassinate the King. It was also revealed that Hadfield had suffered a head wound while serving in the army.

LORD KENYON: Mr Erskine, have you nearly finished your evidence?

MR ERSKINE: No my lord; I have twenty more witnesses to examine.

LORD KENYON: Mr Attorney-general, can you call any witnesses to contradict these facts? With regard to the law, as it has been laid down, there can be no doubt upon earth; to be sure, if a man is in a deranged state of mind at the time, he is not criminally answerable for his acts; but the material part of this case is, *whether at the very time when the act was committed this man's mind was sane.* I confess, the facts proved by the witnesses (though some of them stand in near relationship to the prisoner, yet others do not) bring home conviction to one's mind, that at the time he committed this offence, and a most horrid one it is, he was in a very deranged state. I do not know that one can run the case very nicely; if you do run it very nicely, to be sure it is an acquittal. His sanity must be made out to the satisfaction of a moral man, meeting the case with fortitude of mind, knowing he has an arduous duty to discharge, yet if the scales hang any thing like even, throwing in a certain proportion of mercy to the party.

Mr Attorney-general, you have heard the facts given in evidence; to be sure such a man is a most dangerous member of society, and there are some doctrines and points laid down in a speech which has been alluded to, that are very well worthy the attention of every body, – I believe in the speech of a very illustrious member of our profession, Mr Yorke, in the prosecution of Lord Ferrers. It is impossible that this man with safety to society can be suffered, supposing his misfortune is such, to be let loose upon the public. But in a criminal prosecution, I will, in this part of the business, throw it out for your discretion and that of the other gentlemen who give you their assistance upon this occasion, whether it is necessary to proceed farther. If this shall appear to be an assumed case, – if you can shew it to have been a case by management, in order to give a false colour and complexion to the real transaction, then assuredly this case vanishes.

MR ATTORNEY GENERAL: I must confess, that I have certainly no reason to imagine that this is a coloured case: on the contrary, I stated that I apprehended the prisoner had been originally discharged from the army upon the ground of his insanity. With respect to his sanity immediately preceding and subsequent to the act, I have offered the evidence I had; unquestionably, the circumstances which have now been stated, were perfectly unknown to me.

LORD KENYON: Your conduct, Mr Attorney-general, has been extremely meritorious; no man living has an idea of reproaching any that took any part in the prosecution; it was most fit and absolutely necessary to make the inquiry; the result of the inquiry being such as it is, in the present posture of the cause, I will put it to you whether you ought to proceed.

MR ATTORNEY GENERAL: I am certainly much obliged to your lordship, for having done what you have been so good as to do: your lordship will feel how much it was necessary for me to wait until I should have some intimation upon the subject.

LORD KENYON: It was necessary for us all to wait till the cause was arrived at a certain point of maturity. The prisoner, for his own sake, and for the sake of society at large, must not be discharged; for this is a case which concerns every man of every station, from the king upon the throne to the begger at the gate; people of both sexes and of all ages may, in an unfortunate frantic hour, fall a sacrifice to this man, who is not under the guidance of sound reason; and therefore it is absolutely necessary for the safety of society, that he should be properly disposed of, all mercy and humanity being shown to this most unfortunate creature. But for the sake of the community, undoubtedly, he must somehow or other be taken care of, with all the attention and all the relief that can be afforded him.

MR ATTORNEY GENERAL: I most perfectly acquiesce in what your lordship has said.

LORD KENYON: Gentlemen of the Jury; The attorney-general's opinion coinciding with mine, and with that great assistance I have on my right and left, I believe it is necessary for me to submit to you, whether you will not find that the prisoner, at the time he committed the act, was not so under the guidance of reason, as to be answerable for this act, enormous and atrocious as it appeared to be.

A case is put into my hand of a person tried for felony, who, appearing to the Court to be mad and dangerous to society, was ordered to be removed to a proper place of confinement. I do not think that is the thing to be done here; I apprehend he should be at present confined, till properly disposed of.

MR ERSKINE: My lord, we, who represent the prisoner, are highly sensible of the humanity, justice, and benevolence of every part of the Court; and I subscribe most heartily to the law as it has been laid down by my learned friend the attorney-general; most undoubtedly the safety of the community requires that this unfortunate man should be taken care of.

LORD KENYON: Something must be done that he may be prevented from committing farther mischief.

MR JUSTICE GROSE: At present he must not be discharged.

MR ATTORNEY GENERAL: It is laid down in some of the books, that by the common law the judges of every court are competent to direct the confinement of a person under such circumstances.

LORD KENYON: That may be, Mr Attorney-general; but at present we can only remand him to the confinement he came from; but means will be used to confine him otherwise, in a manner much better adapted to his situation.

MR GARROW: Would it not be for the benefit of posterity, if the jury would state in their verdict the grounds upon which they give it, namely, that they acquit the prisoner of this charge, he

appearing to them to have been under the influence of insanity at
the time the act was committed? there would then be a legal and
sufficient reason for his future confinement.

VERDICT

FOREMAN OF THE JURY: We find the prisoner is Not Guilty; he
being under the influence of Insanity at the time the act was
committed.

Hadfield's Case (1800)

=

*Lawyers and physicians have been required to adjudicate a person's
sanity. At issue has been whether the party should be certified, sent
to an asylum, or permitted to make a will or to inherit. James
Parkinson, the early nineteenth-century doctor after whom Parkinson's disease is named, illustrates some of the difficulties in distinguishing true insanity from mere idiosyncrasy.*

A second interesting case of insanity is described in Parkinson's
own words. 'A gentleman farmer was brought to a house for the
reception of lunatics, his friends grounding the necessity for his
confinement on his conducting his affairs in such a manner as must
soon bring him to ruin. On speaking to the patient, he said, if his
friends could state any circumstance which he could not defend on
principles of reason and equity he would consent to be confined for
the rest of his days. He was then asked:

Do you not give more wages than other farmers? Yes. Why do
You? Because I am of opinion that the standing wages of
labourers is much too small; and the neighbouring farmers agree
with me in that opinion, but have not integrity enough to follow
my example, although they know their labourers to be almost
starving.
But have you not had it clearly demonstrated to you, that this
preceding must terminate in your ruin? Yes, but – a question in
my turn. Am I to be deemed a madman because I will not save
myself from ruin by starving a number of my fellow creatures?
Well, but your friends say, that you have thoughts of leaving

your farm to your servants, and to make a tour over Scotland, setting out with only a crown in your pocket. Is that a rational intention? Yes, I have certainly a right to make what tour I please; it will be a more rational tour than your sparks of quality make, for I go to inform myself of the agriculture of the country I pass through.

But you leave your farm at the mercy of your servants? So do other farms, and more madly than I should, since, by generosity I have assured myself of the fidelity of my servants. But was it not madness to think of setting out on this excursion with only a crown in your pocket? So, extravagant generosity is first brought as proof of my madness, and, this failing, you mean to prove it by my parsimony.

But I can explain this part of my conduct also. I know I injure myself by the wages I pay, and therefore can spare but little for myself – so much for my parsimony. But how is this crown to carry you through? Thus – I shall take one of my horses for the first thirty miles, and then travel on foot for the next twenty; and thus, with care, my five shillings will carry me fifty miles from home. Now the object of my journey is agricultural knowledge, and my wish is to obtain it as cheap as I can; therefore I will hire myself as a labourer until I have got five shillings more, and then set off again. I have got such recommendations as will ensure my employ and extra wages. In this manner, I shall perform my tour; and get, perhaps, as much useful knowledge as will enable me to pay my men without incurring ruin.

Staggered by the acuteness of these answers, the medical gentleman was with difficulty induced to sign the certificate of his lunacy, and, at last, did it with that want of strong conviction which left it a burden on his mind.

A. D. Morris, *James Parkinson, His Life and Times* (1989)

=

How odd do you have to be to be judged insane in the eyes of the law?

Sir Thomas George Apreece, Bart., died by his own hands on the 30th December, 1842, aged fifty-one, possessed of realty to the amount of between 200,000l. and 300,000l., and personalty to the amount of 20,000l.

By his will, executed in June, 1836, the whole of his property, save 100l. to each of his executors, Messrs Frere and Foster, was devised and bequeathed to trustees for sale for the benefit of St George's Hospital.

The will was propounded by Mr Frere, and opposed by Mrs Peacocke, the sister, and only next of kin of the deceased.

Four allegations were admitted in the cause, on which ninety-one witnesses were examined, and, in addition, there was an almost countless number of exhibits.

The general purport of the case, as set up against the will, was to shew that the deceased was, if not from the date of his birth, yet at least from a period shortly after commencing, of unsound mind, and that he continued in that state through life.

The eleventh article of Mrs Peacocke's allegation pleaded: 'That at all times, but more particularly after the death of his [Sir T. G. Apreece's] mother [in 1823], the deceased evinced evident gratification in causing inconvenience and annoyance to others. That he took an insane delight in inducing poor people whom he met on the road, and in particular the aged and infirm, to get into his carriage as if for the benevolent purpose of helping them on their way, but, as soon as they were therein, driving at a rapid pace for several miles, and, as long as the horses could be kept at their speed, far beyond their place of destination, refusing them any assistance in the way of money or otherwise for their conveyance back, and insanely rejoicing in the suffering he had caused them. That in like manner he had an irrational pleasure in teasing and tantalizing his inferiors by insincere offers of gifts, whether of raiment or money. That he also took an unnatural and childish pleasure in speaking and hearing of the pain or suffering of his fellow-creatures, rubbing his hands, grinning, and otherwise evincing an irrational gratification at any evil tidings respecting them.'

The thirty-sixth article pleaded: 'That the said deceased never appeared to have any sense of religion, or ever attended any place of divine worship, and was eminently uncharitable all his life, and generally so known to be by all his acquaintances, and that neither

St George's, nor any other hospital, nor any such or similar institution, was either subscribed to by, or even apparently any object of
interest to, the deceased at any period of his life.'

[Sir George was found eccentric, not insane.]

Headnote to *Frere v. Peacocke* (1846)

=

*Daniel M'Naghten was a Glasgow tradesman convinced that his
business was being ruined by the Prime Minister, Robert Peel. He
came to London to slay Peel, but succeeded only in killing his
secretary. At his trial he was found insane, on the grounds of his
delusions of persecution. In the ensuing brouhaha, the law lords
were required to clarify the grounds upon which a defendant
should be deemed to lack the* mens rea *necessary to establish legal
guilt. The 'M'Naghten Rules' have, in effect, never been
superseded.*

The prisoner had been indicted for that he, on the 20th day of
January 1843, at the parish of Saint Martin in the Fields, in the
county of Middlesex, and within the jurisdiction of the Central
Criminal Court, in and upon one Edward Drummond, feloniously,
wilfully, and of his malice aforethought, did make an assault; and
that the said Daniel M'Naghten, a certain pistol of the value of 20s,
loaded and charged with gunpowder and a leaden bullet (which
pistol he in his right hand had and held), to, against and upon the
said Edward Drummond, feloniously, wilfully, and of his malice
aforethought, did shoot and discharge; and that the said Daniel
M'Naghten, with the leaden bullet aforesaid, out of the pistol
aforesaid, by force of the gunpowder, etc., the said Edward Drummond, in and upon the back of him the said Edward Drummond,
feloniously, etc. did strike, penetrate and wound, giving to the said
Edward Drummond, in and upon the back of the said Edward
Drummond, one mortal wound, etc., of which mortal wound the
said E. Drummond languished until the 25th of April and then
died; and that by the means aforesaid, he the prisoner did kill and
murder the said Edward Drummond. The prisoner pleaded Not
guilty.

Evidence having been given of the fact of the shooting of Mr Drummond, and of his death in consequence thereof, witnesses were called on the part of the prisoner, to prove that he was not, at the time of committing the act, in a sound state of mind. The medical evidence was in substance this: That persons of otherwise sound mind, might be affected by morbid delusions: that the prisoner was in that condition: that a person so labouring under a morbid delusion, might have a moral perception of right and wrong, but that in the case of the prisoner it was a delusion which carried him away beyond the power of his own control, and left him no such perception; and that he was not capable of exercising any control over acts which had connexion with his delusion: that it was of the nature of the disease with which the prisoner was affected, to go on gradually until it had reached a climax, when it burst forth with irresistible intensity: that a man might go on for years quietly, though at the same time under its influence, but would all at once break out into the most extravagant and violent paroxysms.

Some of the witnesses who gave this evidence, had previously examined the prisoner: others had never seen him till he appeared in Court, and they formed their opinions on hearing the evidence given by the other witnesses.

Lord Chief Justice Tindal (in his charge): – The question to be determined is, whether at the time the act in question was committed, the prisoner had or had not the use of his understanding, so as to know that he was doing a wrong or wicked act. If the jurors should be of opinion that the prisoner was not sensible, at the time he committed it, that he was violating the laws both of God and man, then he would be entitled to a verdict in his favour: but if, on the contrary, they were of opinion that when he committed the act he was in a sound state of mind, then their verdict must be against him.

Verdict, Not guilty, on the ground of insanity . . .

Your Lordships are pleased to inquire of us, secondly, 'What are the proper questions to be submitted to the jury, where a person alleged to be afflicted with insane delusion respecting one or more particular subjects or persons, is charged with the commission of a crime (murder, for example), and insanity is set up as a defence?'

And, thirdly, 'In what terms ought the question to be left to the jury as to the prisoner's state of mind at the time when the act was committed?' And as these two questions appear to us to be more conveniently answered together, we have to submit our opinion to be, that the jurors ought to be told in all cases that every man is to be presumed to be sane, and to possess a sufficient degree of reason to be responsible for his crimes, until the contrary be proved to their satisfaction; and that to establish a defence on the ground of insanity, it must be clearly proved that, at the time of the committing of the act, the party accused was labouring under such a defect of reason, from disease of the mind, as not to know the nature and quality of the act he was doing; or, if he did know it, that he did not know he was doing what was wrong. The mode of putting the latter part of the question to the jury on these occasions has generally been, whether the accused at the time of doing the act knew the difference between right and wrong: which mode, though rarely, if ever, leading to any mistake with the jury, is not, as we conceive, so accurate when put generally and in the abstract, as when put with reference to the party's knowledge of right and wrong in respect to the very act with which he is charged. If the question were to be put as to the knowledge of the accused solely and exclusively with reference to the law of the land, it might tend to confound the jury, by inducing them to believe that an actual knowledge of the law of the land was essential in order to lead to a conviction; whereas the law is administered upon the principle that every one must be taken conclusively to know it, without proof that he does know it. If the accused was conscious that the act was one which he ought not to do, and if that act was at the same time contrary to the law of the land, he is punishable; and the usual course therefore has been to leave the question to the jury, whether the party accused had a sufficient degree of reason to know that he was doing an act that was wrong: and this course we think is correct, accompanied with such observations and explanations as the circumstances of each particular case may require.

M'Naghten's Case (1843), 10 Clark & Finnelly

=

Claims to rival expertise have sparked a long history of animosity between legal officials and psychiatrists in the courtroom. Judges have often felt they were being bamboozled by the technical jargon of the doctors. Here the Court of Appeal comes down on the side of laymen's understanding in matters of lunacy.

LAWTON L.J.   Like Lord Denning M.R. and Orr L.J., I agree that this appeal has called attention to the difficulties which arise under the Mental Health Act 1959 from the definition of 'mental disorder', which is set out in section 4 of the Act. For the purpose of seeing what was the intention of the Act, the court has looked at the Report of the Royal Commission on the Law Relating to Mental Illness and Mental Deficiency, 1957. The Royal Commission seem to have overlooked that their recommendations would not result in a definition of 'mental disorder' which would meet the requirements of doctors. The view seems to have been taken that doctors and others who had to apply their recommendations would not in practice have much difficulty in fitting any particular case into its appropriate classification. The facts of this case show how difficult the fitting of particular instances into the statutory classification can be. Lord Denning M.R. and Orr L.J. have pointed out that there is no definition of 'mental illness'. The words are ordinary words of the English language. They have no particular medical significance. They have no particular legal significance. How should the court construe them? The answer in my judgment is to be found in the advice which Lord Reid recently gave in *Cozens* v. *Brutus* [1973] A.C. 854, 861, namely, that ordinary words of the English language should be construed in the way that ordinary sensible people would construe them. That being, in my judgment, the right test, then I ask myself, what would the ordinary sensible person have said about the patient's condition in this case if he had been informed of his behaviour to the dogs, the cat and his wife? In my judgment such a person would have said: 'Well, the fellow is obviously mentally ill.' If that be right, then, although the case may fall within the definition of 'psychopathic disorder' in section 4 (4), it also falls within the classification of 'mental illness'; and there is the added medical fact that when the EEG was taken there were indications of a clinical character showing some abnormality of the brain. It is that application of the sensible person's assessment of the condition, plus the medical indication, which in my judgment brought the case within the classification of mental illness and justified the finding of the county court judge.

The Court of Appeal (23, 24 May 1973)

=

Psychiatrists are wont to pronounce upon the national mental health. Many, early this century, deplored the tendency of British liberality to permit this country to become the asylum of the world.

With regard to the future, it is to be hoped that the mentally perverted who are still amenable to social observances may have their own special 'retreats', where they can pursue their intellectual, æsthetical, or industrial bents in safety; that the morally perverted, who are a danger to themselves or to the community, may be relegated to 'Homes of Detention', where special provision can be made for their care and safety; and lastly, that Great Britain should deny itself the thankless task of offering itself as an 'asylum' for alien perverts and subversivists. Certain it is that England has been in danger of becoming the dumping ground, or 'Asylum of the World', owing to the misguided hospitality it has extended hitherto to alien degenerates, irresponsibles, and undesirables. When these changes are effected, and not till then, will justice be done to the various types of our afflicted fellow-beings.

Theo B. Hyslop, *The Great Abnormals* (1925)

=

There was, of course, nothing new in the notion that England was the homeland of the mad.

HAMLET: . . . How long hast thou been a grave-maker?
1ST CLOWN: Of all the days i' th' year, I came to't that day that our last King Hamlet overcame Fortinbras.
HAMLET: How long is that since?
1ST CLOWN: Cannot you tell that? Every fool can tell that: it was that very day that young Hamlet was born – he that is mad, and sent into England.

HAMLET: Ay, marry, why was he sent into England?

1ST CLOWN: Why, because 'a was mad: 'a shall recover his wits there; or, if 'a do not, 'tis no great matter there.

HAMLET: Why?

1ST CLOWN: 'Twill not be seen in him there: there the men are as mad as he.

HAMLET: How came he mad?

1ST CLOWN: Very strangely, they say.

HAMLET: How strangely?

1ST CLOWN: Faith, e'en with losing his wits.

HAMLET: Upon what ground?

1ST CLOWN: Why, here in Denmark. I have been sexton here, man and boy, thirty years.

William Shakespeare, Hamlet (1604)

=

Good explanations were to hand. Early in the eighteenth century, the Scots physician, George Cheyne (see page 68), offered a double-edged account of the prevalence of 'The English Malady', by which he meant a tendency to nervous disorders, madness, and suicide.

The Title I have chosen for this Treatise, is a Reproach universally thrown on this Island by Foreigners, and all our Neighbours on the Continent, by whom nervous Distempers, Spleen, Vapours, and Lowness of Spirits, are in Derision, called the ENGLISH MALADY. And I wish there were not so good Grounds for this Reflection. The Moisture of our Air, the Variableness of our Weather, (from our Situation amidst the Ocean) the Rankness and Fertility of our Soil, the Richness and Heaviness of our Food, the Wealth and Abundance of the Inhabitants (from their universal Trade) the Inactivity and sedentary Occupations of the better Sort (among whom this Evil mostly rages) and the Humour of living in great, populous and consequently unhealthy Towns, have brought forth a Class and Set of Distempers, with atrocious and frightful Symptoms, scarce known to our Ancestors, and never rising to such fatal Heights, nor afflicting such Numbers in any other known Nation. These nervous Disorders being computed to make almost

one third of the Complaints of the People of Condition in
England . . .

George Cheyne, *The English Malady; or, A Treatise of Nervous Diseases
of all Kinds, with the Author's Own Case* (1733)

=

*In the guise of a visiting Spaniard, Robert Southey implies that the
Devonshire 'prophetess', Joanna Southcott, was raving mad and
should have been subjected to appropriate treatment.*

Joanna talked Satan out of all patience. She gave him, as he truly
complained, ten words for one, and allowed him no time to speak.
All men, he said, were tired of her tongue already, and now she had
tired the Devil. This was not unreasonable; but he proceeded to
abuse the whole sex, which would have been ungracious in any one,
and in him was ungrateful. He said no man could tame a woman's
tongue – the sands of an hour-glass did not run faster – it was better
to dispute with a thousand men than one woman. After this dispute
she fasted forty days; but this fast, which is regarded by her
believers as so miraculous, was merely a Catholic Lent, in which
she abstained from fish as well as flesh.

The Moon which is under her feet in the Revelation, typifies the
Devil: for the moon, it seems, having power to give light by night
but not by day, is Satan's kingdom, and his dwelling-place; he, I
conclude, being the very person commonly called the Man in the
Moon, a conjecture of my own, which, you must allow, is strongly
confirmed by his horns. Once, when the Lord made her the same
promise as Herod had done to Herodias, she requested that Satan
might be cut off from the face of the earth as John the Baptist had
been. This petition she was instructed to write, and seal it with
three seals, and carry it to the altar when she received the sacra-
ment! and a promise was returned that it should be granted. Her
dreams are usually of the Devil. Once she saw him like a pig with
his mouth tied, at another time skinned his face with her nails after
a fierce battle; once she bit off his fingers, and thought the blood
sweet, – and once she dreamt she had fairly killed him. But neither
has the promise of his destruction been as yet fulfilled, nor the
dream accomplished.

This phrensy would have been speedily cured in our country; bread and water, a solitary cell, and a little wholesome discipline are specifics in such cases. Mark the difference in England. No bishop interferes; she therefore boldly asserts that she has the full consent of the bishops to declare that her call is from God, because, having been called upon to disprove it, they keep silent.

Robert Southey, *Letters from England*, ed. J. Simmons (1984)

=

Rebels against the system

Almazov gave her a withering glance.

'This is the position. I don't regard you as a doctor. You call this a hospital, I call it a prison to which, in a typically fascist way, I have been sent without trial. So now, let's get everything straight. I am your prisoner, you are my jailer, and there isn't going to be any nonsense about my health or my relations, or about examination or treatment. Is that understood?'

'We'll have to use compulsory methods.'

'You can try.'

'All right. We'll see.'

The other inmates of Ward 7 could hardly have differed more from Almazov in background or temperament, and they had come to their present pass by a variety of ways. But the cross-roads at which their common lot had brought them together was now their home and they made fast friends.

'What we all have in common,' said Paul Zagogulin, 'is that in one way or another we are all here thanks to the Soviet régime. Ultimately it's that that's crippled our lives.' Almazov agreed with him.

Valeriy Tarsis, *Ward 7: An Autobiographical Novel* (1965)

9

Going In

The writings of the severely mentally disturbed leave one thing very clear: the business of being forcibly detached from their regular surroundings and removed into the asylum has proved terribly traumatic. Many patients clearly believe it responsible for a shocking setback in their condition, involving disorientation, demoralization and depression. Only rarely do autobiographical records, such as William Cowper's, reveal any relief on being institutionalized: usually the patient fights this outcome. George Trosse records how he experienced the journey to the madhouse as a descent into Hell.

Patients typically allege they were badly treated upon arrival at the hospital. Perhaps such negative memories may not be surprising, given the confused mental state that must have precipitated their confinement, and here, as throughout this volume, we are under no obligation to take the memories of the mad at face value. Nevertheless, the complaints form a chorus which acquires authority by being so evidently a widespread experience. Reviewing their first few days inside, patients record being left alone for hours at a stretch, and desolating incommunicativeness and off-handedness from the staff – trials which in due course patients had to learn to cope with. The experience of institutionalization was uniformly found forbidding and humiliating.

As John Perceval's memoirs make clear, many patients had no grasp that their new abode was a lunatic asylum. Perceval records the mental agonies produced by the confusion between the world of his delusions and the *dramatis personae* of the asylum itself. The hallucinations persecuting the sick person often 'came true' in the asylum, full of strange, disorderly people, terrifying authority figures, and, not least – as George Trosse was to find – manacles and chains which brought to mind the torture engines so prominent in the imaginations of the demented.

Institutions for the insane began to develop in many parts of Europe in the late Middle Ages. They became sizeable, numerous, and instruments of public policy only from the mid-seventeenth century in a movement called by the French philosopher-historian, Michel Foucault (see page 11), 'the great confinement'. In England, most lunatic asylums were private business speculations until the nineteenth century, when a system of public county asylums was established to meet the needs of the poor. The orthodox psychiatric dictum that the asylum was the right place for the disturbed caused numbers to swell. By the mid-twentieth century, there were some 150,000 patients in asylums in Britain, and around half a million in the USA. Since then, the development of new drugs and 'community care' policies have led to a dramatic fall in the asylum population.

=======

From the Ancient Greeks until the rise of lunatic asylums within the last three centuries, the custody and care of the insane was typically treated as the responsibility of their family, or, failing that, of their village or parish. Lunatics were generally locked up at home or, if harmless, allowed to wander.

If a man is mad he shall not be at large in the city, but his family shall keep him at home in any way which they can; or if not, let them pay a penalty. . . . Now there are many sorts of madness, some arising out of disease, which we have already mentioned; and there are other kinds, which originate in an evil and passionate temperament, and are increased by bad education; out of a slight quarrel this class of madmen will often raise a storm of abuse against one another, and nothing of that sort ought to be allowed to occur in a well-ordered state.

Plato, *Laws*, Book XI (5th century BC)

=

The legal authority to confine has been fiercely contested. In the State
of Illinois in the mid-nineteenth century, a wife could be sent to an
asylum on the say-so of her husband. Mrs Elizabeth Packard publicly
dissented from the religious opinions of her clergyman husband –
and, by consequence, was perfectly legally institutionalized on his
authority.

And now the fatal hour had come that I must be transported into my
living tomb. But the better to shield himself in this nefarious work,
Mr Packard tried to avail himself of the law for commitment in other
cases, which is to secure the certificate of two physicians that the
candidate for the Asylum is insane. Therefore at this late hour I
passed an examination made by our two doctors, both members of
his church and our bible class, and opponents to me in argument,
wherein they decided that I was insane, by simply feeling my pulse!

This scene is so minutely described in the 'Introduction to my
Three Years Imprisonment', that I shall not detail it here. The
doctors were not in my room over three minutes, conducting this
examination, and without asking me a single question, both said
while feeling my pulse, 'she is insane!'

My husband then informed me that the 'forms of law' were now
all complied with, and he now wished me to dress for a ride to
Jacksonville Insane Asylum. I complied, but at the same time entered
my protest against being imprisoned without a trial, or some chance
at self-defence. I made no physical resistance, however, when he
ordered two of his church-members to take me up in their arms, and
carry me to the wagon and thence to the cars, in spite of my lady-like
protests, and regardless of all my entreaties for some sort of trial
before commitment.

My husband replied, 'I am doing as the laws of Illinois allow me to
do – you have no protector in law but myself, and I am protecting
you now! It is for your good I am doing this, I want to save your soul
– you don't believe in total depravity, and I want to make you right.'

'Husband, have I not a right to my opinions?'

'Yes, you have a right to your opinions, if you think right.'

'But does not the constitution defend the right of religious toler-
ation to all American citizens?'

'Yes, to all citizens it does defend this right, but you are not a citizen; while a married woman you are a legal nonentity, without even a soul in law. In short, you are dead as to any legal existence while a married woman, and therefore have no legal protection as a married woman.' Thus I learned my first lesson in that chapter of common law, which denies to married woman a legal right to her own identity or individuality.

The scenes transpiring at the parsonage, were circulated like wild-fire throughout the village of Manteno, and crowds of men and boys were rapidly congregating at the depot, about one hundred rods distant from our house, not only to witness the scene, but fully determined to stand by their pledge to my son, I.W., that his mother should never leave Manteno depot for an Insane Asylum.

The long two-horse lumber wagon in which I was conveyed from my house to the depot, was filled with strong men as my body guard, including Mr Packard, his deacons, and Sheriff Burgess, of Kankakee city among their numbers. When our team arrived at the depot, Mr Packard said to me, 'Now, wife, you will get out of the wagon yourself, won't you? You won't compel us to lift you out before such a large crowd, will you?'

'No, Mr Packard, I shall not help myself into an Asylum. It is *you* who are putting me there. I do not go willingly, nor with my own consent – I am being forced into it against my protests to the contrary. Therefore, I shall let you show yourself to this crowd, just as you are – my persecutor, instead of my protector. I shall make no resistance to your brute force claims upon my personal liberty – I shall simply remain a passive victim, helpless in your power.' He then ordered his men to transport me from the wagon to the depot in their arms.

Elizabeth Parsons Ware Packard, *The Prisoner's Hidden Life:
Or Insane Asylums Unveiled* (1868)

==

Alexander Cruden protests that he was kidnapped and sent to the madhouse. Author of the standard Concordance to the Bible, Cruden was an Aberdonian religious fanatic who apparently became unhinged after his hopeless love for his landlady met a frosty response.

This day *Oliver Roberts* a Chairman came, as he said, from one
Robert Wightman in *Spring-Gardens*, and told Mr C. that the said
Wightman wanted to speak with him at his lodgings in *Spring-
Gardens*; and *Roberts* taking with him *Anderson* the Coachman,
decoy'd Mr C. into a Hackneycoach; and till the Coach came to
Ludgate-hill Mr C. did not fully discover their wicked Design, for
the Coachwindows were drawn up: Mr C. had asked *Roberts* in
Chancery-Lane which way the Coach was to go to *Spring-
Gardens*? *Roberts* answered Up the *Strand*. And when Mr C. saw
himself thus imposed upon, he expostulated with them in the
following manner: 'Oh! what are you going to do with me? I bless
God, I am not mad. Are you going to carry me to *Bethlehem*? How
great is this Affliction! This is the way to put an end to all my
Usefulness in the World, and to expose me to the highest Degree!
Oh! what shall I do? God help me! I desire to submit to the Will of
God.'

Alexander Cruden, *The London Citizen Exceedingly Injured* (1739)

═

*Raving mad, George Trosse (see page 174) was forcibly taken by
his friends to a private lunatic asylum in Glastonbury. He experienced it as a journey into Hell.*

Being in this miserable distracted Condition, and refusing to make
use of any suitable and proper Means, in order to my Recovery, my
Friends had Intelligence of a Person dwelling in *Glastonbury*, who
was esteem'd very skilful and successful in such Cases. They sent
for him. He came; and engag'd to undertake the Cure, upon Condition that they would safely convey me to his House, where I might
always be under his View and Inspection, and duely follow his
Prescriptions. Hereupon, my Friends determin'd to remove me to
his House; but I was resolv'd *not to move out of my Bed*; for I was
perswaded that if I removed out of it, I should fall into *Hell*, and be
plung'd into the *Depth of Misery*. I likewise apprehended *those
about me*, who would have pluck'd me out of my Bed, to have been
so many Devils, who would have dislodg'd me: Therefore I *stoutly
resisted* them, with *all* my *Might* and *utmost Efforts*, and struggled
with all Violence, that they might not pluck me out of my Bed and

cloath me. When *one* of the Persons about me came behind me to hold me up in my Bed, I was under terrible Apprehensions *it was the Devil that seiz'd me.* And the same Thought I had of *all about me*, that they were *murtherous Devils*; and that they exerted *all their Power* to carry me away into a *Place of Torment*. By their concurrent Strength they at length prevail'd against me, took me out of my Bed, cloath'd me, bore me out between them. They procur'd a *very stout strong Man* to ride before me; and when *he* was on Horseback, they by Force put me up behind *him*, bound me by a strong Linnen-Cloth to *him*; and, because I struggled, and did all I could to throw my self off the Horse, they tied my Legs under the Belly of it. All this while I was full of *Horrours* and of *Hell within*: I neither open'd mine Eyes nor my Mouth, either to see what was done about me or to make any Lamentations: for still I look'd upon this as my *necessary Duty* . . .

Upon the Way, the *Men* stay'd a little to refresh themselves (for I was very troublesome to them by my continual Struggling) and they offer'd me some *Meat*; and altho' I had not *eaten* nor *drunk* for a *long time*, yet then I was perswaded to it. And when they put a Glass into my Hand to *drink* of it, methought I saw in the Glass a *Black Thing*, about the Bigness of a great *black Fly*, or *Beetle*; and *this* I suppos'd to have been the *Devil*; but yet would *drink* it; and, methought, the *Devil* went down my Throat with the *Liquour*, and so *took possession* of me. At which *desperate Madness* of mine, it seem'd to me that all were astonish'd; and I fancy'd, that every Step I stepp'd afterwards, I was making a Progress into the *Depths of Hell*. When I heard the *Bell ring*, I thought it to have been *my Doom* out of *Heaven*; and the Sound of every *Double Stroke* seem'd to me to be, *Lower down; lower down; lower down;* (*viz.*) into the *Bottomless Pit*. This to me *then* was a dismal dejecting Sound. Whatever Noises I heard as I past by, my Fancy gave them *Hellish Interpretations*: For I was now perswaded that I was no longer *upon Earth*, but in the *Regions of Hell*. When we came to the Town, I thought I was in the *midst* of *Hell*: Every House that we pass'd by was as it were a *Mansion* in *Hell*; and it seem'd to me that all of them had their several Degrees of *Torment*; & as we went forward, methought, their *Torments encreas'd*; and I fancy'd I heard some say, as they stood at their Doors with great Wonder,

and somewhat of Pity, *What, must he go yet farther into Hell? O fearful! O dreadful!* and the like.

At last, by God's good Providence, we were brought safely to the *Physician's* House. Methought all about me were *Devils*, and *he* was *Beelzebub*. I was taken off my Horse, and expected immediately to be cast into *intolerable Flames* and *Burnings*, which seem'd to be before mine Eyes.

George Trosse, *The Life of the Reverend Mr George Trosse* (1714)

=

In guilty despair, and having failed in suicide attempts, William Cowper lost his mind, and was pleased to be taken into the secure bosom of the lunatic asylum by his clergyman brother.

Satan plied me closely with horrible visions, and more horrible voices. My ears rang with the sound of torments, that seemed to await me. Then did the pains of hell get hold on me, and, before day break, the very sorrows of death encompassed me. A numbness seized the extremities of my body, and life seemed to retreat before it. My hands and feet became cold and stiff; a cold sweat stood upon my forehead; my heart seemed at every pulse to beat its last, and my soul to cling to my lips, as if on the very brink of departure. No convicted criminal ever feared death more, or was more assured of dying.

At eleven o'clock, my brother called upon me, and in about an hour after his arrival, that distemper of mind, which I had so ardently wished for, actually seized me. While I traversed the apartment, in the most horrible dismay of soul, expecting every moment that the earth would open and swallow me up; my conscience scaring me, the avenger of blood pursuing me, and the city of refuge out of reach and out of sight; a strange and horrible darkness fell upon me. If it were possible, that a heavy blow could light on the brain, without touching the skull, such was the sensation I felt. I clapped my hand to my forehead, and cried aloud through the pain it gave me. At every stroke, my thoughts and expressions became more wild and incoherent; all that remained clear was the sense of sin, and the expectation of punishment. These kept undisturbed possession all through my illness, without interruption or abatement.

My brother instantly observed the change, and consulted with my friends on the best manner to dispose of me. It was agreed among them, that I should be carried to St Alban's, where Dr Cotton kept a house for the reception of such patients, and with whom I was known to have a slight acquaintance. Not only his skill, as a physician, recommended him to their choice, but his well-known humanity, and sweetness of temper. It will be proper to draw a veil over the secrets of my prison house; let it suffice to say, that the low state of body and mind, to which I was reduced, was perfectly well calculated to humble the natural vain-glory and pride of my heart.

These are the efficacious means which infinite Wisdom thought meet to make use of for that purpose. A sense of self-loathing and abhorrence ran through all my insanity. Conviction of sin, and expectation of instant judgment, never left me from the 7th of December, 1763, until the middle of July following. The accuser of the brethren was ever busy with me night and day, bringing to my recollection in dreams the commission of long forgotten sins, and charging upon my conscience things of an indifferent nature, as atrocious crimes.

William Cowper, *Memoir of the Early Life of William Cowper, Esq.*
(1816)

=

The Victorian novel Hard Cash *(significantly subtitled, see page 207) paints a vivid picture of an unscrupulous parent's attempt to certify his son as insane, and of the contemporary psychiatric and legal treatment of insanity.*

The tenacity of a private lunatic asylum is unique. A little push behind your back and you slide into one; but to get out again is to scale a precipice with crumbling sides. Alfred, luckier than many, had twice nearly escaped: yet now he was tighter in than ever. His father at first meant to give him but a year or two of it, and let him out on terms, his spirit broken, and Julia married. But his sister's death was fatal to him. By Mrs Hardie's settlement the portion of any child of hers dying a minor, or intestate and childless, was to go to the other children; so now the prisoner had inherited his sister's

ten thousand pounds, and a good slice of his bereaved enemy's and
father's income. But this doubled his father's bitterness, – that he,
the unloved one, should be enriched by the death of the adored one!
– and also tempted his cupidity: and unfortunately shallow legislation conspired with that temptation. For, when an Englishman,
sane or insane, is once pushed behind his back into a madhouse,
those relatives who have hidden him from the public eye, i.e. from
the eye of justice, can grab hold of his money behind his back, as
they certified away his wits behind his back, and can administer it
in the dark, and embezzle it, chanting 'But for us the "dear deranged" would waste it.' Nor do the monstrous enactments, which
confer this unconstitutional power on subjects, and shield its exercise from the light and safeguard of Publicity, affix any penalty to
the abuse of that power, if by one chance in a thousand detected. In
Lunacy Law extremes of intellect meet; the British senator plays at
Satan; and tempts human frailty and cupidity beyond what they are
able to bear.

So behold a son at twenty-one years of age devoted by a father to
imprisonment for life. But stop a minute; the mad statutes, which
by the threefold temptation of Facility, Obscurity, and Impunity,
ensure the occasional incarceration and frequent detention of sane
but moneyed men, do provide, though feebly, for their bare libera-
tion, provided they don't yield to the genius loci, and the natural
effect of confinement plus anguish, by going mad, or dying. The
Commissioners of Lunacy had power to liberate Alfred in spite of
his relations. And that power, you know, he had soberly but
earnestly implored them to exercise.

After a delay that seemed as strange to him as postponing a hand
to a drowning man, he received an official letter from Whitehall.
With bounding heart he broke the seal, and devoured the contents.
They ran thus:

'SIR, – By order of the Commissioners of Lunacy I am directed to
inform you that they are in the receipt of your letter of the 29th
ultimo, which will be laid before the Board at their next meeting.
                                                    'I am, &c.'

Alfred was bitterly disappointed at the small advance he had made.
However, it was a great point to learn that his letters were allowed

to go to the Commissioners at all, and would be attended to by degrees.

Charles Reade, Hard Cash: A Matter-of-fact Romance (1864)

=

More than with any other theme, the autobiographies of the mad are preoccupied with the evils of being confined to the madhouse against their wishes, vainly seeking an answer to the constantly recurring question: Why must I go in?

The two doctors insisted that I must go into a mental hospital. I pleaded with them. I argued that I was in no way a subject for a mental hospital – I would go anywhere else for recuperative treatment and a rest. 'Why not ask my husband to send me away to the seaside for a while?'

No, I must go, they said.

'Well,' I continued, 'give me one reason why you think I ought to go.'

'You are suffering from delusions,' they told me.

But when I asked them to be specific they would not. Our doctor then proceeded to console me by saying that I could return home within three days. This statement the other doctor corrected, saying, 'She may give three days' notice and return at any time.' With that I had to be content.

I do not remember my actual admission. My husband tells me that I walked into the ambulance. I have no recollection of reaching my destination, nor of going through the formalities of reception.

From then on it was a case of drugs, and still more drugs, drugs to break down one's resistance, drugs to loosen one's tongue, drugs to make one remember and then to make one forget. That, during that time, I became mentally unbalanced, I cannot deny. I believe that my unbalance was induced by drugs. Finally I became unconscious. For how long I do not know. My husband tells me that I did not know him for ten weeks.

When I came to, I had lost my identity, although strangely enough, I remembered right away my child and asked where she was, and was reassured. More weeks went by and I regained my strength, but I still could not remember who I was, nor how I came to be there, locked up in this vast strange building; sometimes sleeping in a long dormitory, sometimes in a small side room off a long corridor, at others in a padded cell on the floor. Always the doors were locked. One could tell when nurses passed by the jingle of keys at their waists. Never had I felt so frightened, lost, lonely or desolate.

D. McI. Johnson and Norman Dodds (eds), *The Plea for the Silent*
(1957)

=

John Home, a patient in Morningside Asylum, Edinburgh (see page 225), complains against the circumstances of his confinement to the asylum.

Noctes insomni et dies miserabilissimae, the experiences of an Edinburgh Writer to the Signet, who, owing to the malignity of an unnatural Sister, whose disposition like her Womb is as hard as flint, and the injudiciousness of a weak minded incapable medical man, devoid of practice, was confined for one night in the Police Cells, and afterwards forcibly and illegally detained for upwards of four weeks in Morningside Asylum.

On the afternoon of Thursday 25th November, while sitting in a room in the University Club smoking a cigarette and sipping a cup of cocoa, I am a total abstainer, two members of the Civic force, belted & spurred, B134 and 136B suddenly appeared on the lapis [?] and said they had been sent to apprehend me. I asked at whose instance I was charged and to be shown the Warrant for my apprehension but no attention was paid to either of these requests. I was then seized by the arms & forced into a Cab in waiting at the back door – On the way to the Cab managed to inflict one or two well directed kicks on the shins of the horney handed civics, who I apprehend must have been got by an alligator out of a rhianocheros [sic], and indulged in language scarcely parliamentary. The Cab was then driven to the Police Office. Shortly after my arrival I was taken before the Lieutenant on duty, I again asked to be informed at whose instance I was charged and to be shown the warrant for my apprehension, but these requests were not complied with. Two miserable looking specimens of the genus homo then appeared and whispered a few sentences in the ear of the Lieutenant which he entered in a book. I asked that the evidence against me should be read over and that I be allowed to cross examine the Witnesses but these requests were in like manner not complied with. I was then seized roughly by the arms by the horney handed ones and jostled down a flight of stairs and shoved into a cell the door of which was banged in my face and locked. The Cell contained no furniture not even a blanket or a rug. Feeling it rather close and stuffy I succeeded in breaking a pane of glass in the Window and a warder thereupon entered and opened the Window. About midnight a female warder appeared and asked if I should like anything. I asked for a cup of Cocoa & some tobacco. She brought the former but expressed regret that she was unable to supply me with the latter. A male warder however shortly afterwards appeared and offered one his pipe. As however I never smoke another man's pipe or allow another man to smoke mine I declined the kind offer. Four hours afterwards the female warder again appeared and brought one another cup of Cocoa and a little cake. So the dreary night went on until at last I began to discern streaks on the Eastern horizon & shortly thereafter the Sun bright harbinger of the coming day. Shortly afterwards I asked when the beak would arrive and was informed that he was expected about 1 o'clock. After a while I heard footsteps outside my door and through a small hole in the door of my Cell about the size of a shilling I discerned the magnificent figure of that utter little Cad Littlejohn the Police Surgeon and another medico with whom I was unacquainted. I immediately saluted the little Cad in most unparliamentary language and choosing my opportunity spat in his face. The two medicos continued to inspect me for about half an hour through the aforesaid small hole but I solemnly affirm on soul and conscience that they neither of them opened the door entered my Cell or engaged in conversation with me although I have never seen or spoken to either of them before. They then left and I presume wrote and signed a Certificate to the effect that I was a lunatic. I again demanded to be taken before the beak but no attention was paid to my request. Some hours afterwards the door of my Cell was opened and there appeared on the scene two of the most repulsive looking men it has been my misfortune to meet. One of them Gregory evidently got by

Satan out of a rotten whore. They told me they were attendants or
keepers at Morningside Asylum and had come by the orders of the
Sheriff to remove one to that palatial residence in the suburbs of
Edinburgh. They seized me by the arms and dragged me into a Cab
waiting at the door and drove off to the Asylum. I indulged in most
unparliamentary language and spat in the face of Gregory. He
thereupon assaulted me most unmercifully to the effusion of blood
in the presence of Alexander Crockatt the other keeper and for this
I shall have him apprehended and charged with assault on
obtaining my freedom. On arriving at the Asylum I was almost
immediately visited by the wooden headed most incompetent Cad
in the establishment who proceeded to examine me. After this was
over I demanded that the Commissioners in Lunacy, most incompetent men, who because they could obtain no private practice got
themselves appointed Commissioners, should be immediately sent
for, and this the wooden headed promised to do but of course did
not. As I afterwards came to know he was the most damnable liar
that ever walked, and the same may be said of the Drs and of the
attendants or keepers. In fact I came to be convinced that the Father
of Lies must have been reared and brought up in a Madhouse.

John Home Letters, Medical Archive Centre MSS
(Edinburgh University Library)

=

*Daniel Schreber protests against his treatment. Schreber was a German
judge who suffered nervous collapse. His* Memoirs *form one of the
most remarkable accounts of madness from the patient's viewpoint.*

About the fourth or fifth night after my admission to the Asylum, I
was pulled out of bed by two attendants in the middle of the night
and taken to a cell fitted out for dements (maniacs) to sleep in. I was
already in a highly excited state, in a fever delirium so to speak, and
was naturally terrified in the extreme by this event, the reasons for
which I did not know. The way led through the billiard room;
there, because I had no idea what one intended to do with me and
therefore thought I had to resist, a fight started between myself clad
only in a shirt, and the two attendants, during which I tried to hold
fast to the billiard table, but was eventually overpowered and

removed to the above-mentioned cell. There I was left to my fate; I spent the rest of the night mostly sleepless in this cell, furnished only with an iron bedstead and some bedding. Regarding myself as totally lost, I made a naturally unsuccessful attempt during the night to hang myself from the bedstead with the sheet. I was completely ruled by the idea that there was nothing left for a human being for whom sleep could no longer be procured by all the means of medical art, but to take his life. I knew that this was not permitted in asylums, but I laboured under the delusion that when all attempts at cure had been exhausted, one would be discharged – solely for the purpose of making an end to one's life either in one's own home or somewhere else.

Daniel Paul Schreber, *Memoirs of My Nervous Illness* (1903)

=

On admission

I was taken down the hall by my attendants, and found a bath awaiting me. After much unnecessary scrubbing, all done by my attendants, I was at last taken back to my room. The door was closed and once more I got wearily into bed, but I had hardly got settled when the door was opened and I was handed my bathrobe and asked to follow. I thought, 'Will this ever stop and will I ever get to sleep?' It appeared that I was to move already to another room.

So here I was in exactly the same kind of quarters, with exactly the same furniture and bars. Again I crawled wearily into bed. As I closed my eyes with a sigh there came a knock on the door.

In walked not a nurse or doctor but a young girl, dressed in regular street clothes. She came over and sat down on the edge of my bed.

'So you are the King; well, I am the Princess. I knew your sister, I knew your brother, I knew your mother and I used to work on a charity board with them. I never knew though that they ever had a child in the family by your name, and I never knew that their child was a Nut.'

'A NUT!' I exclaimed.

'Yes,' she replied. 'Where do you think you are?'

'I am in a general hospital, but I do not know the name of the place yet.'

'Like Hell you are! You are in the Bug House!'

A sudden clutching darkness closed in on me. My breath came short and quick and I opened dry lips. But words would not come.

Marian King, *The Recovery of Myself: A Patient's Experience in a Hospital for Mental Illness* (1931)

On the Inside

If committal to the asylum was disturbing, living inside evidently proved a very mixed experience. Patients made what they could of asylum life. Some, like John Perceval or later Clifford Beers, evidently loathed every minute, decided that the only honourable recourse for them was a declaration of total war, and rationalized (at least after the event) their animosities by claiming that the fight against the evil madhouse system developed the strength of will and qualities of character requisite for overcoming madness itself. Judge Schreber found his years in the asylum unremitting torture.

Others achieved true asylum. Following unsuccessful suicide attempts, William Cowper was placed in the elite St Alban's asylum run by a certain Dr Nathaniel Cotton, and had nothing but praise for the humanity of the treatment which speeded his recovery. Some had mixed experiences. Kit Smart wrote his finest poetry while in a private asylum in London; so did John Clare while a patient at High Beech in Epping Forest, though he hated being confined, and made escape attempts. James Tilly Matthews battled against the Bethlem authorities, yet was allowed to acquire such skill at technical drawing as to be able to produce creditable architectural designs for a new hospital building.

In the asylum, as in everyday life on the outside, processes of accommodation were evidently at work. Inmates made friends with certain, but not all, fellow inmates – and patched up alliances with, or against, various members of the staff. Patients operated their own informal 'psychiatry' – their perceptions as to which of their fellows were truly crazy, and which of the attendants were psychopaths and sadists.

Overall, the annals of the asylum convey a sense of degradation

and demoralization: drabness, squalor, penny-pinching, the perception that the whole order of the institution smacks more of punitive
than curative intentions. Over the last generation, powerful liber-
tarian voices have been raised against the psychiatric institution,
and a philosophy decrying compulsory institutionalization has
gained ground. Arguably, in the eyes not of reformers but of
patients, the real crime committed against them has not been the
enforcement of confinement and treatment, but the poor or almost
non-existent nature of the treatment and care thus forced upon
them.

*Bethlem Hospital emerged from the thirteenth-century priory of St
Mary of Bethlehem, founded on the eastern outskirts of London.
By the fifteenth century it was specializing in accepting the insane.
It acquired, perhaps unfairly, the reputation of 'Bedlam', a mis-
managed dump for uncontrollable lunatics. The poet here trades
upon the image of the bestialization of the inmates to point a moral
for his readers.*

> Where proud Augusta, blest with long Repose,
> Her ancient Wall and ruin'd Bulwark shows;
> Close by a verdant Plain, with graceful Height
> A stately Fabric rises to the Sight.
> Yet, though its Parts all elegantly shine,
> And sweet Proportion crowns the whole Design;
> Though Art, in strong expressive Sculpture shown,
> Consummate Art informs the breathing Stone;
> Far other Views than these within appear,
> And Woe and Horror dwell for ever here.
> For ever from the echoing Roofs rebounds
> A dreadful Din of heterogeneous Sounds;
> From this, from that, from ev'ry Quarter rise
> Loud Shouts, and sullen Groans, and doleful Cries;
> Heart-soft'ning Plaints demand the pitying Tear,
> And Peals of hideous Laughter shock the Ear.
>   Thus, when in some fair Human Form we find

The Lusts all rampant, and the Reason blind,
Griev'd we behold such Beauty given in vain,
And Nature's fairest Work survey with Pain.
   Within the Chambers which this Dome contains,
In all her frantic Forms Distraction reigns.
For when the Sense from various Objects brings,
Through Organs craz'd, the Images of Things,
Ideas, all extravagant and vain,
In endless Swarms croud in upon the Brain:
The cheated Reason True and False confounds,
And forms her Notions from fantastic Grounds.
Then, if the Blood impetuous swells the Veins,
And Choler in the Constitution reigns,
Outrageous Fury straight inflames the Soul,
Quick beats the Pulse, and fierce the Eyeballs roll;
Rattling his Chains the Wretch all raving lies,
And roars, and foams; and Earth and Heav'n defies.
Not so, when gloomy the black Bile prevails,
And lumpish Phlegm the thick'ned Mass congeals,
All lifeless then is the poor Patient found,
And sits for ever moping on the Ground;
His active Pow'rs their Uses all forgo,
Nor Senses, Tongue, nor limbs, their Functions know.
In Melancholy lost, the vital Flame
Informs, and just informs the listless Frame,
If brisk the circulating Tides advance,
And Nimble Spirits through the Fibres dance,
Then all the Images delightful rise,
The tickled Fancy sparkles through the Eyes;
The Mortal, all to Mirth and Joy resign'd,
In ev'ry Gesture shews his freakish Mind;
Frolic and free, he laughs at Fortune's Pow'r,
And plays ten thousand Gambols in an hour.
   The Muse forbears to visit ev'ry Cell,
Each Form, each Object of Distress to tell;
To shew the Fopling curious in his Dress,
Gayly trick'd out in gaudy Raggedness:
The Poet, ever wrapt in glorious Dreams

Of Pagan Gods, and Heliconian Streams:
The wild Enthusiast, that despairing sees
Predestin'd Wrath, and Heav'n's severe Decrees;
Thro' these, thro' more sad Scenes she grieves to go,
And paint the whole Variety of Woe.
   Mean time, on These reflect with kind Concern,
And hence this just, this useful Lesson learn:
If strong Desires thy reasoning Pow'rs control;
If arbitrary Passions sway thy Soul,
If Pride, if Envy, if the Lust of Gain,
If wild ambition in thy Bosom reign,
Alas! thou vaunt'st thy sober Sense in vain.
In these poor Bedlamites thy Self survey,
Thy Self, less innocently mad than They.

Thomas Fitzgerald, 'Bedlam' (1733)

=

In his raving state, George Trosse interprets the asylum as Hell.

I lay upon my Bed, every Instant expecting to be *rack'd* or *cut in Pieces*, and to have all Manner of *Cruelties* to be us'd towards my Body. Every *Person* I saw seem'd to me to be an *Executioner*; and I thought *every Thing* either an *Instrument* of, or a *Preparation* for, my Misery and Torture. I apprehended *Self-Murther* to be the only wise and charitable Act that I could do for my self, as the only Prevention of all expected and dreaded Torment. In Expectation of a *necessary* and *inevitable Injection* into the *Lake* of *Fire* and *Brimstone*, I presum'd that the *longer* I was *out* of it, the *deeper* I should at last *sink into* it, and the more *intolerable* would be my *Torment* there; because, I did nothing but Sin continually, and so every Minute of mine Abode on *Earth*, would be a great Increase of the Intenseness of my Misery in *Hell*. Hereupon, I was also fully convinc'd, that there was nothing so *good* and *beneficial* to me as *immediately* to *cast my self into the Burning Lake*, since there was an utter Impossibility of escaping it; and I conceiv'd, that the *sooner* I was in it, the *easier* I should be, and so prevent *greater* Degrees of my *everlasting Burnings* there. Thus the *Murderer* had got the *Assent of Carnal Self*, the grand Ruling Principle which had influenc'd me all my Days, and was the Chief Cause of all my *Wickedness* and *Rebellion* against God, prompting me to *Self-Destruction*, and *Self-Damnation*: But my God and Saviour would not permit it to have such a fatal Influence upon me.

George Trosse (see page 217), *The Life of the Reverend Mr George Trosse* (1714)

==

The value of the asylum, according to its advocates, was that it could catch cases of insanity early, isolate them from further exacerbating pressures, and permit the rigorous pursuit of a cure. William Perfect, who ran an asylum at West Malling in Kent, was one of the more energetic asylum proprietors of the late eighteenth century. Perfect here uses many of the 'cures' popular in the time: warm bathing, paregoric (opium) and camphor as sedatives, and darkened rooms to reduce nervous over-excitation. He obviously rejected 'issues' and 'setons', forms of skin irritants designed to bring supposedly internal sources of illness to the surface.

CASE I

A Gentleman, aged fifty-eight, was, in the beginning of January, 1770, put under my care for insanity. The cause of his disorder was attributed to a sudden transition in his circumstances, which, from being easy and comfortable, were become doubtful and precarious; his complaints were great pain in the head, almost a continual noise in his ears, and, at intervals, a melancholy depression, or a frantic exaltation of spirits; he was inclined to be costive, his water was very high-coloured, he passed whole nights without sleep, sometimes raved and was convulsed, and his attention was invariably fixed to one object namely, that he was *ruined, lost,* and *undone!* which was his incessant exclamation both by night and day. Strong purges, antimonial vomits, ammoniac draughts, sagapenum, steel, and both kinds of hellebore had alternately been exhibited; issues, venæsection, a seton, and vesicatories had been tried for a series of time; bathing, and, in short, almost every thing, seemed to have been done without the least visible alteration for the better ... When I undertook the care of this person, he appeared very impatient of contradiction; and, even discoursing with him in the most easy and gentle manner, would often ruffle him into a misconstruction of all that was said: I therefore forbade all sorts of intercourse with his relations and acquaintance, till such time, as, in my opinion, it might be admitted without any manifest injury to the patient . . . my curative plan . . . begun by making a seton between his shoulders, and confining the patient to a still, quiet, and almost totally darkened room: I never suffered him to be spoken with, either by interrogation or reply, nor permitted any one to visit him but such whose immediate business it was to supply him with his aliment, which was light, cooling and easy of digestion; at the same time his constant drink was weak and diluting . . . For twelve nights successively he used the warm pediluvium, by which having rested something better than he had long before done, I was induced to go a step farther, and, after two purges, to try the effects of opium, which I began in the evening of the thirteenth day after he came to me, in the quantity of fifteen drops of the *elixir paregoricum* in two ounces of a weak *camphorated julep*, which caused him to sleep an hour at a time; and, through the whole of the day following he appeared much easier and less anxious than usual; the elixir was now repeatedly increased, till his nights became thoroughly still and composed, and his days rendered so free from perturbation of spirits and hurry and confusion of thoughts, that he talked rationally and just, seldom breaking out into any frantic rhapsodies, or passionate expressions whatever. In this course I invariably persevered for nearly four months, occasionally administering a sufficient dose of lenitive electuary to prevent too great a constipation of the bowels from the reiterated use of the paregorics; his reason now returned, his imagination grew stronger, his ideas were more collected, and he spoke of things as they really were, and of the primary cause of his mental infirmity, with philosophic coolness, and resigned moderation. The seton was continued, but the opiate and pediluvium were gradually decreased, and entirely left off on the second of June following; when, after having been with me nearly five months, I restored him to his friends in that state of sanity, which he has happily preserved to the present period.

William Perfect, *Select Cases in the Different Species of Insanity* (1787)

=

Before the nineteenth century, most madhouses were privately owned, some good, many bad. Here David Irish, something of a quack doctor, advertises the superior facilities of his Guildford asylum.

This is to inform all Persons whom it may concern, That D. Irish doth and will (if God permit) instruct his Son in the best and speediest way of curing *Melancholy* and *Madness*. And likewise, those *Lunaticks* which are not Curable, he will take them for term of Life, if paid Quarterly; such, and all others, he takes on Reasonable Terms, allowing them good Fires, Meat, and Drink, with good attendance, and all necessaries far beyond what is allow'd at *Bedlam*, or any other place he has yet heard of and cheaper, for he allows the *Melancholly, Mad,* and such whose Consciences are Opprest with the sense of Sin, good Meat every day for Dinner, and also wholesome Diet for Breakfast and Supper, and good Table-Beer enough at any time: They have also good Beds and Decent Chambers, answerable to their Abilities; all which necessaries are daily allow'd and given them according to agreement during the time agreed for; they are all carefully look'd after by himself at his House in Stoke near Guildford in Surry, being a pleasant place and good Air; and such as please to be at Thorp, his Son looks after them by his Fathers directions, who comes every *Tuesday* to see them, and instruct his Son in the true Method of curing such distemper'd People.

David Irish, *Levamen Infirmi; or, Cordial Counsel to the Sick and Diseased* (1700)

=

Until quite recently, a patient's treatment and standing inside the psychiatric hospital has depended much upon whether he is a compulsory or a voluntary patient. From the early part of this century, an increasing proportion of patients were not 'sectioned', that is, sequestrated under legal compulsion, but became patients of their own accord. Believed to be less dangerous and more compliant, they often received more privileges. Jim Curran suffered from alcohol problems. His business had crashed during the Depression. It was of importance to him that he had been 'admitted' not 'committed'.

I sat in Dr Carlsen's office, and he told me that I was crazy. He did not say it that way. He said: 'There is no such thing as a nervous breakdown. No. It is a mental upset: and right now you are in a state of emotional depression.

'But,' he added in a cheerful voice, 'the encouraging angle of that is that depressive patients practically always get well.'

He smiled at me with his kind brown eyes, but I did not smile back because I was not doing any smiling in those days. I had not smiled much for two years, and now I did not smile at all.

And here I was at St Charles – called a 'State hospital' officially, but referred to by most people as 'the asylum,' or, more flippantly, as the 'nut house.' I had come of my own volition.

Now there's a technicality. It meant that I was rated as 'admitted,' not 'committed.' It meant that I did not lose my citizenship. It meant that if I wished to leave I could be held for only three days after I had given written notice. That is, if – *if* the Superintendent decided I was ready to leave. If he did not think so, however, he might make recommendations which might probably result in my being 'committed,' after all.

So, you see, I knew that I might possibly be there for a long, long time – for life maybe. And I felt terrified. Not strange, is it?

Yes, here I was. Shut in. Those doors were forever locked. That locking of the doors from the inside all during the day and night was what got me. That, and the windows with latticed bars. Oh, I knew where I was, all right. I was in the admission ward of a large State hospital for the insane.

Elsa Kraugh, A Mind Restored: The Story of Jim Curran (1937)

=

The ward routine

There were four washbowls and you waited in line to brush your teeth and wash your face. Virginia found soap in her bag and so could ignore the questionable piece that lay beside the bowl. Next to her a woman sat in the wash-bowl to give herself an intimate bath. Virginia rushed through her washing just in case the plumbing should collapse. She supposed they wouldn't blame her but it was as well to be in another part of the room.

'Meditation, ladies,' announced Miss Hart.

This was too much. You would not join them in evening prayers. Virginia had nothing against prayers, but she did not care to be included. She was extremely tired. The others could run along and pray if they wished.

But the ubiquitous, mind-reading Grace spoke up. 'You've got to take medication, Virginia. You have got to take it as long as you are on the list.'

'Medication? I thought she said meditation.'

'Sue,' said Grace, 'you take Virginia to medication. I'm not on the list any more.'

'Sure,' said a woman who was almost fat enough for the prison gown. 'Come on.' She had a Dutch bob, always the favourite of square-faced, dark, fat women. She looked as if she might make trouble if you didn't come on, and although Virginia felt she would almost rather meditate than medicate, she came on.

Mary Jane Ward, The Snake Pit (1947)

=

The quality of asylum life

The patients housed in this block formed, with some few exceptions, as decent and as well-behaved a company as one would meet in any normal circle. Indeed, their standard of behaviour was above the normal average. I go so far as to assert that frequently in later years I would most willingly have exchanged the society of some of my business associates for that of those incarcerated 'lunatics'. Where 'envy, hatred, malice and uncharitableness', when displayed, are seen by watchful eyes – and noted down – self-discipline becomes self-interest. Few of these men, accordingly, betrayed the minor pettinesses and idiosyncrasies that are met with in ordinary walks of life. Among these patients I made many friends. Many more won my respect alike for patience in adversity, cheerfulness and self-control.

This may seem scarcely credible to a public accustomed to regard Broadmoor as peopled solely with notorious murderers. I can only repeat that what I have set down is literally true. There were, of course, a number of patients who had committed homicide, but the range of offences which can lodge a man in Broadmoor, if he should either plead or manifest mental disturbance, is unlimited. In this same block, for instance, lived an aged man whose bitter boast it was that he had been detained for forty-three years, though charged originally with stealing goods worth only 2s. 6d. He had, however, a perverse, unruly disposition which had destroyed his chances of release.

'Warmark', *'Guilty but Insane': A Broadmoor Autobiography* (1931)

=

A world within a world

I did not stay long in the observation ward. While I was in bed Mrs Pilling and Mrs Everett, for old acquaintance' sake, contrived to send me small delicacies along on the dormitory tea trolley, and sometimes came to talk to me and remark, wistfully, 'No one polished the corridor like you Istina.' They told me excitedly that the old days of the 'rubber-up' were past, that Dr Portman was going to modernize the hospital and had begun by installing a wonderful machine, an electric polisher which also scrubbed provided you remember to turn the correct switch, but none of the patients these days had any sense of ward responsibility, nobody seemed to give the machine its proper care and it was always up in the machine shop being mended, so that the rubbers-up had to be used after all; and that just went to show, didn't it? And the daily meals were delivered to the wards now in closed vans instead of being rattled along, slopping about and gathering dust, on the backs of open lorries. And the old men didn't pull the coal carts any more, leaning and straining, two by two, like old horses between the shafts with the neat attendants walking briskly behind the cart and shouting orders: the coal was delivered by lorries with the strong young men riding on the back; and the old men stayed locked in their dayroom and fussed about, not understanding, and getting ready every morning at eight o'clock to be called to pull the carts, and some crying when no one came for them and shouted at them, 'Coal! Spring to it.'

Janet Frame, *Faces in the Water* (1961)

=

It takes all sorts. Jimmy Laing's vivid memoir covers half a century
of institutionalization: initially detained in borstal as a juvenile
delinquent, he was assigned to an asylum for attempting to escape.

Murthly was a good example of the different kinds of mental
patients that you got under one roof. They weren't completely
mental, certainly not in the criminal sense; I would describe them as
more of a nuisance value. Some certainly would sit around and
vegetate but others would become self-deluded and create their
own characters. There weren't many but I've seen a number who
each claimed to be Jesus Christ and we had Popes and Kings. Now I
see no harm in someone in their fifties, sixties or seventies thinking
themselves to be the British Monarch or President of the United
States. Not at their stage of life stuck in an asylum. When these
people thought themselves King or Queen they were happy. We
learned to live with it saying, 'Good morning, Your Highness,' and
there was no harm in that. Maybe that isn't insanity. Maybe it's a
choice in life. Who are we to say it's wrong when someone at a
particular stage in their life, who is in an asylum, says, 'To hell with
it. I'm here and I'm going to enjoy myself. I'm going to create a
position for myself here'? No one questions this properly when
someone says, 'To hell with it, I'm going to be the Provost of Perth.'
How we sit back and, with a shake of the head, say, 'Delusions of
grandeur, madness.' It's maybe a cool, calculated course of action
they have taken to get away from the humdrum life they are
leading. But what was the reaction of the authorities? They would
come along and give them tranquillizers. After that they sat, day
after day. Their lives, their kingdoms, their mansions were no more.
Now that to me is cruel. A psychiatrist will tell a visiting member of
the family, 'Oh yes, John thinks he's a king and we've had to put
him on tranquillizers for his own good.' But did anyone ever try to
talk to John about it and if he was happy then why not let him be?
Tranquillizers are the ruination of man but also, as far as the system
is concerned, the easy way out. At Murthly they used a variety of
tablets and medicines such as Phenobarbitone and, for epileptic
patients, Epineuton. And, of course, there was the old favourite,
bromide. Bromide we used a lot at that time. You could always tell
those who used it – they came out in spots. At night when the night

nurse would come on there would be a large Winchester bottle full of bromide. By morning it had all gone and no one asked any questions. It seems quite amazing looking back, that here we were in the late Forties and early Fifties, and there was still no real progress in the way that mental patients were treated for their illness. It was still just a case of admitting a patient to an institution and as long as he or she was quite well behaved there would be no trouble. The authorities simply wanted to get through the day without any hassle.

Jimmy Laing and Dermot McQuarrie, *Fifty Years in the System* (1989)

=

Rejoicing in confinement. Kit Smart, perhaps the most original poet of the mid-eighteenth century, became religiously insane and was confined for a time in London.

Let Elizur rejoice with the Partridge, who is a prisoner of state and
    is proud of his keepers.
Let Shedeur rejoice with Pyrausta, who dwelleth in a medium of
    fire, which God hath adapted for him.
Let Shelumiel rejoice with Olor, who is of a goodly savour, and the
    very look of him harmonizes the mind.
Let Jael rejoice with the Plover, who whistles for his love, and foils
    the marksmen and their guns.
Let Raguel rejoice with the Cock of Portugal – God send good
    Angels to the allies of England!
Let Hobab rejoice with Necydalus, who is the Greek of a Grub.
Let Zurishaddai with the Polish Cock rejoice – the Lord restore
    peace to Europe.

For I am not without authority in my jeopardy, which I derive
    inevitably from the glory of the name of the Lord.
For I bless God whose name is Jealous – and there is a zeal to
    deliver us from everlasting burnings.
For my existimation is good even amongst the slanderers and my
    memory shall arise for a sweet savour unto the Lord.
For I bless the PRINCE of PEACE and pray that all the guns may be
    nail'd up, save such as are for the rejoicing days.

For I have abstained from the blood of the grape and that even at
   the Lord's table.
For I have glorified God in GREEK and LATIN, the consecrated
   languages spoken by the Lord on earth.
For I meditate the peace of Europe amongst family bickerings and
   domestic jars.
For the HOST is in the WEST – the Lord make us thankful unto
   salvation.
For I preach the very GOSPEL of CHRIST without comment &
   with this weapon shall I slay envy.
For I bless God in the rising generation, which is on my side.

> From Christopher Smart, *Jubilate Agno* (1758/9)

=

Culture in Broadmoor

Among more individual sources of recreation reading undoubtedly
came first. Book-shelves in most of the day-rooms were replenished
at intervals from the central library of eight thousand volumes, and
there was a good supply of reasonably modern works available.
The Librarian, a patient of many years' standing, was a widely-read
and cultured man whose ability may be gauged from the fact that
he not infrequently won prizes in the literary acrostic competitions
of the *Daily Telegraph*.

> 'Warmark', *'Guilty but Insane': A Broadmoor Autobiography* (1931)

=

*Morningside was the showcase asylum of late Victorian Scotland,
under the firm, paternalistic hand of Dr Thomas Clouston. The
very existence of an asylum newspaper shows the energetic
attempts made to turn the asylum into a community. Perhaps they
did not always succeed.*

For the last five years I have conducted as well as I have been able
one of the very worst library systems in the universe. There was
hardly any kind of rules at all, except a use and wont one that I had
to search for from the patients, for the printed set of rules had long
been a dead letter; and every attempt that I made to frame new

rules to meet the difficulties of the case seemed to meet the opposition of my superiors. The librarian had hardly any authority whatever, and yet was expected to maintain order among his library
visitors, many of whom acted as if they were trained to insult and
annoy him as they pleased, and was at the same time held responsible for the tear and wear of books that everybody was allowed to
destroy *ad libitum*. Consequently, by reason of the strict and but
half-authorized discipline that I was compelled to introduce, in
order, on the one hand, to prevent the library from going wholesale
to destruction, and, on the other, to curb incipient library disorders
before they culminated in what I perceived to be their real object,
an assault upon my person, I became an object of thorough dislike
and hatred to almost all the patients of the Asylum. Now any one
who is at all acquainted with the nature of asylum patients is aware,
that their hatred is always associated with a desire of vengeance,
which nothing but the power of fear will prevent them from gratifying; and my design in the rest of this letter is to sketch the special
direction of their vengeance against myself for the unavoidable
strictness of my library discipline. Dr Clouston says that my story is
a tissue of delusions, but to this assertion my answer seems easy
enough. For, by the laws of the mental science in which he has the
reputation of being an authority, this *animus* of the patients must
have taken some direction or other, there being no restraining
element of fear in the case; and if it did not take the direction that I
am about to describe, let him tell the direction that it really took.
Doubtless there may have been sham-insane patients among the
others as their ringleaders, but that is nothing to the point; and, I
repeat, almost every asylum scheme against me had its origin in this
hatred, and placed my life in peril day by day, until the desire of
vengeance gradually subsided into little more than a mere love of
amusement at my expense – their fun being all the greater that they
thought themselves clever enough to cheat the doctors into
believing that I was subject to delusions.

Gentlemen, my story is told. When patient-librarians are selected
because of their skill in bookbinding or the excellence of their
penmanship, which has usually been the case in the R. E. A., the
chances are that they will have little or none of the delicacy of
nervous temperament that usually accompanies mental and moral

culture; but when patient-librarians are really worthy of their office, the chances are that they will need the protection of the single dormitory.

    I am, Gentlemen,
       Yours respectfully,
        X. Y. Z

                            Morningside Mirror (1884)

=

John Home, however (see page 208), continues to protest against his detention in Morningside Asylum.

I was then removed to what is called the Upper Gallery and shortly afterwards at 2 o'clock went down to dinner in the Dining Hall of the Second Gallery. The repast, to one accustomed to the best of cooking, I need not say was simply filthy, the meat tough as leather and insufficiently cooked. Tea subsequently followed then Supper and to bed at 9 o'clock. Called next morning at 7 30 and breakfast 8. A very plain meal. Then began the day's routine. Three treadmill walks round the grounds about a mile round were a daily occurrence, all, old and young, halt and lame, weak or strong were herded round like a herd of Cattle, if any poor old devil were unable or unwilling to walk then he was shoved along, digged in the ribs or kicked on the bottom. No matter what the weather was foul or fair, frost or snow, rain or sleet round we must go. Remember one day in particular, the Wednesday or Thursday after my arrival, it was raining heavily, yet out I had to go twice. The second time I resisted and so was forced round. I arrived soaked with perspiration and wet to the skin and naturally asked to be allowed to change my clothes but was promptly told I must remain as I was until bedtime. The consequence was that I was severely chilled and this was followed by an attack of incipient pleurisy which however fortunately did not become chronic. On another occasion I elected to vary my walk a little when I was immediately seized by the attendant who shouted to a laboring gardener to assault me which he did by twisting my arm nearly round and causing me excruciating agony. I shall of course charge this man with assault when I leave and the Attendant as art and part. I was not long in discovering that my Attendant who was known by the alias of John Argo was an exprisoner who five years ago was convicted of the hateful crime of rape and sentenced to four years' imprisonment to be followed by four years' police supervision. I lost no opportunity of letting this be widely known. Just fancy in a place like this where there are a number of female patients attendants and servants a man of this character being allowed to go amongst them at large. One morning at breakfast I had four hunks of ham placed before me. These I refused to eat and asked for an egg. The Superintendent was most insolent and said I had had an egg. I told him he was a damned liar, he applied the same to me. I then indulged in unparliamentary language and was removed from the Hall to which I refused to return. I was consequently transferred to the Lower Gallery and a more filthy slum I hope I shall never enter. It was 15 by 4 and there were 9 patients, three of whom openly indulged in the hideous vice of masturbation and another of whom was covered with poxy sores, some of which were continually bursting and besmearing the place with poxous matter, one of the most virulent poisons. The cooking was imply abominable, the meat as tough as leather and the knives perfectly blunt. I was forced to go to bed many nights at 8 o'clock never later than 9 o'clock and my bedroom door was trebly locked.

Finding that the Commissioners did not turn up I wrote them on the 1st and again on the 2nd Decr and at last on the 8th. Silebald, one of their number, a very weak brother, who never had any private practice and whose Cousin sells pots and pans turned up. He conversed with me for about half an hour and seemed perfectly satisfied and said he would report the matter. After waiting several days however no report arrived. I accordingly wrote to the Lord Advocate and insisted that he would either take the necessary steps to [?] a jury to me [?] a lunatic or not or appoint two neutral medical mén of eminence Dr Henry Watson and Dr Tuke [Daniel Hack Tuke, see page 100] to examine me but neither of these requests were attended to. I then wrote to the Home Secretary and then my last and boldest move. I wrote to the famous Editor of 'Truth' & implored the help of his powerful pen and parliamentary influence on my behalf which I have every confidence will be vouchsafed me, but I am still a prisoner here on Sunday the 26th day of December 1886. A rather curious episode occurred this afternoon. After the service in the Chapel the parson went his rounds and accosted me remarking he had not noticed me at Chapel. I told him I never wasted my time by going to church as I was an Agnostic. He asked me to conjugate Agnos which I did. He then remarked you are wrong in one of your quantities the supine is agnŏtum and not agnōtum. I fairly collapsed with laughter and advised him to go & consult his dictionary. He was slim [?] innocent sort of a party not strikingly different from the rest of the Order.

The whole system of Madhouse management is simply infamous, the extent to which red tapeism attains is inconceivable. The attendants as a class are a lot of wooden headed ignorant bullies who are strictly tied down by rule from which they cannot deviate one iota, the head attendant has a trifle more power but the Dr is supreme. One sees him for about three minutes when he rushes through the place about 11 o'clock in the forenoon. The rest of the day he devotes to his private practice and yet he receives a salary of £1200 a year and a free house. He is utterly and entirely unsuited and unfitted for his position, hideous in appearance and repulsively disagreeable in manner, evidently a man of humble origin who has made his way in the world.

I maintain that never in the days before Convents were opened up to inspection, in the foulest and vilest Convent that ever existed were scenes enacted for a moment to be compared to the hideous & almost untellable enormities that daily occur and are witnessed within these walls. As I said before the Attendants with a few exceptions are a class of uneducated coarse Cads about the rank of stable helpers who perform their duties in the most infamous manner, bullying tyrannizing over and openly insulting the poor creatures committed to their charge who are in bodily terror of them and completely under their control. Again again and yet again I have seen poor weak feeble helpless creatures knocked about and abused in a most shameful manner.

Whenever I regain my liberty it is my intention to agitate for a public Enquiry and to insist on the appointment of a Royal Commission. One of the first and most abuses to be set right is the entire suppression of male Drs and attendants or keepers and the substitution for them of members of the gentler sex and were this to be done I boldly proclaim that the Cures would be increased 50 per cent. And

I boldly Assert and loudly proclaim that under the present system cases of recovery hardly if ever occur at all events in this den of infamy.

I am hopeful that the Editor of Truth will join me in the Crusade and that I shall also have the help of those grand intelligent hard working members of the gentler sex who shed a lustre on their sex and aid so nobly every good work and may that Great Unknown Power who has yet to be revealed to us guide direct and assist us in all that we do.

John Home Letters, Medical Archive Centre MSS
(Edinburgh University Library)

=

Brief encounters: two young patients meet in the grounds.

But he was not listening.

'I'm here because of tension. Nervous tension,' he was telling me. He laughed. He seemed to laugh a lot. His teeth flashed in and out. His hair bobbed up and down. 'Anxiety neurosis. On the ward they call it "me noives". Too many emotional crises in my life I suppose. I'm having analysis.' He put on a deep, thundering voice like Dr Clements, 'Deep, profound searching, lasting, enduring analysis'.

'I'm sorry to hear it.'

'Thank you, not at all, don't mensh. It's obvious you are not here on account of too many emotional crises.'

'Emotional crises? It's a year since Mother died if that's what you mean.'

'No, I mean *crises d'amour*. Women,' he giggled, 'or rather men.'

'A man once kissed me, but it hurt. I think his teeth were rather too large or too protruding, or something.'

He giggled again. 'You cold pebble! Get thee to a nunnery! The trouble with me is that I lose my head each time, and let women down. I've let women down once too often.' The *dendrex* at last slipped from his shoulder back to its own. 'My performance is so poor.'

'Your performance?' I thought of amateur theatricals, but I did not want to interrupt him.

'My performance. So my GP stuck me in here for "profound, lasting and searching analysis", along with a lot of depressives and schizies.'

'Schizies. What are they?'

He was sitting upright, cross-legged, and pulling up tufts of the grass. 'Oh, you know, schizophrenics, split personalities smitten with *la belle indifférence*. One of them talks about his messages and complains about the jam at breakfast in the same breath. Then there's the famous Miss Beauchamp case. A classic!'

'And the children I've seen playing at your windows, are they schizies?'

'David certainly is, but Jocelyn's epileptic.'

'And do they cure them, the schizies?'

'Not really. They prop them up a bit and make *some* improvement. They give them insulin and that does some good. But I got all this from the male nurse and "Meyer-Gros", so maybe it's not the last word. What treatment did you have by the way? Just pills and heart to hearts, or the high-jump?'

'I had insulin, but I daresay they give it for other things as well as what you said. I expect they do. I feel sure of that.'

'I'm sure they do.' He was sympathetic. 'I'm sure they do. But still it must have been very nasty.'

'I don't think about it. Mother used to say there were some things it was just not right to remember.'

Jennifer Dawson, *The Ha-Ha* (1961)

==

Batman in Broadmoor

With the acquisition of a private room I also became entitled to engage the services of a fellow-patient as a 'batman'. This was a post in some demand among the poorer inmates of Block II, as it provided them with a welcome addition to their scanty resources. It was a Yorkshire miner from the Rotherham district who offered me his services. He proved an acquisition. I found him from the first well-balanced, willing and efficient. For the authorized remuneration of 5s a month – wealth to a penniless and friendless pauper – he daily made my bed and cleaned my room, mended my clothes and generally performed such minor duties as concern a valet.

'Albert', as he was generally known, had a history of a type far from uncommon at Broadmoor. His early childhood, spent in great poverty and hardship, had been succeeded by a wild, ill-regulated youth. Excess, reacting on a system undermined by early privation, led to derangement and a criminal charge. But years of discipline and simple living had completely altered the man. He came to me a sober, steady fellow in obvious good health, with a turn of mind it was no exaggeration to term pious and a cheerful outlook that often put my own to shame.

He had made many efforts to secure release, but having no friends or relatives inclined to help him, had turned for assistance to the Salvation Army, with whom he was in constant touch. Whether he eventually secured release I have never heard. He was a good and trusty servant and I remember him with gratitude.

'Warmark', *'Guilty but Insane': A Broadmoor Autobiography* (1931)

=

Lady visitors in a strange country

Every month a group of women whom we called 'The Ladies' arrived from an Institute in the city to visit us. They were mostly middle aged with felt hats stout shoes and large handbags uniformly brown and shut with scrolls of dim brass that demanded a strong switch of the hand, like the turning on of a tap, to open. The ladies smelled like retired schoolteachers, with a mixture of loss and love and arrowed diagrams and small print with asterisks to indicate the foot of the page where someone has erased the reference. They were timid and kept in a flock as they toured the dayroom, and before they addressed each patient they looked about them with a furtive embarrassed air. They were not sure how to talk to us or what to say; they had learned somewhere that a fixed smile was necessary, therefore they smiled.

We felt our power over them and some of us uncharitably despised them, for they did not seem to be able to make up their minds whether we were deaf or dumb or mentally defective or all three, so that when they spoke they raised their voices and moved their lips with exaggerated care, and their vocabulary was the simplest, in case we did not understand. Sometimes they gesticulated as if we were foreigners and they were the visitors to our land who needed to try and talk our language. They wanted so much to feel at home with us, to be accepted among us, to sit and chat with us in a friendly cozy manner. They were pathetically eager to be surrounded with smiles and cheerful cries of welcome. It was not difficult to imagine 'The Ladies' themselves clinging to their bags, sitting all day in the hospital sewing room or wandering in the park or yard; sometimes it seemed that they came to visit us because they had a secret affinity with us.

'Hello,' they would exclaim with a heartiness that did not conceal their apprehension. 'Would you like a sweetie?' And they would produce a bag of sweets, offering trustfully the whole open bag and looking shocked, tutting and finally quivering with the necessary smile, when sometimes the whole bag was snatched from them.

Janet Frame, Faces in the Water (1961)

=

Urbane Metcalf, an ex-patient of Bethlem in the early nineteenth century, complains of corruption within.

In each of the galleries the keepers pick out one of their patients whose strength fits him for the situation of bully, and when it is not convenient to be at the patients themselves, they cause him to do it, this is a great abuse.

Another existing evil is the prevention of patients friends from seeing them, when it is their pleasure to say he is so much disordered that they cannot possibly bring him to the visiting room ... I have suffered confinement in the establishment, and am fully acquainted with the practices of the keepers, and advise such persons as have friends confined to insist on seeing them, if they leave any thing it is a matter of chance whether it is given them, the porter takes what he pleases in the first instance, and the keeper the remainder in the last, but the patient invariably comes off with short commons ... The steward and officers have men on each gallery whom they bribe, for the purpose of deceiving those gentlemen who benevolently use their exertions to discover the malpractices carried on in our public institutions, it is only by sheer accident that a solitary case now and then comes before the public, which by threatening an exposure, procures an amelioration in the condition of those persons confined through indisposition.

It would extend far beyond the limits of this little work to pourtray the villainies practised by the Jacks in office, bribery is common to them all; cruelty is common to them all; villainy is common to them all; in short every thing is common but virtue, which is so uncommon they take care to lock it up as a rarity. Like other establishments this appears to be erected too much for the purpose of making lucrative places; the apartments appropriated to the use of the officers are elegant in the extreme, every thing which luxury can covet is at their command; they eat, they fatten, while the poor creatures under their charge are left to all the miseries which confinement and privation can inflict; good God; in England, in this country, so famed for its munificence, surely the miseries of the wretched inmates of this humane institution are totally unknown to the exalted characters who support it, they should not sleep till the abuses are altogether removed; their supiness is the villain's security, their activity alone can prevent the new establishment falling a prey to the miseries and cruelties which disgraced Old Bethlehem.

Urbane Metcalf, *The Interior of Bethlehem Hospital* (1818)

=

Antonia White spent a year in Bethlem Royal Hospital (see page 1), often under restraint, after being certified insane. Beyond the Glass, *the third novel in her 'Clara' trilogy (preceded by* Frost in May *and* The Sugar House*), describes her experiences in Bethlem, which she calls 'Nazareth'.*

Then two nurses dragged her, one on each side, to an enormous room filled with baths. They dipped her into bath after bath of boiling water. Each bath was smaller than the last, with gold taps that came off in her hands when she tried to clutch them. There was something slightly wrong about everything in this strange bathroom. All the mugs were chipped. The chairs had only three legs.

There were plates lying about with letters round the brim, but the letters never read the same twice running. After the hot baths, they ducked her, spluttering and choking, into an ice-cold one. A nurse took a bucket of cold water and splashed it over her, drenching her hair and half blinding her. She screamed, and nurses, dozens of them, crowded round the bath to laugh at her. 'Oh Clara, you naughty, naughty girl,' they giggled. They took her out and dried her and rubbed something on her eyes and nostrils that stung like fire. She had human limbs, but she was not human; she was a horse or a stag being prepared for the hunt. On the wall was a looking-glass dim with steam.

'Look, Clara, look who's there,' said the nurses.

She looked and saw a face in the glass, the face of a fairy horse or stag, sometimes with antlers, sometimes with a wild golden mane, but always with the same dark stony eyes and nostrils red as blood. She threw up her head and neighed and made a dash for the door. The nurses caught and dragged her along a passage. The passage was like a long room; it had a shiny wooden floor with double iron tracks in it like the tracks of a model railway. The nurses held her painfully by the armpits so that her feet only brushed the floor. The passage was like a musty old museum. There were wax flowers under cases and engravings of Queen Victoria and Balmoral. Suddenly the nurses opened a door in the wall, and there was her cell again. They threw her down on the mattress and went out, locking the door.

She went to sleep. She had a long nightmare about a girl who was lost in the dungeons under an old house on her wedding-day. Just as she was, in her white dress and wreath and veil, she fell into a trance and slept for thirty years. She woke up, thinking she had slept only a few hours, and found her way back to the house, and remembering her wedding, hurried to the chapel. There were lights and flowers and a young man standing at the altar. But as she walked up the aisle, people pushed her back, and she saw another bride going up before her. Up in her own room, she looked in the glass to see an old woman in a dirty satin dress with a dusty wreath on her head. She herself was the girl who had slept thirty years. They had shut her up here in the cell without a looking-glass so that she should not know how old she had grown.

Then she was Richard, endlessly climbing up the steps of a dark tower by the sea, knowing that she herself was imprisoned at the top. She came out of this dream suddenly to find herself being tortured in her own person. She was lying on her back with two nurses holding her down. A young man with a signet ring on his finger was bending over her, holding a funnel with a long tube attached. He forced the tube down her nose and began to pour some liquid into the funnel. There was a searing pain at the back of her nose, she choked and struggled, but they held her down ruthlessly. At last the man drew out the tube and dropped it coiling in a basin. The nurses released her and all three went out and shut the door.

This horror came at intervals for days. She grew to dread the opening of the door, which was nearly always followed by the procession of nurses and the young man with the basin and the funnel.

Antonia White, Beyond the Glass (1954)

=

The memory of 'Nazareth'/Bethlem remained with Antonia White all her life, as her daughter, Lady Susan Chitty, recalls in her memoir.

The nightmares of last summer began again. They were always about the asylum, but now Antonia was an old woman being dragged protesting to 'the wire machine and the clippers'. In another dream she was her present age, lying naked and mad, on the pavement. The little street boys 'were looking at her and touching her, curious and rather frightened, saying "she's a sleazy lady"'.

Her mother wrote her a letter, almost illegible with distress, from Binesfield.

The agony of your life pierces my head like a sharp sword.

If I could die alone for you I would, if by dying I could give you happiness. I would, and that is true.

I never have told you all this, not wishing to depress you, my dearest child.

A crisis occurred in Antonia's analysis on 6 July. She discovered the source of the mysterious clicking sound. One day Carroll pulled his bunch of keys from his pocket and shook them. The result was 'convulsive horror'. The click was the imagined sound of her father's latchkey when he returned home to 22 Perham Road. Antonia had become hysterical before at Carroll's; she had screamed and wept and used bad language; but she was never again to be in such a state as this. The effect did not wear off for many days.

Susan Chitty, *Now To My Mother* (1985)

Doctors and Patients

There is a popular genre of psychiatrist joke in which the professional is made to seem madder than the mad. Doctors dealing with the insane have long lamented that they get tarred with their patients' brush, and are popularly associated with lunacy itself: words like 'shrink' or 'trick cyclist' say it all. It was not unknown for Victorian asylum superintendents or nurses to succumb to insanity's contagion and end up as patients in their own asylum. Mental doctor and mental patient readily change places or become doubles in the public imagination, involved in some bizarre form of psychological power struggle or *folie à deux*: the theme of Ingmar Bergman's film, *Persona*. Perhaps this merely proves what a trying vocation the psychiatric doctor embarks upon – and a cussed popular fondness for the underdog!

The interplay between psychiatric patient and doctor takes many forms. Particularly in the grand environment of the asylum, the successful doctor has often sought to project himself as a figure of benign paternal authority (his ineffective double being the physician who is merely aloof, apparently deaf to the daily needs of his charges). In office psychiatry, the psychotherapist must achieve a more intimate rapport – not easy, as the extract from Joyce Delaney's memoirs shows, what with tremendous time pressure and patients eager to exploit the psychiatrist. The client may, for example, seek to use the therapist as a surrogate parent or lover, but intimacy may need to be balanced against authority or objectivity, especially in the extremely emotionally charged liaison between Freudian psychoanalyst and patient, with all the complexities of transference and counter-transference that are involved.

In perhaps the very first deployment of the psychoanalytical technique, Freud's colleague, Josef Breuer, allowed himself to become emotionally and erotically involved with his client 'Anna O.', with untoward consequences all round. Thereafter Freud contended that the analyst should severely keep his distance. Later followers such as Sandor Ferenczi counterargued for the therapeutic benefits of closer emotional involvement; and such views have been taken further in the experiments with 'therapeutic communities' developed by R. D. Laing and others. Laing's so-called 'anti-psychiatry', which suggested that society was often sicker than its patients, implied that madness could be a way of coping with crazy situations, and deplored the callous authoritarianism of routine psychiatry, attempting to break down the sterile divide between doctor and mental patient. As can be seen from the relationship between Mary Barnes and Joseph Berke, the results have sometimes been explosive.

There is nothing new, however, in dramatic encounters between mad doctor and patient. In the early days of specialist psychiatry, back in the late eighteenth century, 'heroic' psychiatrists would routinely transfix their patients with a Mesmeric eye, or would seek to outwit madness by being more devious than the devious, tricking them into the abandonment of their hard-held delusions. Psychiatry has always been a power game.

A patient turns psychiatrist.

'I'm going to be a psychiatrist.'

Joan spoke with her usual breathy enthusiasm. We were drinking apple cider in the Belsize lounge.

'Oh,' I said dryly, 'that's nice.'

'I've had a long talk with Doctor Quinn, and she thinks it's perfectly possible.' Doctor Quinn was Joan's psychiatrist, a bright, shrewd, single lady, and I often thought if I had been assigned to Doctor Quinn I would be still in Caplan or, more probably, Wymark. Doctor Quinn had an abstract quality that appealed to Joan, but it gave me the polar chills.

Joan chattered on about Egos and Ids, and I turned my mind to something else, to the brown, unwrapped package in my bottom drawer. I never talked about Egos and Ids with Doctor Nolan. I didn't know just what I talked about, really.

'. . . I'm going to live out, now.'

I tuned in on Joan then. 'Where?' I demanded, trying to hide my envy.

Doctor Nolan said my college would take me back for the second semester, on her recommendation and Philomena Guinea's scholarship, but as the doctors vetoed my living with my mother in the interim, I was staying on at the asylum until the winter term began.

Even so, I felt it unfair of Joan to beat me through the gates.

'Where?' I persisted. 'They're not letting you live on your own, are they?' Joan had only that week been given town privileges again.

'Oh no, of course not. I'm living in Cambridge with Nurse Kennedy. Her room-mate's just got married, and she needs someone to share the apartment.'

'Cheers.' I raised my apple cider glass, and we clinked. In spite of my profound reservations, I thought I would always treasure Joan. It was as if we had been forced together by some overwhelming circumstance, like war or plague, and shared a world of our own. 'When are you leaving?'

'On the first of the month.'

'Nice.'

Joan grew wistful. 'You'll come visit me, won't you, Esther?'

'Of course.'

But I thought, 'Not likely.'

Sylvia Plath (see page 41), The Bell Jar (1963)

=

A doctor turns patient.

Perhaps the most striking figure of all was an aged man with a white, flowing beard of patriarchal appearance, and deep-set smouldering eyes. Originally a doctor, he had spent over forty years in custody and was the recognised *doyen* of Block II. He suffered from delusions and spent much time in composing letters to members of

the Royal Family, in which he offered fabulous sums for the endow-
ment of hospitals and clinics. From time to time his sense of identity
became confused. Every Good Friday, for instance, he would plead
indisposition and retire to bed, remaining invisible in his room till
early on Easter Sunday morning he would make a dramatic
reappearance.

'Warmark', *'Guilty but Insane': A Broadmoor Autobiography* (1931)

==

How to cure a crazy woman

Goodwife Jackson, aged 39, of a burnt high-coloured sanguine
Complexion, black Hair, 12 Years since fell mad, ran up and down
the Streets, bare footed, Cloaths torn, Hair loose, was ready to lye
down and pull up her Cloaths to every one, pretended Love to one
Mr Holland her Master, then a Prisoner in the King's Bench; at last
she tore all things, and struck every one, and was raving mad; being
poor, I gave her of Glass of Antimony a Scruple in Beer, each other
Morning for 14 Days, then ... sometimes of Scamony in Beer or
Ale, with Nutmeg and Sugar, each other Morning for as long, not
omitting Bleeding and Sleepers; and I gave her Broth and Posset-
Drink, with much Plantane boiled in it, and this cured her, and she
is well to this Day, having been half a Year mad to a high Degree.

Daniel Oxenbridge, *General Observations and
Prescriptions of the Practice of Physick* (1715)

==

*Outsmarting a perverse patient. Note how the early nineteenth-
century madhouse keeper resorts not to the physical violence of
whips and chains but to psychological tactics.*

Female, single. Age, 25. Had been six months under the care of
another Keeper, when brought to me. I often said, that if ever the
devil was in woman, he was surely in this. Good heavens! when I
look back upon the trouble and anxiety I underwent with this
creature, I wonder how ever I got through it; her filth, her fury,
disgusting language, and her almost constant nakedness for nearly
two months, it being totally impossible to keep any clothes upon

her, and it was scarcely possible to keep her from tearing her own
flesh to pieces, as well as others; these altogether left her almost
without the appearance of a human being: till I had her, I thought I
could manage any with the strait waistcoat; but her teeth bid
defiance to every attempt to keep even that upon her. But all our
extraordinary trouble arose from our not making the discovery
sooner, that her particular hallucination was, a determined opposition to the wishes of those about her; and we had only to express
the opposite of our wishes, and it was immediately done; as, Miss,
you must not eat that food, it is for another person; and it was
immediately taken and eaten up. Miss, you must not take that
medicine, it is for such a lady, this is your's; and it was gone in an
instant. Miss, you must lie still to-day; you must not get up, and
wash you, and dress you very neatly; and up she got, and did all we
bid her not to do. We therefore took care to bid her be sure to tear
her clothes all to pieces, and she remained dressed. This was certainly a departure from my usual plan of treating my patients as
rational beings; but it was a case of necessity. Purgatives, tonics,
chalybeates, the warm bath, cold effusion, and embrocations to the
head, were put in requisition: industry and determined per-
severence may do wonders; she got quite well, and became the
well-dressed, well-bred lady ... After this case, I shall never think
any too bad for recovery; she was under my care six months.

Thomas Bakewell, *A Letter Addressed to the Chairman of the
Select Committee of the House of Commons, Appointed
to Enquire into the State of Madhouses* (1815)

=

The first patient of the day

'There's young Gary Timson first,' she said bustling out, her uniform crackling with starch.

He came in smoking. Punk hair style, earring in one dirty ear and
wearing black leather. There was a badge with 'Try Me' on it
pinned in his lapel. It seemed to sum up his air of cheeky aplomb.

'Don't know how you stand this room. It's like a bloody oven.'

He eased his collar while I scanned Dr Hamil's letter which
wasn't at all informative. 'Says he gets tense as if he was going to

explode and all the time he is worrying and unable to meet or mix with people.'

'Are you going to psycho-analyse me?' he asked, as I shifted in the cheap plastic chair which was stuck to my bottom.

'Let's find out the real problem first,' I said. 'What is your trouble, Gary?'

He stubbed out his cigarette and I saw the letters L-O-V-E tattooed on four of his stubby fingers. 'That's what I come to find out, in't it?' He shoved a stick of gum in his mouth and chewed ruminatively.

Oh, one of those, I thought. I could have reminded him that I'd fitted him in as a favour, that he hadn't an appointment, but I knew it would be no use. In his plastic world I was a psychiatrist, the new folk hero who was supposed to work the miracles that God used to perform, only He couldn't now because in Gary's terms God didn't, had never, existed.

The family history? Previous illnesses? After fifteen minutes Gary had lit another cigarette and I had only gleaned that his sister had asthma, his father had died in early life and his mother was doing three jobs and never at home. Schooling, how about that? I asked.

'Proper old load of rubbish they gave us there. Waste of time. Course, when I went to the Approved School I learned a few things,' he smirked.

'Why were you sent to an Approved School?'

'Well, I had to, didn't I? I was caught stealing a car along with a few other things I done with the gang. I had the social worker, the probation officer and two psychologists working on me. It was great. They was a great bunch of lads at the Approved School and that's where I learnt me trade.'

His trade? I'd thought he was unemployed except for a brief spell of a few months as casual labourer.

'What is your trade, Gary?' I asked.

He transferred the gum from one bulging cheek to another. 'I'm a burglar,' he said, with the triumphant air of a Bugsy Malone.

I could feel sweat forming snakes down my face. I tried shifting my chair to get some respite from the glare of the window. Gary stared at me impassively, almost pityingly.

'It's a bugger that window. You want to get something done about it.'

'Have you . . .' I sought for the words. 'Done much burgling' or 'done any big jobs' sounded wrong, so I said, 'You mean you've made your living by burgling?'

'I told you, didn't I?'

'Are you in trouble now?'

'I'm due in court a fortnight today, aren't I? The police have it in for me see, what with me record and that.'

So that was it. He was fly enough to know that it might be worth trying to get a sympathetic psychiatric report to be read out to the court. Maybe that, too, was part of the training at the Approved School.

'Yeah,' he said. 'I got done for breaking and entering.'

Gary and I were never going to establish a rapport. Why hadn't he told Doctor Hamil about this?

'He never asked did he? Anyway, the bloke don't speak English right. He's a real Ying Tong like. Anyway, even if they send me down I don't mind doin' me porridge, it'll give me fiancay a chance to save. And with me nerves bad and that, I can be sent to the hospital during me stretch.'

Before I got him to give me more details of his absurd 'nerves', I found out more about his burgling career. He'd been in prison twice before, that was after some time in Borstal, and his previous brushes with the law were because of stealing a car, breaking into a factory and also some houses in Honeyacre, the rich part of York- ely. He told me about the break-ins with bravado, dwelling on each as if they were proud notches on his gun, a proof of his virility and manhood. Grievous bodily harm and mugging were for the real yobs, not the Raffles figure which Gary seemed to think he was, putting himself on a high echelon of prestige in the underworld.

But his nerves, how did he consider he had nerves? Although I knew there were two new patients waiting outside, and I hated keeping new patients waiting because they were usually so strung up that a wait was horrific for them, Gary's preposterous boasting had a sort of social fascination. So, prison was the 'in' thing with trendy youth? I didn't hear much about drugs now, and sexual exploits were done to death, so maybe lads like Gary thought that gaols went with the Punk era.

'You wanted to know about me nerves like. Well, I get dizzy, fall about like, and me heart starts pounding. Then me insides churn and I come over all queer. Mum used to have nerves, see. Me face goes all red like hers used.'

Yes, and his description of what he imagined to be 'nerves' sounded as unlikely as his mother's menopausal flushes which, I imagined, gave him his idea of what mental illness was. He had no psychiatric symptoms I said firmly, none at all, and sorry, I couldn't give him any more of my time. I could have said that it was a wonder his victims didn't have nerves when they were burgled and that surely they were entitled to pity and attention. I had no intention of writing to any court and it was up to him to decide whether he was going to give up crime or take the consequences.

'I'll write to Doctor Hamil and tell him that you have no sign of any mental illness and don't require any psychiatric help,' I said firmly.

'What do you mean?' the baby face twisted, snarled and became very nasty. 'You never examined me. Never sounded me, not nothing.'

'I've been watching you, observing you for nearly an hour and carefully listening to everything you've said.' I tried to keep my voice as professionally cool as possible, and it was quite a job because I was beginning to get very tired of Gary with his non-problems. 'You probably cause other people to feel nervous,' I went on. 'Breaking into houses and frightening people.' God, I hoped he didn't find out that I lived on my own and burgle me!

'Listen,' he shouted. 'I come here for help. What about them shaking turns I get? And I 'eave after meals. And I don't sleep.'

'Then take up something else other than a life of crime,' I said. 'Now I have to get on with my work.'

'Bleedin' 'ell,' he shouted, getting up. 'Me mates told me I'd get 'elp from you but you're kicking me out! It's us who pays your bloody wages you know.'

I thought he was going to hit me and I prepared myself to say that if he didn't leave quietly I'd send for the police. But I didn't have to say anything. He deflated fairly rapidly and became wheedling. Couldn't he have a few 'sleepers' to keep him going? His 'fiancay' didn't like the Pill and would I fix her up with something else?

He must have seen by my face that there was nothing doing

because he got up and said as a parting shot at the door, 'I'm going to report you. I'll tell my Probation Officer about you, that's what.'

He could do as he liked, I said, and he shot out slamming the door.

Joyce Delaney, *It's My Nerves, Doctor* (1980)

=

John Perceval (see page 23) complains that he was treated like a child. This may have been deliberate policy on the part of the asylum management. The enlightened and popular technique known as 'moral therapy' believed that the ideal psychotherapeutic rapport between doctor and patient should resemble the relations between parent and child.

The first symptoms of my derangement were, that I gazed silently on the medical men who came to me, and resolutely persisted in acts apparently dangerous. No doubt there were also symptoms of bodily fever. But from that moment to the end of my confinement, men acted as though my body, soul, and spirit were fairly given up to their control, to work their mischief and folly upon. My silence, I suppose, gave consent. I mean, that I was never told, such and such things we are going to do; we think it advisable to administer such and such medicine, in this or that manner; I was never asked, Do you want any thing? do you wish for, prefer any thing? have you any objection to this or to that? I was fastened down in bed; a meagre diet was ordered for me; this and medicine forced down my throat, or in the contrary direction; my will, my wishes, my repugnances, my habits, my delicacy, my inclinations, my neces-sities, were not once consulted, I may say, thought of. I did not find the respect paid usually even to a child. Yet my mind was at first sound, except as far as it was deceived by preternatural injunctions; in a certain respect, it remained sound throughout my illness, so that it faithfully recorded the objects and the events that took place around me; but I looked to the inspirations I received for the interpretation of them. If at any time my ear could have been closed to my delusions, I was then fit to be at liberty; but the credit I gave to my delusions, rather than to my judgment, was my disease. I was not, however, once addressed by argument, expostulation, or persuasion. The persons round me consulted, directed, chose, ordered, and force was the unica and ultima ratio applied to me. If I were insane, in my resolution to be silent, because I was sure that neither of the doctors, or of my friends, would understand my motives, or give credit to facts they had not themselves experienced; they were surely no less insane, who because of my silence, forgot the use of their own tongues, – who, because of my neglect of the duties I owed to them, expunged from their consciences all deference to me; giving up so speedily and entirely all attempt at explanation; all hope of sifting the cause of my delusions; all hope of addressing my reason with success; all hope of winning me to speak. If I needed medicine and light diet, still, I say to myself, surely that was not all; surely air and exercise, and water, and occupation or amusement, and a little solid food, would have done me no harm.

> John T. Perceval, *A Narrative of the Treatment Received by a Gentleman, During a State of Mental Derangement* (1838/40)

=

Infantilized by the asylum

And one of its permanent, dominant overtones was this back-to-childhood, back-to-the-kindergarten element. We were handled as children – not as delinquent or bad children, necessarily – but, rather, as potentially decent, irresponsible children who didn't know what was good for us, and therefore frequently had to be told. It was a 'mamma knows best' or 'teacher knows best' atmosphere, protective and generally kindly, but backed up with 'mamma will spank' when children became unmanageable and just had to be dragged kicking to bed without their suppers. Dirk's making me brush my hair whether I wanted to or not, then beaming blandly, seemed to be the essence of it. What gave it sometimes a crazy-dream quality – quite apart from the fact that some of us were crazy – was the fact that all of us were grown men, many of us middle-aged or elderly men of the type which generally bosses and orders other people around in the outside world.

> William Seabrook, *Asylum* (1935)

=

Learning from children

Over the years, through my work at the Sonia Shankman Orthogenic School of the University of Chicago, I learned to understand psychotic children, and I appreciated the importance of this lesson about time even more. Only when given unlimited time did these children come to trust I was on their side, and not against them, as they perceived the rest of the world to be in trying to have them change their ways. Encouraging them to proceed on the basis of their sense of time was demonstration to them that, given their experience of the world, their reactions were taken by us to be as valid for them as were ours for us. When, on occasion, I got restless after having sat silently for hours, trying to reach a catatonic, I had only to recall Johnny's statement. Then time again became totally unimportant, and I was once more in contact with the patient. It worked like a charm. As soon as I stopped worrying that time was passing and nothing was happening, I also stopped making inner demands on myself and on the patient, and stopped wishing his silence would end. In response, eventually the patient did something significant that permitted gaining a better understanding of his experience of the world, and of what it had been in me that had prevented him from relating.

Other parts of the lesson Johnny taught me took much longer to sink in. Off and on I pondered why Johnny had spoken so clearly to me only on this single occasion, and in a complete sentence to boot. After years of working with psychotics I came to understand the crucial difference my motive in relating to them made in their ability to relate, and in their view of themselves. I could elicit no response if my motive was to 'help' them. But if I sincerely wanted them to enlighten me about something of great importance about which they possessed knowledge unavailable to me, they could respond. My belief that Johnny could give me information (about the value of psychoanalysis) I did not possess put us on an equal footing that allowed this completely unrelating child to relate to me, at least for the time of this interaction. That something crucial in his experience was also so in mine established a bond of common humanity. While in all other encounters I had never taken Johnny for my equal, this one time I had done so, by accepting that as patients in analysis, we had experiences which were parallel. This is what made significant communication possible. From many experiences with other psychotic individuals, I learned later that it was this kind of relating which permits extension to other experiences and finally the establishment of true personal relations.

Only in this one encounter had I treated Johnny as a person who had superior knowledge on a matter of greatest significance – was psychoanalysis doing much good? At all other times when we met, I had felt superior to him. This time I had unconsciously hoped that this crazy child would solve my most pressing problem. And so he proceeded to do exactly that.

Bruno Bettelheim, *Recollections and Reflections* (1990)

=

This patient's contempt for the asylum doctor was widely shared. The professional staff of the madhouse were widely seen as a crossbreed between the magician and the jailer.

At last I reached the lowest rung of the medical ladder indeed; for what the wine-trade is to the man who has failed generally, so I take it is the lunacy trade (with marked and fine exceptions, of course) to the doctor who is no good for any other 'specialty,' and knows he is not. His province is the unknown; the law works for him; he is in charge of a certain number of unfortunates, whom others – not he – have pronounced 'mad,' he argues, when he argues at all, backwards. He has not to say to his patients, 'Your words and thoughts are inconsecutive, your eye is wandering, &c.; therefore you are mad;' but, 'You are mad; therefore your words and thoughts are inconsecutive, and your eye is wandering.' This argument has been absolutely used in that shape with me; and I leave honesty to judge what the effect was.

'A Sane Patient', *My Experiences in a Lunatic Asylum* (1879)

=

Successful psychiatry as a battle of wits. It is of course noteworthy that ancient therapeutics, such as vomiting, condemned as long ago as the eighteenth century, were still widely in use in recent times.

Some years ago, a good-looking twenty-five-year-old girl was sent to St Thomas's Hospital by her general practitioner for a second opinion. He told us that she claimed to have been outraged by a burglar one night, but that, when he examined her, she proved to be still a virgin, and although she had not menstruated since the alleged incident, this might well be due to the shock. She had visited gynaecological departments. There, in view of the famous Russell legitimacy case when a mother was supposedly proved to have been impregnated by her husband without any rupture of the hymen, she was given the urine tests for pregnancy. The results were always negative but, though everybody there did their best to convince her that she was not with child, she insisted on her claim. She was still unconvinced.

At the end of a year and three months of supposed pregnancy I then, amongst other reassurances, pointed out to her that, since she was a woman and not an elephant, she really must be mistaken. But no, she swore that she could feel the child moving inside her. All our treatments failed to remove what had become a fixed delusional idea. I now remembered that sudden conversions are most likely to occur when the subject is in very poor physical condition – as certainly happened with the Rev. Charles Wesley – also those priests of ancient Greek and Egyptian mystery cults made a habit of 'purging' their candidates by means of heavy laxatives and emetics, before indoctrinating them with the assistance of arranged hallucinatory visions. So we took the girl into our ward and with the failure of all other treatments dosed her heavily with emetics and starved her – of course with her consent – in the hope that after losing so much weight she might become much more suggestible in her artificially induced debilitation. I then suggested to the house physician that if he kept on arguing with her while breaking her down physically and wearing her down emotionally, she might in the end admit that she had been mistaken. After two days of four-hourly injections and arguments he came to me. 'I wonder, Dr Sargant,' he said, 'if we have been wrong, and the patient really is pregnant?' He suggested further tests to make absolutely sure. And it soon grew clear that the patient with her strongly held fixed beliefs, instead of being converted, had put the intelligent normal, sympathetic, now exhausted, therefore more suggestible young doctor into so vulnerable a state that he had fallen for her own impossible obsession. We had ourselves, in fact, been brainwashed by the supposed victim of our carefully thought out technique. We did, however, finally get her better by other treatment.

William Sargant, *The Unquiet Mind: The Autobiography of a Physician in Psychological Medicine* (1967)

==

Trust in doctors, distrust of their treatments

Meanwhile I was now fully rational, and my first action was, paradoxically, one which convinced the staff that I was not. I refused to take my drugs.

My confidence in the basic good intentions of doctors was extremely strong, having been rooted in me no doubt by the quality of the doctors who looked after me in my one serious childhood illness. But I had no confidence at all in the physical treatment given for mental illness. My experience of insulin treatment had given me a lasting impression that psychiatrists prescribed treatments on an empirical basis without any real knowledge of the effects their treatment had, and without sufficiently taking into account the variable reactions of different individuals. The drug I was on now was clearly a potent one. Was it not really hindering me rather than helping me to recover my intellectual grip? I refused to take any more of it until I had seen a doctor. I found that without it I did feel clearer in my mind, so I felt justified in my action.

The resulting interview with Dr Zimmer was a stormy one. He started by telling me that I was now just as ill as I had been in the acute stage of my first mental illness. Having been inside myself on both occasions I could tell the difference, though he of course could not. He went on to say that if I refused drugs again he would discharge me and have me readmitted on an order and would then use any drugs he liked on me by force. That really terrified me. I had recently been insane and knew it. I had recovered my reason and was clinging to it as the most precious thing I had. Some drug that did not suit me might so easily upset my balance again. But it was no use saying that. I controlled my panic as best I could and kept Dr Zimmer talking. Eventually it came through to him that I was now rational. I was able to explain how confused I had been as to where

I was. He produced a pass written out for a patient with the hospital's full address on it and said, still quite angrily, 'Does *that* convince you?' As direct contact between us was built up, his anger subsided. I admitted to a grave anxiety about the fate of someone I cared for who was abroad, and the humanity with which he reacted to that impressed and touched me deeply. In the end I burst into tears and he cut short the interview. But my show of emotion did not mean, as he thought, that I was too upset to talk. I cried from sheer relief at feeling safe at last. I no longer feared the fact of being in his power; I could trust him as a friend.

After that I could have talked to him very freely, and indeed I longed to do so, but there was no opportunity. It was some weeks before he had time to see me again; later interviews were short and kept to immediate practical matters on which decisions needed to be made.

Morag Coate, *Beyond All Reason* (1964)

=

A psychiatric dialogue between Perceval the patient (see page 23) and Mr Newington, the proprietor of Ticehurst House

In the same evening he returned to my room, saying to me 'Well, now sir, what am I to do? Your servant told me that you attempted to strangle him, and he is afraid to sleep with you, and so are all the servants of the house.'

I interrupted him, seeing what was coming, and said, 'Then, sir, that will just do; you know I do not wish to have any one to sleep with me, I have told you so, long ago and often, and it is one of my objections to continuing under your care.'

He said, 'No, that will not do, I must have you fastened in your bed, or two servants must sleep with you, one is afraid to sleep with you alone.'

I said, 'That is, sir, to offer me an additional insult for no reason; but I must submit to it, I suppose. Why should I not, however, have my room to myself?'

Mr Newington. – 'You'll try to effect your escape, sir, during the night.'

Lunatic! – 'How so, sir,' said I, 'I cannot fly through the bars, and you know it: besides there is a bolt, as you also know, outside my door, which can be bolted.'

Mr N. – 'Ay, sir, but you'll try to break through the walls of the house.'

Lunatic! – 'How can I, sir? What! do you think that I can do this with my earthenware pitcher and glass decanter? No, sir; but you are now a lunatic yourself, and are mocking me, and determined to insult my weakness.'

John T. Perceval, *A Narrative of a Treatment Received by a Gentleman, During a State of Mental Derangement* (1838/40)

=

It was widely believed that it was counter-productive for doctors to reason with lunatics. The practice would only make them more stubbornly entrenched in their delusions, and would increase their often already exaggerated sense of self-importance.

To reason with a lunatic is folly; to oppose or deny his hallucinations is worse, because it is sure to exasperate. If we wish to make an impression on him, it must be by talking *at*, not *to* him. Though he will not listen to what we address to him, yet he will notice what is said to others, and, if applicable at all, will apply the argument or point of your observation more forcibly to his own situation or delusions than we can.

To convince them, or break the catenation of their morbid ideas by fraud, trick, terror or surprise, is always attended with hazard. The chances are great that it will not succeed; and if it fail, the case is inevitably rendered more intractable; and perhaps the painful reflection is left, that our own imprudent and precipitate conduct prevented the recovery which patience might have insured.

Authors relate cases where this sort of hap-hazard practice has succeeded, and they justify it on the ground that desperate diseases require desperate remedies. But as I never could forgive myself were I frustrated in such an experiment; and as I think the proportion of cures in cases of insanity are as numerous, or more so, than in many active diseases, I shall proceed in that cautious course which experience has satisfied me is to be preferred.

The confidence of his patients is the sure basis of the physician's

success; and among none is it more essential than with lunatics. A
cheerful, encouraging, and friendly address; kind, but firm manners; to be patient to hear, but cautiously prudent in answering;
never making a promise that cannot safely be performed, and when
made never to break it; to be vigilant and decided; prompt to
control when necessary, and willing, but cautious in removing it,
when once imposed; – these are qualities which will always acquire
the good-will and respect of lunatics, and a command over them
that will accomplish what force can never attain.

> George Man Burrows (*see page 10*), *Commentaries on the Causes,
> Forms, Symptoms and Treatment,
> Moral and Medical, of Insanity* (1828)

=

The attendant as a case fit for treatment

On [one] occasion the element of personal spite entered into the
assistant physician's treatment of me. The man's personality was
apparently dual. His 'Jekyll' personality was the one most in evidence, but it was the 'Hyde' personality that seemed to control his
actions when a crisis arose. It was 'Doctor Jekyll' who approached
my room that night, accompanied by the attendants. The moment
he entered my room he became 'Mr Hyde.' He was, indeed, no
longer a doctor, or the semblance of one. His first move was to take
the strait-jacket in his own hands and order me to stand. Knowing
that those in authority really believed I had that day attempted to
kill myself, I found no fault with their wish to put me in restraint;
but I did object to having this done by Jekyll–Hyde.

> Clifford Beers (see page 25), *A Mind that Found Itself:
> An Autobiography* (1923)

=

The nurses

The nursing staff at Murthly, like Baldovan, were not 'nurses' in the
true sense of the word. While the majority wouldn't really bother
you, there was a rotten minority. But it was a powerful minority.
Even the good ones would never bear witness against the bad ones.

One of the really sadistic nurses used to enjoy punching patients in the stomach. He took great delight in doing it. If any of the older patients got out of bed or untidied their beds he'd scream at them, 'Lie down and go to bloody sleep.' This went on all day and he didn't want to be disturbed. If the screaming failed he would then punch them repeatedly in the stomach to make them stay in bed.

Of the good ones there was an old chap whom we called Trochry – he came from the village of Trochry in Perthshire. He understood the old men. He would laugh with them and cry with them. You have to know when to say, 'That's enough,' when to laugh and when to cajole. That all comes from understanding human beings and particularly the mental defective.

Jimmy Laing and Dermot McQuarrie,
Fifty Years in the System (1989)

=

Mary Barnes opted to be treated by R. D. Laing's therapeutic community at Kingsley Hall in East London. Her therapist was Joseph Berke. In their stormy but, it seems, ultimately fruitful relationship, Barnes made heavy demands upon Berke.

One day Mary presented me with the ultimate test of my love for her. She covered herself in shit and waited to see what my reaction would be. Her account of this incident amuses me because of her blind confidence that her shit could not put me off. I can assure you the reverse was true.

When I, unsuspectingly, walked into the Games Room and was accosted by foul smelling Mary Barnes looking far worse than the creature from the black lagoon, I was terrified and nauseated. My first reaction was to escape and I stalked away as fast as I could. Fortunately she didn't try to follow me. I would have belted her. I remember my first thoughts very well: 'This is too much, too bloody much. She can damn well take care of herself from now on. I want nothing more to do with her.'

Halfway down the front stairs and nearly out of the house I felt a slight change of heart. 'Stop a minute. What are you getting so worked up about? It's just shit. What's wrong with shit? It ain't any different from the stuff she used in her early wall paintings. Touching her shit won't kill you. Yes it will. No it won't. Stop mixing up her shit with your shit. Her shit is just shit. Ain't going to hurt you none to go back and help her get cleaned up, and if you don't you will never have anything to do with her again. Is that what you want?'

The last point was the clincher. I liked Mary and did not want to give up my relationship with her. I knew that if I didn't turn around and face that poor, sorry, shit-covered creature, I would never be able to face her or anybody like her again.

It wasn't easy. I practically had to push myself back up the stairs. Mary was still in the Games Room, her head bowed, sobbing. I muttered something like, 'Now, now, it's all right. Let's go upstairs and get you a nice warm bath.'

It took at least an hour to get Mary cleaned up. She was a right mess. Shit was everywhere, in her hair, under her arms, in between her toes. I had visions of the principal character in an oldie terror movie, *The Mummy's Ghost*, of the Mummy as he (she?) rose up out of a swamp.

You have to hand it to Mary. She is extraordinarily capable of conjuring up everyone's favourite nightmare and embodying it for them. Until that day, however, she hadn't succeeded with me. When she did, she came over with a bang.

Mary Barnes and Joseph Berke, *Mary Barnes: Two Accounts of a Journey Through Madness* (1973)

=

Berke for his part was also capable of unorthodox counters.

Twice I completely lost my temper and bashed her. I remember one of these incidents very well. That was when Mary tried to prevent me from going out to the Clinic. The other remains a hazy blur. That is when Mary tried to prevent me from going to talk with Leon Redler, an American psychiatrist and old friend of mine, who had recently moved into Kingsley Hall. My memory seems to have combined these two incidents into one; I am sure this is because I still feel guilty about hitting Mary, and reluctant to publicly reveal this example of my own violence.

After reading Mary's account of my blow-ups, I thought she had made a mistake and divided one drama into two. But I checked with Leon and he confirms the essential features of Mary's version. Nevertheless, I shall report what happened as I remember it. Readers can make their own comparisons.

Even when she was lying in bed all day, even when I had seen her for hours, Mary had the uncanny ability to figure out, almost to the exact moment, when I planned to go out or meet someone at the Hall, and then make a huge fuss about it. Looking back, I suspect that I used to let her know about my plans in advance via subtle changes in my tone of voice or body movement, of which I was not aware, but to which she responded.

In the days after Mary began to realize that my going out did not represent a total abandonment of her, but before she perceived the existence of her intense jealousies, I often found myself in the position of having to sneak out of Kingsley Hall the back way in order to avoid her. Later on, it generally sufficed to tell Mary a few hours ahead of time that I would be meeting someone and didn't want to be disturbed, or that I would be away for a while, for me to be able to be alone or leave the place without too much bother. Still Mary could and did revert back to her obnoxious and most trying ways without warning. Such was the case on the afternoon I exploded at her.

It had been a difficult day. The coke hadn't come for the boiler. The shopping had taken longer than expected. And I had to hurry Mary's lunch in order to get out in time for a clinic appointment.

Everything had seemed OK when I said 'good-bye' to Mary. She didn't seem upset, but a few minutes later, just as I was starting to walk down the front stairs, I heard her tearing after me in nothing but her nightdress, pleading with me not to go out, crying and tugging on my coat.

In no uncertain words I told her to go back to bed and that I would see her when I got back. Still she screamed and screamed. I continued to walk downstairs, Mary holding on with all her might. Halfway down, I stopped and tried to reason with her. This seemed to help matters a bit and I thought she would go back to bed. Then I realized that it was getting very late and I made the mistake of proceeding down the stairs without taking the time to stick her in bed.

Mary tore after me, leapt in front of me just as we got to the door, and in what almost seemed a cold calculated manner, screamed that if I didn't remain with her, she would take off all her clothes, go into the middle of the street, and yell that she wanted to be taken to a mental hospital.

That did it. Without a moment's hesitation. I stood back, made a fist, and hauled off at Mary as hard as I could. The connection felt great, as all my anger, not only from her screaming on the stairs, but all the anger accumulated and held in dozens of similar incidents, was released, all at once. Then I noticed that blood was pouring out of Mary's nose and all over her face and gown. I was horrified, and thought, 'What way is this for a doctor to treat his patient?'

Mary Barnes and Joseph Berke, *Mary Barnes: Two Accounts of a Journey Through Madness* (1973)

═══

Nijinsky fears his wife but is unafraid of his doctors.

I can no longer trust my wife, as I feel that she wants to give this diary to the doctor for examination. I said that no one had the right to touch my books. I do not want people to see them so I hid them, and this part I am going to carry on me. I will hide my notes as people do not like the truth. I am afraid of people, as I think they will hurt me. But I will go on loving them even if they hurt me as they are creations of God's. I love my wife and she loves me, but believes in the doctors. I know doctors, I understand them. They want to examine my brain, but I want to examine their minds. But they cannot examine my brain, for they have not seen it. I wrote some poetry in order that the doctors could observe the working of my brain. I wrote sensibly, but they asked senseless questions. My answers were quick and to the point. They did not want to accept one of the poems, for they did not think it was important from the psychological point of view. They did all this on purpose, thinking that I did not know what I was doing, but I know everything I do and therefore I am not afraid. I pretend on purpose to be mad, in order to be put into an asylum. I know that A. telephoned the doctor about me, but I am not afraid of them. I know the love of my wife. She will not leave me. I am terrified of being locked up and of losing my work.

Romola Nijinsky (ed.), *The Diary of Vaslav Nijinsky* (1937)

=

The tables turned: revolution in the asylum

'But the *danger*, my dear sir, of which you were speaking – in your own experience – during your control of this house – have you had practical reason to think liberty hazardous in the case of a lunatic?'

'Here? – in my own experience? – why, I may say, yes. For example: – no *very* long while ago, a singular circumstance occurred in this very house. The "soothing system," you know, was then in operation, and the patients were at large. They behaved remarkably well – especially so – any one of sense might have known that some devilish scheme was brewing from that particular fact, that the fellows behaved so *remarkably* well. And, sure enough, one fine morning the keepers found themselves pinioned hand and foot, and thrown into the cells, where they were attended, as if *they* were the lunatics, by the lunatics themselves, who had usurped the offices of the keepers.'

'You don't tell me so! I never heard of anything so absurd in my life!'

'Fact – it all came to pass by means of a stupid fellow – a lunatic – who, by some means, had taken it into his head that he had invented a better system of government than any ever heard of before – of lunatic government, I mean. He wished to give his invention a trial, I suppose, and so he persuaded the rest of the patients to join him in a conspiracy for the overthrow of the reigning powers.'

'And he really succeeded?'

'No doubt of it. The keepers and kept were soon made to exchange places. Not that exactly either, for the madmen had been free, but the keepers were shut up in cells forthwith, and treated, I am sorry to say, in a very cavalier manner.'

Edgar Allan Poe, 'The System of Dr Tarr and Prof. Fether' (1845)

=

In Virginia Woolf's novel, Mrs Dalloway, Septimus Smith, who has suffered shell-shock in the First World War, is treated by the pillar of normalcy, Dr Holmes. The scene conveys the author's anger at the way she was patronized by doctors during her own nervous collapses.

When the damned fool came again, Septimus refused to see him. Did he indeed? said Dr Holmes, smiling agreeably. Really he had to give that charming little lady, Mrs Smith, a friendly push before he could get past her into her husband's bedroom.

'So you're in a funk,' he said agreeably, sitting down by his patient's side. He had actually talked of killing himself to his wife, quite a girl, a foreigner, wasn't she? Didn't that give her a very odd idea of English husbands? Didn't one owe perhaps a duty to one's wife? Wouldn't it be better to do something instead of lying in bed? For he had had forty years' experience behind him; and Septimus could take Dr Holmes's word for it – there was nothing whatever the matter with him. And next time Dr Holmes came he hoped to find Smith out of bed and not making that charming little lady his wife anxious about him.

Human nature, in short, was on him – the repulsive brute, with the blood-red nostrils. Holmes was on him. Dr Holmes came quite regularly every day. Once you stumble, Septimus wrote on the back of a postcard, human nature is on you. Holmes is on you. Their only chance was to escape, without letting Holmes know; to Italy – anywhere, anywhere, away from Dr Holmes.

But Rezia could not understand him. Dr Holmes was such a kind man. He was so interested in Septimus. He only wanted to help them, he said. Her had four little children and he had asked her to tea, she told Septimus.

So he was deserted. The whole world was clamouring: Kill yourself, kill yourself, for our sakes. But why should he kill himself for their sakes? Food was pleasant; the sun hot; and this killing oneself, how does one set about it, with a table knife, uglily, with floods of blood, – by sucking a gaspipe? He was too weak; he could scarcely raise his hand. Besides, now that he was quite alone, condemned, deserted, as those who are about to die are alone, there was a luxury in it, an isolation full of sublimity; a freedom which the attached can never know. Holmes had won of course; the brute with the red nostrils had won. But even Holmes himself could not touch this last relic straying on the edge of the world, this outcast, who gazed back at the inhabited regions, who lay, like a drowned sailor, on the shore of the world.

Virginia Woolf, *Mrs Dalloway* (1925)

=

Malvolio persecuted by a false healer

Enter MARIA *and* CLOWN.

MARIA: Nay, I prithee, put on this gown and this beard; make him believe thou art Sir Topas the curate; do it quickly. I'll call Sir Toby the whilst. (*Exit.*)

CLOWN: Well, I'll put it on, and I will dissemble myself in't; and I would I were the first that ever dissembled in such a gown. I am not tall enough to become the function well nor lean enough to be thought a good student: but to be said an honest man and a good housekeeper goes as fairly as to say a careful man and a great scholar. The competitors enter.

(*Enter* SIR TOBY *and* MARIA.)

SIR TOBY: Jove bless thee, Master Parson.

CLOWN: Bonos dies, Sir Toby; for as the old hermit of Prague, that never saw pen and ink, very wittily said to a niece of King Gorboduc 'That that is is'; so I, being Master Parson, am Master Parson; for what is 'that' but that, and 'is' but is?

SIR TOBY: To him, Sir Topas.

CLOWN: What ho, I say! Peace in this prison!

SIR TOBY: The knave counterfeits well; a good knave.

MALVOLIO: (*Within*) Who calls there?

CLOWN: Sir Topas the curate, who comes to visit Malvolio the lunatic.

MALVOLIO: Sir Topas, Sir Topas, good Sir Topas, go to my lady.

CLOWN: Out, hyperbolical fiend! How vexest thou this man! Talkest thou nothing but of ladies?

SIR TOBY: Well said, Master Parson.

MALVOLIO: Sir Topas, never was man thus wronged. Good Sir Topas, do not think I am mad; they have laid me here in hideous darkness.

CLOWN: Fie, thou dishonest Satan! I call thee by the most modest terms, for I am one of those gentle ones that will use the devil himself with courtesy. Say'st thou that house is dark?

MALVOLIO: As hell, Sir Topas.

CLOWN: Why, it hath bay windows transparent as barricadoes, and the clerestories toward the south north are as lustrous as ebony; and yet complainest thou of obstruction?

MALVOLIO: I am not mad, Sir Topas. I say to you this house is dark.

CLOWN: Madman, thou errest. I say there is no darkness but ignorance; in which thou art more puzzled than the Egyptians in their fog.

MALVOLIO: I say this house is as dark as ignorance, though ignorance were as dark as hell; and I say there was never man thus abus'd. I am no more mad than you are; make the trial of it in any constant question.

CLOWN: What is the opinion of Pythagoras concerning wild fowl?

MALVOLIO: That the soul of our grandam might haply inhabit a bird.

CLOWN: What think'st thou of his opinion?

MALVOLIO: I think nobly of the soul, and no way approve his opinion.

CLOWN: Fare thee well. Remain thou still in darkness: thou shalt hold th' opinion of Pythagoras ere I will allow of thy wits; and fear to kill a woodcock, lest thou dispossess the soul of thy grandam. Fare thee well.

MALVOLIO: Sir Topas, Sir Topas!

SIR TOBY: My most exquisite Sir Topas!

CLOWN: Nay, I am for all waters.

MARIA: Thou mightst have done this without thy beard and gown: he sees thee not.

William Shakespeare, Twelfth Night (c. 1600)

=

A patient instructs his doctor. James Carkesse worked under Samuel Pepys in the Navy Office, until religious enthusiasm, it seems, turned his mind. He was confined in Bethlem and in Dr Allen's private asylum. He mistakenly hoped that his poetic efforts would convince the authorities of his sanity.

Says He, who more *Wit* than the *Doctor* had,
Oppression will make a wise man Mad;
One of his senses, fierce, untame, and vext,
Means *Solomon* the Preacher in the Text:
Therefore, *Religio Medici* (do you mind?)
This is not Lunacy in any kind:
But naturally flow hence (as I do think)
Poetick Rage, sharp Pen, and Gall in Ink.
A sober Man, pray, what can more oppress,
Then force by Mad-mens usage to confess
Himself for Mad? Reduc'd to this condition,
He may defie the Rack and Inquisition.
Beyond all *darkness*, *chains*, and *keepers* blows,
Sir Madquack, is the *Physick* you impose;
Threatning, because my *Satyres* frisk & dance,
With *Purge* and *Vomit* them to tame and *Lance*.
Quack, you're deceiv'd; thus lies the *argument*;
One God (the *Antients* say) is *President*
Of *Poetry* and *Medicine* too; one Father
Of *Esculapius*, and the *Nine* together:
If Verses then can't *Doctors Bills* defie,
And *Helicon* all Potions else out-vie;
If Poets are not Physick proof, *Apollo*
At War is with himself, 'twill plainly follow:
But *Phœbus* holds the Scale with equal hand,
And does, to keep his *own bounds*, each *command*.
Hence *Poets*, when *Quack* dares *Physick* in their rage,
They vent more sharply choler on the Stage:
Poison, the Body only does torment;
This strangely makes the very Soul ferment.
Let me prescribe then; *Phys* withdraw, & soon
You'l my *new Madness* cure, you call *Lampoon*.

                    James Carkesse, *Lucida Intervalla* (1671)

                    =

Laing and Basaglia, two leaders of the anti-psychiatry movement (see page 5), discuss the therapists' need for therapy.

LAING: Someone has to overcome this fear, this flight from the pain of others that reminds us of our own unhappiness, our own limits and desperation. Someone has to manage to stay with someone whom they realize they absolutely cannot help, without experiencing a sense of failure. This negative capacity is fundamental and important for our analysis. To face uncertainty and doubt when it comes, and to be totally disoriented by it, constitutes a falsely positive ideological position. It is a defensive escape from exercising that negative capacity I spoke of before, and it is completely nondialectical. The young psychiatrist who possesses a new language, internalized as ideology, develops a kind of agitation syndrome. His sense of guilt and personal fear means he can be dishonest with himself, often resulting in the adoption of an air of purity and superiority simply because he belongs to the New Left or the post New Left, and that he isn't a fascist. In practice, however, he may not be better or worse than some idealistic bourgeois psychotherapist who makes his patients pay for their sessions, but perhaps does a serious job.

I think the best solution is that experienced psychiatrists who haven't chosen one of these false solutions teach young students by their example, and not with words or seminars. . . .

BASAGLIA: That is what we're trying to do and if we succeed, the institution should be therapeutic at all levels, even for the therapists. This is what constitutes training. However, it's also necessary to understand the real constraints on our work. In terms of young students, is there an analogous problem in England, since the phenomenon is happening in many other European countries?

LAING: It isn't a problem for us because whoever comes to us for training lives with the patients. They don't just spend a part of their time there – they all live together.

BASAGLIA: In a psychiatric institution, however, there might be a thousand patients and seven hundred nurses, and the body of rules governing the organization of the hospital complicates matters.

Nancy Scheper-Hughes and Anne M. Lovell (eds),
Psychiatry Inside Out: Selected Writings of Franco Basaglia (1987)

=

*I will be revenged upon the whole pack of you: James Tilly
Matthews, an early nineteenth-century Bethlem patient, issues his
death threat against the doctors and their accomplices.*

WRIT BY JAMES TILLY MATTHEWS, PROBABLY
INTENDED TO BE USED BY HASLAM AS EVIDENCE IN
THE KING'S BENCH CASE

James, Absolute, Sole, & Supreme Sacred Omni Imperious Arch
Grand Arch Sovereign Omni Imperious Arch Grand Arch Proprietor
Omni Imperious Arch-Grand-Arch-Emperor-Supreme etc. March
the Twentieth One Thousand Eight hundred & four

The following are the Rewards by Me offered so long ago Issued for
the putting to Death the Infamous Usurping Murderers and their
Families & Races, agreeable to the Just Sentence by Me pronounced
against them and their Agents & Adherents, Under the special
Conditions That neither Machines of Art, Air-Looms, Magnets,
Magnet or other Fluids-Effluvias whether of Poisons or otherways are
made Use of: Nor any Poisons or any Dastardly, Secret, or Cowardly
Act be Used – . That none of the Guards, Household or Servants to
them be made Use of either For if any such take part in putting them
to Death I will cause them to be put to Death as Assassins on the Just
Principle that although They have not any Right to Existence much
less to have Guards, Households, Servants etc and although they
have by their Agents been Endeavouring so many years by every
Cowardly, Dastardly, poisonous, Secret, Violent, and dreadful
means been Endeavouring to Murder Me and My Family; and have
by such means Really Murdered My dear only Son and one of My
Brothers; I will not be Assassin like their Usurping Murderous Selves
nor connive at any Servant, or Person of Household, or Guard etc
lifting up their hand or thought against those who have Committed
themselves in Confidence to their Case etc – *But I have and hereby I
do Omni Imperiously and Most Absolutely Charge and Command
All Persons whomsoever Acting as Guard Household or Servants etc
to any of all the said Usurping Murderers – their Families or Races by
Me Pronounced against or Condemned so to declare. Respectfully
and Modestly to them etc That They are Usurpers That the Territories, Sovereignty, Dominion, Power, Authority, Property etc. by*

them possessed or held by others for or under them etc hath belonged Originally and Antiently to My Ancestors & Family Relatives and wholly since My Birth to Me Sole and Justly; And that I have Pronounced Sentence of Death Justly against them and Commanded the Execution of such Sentence upon them; having offered Rewards for such Executing them but generously prohibited their Guards, Households & Servants etc from being made use of or taking part therein, But to disband and Return to their Own Homes and not to Serve them any Longer Under Pain of being Adjudged their Adherents & Supporters and being put to Death for the same – And I do so further Charge and Command all such Guards, Households, Servants etc to disband themselves and Return from the Service of the said condemned; on Pain of being themselves punished with Death for the Neglect or Refusal hereof.

All Such so Refusing or Neglecting to disband themselves & Retire shall be put to Death as Supporting and Adhering to the Usurping Murderers, their Families, Races, etc And whoever Executes Death upon such as being of any of the Condemned Persons Guards, Households, or their Servants and Refusing so to disband & Retire but Persisting in their Adherence to & Support of such Usurping Murderers their Families & Races &c Shall have and Receive the Sum of One Hundred Pounds Sterling British Money or the Value thereof in other Monies paid within Three Months after My Absolute Possession of that Part of My Omni-ArchEmpire of which such so Executed were Supporting in Adhering to the Usurpation of, &c – The Awards for Executing any others so Adhering to or Supporting any of the Said Usurpers, Their Families, Races &c and of all who take possession or even Claim Possession thereof (Myself Solely Excepted) Is and shall be Twenty Pounds Sterling or the Value of other Monies to be paid for the Executing each, within Six Months at farthest after My Absolute Possession of that part of My Omni ArchEmpire in which they rendered themselves Culpable – Providing always *as a Primary Condition to all the others That every Person so Executing such Sentences has previously and publickly made his Declaration of Allegiance & Duty to Me by so Declaring That I was Born Their Absolute Sovereign, Absolute Proprietor, &c; and* that they always Persevere in such declaration And to their Utmost Assist and protect all others having so alike

declared, & so alike Persevering, &c – That if any of the Usurping
& Condemned are destroyed by any of the Prohibited or dastardly
means, Such Part of the Awards as would have been for the Putting
such so Contrary to My Commands destroyed, shall lapse from the
amount one Share for each according to the Number to be Executed; And shall be distributed among the poor or withheld and not
possibly be obtained by those who Receive the Remainder for
Executing the others – because I will not countenance any Act
which shall not be in My Estimation fair & Honourable according
to My Commands – nor any Working of Secret Assassins – But for
the Executing the said Usurper fairly as by Me Commanded or
Permitted of all which fair Modes I shall Prefer the Hanging them
by the Neck till Dead and afterwards Publickly burning them or
Severing their heads from their Dead Bodies to assure that they are
Dead to be proved. The Executors shall Receive the Rewards hereafter against each Class specified, in those for each to be Executed;
within Thirty days after My Absolute Possession of the said part of
my OmniEmpire Territories &c

Viz: Denmark Norway &c .... Three Hundred Thousand Pounds
Sterling

    Sweden &c .... Six Hundred Thousand Pounds Sterling

    All the Russias .... One Million Pounds Sterling

    China .... One Million Pounds Sterling

All between China and Persia One Years amount of their Civil List
for each –

    Persia .... One Million Pounds Sterling

    Turkey .... One Million Pounds Sterling

Africas one Years Amount of their Civil List for each; but if the
Civil List of Morocco does not amount to

    Three Hundred thousand pounds Sterling: Algiers to Two Hun-
    dred Thousand Pounds Sterling; and Tunis & Tripoli to One
    hundred thousand pounds Sterling each; Such shall be the Sums –

Spain .... One Million Pounds Sterling

Portugal .... Three hundred thousand pounds Sterling

France – Comprizing all those who have been Actually possessed of
    the Sovereign & Administrative Power or pretending Right
    thereto Since the Eighth day of March which was in the Year One

thousand Seven hundred and Sixty Six including the Soi disant
Legislative & National Assemblies, Conventions, Councils,
Directory, Consulate, Chief Departments of Administration and
Ambassadors; Reasoning to Myself to determine respecting those
who did Publicly Renounce and all Secondary & Subordinates;
The Reward is Two million and a half Pounds Sterling or Sixty
Millions of Livres Tournois – Supposing the Number was but
Sixty it would be one Million Livres Tournois for Executing each
OR if the Number was so Great as One Million (which would be
less than they have destroyed!) It would be but Sixty Livres each,
so that any one will befinding the Number be able to Judge what
the share for each Condemneds Execution is: But this is to be
Noticed That though it appears Certain that each Share in France
and many other Parts will be some Hundred Pounds Sterling for
Each Condemned being Executed; being somewhere between Six
and Twenty thousand Livres each Share; I have provided, That
wherever the Number of Usurping Condemned is so great as that
the Reward will not apportion One Hundred & Fifty Pounds
Sterling for the Death of each; It shall be made up and so paid at
least One hundred and Fifty Pounds Sterling or Three thousand
& Six hundred Livres Tournois for the Death of each – So that If
one Person Execute Ten Persons He will receive the number of
Shares; And if Ten or Twenty Execute but one of the Con-
demned, they will have but one Share among them all.
Switzerland – those persisting in the Usurpation or pretending
   Right to the Exercise of Sovereignty Dominion, Power, Authority
   or absolute Property, or other than Subject to Me; Three hun-
   dred thousand pounds Sterling.
Austria, Bohemia Hungary, & Venice, Tyrol, and so on &
Sovereignty of Germany One Million of pounds Sterling
Naples & Sicily .... Five hundred thousand Pounds Sterling
Tuscany &c .... One Hundred Thousand Pounds Sterling
Popedom .... One Hundred Thousand Pounds Sterling
Sardinia &c .... One Hundred Thousand Pounds Sterling
Genoa .... One Hundred Thousand Pounds Sterling
Germany – One Years Civil List Amount of each Separate State for
   the Execution of the Usurpers thereof, their Family & Race. But
   for Wisternberg It is a Sum of Three hundred Thousand Pounds

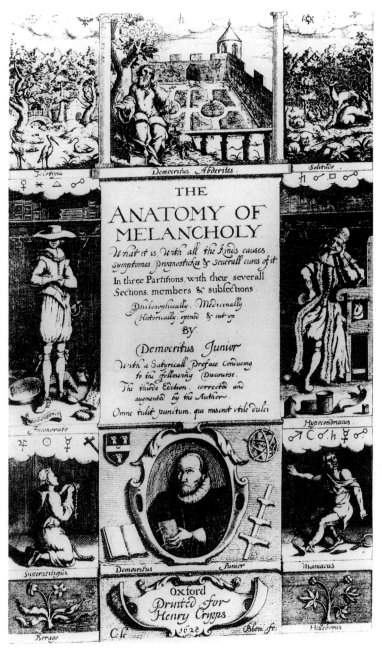

1 Frontispiece to Robert Burton, *The Anatomy of Melancholy* (1621). Burton's vast *Anatomy* shows the polar division, so common in his time, of madness into mania and melancholia, as well as revealing the subdivisions of melancholy (religious melancholy, love melancholy, hypochondria, and so forth). *Wellcome Institute Library*

The Author run Mad

2 (top) Bethlem Hospital. Engraving (1677). At Moorfields, then on the northern outskirts of London, this was the second Bethlem building, replacing the structure at Spitalfields. Its architect was the distinguished scientist Robert Hooke, and its French palatial style provoked much comment – it seemed that the French housed kings in buildings like this; the English, lunatics. *Wellcome Institute Library*

3 (left) Ward in Bethlem Hospital (c. 1745), from D. H. Tuke, *Chapters in the History of the Insane* (London: Kegan Paul, 1882). The image clearly derives from the Bedlam scene in Hogarth's *Rake's Progress*: the representation of the mad as shaven-headed and near-naked was typical of the period. *Wellcome Institute Library*

4 Paul Sandby, *The Author Run Mad*. Engraving (1753). A contemporary of William Hogarth, Sandby caricatures his rival as the classic mad artist suffering from grandiosity. It is a nice joke, since Hogarth himself had portrayed a mad artist in Bethlem in his *Rake's Progress* sequence. *British Museum*

5 (*top*) Thomas Rowlandson, *Doctor and Lunatic*. Unpublished drawing. The histrionics of Rowlandson's lunatic capture the theatrical conventions of the 'presentation' of madness so common in traditional psychiatry. Lunacy was believed to reveal itself through a standard repertoire of poses and gestures. *Clements Fry Collection, Yale*

6 William Blake, *Nebuchadnezzar*. Printed drawing, issued by the artist (1795). The divine punishment of Nebuchadnezzar, reduced to the condition of a wild beast, was a favourite emblem of the madness of pride and ambition through the Middle Ages. Blake's image plays upon the equation of madness and brutishness so common in the eighteenth century. *Tate Gallery*

Pl. II. N.º 2.

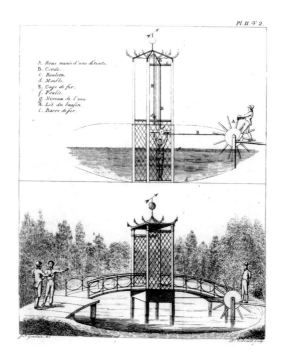

A. Roue munie d'une détente.
B. Corde.
C. Roulette.
d. Moufle.
E. Cage de fer.
f. Poulie.
g. Niveau de l'eau.
h. Lit du bassin.
i. Barre de fer.

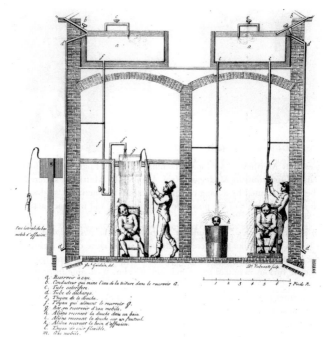

a. Reservoir à eau.
b. Conducteur qui mene l'eau de la voiture dans le reservoir a.
c. Tube calorifere.
d. Tube de décharge.
e. Tuyau de la douche.
f. Tuyau qui aliment le reservoir g.
g. Bac, ou reservoir d'eau mobile.
h. Aléine recevant la douche dans un bain.
i. Aléine recevant la douche sur un fauteuil.
k. Aléine recevant le bain d'affusion.
l. Tuyau de cuir flexible.
m. Axe mobile.

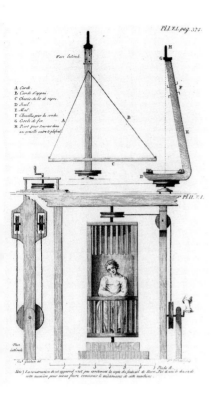

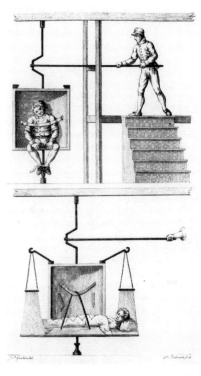

13 (*opposite and above*) Various restraints and treatments (1818–26), from Joseph Guislain, *Traité sur l'aliénation mentale* (Amsterdam: J. van der Heyet et fils, 1826). The age of industrialization produced more ingenious mechanical forms of restraint and therapy. Cold water baths and showers were believed to work on the principle of shock: swing chairs excited fear and produced (so it was hoped) salutary disorientations of disturbed senses. *Wellcome Institute Library*

14 (*right*) 'Lypemania', from J.-E.-D. Esquirol, *Des Maladies mentales considérées sous les rapports médicaux, hygiéniques et médico-legaux* (Paris: Baillière, 1838). Esquirol was the most eminent French psychiatrist of his generation. True to Renaissance artistic prototypes, the lypemaniac (another word for melancholic) is here portrayed listless, and with her hands hidden, signifying that they do no useful work. *Wellcome Institute Library*

PL. II.

Gravé par Ambroise Tardieu.

15 (*below*) Charcot lecturing on hysteria. Etching, after a painting by André Brouillet (1887), Musée de Nice. Jean-Martin Charcot is here portrayed demonstrating to his medical students a swooning hysterical patient. Note, in the top left corner, an illustration of a patient in a similar posture. *Wellcome Institute Library*

Sterling; For Bavaria Three Hundred Thousand Pounds Sterling: For Saxony Three hundred Thousand Pounds Sterling: And for Hanover & Bavaria separate from England Three hundred thousand Pounds Sterling – or their one Years Civil List amount at the option of the Executors Hesse Cassell also Three hundred thousand pounds

Holland as for Switzerland Three hundred thousand Pounds Sterling Prussia & Brandsburg, &c Six hundred Thousand pounds Sterling Poland is Comprized in Russia & Austria, and Prussia America the Soi disant State – Five hundred Thousand Pounds Sterling British East India Company Chief in India and Soi disant Directors in England Five hundred thousand Pounds Sterling including the Commander in Chief in India & the Colonels of their Regiments in England.

British Empire; Including as follows – The Infamous Usurping Murderer George Guelph and His Family and Race –
And all those calling themselves Parliament Lords & Commons of Great Britain, Ireland &c on or since the Eight day of July which come in the Year One Thousand Seven hundred and Ninety Eight – And all which upon of the Soi disant Privy Council, Cabinet, or Embassies at the said Period or have been since then And all those Soi disant Magistrates either of Union Hall in the Borough or of Bow Street Westminster at the End of the Year One thousand Seven Hundred & Ninety Six, or Since then, with all those who were calling themselves either Lord Mayor, Aldermen, Common Council, Governors, doctor, Apothecary, Steward, Clark, Surgeon &c of Bethlehem Hospital on the Twenty Eight day of January which was in the Year One thousand Seven hundred and Ninety Seven Including those calling themselves Secretaries of State and Police Officers of Westminster & London on the said day or Since – Including those of the Porter Keeper at Bethlehem Hospital whom I have Condemned for Ill treating Me, Insulting me, & Including also all those Acting as Judges of Soi disant Law of Equity Courts Since the said Day Including also all those Concerned in Imprisoning or [interfering?] with me or either of My Family and those Exercising Power or Authority in the calling itself College of Arms

who have Witheld the [Pedigree?] of My Family from Me & all those Concerned in Mutilating it or who have been Suborned [?] by the Usurpers or their Agents &c – Including also the Directors of the Bank of England, the Stock Brokers and Loan Contractors, the Commander in Chief of the [so] called [?] London Volunteer &c those Sycophants of Courtiers who in defiance of My prohibiting any to go to Court Upholding the Usurping Guelphe &c after the Thirtieth day of January which was in the Year One thousand and Eight hundred; have since their being dissipating My Properties, Insulting my Right, and Publickly Courting the said Usurping Murderous Guelphe etc and which Comprizes their Household, & Guards refusing to Retire disband etc but for the Execution of which Guards so Persisting in Supporting the said Usurper Three Hundred Pounds Sterling for the Death of each is more Viz Extra The only Condition left them being so fairly to make the declaration & Retire from their Service Ever in which Case though they are at Liberty to take part in Extirpating the Infamous Usurping Assassins calling themselves Lords & Commons of Parliament who have so Plotted at the Murder of My only Son and one of My Brothers and the Uncommon Efforts to Murder Me; and though such [so] called Guards are Capable of Receiving the Rewards for Executing such Soi disant Parliamentaries, They were totally prohibited from any Interference for or against the Infamous Guelphe & Race &c render the penalties of Death itself as mentioned – The Private Individuals who by their besetting & Ill treating Me have Encouraged the Usurpers in their dreadful Murdering Audacities against Myself & Family are also included in the Sentences to be Executed for which purpose I shall Eventually Cause them to be brought forward: But there is the Extra for Executing each.

Unfortunate for Me as it is to have to put to Death any one whomsoever; and especially such a Number; Yet it is Certain that great as this 'Number' appears, It is not half so many Persons as are literally Murdered in one Year in the Island of Great Britain only from the Effect of Machine of Art, Air Looms, Magnet, Poisons, Fluid & Effluvia etc Assortments &c in the System of Eventworking to Support there any Condemned in their Usurpation against Me – And as We all Know that every

Mortal would die sometimes in Course, I Notify to all my good Subjects That whenever any of the Condemned pretend That such as are Murdered by such Eventworking Infamies would die in their Turn as well as others; & That they should not Waste many Words in replying, but merely say And so would You die sometime or other if you were not now Executed – As You would live longer if Death was not Executed as a Punishment upon you, So they would have lived longer if Your Agents Assailments had not produced to them Death more early.

As for the Workers themselves especially those Gangs who have been Concerned in their Attacks on Myself and My Family; It is with me a Great Object to have them delivered up to Me alive and in their Perfect Senses, And to have their Apparatus unbroken [very?] Whole and in the State they Used it, with their Modes &c Publickly Exhibited – There is 13 or 14 in the Gang Assassinating Me, and they say Five or Six others who took part in Murdering My only Son: Several others Concerned in Murdering My Brother William and distinct Parties, who murdered My Mother & only Sister during my Infancy & Youth & Endeavoured to Murder my Father & Myself these and Four or Five Women who Endeavoured to Murder Her Omni Arch Majesty at these distant times – In order to prevent their further Atrocities & to have them delivered up to Me in their Senses Untouched, and their Machinery, Air Looms, Magnets, & whole that all My Subjects may have the Sight of them and know such weapons of Murder wherever they may be, I have determined a Separate Reward for these Purposes and so liberally as whether Ten, Twenty, Thirty, Forty, or Fifty thousand Pounds Sterling shall be tolerable Fortune among those who Effect the apprehending & so deliver them in their Senses, and preventing their atrocities in the meanwhile.

The dreadful gang of 13 or 14 Monster Men & Women who are so making their Efforts on Me; dare every one, and boast that they have what they call Beat out of the Field Viz fairly frightened those who have approached them with a view of molesting them or even Observing them Preparatory to dragging them forth: For so dreadful are they that they would Stab mortally Virtue itself and Abash it – when any Person appears not to approve their ways much more goes near them as they say some have, they Menace them to Accuse them or their Families Wives, Daughters, Sisters, Brothers, Fathers, Sons, Selves or Relations with Murder or Concerned therein or Sodomy or Whoredom or any dreadful such like; and they say they will Revenge themselves in such manner on whoever takes part against them if they are prevented attacking them with their Machines, Air Looms, Magnets, Poisonous Effluvias &c And that if all wont believe them some will for such things uttered once are sure to find Partizans and never can be Unsaid again – Now I am of opinion that I ought to Punish instead of Pitying whoever is afraid of them or their Assassin Utterance either; for it is by such means they have arrived at that pitch of very Uncommon depravity which they have attained – Verily their common discourse much more their Furious Malice is of such Unparalelled Obscene, Filthy, dreadful Expressions & nature, as makes human Nature Shudder: But the only Cure for such Evil is to drag them forth to Public View – As the Vampiring Consequentials calling themselves the better sort but who prove to be the worst sort, are so afraid of them; the Road is open for any good Resolute fellow not Comprized in the Sentence to make His Fortune & several others also. Thus – Any such one taking about a Score good hardy Carmen, Dragmen or Countrymen; and Suddenly presenting himself and Companions at their Cavern of Rendezvous might surely be Sufficient to Outscramble such desperadoes and bring them forth – They themselves have very often declared to me, that they are in a Cellar behind the houses forming the otherside of the Street called – – – – – London Wall opposite the Middle part of Bedlam – and very often indeed Several of them have pretended that they are in an Old Subterranean place which was a pass out of the City underground when the Walls of London were existing, and that when Bedlam was Built, it was so Contrived that such Subterrane should Serve for the Workers Rendezvous and that their Apparatus is therein – that it extends under some Parts of the Building – there being an Entrance to it from some little distance through a Cellar – Sometimes others have said that they were in Upper Rooms of a house not far distant, and that their Apparatus had Conductors to every part of Bedlam and the Neighbourhood even as far as to the Excise Office – Some of them Sometime ago also Averred that some of them calling themselves Governors of Bedlam Knew where they were well enough: but they then and at this moment say None will touch them for that all Say I am a Dangerous Man. They will find Me so to all such Assassins as themselves, their Employers and those who have Connived at their Existence: Supplied them &c. – However there cannot be a doubt but the Place of Entrance to their Rendezvous may be found – And if all other Methods fail, the letting the Water into it if it is below Ground will prevent their Using their Machine so Completely as to Injure any one – In the Magazine termed Annual Register for October Ninety one, There is an Account of the River Clyde having overflowed its Banks and I believe at Glaskow filled all the lower parts of the houses &c with Water which, reaching the lower Cells of the Madhouse where all the called Raving were, they at its approach immediately became quite Calm, even those who were the most Furious, And not only Suffered the Keepers &c to remove them up into the Upper Rooms, but remained quite Composed as long as the Water or Inundation remained – The True Secret of this was that the Water having found its way into the Place of Rendez-vous of the Gang Working that Madhouse as they term it, obliged them to quit their Assassins Employ till the Water had Subsided; during which the Poor oppressed Racked, Tortured and Machine driven called Lunaticks not being assailed became as much them-selves as their Machine & Magnet Agitated Rarified &c Fluids & Juices would so Immediately Admit – Their Arrivals as well as what I can Perceive prove the Certainty that this dreadful Scene of Villany of Eventworking by Working the Fluids, Juices, Brain, Vitals, Muscles, Nerves &c of Persons & their Circulations etc, is Extended to that point that in many places a Groupe of Workers are Employed in the Neighbourhoods of Private Individuals called Madmen; And that there is not a Madhouse of any Kind but to Work which there is a Gang – These Gangs have a sort of Ambassa-dors with other Gangs to Manage their Interests in the Actuating persons to produce Events therefrom for such of the Usurping Families, Individuals, Nations, parties, persons, &c as through their Secret Agents Six or Eight fold between them and the Dirty Workers pay them Cash.

From Roy Porter's introduction to John Haslam,
Illustrations of Madness (1810)

=

Should Matthews have been detained in Bethlem? The House of Commons set up its first systematic inquiry into madhouses in 1815, and here its Committee takes evidence on the case.

MERCURII, 3° DIE MAII, 1815

The Right Honourable GEORGE ROSE in the Chair
Mr Richard Staveley, called in, and Examined.

What do you know respecting the situation of Mr James Tilley Matthews, during the time he was confined in Bethlem? – MR R. STAVELEY: My knowledge of him has been principally within the last eight years, when, in consequence of his declining state of health, and the sufferings he was labouring under from the manner in which he was confined, I made application, with another relative, who is since dead, Mr Dunbar, to the committee several times, that he might be removed from the Hospital to be in the care of his friends. I grounded this application on the information and evidence of two physicians of the highest respectability, Dr Birkbeck and Dr Clutterbuck, who authorized me to state to the committee, that he was not by any means in that insane state of mind to render confinement necessary to him; that his mind was certainly affected on one point, but that was more on a philosophical point with respect to an air-loom system, as to which he fancied there were certain agents employed by the Hospital to annoy him by different modes, and they were of opinion that if he was removed from the scene this would cease; that he was by no means considered as a dangerous Lunatic, for from the evidence of their own officers who attended (the different keepers) that for the whole time of his being there, the man, so far from interrupting the peace of the house or creating disturbance, was the man to whom all parties, whether patients or servants of the house, if there were any grievances, made their reference for redress; but there appeared on the part of Mr Haslam, which I have told him himself, and which I told to Dr Monro, a violent animosity against this man. With respect to the circumstance of his being chained, I did not see him so myself, but had it as reported by him; it was previous to my having so much intercourse with him; that arose from his disputing the authority by which he had been sent there, or Mr Haslam's authority to treat him in the manner he did. Mr Matthews said to me, that Mr Haslam said in reply, 'you dispute our authority,' (with an oath) 'Sir, we will soon let you know what our authority is;' and the next day he was leg-locked. On enquiry to find the authority by which he was confined, they informed us it was by the parish officers of Camberwell. I went to the parish officers of Camberwell, who were, of course, very desirous of getting rid of an expense which they had been paying for so many years, and of relieving their own funds of it, if Mr Matthews's friends would come forward and take the onus on themselves; they attended the committee of Bethlem Hospital with me, to state the interview they had had with us, and to demand that he might be restored to his friends. The committee adjourned that day the consideration of the subject till the subsequent Saturday; in the interim we took a legal opinion upon the point, as to the parish officers of Camberwell, they saying, We certainly are not authorized to appropriate the funds of the parish to the support of this man in Bethlem, when his friends are willing to come forward and relieve us of that charge. We have the assertions of the medical men, who state that he is by no means a dangerous Lunatic, and therefore we request he may be given up.

Report (1) from the Committee on Madhouses in England,
House of Commons (1815)

==

Should Matthews have been confined? John Conolly, the leading early Victorian psychiatrist, offers his view.

Dr Haslam has related a singular case, at great length, without appearing, during the whole of the narration, once to have thought of the only question with which a medical adviser had any thing to do. The case is that of a Mr Matthews, who, it seems, considered himself to be the especial object of annoyance from a mysterious gang, residing in some unknown apartment near London Wall, who, by their skill in pneumatic chemistry, were enabled to inflict upon him various kinds of torture; of which kinds of torture, and of the persons inflicting it, he would give a very minute account. Sometimes they constricted the fibres of his tongue; sometimes they spread a veil beneath his brain, and intercepted communication between the mind and the heart: they would afflict him with stone in the bladder, introduce ideas at will to float and undulate in his brain, compress him almost to death by magnetic atmosphere, excoriate his stomach, force fluids into his head, lengthen the brain, and produce distortion of all images and thoughts; and now and then they distended his nerves with gas. All these, and other sufferings, sufficiently indicative of disordered sensations having assumed the force of realities, and so having disordered this poor man's understanding, were really little to the purpose for which Dr Haslam appears to have related them. What, in fact, was there in all this to warrant confinement in a lunatic asylum? No danger to others, or to the patient himself; no danger to his property or that of others; no suspicion of meditated violence. It seems indeed highly probable, that the patient indulged in these descriptions chiefly before those who sought to have them fully detailed; and that he enjoyed that perverse pleasure of exaggerating which has been mentioned among the infirmities of the mind. This opinion is strengthened by the circumstance, that the patient was seen by two highly respectable physicians, and that they seem to have heard nothing of the pneumatic chemists. But the important point is, that, admitting the patient to have had implicit faith in his delusions, and to have stated them without exaggeration, there was nothing to show the danger of allowing the individual to be at large. Superintendence and watching might have been advisable, medicine might have been necessary, but confinement in a madhouse was unjustifiable.

John Conolly, *An Inquiry Concerning the Indications of Insanity, With Suggestions for the Better Protection and Care of the Insane* (1830)

=

Victim blaming

The general attitude of this hospital towards insanity recalled the old-time madhouses. Hysteria still seemed to be regarded as a form of self-indulgence, although I have noticed that it is usually people reserved by nature and brought up to hide their feelings who suffer most violently from this complaint. I speak strongly on this subject, for even many medical people seem unable to grasp that self-control can only stave off the trouble and make the outburst the more uncontrollable, when the breaking-point is eventually reached. As a sufferer from this symptom, I can say without exaggeration that the victim feels like nothing so much as a caged tiger that is prodded with sticks until it is goaded to fling itself against the bars in a frenzy, though aware that the only result will be bruises to itself and the derision of the bystanders. I can never understand the common attitude of amused contempt towards a complaint which merely represents an attempt to escape from unendurable conditions by irrational behaviour. Why should a malady common even to dogs be regarded in human beings as exhibitionism?

After a few weeks of shocks and suspense in this hospital, aggravated by seeing other other hysterical patients bullied or consigned to 'refractory' wards, and without the benefit of any doctor or nurse who encouraged me to relieve my feelings, I reached a state that might soon have justified my return to 'J' ward. Only a fortunate meeting with the hospital psychiatric social worker, who always gave me the relief of a sympathetic hearing, even though she was unable to afford me active help, enabled me to maintain even an appearance of normal behaviour. With a few gratefully remembered exceptions, I found the attitude of this hospital towards its patients as one of regarding them as unmitigated nuisances and undeserving malcontents. Within the last few days of my stay there, a sister who slept in her own room in the villa, instead of in the nurses' home, complained that she 'had to put up with you people', and contrasted the price she paid for her room with 'you who get in for nothing'.

Even the deportment of the nurses seemed to lack the dignity common in a general hospital, depriving the patient of a sense of stability so necessary to mental cases. There is little confidence to be found in trying to talk to a sister who habitually flings remarks over her shoulder, and no respect for nurses who are sometimes overfamiliar in their manners and at other times casual to the point of insult.

D. McI. Johnson and Norman Dodds (eds),
The Plea for the Silent (1957)

=

The ambiguities of helping

there is something the matter with him
because he thinks
    there must be something the matter with us
for trying to help him to see
that there must be something the matter with him
to think that there is something the matter with us
for trying to help him to see that
    we are helping him
to see that
    we are not persecuting him
    by helping him
    to see we are not persecuting him
    by helping him
    to see that
    he is refusing to see
    that there is something the matter with him
    for not seeing there is something the matter with him
    for not being grateful to us
    for at least trying to help him
    to see that there is something the matter with him
for not seeing that there must be something the matter with him
for not seeing that there must be something the matter with him
for not seeing that there is something the matter with him
for not seeing that there is something the matter with him

for not being grateful

    that we never tried to make him
    feel grateful

R. D. Laing, *Knots* (1969)

[12]

Treatments

Down the centuries, mental illness has been unfathomed, uncharted, uncertain in its nature, dire in its effects. It has attracted the therapies it deserves. Desperate conditions get desperate remedies. Alongside the banal personal, mechanical restraints of leg-locks and irons, manacles and straitjackets, the standard therapeutic armoury was, of course, always wheeled out against the mentally sick – or rather, against the disease that had supposedly invaded their two yards of skin. Lunatics were purged, bled, and vomited, *ad nauseam*, like their physically ill neighbours. Mass late spring purgings were carried out at Bethlem, and the Monros – a dynasty of doctors who ran Bethlem while the Georges were running Britain – seem to have had particular faith in a good emetic, to the consternation of other, more enlightened, practitioners, such as William Battie, famous for pioneering the slogan that, in mental disorder, management might do more than medicine. Benjamin Rush, the towering Philadelphian physician, believed that madness lay in the blood, and set about relieving the patient of as much of it as possible.

Various alternatives to gross physical restraint and blind medication emerged. In the secure, total environment of the asylum, many superintendents experimented with treatment by forms of conditioning. Place people in a safe milieu, completely controlled (they urged), then act upon them with gentleness and consideration, establish routines of behaviour and discipline, develop occupational therapies and improve social skills, and you will re-train the mad into normalcy, much as you would educate a child at school. This was the therapeutic system pioneered at institutions such as the Quaker York Retreat, opened in 1796 (see page 135). The system seemed to work, but it required dedication, favourable staff–patient ratios, and, perhaps, responsive inmates in the first place.

Instead of this 'softly, softly' way by kindness, cosiness and sweet reason, another attractive alternative, with crude, immediate appeal, was the shock: maybe patients could suddenly be jolted back into normalcy. Probably originally used to drive out devils – or maybe simply to weaken patient resistance – a multitude of different shock tactics had been deployed time out of mind, including whippings and cold-water showers: folklore advocated setting the mad under waterfalls, or throwing them out of a boat at sea, with a rope attached.

In time, shock technologies grew more sophisticated. The industrial age developed swing-chairs and elaborate douche systems (see Plate 13). The present century has seen malaria treatment (the rationale: induce a fever and the heat will fry the disease) and insulin coma therapy (the rationale: deep coma will break the grip of obsessions and *idées fixes*) come and go. Electro-convulsive therapy (ECT) still finds occasional use, though far less than thirty years ago. And lobotomies and leucotomies were in vogue for a time as the 'heroic' contribution of psycho-surgery. All of these have had their enthusiastic advocates amongst the medical community, and even occasional supporters amongst patients. But nothing in the literature of madness is so harrowing as the opposition expressed by most patients to compulsory doses of any of these deeply disagreeable and painful shock procedures.

Partly because of hostility to such shock treatments within the institution and in society at large, the new range of psychotropic drugs becoming widely available after the Second World War was greeted with ecstatic enthusiasm. Psycho-pharmacology had long been lumbered with blunt weapons such as bromides and croton oil (an ultra-powerful purge which, in effect, merely put the patient out of action). From the 1950s, psychotropic (mood-influencing) drugs such as Largactil (thorazine) rendered even violent patients tractable, and opened up possibilities of full cures and the restoration of patients to the community, under supervised courses of medication. The response of patients themselves to heavy medication ('the liquid cosh') has been more ambiguous, since they readily induce lethargy, mental vacancy, and the 'zombie' effect.

Healing

MACBETH: Canst thou not minister to a mind diseased,
Pluck from the memory a roothed sorrow,
Raze out the written troubles of the brain
And with some sweet oblivious antidote
Cleanse the stuffed bosom of that perilious stuff
Which weighs upon the heart?

William Shakespeare, *Macbeth* (c.1606)

=

How to cure madness?

LUNACY

Give decoction of agrimony four times a day.

Or, rub the head several times a day with vinegar in which ground-ivy leaves have been infused.

Or, take daily an ounce of distilled vinegar.

Or, boil the juice of ground-ivy with sweet oil and white wine into an ointment. Shave the head, anoint it therewith, and chafe it every other day for three weeks. Bruise also the leaves and bind them on the head, and give three spoonsful of the juice, warm, every morning.

This generally cures melancholy.

The juice alone taken twice a day will cure.

Or, be electrified. (Tried.)

RAGING MADNESS

Apply to the head cloths dipped in cold water.

Or, set the patient with his head under a great water-fall as long as his strength will bear, or pour cold water on his head out of a tea-kettle.

Or, let him eat nothing but apples for a month.

Or, nothing but bread and milk. (Tried.)

John Wesley, *Primitive Physick: Or, an Easy and Natural Method of Curing Most Diseases* (1747)

=

Prevention better than cure, and philosophy the best preventive

For *prevention* of these *distracted Calamities*, since generally, and
most commonly they proceed from excess of *Passion*, and irregular
Desire; Therefore let all Persons Study by Temperance, and Moderating their Affections, to eschew those banefal Evils, and by
hearkening to the *Voyce* of *Wisdom*, they shall assuredly avoid
them, and many other Distempers and Mischiefs: Therefore, O
Man! consider what is before mentioned, keep thy Self to thy Self;
turn thy Eye of thy Understanding *inward*; observe thy *own Center*,
and learn to understand with *David, That thou art Fearfully and
Wonderfully made*, and so by the Conduct and Guidance of the
Divine Light and Love thou shalt come to know the wonderfull
Power of God in thy own Soul, which will open unto thee both the
Mysteries of *Nature*, and the Treasures of *Eternity*.

Thomas Tryon (see page 3), *A Discourse of the Causes, Natures and
Cure of Phrensie, Madness or Distraction* (1689)

=

*Madness, argues David Cooper, a leading spokesman for the anti-
psychiatry movement of the 1960s (see pages 5 and 239), is the cure
for the diseases of alienating capitalist society.*

Madness is the destructuring of the alienated structures of an
existence and the restructuring of a less alienated way of being. The
less alienated way of being is a more responsible way of being.
Responsibility means answering with one's own voice, not with all
the voices and their messages that have been planted in one's mind
throughout one's history (the 'schizophrenic symptom' of alien
ideas being planted in one's mind is a true realization of this
alienation). Alienation is the invasion of what we regard as 'our'
selves' by deformed human otherness – the otherness consisting in
the whole mass of human relations from the micro-social 'personal'
experiences in relationships to the institutional and the macro-
social. The deformation arises because human social existence is
perpetually perplexed and shattered by the relation exploiter/
exploited with the whole zone of mystification that comes in
between the poles. The destructuring I'm talking about involves the

elimination of these traces of otherness which, if thoroughgoing enough, passes a zero-point, a point of emptied out existence, the nullifying of mind that marks the beginning of the next phase; of restructuring.

Destructuring/restructuring follows a dialectical rationality, a rationality of depassment. This is the logic of every form of creative activity; it is also the logic of madness and the language of madness. There is another logic, antagonistic to the logic of destructuring restructuring, which in this age we may call capitalistic logic – a logic of destruction: a state of affairs exists or it is simply negated. In destructuring as in destruction there is negation (or alienated experience in the former case), but inherent in destructuring there is the negation of this negation, the actualization of the 'promise' that leads to restructuring.

David Cooper, *The Language of Madness* (1978)

=

Prospects for cures

I shall now mention the signs of a favourable and unfavourable issue of madness, in all the forms of it which have been described.

The longer its remote and predisposing causes have acted upon the brain, and mind, the more dangerous the disease, and vice versa.

General madness which succeeds tristimania, or that comes on gradually, is more difficult to cure, than that which comes on suddenly. Here we see its affinity to fever.

Madness, which arises from a hereditary predisposition, is said to be more difficult to cure, than that which follows a predisposition to it that has been acquired. It is certainly excited more easily, and is more apt to recur when cured, but in general, its paroxysms yield to medicine as readily as madness from an acquired predisposition.

Madness from corporeal causes is more easily cured than from such as are mental.

The younger the subject, the more easy the cure. Of 467 persons cured in Bethlehem Hospital, between the years 1784 and 1794, who were between 20 and 50 years of age, 200 of them were between 20 and 30.

It is rarely cured in old people. Mr Haslam says, of 31 persons in advanced life, who were admitted into Bethlehem Hospital, but four were cured in the course of ten years.

Persons who have children are more difficult to cure than those who are childless.

It is more easily cured in women than in men. Mania yields more readily to medicine than manicula, or manalgia. An 100 patients in mania in its furious state, and the same number in its chronic state, were selected in the Bethlehem Hospital, in order to determine their relative danger and obstinacy. Of the former 62 were cured, and of the latter but twenty -seven.

A paroxysm of mania succeeding manicula, or manalgia, is favourable.

A fever succeeding bleeding is favourable. It shows a suffocated disease to be changed into a diffused one. A malignant fever, I remarked formerly, once cured a number of maniacs in our hospital.

Remissions and intermissions of violent mental excitement, are always favourable.

Lucid intervals in manicula and manalgia are likewise favourable. They show that torpor has not completely taken possession of the brain.

Abscesses in any part of the body are favourable. I formerly mentioned instances of recoveries which succeeded them.

A running from, or moisture in the nose, after it has been long dry, is favourable.

Warm and moist hands, after they have been long cold and dry, are favourable.

A cessation of burning in the feet is favourable.

Benjamin Rush (see page xiv), *Medical Inquiries and Observations upon the Diseases of the Mind* (1812)

=

Music

Now if it were found practicable in some cases to sooth the turbulent affections, and appease the disorderly rovings of fancy, and
as it were to re-establish the former union of the body and mind, by
the powers of musick, in that interval of time, proper medicines
might be administered to better purpose ... That musick is effective
in most people, and more particularly in some few (from a peculiar
conformation, the force of custom, &c.) of very remarkable alterations seems evident, from its being a kind of universal incentive to
motion or rest. And if we duly attend to the operation of medicines,
we shall find their effects, and evacuations, to depend almost
entirely on the motions, they appease or excite ... But in musick,
providence seems to have favoured us with a much more agreeable
application to the intelligent principle itself, and a most delicious
cordial against the inquietudes and defects, which its imprisonment
in the body has subjected it to. Besides which, as it solaces the mind,
and sooths the passions, it has a considerable tendency to maintain
that blisful union, which gives the sole relish of every enjoyment,
the *Mens sana in corpore sano.*

The power of musick ... may be illustrated by the following
relation of Mr Stanley, a gentleman deservedly eminent in his
profession. A child not two years old, born of musical parents, was
one day remarkable for mirth and good humour, upon hearing
some sprightly airs of musick, this gave occasion to the father and
Mr Stanley to try the effects of different measures; when they had
rais'd the infant's spirits very high by this means. But as the
chromatick and graver strains began, the child grew melancholy
and sad, which temper was remov'd as soon as pleasanter music
was play'd. Thus, as I am inform'd, they could solely by this art
raise, and allay joy and grief, by turns, in the infant's mind.

Richard Brocklesby, *Reflections on Antient and Modern Musick* (1749)

Back in the seventeenth century, it was commonly believed that
lunatics were best handled with physical violence. See also Sir
Thomas More, page 98.

The first Indication, *viz.* Curatory, requires threatnings, bonds, or
strokes, as well as Physick. For the Mad-man being placed in a
House for the business, must be so handled both by the Physician,
and also by the Servants that are prudent, that he may be in some
manner kept in, either by warnings, chiding, or punishments inflicted on him, to his duty, or his behaviour, or manners. And indeed
for the curing of Mad people, there is nothing more effectual or
necessary than their reverence or standing in awe of such as they
think their Tormentors. For by this means, the Corporeal Soul
being in some measure depressed and restrained, is compell'd to
remit its pride and fierceness; and so afterwards by degrees grows
more mild, and returns in order: Wherefore, Furious Mad-men are
sooner, and more certainly cured by punishments, and hard usage,
in a strait room, than by Physick or Medicines.

But yet a course of Physick ought be to instituted besides, which
may suppress or cast down Elation of the Corporeal Soul.
Wherefore in this Disease, Bloodletting, Vomits, or very strong
Purges, and boldly and rashly given, are most often convenient;
which indeed appears manifest, because Empiricks only with this
kind of Physick, together with a more severe government and
discipline do not seldom most happily cure Mad folks ... Further
there are to be used Specifick Remedies, so called, of which is
famous, a Decoction of Pimpernel with the purple flower, also the
tops of Hyperican or St Johns-Wort, and other Decoctions, Opi-
ates, and Powders of Antilyssi are frequently noted among all the
famous Empericks ... Moreover, from Chirurgical Remedies,
besides, opening a Vein, many other helps are wont to be had for
the curing of this Disease. Cupping-glasses with Scarification, often
help. Blisterings, Cauteries both actual and potential are praised of
many. Others commend cutting an Artery, others Trepaning, or
opening the Skull, others Salivation.

Thomas Willis, *Two Discourses Concerning the Soul of Brutes* (1683)

=

Willis does not always seem to have used such violent methods.

A countrywoman, aged about 45, for long melancholic, was seized by mania on the 29th of June; so much so that it was necessary to bind her with chains and ropes to keep her in bed. On the fifth day ½ pint of blood was drawn from the basilic vein. At bedtime she took 2 grains of laudanum in a decoction of barley with an infusion of poppy flowers dissolved in a sweetened cardiac syrup. She slept about 3 hours that night. Early in the morning she had 3 stools from the enema administered the day before. About noon she slept again. In the evening I visited her. She was now shouting wildly, now singing, now weeping. She breathed rapidly, drawing the breath in with a hiss, her lips being drawn inwards. I prescribed a liniment of Vigo's ointment with [word illegible] smeared on a rose cake to be applied to her forehead and temples and a poultice of gently cooked water-hemlock to be put on the region of spleen; and also repeated draughts of a cardiac julep. The next night she died.

Thomas Willis, 'For the wife of H. Bolt of Eaton' (5 July 1650)

=

Officially sanctioned or not, violent methods such as the 'Spread Eagle Cure' here described, have stained the history of the asylum.

It is a term used in all asylums and prisons. A disorderly patient is stripped naked and thrown on his back, four men take hold of the limbs and stretch them out at right angles, then the doctor or some one of the attendants stands up on a chair or table and pours a number of buckets full of cold water on his face until life is nearly extinct, then the patient is removed to his dungeon cured of all diseases; the shock is so great it frequently produces *death*.

If all the persons in this commonwealth found intoxicated and not able to govern themselves in a proper manner should by LAW RECEIVE SUCH MEDICAL TREATMENT, say four buckets full of cold water applied in that way for the first offence, and for the second two more added and so on until the desired reform is accomplished, it would do more to prevent crime and INTEM-PERANCE than any other means. The tax payers would save a vast amount of money collected now to support the paupers of every

grade in this community. Let a steady stream of water seven or
eight feet in height fall down directly on the face of the patient, it
will have the same effect as if he was held under water the same
number of feet for the same time; a person cannot breathe when the
water is falling down directly in his mouth any better than he can
ten feet under water; it is a shock to the whole nervous system, and
it drives the blood from the brain, which has been forced up there in
many ways, which causes the patient to lose his proper balance of
mind.

*

I speak from my own observation on the spot. I have witnessed the
most cruel and barbarous treatment by a nurse in the hospital at
Pine street that could be inflicted on a human being. The person
was brought to the hospital with the mania a potu, and put into a
cell, strapped on an iron bedstead, with a hard mattress under him
– the term familiarly used in the hospital, *made into a spread eagle.*
The person is stretched out flat on his back, with a strap around the
bedstead, up over the breast of the victim, and buckled under the
bedstead; his legs are pulled wide apart and strapped to each corner
at the foot of the bedstead, the arms are pulled out straight from the
body, and strapped down under the bedstead, leaving his head
scarcely room to turn one quarter around; in that position a person
was kept three days and three nights; on the fourth night, at 9
o'clock, death relieved him of his agony.

> Ebenezer Haskell, *The Trial of Ebenezer Haskell, in Lunacy* (1869)

=

Tortures masquerading as treatments

There are several methods of restraint in use to this day in various
institutions, chief among them 'mechanical restraint' and so-called
'chemical restraint.' The former consists in the use of instruments of
restraint, namely, strait-jackets or camisoles, muffs, straps, mittens,
restraint or strong sheets, etc. – all of them, except on the rarest of
occasions, instruments of neglect and torture. Chemical restraint
(sometimes called medical restraint) consists in the use of temporarily paralyzing drugs – hyoscine being the popular 'dose.' By
the use of such drugs a troublesome patient may be rendered

unconscious and kept so for hours at a time. Indeed, very troublesome patients (especially when attendants are scarce) are not infrequently kept in a stupefied condition for days, or even for weeks – but only in institutions where the welfare of the patients is lightly regarded.

After the supper fight I was left alone in my room for about an hour. Then the assistant physician entered with three attendants, including the two who had figured in my farce. One carried a canvas contrivance known as a camisole. A camisole is a type of strait-jacket; and a very convenient type it is for those who resort to such methods of restraint, for it enables them to deny the use of strait-jackets at all. A strait-jacket, indeed, is not a camisole, just as electrocution is not hanging.

A camisole, or, as I prefer to stigmatize it, a strait-jacket, is really a tight-fitting coat of heavy canvas, reaching from neck to waist, constructed, however, on no ordinary pattern. There is not a button on it. The sleeves are closed at the ends, and the jacket, having no opening in front, is adjusted and tightly laced behind. To the end of each blind sleeve is attached a strong cord. The cord on the right sleeve is carried to the left of the body, and the cord on the left sleeve is carried to the right of the body. Both are then drawn tightly behind, thus bringing the arms of the victim into a folded position across his chest. These cords are then securely tied.

When I planned my ruse of the afternoon, I knew perfectly that I should soon find myself in a strait-jacket. The thought rather took my fancy, for I was resolved to know the inner workings of the violent ward.

Clifford Beers (see page 25), A Mind that Found Itself:
An Autobiography (1923)

=

The evils of the straitjacket

No incidents of my life have ever impressed themselves more indelibly on my memory than those of my first night in a strait-jacket. Within one hour of the time I was placed in it I was suffering pain as intense as any I ever endured, and before the night had passed it had become almost unbearable. My right hand was so held that the tip of one of my fingers was all but cut by the nail of another, and soon knifelike pains began to shoot through my right arm as far as the shoulder. After four or five hours the excess of pain rendered me partially insensible to it. But for fifteen consecutive hours I remained in that instrument of torture; and not until the twelfth hour, about breakfast time the next morning, did an attendant so much as loosen a cord.

During the first seven or eight hours, excruciating pains racked not only my arms, but half of my body. Though I cried and moaned, in fact, screamed so loudly that the attendants must have heard me, little attention was paid to me – possibly because of orders from Mr Hyde after he had again assumed the role of Doctor Jekyll. I even begged the attendants to loosen the jacket enough to ease me a little. This they refused to do, and they even seemed to enjoy being in a position to add their considerable mite to my torture.

Before midnight I really believed that I should be unable to endure the torture and retain my reason. A peculiar pricking sensation which I now felt in my brain, a sensation exactly like that of June, 1900, led me to believe that I might again be thrown out of touch with the world I had so lately regained. Realizing the awfulness of that fate, I redoubled my efforts to effect my rescue. Shortly after midnight I did succeed in gaining the attention of the night watch. Upon entering my room he found me flat on the floor. I had fallen from the bed and perforce remained absolutely helpless where I lay. I could not so much as lift my head. This, however, was not the fault of the strait-jacket. It was because I could not control the muscles of my neck which that day had been so mauled. I could scarcely swallow the water the night watch was good enough to give me. He was not a bad sort; yet even he refused to let out the cords of the strait-jacket. As he seemed sympathetic, I can attribute his refusal to nothing but strict orders issued by the doctor.

It will be recalled that I placed a piece of glass in my mouth before the strait-jacket was adjusted. At midnight the glass was still there. After the refusal of the night watch, I said to him: 'Then I want you to go to Doctor Jekyll' (I, of course, called him by his right name; but to do so now would be to prove myself as brutal as Mr Hyde himself). 'Tell him to come here at once and loosen this jacket. I can't endure the torture much longer. After fighting two years to regain my reason, I believe I'll lose it again. You have always treated me kindly. For God's sake, get the doctor!'

'I can't leave the main building at this time,' the night watch said (Jekyll–Hyde lived in a house about one-eighth of a mile distant, but within the hospital grounds.)

'Then will you take a message to the assistant physician who stays here?' (A colleague of Jekyll–Hyde had apartments in the main building.)

'I'll do that,' he replied.

'Tell him how I'm suffering. Ask him to please come here at once and ease this strait-jacket. If he doesn't, I'll be as crazy by morning as I ever was. Also tell him I'll kill myself unless he comes, and I can do it, too. I have a piece of glass in this room and I know just what I'll do with it.'

The night watch was as good as his word. He afterwards told me that he had delivered my message. The doctor ignored it. He did not come near me that night, nor the next day, nor did Jekyll–Hyde appear until his usual round of inspection about eleven o'clock the next morning.

'I understand that you have a piece of glass which you threatened to use for a suicidal purpose last night,' he said, when he appeared.

'Yes, I have, and it's not your fault or the other doctor's that I am not dead. Had I gone mad, in my frenzy I might have swallowed that glass.'

'Where is it?' asked the doctor, incredulously.

As my strait-jacket rendered me armless, I presented the glass to Jekyll–Hyde on the tip of a tongue he had often heard, but never before seen.

Clifford Beers, (see page 25), A Mind that Found Itself:
An Autobiography (1923)

=

The wet pack

My nerves were jangling like cracked fire alarms.

When Paschall came around that night and saw I really needed a dope-pill or a triple bromide, he said, 'I'll leave an order so you can get it if you think you must, but there's a way we think is better. It may not work with you. You may lose your temper. But we might try it. Want to try it?'

'Yes, what?' I said. 'Try anything.'

He went away and pretty soon the prize-fighter and another husky came in, carrying what looked like the hotel wet-wash. They fixed the bed so it wouldn't soak through to the mattress, then laid me straight and naked on the bed with my arms pressed along my sides like a soldier lying at attention and began swathing me, rolling me on one side and then the other, in tight wet sheets, so that the weight of my body rolling back would pull them smoother and tighter, over and over again, until they stood off to smooth any wrinkles out of the job and look at it and see if it was all right. I was flat on my back. Except that my head stuck out and lay comfortably on a pillow, I was the mummy of Rameses. I couldn't bend my elbows or knees. I couldn't even double my fists. My hands were pressed flat. I couldn't move a muscle except by tele-graphing a deliberate local order to it as oriental dancers do. This was the famous 'pack.' It occurred to me that I'd have been willing to bet any amount of money – and I still would – that this would have held Houdini. I had seen strait-jackets on the vaudeville stage, and a strait-jacket was a ten-acre field compared to this cocoon. It was tighter than any kid glove. And the tightness was so uniform that it didn't stop circulation. After they had gone I started to get excited locally, and it stopped even that. They told me I'd sweat a lot presently, and had fixed an ice pack on the top of my head where the skull was thickest. They had turned out all the lights, but had left the door slightly ajar, and had told me that they'd be down the hall somewhere so that if anything went wrong I could let out a yell.

I lay there in the darkness like an Egyptian mummy. After a while my mind began to work, and I discovered that I liked it. It occurred to me that probably I was masochistic or something of the sort. I set about rationalizing it, but of course one always does. I remembered the theories that we all have a subconscious longing to be back in the womb – that we remember subconsciously how nice and safe and warm it was. I remembered poetry about the womb and the grave. There were some distant, ordinary, living, human sounds way down the corridor somewhere, but they didn't disturb or concern me. Perhaps they did disturb me, for I became acutely conscious again of my jangled nerves. I wanted to turn over, to 'toss' about in the bed. I wanted to put my elbow up under the pillow. I wanted to move my arms. I wanted to scratch my forehead. I'd have to yell for help if a fly alighted on my nose. In a little while, the active nervousness decreased, but I was conscious of increasing tension. I tried experimentally to break, or stretch my bonds, by contracting and straining every muscle. I found that I couldn't loosen them at all, and it was this that had excited me and made me like it. I went lax presently and was beginning to sweat. I sweated, time passed, and the tension was gone and the jangling nervousness disappeared too, faded slowly as it does under a strong soporific. I was soon as peaceful as a four-month fetus.

When they came back after a long time and began to unwind me, I was still peaceful. And when they went away I turned on my side, stuck my arm up under my head, and went to sleep without another movement.

I was put to bed that way for five or six successive nights, and then Dr Paschall ordered it stopped. He said I liked it too well – that it could get to be another habit, like dope, veronal or whiskey, and advised me to read *La Séquestrée de Poitiers*.

William Seabrook, *Asylum* (1935)

=

Manacles preferable to straitjackets

The usual contrivance by which a maniac is restrained is the strait-waistcoat; this confines his arms and hands, which are crossed over the region of the stomach, and it is secured by being tied behind. This has been generally found a very convenient instrument of restraint, but it has been more convenient to the Keeper than advantageous to the Patient. As far as his hands are concerned, he is certainly prevented from doing mischief. But the disadvantages which result from the employment of this contrivance overbalance its conveniences. It will readily be seen, when a patient is compacted in this instrument of restraint, that he is unable to feed himself, and also prevented from wiping the mucus from his nose as it accumulates, and which, if long continued, would render him a driveller. He cannot assist himself in his necessary evacuations, and thereby is induced to acquire uncleanly habits. He is incapable of scratching to appease any irritation – If, in the warm season, flies annoy him, he cannot drive them away, and if, from the negligence of the keeper, his person should be infested with other insects, he must submit to their painful vexation: and it is always at the discretion of the keeper how tightly he may chuse to tie it. When several lunatics are confined in a room together, the strait-waistcoat is of little security, as it may be unloosed by any patient whose hands are at liberty, and I have known several ingenious maniacs who alone have been able to extricate themselves from it. It should also be kept in view that a single keeper will have the utmost difficulty in applying the strait-waistcoat if the patient be refractory, he will then be unable to effect his purpose without his most forcible efforts: and should his temper become exasperated in the contest, it is more than probable he will have recourse to undue advantages.

The other mode of restraining a furious maniac is by metallic manicles, which encompass the wrists, and prevent the hands from being separated when the patient may be disposed to strike. In my own opinion this mode of security is the most lenient, and subjects the person wearing them to none of the privations incurred by the strait-waistcoat. They are sooner and less difficultly applied, and cannot be removed by the assistance of another patient. Where the hands of the patient are in constant motion, which often occurs in the active state of the disorder, the friction of the skin against a polished metallic substance does not produce excoriation, which shortly takes place when it is rubbed against any linen or cotton materials. Considerable opposition has been made to the employment of metallic manacles, but the objectors have not condescended to adduce any reasons for their aversion to such mode of security. The sole object is to repress the efforts of a violent maniac with the least inconvenience to himself, and to allow him, under a restraint which shall be protecting to himself and others, a degree of liberty which enables him to assist himself, which exempts him from pressure, and is calculated to obviate those habits and infirmities which result from the fingers being muffled.

John Haslam, *Considerations on the Moral Management
of Insane Persons* (1817)

===

*The restraining chair more beneficial still, argues Benjamin Rush
(see page xiv) and Plate 11).*

Dear Sir,

In attending the maniacal patients in the Pennsylvania Hospital, I
have long seen with pain the evils of confining them, when ungovernable, by means of what is called the mad shirt or straight waistcoat. It generally reduces them to a recumbent posture, which never
fails to increase their disease. In this state they often lie whole days
and nights, and sometimes in a situation which delicacy forbids me
to mention. The straight waistcoat moreover renders it impracticable to feel their pulses or to bleed them without taking off the
greatest part of it. To obviate these evils and at the same time to
retain all the benefits of coercion, I requested, by permission of the
sitting managers of the Hospital, Mr Benjamin Lindall, an
ingenious cabinetmaker in this city, to make for the benefit of the
maniacal patients a strong armchair, with several appropriate peculiarities as noticed in the drawing which I have herewith sent you
for your Museum. From its design and effects I have called it a
Tranquilizer.

It has the following advantages over the straight waistcoat:

1   It lessens the force of the blood in its determination to the head
by opposing its gravity to it; and by keeping the head in a fixed and
erect position, it prevents the interruption of the passage of the
blood to and from the brain by pressure upon any of its blood
vessels.

2   It produces more general muscular inaction and of course acts
more powerfully in weakening the force of the blood vessels in
every part of the body.

3   It places the patient in a situation in which it is possible,
without any difficulty, to apply cold water or ice by means of a
bladder to the head, and warm water to the feet at the same time.

4   It enables a physician to feel the pulse and to open a vein

without relieving any other part of the body from its confinement but a single arm. It enables him likewise to administer purgative medicines without subjecting the patient to the necessity of being moved from his chair or exposing him afterwards to the fetor of his excretions or to their contact with his body.

5 The body of the patient in this chair, though in a state of coercion, is so perfectly free from pressure that he sometimes falls asleep in it.

6 His position in this chair is less irritating to his temper, and much less offensive to the feelings of his friends, than in a straight waistcoat.

I have hitherto employed this chair only as an auxiliary remedy for the cure of the violent state of madness; but I have no doubt it might be employed with advantage in other diseases in which a recumbent posture of the body has been found to be hurtful, particularly in epilepsy, headache, wakefulness and sleepiness, and from too much fullness of the blood vessels of the brain. The back of the chair for such cases might be made to fall back at the pleasure of the patient or to suit the grade of his disease.

I subjoin to the account I have given of the Tranquilizer letters from two of the medical officers of the Hospital, viz., Dr Vandyke and Mr Moore, who have faithfully attended to its effects upon a number of maniacal patients.

From, dear sir, yours very respectfully,

Benjamin Rush
    Benjamin Rush, letter to John Redman Coxe (5 September 1810)

=

In the age of the Industrial Revolution, there was a growing urge to find technological means which would provide quick cures to lunacy. The Swing Chair enjoyed a brief vogue.

This is both a moral and medical mean in the treatment of maniacs. It may be employed in either the oscillatory or common, or the circulating form. The first, or oscillatory, is too generally known to require a description: the second, or circulating, is easily construct-ed by suspending a common Windsor chair to a hook in the ceiling, by two parallel ropes attached to the hind legs, and by two others passing round the front ones joined by a sliding knot, that may regulate the elevation of the patient when seated, who, besides being secured in a strait waistcoat, should be prevented from falling out of the chair by a broad leather strap, passed round the waist and buckled behind to the spars, while another strap to each leg may fasten it to the front ones of the chair. The patient thus secured, and suspended a few inches from the ground; the motion may be communicated by an attendant turning him round according to the degree of velocity required. But a more compleat rotatory swing may be very easily contrived, of which I cannot convey a more accurate idea than in the words of Dr Darwin, with whom I believe the idea first originated. 'Let one end of a perpendicular shaft, armed with iron gudgeons, pass into the floor, and the other into a beam in the ceiling, with an horizontal arm, to which a small bed might be readily suspended'. To this perpendicular shaft a chair may be fixed, and the patient secured in it as above described ... Thus by means of the chair or the bed, the patients may be circulated in either the horizontal or perpendicular position.

On persons in health these swings produce only the common effects; but in proportion to the degree of motion communicated, and sooner by the circulating than by the oscillatory, and in the horizontal than in the perpendicular position. Independent of these more obvious effects in some maniacal cases, swinging, often repeated, has had the singular property of rendering the system sensible to the action of agents, whose powers it before resisted. One of its most valuable properties is its acting as a mechanical anodyne. After a very few circumvolutions, I have witnessed its soothing lulling effects, tranquillizing the mind and rendering the body quiescent; a degree of vertigo has often followed, which has been succeeded by the most refreshing slumbers; an object this the most desirable in every case of madness, and with the utmost difficulty procured ...

The valuable properties of this remedy are not confined to the body, its powers extend to the mind. Conjoined with the passion of fear, the extent of its action has never been accurately ascertained; but I have no doubt it would afford relief in some very hopeless cases, if employed in the dark, where, from unusual noises, smells,

or other powerful agents, acting forcibly on the senses, its efficacy
might be amazingly increased. The employment of such Herculean
remedies requires the greatest caution and judgment, and should
never be had recourse to but in the immediate presence of the
physician ... In every case it appeared that suddenly stopping the
machine, when in full gyration, occasioned a very violent shock
both to mind and body ... I have sometimes seen a patient almost
deprived of his locomotive powers, by the protracted action of this
remedy, who required the combined strength and address of several
experienced attendants to place him in the swing, from whence he
has been easily carried by a single person; the most profound sleep
has followed and this has been succeeded by convalescence and
perfect recovery, without the assistance of any other mean. One of
the most constant effects of swinging is a greater or less degree of
vertigo, attended by pallor, nausea, vomiting, and frequently by the
evacuation of the contents of the bladder ... and ... an obvious
change in the circulation ... these changes necessarily result from
an impression made on those organs of sensibility, the brain and
nervous system, and prove that the remedy acts on the seat of the
disease; though the proximate cause cannot be satisfactorily ascertained.

> Joseph Mason Cox, *Practical Observations on Insanity* (1806)

=

*A rival camp claims that all forms of violence and restraint directed
against lunatics can only prove counter-productive.*

The object of the following Lecture is simply to advocate the Total
Abolition of Severity, of every species and degree, as applied to
Patients in our Asylums for the Insane; and with this view to shew,
– *First*, That such Abolition is in theory highly desirable, and
Secondly, That it is practicable: in proof of which assertions the
present state of the Lincoln Lunatic Asylum is adduced. There such
a system is in actual and successful operation – the theory verified
by the practice. It may be proper to state here, that the principle of
Mitigation of Restraint to the utmost extent that was deemed
consistent with safety, was ever the principle pressed upon the
attention of the Boards of the Lincoln Asylum by its humane and

able Physician, Dr Charlesworth: at his suggestion many of the more cruel instruments of restraint were long since destroyed, very many valuable improvements and facilities gradually adopted, and machinery set in motion, which has led to the unhoped for result of actual Abolition, under a firm determination to work out the system to its utmost applicable limits. To his steady support, under many difficulties, I owe chiefly the success which has attended my plans and labours. He originated the requisite alterations and adaptations in the Building, and threw every other facility in the way of accomplishing the object. Experience has shewn that the mere partial mitigation of restraint is not in itself a safe system, suicides not having diminished under it; if any conclusion may be drawn from the few cases, it would appear on the contrary that there is not any safety, when the Attendants are not compelled to rely wholly upon Inspection. This propensity cannot be counteracted by any other means, than the constant supervision of attendants by day, and a watch by night, aided by the remission of ignorant and cruel usages which no doubt have often driven the insane sufferer to seek in suicide the only means of escape. The disappearance of suicide under the system of Total Abolition has confirmed this opinion. By the annexed Tables it will be seen, that not one fatal accident has occurred in this Asylum since the Total Abolition of Restraints.

But, it may be demanded, 'What mode of treatment do you adopt, in place of restraint? How do you guard against accidents? How do you provide for the safety of the attendants?' In short, what is the substitute for coercion? The answer may be summed up in a few words, viz. – *classification* – *watchfulness* – *vigilant and unceasing attendance by day and by night* – *kindness, occupation, and attention to health, cleanliness, and comfort, and the total absence of every description of other occupation of the attendants* ...

With your kind indulgence, I will trespass on your time and patience only a little longer, while I take a brief view of the *obstacles* to the practical execution of this, my theory ... *First.* The expense of providing a Building having suitable apartments, Galleries, Dormitories, separate Sleeping Rooms, with Airing Courts, Pleasure Gounds, Gardens, and Walks. – and such ample remuneration of Attendants, as may ensure persons of character and respectability ... *Secondly*. The prejudice which this plan (as has been the case with every improvement on its first introduction) has to encounter. *What! Let loose a Madman! Why he will tear us to pieces!* Look a moment at the facts. The following Table, conjoined with the fact, that no serious accident has occurred under this System, will I think, remove this idea from the mind of any impartial person ... *Thirdly*. The unwillingness of attendants, nurses, &c., to undertake the increased trouble, which this system requires. Here I have found my greatest difficulty ... It is stated truly in the Report of this year, that 'it is in the power of an unwilling officer to make any improvements fail in practice'. When a patient is under Restraint, it saves them the trouble of watching him: they can enjoy themselves at leisure, and play at cards, or otherwise amuse themselves as they please. Such was the case formerly, but cannot be tolerated under the new system.

Robert Gardiner Hill, *Total Abolition of Personal Restraint
in the Treatment of the Insane* (1839)

===

Thomas Monro, physician to Bethlem, explains how the therapy of choice often boils down to a matter of class and cost.

Do you not find the use of the strait-waistcoat extremely inconvenient to the patient in hot weather? – Yes, I should think it is; very often.

Of course, if he is annoyed by flies, preventing his delivering himself from them? – Yes.

Are you accustomed to keep the strait-waistcoat on any considerable time? – Only when it is immediately necessary.

That necessity may last for hours and days, may it not? – Then they are taken off and eased.

Are there not many inconveniences, such as the heat, the confinement of the ligature, and the prevention of respiration? – I have no idea of its preventing respiration.

Its degree of tightness is at the mercy of the keeper? – Yes; and they want a great deal of looking after.

What idea do you affix to the words, that a gentleman would not like irons? – In the first place, I am not at all accustomed to gentlemen in irons; I never saw any thing of the kind: it is a thing so totally abhorrent to my feelings, that I never considered it necessary to put a gentleman into irons.

Do you or not think that a man in a superior rank of life is more likely in a state of insanity to be irritated by such a mode of confinement, than a pauper Lunatic? – Most assuredly.

Are you in the habit of visiting any house in which pauper patients are kept? – Not unless I am desired to go and see a patient.

Are there any paupers at the expense of their respective parishes, confined in Bethlem? – Yes.

In point of fact, is more personal restraint imposed upon them than upon other patients? – Not that I know of.

What is your opinion as to the effect of irritation of any kind, in retarding or otherwise the convalescence of the patient? – It certainly retards their convalescence.

If a convalescent patient is subjected to a more rigorous confinement than is absolutely necessary, is that likely to produce such irritation as to retard his convalescence? – I should think it was.

You have informed the Committee that you think the strait-waistcoat, as an instrument of restraint, preferable to manacles; have you not observed at Bethlem, in going round the galleries, that manacles are much more frequently used than a strait-waistcoat? – They are generally chained to the wall with them.

Report (1) from the Committee on Madhouses in England,
House of Commons (1815)

=

How to master a maniac – by psychological means

The *government* of maniacs is an art, not to be acquired without long experience, and frequent and attentive observation. Although it has been of late years much advanced, it is still capable of improvement. As maniacs are extremely subdolous, the physician's first visit should be by surprize. He must employ every moment of his time by mildness or menaces, as circumstances direct, to gain an ascendancy over them and to obtain their favour and pre-possession. If this opportunity be lost, it will be difficult, if not impossible, to effect it afterwards; and more especially, if he should betray any signs of timidity. He should be well acquainted with the *pathology* of the disease – should possess great acumen – a discerning and penetrating eye – much humanity and courtesy – an even disposition, and command of temper. He may be obliged at one moment, according to the exigency of the case, to be placid and accommodating in his manners, and the next, angry and absolute.

I shall subjoin three or four cases, in which *management* seemed to be attended with the most desirable effects.

CASE I

When I was a pupil at St Bartholomew's Hospital, as my attention was much employed on the subject of Insanity, I was requested by one of the sisters of the house, to visit a poor man, an acquaintance of her's, who was disordered in his mind. I went immediately to the house, and found the neighbourhood in an uproar. The maniac was locked in a room, raving and exceedingly turbulent. I took two men with me, and learning that he had no offensive weapons, I planted them at the door, with directions to be silent, and to keep out of sight, unless I should want their assistance. I then suddenly unlocked the door – rushed into the room and caught his *eye* in an instant. *The business was then done* – he became peaceable in a moment – trembled with fear, and was as governable as it was possible for a furious madman to be.

William Pargeter (see page 36), *Observations on Maniacal Disorders*
(1792)

===

The dark side of psychological management: therapy by trickery

Many attendants are not at all averse to being considered demons by the patients; and one of them played some tricks on me in this way, but I saw through him at once, for at the time I was not in any suffering. Long afterwards, I saw another try to 'humour' an old patient by disguising himself one afternoon with a long black cloak, black gloves, and motor-goggles. The patient, who was suffering from general paralysis with excitement and exaltation (a disease fatal in the course of two years), was told by another attendant that someone was waiting for him in the boot-room. He went in, and was startled for a moment, but saw through the disguise. I happened to be passing at the time, and was amused, till I remembered the state I had been in myself. This may seem harmless fun to ignorant or disobedient attendants: it spells perhaps a death of slowly drawn-out terror to a patient. Now though by this very means God's will may be done, and a patient's trial or punishment effected, yet 'those by whom the offence cometh are not guiltless' are words that were not written by a fool; and 'judgement is without mercy to him that hath shewed no mercy' are words whose full significance few realize, and they are not written in a 'gospel of straw'; for He who created all things knows how to give certain agents in the administration of just punishment power to cause suffering which the pen can hardly picture. From what happens to some of us here, we can see more clearly than in a figure what awaits some others of us hereafter. To those who cannot feel for the insane – and many of them, if all were known, are not deserving of the slightest sympathy – the above statements may seem too strong and the patients' terror amusing; but when the 'real thing' comes for them – when they are handed over to be sifted by the King of Terrors – they will not be so amused; and the least touch to the mind and sight, just a little *vice versa*, and you have the real thing, as real as it can be in the flesh. The suffering of the mind and spiritual sensations of bodily torture are presumably less when that mind and spirit are protected by a dense and fleshly case or mortal body, and we can judge by analogy that either joy or suffering can be increased to an unknown infinite degree in a spiritual body not subject to dissolution from even the most violent shock or continued suffering. When one attempts to compare the greatest possible joy on earth with the most awful sorrow and suffering on earth, the other may, perhaps, for a second be dimly imagined.

D. Davidson, *Remembrances of a Religio-Maniac: An Autobiography*
(1912)

=

The use of surgery for mental disorders became common from the mid-nineteenth century, when hysteria and other female disorders were attacked via hysterectomies and occasionally clitoridectomies. The distinguished German psychiatrist, Paul Flechsig, performed psycho-surgery on both sexes.

CASE 3: HYSTEROEPILEPSY; STENOSIS OF THE EXTERNAL CERVICAL OS; SURGICAL DILATATION; PATIENT CURED

This case concerns T.F., eighteen years old, no hereditary taint. She has suffered from convulsions since she started menstruating several years ago (the exact date is unknown). These convulsions occurred frequently before and during bleeding but less frequently during the intervals between periods. At the same time, she suffers from frequent and severe lower back pain, vomiting, urinary retention, etc. She feels perpetually weak, has no appetite, and tends toward constipation. Her sleep is disturbed, and she sometimes suffers from anxiety attacks. She consulted a well-known gynecologist, who diagnosed stenosis of the external cervical os, made repeated attempts at cervical dilatation, and later sent the patient to a spa specializing in mineral waters and baths. Even though the dysmenorrheal symptoms decreased, the convulsions continued and even increased in frequency. The patient was admitted to our mental hospital on October 27, 1883 (not for treatment of mental illness but for treatment of convulsions).

Present status: Somewhat smaller than medium height, the patient is a well-developed girl weighing 54 kilos, with a pale complexion. Except for her genitalia, her organs are normal in every way, with no signs of degeneration. Her nervous symptoms include feelings of pressure and lightning-swift pains in her head, and a tingling in her hands. From the psychological point of view, the only thing out of the ordinary is her somewhat erotic facial expression. Examination with a speculum reveals extreme stenosis of the external cervical os and a copious thin discharge.

A hysteroepileptic attack occurred shortly after admission: it started with jubilant exultations, followed by tonic spasms of the torso and extremities and extreme opisthotonos. Her sensory aspect resembled a moderately deep hypnosis. There continue to be one or more attacks almost daily. They begin like the one described above. Frequently, the tetanic state is followed by a series of clonic spasms. The patient moves her torso violently and rapidly so that she thrusts herself upward in bed. Meanwhile, she rolls her entire body longitudinally and violently. Her sensory perceptions are somewhat dulled, but her intellectual capacity is totally unchanged. The patient attempts to avoid exposing her body during an attack, which occurs most frequently at the sight of men. The patient masturbates and in the company of women frequently speaks of sexual matters in a cynical way. From November 11 to 19, she is given 2.5 grams of sodium bromide three times daily.

On November 17 a surgical dilatation of the external cervical os is performed via a cross-like incision. Several wedge-shaped sections of the cervical canal are extirpated. There is conical dilatation; tamponade with iodoform gauze; antiseptic treatment.

Following this, the patient suffers three more attacks ... On the last of these dates, a totally pain-free menstrual period begins.

Beginning November 19, the patient suffers frequent lower back pain, pain near the bladder, urinary incontinence, vomiting, constipation, headaches, and dizziness, which diminish slowly and disappear altogether around January 8. Her erotic mannerisms gradually abate. Starting at the end of November, we administer vaginal douches with 1/1000 potassium permanganate and lengthy daily sitz baths.

On December 24, the patient is very depressed, claims to be held in contempt by her doctors and others around her, claims to have overheard insulting remarks about her and speaks of suicide. This depression no doubt is due to a remark made by her father that she was considered to be a 'nymphomaniac' in the clinic, that is, to psychological influences having nothing to do with her operation. Her bad mood gradually improves and is gone by January 8. On January 23, the patient is discharged, completely cured. She appears to be in glowing health and has gained four kilos. At last report, she is still well (as of September).

Discussion: I cited the above case only because many psychiatrists reject the gynecological treatment of neurosis. The failure of the first therapeutic method could easily have led to this case being cited as proof of the uselessness of gynecological treatment of erotic hysteria, whereas it actually proves the opposite. Above all, it is necessary to choose the correct method.

  Paul Flechsig, 'On the Gynaecological Treatment of Hysteria' (1884)

=

Around 1940, lobotomy, pioneered by the Portuguese neurologist, Egas Moniz, appeared to be a great psycho-surgical leap forward.

Another experience in Washington was to have a great effect on my psychiatric career. I must record with shame that, only a year before, I had roared with laughter on being told that an eminent neurologist, Dr Egas Moniz of Portugal, had claimed to cure mental disorder by operating on the silent areas of the brain in the frontal lobe region. This was too much even for me to swallow. Nobody then knew what were the functions of the frontal lobes; how on earth could such a complicated psychopathological illness as schizophrenia, with all its multiple and complicated psycho-pathological causes be helped simply by destroying certain tracts of the frontal lobes? It sounded utterly ridiculous. Yet here in Washington, Dr Walter Freeman, a neurologist, and Dr Watts, an eminent neurosurgeon, were following Moniz's methods and claiming impressive help of hitherto hopelessly ill patients. I rang up Freeman, and begged him to let Dr Fraser and myself, visiting doctors from England, examine three of his patients, absolutely alone, so that we could form our own conclusions as to whether or not these operations had been successful. He consented to let us interview at satisfactory length a chronic alcoholic, a chronic schizophrenic and a severe long-standing melancholic. I came away in a state of great excitement: the alcoholic commended the operation highly: he said he could now drink half his ordinary amount of whisky and get twice as tight! Obviously, it had done his alcoholism no good and perhaps a great deal of harm: he was much less tense but of course did badly later on as he continued drinking heavily. I remember his broad smile as he walked into the room, thumbs plunged in his waistcoat pockets, and saying, My! it had been a first-class operation. But we still doubted.

  The second patient, the schizophrenic, had for years been bombarded with threatening voices. Now, she said, she still heard them but they no longer tormented her. She was reasonably happy again.

The chronic melancholic said that she felt remarkably better, that the despair had gone, but that she had noticed a great change in her personality. Before the operation she had been too careful of other people's sensibilities. Now she dared to speak her mind, be bad-tempered, blow off steam at the slightest provocation, and think about herself much more for a change. This alteration in personality had not been so marked in the other two patients. But one thing was obvious: that Freeman and Watts had confirmed the value of an operation which, for the first time in my experience, seemed able to relieve chronic tension and anxiety in whatever psychiatric setting it presented itself. With each of these three very different psychiatric conditions, the chronic anxiety and intense fears of impending disaster had diminished or disappeared.

When I suggested to Freeman that he had not found a cure for either chronic alcoholism, schizophrenia, or depression, but for persistent chronic anxiety and obsessive tension, he was somewhat doubtful – not having thought of his operation in that light. But this has proved to be the correct view. We had, in fact, witnessed a preliminary skirmish in a surgical attack on the supposed 'soul' of man. True, the first operations were sometimes followed by a marked deterioration of the patient's personality, and the next tactical move was to overcome these effects by modifying the surgical technique while still relieving obsessive anxiety. Another two years passed before I could start active research in this field. But as soon as possible after my return to England in 1940, I began planning to try to develop modified techniques of leucotomy.

We have had to find out how to do a modified form of leucotomy that will ease chronic suffering and tension, while all but guaranteeing an avoidance of deleterious side-effects. The only proviso now to achieve this is that the neuro-surgeon must cut in the correct area of the frontal lobes, that is *confine the cut to the lower medial quadrants, a quarter part of the old operation*, and that haemorrhage or other accidents must not complicate the operation, as they very rarely do these days. Yet what moral repugnance this operation still arouses among some psychiatrists who are too prone to deny mental disorders any real physiological basis – believing them to be of mainly psychological, environmental or spiritual origin!

And when they are asked why they object so much even to the new modified leucotomies, the old bogy of 'personality deterioration', long ago minimized by new techniques, is still produced to frighten patients and relatives into choosing other less certain treatment alternatives, or doing nothing at all even if the patient is suffering terribly as well as having been totally incapacitated in a mental hospital for years on end.

> William Sargent, *The Unquiet Mind: The Autobiography of*
> *a Physician in Psychological Medicine* (1967)

=

Rescuing negroes with leucotomies

Central bureaucratic control of medicine cannot easily avoid a special mental sickness of its own. Professor Lyman was using his year's leave of absence to work at Tuskegee Hospital, Alabama, an institution reserved for negro veterans, and on one occasion I went down there to spend a few days with him. My visit to the psychiatric back wards, where I found negroes strapped down in chairs, like poor King George III, or subjected to other fearsome restraining devices, filled me with horror; I morbidly imagined myself confined there as the result of a sudden mental attack, and asked Professor Lyman why some of these pitiably agitated patients could not be given the benefit of modified leucotomy operations. I reminded him that Professor Walter Freeman was successfully practising these operations at Washington, and that the Boston Psychopathic, and two or three other progressive Northern hospitals, also favoured other new modified procedures. And in England this method had been found effective in thousands of cases; so the negro's suffering could certainly not be any worse after the operation than before, even if it failed to cure him. Professor Lyman promised that he would persuade the local Superintendent to do something about all this.

Professor Freeman had, as it happened, just perfected a new modified leucotomy technique that created intense antagonism amongst certain of his colleagues in America. The background was a shortage of properly trained neurosurgeons who could deal with the mass of patients in need of this operation. But Freeman had hit on a far simpler and cheaper method – the value of which has since been repeatedly confirmed – of performing this modified leucotomy. It was first suggested by the Italian Doctor Fiamberti: one cuts the small limited area, in the lower medial quadrant of the frontal lobe, that maintains tension and obsessive thinking, thus relieving the patient without any risk of the 'personality deterioration' which often resulted from the old full operation. Freeman simply pushed a strong needle through the roof of the eye-socket and into the lower part of the frontal lobe; then he manipulated the needle in such a way as to cut the appropriate brain tracts. The needle was then withdrawn, and though the eye itself might be temporarily displaced, it was surprisingly enough never damaged. Nor did the thrusting of a needle into the brain risk brain sepsis, because penicillin and other antibiotics given to the patient before the operation and for several days afterwards, fended off infection. Ordinary psychiatrists could now, if absolutely necessary, undertake a modified leucotomy themselves, without having to summon a neurosurgeon, and, as it proved, with a lower mortality rate into the bargain. I suggested to Lyman that he had a wonderful chance at Tuskegee to use this new 'transorbital' leucotomy and do a controlled experiment. Why not operate on fifty of the chronically agitated patients, whose personalities had not yet deteriorated too far, and compare the results with a group of fifty untreated patients who, if the experiment proved successful, would undergo the operation later on. Lyman took my advice and set up the whole experiment with scientific precision. Patients were specially chosen, so were the matched controls, and permission was obtained from all the relatives concerned, many of whom seemed deeply grateful that at last something would be done for their loved ones. Professor Freeman even volunteered to come down and perform all the operations himself without fee. The sequel was calamitous. The Veterans' Hospital Administration in Washington put a sudden ban on the use of this treatment. The whole negro-rescue plan had to be cancelled.

William Sargant, *The Unquiet Mind: The Autobiography of a Physician in Psychological Medicine* (1967)

=

One morning I was given my clothes and told to get up. My clothes flapped and sucked at my bones like a tent pitched in the snow to shelter the dead explorers from the blizzard as if the dead in their coldness need shelter from cold in the same way that man needs most to hide from the attributes which make him human.

After being for weeks in the small shuttered room I blinked in the harsh gritty sulphur-colored daylight as I followed the nurse out into the park amongst the patients from the dirty dayroom, and sat there on the grass and looked up at the sky at the clouds walking the plank of light. Suddenly the park gate was unlocked and some-one entered; it was a doctor I had never seen before, a short man with a monkey-like face and his head on one side and his white coat too long. I stared at him, everybody stared at him, for no doctor ever came into the park. Didn't he know that doctors could not mingle in this way with the disturbed patients, that even if Matron Glass approved of his lone touring of the ward, and it was certain that she did not approve, he would surely be mobbed by women pleading to go home although they knew nobody wanted them and there was nowhere for them to go; yet they would keep asking, 'When can I get out of here, out of this dump?'

The strange doctor walked slowly into the park and at once was surrounded by women talking to him and taking his arm, and it was astonishing that he took their arms, and talked to them and laughed. He did not reprimand anyone, saying 'Pull down your dress,' when some of the patients lifted their dress to show him, and he did not inquire if missing stockings had been thrust down the lavatory bowl or shoes thrown over the fence. No, he talked and listened with respect and did not seem afraid or hurried or discon-certed in case Matron Glass surprised him walking unescorted in the park among the disturbed patients who were now crowding to him like children to an ice-cream seller on a hot day or like people in lonely outposts wanting news.

'Hello,' he said to me. 'What if I bring you some pictures to look at? Will you tell me stories about them? I hear you've been very naughty.'

I burst into tears. So everybody, even the new doctor called me naughty as if I were a child in disgrace. I ran from him to the top of the park and lay on the grass considering my crime and turning the

imitation judgment that everyone, even myself, seemed to treasure
and no one could part with, like an evil jewel in my hand.

At dinner Carol told us that the new doctor was Dr Trace. 'I told
him about my "gagement ring",' she said.

A few days later Dr Steward asked to interview me in the clinic.

'We don't like to see you here,' he said. 'There's an operation
which changes the personality and reduces the tension, and we've
decided it would be best for you to have the operation. One of your
parents will sign the paper. We've asked your mother to come for
an interview.'

There was a staccato thudding in my chest and I seemed to be
falling away from myself like a tree that, having stood many years
in a caverned reserve of personal space, is suddenly felled yet leaves,
still upright, the force of its habitual life, like an invisible shape
withstanding the greedy inrush of air.

Ha, I thought. I felt myself being packed in layers of ice and I
shivered.

Dr Steward's eyes loped up and down like seals in a round pool.

'You will be changed,' he repeated. 'The tension will be reduced.'

His Adam's apple bulged like plumbing in his throat. His face
was gray. 'The prison camp in Germany,' I thought, and then Miss
Dock, the history teacher who wove in her spare time and made
baskets and raffia stands for teapots, switched on her face before
me like a light and battered the title like a neon advertisement,
Europe in the Melting Pot. She smiled with glee and poured in the
liquid continents and islands and stirred the mixture while Dr
Steward Matron Glass Sister Bridge prepared the new mold.

'What will they do?' I asked.

'It's an operation on the brain of course,' said Dr Steward.

Of course.

I remembered a picture of the brain, how it looked like a shelled
walnut and its areas were marked in heavy print, Concentration,
Memory, Emotion, like the names of cities in a strange allegorical
land.

'I want to go home,' I said. I did not mean to where my parents
were living or to any other house of wood, stone or brick. I felt no
longer human. I knew I would have to seek shelter now in a hole in
the earth or a web in the corner of a high ceiling or a safe nest

between two rocks on an exposed coast mauled by the sea. In the rush of loneliness which overcame me, at the doctor's words, I found no place to stay, nowhere to cling like a bat from a branch or spin a milk-white web about a thistle stalk.

'The tension will be reduced,' Dr Steward repeated in formal tones, like someone announcing the departure of a train.

Then he smiled, 'It's better than staying here all the time, isn't it? Now run along and be good.'

Janet Frame, Faces in the Water (1961)

=

Lobotomy

'Have you seen my scars?'

Valerie pushed aside her black bang and indicated two pale marks, one on either side of her forehead, as if at some time she had started to sprout horns, but cut them off.

We were walking, just the two of us, with the Sports Therapist in the asylum gardens. Nowadays I was let out on walk privileges more and more often. They never let Miss Norris out at all.

Valerie said Miss Norris shouldn't be in Caplan, but in a building for worse people called Wymark.

'Do you know what these scars are?' Valerie persisted.

'No. What are they?'

'I've had a lobotomy.'

I looked at Valerie in awe, appreciating for the first time her perpetual marble calm. 'How do you feel?'

'Fine. I'm not angry any more. Before, I was always angry. I was in Wymark, before, and now I'm in Caplan. I can go to town, now, or shopping or to a movie, along with a nurse.'

'What will you do when you get out?'

'Oh, I'm not leaving,' Valerie laughed. 'I like it here.'

Sylvia Plath (see page 41), The Bell Jar (1963)

=

*In recent times, psycho-pharmaceutical breakthroughs have seemed
to offer the best prospects for the control, if not the cure, of mental
disorders. There is, of course, a long history of pills for mental ills.
The virtues of opium were being explored in the eighteenth century.*

When first I used opium for a *melancholia*, it proved a very successful remedy; so that I doubted not but that it acted as a specific, and
only failed in other peoples hands, because they gave it in too small
doses. I gave six grains in one night to a young gentleman, for a
recent melancholy: he fell into a profound sleep, and sweated much
all night; yet without my orders, he was that morning put into the
cold bath, and again laid in bed to sweat. This was bold, but blind
practice; however, he was well in eight days, tho' I could not
determine whether the opium or the bath had the greatest share in
the cure.

I gave four grains of opium to a gentlewoman who lost the use of
her reason on a sudden, by the barbarous treatment of her husband,
and she was cured by that single dose. Whether a case so recent
would not have been easily cured without medicines, or whether
the profound sleep she fell into might contribute totally to efface
the incoherent set of ideas which possessed her mind before she
took the opium, I will not pretend to determine; but soon after this,
I had some other instances, as I thought, of the good effects of
opium in this disease, which made me fond of it as a specific in the
like cases. At length I had a patient labouring under a religious
melancholy, who talked of nothing but the unpardonable sin, &c.
In short, despair had drove him mad. In one of his mad fits he took
such a dose of *laudanum*, without the knowledge of his physicians,
as had almost killed him. When we found him in that condition, we
discovered that he had taken *laudanum* by the smell of his breath,
but we knew not the quantity; his sleep was so profound, that he
could not be awakened; his breathing was high and laborious,
attended with a profuse sweat, moaning, a florid countenance, and
frequent spasms of the muscles. Tho' he recovered of the opium, his
melancholia continued . . .

George Young, *A Treatise on Opium, Founded upon
Practical Observation* (1753)

=

Happiness pills

I let it pass. To be quixotic at my age would be merely comic.

'So you stick to happiness pills?'

'Yes, exactly. Happiness pills. Andaxin, aminodin and the rest of the muck – our doctors think the world of it.'

'And yet the long-term effects are anything but happy! Damage to memory, to eyesight, reduced sexual potency, apathy and indifference. Can they possibly think these are the things that make for happiness?'

'Why not? It suits our masters that we should have no memory – the less of it we have, the sooner we'll forget what they did to us. The blinder we are the less unattractive we'll find our surroundings. Apathy suits them down to the ground – apathetic people don't fly into rages, they don't protest, they don't hatch conspiracies. And to reduce sexual potency is not such a bad thing either – we are short of food and housing as it is. The whole object of our society is to train robots. In our hospitals, abuse and even blows are part of the treatment! I know hundreds of psychiatrists who are neither doctors nor psychiatrists.'

Valeriy Tarsis, Ward 7: An Autobiographical Novel (1965)

=

Dr Montagu Lomax blew the whistle on malpractices in British asylums early this century. He was particularly shocked by the gross overdosing of strong laxatives, for the sole end of pacifying patients.

As important as the abuse of strong narcotics and sedatives is the abuse of powerful purgatives, such as croton-oil. Chloral, bromide, and croton-oil are the three sheet-anchors of all asylum medicinal treatment, and the worst in its effects of all three is possibly croton-oil. Again I need not repeat what I have already said, that for the vast majority of asylum patients aperients of some sort are at times absolutely necessary. Not only does their confinement render this necessary, but their mental condition. Nearly all insane persons, whether in asylums or not, are habitually constipated. And nothing tends more to clear their heads, improve their tempers, and abort or cut short a mental crisis, than the proper regulation of their bowels. This is a commonplace in the treatment of all mental patients. Nevertheless, the aperients employed should be properly chosen, medically supervised, and their effects carefully noted. They should never be given indiscriminately by the attendants, and the use of 'stock bottles' and routine treatment by the Ward Charges is to be deprecated. Thus employed, aperients are of the greatest service, and many an insane patient owes his recovery in large measure to their careful and conscientious use. But when I have said that I have said everything. In most public asylums aperients are never carefully prescribed or conscientiously employed. In nine cases out of ten they are never personally prescribed by the Medical Officers, but are given at the whim of attendants and as a matter of routine. Ordinary aperients thus given do not do much harm. But it is very different with a powerful drug like croton-oil, which can only be prescribed by medical order. And I have a very grave indictment to bring against the medical usage of most public asylums in this matter. When I first took office I found the use of croton-oil almost universal. This powerful purgative was only dispensed in two-minim capsules (a very strong dose), and not a day passed without the attendants specifying a certain number of cases in each ward that required 'crotons'. In some cases the patients were constipated and really needed an aperient, in most they were simply troublesome or refractory, and this was the recognized method of 'taming' them or keeping them quiet. No doubt, in many cases, croton-oil is a valuable purgative, it acts quickly and thoroughly, and if the patient is young and strong does no harm when occasionally used. But the cases are not carefully selected, the drug is used much too frequently and indiscriminately, and, worse still, often as a 'punishment'. It is in the latter light that all patients regard it. All insane patients are at times exceedingly troublesome; attendants are often harried and at their wits' end to keep them in order; and to give them a 'croton' is such an easy and effectual way of quieting them that it is no wonder that attendants advocate it. They are only human after all. None the less this routine employment of croton-oil as a means of maintaining order is sheer cruelty, and to be sternly deprecated. It is probably responsible for more harm than all the other drugs used in asylums put together. I have little doubt in my own mind that it is the indirect cause of more cases of 'colitis' or 'asylum dysentery' than is ever suspected. The Board of Control are constantly referring in their Reports to the prevalence of 'colitis' in public asylums. I have often wondered whether it has ever occurred to them that among the unsuspected causes of this very serious and infectious disease the abuse of croton-oil may be one. 'Asylum dysentery', of course, is due to a specific organism, but it needs a favourable soil to thrive in, and what more favourable soil for its reception and transmission can be imagined than a bowel weakened and inflamed by constant and drastic purgation? The reader may be ignorant of the effects of croton-oil purgation, for the drug is seldom used in civil life. But I can speak from personal, as well as professional, experience. I once took a two-minim capsule myself, for I was anxious to judge of the effects of a drug in such constant use. The experience was extremely unpleasant, and confirmed me in my profound objection to the drug. The bowels, after a strong croton purge, may be opened ten or even twenty times. Often there is severe griping as well, and the patient may be violently sick. The pulse-rate is markedly lowered, feeble cases may become blue and cyanotic, and may even faint. I was told by one of the Head Attendants in this asylum of a patient being carried off one of the airing-courts into the hospital vomiting and violently purged at the same time, and in a state of complete collapse. This is unusual, no doubt, but it shows the strength and dangerousness of the drug. The more usual result is for the patient to be violently purged a dozen times or more, and his vitality lowered for twenty-four hours, after which, if young and strong, he recovers and is apparently not much the worse. But the reader may imagine its effects upon weak and elderly patients, and I have known attendants recommend such for this treatment, and callous and ignorant Medical Officers prescribe it. Even in young and vigorous patients its effects should be carefully watched, and it should never be repeated except at considerable intervals. For these effects are not simply those of purging, the bowels are not merely opened, they are scoured out, and, as the strips of mucous membrane found in the stools testify, they are not only scoured out but flayed. As I have stated, this is no guesswork on my part, but the result of personal experience. And I would suggest to all Medical

Officers of asylums, who are in the habit of prescribing croton-oil for their patients, that they should repeat my experiment, and learn for themselves what its results are like. 'A fellow feeling makes us wondrous kind', and probably, if they took my advice, they would think twice before prescribing this drug so indiscriminately. Acting upon this principle, I once told an ill-tempered attendant who was always getting into trouble with his refractory cases, and recommending them for 'croton treatment', that if I ordered a croton for anybody it would be for him, as needing it more than the patients did. I shall never forget the man's face. But it had its effect, and for a long time afterwards I had no patients recommended for 'crotons' from the ward.

Montagu Lomax, *The Experiences of an Asylum Doctor, with Suggestions for Asylum and Lunacy Law Reform* (1921)

=

A long tradition assumed that madness was produced or worsened by a build-up of bodily poisons. Remedial methods were needed for this madness in the bowels, and the practice of administering laxatives was one that died hard.

Each Thursday night the charge nurse stood at the foot of the stairs with a large enamel pail of liquorice which was used as a purgative for bowel movement. Nobody had heard of it before and each person was given his dosage as he went up to bed. You see they still had this belief, as it is today, this *obsession* with bowel movements. They had to clean out the wickedness from you. This went on for about five weeks then people started refusing to take it and it was stopped. Well, at Carstairs you don't refuse to do anything.

Jimmy Laing and Dermot McQuarrie (see page 223), *Fifty Years in the System* (1989)

=

Emetics were also a favourite method of relieving the stomach of poisons and providing a 'shock to the system'. Their value had been challenged as early as the eighteenth century by the pioneer English psychiatrist, William Battie.

Lastly with respect to Vomits, tho' it may seem almost haeretical to impeach their antimaniacal virtues; yet, when we reflect that the good effects which can be rationally proposed from such shocking operations are all nevertheless the consequences of a morbid convulsion, these active medicines are apparently contraindicated, whenever there is reason to suspect that the vessels of the brain or nervous integuments are so much clogged or strained as to endanger a rupture or further disunion, instead of a deliverance from their oppressive loads. The same objection equally holds good against such muscular irritation, whenever the vessels are contracted with excessive cold, or when their contents are rarefied by heat, as also in constitutions that are lax and feeble or naturally spasmodic, and in several other circumstances which need no particular description.

William Battie, *A Treatise on Madness* (1758)

===

Vomits vindicated

There is no remedy for the cure of insanity that has been more generally or strongly recommended than vomiting.

Evacuation, says the elder Monro, is the best cure, and vomiting preferable to all others; and if not carried beyond the patient's strength, nor crowded too fast upon him, his health of body will visibly improve so long as vomits are continued. The prodigious quantity of phlegm which accumulates, he observes, is not otherwise to be got rid of; and he adds, that purges do not operate so well till after vomits. Hallaran, however, advises that purging should precede vomiting.

The opinions of Monro are certainly strengthened by the practice of many, before and since his day.

I am disposed, however, to think that the action of emetics when beneficial in cases of insanity, is not conducive to that end simply as an evacuant, but rather from the well-known effect vomiting produces on the circulation.

During the nausea first induced, the circulation is in a condition resembling the cold stage of fever; and when vomiting commences, the whole vascular system is in commotion, and an equality in the circulation ensues, which removes those local determinations to the brain which disturb its functions, and occasion delirium and mental derangement.

Dr Bryan Robinson gave emetics daily for a whole year, and sometimes twice a day, with great success, in the cure of insanity; and Dr John Monro gave a gentleman sixty-one emetics in six months, and also for eighteen successive nights, by which the patient was recovered.

> George Man Burrows (see page 10), *Commentaries on the Causes, Forms, Symptoms and Treatment, Moral and Medical, of Insanity*
> (1828)

=

Copious blood-letting also had its advocates. The great French psychiatrist, Philippe Pinel (see page 12), begged to differ.

Of the continental authors, extracts will first be taken from those of France.

'The blood of maniacs is sometimes so lavishly spilled, and with so little discernment (discrimination,) as to *render it doubtful whether the patient or his physician has the best claim to the appellation of madman.* At the same time, I do not wish to be understood as altogether proscribing the use of the lancet in this formidable disorder; my intention is solely to deprecate its abuse.

Insanity consequent upon the suppression of periodical or habitual discharges of blood will doubtless frequently yield to an artificial evacuation of the same fluid, procured either by venesection or topically by leeches and cupping. A paroxysm of mania is sometimes preceded by symptoms of its approaches which cannot be mistaken; such as heightened complexion, wildness and prominence of the eyes, exuberant loquacity. In such cases the experience of hospitals authorizes the free use of the lancet. It is well established fact, that paroxysms of madness thus anticipated, are in many instances prevented by a copious bleeding. On the other hand, I feel it my duty *to abstain from this practice after the explosion of a paroxysm* or irregular periodical insanity . . .

It frequently happens that bleeding, practised as it is, without rule or bounds, is found to exasperate the complaint, and to cause periodical and curable mania to degenerate into dementia or idiotism. In melancholia, whether simple or complicated with hypochondriasis, bleeding is still less to be recommended.

Philippe Pinel, A Treatise on Insanity (1806)

=

A confident prophecy of the ready cure of insanity, thanks to new drugs, by 1992

Unfortunately we have yet to find medical means for helping lifelong anxiety states – except in certain rare, carefully selected cases where the new modified leucotomy does seem to work; and we can pick out at least some of these cases as suitable by testing for an abnormal forearm blood flow, of all things. Treatments for sexual perversion or for immature and aggressive psychopathic personalities still await discovery; but despite all our many treatment failures to balance some of the successes reported in this book, I feel safe in predicting that in the course of the next twenty-five years nearly all psychiatric patients will be readily cured with simple drugs mostly prescribed by general physicians. As this book will continue to show, many such drugs and other physical treatments are already in use; all that now remains is to train medical students how to use them and future ones selectively and well. This means, of course, that the teaching of skilled psychiatric treatment must figure far more prominently in the ordinary medical curriculum than it does at present. The accompanying research can also best be done in general or psychiatric hospitals where hundreds of new and old patients are always available on which new treatment combinations can be tried and assessed with the care always so necessary in this work.

William Sargant, The Unquiet Mind: The Autobiography of
a Physician in Psychological Medicine (1967)

=

The tranquillizer world

'Well, Miss Gordon, how are you today?' he asked, giving me what seemed to be a significant stare. I felt a familiar heaviness inside when he spoke those words. The man knew everything about me – my loves and my hates, my joys and hurts, my fantasies and fears. And still he called me Miss Gordon.

I looked at the carefully pressed suit, the white shirt, the characterless tie, the angular face, the sterile room. How old was he? I realized I had no idea. He could have been forty-three or fifty-one. He had revealed so little of himself in the past ten years that I knew nothing about him – not so much his private life, but what kind of person he was. That's the way it is supposed to be, I thought; cool, detached. He must remain so distant in order to help me, I told myself. But he seemed so detached that it was hard for me to believe that he was trying to stay distant. God, I thought, maybe he *is* that detached. I knew he didn't sense the urgency I felt. Years before when he was on vacation, I had visited a doctor he had recommended in case I needed to talk to someone. I had remarked to that doctor, You are so engaged, so immediate, I really like talking to you better than Dr Allen. You hear me. But then I had felt terrible, guilty. Dr Allen knew me better. I didn't want to start the whole thing all over again.

I was shocked to hear myself burst into a monologue of almost feverish intensity. 'What's new, Dr Allen, is that I can't walk the streets of the city I love alone. Unless I'm stoned on pills or with someone, I can't do it. I can't function without Valium. I'm growing too dependent on something other than myself to function. I'm growing too dependent on pills. Why? Tell me why!'

He interrupted, 'But I've told you many times, Miss Gordon, they are not addictive. They can't hurt you.' And he crossed his legs and sat back in his chair to hear my response.

Barbara Gordon (see page 76), *I'm Dancing as Fast as I Can* (1981)

=

The new panacea

In the mid-Sixties medicine was the answer to everything at Carstairs. Everybody was on one kind of a medicine or another. And the more you shouted, 'I shouldn't be on this,' the more they gave you. Fortunately I didn't go under as far as some did. I remember one nurse, an Irishman, who told me that I was getting enough to knock out a horse. I wasn't particularly trying to fight it, I just managed to get through it.

It was àt that time that I fell and sustained a severe cut on my chin. They started to worry about me. One of the sweetest things that ever happened in my life, apart from eventually getting out, was the day Dr Neville said that he was concerned about me and that he was going to reduce my dosage of medicine. 'Oh no you're not,' was my reply. 'I either stay on the lot or come off it altogether.' I came off the lot. The withdrawal symptoms were horrendous. There were nights when I was falling off cliffs, drowning or walking through fire. I used to take three nightshirts – there were no pyjamas – to change overnight, owing to the sweating. During the day I was very snappy. The least little thing would set me off. But at the end of the day I conquered it. That showed me that I had the strength to overcome – inner strength. To be in that condition when I was on my own, locked up from seven at night until seven in the morning, with no one to help me, I patted myself on the back at the end of it. No one else did.

Jimmy Laing and Dermot McQuarrie (see page 223),
Fifty Years in the System (1989)

=

Largactil the wonder drug

Largactil (thorazine) really deserves the name of 'wonder-drug' accorded to it by the popular press. Follow-up figures *two years after discharge* recently published show that of all the picked schizophrenics admitted to our ward at St Thomas's – and we were now only obliged to send less than one a year urgently on to mental hospitals – all but 16 per cent had sufficiently recovered after treatment to be still at home.

Another more recent follow-up has now confirmed the fact that in both groups 84 per cent of the patients treated were at home two years after discharge, and if they relapsed meanwhile, they had been quickly sent back home again after further treatment. Also, all these schizophrenic patients in both follow-up groups had initially only spent an average of *six weeks'* treatment in a general hospital unlocked psychiatric ward. In contrast, at the pre-war Maudsley, where we had to rely on psychotherapy, psychoanalysis or spontaneous recovery for a cure, no more than one-third of the most favourable of schizophrenic patients, chosen for their good prognosis in those days, were found, by a three-year follow-up, to have markedly improved. Two-thirds had become inmates of large mental hospitals or were invalids at home; many must be still in those hospitals. Our treatment failures in psychiatry can live on to an eternity of suffering and this is why skilled psychiatric treatment is so important. It has very few dead men, except suicides, who can tell no tales of the subsequent horror of their lives in hospital for years and years afterwards.

More and more patients are now being sent to St Thomas's from all over England for second opinions as to whether or not special treatments, such as modified leucotomy, are advisable. For we have consistently shown in recent years that there is hardly a single acute case of schizophrenia or of suicidal depression that, provided the previous personality is a good one, cannot be treated in a general hospital ward, and got better always provided that treatments are given early enough and intensively enough, and that *all* available methods are finally used, combined if necessary.

Unlike bromides, the new tranquillizers can be taken in massive doses without clouding the patient's consciousness, without any danger to health and are not addictive. This gives the doctor sufficient time to give whatever other effective treatment is needed for his patient's full recovery. Professor Mapother predicted that psychiatry would go ahead only when it was able to cure as many people under general hospital conditions as other medical specialties could. Some students who come to the St Thomas's psychiatric department for six weeks' whole-time work still imagine that they will mainly hear sex talked to patients on couches, and are amazed to watch what seemed the most severely disturbed patients being restored to relative normality often in less than a month by mainly physical means. In fact, we have outrun Mapother's prediction: our record of patients whose troubles we can relieve is now probably higher than those of such general hospital departments as the Cardiac Department, the Dermatological Department and certainly the Neurological Department. This is partly because so many of our cases are liable to spontaneous recovery, if encountered early enough, and assisted by modern physical treatments and the very minimum of psychotherapeutic help. Of course, no psychiatrist can yet make a silk purse out of a sow's ear, so if the patient's basic previous personality was unstable even before his illness started, it is very difficult indeed, and often quite impossible, to repair or remove this brain instability by any treatment. What we lack are any effective treatments as yet for patients who have suffered from anxiety states or schizophrenia since very early childhood; for adolescent and adult immature psychopaths; and for chronic sexual deviates. For mental defectives no cure has yet been envisaged: so many of these are Nature's prenatal errors.

> William Sargant, *The Unquiet Mind: The Autobiography of a Physician in Psychological Medicine* (1967)

=

The wonders of Largactil

In the first few years there was no improvement in the therapeutic treatment. There were new drugs though, which no doubt the system considered to be an improvement on the previous ones. Once again it was trial and error. The great new 'cure-all' was the tranquillizing drug Largactil. That kept them down! It also gave you what we called the Largactil kick. You would see a group of men sitting in a room and all of them would be kicking their feet up involuntarily. Another was Fentazin, which made you walk round all day with your head to the side. 'Don't worry, it'll wear off,' they would say. It didn't.

At that time, the staff ran the show, not the doctors. In many ways it's still the case now as the doctors have to rely on the staff but they have more influence over the nurses today. The doctors were there as figureheads. They would come in and ask, 'How's Jimmy Laing today?' 'Oh, I think he needs some more Largactil, doctor,' the nurse would say. 'It's been a great help to him.' What they meant was that it had given them an easy life with us sitting around in a docile way. The doctor would agree to an increase in the dosage without even checking the patient. Dr Neville did try eventually to get group meetings going in the top wards to discuss, with the patients, benefits which we should have and the treatment we were getting, but all this was very superficial. He never got down to the real problems.

> Jimmy Laing and Dermot McQuarrie (see page 223), *Fifty Years in the System* (1989)

=

Heavy-duty occupational therapy

We are informed by Dr Gregory, that a farmer, in the North of Scotland, a man of Herculean stature, acquired great fame in that district of the British empire, by his success in the cure of insanity. The great secret of his practice consisted in giving full employment to the remaining faculties of the lunatic. With that view, he compelled all his patients to work on his farm. He varied their occupations, divided their labour, and assigned to each, the post which he was best qualified to fill. Some were employed as beasts of draught or burden, and others as servants of various orders and provinces. Fear was the operative principle that gave motion and harmony to this rude system. Disobedience and revolt, whenever they appeared in any of its operations, were instantly and severely punished.

Philippe Pinel (see page 12), *A Treatise on Insanity* (1806)

=

The human touch spells effective psychological management.

Some years ago a man, about thirty-four years of age, of almost Herculean size and figure, was brought to the house. He had been afflicted several times before; and so constantly, during the present attack, had he been kept chained, that his clothes were contrived to be taken off and put on by means of strings, without removing his manacles. They were however taken off, when he entered the Retreat, and he was ushered into the apartment, where the superintendents were supping. He was calm; his attention appeared to be arrested by his new situation. He was desired to join in the repast, during which he behaved with tolerable propriety. After it was concluded, the superintendent conducted him to his apartment, and told him the circumstances on which his treatment would depend; that it was his anxious wish to make every inhabitant in the house, as comfortable as possible; and that he sincerely hoped the patient's conduct would render it unnecessary for him to have recourse to coercion. The maniac was sensible of the kindness of his treatment. He promised to restrain himself, and he so completely succeeded, that, during his stay, no coercive means were ever employed towards him. This case affords a striking example of the efficacy of mild treatment. The patient was frequently very vociferous, and threatened his attendants, who in their defence were very desirous of restraining him by the jacket. The superintendent on these occasions, went to his apartment; and though the first sight of him seemed rather to increase the patient's irritation, yet after sitting some time quietly beside him, the violent excitement subsided, and he would listen with attention to the persuasions and arguments of his friendly visitor. After such conversations, the patient was generally better for some days or a week; and in about four months he was discharged perfectly recovered.

> Samuel Tuke, *Description of the Retreat, an Institution near York for Insane Persons of the Society of Friends* (1813)

=

The therapeutic value of fear

The principle of fear, which is rarely decreased by insanity, is considered as of great importance in the management of the patients. But it is not allowed to be excited, beyond that degree which naturally arises from the necessary regulations of the family. Neither chains nor corporal punishments are tolerated, on any pretext, in this establishment. The patients, therefore, cannot be threatened with these severities; yet, in all houses established for the reception of the insane, the general comfort of the patients ought to be considered; and those who are violent, require to be separated from the more tranquil, and to be prevented, by some means, from offensive conduct, towards their fellow-sufferers. Hence, the patients are arranged into classes, as much as may be, according to the degree in which they approach to rational or orderly conduct.

> Samuel Tuke, *Description of the Retreat, an Institution near York for Insane Persons of the Society of Friends* (1813)

=

Shock treatments – from cold water up to electro-convulsive therapy – have always had a simple psychological appeal to doctors: they promise to jolt the mad out of their private universe. They might also, one could conclude, mask more sinister, punitive attitudes.

It was at first a fiery zeal for Religion or rather a mistaken notion of it too much encourag'd by a certain set of people that disordered his senses and at last made him furiously mad ... He had a few glimpses of Reason when I came first to him, suffered himself to be bled and took what was prescrib'd to him but was so outrageous that 4 men could scarce keep him in bed. ... his fury encreased and his strength augmented so much that double the number of men could not keep hold of him but they were forc'd to make use of ropes and fetter his hands and feet with Iron. Next day I attempted the Cold Bath and ordered him to be plung'd thus bound into an hogshead of water all of a sudden, and throwing 8 or 10 palefulls of water by the force of so many people upon his head all at once, but this had scarce any effect because I neglected to blindfold him, but though he was somewhat calm'd a little after. Upon this I ordered him to be kept dark in fetters and ropes untill next day that I contriv'd a byspout form a Current of water (for a Cornmill) which had 20 foot fall. I plac'd him directly below this in a Cart by whose wheels mov'd it to and from under the water as occasion requir'd. Thus I kept him under this vast pressure of water for 15 minutes until his spirits were fully dissipated and his strength quite exhausted, and it is to be observ'd that he who being blindfolded and led by 2 persons came whistling singing dancing and merrily leaping along about ½ mile to the fall of the mill was fain to be carried home in a Litter I had provided on purpose. Being laid in his bed the fetters put on and the room darkened he fell asleep immediately and slept 19 hours and awoke as sound in his judgement as ever ... Ever since he has continued so well that they put him shortly after to be an aprentice to a brewer where he has led a very sober life.

This unexpected and surprising success encouraged me to make further Improvements on the Practice by the fall of water and since coming to Boston my Endeavours have not been in vain. I was sometime in this place before I understood there was an Engine so fit for my purpose as it has since prov'd to be. It is built at about 1½ mile from hence in order to raise and convey water to serve the Town. There is a wind Engine like that which raises the New River water at London. At some distance is built a Square Tower 35 foot high. The water being forc'd to it by the Engine ascends perpendicularly in a large pipe at one corner and is discharg'd into a cistern on the top of the Tower which will contain about 80 Tun of water. At the opposite corner the water descends directly by another pipe from whence its convey'd to the Town. There are 3 habitable rooms in the bottome of the Tower, the middle of which has a Chimney. I have got a lateral pipe fix'd to the descending one by which I make the water to fall in any part of the middle room I think proper. I have a bathing Tub 6 foot long, I place a Chair in it in which the patient sits. The chair is so fix'd in the Tub and the patient so ty'd to the chair that none of them can move. The Lateral pipe has a cock by which I can stop or let down as much or as little water as I think proper. When the patients have got sufficiently of the fall I have a bed in readiness in the next room where they are laid and sutable care is taken of them as will appear by the following observations . . .

A married Woman . . . became mad, neglected every thing, would not own her husband nor any of the Family, kept her room, would converse with nobody but keept spitting continually, turning from any that turn'd from her and chiding any who put their hand in their sides, telling them she was not a whore . . . These Symptomes requir'd great preparation of the vitiated humors before she could undergo such an operation; frequent bleedings, violent Emeticks, strong purgatives and potent Sudorificks and Narcoticks were not wanting, nor did I fail to let her have sutable and specifik Alteratives, but none of them answered the design nor workt for a wish'd for advantage. In this course I continued her for 1 month, now it was time to come to salivation which I usually have recourse in such cases . . . she became insensibly to have the use of her Reason and after 5 weeks under this second course of physick she began to enquire more seriously into the state of domestic affairs at the servants who came to see her, spoke more kindly to them, shew'd a desire to be at home, quitted much of her former gestures speeches and behaviour, was obedient when reprov'd because of them and gave all signs of recovery except that of the dislike to her husband and yet she would sometimes allow her self to be called by his name which she could not endure before. Observing these alterations I train'd her into the Engine house putting her in hopes of getting home from thence that night but when she went into the Room in which she was to Lay I ordered her to be blindfolded. Her nurse and other women stript her. She was lifted up by force, plac'd in and fixt to the Chair in the bathing Tub. All this put her in an unexpressable terrour especially when the water was let down. I kept her under the fall 30 minutes, stopping the pipe now and then and enquiring whether she would take to her husband but she still obstinately deny'd till at last being much fatigu'd with the pressure of the water she promised she would do what I desired on which I desisted, let her go to bed, gave her a Sudorifick as usual. She slept well that night but was still obstinate. I repeated the bleeding and other preparatory doses. A week after I gave her another Tryal by adding a smaller pipe so that when the one let the water fall on top of her head the other squirted it in her face or any other part of her head neck or breast I thought proper. Being still very strong I gave her 60 minutes at this time when she still keept so obstinate that she would not promise to take to her husband till her spirits being allmost dissipated she promised to Love him as before. Upon this she was laid a bed as formerly but next day she was still obstinate. Evacuations being endeavoured for 2 or 3 dayes more I gave her the 3d Tryal of the fall and continued her 90 minutes under it, promised obedience as before but she was as sullen and obstinate as ever the next day. Being upon resentment why I should treat her so, after 2 or 3 dayes I threatned her with the fourth Tryal, took her out of bed, had her stript, blindfolded and ready to be put in the Chair, when being terrify'd with what she was to undergo she kneeld submissively that I would spare her and she would become a Loving obedient and dutifull Wife for ever thereafter. I granted her request provided she would go to bed with her husband that night, which she did with great chearfullness ... About 1 month after- wards I went to pay her a visit, saw every thing in good order ... Being thus successful I was willing to know the pondus of water and the pressure of her strength was able to undergo ... By ... Calculation it appear'd that in 90 minutes there was 15 Ton of water let fall upon her ...

In a word I have made such an Improvement of this Cataractick way of cold Bathing that as its the most effectual so its the safest method of curing mad people for I can calculate or measure the water as it falls to the weight of 1 oz. and sink the patients spirits even to a deliquium without the least hazard of their Lives which

dare not be ventured by plunging or immersion which they have
hitherto made use of in such cases.

Patrick Blair, *Some Observations on the Cure of Mad Persons* (1725)

=

The heroine of J. S. Lefanu's Victorian Gothic novel, wrongfully
assigned by her scheming mother to an asylum, is forced by the
sinister Dr Antomarchi to witness a horrific 'cure by water' admin-
istered to one of her unfortunate fellow inmates.

Maud was shocked to recognize in this melancholy transformation,
the pseudo-Duchess of Falconbury. Poor thing! her grace was in a
sorry plight, strapped down in the iron chair, and, spite of all her
writhings and tuggings, unable to alter her position by a hair's-
breadth, or even to jolt one leg of the heavy chair the smallest
fraction of an inch off the ground.

She was talking at a screaming pitch, without a moment's rest.
But not many moments were allowed her. The chair, with its
burden, was rolled quickly into the bath, and the door shut. The
shrilly uproar continued, but so muffled that Maud could now hear
without effort, distinctly, all the doctor said.

'You have taken an ordinary shower-bath, I dare say, Miss
Vernon, and found it quite long and heavy enough? This, from its
greater height, has a fall more than twice as heavy. Yours lasted
only a fraction of a minute, this will descend, without interruption,
for exactly thirty-five minutes. Yours, probably, contained between
two and three stone weight of water; this will discharge between
eight and nine tons. You observe, then, that it is very different from
anything you have experienced. Are you ready?'

'Yes, sir,' answers Mercy Creswell, who looks a little pale. 'How
long, please, sir?'

'Thirty-five minutes,' said the doctor.

'But please, sir,' said Creswell, growing paler, 'that is five minutes
longer than the longest.'

The doctor nodded.

'She never had it before, sir.'

'Better *once* effectually, than half-measures repeatedly,'
remarked the doctor to Miss Vernon, with his watch in his hand.

'Take the winch,' he said to Mercy Creswell. 'When the minute-hand reaches half-past (keep your eye on the clock) you turn it on; and when it reaches five minutes past, you turn it off. You are ready? stay – wait – look to the minute-hand – now.' ... The monotonous down-pour grew louder and louder, as minute after minute passed. The yells became sobs, and the sobs subsided. And still the rush of water thundered on.

'Oh! my God! She's drowning!' cried Maud.

'You perceive,' said the doctor, 'when treatment of this kind becomes necessary, we don't flinch.'

'It is cruel; it is horrible; it is frightful cruelty!' cried Maud.

'Cruelty! My dear Miss Vernon, have you no compassion for an honest keeper whom she would have killed, if she could?' replied the doctor, on whose stern lips she sees, or fancies, something like a smile, a cruel pride that is vindictive.

'But her voice is gone! For God's sake, let her out,' pleads Maud.

'She has got through twelve minutes,' said Antomarchi; 'she has twenty-three still to go through. She will be taken out when the time is accomplished, not sooner.'

'She can't live through it,' Maud almost screamed. 'It is quite impossible. Mercy Creswell, let her out. You are killing her, I command you, let her out. Must I stay here to see her *killed*?'

Mercy Creswell makes no sign. She does not glance towards her mistress. She stares darkly, straight before her, very pale, and looks in a sort of 'sulk'.

One of the younger women is crying, with her face toward the wall, and her apron to her eyes.

If one could get rid of the idea of extreme suffering, ay, and of danger, for it has turned out there *is* danger, this scene has its ludicrous side, and might be witnessed as merrily as, in old times, men stood by and laughed at the ducking of a witch.

The descent of the water thunders on like the roll of a hundred muffled drums; no sound of life, ever so suffering, ever so faint, ever so intermittent, is now heard from within.

Will that dragging minute-hand never make its appointed course and point to the second of her release?

At length the dreadful half-hour has passed; that seems like half a day; four minutes remain – the hand is measuring the last minute.

Antomarchi's eye is on the second-hand of his watch – the last second is touched. 'Stop,' cries his loud voice, and the winch is turned.

The noise of the falling water has ceased. The door is open, the room is as still as the dead-house of an hospital. A great silence has come. In a whisper Mercy directs the women, who obey in silence.

The straps are unbuckled, and the 'patient' is lifted out, and laid on another chair in the midst of the room. She looks lifeless. Her long dark hair clings about her shoulders. Her arms hang helplessly, and the water streams over her; over her hair, over her closed eyes, in rivulets; over her pretty face, that looks in sad sleep; over her lace and vanities; over her white slender hands that hang by her sides, and over her rings, making little rills and pools along the tiles.

The imperturbable doctor, his watch in his hand, approaches and takes her wrist, and tries her pulse.

Mercy Creswell gently drew back her hair, and Antomarchi with a handkerchief dried her face.

The others drew a cord that opened the window, and admitted the fresh air.

After a time there was a little sob; and after an interval another; and then a great sigh, and then again another, and another, long-drawn as that with which life departs.

There must be the agonies of drowning in all this; worse than common drowning, drowning by a slower suffocation, and with a consciousness horribly protracted.

And now there is the greater agony of recovery.

The doctor had returned to the side of the poor duchess, who was now breathing, or rather sighing, heavily, and staring vaguely before her.

His fingers were again on her pulse.

'Give her the white mixture,' he said to Mercy Creswell, glancing at a phial which stands beside a cup on a table a little way off.

'Oh, sir, please, doctor, not this time, sir,' faltered Mercy Creswell. 'She eat no breakfast, I hear, sir, and she'll be very bad for hours after she takes the mixture.'

'Shake it first; pour it into the cup; and administer it to the patient. Do your duty, Creswell.'

She shook the bottle, poured its contents into the cup, and, with a frightened face, did as she was ordered.

This peculiar use of the shower-bath in the treatment of the insane is no fiction. The Commissioners in Lunacy preferred an indictment against the medical superintendent of an English asylum, for having, as they alleged, caused the death of a pauper patient, by subjecting him to a continuous shower-bath of *thirty* minutes' duration, and for having administered to him, soon after his removal from the bath, and whilst in a state of vital depression, a dose of white-coloured mixture, alleged to have contained two grains of tartar emetic.

The physician in this case resembled Antomarchi in no respect, except in being a man of attainments and experience. He was perfectly conscientious. The grand jury threw out the bill. A commission of medical men of eminence reinstated him in his office. But his theory was this, that in the awfully depressing malady of madness, if a patient is 'violent', 'noisy', 'excited', and 'destructive', 'quiet' and 'docility' are legitimately to be induced by 'overpowering' him,. and 'prostrating the system', by a continuous shower-bath of monstrous duration, followed up on his release from the bath by a nauseating emetic, still further to exhaust an already prostrate system. That practice is no longer countenanced by the faculty.

Antomarchi now said: 'The patient may go, Creswell; you are to attend Miss Vernon as before. Miss Vernon, you can return to your rooms.'

He made her a bow, and in a moment more Maud and her femme de chambre had left the room.

'Miss Vernon, a spirited young lady,' mused Antomarchi. 'She has had her first lesson.'

Joseph Sheridan Lefanu, *The Rose and the Key* (1871)

=

One of the most controversial of the shock therapies has been ECT (or, as it is known in the United States, EST, electro-shock therapy). The Italian psychiatrist, Ugo Cerletti, describes his courage in persisting with experiments with it.

This subject was chosen for the first experiment of induced electric convulsions in man. Two large electrodes were applied to the frontoparietal regions, and I decided to start cautiously with a low-intensity current of 80 volts for 0.2 seconds. As soon as the current was introduced, the patient reacted with a jolt and his body muscles stiffened; then he fell back on the bed without loss of consciousness. He started to sing abruptly at the top of his voice, then he quieted down.

Naturally, we, who were conducting the experiment were under great emotional strain and felt that we had already taken quite a risk. Nevertheless, it was quite evident to all of us that we have been using a too low voltage. It was proposed that we should allow the patient to have some rest and repeat the experiment the next day. All at once, the patient, who evidently had been following our conversation, said clearly and solemnly, without his usual gibberish: 'Not another one! It's deadly!'

I confess that such explicit admonition under such circumstances, and so emphatic and commanding, coming from a person whose enigmatic jargon had until then been very difficult to understand, shook my determination to carry on with the experiment. But it was just this fear of yielding to a superstitious notion that caused me to make up my mind. The electrodes were applied again, and a 110-volt discharge was applied for 0.2 seconds.

Ugo Cerletti, 'Electroshock Therapy' (1956)

=

Finding out about the Shock Shop

'And, my friend, if you *continue* to demonstrate such hostile tendencies, such as telling people to go to hell, you get lined up to go to the Shock Shop, perhaps even on to greater things, an operation, an – '

'Damn it, Harding, I told you I'm not up on this talk.'

'The Shock Shop, Mr McMurphy, is jargon for the EST machine, the Electro Shock Therapy. A device that might be said to do the work of the sleeping pill, the electric chair, *and* the torture rack. It's a clever little procedure, simple, quick, nearly painless it happens so fast, but no one ever wants another one. Ever.'

'What's this thing do?'

'You are strapped to a table, shaped, ironically, like a cross, with a crown of electric sparks in place of thorns. You are touched on each side of the head with wires. Zap! Five cents' worth of electricity, through the brain and you are jointly administered therapy and a punishment for your hostile go-to-hell behaviour, on top of being put out of everyone's way for six hours to three days, depending on the individual. Even when you do regain consciousness you are in a state of disorientation for days. You are unable to think coherently. You can't recall things. Enough of these treatments and a man could turn out like Mr Ellis you see over there against the wall. A drooling, pants-wetting idiot at thirty-five. Or turn into a mindless organism that eats and eliminates and yells "fuck the wife," like Ruckly. Or look at Chief Broom clutching to his namesake there beside you.'

Harding points his cigarette at me, too late for me to back off. I make like I don't notice. Go on with my sweeping.

Ken Kesey, *One Flew Over the Cuckoo's Nest* (1962)

=

The French poet, theatre director and artist, Antonin Artaud, suffered a long history of mental disorder, probably worsened by drug habits. He underwent ECT.

ELECTROSHOCK [FRAGMENTS]

I died at Rodez under electroshock.

I died. Legally and medically died.

Electroshock-coma lasts fifteen minutes. A half an hour or more and then the patient breathes.

Now one hour after the shock I still had not awakened and had stopped breathing. Surprised at my abnormal rigidity, an attendant had gone to get the physician in charge, who after examining me with a stethoscope found no more signs of life in me.

I have personal memories of my death at that moment, but it is not on these that I base my testimony as to the fact.

I limit myself strictly to the details furnished me by Dr Jean Dequeker, a young intern at the Rodez asylum, who had them from the lips of Dr Ferdière himself.

And the latter asserts that he thought me dead that day, and that he had already sent for two asylum attendants to instruct them on the removal of my corpse to the morgue, since an hour and a half after shock I had still not come to myself.

And it seems that just at the moment that these attendants arrived to take my body out, it gave a slight shudder, after which I was suddenly wide awake.

Personally I have a different recollection of the affair.

But I kept this recollection to myself, and secret, until the day when Dr Jean Dequeker on the outside confirmed it to me.

And this recollection is that everything which Dr Jean Dequeker told me, I had seen, but not from this side of the world but from the other, and quite simply from the cell where the shock took place and under its ceiling; although for moments there was neither cell nor ceiling for me, but rather a rod above my body, floating in the air like a sort of fluidified balloon suspended between my body and the ceiling.

And I shall indeed never forget in any possible life the horrible passage of this sphincter of *revulsion* and asphyxia, through which the criminal mob of beings forces the patient in extremis before letting go of him. At the bedside of a dying man there are more than 10,000 beings, and I took note of this at that moment.

There is a conscious unanimity among all these beings, who are unwilling to let the dead man come back to life before he has paid them by giving up his corpse totally and absolutely; for existence will not give even his inert body back to him, in fact especially his body.

And what do you expect a dead man to do with his body in the grave?

Jack Hirschman (ed.), *Artaud Anthology* (1965)

＝

Twentieth-century patients have been more vocal about the horrors of involuntary ECT than any other issue.

So much care is taken in the home to avoid the slightest electric shock from appliances in everyday use, and yet much larger doses are applied direct to people in the cause of health, systematically once, or sometimes twice, a week.

In all, I had sixteen of these doses of electrical treatment, every one under protest. But, had they given me sixty, the memory of the ninth will always remain. For that was the one and only time I said to myself as I came round 'that is what it must feel like to be dead'. I am fairly certain that my heart had ceased to beat for at least a few seconds. I cannot describe the feeling. There are no words – the nearest which come to mind are those from the scriptures of 'a peace which passeth all understanding'. When I tried to stand, for several seconds I could not, and only succeeded in staggering to the next bed and falling on my knees in a passion of tears. Despite all my pleadings, the treatments were continued.

I hated every moment of them. The waking in the morning with the consciousness that I would be one of those on the doctor's list for treatment that day. The sister in charge of the ward read the names in a stentorian voice when the breakfast trolley arrived. Those due for treatment were allowed only one cup of tea and a piece of bread and butter. Then came the wait for treatments, which were carried out reasonably early in the morning, but for which the waiting nevertheless seemed long. A kind of sleeping tablet was given to each patient about half an hour before, and then, stripped of such metal things as hair-grips or rings and teeth, we were led to the waiting room which adjoined the theatre to await our turn to be 'shocked'.

To my dying day I will remember these waits, the black marble lino on the floor, the deathly quiet of the room, and the red, serpent-eye of the light which showed the current was 'on' and the job in progress in the adjoining room. Occasionally one heard the muffled shout of the 'victim' as she went 'out'. Most endured these treatments stoically; I was always very quiet at the actual time. My protesting had been done vocally beforehand, or in a written letter to the doctor, all of which were ignored. Sometimes one saw the shock treatment patients returning on stretchers, or being put into wheelchairs to be taken back to the ward, their heads lolling, their eyes staring unseeingly. Back in the ward we were allowed to sleep, but were always roused for luncheon, which, on these days, usually consisted of rather dry fish, bullet peas and potatoes. We then spent the rest of the day in a dazed condition in chairs in the day room. I always wondered why we were not allowed to continue sleeping and would have much preferred to do so, but no doubt there was some good reason for rousing the patients.

D. McI. Johnson and Norman Dodds (eds), *The Plea for the Silent*
(1957)

=

And as Doctor Gordon led me into a bare room at the back of the house, I saw that the windows in that part were indeed barred, and that the room door and the closet door and the drawers of the bureau and everything that opened and shut was fitted with a keyhole so it could be locked up.

I lay down on the bed.

The wall-eyed nurse came back. She unclasped my watch and dropped it in her pocket. Then she started tweaking the hairpins from my hair.

Doctor Gordon was unlocking the closet. He dragged out a table on wheels with a machine on it and rolled it behind the head of the bed. The nurse started swabbing my temples with a smelly grease.

As she leaned over to reach the side of my head nearest the wall, her fat breast muffled my face like a cloud or a pillow. A vague, medicinal stench emanated from her flesh.

'Don't worry,' the nurse grinned down at me. 'Their first time everybody's scared to death.'

I tried to smile, but my skin had gone stiff, like parchment.

Doctor Gordon was fitting two metal plates on either side of my head. He buckled them into place with a strap that dented my forehead, and gave me a wire to bite.

I shut my eyes.

There was a brief silence, like an indrawn breath.

Then something bent down and took hold of me and shook me like the end of the world. Whee-ee-ee-ee-ee, it shrilled, through an air crackling with blue light, and with each flash a great jolt drubbed me till I thought my bones would break and the sap fly out of me like a split plant.

I wondered what terrible thing it was that I had done.

Sylvia Plath, *The Bell Jar* (1963)

=

It is nearly my turn. I walk down to the treatment room door to wait, for so many treatments have to be performed that the doctor becomes impatient at any delay. Production, as it were, is speeded up (like laundry economics – one set of clothes on, one set clean, one in the wash) if there is a patient waiting at the door, one on the treatment table, and another being given a final 'rub-up' ready to take her place at the door.

Suddenly the inevitable cry or scream sounds from behind the closed doors which after a few minutes swing open and Molly or Goldie or Mrs Gregg, convulsed and snorting, is wheeled out. I close my eyes tight as the bed passes me, yet I cannot escape seeing it, or the other beds where people are lying, perhaps heavily asleep, or whimperingly awake, their faces flushed, their eyes bloodshot. I can hear someone moaning and weeping; it is someone who has woken up in the wrong time and place, for I know that the treatment snatches these things from you, leaves you alone and blind in a nothingness of being and you try to fumble your way like a newborn animal to the flowing of first comforts; then you wake, small and frightened, and the tears keep falling in a grief that you cannot name.

Beside me is the bed, sheets turned back pillow arranged where I will lie after treatment. They will lift me into it and I shall not know. I look at the bed as if I must establish contact with it. Few people have advance glimpses of their coffin; if they did they might be tempted to charm it into preserving in the satin lining a few trinkets of their identity. In my mind, I slip under the pillow of my treatment bed a docket of time and place so that when and if I ever wake I shall not be wholly confused in a panic of scrabbling through the darkness of not knowing and of being nothing. I go into the room then. How brave I am! Everybody remarks on my bravery! I climb on to the treatment table. I try to breathe deeply and evenly as I have heard it is wise in moments of fear. I try not to mind when the matron whispers to one of the nurses, in a hoarse voice like an assassin, 'Have you got the gag?'

And over and over inside myself I am saying a poem which I learned at school when I was eight. I say the poem, as I wear the gray woolen socks, to ward off Death. They are not relevant lines because very often the law of extremity demands an attention to irrelevancies; the dying man wonders what they will think when they cut his toenails; the man in grief counts the cups in a flower. I see the face of Miss Swap who taught us the poem. I see the mole on the side of her nose, its two mounds like a miniature cottage loaf and the sprout of ginger hair growing out the top. I see myself standing in the class-room reciting and feeling the worn varnished desk top jutting against my body against my bellybutton that has specks of grit in it when I put my finger in; I see from the corner of my left eye my neighbor's pencil case which I coveted because it was a triple decker with a rose design on the lid and a wonderful dent thumb-size for sliding the lid along the groove.

'Moonlit Apples,' I say. 'By John Drinkwater.'

> At the top of the house the apples are laid in rows
> And the skylight lets the moonlight in and those
> Apples are deep-sea apples of green.

I get no further than three lines. The doctor busily attending the knobs and switches of the machine which he respects because it is his ally in the struggle against overwork and the difficulties depressions obsessions manias of a thousand women, has time to smile a harassed Good Morning before he gives the signal to Matron Glass.

'Close your eyes,' Matron says.

But I keep them open, observing the secretive signal and engulfed with helplessness while the matron and four nurses and Pavlova press upon my shoulders and my knees and I feel myself dropping as if a trap door had opened into darkness. I imagine as I fall my eyes turning inward to face and confound each other with a separate truth which they prove without my help. Then I rise disembodied from the dark to grasp and attach myself like a homeless parasite to the shape of my identity and its position in space and time. At first I cannot find my way, I cannot find myself where I left myself, someone has removed all trace of me. I am crying.

A cup of sweet tea is being poured down my throat. I grasp the nurse's arm.

'Have I had it? Have I had it?'

'You have had treatment,' she answers. 'Now go to sleep. You are awake too early.'

But I am wide awake and the anxiety begins again to accumulate.

Will I be for treatment tomorrow? . . .

Janet Frame, *Faces in the Water* (1961)

Her name was called and she left the room.

'Ladies first,' I thought.

A minute later I heard my name and jumped up to obey the voice. It must be that the treatment is over very quickly, I thought.

In the neighbouring room was a kind of table, like an operating table. Obediently I climbed on when someone told me to. A smiling lady nurse took off my shoes and placed gauze in my mouth. Everyone was so cheerful. They must enjoy their work.

Something was being screwed or clamped against my temples. There was a kind of pillow under the small of my back. My hands were folded on top of my stomach. I stared at the ceiling and wondered what was going to happen when . . .

I was upstairs sitting in the dayroom. My shoes were back on. The treatment was over some time ago. The doctor had turned on the electricity, which knocked me out so fast and so completely that I could not remember anything until after I had come to and walked back upstairs.

'We'll knock those ideas out of your head,' the doctor announced cheerfully.

You think so, doctor? Well, I don't want them to be knocked out, because they are true ideas. Why, I'll bet you couldn't knock them out with a dozen shock treatments!

Which turned out to be true, too. It was true after a dozen treatments and many more. It is still true.

William L. Moore, *The Mind in Chains: The Autobiography*
of a Schizophrenic (1955)

=

Next day, under the guise and excuse of medical investigations, I was electrocuted. At all events, I felt pretty sure that was the purpose of the exercise when I was put in the chair in the secret room and the bands strapped round my head. No ordinary electro-encephelograph could require such an enormous machine; besides, I recognized it. It was part of the science-fiction equipment of a novel I had once written, and the girl who was working it was me – though a very different version of me from the one sitting in the chair in the same space as the condemned person whose execution I was now voluntarily sharing. Perhaps because I made no fuss, I was only examined and not electrocuted after all. It took longer than I expected. After the current had been turned on, different associations of ideas were touched off in series in my mind, and geometrical patterns flashed before my eyes, some of them in brilliant colour. At last the machine was switched off, I was released and taken back to the ward. I accepted drugs from the day staff quite trustfully, but a night nurse that evening was unnecessarily rough; I promptly distrusted her and the drugs she brought, and a spirited fight ensued in which I was eventually worsted. I fell asleep and dreamed that the night nurses had become tigers and were leaping over and over the beds all down the ward.

Next day I had a heart operation. This was performed by spiritual surgeons in the unseen ... They removed my heart and divided it in two to make one for someone else, and then returned it to me. Afterwards my heart was linked to the other one so that they could beat in unison, with mine acting as pacemaker. It was important that I should not become over-anxious, or the result would show in my pulse rate and be transmitted to the other. I kept as calm as I could. When it was all over, Linda arrived at my bedside and pinned onto my jacket a tiny pair of twin hearts made out of felt. I was very proud of my 'decoration.'

Morag Coate, *Beyond all Reason* (1964)

=

In the 1960s and 1970s Doris Lessing was associated with R. D. Laing's circle, and some of his associates are supposed to appear in her novels.

I'm going on. Or you can agree to have shock therapy. I've already gone into the pros and cons pretty thoroughly. It has to be shock, because you haven't responded to the alternative drugs.

Tell me.

The essence of it in my opinion is that I don't think it would do you any harm, and it may have the effect of making you remember.

Remember what, that's the point!

Or it may leave you exactly as you are now.

When you give people electric shock treatment you don't know, not really, what it does.

No. But we do know there are thousands, probably millions by now, of people who would be too depressed to go on living without it.

I'm not depressed, Doctor. I am not.

Well, well.

And if you were in my place, you'd have the electric shock treatment?

Yes, I would. You'll probably come to that in the end. That's my view. It is also the view of Doctor X. You have had the drugs we use instead of shock. None has worked with you. Nothing has worked. You had lost your memory when you came in, and you still have no memory. So what shall we do?

But I have two weeks more here?

Yes.

Of course I might remember in that time.

Yes, you might. Would you like to try writing things down again? A tape recorder?

> Doris Lessing, *Briefing for a Descent into Hell* (1971)

=

Some patients, however, comment upon the benefits of ECT.

During my second illness I had a longer course of ECT, and no other treatment. This dramatically cured my symptoms and left me with excellent intellectual grip; it spared me the miseries of the recovery stage of the other illnesses. The disadvantage was that it gave me a sense of false security and led me to believe that spiritual disturbances were not relevant. It is more likely that during the preceding months, after I had broken off my attempt at a relationship with

God, the impulse was driven deeply underground and erupted finally
from an unconscious level where I had no control over it.

Morag Coate, *Beyond All Reason* (1964)

=

*Desperate disorders need desperate remedies, it is often said, and to
an outsider it easily seems that treatments for mental illness have a
bizarre quality, marked by a 'try anything' philosophy. A couple of
generations ago, it was hoped that putting patients into deep coma
would somehow shake them free of their confusions.*

Already before World War II, schizophrenia, especially in the early
stages of the disease, was being successfully treated by insulin shock
therapy. This method is to give a patient large doses of insulin to
lower the amount of sugar in his blood, thus producing a state of
mental confusion and excitement. For an hour or more, perhaps, he
lies in a semi-conscious state, twitching, jerking, and perhaps talking
incoherently, until a deep coma supervenes. When using this treatment for the relief of schizophrenia, the psychiatrist may keep the
patient in coma for half an hour. Sugar is then administered by
means of a stomach-tube or intravenous injection, and he quickly
wakes up. Symptoms may disperse after a course of such treatments
given daily and with little additional psychotherapy. So here is one
more treatment involving an initial stage of often uncontrolled brain
excitement, and ending in temporary brain inhibition and stupor.

Both electric shock and insulin shock treatments tend to disperse
recent abnormal behaviour patterns, though seldom proving
efficacious in cases where these are too long established. The useful
fields of these various treatments are now becoming more clearly
differentiated; for instance, it is generally recognized that severe
cases of early schizophrenia may respond best to the more complicated insulin therapy, combined sometimes with electric shock
treatment, whereas states of mental depression perhaps brought
about by prolonged petty anxiety, can often be cured by electric
shock alone; and war neuroses, again, with depressive symptoms
caused by more violent mental stress, may respond to much less
severe abreactions under drugs.

William Sargent, *Battle for the Mind: A Physiology of
Conversion and Brain-Washing* (1957)

Deep insulin treatment is given after fasting for about fourteen hours. Rubber-sided beds are used, as a protection to the patient during the convulsions produced by the drug.

A young lady seemed to be in charge, and I was soon to witness the results of one of her experiments on my co-patient. He was, I heard, being given a daily dose of 400 units. I was opposite in an unscreened bed. There were screams and groans from the adjoining room, and I later found that several female patients were being treated there.

My friend's dose was heavily increased one day (I was told to 600 units). This resulted in his relapsing into a stage beyond coma, where the usual revival injection into the vein had no effect. There was a terrific scramble when his condition was noted, and oxygen revival had to be organized. His mouth was badly damaged in the efforts to save him, and his wife was told, on enquiry, that this was 'only the result of the treatment'.

He was due to go home for Christmas in a few days, but, whilst still semi-conscious, he was 'persuaded' that he would prefer to stay in the hospital. I helped him back to his quarters that evening, and managed to explain what he was supposed to have agreed to. He wrote to his wife, and I saw her when she visited. He did go home that Christmas.

A friend – I can say no more – told me of a method to counter the increasing dosage of insulin, but this involved the eating of chocolate at a certain time, and, rationing being still in force, I knew I could not do this indefinitely. The Christmas break saved me from the worst effects – 90 units being my maximum to date; the strain was telling.

D. McI. Johnson and Norman Dodds (eds), *The Plea for the Silent*
(1957)

=

Value of insulin coma therapy

When, in November 1938, we were finally permitted to use deep insulin-coma at the Maudsley, some patients who for perhaps six to nine months had proved wholly irresponsive to other treatments made rapid recoveries. I have come to distrust statistical reports on psychiatric treatment techniques by any writer for whose judgment and lack of bias I cannot personally vouch, and always make a point of treating patients myself and watching the actual results obtained at the bedside before I can decide on the efficacy of any method suggested. It remains to add that even a generation later, insulin-coma treatment still remains an intensely controversial subject. All sorts of bizarre reasons and red herrings were put forward to explain a patient's recovery. These reasons have included the social effects of the treatment, the subconscious death-wish, the mothering of the patient during and after the induced coma. One unit went so far as to recommend nurses with big breasts so that when the patient came out of his death-like coma, he or she was greeted on rebirth with this invitingly maternal sight. Fortunately better treatments of schizo-phrenia than insulin-coma have now been found and the arguments for and against it have in the main a historical rather than practical value. But it seemed to me at the bedside the most helpful treatment we had, especially when combined with electroshock; that is before the discovery of largactil (thorazine).

William Sargant, *The Unquiet Mind: The Autobiography of a Physician in Psychological Medicine* (1967)

=

MONDAY, 23 NOVEMBER

Treatment 6
About six minutes and two or three treatments later (i.e., after two or three other patients have had treatment):

Still 8 cc's, they said. They said some leaked out of the vein last time. It felt more – but I didn't go out. I came out and played half a hand of cards. But it was hard to be interested.

PS A few minutes later I sat down between two shock patients and helped them stare into space.

This treatment almost got me. There was no pain but I moved in the bed, which probably was the beginning of a seizure, and I felt as though I was relieving myself, or something.

Afterwards my jaw felt stiff. My head felt as if the nerves had been tightened or strengthened. It was like post-shock treatment last spring. And during the week end it felt that way, too, though then I began to wonder: what if my brain did go?

WEDNESDAY, 25 NOVEMBER

About 7 hours after treatment:

Dr List spoke to me before the treatment. He asked about my book. I told him he could see the letters from the literary agent if he wanted to.

'No, that isn't necessary. I believe you.'

I happened to mention that the agent recommended I sell my book as a fiction story.

'You see,' he exclaimed. 'As a fiction story it would be a best seller.'

But as a true story it would not, he implied.

So you don't believe me after all, I thought.

'How much this time?' I asked while waiting for the injection.

No one answered.

The gauze went into my mouth. An attendant held his hand to my jaw just in case.

The next thing I remember I was tossing on the bed.

'What day is it?'

'You know.'

'No, I don't.'

I knew it was treatment day but that was all.

'It's Wednesday.'

'Did I have a seizure?'

'Yes.'

'How long have I been out?'

'Forty-five minutes.'

I came out to the dayroom, tried to lie down on a bench. Then they let me go back to the bedroom. I skipped the noon meal and slept off and on the whole day. After I had vomited on the floor, they brought a bucket with water in it for me to use. I used it a few times, though little came out each time. My lip had been bitten, though not enough to be sore. I had a headache. And I kept feeling stuffy hot or chilly cold.

PS Later I threw up my supper.

NOTE: I don't know of anyone else so hard to knock out and who got so sick afterward. An attendant said the reason it took so long to knock me out only meant that my system was more tolerant of that particular drug. But when it got me, it really took hard.

MONDAY, 30 NOVEMBER

Treatment 8:
  Knocked cold again. Headache. Ate next to nothing. Slept all day.

WEDNESDAY, 2 DECEMBER

Treatment 9:
  Vomited several times.
  Recovered better, went bowling with a group of other patients.

FRIDAY, 4 DECEMBER

Treatment 10:
  Still nine cc's, but building resistance and wasn't quite knocked out, though eyelids fluttered and I was on the edge. Dr Schultz tapped my stomach for reaction.

MONDAY, 7 DECEMBER

Treatment 11:
  Nine and a half cc's.
  Knocked out.

FRIDAY, 11 DECEMBER

Treatment 12:
  Nine and a half cc's.
  Not quite knocked out.

MONDAY, 14 DECEMBER

Treatment 13:
  Knocked out and sick all day, though they said the amount given me wasn't increased.
  (PS Larger opening in needle so I got the shot faster.)

WEDNESDAY, 16 DECEMBER

Treatment 14:
  Not quite knocked out. Needle in smoking room. Wheeled me out to bedroom this time.

FRIDAY, 18 DECEMBER

Treatment 15
About five minutes after:
  Dr List.
  Hurt my arm but didn't quite knock me out.
                    William L. Moore, *The Mind in Chains: The Autobiography*
                                        of a Schizophrenic (1955)

=

A man's best therapist

We have institutes of mental hygiene in these days. I trust they have
included in their syllabus 'The Dog', for it is really a mental antiseptic and tonic of incalculable value. Many a man has been saved
from madness by a Dandy Dinmont, or a fox terrier. The solitary
student perhaps more than anyone else profits by it. It becomes his
enlivening and beloved companion. It pulls him down from the
heights of speculation, reminds him that he must not neglect his
meals, induces him to take exercise. It betrays him into frivolous
conversation and even frolics, and keeps alive his altruistic sentiments, for if it is threatened with distemper, he is more solicitous
about it than about the fate of his next book.
    Sir James Crichton-Browne, *The Doctor's Second Thoughts* (1931)

13

What Should Be Done with the Asylums?

In the literature of insanity, no issue has so concentrated the mind as the asylum, its potential, its progress, its problems. After all, from the eighteenth to the middle of the present century, the madhouse, asylum or psychiatric hospital – call it what you will – was the model for treating the disturbed, the normative institution, by far the greatest source of expenditure in the treatment of the insane; it was the bricks-and-mortar of psychiatry, its great white hope. By 1950, psychiatric institutions were housing some 150,000 patients in the United Kingdom, and up to half a million in the United States.

Yet official enthusiasm had long since evaporated. As early as mid-Victorian times, when the asylum-building programme was still in its infancy, even scions of the psychiatric profession were themselves prepared to admit that a gigantic asylum was a gigantic evil. A full century before the modern anti-psychiatry movement, the Victorians had seen and began to criticize the untoward effects of institutionalization. Many psychiatric disorders were being recognized as the products of that very institution which psychiatry was claiming would be their cure.

Some of the most vocal and effective critics of the asylum were its patients. In the eighteenth century, there were two standard complaints. On the one hand, illegal or improper confinement – the forcible locking up of the sane, usually at family instigation, for underhand purposes, such as to overturn a will, or get rid of an ugly wife. On the other, gross brutality.

Such complaints led to reforms, legal and administrative, but with the increased size and scale of public asylums in the nineteenth century – in the United Kingdom they could run to over 3,000 beds, in the United States to up to 10,000 – the new criticism was that they had, in effect, been transformed into mere warehouses, capable of doing nothing more ambitious for their patients than feeding, clothing and sheltering them, and (for the taxpayer) than undertaking these custodial functions as cheeseparingly as possible. The York Retreat, one of the premier asylums in Britain, set up by Quakers in the late eighteenth century, was often offered as a successful proof that 'small was effective'. Beginning with only about thirty patients, it was able to maintain good staff–patient ratios.

Patients – surely the best judges, unless their mental conditions automatically invalidate their criticisms – have complained throughout the entire history of mental hospitals that institutions themselves bred attitudes and behaviours amongst staff that robbed patients of their essential humanity, and thereby thwarted any possible constructive psychiatric achievement. Deny patients their individuality, and how can you expect (demanded John Perceval) that they will regain it?

Officially, the insane were incapable of proper responses: no sense, no feeling. Perceval countered that it was the asylum staff who were evidently utterly incapable of putting themselves into their patients' shoes, and of understanding their needs. His allegation has found many echoes over the years.

For decades there was a paralysis in policy. No one grasped the nettle of the great 'bins'. Since the middle of this century, the advent of new psychotropic drugs, such as Largactil, the rise of the anti-psychiatry movement, and the allure of economies, have together triggered a new policy of replacing the traditional asylum with acute psychiatric units on the one hand, and 'community care' on the other. Until now, 'community care' has been something of a mirage. Will the new policies in their turn produce a new literature of protest?

The perfect asylum

In place of multiplying individual examples of excellence, let me conclude by describing the aspect of an asylum as it ought to be. Conceive a spacious building resembling the palace of a peer, airy, and elevated, and elegant, surrounded by extensive and swelling grounds and gardens. The interior is fitted up with galleries, and workshops, and music-rooms. The sun and the air are allowed to enter at every window, the view of the shrubberies and fields, and groups of labourers, is unobstructed by shutters or bars; all is clean, quiet, and attractive. The inmates all seem to be actuated by the common impulse of enjoyment, all are busy, and delighted by being so. The house and all around appears a hive of industry. When you pass the lodge, it is as if you had entered the precincts of some vast emporium of manufacture; labour is divided, so that it may be easy and well performed, and so apportioned, that it may suit the tastes and powers of each labourer. You meet the gardener, the common agriculturist, the mower, the weeder, all intent on their several occupations, and loud in their merriment. The flowers are tended, and trained, and watered by one, the humbler task of preparing the vegetables for table, is committed to another. Some of the inhabitants act as domestic servants, some as artizans, some rise to the rank of overseers. The bakehouse, the laundry, the kitchen, are all well supplied with indefatigable workers. In one part of the edifice are companies of straw-plaiters, basket-makers, knitters, spinners, among the women; in another, weavers, tailors, saddlers, and shoemakers, among the men. For those who are ignorant of these gentle crafts, but are strong and steady, there are loads to carry, water to draw, wood to cut, and for those who are both ignorant and weakly, there is oakum to tease and yarn to wind. The curious thing is, that all are anxious to be engaged, toil incessantly, and in general without any other recompense than being kept from disagreeable thoughts and the pains of illness. They literally work in order to please themselves, and having once experienced the possibility of doing this, and of earning peace, self-applause, and the approbation of all around, sound sleep, and it may be some small remuneration, a difficulty is found in restraining their eagerness, and moderating their exertions. There is in this community no compulsion, no chains, no whips, no corporal chastisement, simply because these are proved to be less effectual means of carrying any point than persuasion, emulation, and the desire of obtaining gratification. But there are gradations of employment. You may visit rooms where there are ladies reading, or at the harp or piano, or flowering muslin, or engaged in some of those thousand ornamental productions in which female taste and ingenuity are displayed. You will encounter them going to church or to market, or returning from walking, riding, and driving in the country. You will see them ministering at the bedside of some sick companion. Another wing contains those gentlemen who can engage in intellectual pursuits, or in the amusements and accomplishments of the station to which they belong. The billiard-room will, in all probability, present an animated scene. Adjoining apartments are used as news-rooms, the politicians will be there. You will pass those who are fond of reading, drawing, music, scattered through handsome suits of rooms, furnished chastely, but beautifully, and looking down upon such fair and fertile scenes as harmonize with the tranquillity which reigns within, and tend to conjure up images of beauty and serenity in the mind which are akin to happiness. But these persons have pursuits, their time is not wholly occupied in the agreeable trifling of conning a debate, or gaining so many points. One acts as an amanuensis, another is engaged in landscape painting, a third devolves to himself a course of historical reading, and submits to examination on the subject of his studies, a fourth seeks consolation from binding the books which he does not read. In short, all are so busy as to overlook, or all are so contented as to forget their misery.

Such is a faithful picture of what may be seen in many institutions, and of what might be seen in all, were asylums conducted as they ought to be.

W. A. F. Browne, *What Asylums Were, Are, And Ought to Be* (1837)

=

Before 1774, there was no legislation in England governing the conditions under which patients might be institutionalized. The result? It was widely alleged, by reformers such as Daniel Defoe, that sane people were despatched to madhouses by scheming relatives.

This leads me to exclaim against the vile Practice now so much in vogue among the better Sort, as they are called, but the worst sort in fact, namely, the sending their Wives to Mad-Houses at every Whim or Dislike, that they may be more secure and undisturb'd in their Debaucheries: Which wicked Custom is got to such a Head, that the number of private Mad-Houses in and about London, are considerably increased within these few Years. This is the height of Barbarity and Injustice in a Christian Country, it is clandestine Inquisition, nay worse. How many Ladies and Gentlewomen are hurried away to these Houses, which ought to be suppress'd, or at least subject to daily Examination, as hereafter shall be proposed? How many, I say, of Beauty, Vertue, and Fortune, are suddenly torn from their dear innocent Babes, from the Arms of an unworthy Man, who they love (perhaps too well) and who in Return for that Love, nay probably an ample Fortune, and a lovely Off-spring besides; grows weary of the pure Streams of chaste Love, and thirsting after the Puddles of lawless Lust, buries his vertuous Wife alive, that he may have the greater Freedom with his Mistresses?

If they are not mad when they go into these cursed Houses, they are soon made so by the barbarous Usage they there suffer, and any Woman of Spirit who has the least Love for her Husband, or Concern for her Family, cannot sit down tamely under a Confinement and Separation the most unaccountable and unreasonable. Is it not enough to make any one mad to be suddenly clap'd up, stripp'd, whipp'd, ill fed, and worse us'd? To have no Reason assign'd for such Treatment, no Crime alledg'd, or Accusers to confront? And what is worse, no Soul to appeal to but merciless Creatures, who answer but in Laughter, Surliness, Contradiction, and too often Stripes? All conveniences for Writing are denied, no Messenger to be had to carry a Letter to any Relation or Friend; and if this tyrannical Inquisition, join'd with the reasonable Reflections, a Woman of any common Understanding must necessarily make, be not sufficient to drive any Soul stark staring mad, though before they were never so much in their right Senses, I have no more to say . . .

How many are yet to be sacrificed, unless a speedy Stop be put to this most accursed Practice I tremble to think; our Legislature cannot take this Cause too soon in hand: This surely cannot be below their Notice, and 'twill be an easy matter at once to suppress all these pretended Mad-Houses. Indulge, gentle Reader, for once the doting of an old Man, and give him leave to lay down his little System without arraigning him of Arrogance or Ambition to be a Law-giver. In my humble Opinion all private Mad-Houses should be suppress'd at once, and it should be no less than Felony to confine any Person under pretence of Madness without due Authority. For the cure of those who are really Lunatick, licens'd Mad-Houses should be constituted in convenient Parts of the Town, which Houses should be subject to proper Visitation and Inspection, nor should any Person be sent to a Mad-House without due Reason, Inquiry and Authority.

Daniel Defoe, *Augusta Triumphans* (1728)

=

John Conolly was still drawing attention to these dangers over a century later. Husbands were at risk too.

With what improper motives medical men are sometimes consulted, I have myself had some opportunities of knowing. Very few months have elapsed since I was requested to see a tradesman, whose wife was desirous of shutting him up in a Lunatic asylum. It happened that my visit was paid at an unexpected hour, and the lady of the house was absent. I met her husband on the stairs, and with some difficulty persuaded him to go into his parlour, that I might talk to him. He had evidently become suspicious of the intentions of strangers, but after a little quiet conversation he became more confident, and entered into a detail of domestic affairs of a nature calculated to make any man insane. His present affectionate wife, it appeared, was the second to whom he had been united; his first having been a woman of abandoned character, who had wasted much of his property. He was proceeding to the second chapter of his matrimonial accidents, when his present wife broke in upon us, and, apparently suspecting the tenor of her husband's communication, began to abuse him very vehemently. His manner had, before this interruption, plainly evinced that his intellects were weakened, but his wife's mode of accosting him gave him immense disturbance; instead of allaying this, she persevered in a course of invective and abuse, after the manner of irritated women, until the poor man became perfectly frantic, and bounced out of the room, slamming the door after him with violence almost sufficient to bring down the house. 'Now,' exclaimed the ready wife, 'you see what a state he is in: he does this twenty times a day; there is no living with him.' To all this I made the best reply I could; and only requested permission to invite the poor man upstairs again, and to talk to him without the addition of a word from herself. I found, however, that as my mode of talking to the patient was calculated to soothe him, his wife could not avoid throwing in a provoking word from time to time, until at last the patient jumped up again, and after venting a few well deserved curses on his tormentor, made his exit in the same manner as before. The facts of the case were, that this unfortunate tradesman had always been a person of weak intellects; that his first wife had almost broken his heart; and his second had married him for his money; and finding that he was troublesome, or perhaps a little in the way, and that his weak intellects were thrown into utter confusion by passion, had learnt her part so well, as to have had him confined in Lunatic houses three or four times before I saw him, and each time with a regular certificate. The paper was lying on the table to be signed, and if the good lady on the joyful occasion had not taken a little more gin than usual, (for this was the apology of her friends for her violent behaviour,) it is possible I might myself have been guilty of consigning to an asylum a poor unprotected creature, whom ill-treatment had driven half mad, and whom further confinement in a Lunatic asylum will probably drive wholly so. As I refused to testify to his being in a state to justify such confinement, and signified that in my opinion his wife was the maddest of the two, I was troubled no more about him. When I called one day, subsequently, to inquire about him, he was not to be seen, and I fear he is at this moment in one of the establishments in the neighbourhood.

John Conolly, *An Inquiry Concerning the Indications of Insanity, with Suggestions for the Better Protection and Care of the Insane* (1830)

=

In the minds of idealists, the asylum appeared a positive haven for the insane, meeting their needs for shelter and care, secure from the pressures of the wider world.

The first requirement of a mental hospital is that it should be an asylum in the true sense of the word; as far as is humanly possible it should not only be but should appear to be a place of safety and protection. This is naturally difficult and sometimes impossible to ensure. Acutely disturbed patients whose inner world is divorced from outer reality may need to be forcibly restrained in their own interests and in the interests of other people; they may need to be cared for alongside other patients whose different disturbances reactivate and intensify their own; the nature of their illness may be such that hospital is inevitably an unhappy and a frightening place. The important thing to remember is that they are still human people, and the factors that make for happiness and security in a general hospital apply no less, but in fact much more, in a mental hospital.

I have never been in a mental hospital where the staff were deliberately unkind; on the other hand the contrasts between them were considerable. The striking contrast provided by the general hospital where I had an acute physical illness gives an additional basis for comparison.

In the general hospital I was treated in a warm and friendly manner as a person, and at the same time I was cared for. Those things which, by reason of severe illness, I could not do for myself, were done for me. That gave me a wonderful sense of security; I was relieved of a struggle with my physical environment which was, in the circumstances, too much for me, and at the same time I felt at home. Both doctors and nurses showed a simple human friendliness towards me as a person which was separate from and additional to the professional skill with which they attacked the problem of my illness. Mental illness makes this approach harder to achieve, but it is not in fact so impossible as might at first be thought, and it is of such paramount importance that it deserves to be considered with especial care.

To treat psychotics as persons is especially difficult because in acute mental illness the person may be to all intents and purposes

invisible. The mental nurse's problem is in a different way comparable with that of the nurse on an accident ward who has to deal
with a patient who is bandaged all over his face. It needs much
more skill and patience in such a situation to elicit and to interpret
personal responses and to gain a reasonable picture of the person
inside; and it is in such a situation all the more important to do this
in order to establish mutual confidence and rapport.

Two things are especially important to remember. Psychotics
may take in more of what is said and done around them than those
who care for them realise. On the other hand they are much less
able to make sense of their environment than normal people.

Morag Coate, *Beyond All Reason* (1964)

=

*Amidst the dross, the House of Commons Committee on Mad-
houses in England (1815) (see page 274) found a number of well-
run institutions. James Tilley Matthews (see page 123) was moved
from Bethlem to London House, Hackney, after contracting tuber-
culosis.*

What Private Houses have you visited within the Bills of Mortality?
– The first house that I applied to see, was kept by Peter Gilles
Briant, at Gore-house, *Kensington*, who refused letting any person
see a patient within his house or the house itself, or any thing in it.
The next was kept by a person of the name of Pearce, at *Chelsea*; in
that house there were four patients only, all of whom I saw; they
were idiots, without any coercion; the house generally dirty; but
otherwise, from the superficial glance I had of it, I saw no reason to
find any fault with it. The next place I went to was *Norman House*,
at Fulham; this was a house kept by a man of the name of Talfourd,
for females only; there were in it fourteen ladies, all of whom I saw,
and was delighted with the manner in which they were treated, and
with the degree of happiness which they appeared to enjoy; I
remained with them nearly two hours; conversed with every individual; and could not find, that either hand-locks or leg-locks were
ever used: Some of them stated, that they frequently went to
church; that they attended a fair in the neighbourhood (Brook
Green fair); and two had walked to Walham Green, to see Louis

XVIII. I think it difficult to speak too highly of Norman House generally; I believe there was no man in the house, except the husband of the woman who kept it, and there was the greatest kindness towards the patients. I next visited Mr Fox's, London House, *Hackney*; this is a house that I think admirably conducted: Mr Fox himself is an apothecary, living in Norton Falgate, and it is managed by his wife, who is a judicious good-natured woman, whom all the patients seemed very much to respect; every time that I was there, Mr Tilley Matthews was living, and in point of fact was the advising manager of the conduct of the patients in that house; it is a large house, capable of the sexes being kept distinct and separate, and they were here classed, according to their habits in life; one lady, who conceived herself to be Mary Queen of Scots, acts as preceptress to Mrs Fox's little children, and takes great pains in teaching them French, &c.

Report (1) from the Committee on Madhouses in England,
House of Commons (1815)

=

Like most of his contemporary psychiatric doctors, John Conolly regarded the eighteenth-century madhouse as little better than a torture chamber.

Indeed it would almost seem as if, at the period from the middle to near the end of the last century, the superintendents of the insane had become frantic in cruelty, from the impunity with which their despotism was attended. Some of the German physicians meditated even romantic modes of alarm and torture; wished for machinery by which a patient, just arriving at an asylum, and after being drawn with frightful clangour over a metal bridge across a moat, could be suddenly raised to the top of a tower, and as suddenly lowered into a dark and subterranean cavern; and they avowed that if the patient could be made to alight among snakes and serpents it would be better still. People not naturally cruel became habituated to severity until all feelings of humanity were forgotten. I used to be astonished, even seventeen years ago, to see humane physicians going daily round the wards of asylums, mere spectators of every form of distressing coercion, without a word of sympathy, or any

order for its mitigation. But men's hearts had on this subject become
gradually hardened. In medical works of authority the first principle
in the treatment of lunatics was laid down to be fear, and the best
means of producing fear was said to be punishment, and the best
mode of punishment was defined to be stripes. The great authority of
Dr Cullen, certainly one of the most enlightened physicians of his
time, was given to this practice, although his theory of madness was
that it depended upon an increased excitement of the brain.

John Conolly, *The Treatment of the Insane
Without Mechanical Restraint* (1856)

=

*An ex-patient, Urbane Metcalf, took the lid off Bethlem early in the
nineteenth century.*

The case of Kemp, a patient now in the house, a man of good
education, and who has lived in respectable circumstances, who has
not only the misfortune of being disordered, but of being poor; on his
admittance he was put in Blackburn's gallery, but not suiting him, he
contrived to get him removed into the basement by the following
means: he (Blackburn) complained to Dr Tothill (Kemp's physician)
that he of a night made so much noise that he disturbed the other
patients and prevented their recovery and got other patients to
corroborate his assertion, for this he was removed into the basement,
but I know if he had money, or been a good cleaner all would have
been well, and he might have remained there, as there are patients
who make far more noise now in his gallery; the villain without any
provocation had the cruelty to say to Kemp, *had I a dog like you I
would hang him*. Another patient named Harris, for the trifling
offence of wanting to remain in his room a little longer one morning
than usual, was dragged by Blackburn, assisted by Allen, the basement keeper, from No. 18, to Blackburn's room, and there beaten by
them unmercifully; when he came out his head was streaming with
blood, and Allen in his civil way wished him good morning.

  The case of Morris; this man had some pills to take, which he
contrived to secrete in his waistcoat pocket, this Blackburn discovered, and by the assistance of Allen, they got him to his room and
there beat him so dreadfully for ten minutes as to leave him totally

incapable of moving for some time, Rodbird was looking out to give them notice of the approach of any of the officers; they are three villains. A man by the name of Baccus, nearly eighty years of age, was this summer admitted into the house; one very hot day he had laid down in the green yard, another patient named Lloyd, very much disordered, trod on the middle of his body purposely, this Blackburn the keeper encouraged by laughing, and Lloyd would have repeated it, but something diverted his attention: Baccus is since dead.

Coles, a patient of Blackburn's, one day, for refusing to take his physic, was by Blackburn and Rodbird beat and dashed violently against the wall several times, in the presence of the steward, though from the general tenor of this man's conduct it is probable a little persuasion would have been sufficient to induce him to take the medicine quietly, Coles is since put upon the long list, and is now in the upper gallery.

Urbane Metcalf, *The Interior of Bethlehem Hospital* (1818)

=

Oppression in the asylum: Maria Acland, a patient in Fishponds Asylum, Bristol, in the 1830s, pleads with her uncle.

'Dr Bompas', Fishponds, near Bristol, Sept. 1838.
Oh dearest Uncle, I implore you to interpose for me. Mamma has been to see me but once in 10 months. She disregards or disbelieves all my statements. You know how often she has been misled. She is completely imposed upon. Oh bitterly will she repent her fatal error when it is even too late.

To communicate this to her would be perfectly useless, but by all the memory of your past kindness, interpose yourself for your wretched agonized dying niece.

Dr B. is considered even by his own people incompetent, unfeeling, thoroughly false, and actuated only by selfish interest in endeavouring to keep his patients ... and in denying all means of enquiry or free communication. The servants treat the patients most brutally and complaints are seldom attended to.

As to the nominal inspection of magistrates occasionally, that is a mere farce, everything is prepared beforehand and the statements of the patients utterly disregarded. The dreadful society to which I am exposed, the daily scenes and sounds of suffering, horror, cruelty and despair, surpass description. I have been chained, handcuffed, tortured, bitterly reviled, yet never offered the slightest resistance to all their cruelty. I am forced to exertions far beyond my strength and abused and threatened when I fail.

They also force me by threats and violence to take much more food (and that of the coarsest kind) than I could ever digest even in health, and my consequent disease and sleeplessness night and day are dreadful, constantly increasing and make me pray for death in which the present treatment must end.

My objecting to eat so much and my expectation of suffering are the only alleged ground for treating me as insane – is this legal? Dr Prichard has in many cases been fatally mistaken. Oh do write to him yourself (Park Row, Bristol) and demand his legal grounds for certifying insanity. At least insist on my being allowed to call in another physician or to choose another asylum.

If you (or Uncle John) could but come and see me yourself, and examine into my state and into the truth of the whole account which I shall then be able to give you, you might perhaps save my wretched life. Ah, do not listen to the objections which Mamma or Dr B. might raise. The former is misled and the latter evidently cheats the truth being known. There are many here who will bear witness to the truth of all and more than all my statements. My bodily sufferings . . . weary . . . are such a . . . to convey any idea of, and may account for any seemingly strong expressions respecting them. Considering poor Mamma's fatally erroneous views respecting me, I dare not even if I were removed home, confide myself solely to her protection.

Maria Acland, letter to her uncle (September 1838), in H. Temple Phillips, 'The History of the Old Private Lunatic Asylum at Fishponds, Bristol, 1740–1859' (1973)

=

The oppressive silence of the asylum

I was not allowed to write to my employers to notify them of my inability to continue my work, and I was not allowed to write to my best friend to tell her where to locate me. No reason was ever given for this breach of the rules; and no harm could possibly have resulted from my correspondence, since the ward sister read every letter written by patients, and failed to post those of which she, or the doctor, disapproved.

Apart from replying to questions, and providing me with food, the staff ignored me. There I lay, perfectly quietly in bed, without a soul to whom I could voice the awful terror which consumed me, and with no knowledge of the staff's next step. It appeared that I was expected to lie in bed all day long, with nothing whatever to do, but suffer from the shock of certification and my terror of the future.

I thought that this technique must be a new method devised for the study of mental illness; but I was soon to learn that it appeared to be nothing but a callous belief that the insane do not suffer and that any problems they may express are bound to be 'imaginary'. I heard, with mounting horror, the attempts of other new patients to get their needs satisfied and their efforts to obtain information; and I noted the evasions of the staff. No one ever seemed to be able to get a sensible reply to any question.

It arose from two causes. The first was clearly a well-fixed belief of nearly the whole staff that the patients were something less than human beings, and need not be handled as though they had human rights, or normal feelings, like other people. 'Where there is no sense there is no feeling', was a favourite saying of these nurses. The fact that they constantly said it about patients in the hearing of patients proves that they believed it to be true.

D. McI. Johnson and Norman Dodds (eds), *The Plea for the Silent* (1957)

=

The evils of 'institutionalization' are no modern discovery, but were well known to patients and reforming doctors alike in the nineteenth century. John Perceval (see page 23) blamed the habitual violence of the asylum on the staff.

Here let me observe, if you want any proof of the madness as well as cruelty of applying a system such as this to insane patients, where can you find one more perfect than in the fact, that you drive them in self-defence to conduct which in ordinary circumstances a man

cannot fail to look upon as a sign of unsettled mind? You look upon
the unfortunate object of your pretended concern, and of your
occasional malevolence, with pity for irregularities and extravagances, which however singular, however extravagant, are alas in him
but too reasonable, through your own unreasonableness; or putting
him in circumstances of extraordinary trial; do you expect from him,
from him whom you confine expressly for his weakness and
deficiency, an example of fortitude, a pattern of self-denial, perhaps
not to be found in the annals of human nature? By reason of your
own conduct, your judgment if honest and scrupulous must be in
ambiguity; for you can never tell if the patient's eccentricities, are the
symptoms of his disorder, or the result of antipathy to the new
circumstances in which you have placed him; and he, who is
struggling against the guilty tyranny and oppression of the doctor; he
who is dying daily to hope – to life – to the desire to exercise those
qualities of the mind, which for the sake of woman endear a man to
society, and society to man; he in whose breast the seeds even of a
divine nature, in spite of your cruelty and contempt, rise to new life
hourly, hourly to be crushed and murdered, acknowledges amongst
the cruelest of his wrongs, and the hardest of his chains, that he must
either tempt his nature to bear more than he can endure, or be
condemned as insane, for actions and conduct arising from the
faultiness of the conduct pursued towards him, the childishness of
those who deal with him, and judge of him, forgetting his actual
situation. To prefer walking in a cold drizzling rain, to sitting by a
warm fire side, were folly, if your kindness were not coupled with
that mockery, which makes the inclemency of the season and
weather comparatively less cruel. To be silent and incommunicative
is a singularity; but that singularity becomes reasonable, when a man
is denied liberty of expression and action, and confined with perfect
strangers, amidst those whose interest it is to suspect and pervert his
ways; aware of that which you, enthroned in the conceit of a more
sound understanding, are daily forgetting, that the weakness of his
mind renders it peculiarly improper for him to open the secrets of his
heart to men with whom he has even no acquaintance. To halloo, to
bawl, to romp, to play the fool, are in ordinary life, signs of
irregularity, but they become necessary to men placed in our position, to disguise or drown feelings for which we have no relief; too

great for expression, too sacred for the prying eye of impertinent, impudent, and malevolent curiosity. I will be bound to say that the greatest part of the violence that occurs in lunatic asylums is to be attributed to the conduct of those who are dealing with the disease, not to the disease itself; and that that behaviour which is usually pointed out by the doctor to the visitors as the symptoms of the complaint for which the patient is confined, is generally more or less a reasonable, and certainly a natural result, of that confinement, and its particular refinements in cruelty; for all have their select and exquisite moral and mental, if not bodily, tortures.

John T. Perceval, *A Narrative of the Treatment Received by a Gentleman, During a State of Mental Derangement* (1838/40)

=

A gigantic asylum is a gigantic evil.

Many asylums have grown to such a magnitude, that their general management is unwieldy, and their due medical and moral care and supervision an impossibility. They have grown into lunatic colonies of eight or nine hundred, or even of a thousand or more inhabitants, comfortably lodged and clothed, fed by a not illiberal commissariat, watched and waited on by well-paid attendants, disciplined and drilled to a well-ordered routine, gratified by entertainments, and employed where practicable, and, on the whole, considered as paupers, very well off; but in the character of patients, labouring under a malady very amenable to treatment, if not too long neglected, far from receiving due consideration and care.

Although the aggregation of large numbers of diseased persons, and of lunatics among others, is to be deprecated on various grounds, hygienic and others, yet the objections might be felt as of less weight, contrasted with the presumed economical and administrative advantages accruing from the proceeding, were the medical staff proportionately augmented, and the mental malady of the inmates of a chronic and generally incurable character. But, in the instance of the monster asylums referred to, neither is the medical staff at all proportionate to the number of patients, nor are their inmates exclusively chronic lunatics. The medical officer is charged with the care and supervision of some three, four, or five hundred insane people, among whom are cases of recent attack, and of bodily disease of every degree of severity, and to whom a considerable accession of fresh cases is annually made; and to his duties as physician are added more or fewer details of administration, and all those of the internal management of the institution, which bear upon the moral treatment of its inmates, and are necessary even to an attempt at its harmonious and successful working.

Now, little reflection is needed to beget the conviction, that a medical man thus surcharged with duties cannot efficiently perform them; and the greater will his insufficiency be, the larger the number of admissions, and of recent or other cases demanding medical treatment. He may contrive, indeed, to keep his asylum in good order, to secure cleanliness and general quiet, to provide an ample general dietary, and such like, but he will be unable to do all that he ought to do for the cure and relief of the patients entrusted to him as a physician. To treat insane people aright, they must be treated as individuals, and not *en masse*; they must be individually known, studied, and attended to both morally and medically. If recent insanity is to be treated, each case must be closely watched in all its psychical and physical manifestations, and its treatment be varied according to its changing conditions. Can a medical man, surrounded by several hundred insane patients, single-handed, fulfil his medical duties to them effectively, even had he no other duties to perform, and were relieved from the general direction of the asylum? . . .

The inadequacy of the medical staff of most asylums is a consequence, in part, of the conduct of superintendents themselves, and in part of the notions of economy, and of the little value in which medical aid is held by Visiting Justices in general. The contrast of a well-ordered asylum at the present day, with the prison houses, the ill-usage and neglect of the unhappy insane at a period so little removed from it, has produced so striking an effect on mankind at large, that public attention is attracted and riveted to those measures whereby the change has been brought about; in other words, to the moral means of treatment, – to the liberty granted, the comforts of life secured, the amusements contrived, and the useful employment promoted, – all which can, to a greater or less extent, be carried out equally by an unprofessional as by a professional man. It is therefore not so surprising that the import-ance of a medical attendant is little appreciated, and that the value of medical treatment is little heeded . . .

In a colossal refuge for the insane, a patient may be said to lose his individuality, and to become a member of a machine so put together as to move with precise regularity and invariable routine; – a triumph of skill adapted to show how such unpromising materials as crazy men and women may be drilled into order and guided by rule, but not an apparatus calculated to restore their pristine condition and their independent self-governing existence.

John Thomas Arlidge, *On the State of Lunacy,*
and the Legal Provision for the Insane (1859)

=

Terrifying cases of cruelty and neglect were brought to light by the House of Commons Committee of 1815. James Norris (see Plate 12) was an American marine who had been continuously restrained for many years in an iron harness which denied him almost all move-ment. The Bethlem apothecary, John Haslam, is being questioned.

Have you any objection to mention the name of the person to whom you alluded as having been under restraint for twelve years? – His name was Norris.

Do you know of many other instances of the same nature? – I feel great difficulty in recollecting the names of all the patients who have been in our house for twenty years.

Do you recollect other persons having been in that situation? – We had a man in our house for many years, of the name of Abbott, who had murdered three or four people in one morning, and he was confined by the chain round one arm, and a hole made through from the other cell, by which, when he became furious, he could be drawn down until the keeper came to apply the hand-cuffs; but in general he was at liberty, only this chain round his hand always ready, as he was a man of extreme power.

Did Norris remain in that state of ferocity and consequent con-finement till the period of his death? – No; he was released some weeks previously to his death.

Can you recollect about what time that was? – I think he died in February.

Do you recollect at what period he was released from his confinement? – I would say, on guessing at the thing, three weeks or a month before his death.

Are you quite certain it was not longer than that? – It might be longer, I will not be sure; the sum total I recollect very well of every thing, but I cannot charge my memory with particular names.

Was the release in consequence of any alteration in his mind? – He was weaker in his body, and he promised to behave well.

He died of a decline? – Yes, and an affection of the lungs.

What age was he? – I should presume fifty-seven or fifty-eight.

What do you mean by released? – He was suffered to walk about the gallery.

Without chains? – He requested first of all to have a pair of hand-cuffs on to walk about; it was a request of his own.

Did his less degree of dangerousness arise from any alteration in the state of his mind, or from his body having become infirm? – I believe more from the feebleness of his body.

Do you believe that the degree of restraint that Norris was in, was less painful and disagreeable to him than a strait-waistcoat would have been? – Much more easy; a strait-waistcoat would not have been efficient.

Is there not in the books of Bethlem a minute, entered by the governors and signed by some of them, in which there is a narrative of the case of Norris? – There was, after the case of Norris had made some noise, a committee assembled, convened by the president and the treasurer of our hospital, inviting all those Members of the Lords and Commons who were governors of our hospital to the investigation of the case of Norris, and the subject was gone into by them, and a report prepared thereon.

Was that report made? – That report is in existence in the books at Bridewell.

When did that investigation take place? – I think it was last June.

You say that was about the time that a noise was made about the case of Norris? – The public papers abounded with it.

Is there not a minute entered in that book of the hospital some years back, in which the reasons that were supposed to warrant the nature of the confinement of Norris, are entered? – That minute is therein recorded, speaking of the report.

That is to say, the report that you suppose was made last June contains within it the minute to which the Committee allude? – It does.

There would be no objection to produce a copy of it? – I should conceive not the slightest objection; there is nothing to require a moment's secrecy.

Can you state what were the circumstances that led to the alteration in Norris's restraint? – It was mentioned to me by the servant, that the iron which encompassed him did not answer the purpose, for he could get his hands out of it; and immediately on such representation, I desired it might be taken off; and that there might be no doubt of the order being given, I wrote it down, and a copy of that order written by me forms a part of the record in the report I have mentioned.

Did that arise entirely from the representation of a keeper only? – Certainly, the thing being inefficient of course was taken off.

Then, in point of fact, the alteration in the restraint upon Norris, arose from the restraint being insufficient? – It having been represented to me, by the keeper who had the care of Norris, that he could get his arms out, it no longer became a security, I accordingly gave him an order to take it off immediately.

Then you are understood to say, he had been under that inefficient restraint for twelve years? – I do not say that by any means.

Then how long had Norris been under that inefficient degree of restraint? – That I cannot tell.

Can you form any recollection of the time; was it a year? – More than one, two three or four years certainly. You will be able to collect the precise time from the date of the resolution of the committee that he should be so secured, connected with the order for the release from it, that will give the time, but that time I do not recollect.

Then your answer is, that Norris had been under the same degree of restraint from which he was released, for several years? – Certainly.

And the discovery that it was insufficient was not made till a noise was made about his case? – No, I did not say that; I say the meeting to enquire into it was the result of reports that had gone abroad and appeared in the papers.

Was the order for the release of Norris, so signed by you, given prior to those gentlemen visiting Bethlem who drew the picture of Norris, and who found him in the situation in which he was? – I never saw any picture, or knew of any picture being drawn; nor did I know of any visitation having been made when this apparatus or restraint was taken from him; he was confined by a chain round the neck, and a cord affixed to a stantion, which is an iron bar.

In consequence of whose report was it, that the order was originally given to confine Norris in that manner? – When he had committed various acts of desperation, I suggested that he should be confined in a double cell; that this man, being the most mischievous patient perhaps that ever I saw, should have two cells, a door communicating between them, so that he should have a sitting-room and a bed-room; he should go into his bed-room without his cloaths, that would enable the keeper to clean out the sitting-room, and to examine daily his pockets, to see that he had no offensive weapon or any thing with which he could do mischief; that when he retired from his bed-room into the other room the keeper would be enabled to ventilate and sweep the bed-room: this was my proposition, and this forms part of the report alluded to; this was overruled and the present apparatus, by whom contrived I do not know, was exhibited, and its imposition agreed on.

This was the advice you gave to the then committee? – Yes; and that forms a part of the report alluded to.

By whom was that advice of yours overruled? – I cannot say that it was overruled; they did not consent to it.

It was overruled by the governors? – By some existing committee at that time, to whom it was proposed.

It was overruled by the committee to whom it was proposed? – Certainly.

Who composed the committee to whom that advice was given by you? – I cannot tell, after a lapse of fifteen years.

How many governors? – It was an open committee; and sometimes it is one half dozen and sometimes another.

As this was a very remarkable case, did not it make any impression on you; did not the circumstance of his case coming before the committee make a greater impression upon your mind than the case of any ordinary patient? – Certainly; and therefore I proposed additional security, which was what I had the honour to submit to the committee, of his having two cells.

And that proposal was overruled by the committee; of whom was that committee composed? – That I cannot tell.

Will it appear upon the minutes, of whom the committee was composed in which Norris's case was discussed? – I cannot say whether the clerk made a minute of that. When this apparatus was fixed on him I took care that a minute should be made that I might know who was present.

Do you know by whom the plan of confinement was devised to which he was afterwards subjected? – Not certainly; but I did hear, as a matter of report, that they had some dangerous man in Newgate for whom this iron had been made, and this was brought from there; but it is mere report.

Did you approve of that mode of confinement? – My other proposition being overruled; this, for reasons which ought to be explained, and that form a part of the report, that it met with the concurrence of Doctor Monro, and the medical officers.

Among whom was Mr Haslam? – Certainly.

Then you mean to say, that the plan of confinement by two cells, being disapproved by the committee, no other or better mode of confining the patient than that which was adopted, was recommended by the medical officers, but that they consented to and approved the adoption of that which has been already alluded to? – I have no great genius myself for any contrivance of this kind. It is recorded in the minute that the physicians and the medical officers approved of it. I presume that is correct.

They approved specifically of this mode? – The apparatus was brought into the committee-room and exhibited.

Will you give your own description of what that mode of confinement was? – There was a sort of frame through which the arms went.

What sort of frame was it? – Iron.

There was an iron frame which went round his body, and to which his arms were confined; was there not? – His arms went through some part of this contrivance; but the machine is particularly described in the report of the committee.

Have you any thing to say, explanatory of the reasons on account of which the medical officers agreed to this mode of confinement? – I have; Norris's wrists were so constructed that handcuffs or manacles were of no service, the bones of his hands were smaller than his wrists; and on many and repeated occasions where the manacles had been imposed, he slipped them off and converted them into weapons of offence; so that the ordinary mode, the ultimatum of restraint to which we had hitherto resorted, was unavailing in Norris's case; and that was the reason for further means of coercion.

Do you know whether he was capable of slipping his feet out of the foot locks? – Certainly he was not.

Was he not confined by an iron collar round his neck, exclusively of that which went round his body, which has been already alluded to, and which neck-collar was fastened by a chain to an upright bar behind his bed? – Yes.

What was the reason for this additional confinement of the neck-collar and chain? – He was inclined to dart forward, and he would not have been secure in his bed-place.

Is it your opinion, that if this man had been confined in foot-locks, with manacles on his wrists and his arms fastened behind him, that he would have been able to have darted forwards, and done the mischief that seems to have been apprehended? – I have previously stated, that handcuffs or manacles were unavailing, from repeated experience.

Have not you had much experience, in the confinement of Maniacs? – Certainly.

Do you conceive yourself incapable of contriving a handcuff, from which a man should not be able to extricate his hands, even though they should be formed as Norris's were? – No; I have no contrivance of that kind; nor do I know of any that would have answered.

Was the strait-waistcoat ever tried upon Norris? – It was.

For what reason was it left off? – It answered no purpose; he burst it to pieces.

Do you know of any contrivance attempted for securing Norris, other than those which have been described already? – None; with the exception of the two cells which were proposed, and not adopted.

Do you mean to say, that a strait-waistcoat could not have been made of sufficient strength to have prevented Norris from extricating himself from it? – That is a question I cannot answer.

Do you believe that a strait-waistcoat might not have been easily constructed, of so much strength as that Norris could not have burst it open? – I cannot tell.

Do you know for how long a time Norris was confined to his bed, manacled in the manner already described? – I have previously said I could not judge of the exact time.

Do you think that his confinement in that manner, during the whole of that period, was necessary? – Certainly.

At what intervals were you accustomed to see Norris during those years? – Frequently; very frequently.

How came it then, that it was not till the month of June last you were acquainted with the circumstance of his withdrawing his hands from that confinement which was imposed upon him as necessary to his safety, because a handcuff was not a sufficient confinement? – That information I had from the keeper who attended him.

How came it, that it was not till the month of June last you were acquainted with the circumstance of his withdrawing his hands from that confinement which was imposed upon him as necessary to his safety, because a handcuff was not a sufficient confinement? – I only know his capability of so extricating himself from the report of the keeper; he might be thinner, and therefore could more easily extricate himself; but I cannot pretend to say.

Did that discovery ever take place, till the noise about his case, of which you have already spoken, had happened? – The dates will prove that.

Is that, or is it not, within your knowledge? – I think it was before, but I will not be sure; it was before our inquisition at Bethlem Hospital.

Do you know, or believe, that the report of the keeper, in consequence of which Norris was released from that species of confinement in which he had been so long kept, was made to you before the visits which took place to Bethlem Hospital? – I know nothing of the time when the visits did take place.

Before the case of Norris became the subject of common conversation? – I really cannot tell.

You have been asked, whether you know, or believe, that the report of the keeper, in consequence of which Norris was released from the species of confinement in which he had been so long kept, was made to you before Norris's case had become the subject of public conversation? – That the keeper can tell better than I can.

You are only asked, whether you know, or believe, it was before those visits? – I cannot tell.

Do you know, or believe, that the report of the keeper, in consequence of which Norris was released from that species of confinement in which he had been so long kept, was made to you before the visits which took place to Bethlem Hospital? – I cannot connect dates in my recollection in that way.

Have you really no belief on the subject? – I cannot say that I have a belief on the subject; I cannot fix the epoch of the public conversation any further than from reading something of it in the newspapers.

Have you any belief on the subject, or not? – I have not.

> Report (1) from the Committee on Madhouses in England,
> House of Commons (1815)

=

Violence has not been unknown in more recent times.

At the north end of the building there was a small ward of eight people who were considered to be 'very disturbed'. There was one lad who came from Dundee. He had been at West Green Hospital (now known as the Royal Liff Hospital). His mother had had him transferred from West Green because of his treatment there. At night these patients, like ourselves, went upstairs to bed: we at one end of the building, they at the other. The routine was that the night nurse – I use the term loosely – would come on duty, get the handover from his day counterpart, then settle himself down on a couch with a blanket round him and go off to sleep. Well you never dared disturb the night nurse, but the lad from Dundee did. He shook the nurse to waken him saying, 'You're not supposed to be doing that. You're supposed to be looking after us.' The nurse, together with another from the next ward, turned on him and started to kick the living nightlights out of him. This was the first of many such beatings I was to witness in the years to come. Fortunately, one of the nurses, Geordie, was a bit better than the other. I said, 'For God's sake, stop it. You'll kill him.' The other nurse told me to 'Fuck off' or I would get the same but I said to Geordie, 'Come on, that's no' like you, you'll kill him.' His face turned white as a sheet. He now knew that should anything happen there was a witness. They stopped beating the lad from Dundee. My cold baths and hammerings at Baldovan were nothing compared to this. And this happened when I had been in the place less than two weeks.

Later that week I was sitting on a bench beside the cricket pitch when a senior member of staff came along. I asked why two or three nurses would want to beat up a patient. Without answering he got up and walked away. He didn't want any trouble.

Jimmy Laing and Dermot McQuarrie (see page 223),
Fifty Years in the System (1989)

=

The song of captivity

A CAPTIVE SONG-BIRD

To-day amid the grime I heard
   A thrush that carolled in his cage
So blithe, so pitiful, it stirred
   My human heart almost to rage
      That God should let His woodland creatures free
      So languish on in drab captivity.

Then, as I listened, out there thrilled
   The answer from that shameful box
Of wire and wood, where Bravery trilled
   Loud to the world this paradox:
      Souls oft soar highest on a grief-clipped wing;
      And many a heart must break, ere it can sing.

'Warmark', *'Guilty but Insane': A Broadmoor Autobiography* (1931)

=

Emotional straitjacketing

Tears are taboo in mental hospitals. Everything possible is done to prevent them, check them, hush them up. There seems to be no understanding of the fact that the patients who are unbearably tense or most deeply depressed may be suffering both mentally and physiologically from the fact that they cannot cry. Some patients do cry all over the place and don't mind or can't prevent it, and if these cry when they are with the doctor they need kind firmness and some bracing up. But others cannot or will not allow themselves to cry in public, and some are hurt so deeply that without help they cannot cry at all. These are the ones the doctor may unexpectedly get to cry. Perhaps he makes some chance remark and sees, by the reaction, that he has inadvertently touched a very painful spot. Quickly, instinctively he changes his tone to warmth and sympathy to ease the pain he caused. Tears follow; he feels at a loss, uneasily conscious that his probing has made the patient cry. It did nothing of the sort. He has done all the right things, and all he needs now is to understand this and relax. The remark that caused the pain gave him a clue; his readiness to pick up the clue and his show of genuine concern for the other person's suffering provided the warmth and support which alone could enable the sufferer to bring deep distress to the forefront of consciousness and disperse it into tears.

Morag Coate, Beyond All Reason (1964)

=

A more humane asylum? Psychiatric hospitals might be improving, Jimmy Laing suggests, but eradicating their abuses remains next to impossible.

About two weeks before my release date an incident occurred that I have lived with since and which has tormented me ever since it happened. We had a particular patient in the admission ward who was in Carstairs as one of the many patients who was dumped there. He had a habit of keeping some of his bread from his meals and throwing it out of the window in his room for the birds. This was frowned upon. One day he was caught throwing the bread out by an enrolled nurse who called in another nurse, saying, 'Come and see this. What a bloody mess you've made outside.' Then I heard them slapping the patient and eventually beating him up. The next day, Thursday, was bathing day, and one of the nurses announced that we would get as many bathed as possible in the morning as there was a good film on television that afternoon. I hadn't said anything to anybody about the beating but Jock Reid came on duty and he saw that the patient was black and blue with bruises. Jock immediately called his superior officer, George Tait, who was the group charge nurse. George arrived and said that he was having nothing to do with it and called in the principal nursing officer Ian MacKenzie. He in turn called in Dr McDonald who called in the local GP from Carnwath who gave the patient a full examination. He pronounced that there was evidence the patient had been badly beaten. Dr McDonald called in the police. What a difference to the old days. In times past the whole incident would have been hushed up, but not in modern times, thank God. When the police arrived the patient told them that he had been beaten up for throwing bread out of the window to the birds. 'I feed them every day,' he said. He was a poor soul. However, an inquiry was immediately started and the union agreed that it would co-operate.

The police organized an identity parade of eight nurses from around the hospital and the patient was asked to pick out the nurse involved. He went up and down the line and picked out the one who had beaten him up. The other one wasn't there and as he hadn't actually taken part in the beating he was allowed to go free. The nurse involved was immediately suspended from duty. The police then began to question the other patients in the ward about the beating. Eventually they came to me. 'Good afternoon, Mr Laing,' said the policeman. 'We are making inquiries into the alleged beating that took place and we want to know if you have any knowledge of it. Did you hear any noises, screams or shouts?' My life flashed in front of me. I had just come from the bedside of a very young patient called Sammy. He had been sent to Carstairs as he was unmanageable at the other hospital he had been in. I had spent a lot of time with him as his story was so close to my own. I thought of him and the future that lay ahead. I thought of my own future and the fact that I was getting out in two weeks' time.

Later my reply was to tear holes inside me. 'I don't know

anything about any beatings, sir,' I replied. 'I didn't hear anything at all. We have a patient here who tends to shout a lot, perhaps that's what I heard.' I actually wanted to believe that. My God, what a coward. All those years fighting for my own rights and those in the system and at the end I let myself and the others down. Why did I do it? Yes, I did it for myself but I also did it for Sammy. If I had told the truth all hell would have broken loose. The system, by this time, was changing, it had changed a lot, and was still progressing. I was leaving. Was I going to leave that young boy behind to the life I had suffered? No, I had to leave him to survive in a system which, I hoped, would provide him with a better life than I had ever had inside. But I was sick within myself. I excused myself and went to my room where I wept my heart out. In spite of my good intentions to help Sammy, I had betrayed my fellow patients. Self-preservation had eventually taken me to this awful stage. If I had spoken out I could have been kept at Carstairs for months afterwards for internal inquiries.

Eventually the inquiry gave its result. No action was taken against the nurse in question as the case against him could not be proved. A whitewash.

Jimmy Laing and Dermot McQuarrie (see page 223),
Fifty Years in the System (1989)

=

The asylum is un-English, a disgrace to the nation.

Tie an active limbed, active minded, actively imagining young man in bed, hand and foot, for a fortnight, drench him with medicines, slops, clysters; when reduced to the extreme of nervous debility, and his derangement is successfully confirmed, manacle him down for twenty-four hours in the cabin of a ship; then for a whole year shut him up from six A.M. to eight P.M. regardless of his former habits, in a room full of strangers, ranting, noisy, quarrelsome, revolting, madmen; give him no tonic medicines, no peculiar treatment or attention, leave him to a nondescript domestic, now brushing his clothes, sweeping the floors, serving at table, now his companion out of doors, now his bed-room companion; now throwing him on the floor, kneeling on him, striking him under all these distressing and perplexing circumstances; debar him from all conversation with his superiors, all communication with his friends, all insight into their motives, every impression of sane and well-behaved society! surprise him on all occasions, never leave harassing him night or day, or at meals; whether you bleed him to death, or cut his hair, show the same utter contempt for his will or inclination; do all in your power to crush every germ of self-respect that may yet remain, or rise up in his bosom; manacle him as you would a felon; expose him to ridicule, and give him no opportunity of retirement or self-reflection; and what are you to expect? And whose agents are you; those of God or of Satan? And what good can you reasonably dare to expect? and whose profit is really intended?

Gentlemen of England, the system I have described is not only the system of English men, it is the disgrace of English surgeons or English physicians. It is practised or connived at by the innocent simplicity of that race of presuming upstarts, who in various guises admitted by your condescension to terms of familiarity, sit at your tables, hiding their conceit in a false humility and in silky smiles; whilst they ape your manners and dupe your generosity. Be assured, whoever ye are, who have to deal with children or lunatics, if you are not looking after them yourselves, you are not respecting them. The doctors know that, and take advantage of it, to construe your disrespect into worse even than it is. Their servants take advantage of it. Bystanders draw false conclusions from it, much rather the poor object of it. His nature resents it; though he is not always aware of anything but his delusions: and his delusions contending with his feelings for the mastery over him, make him a madman. His self-respect, also, for so he respected himself partly for your sakes, is destroyed; and he delivers himself up to every grovelling thought and lewd idea, reckless on account of your ingratitude; even if his weakness and total want of wholesome exercise, wholesome occupation, and wholesome repose, does not render such a surrender inevitable. If, however, he has sense to resent consciously your desertion, he has also ten to one the high-mindedness to do it by scorn, contempt, and silence on his part; perhaps he does so by expressions of hatred and attempts at violence in your presence, devoid of discretion, and impotent over his revenge. These the doctor, consciously or not, easily gets you to interpret into signs of the complaint, when they are in truth the signs of his devilish treatment, and of the patient's unguarded honesty: which, also, a few respectful words of repentance from you might make vanish like the morning mists. Not however, if you repent only to offend again; if you mock at one who, whatever may be the source, is preternaturally enlightened. I am sure that no lunatic who has undergone the trials I describe, can meet his family on terms of cordiality, but through practising dissimulation, or through being a simpleton. At this distance of time, I cannot forgive my family the guilt they incurred by their abandonment of me. I am at a loss to find any argument which will justify me in doing so: I dare not expect to be able to do so. But if haply perfection requires this moral excellence, by what happy fortune are you entitled to look for it in the inmates of a lunatic asylum?

I have complained that the behaviour adopted towards me, was calculated to humour the state of mind I was then in, not to correct. The servant, for instance, whom I used to call Jesus, and Herminet Herbert, ran with me, jumped, joked, walked arm in arm with me, rattled the spoons in my face as he put them into the cupboard, pulled me by the nose, &c. &c. If I was not insensible to the impropriety of this familiarity, at least, I could not express my sense of it. But it will be evident, this was not the way to correct a gentleman's diseased mind. This conduct may be partly accounted for by having been placed under a quondam Quaker, to whom in theory and in practice, as far as it only interfered with others, and suited his interests, perfect equality of rich and poor was a matter of faith. There was, however, this unfairness in it, that I observed the joke ceased whenever the domestic had had enough of it. The lunatic's presence of mind and tranquillity might be broken in upon, but not so the keeper's. There was but one step from joking with them to violence and objuration. Later in the year, a young handsome lad used to invite me to box with him every evening in my bed-room, striking me in sport a few blows: at length, I expressed a kind of awkward resentment at it. I have perhaps written enough on this subject.

John T. Perceval, *A Narrative of the Treatment Received by a Gentleman,
During a State of Mental Derangement* (1838–40)

=

In David Cooper's view (see page 5), the only solution is the replacement of psychiatry with non-psychiatry.

Non-psychiatry is coming into being. Its birth has been a difficult affair. Modern psychiatry, as the pseudo-medical action of detecting faulty ways of living lives and the technique of their categorization and their correction, began in the eighteenth century and developed through the nineteenth to its consummation in the twentieth century. Hand in hand with the rise of capitalism it began, as a principal agent of the destruction of the absurd hopes, fears, joys and despair of joy of people who refused containment by that system. Hand in hand with capitalism in its death agonies, over the coming years (it might be twenty or thirty years), psychiatry, after familialization and education one of the principal repressive devices (with its more sophisticated junior affiliate psychoanalysis) of the bourgeois order, will be duly interred.

The movement, schematically, is very simple: psychiatry, fully institutionalized (put in place) by a state system aimed at the perpetuation of its labour supply, using the persecution of the non-obedient as its threat to make 'them' conform or be socially eliminated, was attacked in the year 1960 – by an anti-psychiatric movement which was a sort of groping anti-thesis, a resistance movement against psychiatric hospitals and their indefinite spread in the community sectors, that was to lead dialectically to its dialectical issue which we can only call non-psychiatry, a word that erodes itself as one writes it.

Non-psychiatry means that profoundly disturbing, incomprehensible, 'mad' behaviour is to be contained, incorporated in and diffused through the whole society as a subversive source of creativity, spontaneity, not 'disease'. Under the conditions of capitalism, this is clearly 'impossible'. What we have to do is to accept this impossibility as the challenge. How can any challenge be measured by less than its impossibility? The non-existence of psychiatry will only be reached in a transformed society, but it is vital to start the work of de-psychiatrization now.

David Cooper, The Language of Madness (1978)

=

14

Mental Diseases

In recent years it has been argued by various critics, but most forcibly by the psychiatrist Thomas Szasz, that to talk about *mental disease* is a misnomer. Disease properly speaking – smallpox, for instance – is a tangible, physical entity, affecting the body. So-called mental illnesses lack such qualities: no one has ever isolated a manic-depressive virus. They are thus, properly speaking, not *diseases* at all, but abnormalities in conduct, views and values, which should be handled (or not handled, as the case may be) like any other unconventional mode of behaviour. Szasz has long campaigned against the evils of spurious 'medicalization', prime amongst which he sees the policy of compulsory psychiatric institutionalization.

In a somewhat similar way, many sociologists of illness have denied that mental 'diseases' are objective scientific realities, regarding them as 'labels' pinned on for reasons of social and professional convenience: the disturbing get called 'disturbed'.

During the long history of its dealings with the mad, the medical profession has mainly upheld the contrary view, asserting the reality of mental illness, and assimilating such conditions to regular disease models (for example, delirium is not a scream of protest; it is a sign of fever). The aim of psychological medicine has been to construct epidemiologies of psychiatric disorders, and to locate their organic aetiologies, as with any other disease.

Nevertheless, psychiatric conditions have proved highly resistant to being assimilated within the model of general bodily disorders. Over the centuries, there has been little agreement as to how precisely the whole mental illness cake should best be sliced up into pieces, with different names usefully distinguishing diverse conditions.

A few centuries ago, doctors tended to make do with the simplest of dichotomies. On the one hand, mania, the disorder of excess (rage, lust, violence, fever); on the other, melancholy, the disorder of deficit (lethargy, silence, solitude, self-destructiveness).

In some ways, the accent today is once more upon a quest for simplicity. Psychiatry this century has been disposed to make a grand differentiation between the 'neuroses' (relatively mild conditions, perhaps with no organic base), and the 'psychoses' (severer disturbances, probably with a physical aetiology). And then, within the psychoses, a further grand distinction has been drawn between manic-depressive (or 'bipolar') conditions, and, on the other hand, schizophrenia. Nevertheless, the simplicity is deceptive, as a glance at *DSMIII* (*Diagnostic and Statistical Manual III*), the profession's diagnostic handbook, will show. Requiring energetic revision every few years, and itself the subject of bitter controversy, *DSM* reveals an extraordinary proliferation of different and often incompatible or overlapping terminologies, many of which disappear and reappear from edition to edition. A notorious postal-vote poll, held by the American Psychiatric Association in 1975, led to homosexuality being belatedly removed from its list of mental afflictions.

Behind this confusion lies a long story. Much of the energies of psychiatrists over the last two centuries has been channelled into attempts to provide a scientific inventory of mental disorders. This has involved two principal tasks: on the one hand, attempts to provide stable and comprehensive descriptions of the signs and symptoms of differentiated conditions, on the other, attempts to place the range of individual conditions within an intellectually satisfying taxonomy or classification, within the framework of broader categories such as 'compulsions', 'phobias', 'manias', 'dementia', and so forth.

Both procedures have produced as much chaos as clarification. For one thing, in their attempts to describe the diseases afflicting patients, psychiatrists have always been liable to the 'uncertainty principle' objection. The disorder may not be 'real', in nature, but an artefact of the psychiatric encounter itself. Charcot's depiction of 'hysteria' and (perhaps less obviously) Kraepelin's demonstration of *dementia praecox* cannot escape this objection. When Kraepelin begins to build up his picture of the 'negativism' of the patient suffering from *dementia praecox*, it is hard to tell how far he is depicting an authentic condition, or merely inadvertently recording his own difficulties in dealing with such patients.

Also, mental disorders are so protean that they seem to resist the kind of systematic taxonomic labelling so successful with plants within the Linnaean system. In the excerpts below, Benjamin Rush, writing some 200 years ago, mocks the temptation to discover a new diagnostic label for evey human idiosyncrasy. A century later, Max Nordau found he was still needing to make the same point, implying that the psychiatrists of the *fin de siècle* era were themselves subject to the mental peculiarities they identified in their own age (every era evidently gets both the madmen and the psychiatrists it deserves).

═══════════════

The great French neurologist, Jean-Martin Charcot (see Plate 15), demonstrates to his students the symptomatology of hysteria.

A female patient on a stretcher is brought into the amphitheater.
CHARCOT: Here is a patient whom you saw last Friday. After a fall she developed a lower extremity contracture with a deformity of her right foot. Nothing is more frequent in hysterics than post-traumatic contractures. What could one make of such a case? I told you last time how important it is to treat and cure these contractures as soon as they appear. But now here we have an exception to this rule, and we have waited and watched this woman three or four days without interfering. I told you why we did this – with cases like this woman's, you may, in fact, be able to treat this through provoking a second sort of attack. Often with such attacks, a change occurs in the patient and a contracture that seemed permanently fixed before can completely disappear. You may say to me, 'Isn't there something immoral about waiting and provoking such crises?' Surely not, if one can offer a treatment for a disorder that otherwise has no cure.

And I have shown you how there is a parallel relationship between transient hysteric attacks and the forms of hysteria like this one that last longer, five or six months. Often, those patients with contractures are not those who have fleeting hysteric attacks and vice versa. It is because of his doctrine, so soundly described by Dr Pitres, that we can make use of hysterogenic points to provoke a transient attack as a form of therapy in the treatment of static hysteric signs. Now, this patient will be useful for demonstration. I will tell you, however, that although I am practically certain of the outcome of the experiment, man is less predictable than machinery, and I will not be totally surprised if, in fact, we do not succeed. I have also heard that animal experiments performed before an audience often give different results from those seen in the laboratory. This may be the case here, since this is, in fact, a comparable clinical experiment. If we do not get the desired result, it will still be a significant lesson for you.

This patient has a hysterogenic point on her back, another under her left breast, and a third on her leg. We will focus on this latter one. If the attack proceeds as I believe it will, I will want you to focus on all its phases. This is not an easy task, and it took me many years to analyze the phenomena you will see. I first came to the Salpêtrière 15 or 20 years ago and inherited the well-run service of Dr Delasiauve. From my first days I witnessed these hysteroepileptic attacks, and was very circumspect in making my early diagnoses. I said myself, 'How can it be that such events are not described in the textboooks? How should I go about describing these events from my first-hand experience?' I was befuddled as I looked at such patients, and this impotence greatly irritated me. Then one day, when reflecting over all these patients as a group. I was struck with a sort of intuition about them. I again said to myself, 'Something about them makes them all the same.' Indeed we have a particular disease before us – primary hysteria beginning with an epileptic-like attack that resembles so closely real epilepsy that it may be called hysteroepilepsy, even though it has nothing at all to do with true epilepsy. The epileptoid phase can be divided into a tonic and clonic portion. Then, after a brief respite, the phase of exotic movements begins, under one of two predominant forms, either vocalizations or extreme opisthotonus (*arc en cercle*). Then, the third phase supersedes, and suddenly the patient looks ahead at an imaginary image – indeed a hallucination, which will vary according to the setting. The patient may look with great fear or with joy, depending on what she sees. You saw this in a woman the other day when I touched her abdomen in the ovarian region. She rose from her bed, hurried into the corner, and said the most distressing things.

But I want you to appreciate especially the unfolding of an attack. I tell you all this beforehand so that you can mark each phase, since they are hard to appreciate without preparation. Importantly, the attack is not a series of individual small attacks, but a single event that unrolls sequentially. I use here the method of describing an archetype with the most complex and fully developed features described. This system is essential for all neurologic diagnosis; one must learn to identify the archetype. The epileptoid phase can be lacking and the attack begin with the movement phase, either vocalizations or back arching. Sometimes the movements never appear, and one only has hallucinations. There are as many as 20 variations, but if you have the key to the archetype, you immediately focus on the disease at hand and can say with confidence that in spite of the many possible variations, all these cases represent the same disorder. So, here we have this contracted foot that reportedly cannot be reduced either during the day or night. I have not specifically examined it at all times, but I surmise that this is in fact true. We are not dealing here with simulation, one of the greatest obstacles to neurology.

(*The intern touches the hysterogenic point under the left breast. Immediately, the attack begins.*)

CHARCOT: Now, here we have the epileptoid phase. Remember this sequence – epileptoid phase, arched back, then vocalizations. the arched back that you now see is rather pronounced. Now here comes the phase of emotional outbursts, which fuses with the back arching, and now there is a contracture phase. Such contractures can persist occasionally, and if this occurs in our patient, we will hardly have helped her. Now the epileptoid period starts again. Focus your attention this time on the two distinct epileptoid movement phases – first, the tonic, then the clonic. Note how this resembles true epilepsy. Now let us see if she is ovarian.

(The intern comes forward and compresses the ovarian region.)

CHARCOT: Do this in a real epileptic and nothing will happen, showing you immediately the difference between epilepsy and hysteroepilepsy. In contrast to this situation, epilepsy has no direct link with the ovary. See how the attack is momentarily suspended by abdominal compression. Is it true that ovarian compression actually aborts the attack? This maneuver is contested in a number of textbooks, where the authors act as if they know what they are talking about. In both England and Germany there are some people who say they have never seen ovarian compression work, but these same people are those who are all too eager to generalize from their very limited experience. In that the phenomenon has been unequivocally demonstrated to occur in Paris, I find it only reasonable to believe it also occurs elsewhere.

Now we will release the compression, and you will see how the attack promptly recommences. Here comes the epileptoid phase again. Often outside of France, epileptoid behavior is still called epilepsy. I disagree with such terminology and distinctly call this hysteroepilepsy or hysteria major. Here now comes the arched back. Note the consistent pattern, always predictable and regular.

Her contracture persists throughout this entire period. If we do not succeed in relieving it, we will try another tack later. A therapeutic crisis like this one will have primed her for this next therapy, which is more likely to be beneficial than if we had just tried it alone. These attacks can last quite a time, perhaps all day. But the patient recovers curiously without being the least bit tired or spent. This represents another distinction between hysteroepilepsy and epilepsy itself. When true epileptic fits merge with one another, this is called status epilepticus. This is a severe disease often with a fatal outcome. With hysteroepilepsy, on the other hand, attacks can follow one another and fuse together for one, two, or even three days and still be of no danger to the patient. Status hysteroepilepticus is entirely different from status epilepticus.

Let us press again on the hysterogenic point. Here we go again.

Occasionally subjects even bite their tongues, but this would be rare. Look at the arched back, which is so well described in the textbooks.

PATIENT: Mother, I am frightened.

> Jean-Martin Charcot, *Charcot the Clinician: The Tuesday Lessons –*
> *Excerpts from Nine Case Presentations on General Neurology*
> *Delivered at the Salpêtrière Hospital in 1887–8*

=

Although Charcot saw hysteria as a male as well as a female condition, many psychiatrists have argued the existence of a distinctive female psyche susceptible to distinctive psychiatric disorders.

The reason of women is not receptive to masculine demonstrations, that is, it cannot be swayed by them, but only by senses, emotions, or imagination; and their will can be swayed through this reason or without it. Whoever wishes to guide women must have one of these moments on his side, depending on whether the woman is of a superior or inferior type. Feminine stubbornness, popularly known as 'women's pigheadedness,' from which no woman is exempt, is probably the result of the fact that members of our own sex appeal to the intellect or to the will of women directly in order to reassert what they consider to be their rights.

> Johann Christian August Heinroth, *Textbook of Disturbances of*
> *Mental Life, or Disturbances of the Soul and their Treatment* (1818)

=

A puzzling disorder which rose to prominence in the last years of the nineteenth century was multiple personality. In a major study the American psychiatrist Morton Prince discovered that his patient, 'Miss Christine Beauchamp', possessed a whole deck of mutually exclusive personae.

Miss Christine L. Beauchamp, the subject of this study, is a person in whom several personalities have become developed; that is to say, she may change her personality from time to time, often from hour to hour, and with each change her character becomes transformed and her memories altered. In addition to the real, original

or normal self, the self that was born and which she was intended
by nature to be, she may be any one of three different persons. I say
three different, because, although making use of the same body,
each, nevertheless, has a distinctly different character; a difference
manifested by different trains of thought, by different views, beliefs,
ideals, and temperament, and by different acquisitions, tastes,
habits, experiences, and memories. Each varies in these respects
from the other two, and from the original Miss Beauchamp. Two of
these personalities have no knowledge of each other or of the third,
excepting such information as may be obtained by inference or
second hand, so that in the memory of each of these two there are
blanks which correspond to the times when the others are in the
flesh. Of a sudden one or the other wakes up to find herself, she
knows not where, and ignorant of what she has said or done a
moment before. Only one of the three has knowledge of the lives of
the others, and this one presents such a bizarre character, so far
removed from the others in individuality, that the transformation
from one of the other personalities to herself is one of the most
striking and dramatic features of the case. The personalities come
and go in kaleidoscopic succession, many changes often being made
in the course of twenty-four hours. And so it happens that Miss
Beauchamp, if I may use the name to designate several distinct
people, at one moment says and does and plans and arranges
something to which a short time before she most strongly objected,
indulges tastes which a moment before would have been abhorrent
to her ideals, and undoes or destroys what she had just laboriously
planned and arranged.

. . . I hastened to follow up the lead offered and asked, as if in
ignorance of her meaning, who 'She' was. The hypnotic self was
unable to give a satisfactory reply.

'You are "She,"' I said.

'No, I am not.'

'I say you are.'

Again a denial.

Feeling at the time that this distinction was artificial, and that the
hypnotic self was making it for a purpose, I made up my mind that
such an artifact should not be allowed to develop. I pursued her
relentlessly in my numerous examinations, treated the idea as

nonsense, and refused to accept it, but with what success will be noted. Finally:

'Why are you not "She"?'

'Because "She" does not know the same things that I do.'

'But you both have the same arms and legs, haven't you?'

'Yes, but arms and legs do not make us the same.'

'Well, if you are different persons, what are your names?'

Here she was puzzled, for she evidently saw that, according to her notion, if the hypnotic self that was talking with me was Miss Beauchamp, the waking self was not Miss Beauchamp, and *vice versa*. She appeared to be between the horns of a dilemma, was evasive, unable to answer, and made every effort not to commit herself. On another occasion, in answer to the question why she (the *apparently* hypnotic state) insisted that Miss Beauchamp in her waking state was a different person from herself at that moment, the contemptuous reply was: 'Because she is stupid; she goes round mooning, half asleep, with her head buried in a book; she does not know half the time what she is about. She does not know how to take care of herself.' The contemptuous tone in which she spoke of Miss Beauchamp (awake) was striking, and her whole manner was very different from what it formerly had been when hypnotized. The weary, resigned, attitude was gone; she was bold, self-assertive, unwilling to accept suggestions, and anything but passive. A few days after this, when hypnotized, all became changed again; the former hypnotic manner returned.

'Who are you?' I asked.

'I am Miss Beauchamp.'

Then, after a number of questions on another point:

'Listen: now you say you are Miss Beauchamp.'

'Yes.'

'Then why did you say you were not Miss Beauchamp?'

[Surprised] 'Why, I never said so.'

'The last time we talked you said you were not Miss Beauchamp.'

'You are mistaken. I did not. I said nothing of the sort.'

'Yes, you did.'

'No.'

Morton Prince, The Dissociation of Personality: The Hunt for
the Real Miss Beauchamp (1978)

=

Modern neurology has made dramatic steps forward in understanding how abnormalities of the brain – not least, the imbalance between left and right hemispheres – account for peculiarities of perception and behaviour in otherwise highly intelligent and capable people.

'Can I help?' I asked.

'Help what? Help whom?'

'Help you put on your shoe.'

'Ach,' he said, 'I had forgotten the shoe', adding, *sotto voce*, 'The shoe? The shoe?' He seemed baffled.

'Your shoe,' I repeated. 'Perhaps you'd put it on.'

He continued to look downwards, though not at the shoe, with an intense but misplaced concentration. Finally his gaze settled on his foot: 'That is my shoe, yes?'

Did I mis-hear? Did he mis-see?

'My eyes,' he explained, and put a hand to his foot, '*This* is my shoe, no?'

'No, it is not. That is your foot. *There* is your shoe.'

'Ah! I thought that was my foot.'

Was he joking? Was he mad? Was he blind? If this was one of his 'strange mistakes', it was the strangest mistake I had ever come across.

I helped him on with his shoe (his foot), to avoid further complication. Dr P. himself seemed untroubled, indifferent, maybe amused. I resumed my examination. His visual acuity was good: he had no difficulty seeing a pin on the floor, though sometimes he missed it if it was placed to his left.

He saw all right, but what did he see? I opened out a copy of the *National Geographic Magazine*, and asked him to describe some pictures in it.

His responses here were very curious. His eyes would dart from one thing to another, picking up tiny features, individual features, as they had done with my face. A striking brightness, a colour, a shape would arrest his attention and elicit comment – but in no case did he get the scene-as-a-whole. He failed to see the whole, seeing only details, which he spotted like blips on a radar screen. He never entered into relation with the picture as a whole – never faced, so to speak, *its* physiognomy. He had no sense whatever of a landscape or scene.

Oliver Sacks, *The Man Who Mistook His Wife for a Hat* (1985)

=

A key modern diagnostic term is schizophrenia. The concept emerged out of the characterization of dementia praecox (literally: precocious dementia) by the great German psychiatrist, Emil Kraepelin.

Gentlemen, – You have before you to-day a strongly-built and well-nourished man, aged twenty-one, who entered the hospital a few weeks ago. He sits quietly looking in front of him, and does not raise his eyes when he is spoken to, but evidently understands all our questions very well, for he answers quite relevantly, though slowly and often only after repeated questioning. From his brief remarks, made in a low tone, we gather that he thinks he is ill, without getting any more precise information about the nature of the illness and its symptoms. The patient attributes his malady to the onanism he has practised since he was ten years old. He thinks that he has thus incurred the guilt of a sin against the sixth commandment, has very much reduced his power of working, has made himself feel languid and miserable, and has become a hypochondriac. Thus, as the result of reading certain books, he imagined that he had a rupture and suffered from wasting of the spinal cord, neither of which was the case. He would not associate with his comrades any longer, because he thought they saw the result of his vice and made fun of him. The patient makes all these statements in an indifferent tone, without looking up or troubling about his surroundings. His expression betrays no emotion; he only laughs for a moment now and then. There is occasional wrinkling of the forehead or facial spasm. Round the mouth and nose a fine, changing twitching is constantly observed.

The patient gives us a correct account of his past experiences. His knowledge speaks for the high degree of his education; indeed, he was ready to enter the University a year ago. He also knows where he is and how long he has been here, but he is only very imperfectly acquainted with the names of the people round him, and says that he has never asked about them. He can only give a very meagre account of the general events of the last year. In answer to our questions, he declares that he is ready to remain in the hospital for the present. He would certainly prefer it if he could enter a profession, but he cannot say what he would like to take up. No physical disturbances can be definitely made out, except exaggerated knee-jerks.

At first sight, perhaps the patient reminds you of the states of depression which we have learned to recognize in former lectures. But on closer examination you will easily understand that, in spite of certain isolated points of resemblance, we have to deal with a disease having features of quite another kind. The patient makes his statements slowly and in monosyllables, not because his wish to answer meets with overpowering hindrances, but because he feels no desire to speak at all. He certainly hears and understands what is said to him very well, but he does not take the trouble to attend to it. He pays no heed, and answers whatever occurs to him without thinking. No visible effort of the will is to be noticed. All his movements are languid and expressionless, but are made without hindrance or trouble. There is no sign of emotional dejection, such as one would expect from the nature of his talk, and the patient remains quite dull throughout, experiencing neither fear nor hope nor desires. He is not at all deeply affected by what goes on before him, although he understands it without actual difficulty. It is all the same to him who appears or disappears where he is, or who talks to him and takes care of him, and he does not even once ask their names.

This peculiar and fundamental want of any *strong feeling of the impressions of life*, with unimpaired ability to understand and to remember, is really the diagnostic symptom of the disease we have before us. It becomes still plainer if we observe the patient for a time and see that, in spite of his good education, he lies in bed for weeks and months, or sits about without feeling the slightest need of occupation. He broods, staring in front of him with expressionless features, over which a vacant smile occasionally plays, or at the best turns over the leaves of a book for a moment, apparently speechless, and not troubling about anything. Even when he has visitors, he sits without showing any interest, does not ask about what is happening at home, hardly even greets his parents, and goes back indifferently to the ward. He can hardly be induced to write a letter, and says that he has nothing to write about. But he occasionally composes a letter to the doctor, expressing all kinds of distorted, half-formed ideas, with a peculiar and silly play on words, in very fair style, but with little connection. He begs for 'a little more *allegro* in the treatment,' and 'liberationary movement with a view to the widening of the horizon,' will '*ergo* extort some wit in lectures,' and '*nota bene* for God's sake only does not wish to be combined with the club of the harmless.' 'Professional work is the balm of life.'

These scraps of writing, as well as his statements that he is pondering over the world, of putting himself together a moral philosophy, leave no doubt that, besides the emotional barrenness, there is also a high degree of *weakness* of *judgment* and *flightiness*, although the pure memory has suffered little, if at all. We have a *mental and emotional infirmity* to deal with, which reminds us only outwardly of the states of depression previously described. This infirmity is the incurable outcome of a very common history of disease, to which we will provisionally give the name of *Dementia Praecox*.

The development of the illness has been quite gradual. Our patient, whose parents suffered transitorily from 'dejection,' did not go to school till he was seven years old, as he was a delicate child and spoke badly, but when he did he learned quite well. He was considered to be a reserved and stubborn child. Having practised onanism at a very early age, he became more and more solitary in the last few years, and thought that he was laughed at by his brothers and sisters, and shut out from society because of his ugliness. For this reason he could not bear a looking-glass in his room. After passing the written examination on leaving school, a year ago, he gave up the *vivâ voce*, because he could not work any longer. He cried a great deal, masturbated much, ran about aimlessly, played in a senseless way on the piano, and began to write observations '"On the Nerve-play of Life," which he cannot get on with.' He was incapable of any kind of work, even physical, felt 'done for,' asked for a revolver, ate Swedish matches to destroy himself, and lost all affection for his family. From time to time he became excited and troublesome, and shouted out of the window at night. In the hospital, too, a state of excitement lasting for several days was observed, in which he chattered in a confused way, made faces, ran about at full speed, wrote disconnected scraps of composition, and crossed and recrossed them with flourishes and unmeaning combinations of letters. After this a state of tranquillity ensued, in which he could give absolutely no account of his extraordinary behaviour.

Besides the mental and emotional imbecility, we meet with other very significant features in the case before us. The first of these is the silly, vacant *laugh*, which is constantly observed in dementia praecox. There is joyous humor corresponding to this laugh; indeed, some patients complain that they cannot help laughing, without feeling at all inclined to laugh. Other important symptoms are *making faces* or grimacing, and the fine muscular twitching in the face which is also very characteristic of dementia praecox. Then we must notice the tendency to peculiar, distorted turns of speech – *senseless playing with syllables and words* – as it often assumes very extraordinary forms in this disease. Lastly, I may call your attention to the fact that, when you offer him your hand, the patient does not grasp it, but only *stretches his own hand out stiffly to meet it*. Here we have the first sign of a disturbance which is often developed in dementia praecox in the most astounding way.

As the illness developed quite gradually, it is hardly possible to fix on any particular point of time as the beginning. In such cases, the change which is taking place is easily referred to some culpable looseness of morality, which it is sought to combat by educational means. Onanism in particular, which is very common in our patients, is usually held to be the source of the disease, so that cases of this kind were formerly spoken of as the insanity of onanism. I am nevertheless inclined to see in onanism a symptom, rather than the cause, of the disease. We often see the whole severe mental and physical condition arise, without any striking degree of onanism, and we also know degenerate onanists who present quite different symptoms. Hence there cannot well be any question of a regular causal connection between onanism and dementia praecox. Besides, the disease is just as common among women, in whom the weakening effect of onanism must be much slighter. Lastly, it is to be observed that the disease often sets in quite suddenly, another circumstance not exactly adapted to confirm the supposition of its onanistic origin.

Emil Kraepelin, *Lectures on Clinical Psychiatry* (1894)

=

But is schizophrenia what it seems? Joseph Berke comments.

More often than not, a person diagnosed as 'mentally ill' is the emotional scapegoat for the turmoil in his or her family or associates, and may, in fact, be the 'sanest' member of the group. The disturbance may express itself slowly or rapidly, quietly or explosively, immediately or after many years.

In medical school I had been taught that the gravest form of 'mental illness' was something called 'schizophrenia'. I say 'something' because I could never match the definition of this 'illness' with the reality of the people who were supposed to manifest it. So, I shall begin my contribution to this book by telling you how I began to understand that 'schizophrenia' is a career, not an illness. This career always involves at least two professionals, a patient and a psychiatrist. More often than not it is launched with the aid and encouragement of one's immediate family. Furthermore, the experiences that occur in the person labelled 'schizophrenic', and are commonly subsumed under the term 'psychosis', are not at all unintelligible, that is, crazy. They simply occur at a different order or reality, akin to a waking dream. The social invalidation of such experiences by calling them 'sick' or 'mad' is a basic interpersonal manoeuvre among peoples in Western cultures where dreams and dream-like states are not considered a valid vehicle for conveying reality, no matter how much truth they may express.

Mary Barnes and Joseph Berke, *Mary Barnes: Two Accounts of a Journey Through Madness* (1973)

=

What is schizophrenia?

In the face of the above, I propose to take a step back, and start from the following. *Schizophrenia is the name for a condition that most psychiatrists ascribe to patients they call schizophrenic.* This ascription is a system of attributions that has a variable internal consistency, and is predominantly derogatory. It is frequently in a mixture of clinical–medical–biological–psychoanalytical psychiatrese, which vies with schizophrenese itself in its apparent profound confusion.

Hypothesis: this set of ascriptions to a person, and this induction into the role of schizophrenic, themselves generate much of the behaviour that is classifid as 'symptomatology' of schizophrenia.

Experiment: Take a group of normal persons, group N (by agreed criteria)
Treat them as schizophrenic
Take a group of 'early' schizophrenics, group X (by agreed criteria)
Treat them as normal.

Prediction: Many of N will begin to display the agreed criteria of schizophrenia
 Many of X will begin to display the agreed criteria of normality

Experiment: Take a group of 'early' schizophrenics
(i) treat them in role as crazy
(ii) treat them like oneself as sane
Prediction: In (i) the 'symptomatology' of schizophrenia will be very much greater
(ii) the symptomatology of schizophrenia will be greatly diminished

An experiment of such a kind is feasible, and as far as I know has not been done. How extraordinary.

R. D. Laing, *The Politics of the Family* (1971)

=

Lycanthropy

Lycanthropy, Wolf-madness, is a disease, in which men run barking and howling about graves and fields in the night, lying hid for the most part all day, and will not be perswaded but that they are Wolves, or some such beasts. *Donatus ab Altomari* saith, they have

usually hollow eyes, scabbed legs and thighs, very dry and pale, and
that he saw two of them in his time. *Wierus* tells a storie of such a
one at *Padua*, 1541, that would not believe to the contrary, but that
he was a Wolf: He hath another instance of a Spaniard, who
thought himself a Bear. *Forestus* confirms as much by many
examples; one amongst the rest, of which he was an eye-witness, at
Alcamer in *Holland*; a poor Husbandman, that still hunted about
graves, and kept in Church-yards, of a pale, black, ugly, and fearful
look. This malady, saith *Avicenna*, troubleth men most in February, and is now adayes frequent in *Bohemia* and *Hungary*,
according to *Heurnius*. A certain young man, in this City, tall,
slender, and black, of a wild and strange look, was taken with this
kinde of malady, for he run barking and howling about the room
where he was, and would make to get out; so that its most like, if he
had got abroad, he would have haunted some solitary place: I
remember I opened a vein, and drew forth a very large quantity of
blood, black like Soot.

Robert Bayfield, *A Treatise De Morborum Capitis* (1663)

=

Such disorders were still to be seen in Esquirol's day. He termed
them Zoanthropy.

Connected with demonomania as a sub-variety, is Zoanthropy; a
deplorable aberration of the mind, which perverts the instinct even,
and persuades the lypemaniac that he is changed into a brute. This
strange form of insanity has been observed from the highest
antiquity; and was connected with the worship of the ancient
pagans who sacrificed animals to their gods. Lycanthropy was
described by Ætius and the Arabians. It has been known since the
fifteenth century, and they have given in France, to those afflicted
with this disease, the appellation of wolf-men. These wretched
beings fly from their fellow men, live in the woods, church-yards
and ancient ruins, and wander, howling, about the country at night.
They permit their beard and nails to grow, and thus become confirmed in their deplorable conviction, by seeing themselves covered
with long hair, and armed with claws. Impelled by necessity or a
cruel ferocity, they fall upon children, tear, slay and devour them.

Roulet, at the end of the sixteenth century, was arrested as a
wolf-man, and confessed, that with his brother and cousin, after
having rubbed the body with an ointment, they were changed into
wolves, and that they then ran about the fields, and devoured
children. Justice, more enlightened than in the preceding ages of the
world, sent these unfortunate men to a hospital for the insane.

J.-E.-D. Esquirol (see page 149), Mental Maladies:
A Treatise on Insanity (1845)

=

Syphilophobia

In this Disease more particularly, we have two sorts of People to
deal with, the Fool-hardy on the one hand, who cannot be persuaded they have occasion for taking any Medicine, nor will be
confin'd to any proper Regimen; and the poor Melancholic on the
other, who, how free soever from the same, will not be convinc'd
that he is so, nor easy any longer than whilst under a Course of
Physick.

A Tradesman in good Business, of a thoughtful Temper, or
inclining to Melancholy, having, in his younger Days, been too
familiar with a Wench living in the same House as a Servant, grew
soon after very pensive, as fancying he had got the Foul Disease,
upon a Belief, as it seemed, that every Woman playing the Whore
must surely be distemper'd. Under these Jealousies he continued for
some Years, without making his Complaint to any one, till at length
happening to marry, his Discontent of Mind soon after encreased,
which was observ'd in his Family; yet his Wife could get nothing
out of him, but that he had been a wicked Man, and had ruin'd her
and her Child ... At length Matters were brought to that pass, that
not caring to come into his Shop, he betook himself to his Chamber, where he was usually poring on some Books of Devotion, and
desir'd not to see his old Acquaintance ... This poor crazy-headed
Person came one Evening to my House, and desir'd a Word in
private: Where, by his very Aspect, before he began his Story, I
suspected what kind of a Chapman I had got. He sat down and fell
into Tears, wringing his Hands, and telling me he was ruin'd, that
he had got an ill Disease; and his Concern was not so much on his

own Account but for that he had given the same to his Wife and Child. I ask'd him how long it was since he was clap'd; he answer'd me, nine Years; I then enquir'd, unto whom he had apply'd for Cure, and he said, being asham'd, he had consulted no body, till long time after, when he took as much Physick as had cost him twenty Pounds, from a Doctor upon Ludgate-Hill. I now wanted to know the Symptoms; and therefore suspecting he had been impos'd upon, ask'd him whether he had any Running, with Heat of Urine, or Breakings out, after he had been concern'd with the Woman, who he said gave him the Distemper; to which he reply'd, neither the first, nor the last . . . his Doctor . . . told him it was an inward Pox; and that if it had been attended with Running, or Blotches on the outside of his Body, he could have cur'd him for half the Money.

Daniel Turner, *Syphilis: A Practical Dissertation on the Venereal Disease* (1724)

=

Naming the phobias

A form of morbid fear that I have lately described, and of which I have seen a large number of cases, is *Anthropophobia*, derived from the Greek *anthropos*, man, and *phobos*, fear. This term applies to aversion to society, a fear of seeing, encountering, or mingling with a multitude, or of meeting any one besides ourselves. This phase of morbid fear has different varieties. In quite a number of cases, this fear of man is so severe as to compel patients to give up business entirely; and I know a number of cases where men of strong muscles and having the appearance of great physical strength have been compelled, through this symptom alone, to withdraw from the occupations in which they were engaged; they could not face men, deal with them, persuade them to buy or sell, or have any influence over them; they dreaded to meet a human being. This form of morbid fear is often accompanied with turning away of the eyes and hanging down of the head, but not necessarily so, and usually so only in the severer cases. The world over, aversion of the eyes with a turning away of the face is an expression of the emotion of humility and bashfulness, that is, of a feeling of weakness as compared with the person in whose presence we stand – an instinctive and involuntary recognition of the fact that, for the moment, our force is inferior to his. In neurasthenia this same principle appears as a pathological symptom – an expression of debility, of inadequacy, of incompetence. This aversion of the eyes is so constant a symptom in these neurasthenic patients that I often make the diagnosis as soon as they enter the office, before a word has been spoken by either party, and even before the patient has had time to be seated. I have now under my care a young man who is so badly anthropophobic that, even when I take his head in my hands and hold it up, it is impossible to keep his eyes fixed on mine for more than an instant . . . forms of morbid fear, whatever the cause may be; and as such it should be studied and treated.

There is a manifestation of morbid fear which is not uncommon, and to which we might perhaps give the term *pantaphobia*, or fear of everything; all responsibility, every attempt to make a change of movement being the result of dread and alarm. The wife of one of my patients has a morbid fear in reference to one of her sons, a lad of about fifteen years of age; and so distressed is she by it that she cannot allow him to go out of the house, or out of her sight; fearing lest he may be kidnapped, or some harm may come to him, as in the case of Charlie Ross. The poor fellow is thus kept a prisoner most of the time, and the whole family is disturbed and annoyed. He must remain in the city during the summer, as she cannot allow him to leave town; and at no season can he go anywhere unless accompanied by his tutor.

A lady now under my treatment, who is also *astraphobic*, tells me that she is afraid to go into the street, to do any shopping, or attend to any business; that it is an affliction for her to see a physician; everything is a dread to her, even when there is no draft made upon her physical strength.

The expression, *phobophobia*, fear of fears, might possibly apply to a certain class of nervous patients who fear they may fear, provided they make an attempt to move or go in any direction where their morbid fear is in the way; they are afraid even when they do and say nothing. These persons fear when they are entirely still and inactive, from a fear that if they attempt to do anything they will be attacked with their especial morbid fear. One of my patients – a stout and large man – in addition to topophobia (fear of places) had at one time a fear of committing some crime that would disgrace him. He was ashamed of his fear; he could not help it, although he has now entirely recovered,

Siderodromophobia – 'This is a form of intense spinal irritation, described by Rigler of Germany, coupled with a hysterical condition, and morbid disinclination for work, which is the result of shock, and occurs among railroad men; most commonly seen in cases of railway-engine mechanics who have some altered nerve condition, or irritation of the nerve-centres. It is the perpetual jarring, shaking, and noise which lead by degrees to this change, and which under the influence of some unexpected shock completely breaks up the nervous equilibrium.'

George Beard, *Practical Treatise on Nervous Exhaustion* (1890)

=

The modern manias: is their proliferation itself a form of mental aberration?

Recent clinical observation has discovered a long series of similar fixed ideas or 'monomanias,' and recognized the fact that they are one and all the consequence of a fundamental disposition of the organism, viz, of its degeneration. It was unnecessary for Magnan to give a special name to each symptom of degeneration, and to draw up in array, with almost comical effect, the host of 'phobias' and 'manias.' Agoraphobia (fear of open space), claustrophobia (fear of enclosed space), rupophobia (fear of dirt), iophobia (fear of poison), nosophobia (fear of sickness), aichmophobia (fear of pointed objects), belenophobia (fear of needles), cremnophobia (fear of abysses), trichophobia (fear of hair), onomatomania (folly of words and names), pyromania (incendiary madness), kleptomania (madness for theft), dipsomania (madness for drink), erotomania (love madness), arithmomania (madness of numbers), oniomania (madness for buying), etc. This list might be lengthened at pleasure, and enriched by nearly all the roots of the Greek dictionary. It is simply philologico-medical trifling. None of the disorders discovered and described by Magnan and his pupils, and decorated with a sonorous Greek name, forms an independent entity, and appears separately; and Morel is right in disregarding as unessential all these varied manifestations of a morbid cerebral activity, and adhering to the principal phenomenon which lies at the base of all the 'phobias' and 'manias,' namely, the great emotionalism of the degenerate. If to emotionalism, or an excessive excitability, he had added the cerebral debility, which implies feebleness of perception, will, memory, judgment, as well as inattention and instability, he would have exhaustively characterized the nature of degeneration, and perhaps prevented psychiatry from being stuffed with a crowd of useless and disturbing designations. Kowalewski approached much nearer to the truth in his well-known treatise, where he has represented all the mental disorders of the degenerate as one single malady, which merely presents different degrees of intensity, and which induces in its mildest form neurasthenia; under a graver aspect impulsions and groundless anxieties; and, in its most serious form, the madness of brooding thought or doubt. Within these limits may be ranged all the particular 'manias' and 'phobias' which at present swarm in the literature of mental therapeutics.

Max Nordau, *Degeneration* (1895)

=

Benjamin Rush (see page xiv) mocked what seemed the irresistible urge amongst modern doctors to multiply disease conditions.

Dr Cullen has divided Hydrophobia into two species. The principal species is that disease which is communicated by the bite of a mad animal, and which is accompanied with a dread of water. Without detracting from the merit of Dr Cullen, I cannot help thinking that the genus of the disease which he has named Hydrophobia, should have been PHOBIA, and that the number, and names of the species, should have been taken from the names of the objects of fear or aversion. In conformity to this idea, I shall define Phobia to be 'a fear of an imaginary evil, or an undue fear of a real one'. The following species appear to belong to it.

   1. The CAT PHOBIA. It will be unnecessary to mention instances of the prevalence of this distemper . . . 2. The RAT PHOBIA is a more common disease than the first species that has been mentioned: it is peculiar, in some measure, to the female sex . . . 3. The INSECT

PHOBIA. This disease is peculiar to the female sex. A spider – a flea – or a musqueto, alighting upon a lady's neck, has often produced an hysterical fit ... 4. The ODOR PHOBIA is a very frequent disease with all classes of people ... 5. The DIRT PHOBIA. This disease is peculiar to certain ladies ... They make every body miserable around them with their excessive cleanliness: the whole of their lives is one continued warfare with dirt ... 6. The RUM PHOBIA is a very *rare* distemper ... If it were possible to communicate this distemper as we do the small-pox, by inoculation, what an immense revenue would be derived from it by physicians ... 7. The WATER PHOBIA. This species includes not the dread of swallowing, but of *crossing* water. I have known some people, who sweat with terror in crossing an ordinary ferry ... 8. The SOLO PHOBIA; by which I mean the dread of solitude ... 9. The POWER PHOBIA. This distemper belongs to certain demagogues. Persons afflicted with it, consider power as an evil – they abhor even the sight of an officer of government ... 10. The FACTION PHOBIA. This disease is peculiar to persons of an opposite character to those who are afraid of power ... 11. The WANT PHOBIA. This disease is confined chiefly to old people ... 12. The DOCTOR PHOBIA. This distemper is often complicated with other diseases. It arises, in some instances, from the dread of taking physic, or of submitting to the remedies of bleeding and blistering. In some instances I have known it occasioned by a desire sick people feel of deceiving themselves, by being kept in ignorance of the danger of their disorders ... 13. The BLOOD PHOBIA. There is a native dread of the sight of blood in every human creature, implanted probably for the wise purpose of preventing our injuring or destroying ourselves, or others ... 14. The THUNDER PHOBIA. This species is common to all ages, and to both sexes: I have seen it produce the most distressing appearances and emotions upon many people ... 15. The HOME PHOBIA. This disease belongs to all those men who prefer tavern, to domestic society ... 16. The CHURCH PHOBIA This disease has become epidemic in the city of Philadelphia ... 17. The GHOST PHOBIA. This distemper is most common among servants and children ... 18. The DEATH PHOBIA. The fear of death is natural to man – but there are degrees of it which constitute a *disease*.

Benjamin Rush, 'On the Different Species of Phobia' (1798)

=

The futility of diagnosis

Face to face with the patient, it is futile to waste time in considering whether he is a case of neurasthenia, psychosthenia, anxiety neurosis, or hysteria. The war has unfortunately increased the universal love of labels. Medicine is particularly thought to be based on the principles of a penny-in-the-slot machine. Make a so-called 'diagnosis' and the rest follows mechanically. Hysteria is treated with electricity and massage; an anxiety neurosis needs a 'rest cure'; obsessions require fresh air and cheery companions. Nothing is more pitiful than the condition of the medical man who finds that these rules of practice break under him. *He is filled with mingled anger and despair, which frequently lead him to vent his impotence on the patient*; he expresses his opinion that 'the fellow is a rotter,' and he 'would like to see all his sort on the parade ground.' He has made no attempt to investigate the forces at work that produce the condition he does not understand. His 'diagnoses' are but camouflaged ignorance. The only diagnosis that is of the slightest value, or is worthy of the dignity of our profession, is the laying bare of the forces which underlie the morbid state and the discovery of the mental experiences which have set them in action. *Diagnosis of the psycho-neuroses is an individual investigation; they are not diseases, but morbid activities of a personality which demand to be understood.* The form they assume depends on the mental and psychological life of the patient, his habits, and constitution.

Henry Head, 'Observations on the Elements of the Psycho-Neuroses'

(1920)

15

Freud and His Followers

Unquestionably the greatest single figure in the history of psychiatry, Freud is intriguing as a patient as well as a therapist. As is documented in his correspondence with his fellow physician, Wilhelm Fliess, he personally underwent a severe mental and emotional crisis, sparked by the death of his father; this precipitated a lengthy self-analysis, at the conclusion of which Freud emerged, as from a cocoon, equipped with the key theories of psychoanalysis, above all, the Oedipus complex.

Quite apart from his therapeutic labours with patients and his founding of the psychoanalytic movement, Freud's enduring importance is utterly bound up with his extraordinary literary artistry: even were his psychodynamic theories to become wholly scientifically and therapeutically discredited, his talent for depicting the self-deceptions of the psyche, the tensions of the family, and the rich ambiguities of the psychopathology of everyday life, both in his case-histories and in his later, speculative writings, would ensure his immortality as a chronicler of the human comedy.

Moreover, the reader cannot resist applying Freudian methods to Freud's own writings, and, by extension, his life. There are times – as with his published autobiography – when the founder of psychoanalysis's apparent failure to apply Freudian insights to himself – to set himself on the couch – seems little less than wilful. Ruthless and acute with the self-deceptions of his patients, how well Freud understood himself is more open to debate.

Some indications are perhaps afforded by the accounts left by his analysands of treatment in Freud's consulting rooms in his home at Berggasse 19. All testify to Freud's charisma and his dazzling insights. But many, such as the Russian aristocrat known as the

'Wolf-Man', were to find Freud's reading of their life experiences dogmatic and far-fetched. Abraham Kardiner, himself later a distinguished psychoanalyst, thought that Freud habitually projected his own psychological turmoils on to his patients (or, roughly, that the creator of the idea of transference never showed adequate understanding of counter-transference).

Freud prescribed the protocols for analysis. The therapist, he suggested, should be aloof, dispassionate, scientific. The informal analytical contract stipulated that the patient should say everything that came into his head, and that the analyst should listen and, as necessary, encourage the therapeutic flow of free associations. The signs are that Freud hardly practised what he preached. His own write-up of the Dora case leaves the reader in no doubt that the analyst fought his teenage patient tooth-and-nail. It is equally clear, from the memoirs of Hilda Doolittle, Sergius P. and others, that Freud often assumed a combative stance *vis-à-vis* his clients, and became emotionally involved with them.

A giant in every way, Freud has overshadowed his co-workers, followers, and competitors. Jung, Adler, Ferenzi and those younger colleagues, such as Wilhelm Reich, whose connections were slightly more oblique, all subscribed to certain basic tenets, yet developed depth psychiatry in different directions according to their own temperaments and insights. The last half-century has seen an enormous proliferation of psychodynamic philosophies and practices, from the ultra-biologistic dynamics of Reich (with its attractively simplistic assumption that orgasm contains the answer to all emotional problems) to the upbeat, folksy optimism of Carl Rogers.

Accepted for analysis

Late in April 1921, I received a letter from Freud which read as follows:

Dear Dr Kardiner,

I am glad to accept you for analysis especially since Dr Frink has given so good an account of you. He is strongly confident of your chances as an analyst, and spoke highly of your character.

Six months are a good term to achieve something both theoretically and personally. You are requested to be in Vienna on the first of October, as my hours will be given away shortly after my return from the vacation, and give me definite assurance of coming some time before – let us say, in the beginning of September.

My fees are $10.00 an hour or about $250 monthly to be paid in effective notes, not in checks which I could only change for crowns.

If you understand German, it would be a great help to our analysis.

With kind regards,

Yours truly,
FREUD

This letter changed my fate and my world. To be an apprentice to one of the great figures of our time! I had been in psychoanalytic practice for a little over a year and was also medical examiner at the Children's Court. At the time, there were all of eight practicing psychoanalysts in New York.

A. Kardiner, *My Analysis with Freud* (1977)

=

In the thick of attempting to unravel the mysteries of hysteria, Freud confides in his friend Wilhelm Fliess.

Vienna, October 16, 1895

Dearest Wilhelm,

Fortunately I had mailed the little box as well as the letter *before* I received your reproachful lines. Nevertheless, you are right, but I could explain everything to your satisfaction. The feverish work of these last weeks, the enticing hopes and disappointments, a few genuine findings – all that against a background of feeling miserable physically and the usual everyday annoyances and difficulties. If on top of all that I send you a few pages of philosophical stammering (not that I think they are successful), I hope to have put you in a conciliatory mood again.

I am still all mixed up. I am almost certain that I have solved the riddles of hysteria and obsessional neurosis with the formulas of infantile sexual shock and sexual pleasure, and I am equally certain that both neuroses are, *in general*, curable – not just individual symptoms but the neurotic disposition itself. This gives me a kind of faint joy – for having lived some forty years not quite in vain – and yet no genuine satisfaction because the psychological gap in the new knowledge claims my entire interest.

I naturally have not had a moment left for the migraine, but that will still come. I completely gave up smoking again, so as not to have to reproach myself for the bad pulse, and to be rid of the miserable struggle against the craving for the fourth and fifth [cigar]; I prefer struggling right away against the first one. Abstinence probably is not very conductive to psychic contentment either.

Enough about myself now. The result is perhaps still gratifying – that I consider the two neuroses essentially conquered and am looking forward to the struggle with the psychological con- struction.

Sigmund Freud, letter to Wilhelm Fliess (16 October 1895)

=

The Wolf-Man's analysis begins

When, in January 1910, we arrived in Vienna and met Freud, I was so impressed and inspired by his personality that I told Dr D. I had definitely decided to be analyzed by Freud, so there was no point in continuing our journey to Dubois in Geneva. Dr D. agreed.

Of course I told Professor Freud of my stormy courtship of Therese in Munich, and of Therese's visit to Berlin which had had such an unexpected and fateful end. Freud's judgment of the former was a positive one, but he called the latter a 'flight from the woman,' and in accordance with this he answered my question whether I should return to Therese with a 'yes,' but with the condition that this could take place only after several months of analysis.

During these first months in analysis with Professor Freud, a completely new world was opened to me, a world known to only a few people in those days. Much that had been ununderstandable in my life before that time began to make sense, as relationships which were formerly hidden in darkness now emerged into my consciousness.

Muriel Gardner (ed.), *The Wolf-man and Sigmund Freud* (1972)

=

Freud's greatest book

With the appearance of *The Interpretation of Dreams* in 1900, psychoanalysis became established. This greatest of Freud's works is one of introspection; in it all interest is devoted to the innermost self of man, to the neglect of the external world, which pales in comparison to the fascination of this inner world. That this turn-of-the-century Viennese *chef d'oeuvre* was indeed the result of desperation at being unable to change the course of the external world, and represented an effort to make up this deficiency by a single-minded interest in the dark underworld, is attested to by the motto which Freud put at its beginning: Virgil's line *Flectere si nequeo superos, Acheronta movebo* ('If I cannot move heaven, I will stir up the underworld'). This motto was a most succinct suggestion that turning inward toward the hidden aspects of the self was due to a despair that it was no longer within one's ability to alter the external world or stop its dissolution; that therefore the best one could do was to deny importance to the world at large by concentrating all interest on the dark aspects of the psyche.

Bruno Bettelheim, *Recollections and Reflections* (1990)

=

If dreams are wish fulfilments, why do we have unpleasurable dreams?

Unpleasurable dreams may also be 'punishment-dreams'. It must be admitted that their recognition means in a certain sense a new addition to the theory of dreams. What is fulfilled in them is equally an unconscious wish, namely a wish that the dreamer may be punished for a repressed and forbidden wishful impulse. To that extent dreams of this kind fall in with the condition that has been laid down here that the motive force for constructing a dream must be provided by a wish belonging to the unconscious. A closer psychological analysis, however, shows how they differ from other wishful dreams. In the cases forming Group B the dream-constructing wish is an unconscious one and belongs to the repressed, while in punishment-dreams, though it is equally an unconscious one, it must be reckoned as belonging not to the repressed but to the 'ego'. Thus punishment-dreams indicate the possibility that the ego may have a greater share than was supposed in the construction of dreams. The mechanism of dream-formation would in general be greatly clarified if instead of the opposition between 'conscious' and 'unconscious' we were to speak of that between the 'ego' and the 'repressed'. This cannot be done, however, without taking account of the processes underlying the psychoneuroses, and for that reason it has not been carried out in the present work. I will only add that punishment-dreams are not in general subject to the condition that the day's residues shall be of a distressing kind. On the contrary, they occur most easily where the opposite is the case – where the day's residues are thoughts of a satisfying nature but the satisfaction which they express is a forbidden one.

Sigmund Freud, *On the Interpretation of Dreams* (1900)

＝

The meaning of dreams

Before joining the Navy I bought Freud's *Introductory Lectures* because I heard it was sexy. It proved disappointing. Some of his ideas are screwy, like 'steeple' in dreams meaning 'penis,' so I put it out of my mind. I dream about steeples all the time. A pal saw the book on my dresser, asked if I could understand it. I felt ashamed to admit it was mine and said it was Carl's.

Met a girl named Josephine for the third time last Friday at a dance. She was standing at the dance-hall bar. Since she only took a Coke, she may be a good girl, but I don't know.

At night I have trouble praying. I have no right to pray for things, for I feel unworthy, a nobody. Why should God waste His time and listen to me? All my actions are selfish; I've accomplished nothing. All day long I just fool around and daydream. I fantasy being a scout leader to help little boys develop, but I never do anything about it ...

I wear glasses to relieve fatigue and eyestrain. They don't really magnify much. I use them mainly for reading. When I'm tired I can't see clearly, and my eyes blur without them.

[*Pedro was reminded to mention his dreams during session.*] I have a lot of trouble remembering my dreams. You said I'd dream, and I do now, but I don't recall them properly. As I reach for paper and pencil by my bed, my arm gets numb. I feel so tired that I flop over like a fish, dead to the world. Or I write in the dark with my eyes still closed and can't make it out the next day . . .

Harold Kenneth Fink, *Long Journey: A Verbatim Report of a Case of Severe Psychosexual Infantilism* (1954)

=

Freud's skill as an analyst: the Wolf-Man's view, as told to a Viennese journalist, Karin Obholzer

w: Everything was so new and interesting for me, you understand. I was used to the old psychiatrists . . . He said that one should say out loud whatever came into one's mind, just the way the thoughts came.

o: He said, 'Treatment means that you have to say everything that occurs to you'?

w: Everything that occurs to you.

o: Did he explain why?

w: No, he did not go into details. He must have thought that the important things are in the subconscious and that they emerge through free association. When he had explained everything to me, I said to him, 'All right then, I agree, but I am going to check whether it is correct.' And he said: 'Don't start that. Because the moment you try to view things critically, your treatment will get nowhere. I will help you, whether you now believe in it, or not.' So I naturally gave up the idea of any further criticism.

o: Why?

w: Well, because he said that if I continued to criticize I would make no progress, because I always want to prove something. He writes somewhere that I had the tendency to clear up contradictions. But that may be the very opposite of my character, because contradictions are constantly battling each other inside me. And precisely in those cases where I should be logical, I fail. In

theoretical matters, I am logical. I would rather be logical where
feelings are concerned . . . But it is interesting that he should have
said, 'Don't criticize, don't reflect, don't look for contradictions,
but accept what I tell you, and improvement will come by itself.'
That's how he succeeded in bringing about a total transference to
himself. Is that a good thing, do you suppose? That's the question. Too strong a transference ends with your transferring to
individuals who replace Freud, as it were, and with your
believing them uncritically. And that happened to me, to a
degree. So transference is a dangerous thing.

Karin Obholzer, The Wolf-Man Sixty Years After (1982)

=

A Freudian slip?

Is this what they call a 'Freudian slip?' Cousin Juan and I were
discussing girls in the kitchen one day when I was eleven. Although
the bathroom was nearby, I lost my head and impulsively opened
the garbage pail to piss in it. Catching myself, I tried to cover up by
keeping the conversation going. But in a little while I did it again,
shook myself, closed my pants quickly, and tried to laugh it off,
saying like a big fellow, 'What the hell am I doing!' But Juan neither
laughed nor seemed to notice anything unusual. Perhaps he was
convinced that all Laveros used the pail for that purpose, or maybe
he kept a pot under his bed at night. I had a vague desire to seduce
Juan, like the time we touched pricks, but I got cold feet.

I've discovered that I play with myself more often when I feel
frustrated or impotent. Sunday I bought some magazines about the
nudist movement, put my balls between my legs while drinking in
the picture of a beautiful naked girl. I thought to myself, 'Something missing here!' She had a boyish face that bothered me, and
large pointed breasts out of proportion to her thin body. Her sex
triangle annoyed me the most; it wasn't all there!

Harold Kenneth Fink, Long Journey: A Verbatim Report of a Case of
Severe Psychosexual Infantilism (1954)

=

*Freud sees parallels between the witches of earlier centuries (see, for
example, pages 159–60) and his own hysterical female patients.*

January 17, 1897
IX., Berggasse 19

My dear Wilhelm,
    You are obviously enjoying the goings-on in my head; that is why
I shall let you know every time there is something new. I still think
highly of the determination of the psychoses and shall present the
material to you soon. You caused me to doubt my explanation of
epilepsy, but it is not yet entirely shattered. What would you say, by
the way, if I told you that all of my brand-new prehistory of
hysteria is already known and was published a hundred times over,
though several centuries ago? Do you remember that I always said
that the medieval theory of possession held by the ecclesiastical
courts was identical with our theory of a foreign body and the
splitting of consciousness! But why did the devil who took possession of the poor things invariably abuse them sexually and in a
loathsome manner? Why are their confessions under torture so like
the communications made by my patients in psychic treatment?
Sometime soon I must delve into the literature on this subject.
Incidentally, the cruelties make it possible to understand some
symptoms of hysteria that until now have been obscure. The pins
which make their appearance in the oddest ways; the sewing
needles on account of which the poor things let their breasts be
mutilated and which are not visible by X-ray, though they can no
doubt be found in their seduction stories! Eckstein has a scene [that
is, remembers] where the diabolus sticks needles into her fingers
and then places a candy on each drop of blood. As far as the blood
is concerned, you are completely without blame! A counterpart to
this: fear of needles and pointed objects from the second psychic
period. In regard to cruelty in general: fear of injuring someone
with a knife or otherwise.
    Once more, the inquisitors prick with needles to discover the
devil's stigmata, and in a similar situation the victims think of the
same old cruel story in fictionalized form [helped perhaps by dis-
guises of the seducers]. Thus, not only the victims but also the

executioners recalled in this their earliest youth.

On Saturday I fulfilled my duty of giving an account of your work on the nose in my course on neuroses, and on Thursday I shall continue it. The five boys properly pricked up their ears. Indeed, it already makes enthralling [material].

As you see, I am doing very well. Why are you not feeling lively now? Oscar and Melanie recently paid us a pleasant visit.

Cordial greetings to your wife and your boy.

Yours
Sigm.

Sigmund Freud, letter to Wilhelm Flieess (17 January 1897)

=

Freud saved from a fatal error

Before going further into the question of infantile sexuality I must mention an error into which I fell for a while and which might well have had fatal consequences for the whole of my work. Under the pressure of the technical procedure which I used at that time, the majority of my patients reproduced from their childhood scenes in which they were sexually seduced by some grown-up person. With female patients the part of seducer was almost always assigned to their father. I believed these stories, and consequently supposed that I had discovered the roots of the subsequent neurosis in these experiences of sexual seduction in childhood. My confidence was strengthened by a few cases in which relations of this kind with a father, uncle, or elder brother had continued up to an age at which memory was to be trusted. If the reader feels inclined to shake his head at my credulity, I cannot altogether blame him; though I may plead that this was at a time when I was intentionally keeping my critical faculty in abeyance so as to preserve an unprejudiced and receptive attitude towards the many novelties which were coming to my notice every day. When, however, I was at last obliged to recognize that these scenes of seduction had never taken place, and that they were only phantasies which my patients had made up or which I myself had perhaps forced upon them, I was for some time completely at a loss. My confidence alike in my technique and in its results suffered a severe blow; it could not be disputed that I had arrived at these scenes by a technical method which I considered correct, and their subject-matter was unquestionably related to the symptoms from which my investigation had started. When I had pulled myself together, I was able to draw the right conclusions from my discovery: namely, that the neurotic symptoms were not related directly to actual events but to phantasies embodying wishes, and that as far as the neurosis was concerned psychical reality was of more importance than material reality. I do not believe even now that I forced the seduction-phantasies upon my patients, that I 'suggested' them. I had in fact stumbled for the first time upon the *Oedipus complex*, which was later to assume such an overwhelming importance, but which I did not recognize as yet in its disguise of phantasy. Moreover, seduction during childhood retained a certain share, though a humbler one, in the aetiology of neuroses. But the seducers turned out as a rule to have been older children.

It will be seen, then, that my mistake was of the same kind as would be made by someone who believed that the legendary story of the early kings of Rome (as told by Livy) was historical truth instead of what it is in fact – a reaction against the memory of times and circumstances that were insignificant and occasionally, perhaps, inglorious. When the mistake had been cleared up, the path to the study of the sexual life of children lay open. It thus became possible to apply psychoanalysis to another field of science and to use its data as a means of discovering a new piece of biological knowledge.

Sigmund Freud, *An Autobiographical Study* (1925)

=

Freud's way with women. The writer Hilda Doolittle underwent analysis with Freud – a moving, if sometimes stormy, experience.

This was the homely historical instrument of the original scheme of psychotherapy, of psychoanalysis, the science of the unravelling of the tangled skeins of the unconscious mind and the healing implicit in the process. *Consciously*, I was not aware of having said anything that might account for the Professor's outburst. And even as I veered around, facing him, my mind was detached enough to wonder if this was some idea of *his* for speeding up the analytic content or redirecting the flow of associated images. The Professor said, 'The trouble is – I am an old man – *you do not think it worth your while to love me.*'

The impact of his words was too dreadful – I simply felt nothing at all. I said nothing. What did he expect me to say? Exactly it was as if the Supreme Being had hammered with his fist on the back of the couch where I had been lying. Why, anyway, did he do that? he must know everything or he didn't know anything. He must know what I felt. Maybe he did, maybe that was what this was all about. Maybe, anyway, it was just a trick, something to shock me to break something in myself of which I was partially aware – something that would not, must not be broken. I was here because I must not be broken. If I were broken, I could not go on here with the Professor. Did he think it was easy to leave friendly, comfortable surroundings and come to a strange city, to beard him, himself, the dragon, in his very den? Vienna? Venice? My mother had come here on her honeymoon, tired, having 'done' Italy as a bride. Maybe my mother was already sheltering the child, a girl, that first child that lived such a very short time. It was the bread she talked of, Vienna and how she loved the different rolls and the shapes of them and ones with poppy-seeds and Oh – the coffee! Why had I come to Vienna? The Professor had said in the very beginning that I had come to Vienna hoping to find my mother. Mother? Mamma. But my mother was dead. I was dead; that is, the child in me that had called her mamma was dead. Anyhow, he was a terribly frightening old man, too old and too detached, too wise and too famous altogether, to beat that way with his fist, like a child hammering a porridge-spoon on the table.

I slid back onto the couch.

H. D., *Tribute to Freud* (1974)

=

The Wolf-Man's verdict on Freud's analysis of him

O: When you read the 'History of an Infantile Neurosis' for the first time, what did you think?

w: I didn't think much about it.

o: Did you believe at the time that everything Freud had written in that text was correct?

w: I didn't think about it. That was because of transference.

o: And today?

w: There is that dream business. I never thought much of dream interpretation, you know.

o: Why not?

w: In my story, what was explained by dreams? Nothing, as far as I can see. Freud traces everything back to the primal scene which he derives from the dream. But that scene does not occur in the dream. When he interprets the white wolves as nightshirts or something like that, for example, linen sheets or clothes, that's somehow far-fetched, I think. That scene in the dream where the windows open and so on and the wolves are sitting there, and his interpretation, I don't know, those things are miles apart. It's terribly farfetched.

o: But it is true that you did have that dream.

w: Yes, it is.

o: You must have told him other dreams.

Karin Obholzer, *The Wolf-Man Sixty Years After* (1982)

=

Freud deduced that the Wolf-Man could perform sexually only a tergo.

w: That's incorrect.

o: How so?

w: No, it's incorrect.

o: Then why does Freud write it?

w: With Therese, if you insist on details, the first coitus was that she sat on top of me.

o: That would be the precise opposite . . .

w: I ask myself the following: Are we sitting in judgment on psychoanalysis? (*Laughs.*)

Karin Obholzer, *The Wolf-Man Sixty Years After* (1982)

=

Unconscious homosexuality

This set off a train of associations in my mind. I could still see the enigmatic expression on the cat's face. It seemed immovable, unapproachable, indifferent. What did that have to do with my stepmother? While I feared my father, I lacked 'trust' in her. Maybe that was the connection with the cat. Would she be there when I really needed her, especially as a protector against my father? The answer seemed to be in the cat. She was not hostile but immobile!

Out loud, I said to Freud, 'But my stepmother was such a stabilizing force in my life that I will always be grateful to her.'

For the first time in the analysis, Freud raised his voice. 'You are mistaken about your stepmother. While it is true that she gave you a structured environment, she also overstimulated you sexually and thereby augmented your guilt toward your father. You took refuge from this dilemma by fleeing into your unconscious homosexuality by way of identification with your natural mother. The basis for this was that you identified yourself with your helpless mother, for fear of identifying yourself with the enraged, aggressive father.'

I tried to relate to what Freud was telling me. I could understand the identification and the female part. As a child, I remember feeling that it was an extraordinary privilege to be one of these remarkable creatures. They seemed to have so much easier a time of it. All they had to do was take care of the house and the children. The real responsibility was on the father. Having watched my father's efforts to make a bare living, that picture was understandable. In looking at this grown-up giant of a man and seeing his struggles, I, the child, could only feel an ego weakness that made me unequal to the task of performing exploits of great daring, like coming to America or combating a hostile world to eke out a livelihood. So my wish for the female role was really a wish to escape the hardships of being a male. But this had never interfered with my erotic drive toward the female. Therefore Freud's interpretation took me aback. I could not understand what all this had to do with unconscious homosexuality, and I asked Freud to explain.

'What do you mean,' I asked Freud, 'by unconscious homosexuality?'

He explained, 'By identifying himself with the mother, the child surrenders his identification with the father, thereby discontinuing his role as rival to the father. This guarantees him the continued protection of the father, thereby answering his dependency needs.'

'What can I do about this?'

Freud's answer was, 'Well, just as with the Oedipus complex, you come to terms with it. You reconcile yourself to it.'

In comparing notes with other students, I discovered that, as with the Oedipus complex, unconscious homosexuality was a routine part of everyone's analysis. It consumed a good part of the rest of my analysis.

Freud's perspective on the whole problem of development was constricted by his emphasis on unconscious homosexuality and the Oedipus complex. He could have helped me develop self-assertion and, with a little encouragement, this would have been easy because I had a good deal of drive. By making it into a problem of unconscious homosexuality, he turned my attention to a nonexistent problem and away from a very active one. In his use of the insights of the rag dream (as well as the three Italians), he overlooked the fact that in my relations to him I was doing the same thing I had done with my father. He had sent me into a panic when he informed me of my fear of uncovering a repressed hostility to my father, but failed to point out that this was a pattern that was now operative in the present with Freud and other male authority figures. As with my father, I would repress my self-assertion with Freud in order to maintain his favor and support. The central fact in the transference situation was overlooked by the man who had discovered the very process of transference itself.

A. Kardiner, *My Analysis with Freud* (1977)

=

Jung

Jung was already a man of international fame in psychiatry. Two years before he had published his great *Studies in Association*, perhaps his most original contribution to science, which had provided confirmation from the side of experimental psychology of the theory underlying Freud's empirical 'free association method', and in the present year his book on the *Psychology of Dementia*

Praecox had just appeared. Nothing that he wrote later ranked, in my opinion, with these, and in three or four years he was to begin his descent into a pseudo-philosophy out of which he has never emerged. At that time I could best describe Jung as a breezy personality. He had a restlessly active and quick brain, was forceful or even domineering in temperament, and exuded vitality and laughter; he was certainly a very attractive person. He cherished the notion, rightly or wrongly, that his descent owed something to one of Goethe's love affairs, and I feel sure his career was influenced by a medley of scientific, literary, and philosophical pretensions in which he tried to emulate his great ancestor. With all his intelligence and learning, however, Jung lacked both clarity and stability in his thinking; I was not surprised when, not very long ago, someone who was in school with him recollected as a prominent feature that he had a confused mind. My first observation of this was his attempt to combine his important discoveries in the psychology of dementia praecox with the pathological findings in that condition by postulating a 'psychical toxin' whereby the mind poisoned the brain. His grasp of philosophical principles was so insecure that it was little wonder that they later degenerated into mystical obscurantism.

Ernest Jones, *Free Associations: Memories of a Psycho-Analyst* (1959)

=

The tense relationship between Freud and Jung

The year 1909 proved decisive for our relationship. I had been invited to lecture on the association experiment at Clark University in Worcester, Massachusetts. Independently, Freud had also received an invitation, and we decided to travel together. We met in Bremen, where Ferenczi joined us. In Bremen the much-discussed incident of Freud's fainting fit occurred. It was provoked – indirectly – by my interest in the 'peat-bog corpses.' I knew that in certain districts of Northern Germany these so-called bog corpses were to be found. They are the bodies of prehistoric men who either drowned in the marshes or were buried there. The bog water in which the bodies lie contains humic acid, which consumes the bones and simultaneously tans the skin, so that it and the hair are

perfectly preserved. In essence this is a process of natural mummifi-
cation, in the course of which the bodies are pressed flat by the
weight of the peat. Such remains are occasionally turned up by peat
diggers in Holstein, Denmark, and Sweden.

Having read about these peat-bog corpses, I recalled them when
we were in Bremen, but, being a bit muddled, confused them with
the mummies in the lead cellars of the city. This interest of mine got
on Freud's nerves. 'Why are you so concerned with these corpses?'
he asked me several times. He was inordinately vexed by the whole
thing and during one such conversation, while we were having
dinner together, he suddenly fainted. Afterwards he said to me that
he was convinced that all this chatter about corpses meant I had
death-wishes towards him. I was more than surprised by this interpretation. I was alarmed by the intensity of his fantasies – so strong
that, obviously, they could cause him to faint.

In a similar connection Freud once more suffered a fainting fit in
my presence. This was during the Psychoanalytic Congress in
Munich in 1912. Someone had turned the conversation to Amenophis IV (Ikhnaton). The point was made that as a result of his
negative attitude towards his father he had destroyed his father's
cartouches on the steles, and that at the back of his great creation of
a monotheistic religion there lurked a father complex. This sort of
thing irritated me, and I attempted to argue that Amenophis had
been a creative and profoundly religious person whose acts could
not be explained by personal resistances towards his father. On the
contrary, I said, he had held the memory of his father in honour,
and his zeal for destruction had been directed only against the name
of the god Amon, which he had everywhere annihilated; it was also
chiselled out of the cartouches of his father Amon-hotep. Moreover, other pharaohs had replaced the names of their actual or
divine forefathers on monuments and statues by their own, feeling
that they had a right to do so since they were incarnations of the
same god. Yet they, I pointed out, had inaugurated neither a new
style nor a new religion.

At that moment Freud slid off his chair in a faint. Everyone
clustered helplessly round him. I picked him up, carried him into
the next room, and laid him on a sofa. As I was carrying him, he
half came to, and I shall never forget the look he cast at me. In his

weakness he looked at me as if I were his father. Whatever other causes may have contributed to this faint – the atmosphere was very tense – the fantasy of father-murder was common to both cases.

At the time Freud frequently made allusions indicating that he regarded me as his successor. These hints were embarrassing to me, for I knew that I would never be able to uphold his views properly, that is to say, as he intended them. On the other hand I had not yet succeeded in working out my criticisms in such a manner that they would carry any weight with him, and my respect for him was too great for me to want to force him to come finally to grips with my own ideas. I was by no means charmed by the thought of being burdened, virtually over my own head, with the leadership of a party. In the first place that sort of thing was not in my nature: in the second place I could not sacrifice my intellectual independence; and in the third place such lustre was highly unwelcome to me since it would only deflect me from my real aims. I was concerned with investigating truth, not with questions of personal prestige.

C. G. Jung, *Memories, Dreams, Reflections* (1963)

=

In memory of Sigmund Freud

(d. SEPT. 1939)

When there are so many we shall have to mourn,
when grief has been made so public, and exposed
    to the critique of a whole epoch
    the frailty of our conscience and anguish,

of whom shall we speak? For every day they die
among us, those who were doing us some good,
    who knew it was never enough but
    hoped to improve a little by living.

Such was this doctor, still at eighty he wished
to think of our life from whose unruliness
    so many plausible young futures
    with threats or flattery ask obedience,

but his wish was denied him: he closed his eyes
upon that last picture, common to us all,
    of problems like relatives gathered
  puzzled and jealous about our dying.

For about him till the very end were still
those he had studied, the fauna of the night,
    and shades that still waited to enter
  the bright circle of his recognition

turned elsewhere with their disappointment as he
was taken away from his life interest
    to go back to the earth in London,
  an important Jew who died in exile.

Only Hate was happy, hoping to augment
his practice now, and his dingy clientele
    who think they can be cured by killing
  and covering the gardens with ashes.

They are still alive, but in a world he changed
simply by looking back with no false regrets;
    all he did was to remember
  like the old and be honest like children.

He wasn't clever at all: he merely told
the unhappy Present to recite the Past
    like a poetry lesson till sooner
  or later it faltered at the line where

long ago the accusations had begun,
and suddenly knew by whom it had been judged,
    how rich life had been and how silly,
  and was life-forgiven and more humble,

able to approach the Future as a friend
without a wardrobe of excuses, without
    a set mask of rectitude or an
  embarrassing over-familiar gesture.

No wonder the ancient cultures of conceit
in his technique of unsettlement foresaw
    the fall of princes, the collapse of
  their lucrative patterns of frustration:

if he succeeded, why, the Generalised Life
would become impossible, the monolith
    of State be broken and prevented
  the co-operation of avengers.

Of course they called on God, but he went his way
down among the lost people like Dante, down
    to the stinking fosse where the injured
  lead the ugly life of the rejected,

and showed us what evil is, not as we thought,
deeds that must be punished, but our lack of faith,
    our dishonest mood of denial,
  the concupiscence of the oppressor.

If some traces of the autocratic pose,
the paternal strictness he distrusted, still
    clung to his utterances and features,
  it was a protective coloration

for one who'd lived among enemies so long:
if often he was wrong and, at times, absurd,
    to us he is no more a person
  now but a whole climate of opinion

under whom we conduct our different lives;
Like weather he can only hinder or help,
    the proud can still be proud but find it
  a little harder, the tyrant tries to

make do with him but doesn't care for him much:
he quietly surrounds all our habits of growth
    and extends, till the tired in even
  the remotest miserable duchy

have felt the change in their bones and are cheered,
till the child, unlucky in his little State,
    some hearth where freedom is excluded,
  a hive whose honey is fear and worry,

feels calmer now and somehow assured of escape,
while, as they lie in the grass of our neglect,
    so many long-forgotten objects
  revealed by his undiscouraged shining

are returned to us and made precious again;
games we had thought we must drop as we grew up,
    little noises we dared not laugh at,
  faces we made when no one was looking.

But he wishes us more than this. To be free
is often to be lonely. He would unite
    the unequal moieties fractured
  by our own well-meaning sense of justice,

would restore to the larger the wit and will
the smaller possesses but can only use
    for arid disputes, would give back to
  the son the mother's richness of feeling:

but he would have us remember most of all
to be enthusiastic over the night,
    not only for the sense of wonder
  it alone has to offer, but also

because it needs our love. With large sad eyes
its delectable creatures look up and beg
    us dumbly to ask them to follow:
  they are exiles who long for the future

that lies in our power, they too would rejoice
if allowed to serve enlightenment like him,
    even to bear our cry of 'Judas',
  as he did and all must bear who serve it.

One rational voice is dumb. Over his grave
the household of Impulse mourns one dearly loved:
    sad is Eros, builder of cities,
  and weeping anarchic Aphrodite.

W. H. Auden, 'In Memory of Sigmund Freud' (1939)

=

Freud: the master of the feelings

Read Freud's *Mourning and Melancholia* this morning after Ted
left for the library. An almost exact description of my feelings and
reasons for suicide: a transferred murderous impulse from my
mother onto myself: the 'vampire' metaphor Freud uses, 'draining
the ego': that is exactly the feeling I have getting in the way of my
writing: Mother's clutch. I mask my self-abasement (a transferred
hate of her) and weave it with my own real dissatisfactions in
myself until it becomes very difficult to distinguish what is really
bogus criticism from what is really a changeable liability. How can
I get rid of this depression: by refusing to believe she has any power
over me, like the old witches for whom one sets out plates of milk
and honey. This is not easily done. How is it done? Talking and
becoming aware of what is what and studying it is a help.

Sylvia Plath, journal entry (27 December 1958)

16

Psychoanalysis

Amongst the lay public – far more than within the wider psychiatric profession itself – psychoanalysis was to acquire an extraordinary aura. In countless novels and films from the interwar years onwards, the 'shrink' was standardly depicted as the sage of the psyche, a wise man, magician, miracle worker, yet also a doctor: in short, the new priest of the twentieth century.

Freudian psychoanalysis claimed that the disturbed behaviour of neurotics typically stemmed from unresolved sexual conflicts experienced in early childhood and subsequently unhealthily repressed. Consigned to the unconscious, these conflicts were destined to find outlet in psychologically morbid ways. The healthy release of what had been repressed – *par excellence* through the so-called 'talking cure', or the patient and protracted discipline of free association on the couch – would eventually free the sufferer from these unwanted ghosts.

In so teaching, psychoanalysis – at least in the diluted and more palatable forms popularized in the United States – told the educated public of the first half of this century what it wanted to hear. It was possible to achieve better self-understanding, to deploy one's own powers more harmoniously and effectively, and, above all, to free oneself from the shackles of one's past, achieving true autonomy. Sexual inhibition, as supposedly ordained by the Victorians, was sick; erotic emancipation therapeutic. To the progressive mind, psychoanalysis became associated with individual self-realization and sexual emancipation – albeit occasionally, as Barbara O'Brien's extract here shows, in ways that seemed to the patient less than apposite. Not least, it was a daring and exhilarating star to follow.

The experiences of patients undergoing psychoanalysis excerpted in this book typically read very differently from the experiences of those who received other forms of psychiatric treatment. Analysands have *opted* to be treated. They have relished the direct, personal encounter with the therapist; above all, they have welcomed the opportunity to talk and to be heard. Most write enthusiastically about their experiences – indeed, they write *within the language of analysis itself* (or, as the organic psychiatrist William Sargant tartly observes, psychoanalysis has a great potential for brainwashing).

Having created high, perhaps exaggerated, expectations, an element of 'the god that failed' disillusionment also surrounds those who have written about their encounters with psychoanalysis. Some people's experiences have been no less than calamitous. And, as the journalist Janet Malcolm was to discover, orthodox Freudianism in the United States is, in some ways, unhealthily preoccupied with professional navel-gazing (perhaps with good reason: it seems that about one in six American analysts have slept with their patients). Being so introspective, and concerned with hidden meanings, many (including many psychiatrists) wonder whether psychoanalysis does not create more problems than it solves.

═══

Psychoanalysis may or may not be, in the words of Karl Kraus's witticism, the disease of which it claims to be the cure. But its processes carry with them an element of the occult.

It had taken the first four years of analysis, such a great number of sessions, to begin to understand that I was in the process of being psychoanalysed. Until then I had handed myself over to the treatment as if it were a form of witchcraft, a sort of magic trick to give me refuge from the psychiatric hospital. I had progressed well, but I could not convince myself that mere words were going to definitively drive away my disorder, this sickness which was so profound, this devastating disorder, this ongoing fear in me . . . From one minute to the next, I expected everything to begin again: the blood, the anxiety, the sweat, and the tremors. I was so astonished to see the

respite continue that I did not understand I had changed profoundly. I was less and less at the mercy of others.

The dead end became the laboratory and, at the same time, the
castle of the locked doors. The little doctor was my safety net and
the witness of my journeys into the unconscious. My trail was
ablaze with landmarks as familiar to the doctor as to myself. I could
no longer lose my way.

Marie Cardinal, *The Words to Say It: An Autobiographical Novel*
(1984)

=

'This seems sort of silly!'

I suggested to Pedro that he lie down on the couch, as a means of
encouraging him to relax rather than watch and compete with me,
and to ease free association about his beliefs, fears, hopes, joys, and
problems. 'This seems sort of silly!' was Pedro's reaction; 'but I
guess you know what you're doing.' I advised him to try it and see
how it worked. Thus began psychotherapy, and Pedro's long
journey.

Harold Kenneth Fink, *Long Journey: A Verbatim Report of a Case of
Severe Psychosexual Infantilism* (1954)

=

How I learned about psychoanalysis

Seventy years ago, in the early days of psychoanalysis, one's introduction to it was likely to be very different from what it typically is
today. It was usually a highly personal matter, rather than a chosen
course of study.

I did come to psychoanalysis originally because of what it had to
offer people in need of therapy, nor out of intellectual curiosity, nor
as part of my academic studies. Least of all did it occur to me that
psychoanalysis could become my vocation. Although it eventually
became the most important ingredient of my intellectual life and my
main profession, this was actually a matter of pure chance and due
to most personal experiences.

In the spring of 1917, the third year of the First World War, I was thirteen years old and I joined the Viennese radical youth movement called Jung Wandervogel, which was both socialist and pacifist. The group called itself the 'Young' Wandervogel to emphasize its divergence from the prewar German Wandervogel movement, which had been strongly nationalistic and patriotic. But the Jung Wandervogel shared with the older youth movement an interest in radical educational reform. Ours was a small group of some fifty to a hundred adolescents. An important part of our activities during these war years was regular Sunday outings into the Viennese woods, excursions which were equally conducive to play and to the exploration of radical ideas concerning politics and human relations, including those within the family. From exploring what seemed to us new ideas about human relations, it was only a short step to forming affectionate attachments, the nature of which we so earnestly discussed.

It was in this context that I formed my first adolescent attachment to a girl my age. All seemed to go well, until one Sunday when a young man in uniform named Otto Fenichel joined our group, of which he had been an important member before he was drafted into the army. He was only a few years older than we, and had been given leave from military duties to finish his study of medicine. Much to my dismay, he concentrated his interest on the girl whom I considered to be my own.

Otto was at the time attending Freud's lectures at the University of Vienna. They were the lectures which under the title *Introductory Lectures on Psychoanalysis* subsequently became world-famous. These lectures had fascinated Otto. Like many new converts, he was not only all excited about the arcane doctrines of Freud, but felt obliged to propagandize them. While we had heard vaguely about these theories in our circle, which was eagerly taking up all new and radical ideas, we knew nothing of substance about them. So what Otto told us about Freud's teachings was all news to us.

Mostly Otto asked us about our dreams and tried to tell us their meanings, very much including their sexual meanings. This was a most alluring topic to his young listeners, particularly in view of our ambivalent attitude toward sex, characteristic of the youth movement in that period. Rejecting what we considered the stuffy bourgeois prejudices about sex of our parents' generation, and the prevailing double standard in regard to it, we were committed to sexual freedom in theory. In actuality, we repressed our sexual strivings, pretending that in doing so we were following the principles of a superior morality, thus hiding from ourselves our sexual anxieties. Holding such ambivalent attitudes about sex, we found what Otto told us of Freud's ideas concerning sex and its important role in man's life both exciting and perturbing.

The situation that day was particularly perturbing to me, as I observed that the girl I had considered my 'girlfriend' gave apparent signs of being more and more interested not only in what Otto had to say but also in him as a person. The more captivated she seemed, the more furious I became, feeling badly outclassed by all the new and exciting knowledge the young medical student spouted. But since my self-love did not permit me to believe that Otto might be more interesting to her than I was, I attributed all his success to his knowledge of psychoanalysis, which by the end of the day I thoroughly hated and despised. It was psychoanalysis which I thought had alienated my girl and made her turn her affection toward my competitor. Thus we parted at the end of this, for me, fateful Sunday.

My intense anger at and scorn for psychoanalysis prevented me from falling asleep that night until finally, early in the morning, I hit on a solution. I decided that if Otto F., as he was known in the circle of the Jung Wandervogel, could win my friend by talking about psychoanalysis, I might be able to beat him at his own game by winning her back with the same method. All I had to do was to become knowledgeable about psychoanalysis, and this I would do. The decision made, I finally could fall asleep.

On Monday as soon as school let out, I went to the only bookstore in Vienna which stocked psychoanalytic publications, since it was also their publisher, and bought as many of them as I could afford. I acquired some monographs and current psychoanalytical journals and immediately began reading them. The more I did, the more surprised I became at what I was reading. I soon realized that my Victorian family, although personally acquainted with members of the Freud family, would be utterly shocked to find me perusing such obscene literature. My solution was to hide it from them by taking it to school and reading it there surreptitiously while I was supposed to be attending to studies which, by comparison, were utterly boring.

The works that impressed me most were *The Psychopathology of Everyday Life, Wit and the Unconscious*, and, because of my interest in art, the papers on Leonardo and Moses. The two first mentioned are still those of Freud's writings which are most easily accessible, so it was a fortunate chance that I was able to acquire them. *The Interpretation of Dreams* was not available to me; I do not recall whether it was out of print at the time, or if it was too expensive for me to buy. But the more I read of Freud, the more interested I became, and the more convinced that through my reading I was gaining an entirely new and most important understanding of man's psyche.

Such was my introduction to Freud and psychoanalysis. While hating it as much as I was able to hate anything because I blamed it for the loss of my girl, I was at the same time utterly fascinated by what I learned from it and certain that by becoming knowledgeable about it I could win her back. I do not know whether one could call this a belief in the practical value of psychoanalysis, but during this week in which I became converted to it, I believed in its power to gain for me what at that moment seemed the most desirable goal. So hatred of psychoanalysis and simultaneous belief in its extraordinary power stood at the beginning of its becoming an important part of my life.

Now I believe that coming to psychoanalysis in such a personal way, becoming so deeply involved emotionally and yet so ambivalently, was a most auspicious beginning.

To finish this part of my story, there was a happy ending in all respects, not just in regard to psychoanalysis gradually becoming my lifelong vocation. The next Sunday, my girlfriend and I got together again to go with the youth group to the Vienna Woods. When I began to unpack my newly acquired knowledge of psychoanalysis, she told me that this subject had been fine for one Sunday, but now we should talk about ourselves. She assured me, to my great relief, that while she had been very interested in what Otto had said about psychoanalysis, not for a moment had she been interested in him as a person or wavered in her affection for me. So now there was no reason for me to go on with psychoanalysis so far as my relation to this girl was concerned. But there was no longer any getting away from it for me. One week of complete concentration on psychoanalysis and I was hooked for life.

The young lady and I lost our romantic interest in each other a while later, but remained good lifelong friends. The reason I recount this story is to highlight the result of our different types of interest in psychoanalysis. Because this young woman's interest in psychoanalysis had been theoretical and more or less abstract, it did not take deep roots and played no significant part in her life. My interest had been anything but theoretical – from the beginning it had been personal and very emotional, characterized by a belief that psychoanalysis could make a most important difference in one's life; and so it did in mine.

Bruno Bettelheim, *Recollections and Reflections* (1990)

=

The talking cure

My business is words. Words are like labels,
or coins, or better, like swarming bees.
I confess I am only broken by the sources of things;
as if words were counted like dead bees in the attic,
unbuckled from their yellow eyes and their dry wings.
I must always forget how one word is able to pick
out another, to manner another, until I have got
something I might have said . . .
but did not.

Your business is watching my words. But I
admit nothing. I work with my best, for instance,
when I can write my praise for a nickel machine,
that one night in Nevada: telling how the magic jackpot
came clacking three bells out, over the lucky screen.
But if you should say this is something it is not,
then I grow weak, remembering how my hands felt funny
and ridiculous and crowded with all
the believing money.

Anne Sexton (see page 86), 'Said the Poet to the Analyst', in
To Bedlam and Part Way Back (1960)

Going into psychoanalysis

There, I had told it all.

I had wanted to talk about the blood and yet it was above all the Thing about which I had spoken. Was he going to send me away? I didn't dare look at him. I felt all right there, in that small space talking about myself. Was it a trap? The last of them? Perhaps I shouldn't have trusted him.

And then he said: 'You were right not to take those pills. They are very dangerous.'

My whole body relaxed. I felt profound gratitude towards this little man. Perhaps there was a path between myself and another. If only it were true I could talk to someone who would really listen to me!

He continued: 'I think I can help you. If you agree, we can begin an analysis together starting tomorrow. You would come three times a week for three forty-five minute sessions. But, should you agree to come here, it is my duty to warn you, on the one hand, of the risk that psychoanalysis may turn your whole life upside down, and, on the other hand, that you will have to stop taking all medication right now, whether for your haemorrhages or for your nervous system. Not even aspirin, nothing. Finally, you must know that an analysis lasts at least three years and that it will be expensive. I'm going to charge you forty francs a session, that is to say one hundred and twenty francs a week.'

His manner of speaking was serious and I felt he wanted me to listen to him and to think about what he was saying. For the first time in a long time someone was addressing me as if I were a normal person. And for the first time in a long while I was behaving like a person capable of assuming responsibilities. Then I understood that little by little they had taken all these reponsibilities away from me. I was no longer a nothing. I began to think about this situation and about what he had just said. How could my life turned upside down be worse than it was? Perhaps I would get a divorce because it was from the time of my marriage that the Thing established itself inside me. Never mind, I'll get a divorce or I won't get a divorce. Besides this, I couldn't see what else could be changed in my life.

As for the money, that was more difficult; I didn't have any. I lived on the money my husband earned and what my parents gave me.

'I have no money, Doctor.'

'You will earn it. You will have to pay for your sessions with the money you have earned yourself. It is better that way.'

'But I can't go out, I can't work.'

'You'll manage. I can wait three months, six months until you find a position. We can arrange something. What I want is for you to know that you will have to pay me and that it will be expensive.'

Marie Cardinal, *The Words to Say It: An Autobiographical Novel* (1984)

=

Entering into treatment with R. D. Laing

By this time I had read *The Divided Self*. I was in no doubt that Dr Laing understood about schizophrenics.

I imagined Ronnie. I imagined his office. His secretary would show me in. He would be standing by a desk. He would turn towards me. He was dark and wore a dark suit. He was not very young. Rather staid. Quiet. Professional. He stood by a flat desk, on the far side of his office. He was medium height, if anything a bit short. He was not fat, but he was solid. So, in my mind I saw Ronnie. His hair was rather dark. The desk was brown. There was a fireplace. I had to rather make a couch come into the picture. Analysts had a couch. I would lie on his. I would go often. I was going to have analysis. He would cure me. Get me right. Make me better. I would tell him all my thoughts. Just how they came, everything in my mind, I would say, I'd read all about it, how you have to tell everything. I thought hard of all the things in my life. Everything I felt ashamed of or frightened of I must tell. Everything I was angry about and all my jealousy I didn't think of. I didn't know, in that way, in my head, that I was jealous and angry. I tried to read a bit more about analysis. Somehow I couldn't read any more. Everything seemed to wander away from me.

At last the day came to see Ronnie. I got there, to Wimpole Street. I was in very good time. I rang the bell, a lady opened the door, Peter was not there. The waiting-room was empty. I sat down. There were magazines. I didn't want to look at them. Walking round the room I very closely inspected everything, touching very carefully, for fear anything should break. Then I sat down, in the same place, facing the window, wrapped in my black velvet coat, watching for Peter.

My thoughts wandered, schizophrenics, my clothes, a mauve and green skirt, they – schizophrenics – dressed 'in bizarre ways' the books said. Would Peter *come*? Oh God, get him here, *get* him – *please* don't let anything stop it now. I get up. I can't see far out. I sit down, back on the sofa, facing the window, I decide. There is nothing I can do. If he doesn't come, he doesn't. I must think what I am going to say. I'm sitting up straight, I can't lean back. I'm holding myself together, I'm afraid of my life. I'm wrapped in my coat, I'm looking out. I feel the moments, I'm here. He's an analyst. He can help us. James Robertson knows. He's an analyst. I like him. He knew this man was the person to help me. Over and over inside me I'm saying, Laing, Laing, Ronald David Laing, Doctor Laing.

> Mary Barnes and Joseph Berke, *Mary Barnes: Two Accounts of a Journey Through Madness* (1973)

=

What good has psychoanalysis done? Crichton-Browne was one of many eminent British psychiatrists of the older generation who treated psychoanalysis with profound scepticism – partly, it seems, because it gave prominence to dirty subjects like sex.

A SPECIMEN WITH COMMENTS

An invalid lady who had been a good performer on the violin, dreamed that the tuner had called to tune the piano. He was engaged in taking out a number of seeds from the inside of the piano.

Well, surely we may leave it at that as a dream reminiscence of a commonplace incident. But not at all. The psycho-analyst must be called in and after an analysis which lasted one hour – Joseph was much more expeditious with the butler's and the baker's dreams –

arrived at the interpretation thereof. He discovered what, in the occult jargon of the cult, is called symbolizations and determinations. The dreamer herself is representative of the piano; she had said the day before that she wanted to go piano for a bit. The desire 'to go piano' (represented symbolically by actually being a piano) is the first and most superficial wish fulfilment of the dream. The tuner is a symbol of the analyst – one indeed that is apt enough, for there is an obvious analogy between the relation of a tuner of a piano and that of psycho-analyst and his patient. The dream therefore contains a reference (as many dreams do) to the analytic situation itself. But why is the tuner (the analyst) removing seeds from the piano (the patient). Probably because they had dropped into it from a canary cage hanging over it. Not at all. 'With this question,' we are told, 'we come to the sexual elements, which are so seldom lacking in dreams' (a statement which most decent people will repudiate), 'for seed here as elsewhere refers to the biological processes of reproduction. But the association made it evident that there were three distinct meanings within this sphere: In the first place, seeds refer to certain sexual desires which, as the analyst was making her realize, she had all unknowingly harboured in her mind. The analyst she hoped would rid her of these, as it seemed to her, evil and unseemly desires. Hence the analyst was symbolically removing them.' But how did he do this? Did he extract them like a decayed tooth, or is he endowed with the power of plenary absolution, and is it the best way to remove evil and unseemly desires to stir them up and bring them from the depths of subconsciousness into the light of common day, from the unknown into the known, and is there not a risk that the analyst may be introducing evil and unruly desires into an entirely innocent mind?

'But there are two further wish fulfilments of a cruder and more instinctive kind. The word seed can be metaphorically used for offspring, and the third meaning of the dream is that the analyst is acting as the patient's accoucheur at the birth of a child. Lest the reader should be astonished and disgusted, let him remember that Socrates, who with his motto "Know thyself", seems to have been in some way the forerunner of Freud.' But notwithstanding this perversion of the dictum of Socrates, whom Freud resembles as much as a toadstool does a British oak, the reader is astonished and disgusted by all this jargon and quest of the unclean, and feels sure that any right-minded father who found out that his daughter had been subjected for an hour to dream interpretation of this kind would kick the piano-tuner out of the house.

I have selected one of the simplest and least offensive illustrations of analytical dream-craft – there are some that one would be ashamed to quote – and it must be confessed that while one wishes to be polite, the exclamations that rise to one's lips are of a very uncomplimentary complexion. The medical man engaged in the treatment of mental disease must occasionally listen to painful confessions and elicit unsavoury truths, but he need not go boring in search of veins of pruriency or suggest it in every simple case. What has psycho-analysis done for us? We are told that, apart from its use in medicine, it is of immense psychological and sociological utility, and has a bearing on our general conception of the human mind and human institutions. One does not notice that in Austria – the cradle and nursery and collegium of its orthodox variety – it has had any highly beneficial social influence, nor has the League of Nations as yet created a special department for psycho-analytical investigation, although, if the claims made for it are correct, it ought to be of the utmost international and ethnical value. Even in medicine, in which it is alleged to find its highest utility, we have no satisfactory evidence of that. No doubt a number of neurotic and psycho-asthenic subjects improve for a time under psycho-analytical treatment, as they do under any kind of new and startling treatment, or none at all. But how long does the improvement last? I have seen in asylum, cases of confirmed insanity that had been cured by psycho-analysis. Has there been any increase in the rate of recovery from mental disease since psycho-analysis was introduced?

Sir James Crichton-Browne, *The Doctor's After Thoughts* (1932)

=

Psychoanalytical fun and games. Alix Strachey, one of the thirty original members of the British Psychoanalytic Society, writes to her husband.

P.B.
Friday 28.11.24

[To James]
    Your Wed. night letter has just arrived. What in GOD'S name is it about? I can't understand a word. My head reels . . . am *I* mad . . . or is it possible . . . what you *seem* to be saying is that JONES (Ernest) – the one & only JONES, Doctor & Psycho-analyst – talked to you over the telephone about a certain X who is a manic-depressive – no, he, Jones, is – & asked your advice as to whom this X should go to for analysis? He went on to say that you had better 'steer clear' of X i.e. not analyse him or what? You suggested Rickman or J. Glover as a possible analyst, & Jones made absurd speeches about R. Well, alright. *But who, for Heaven's sake, is X?* A possible patient? 'Not sent back to him (Jones)' – so an ex-patient of Jones. It looks as if a letter had got lost. The last one from you is dated Monday evg. (& written on best Asprey paper, as usual – currse you!). I'm dying to know. Explain – Explain.

yrs. A.
                Alix Strachey, letter to James Strachey (28 November 1924)

==

The shock value of psychoanalysis

Psychoanalysis has sprung many surprises on us, performed more than one *volte-face* before our indignant eyes. No sooner had we got used to the psychiatric quack who vehemently demonstrated the serpent of sex coiled round the root of all our actions, no sooner had we begun to feel honestly uneasy about our lurking complexes, than lo and behold the psychoanalytic gentleman reappeared on the stage with a theory of pure psychology. The medical faculty, which was on hot bricks over the therapeutic innovations, heaved a sigh of relief as it watched the ground warming under the feet of the professional psychologists.

This, however, was not the end. The ears of the ethnologist began to tingle, the philosopher felt his gorge rise, and at last the moralist knew he must rush in. By this time psychoanalysis had become a public danger. The mob was on the alert. The Œdipus complex was a household word, the incest motive a commonplace of tea-table chat. Amateur analyses became the vogue. 'Wait till you've been analysed,' said one man to another, with varying intonation. A sinister look came into the eyes of the initiates – the famous, or infamous, Freud look. You could recognize it everywhere, wherever you went.

Psychoanalysts know what the end will be. They have crept in among us as healers and physicians; growing bolder, they have asserted their authority as scientists; two more minutes and they will appear as apostles. Have we not seen and heard the *ex cathedra* Jung? And does it need a prophet to discern that Freud is on the brink of a *Weltanschauung* – or at least a *Menschanschauung*, which is a much more risky affair? What detains him? Two things. First and foremost, the moral issue. And next, but more vital, he can't get down to the rock on which he must build his church.

> D. H. Lawrence, *Fantasia of the Unconscious and Psychoanalysis and the Unconscious* (1922)

=

The liberating promise of psychoanalysis

On that same drive Claire and I talked about something else. That conversation, carried on casually, was forgotten for many years, but it had profound significance.

'Do you know much about psychology?' she asked.

'I know what it is. That's about all,' I told her.

'It's a fascinating subject. A lot of people believe that you can never be free of your background unless you have some sort of psychoanalysis.'

'What do you mean by being free of your background?'

'Not carrying around the emotional burdens you pick up in childhood.'

'It seems to me that an intelligent person should be able to cope with his background without getting help from any doctor. All the people I know who ever studied psychology are kind of kooky themselves. I wouldn't want any of them fooling around with me.'

'You don't believe in it at all?'

'Of course I believe in some of it, but only for people who are really sick. For anyone who's able to function I think it's sort of obscene to have someone else poking around in your private life.'

Claire clearly didn't like my point of view. She took a long time repairing her lipstick in her compact mirror.

'You're very prejudiced about all this, aren't you?' she said after a while.

'I'm prejudiced against futility.'

'John, I think you're wrong,' she said, and then smiled. 'But I like you anyway. And John, slow down. You started racing everyone on the Parkway when we began talking about psychiatry.'

John Balt, *By Reason of Insanity* (1972)

=

Psychoanalysis as a mode of brainwashing

Some techniques of psychotherapy do, in fact, show that methods of political and religious conversion have their counterparts in ordinary psychiatric practice, and that the patient can be made to 'see the light,' whatever the particular doctrinaire light may be, without recourse to drugs or specially induced debilitation, or any other artificial aid to abreaction. Drugs speed up the process by bringing about the required physiological changes in brain function; but these can also be produced by the use of repeated psychological stimuli.

A patient under psycho-analytic treatment, for instance, is made to lie on a couch, where daily for months, and perhaps years he is encouraged to indulge in 'free association of ideas.' He may also then be asked: 'What does "umbrella" mean to you?' – 'Uncle Toby.' 'What does "apple" mean to you?' – 'The girl next door.' These answers may perhaps also be found to be of sexual significance. He has to go back over his past sexual peccadilloes, and relive other incidents which aroused intense anxiety, fear, guilt, or aggression, especially in childhood. As the analysis proceeds, and emotional storms perhaps mount, the patient becomes more and more sensitized to the analyst. So-called 'transference situations,' both positive and negative, are built up physiologically; often assisted in the early stages of treatment by the fatigue and debilitation resulting from the anxiety aroused. The patient's tension and dependence on the therapist may be greatly increased. A stage is finally reached when resistance weakens to the therapist's interpretations of a patient's symptoms, and he may start to accept them much more readily. He now believes and acts upon theories about his nervous condition which, more often than not, contradict his former beliefs. Many of the individual's usual patterns of behaviour may also be upset by this process, and replaced by new ones. These changes are consolidated by making the patient's behaviour as consistent as possible with the new 'insight' gained. Attempts are then made, before treatment ends, to reduce the patient's emotional dependence on the therapist. As one patient personally analysed by Freud remarked to me: 'For the first few months I was able to feel nothing but increasing anxiety, humiliation and guilt. Nothing about my past life seemed satisfactory any more, and all my old ideas about myself seemed to be contradicted. When I got into a completely hopeless state, he [Freud] then seemed to start to restore my confidence in myself, and to piece everything together in a new setting.'

Psycho-analytic treatment is much slower in bringing about what more violent or intensive methods often achieve in the psychiatric, political or religious field.

William Sargant, *Battle for the Mind: A Physiology of Conversion and Brain-washing* (1957)

=

Patients' writings suggest very little personal involvement with the concepts of orthodox psychiatry, but often a powerful uptake and internalization of the language of psychoanalysis. In this case, a patient interprets her own troubles within the Freudian schema, and her doctors interpolate their comments.

When a girl doesn't want to walk, it's because she doesn't want to realize that there is nothing swinging between her legs. She would like to be paralyzed from the waist down. If her legs are dead, then her genitals are dead too. She won't have to think of them again. I hated to walk. I could feel my thighs rubbing and that made me remember my genitals. I hated you for making me walk.

Patients dribble and smear their food or smear their BM in an effort to test it out. They want to get to know what is going in and coming out of them. They want to get acquainted and know what it feels like on the outside. Then they can feel safe when it's inside. It's terribly frightening not to know what may go on inside.

I used to beg to go outdoors because I needed to be warmed by the sun. It's terrible to feel empty and cold inside. Rainy weather is very hard on patients because it forces them to look inside themselves for warmth, but they can't find any. It helped me a lot to lie on the beach because then I could feel that mother was holding me and giving me warmth and life.

Joan here gives us some valuable insight into certain psychotic behaviour that had seemed quite inexplicable and annoying to the therapist and hospital personnel.

I had to be able to tease you sexually so that I could be sure that I really was attractive, but before I could do this I had to be sure that nothing bad would come of it. While I lunged and wrestled with you and bit you, it was very close to intercourse. I was thinking of a stallion and a mare and how they rear and kick and bite. It would all be terribly intense and animal and beautiful. The animal part of me would rise to meet the animal part of you. That would be the only way I could have orgasm. It would be too violent to do it as people.

If you had actually screwed me it would have wrecked everything. It would have convinced me that you were only interested in pleasure with my animal body and that you didn't really care about the part that was a person. It would have meant that you were using me like a woman when I really wasn't one and needed a lot of help to grow into one. It would have meant you could only see my body and couldn't see the real me which was still a little girl. The real me would have been up on the ceiling watching you do things with my body. You would have seemed content to let the real me die. When you feed a girl, you make her feel that both her body and her self are wanted. This helps her get joined together. When you screw her she can feel that her body is separate and dead. People can screw dead bodies, but they never feed them.

The problem of handling the sexual drives of a schizophrenic woman can be a very great one. In this case, the 'teasing' consisted of disrobing, erotic posturing and pleading for sexual intercourse. Such advances cannot be rejected roughly or moralistically, since it is vitally important for a woman to be sure that she is physically attractive. She also needs to reassure herself that sexual feelings do not automatically lead to a violent, bestial situation. On the other hand, too much permissiveness, leading to erotic intimacy, convinces the patient that men are animals who are only interested in physical pleasure.

The authors find that these conflicting needs can be satisfied if the therapist will express sincere praise of the patient's physical charms and enter into a warm joint fantasy showing that sexual intercourse with her would be enjoyable. On the other hand, it can be pointed out that intercourse has never cured schizophrenia. Since proper treatment is essential for the patient's welfare, the doctor is not going to take any chances of doing something that might interfere with treatment.

In this passage Joan shows very clearly the schizophrenic split between the 'real' her and the sexual, animal self. It is vitally important for the patient to be able to experience this latter part of herself in a warm, constructive setting, so that all these forces can be accepted and integrated into the total personality. Joan is here describing the period when she was beginning to use the therapist as a good father.

Malcolm L. Hayward and J. Edward Taylor, 'A Schizophrenic Patient
Describes the Action of Intensive Psychotherapy' (1956)

=

Resistance

I remembered how silly a fellow patient named Jake Eckstein had seemed to me when he had gone into hysterical rage because his psychoanalyst had asked him *why* he had wanted to kill his father. Jake was a self-made Ghetto Jew who had learned law at City College without learning much of anything else. He had never heard of Oedipus, Havelock Ellis or D. H. Lawrence. I doubt if he had ever heard of Dr Freud, or the stock commonplaces of the new psychology. I mean, every callow sophomore these days is familiar and bored with the idea that he was in love with his mother and wanted to murder the old man. But to Jake, the idea had been astounding, unspeakable. I remembered how we had heard him screaming at the doctor all the way down the hall through the closed door of his bedroom:

'Why, you wicked degenerate monster! To put such a horrible thought as that into my head!'

Spike had whispered to me afterward, when we heard it all from the outraged Jake himself:

'It's lucky the doctor didn't tax him too with being in love with his mamma, or we'd have had bloody murder right here on the floor.'

It occurred to me now that I didn't want to be as naive as Jake. I decided, after Paschall had left me, that instead of getting mad about it I would think it over. One of the things about being locked up for a long time is that, despite workshops and gymnasium, it gives you plenty of time to think.

William Seabrook, *Asylum* (1935)

=

Learning how to psychoanalyse

I remember when she first came into my office – a short, plump, self-conscious girl, who giggled and gave vapid, inconsequential answers to the questions I asked her. We had a few sessions sitting up, and then one day I said, 'Why don't you lie down on the couch?' She giggled and walked over to the couch and arranged herself on it gingerly, with a lot of tugging at her skirt, and went on taking in her inane, girlish, monosyllabic way. This kept up for three or four sessions. Then one day she walked in and didn't *get* on the couch, she *threw* herself on it. She bounced up and down and began to *rail* me. 'You don't *do* anything for me,' she said. 'You just

sit there and don't *do* anything. You don't tell me anything. What
kind of business is this? Why don't you *do* something for me? Why
do you just sit there?' She went on and on, berating me for my
coldness and passivity and indifference to her sufferings – and that
was the true beginning of the analysis. But I didn't know it. I sat
there cowering under her anger and irked with her for not knowing
that what I was doing as 'I just sat there' was classical Freudian
analysis. I found her in every way disappointing. I had expected a
patient who would free-associate, and here they had sent me this
banal girl who just blathered. I didn't understand – I was so naive
then – that her blathering *was* free association, that blathering is
just what free association is. Worse than that, I thought I had to
instruct her on the nature of her unconscious. I would laboriously
point out to her the unconscious meaning of what she said and did.
Only after years of terrible and futile struggle did it dawn on me
that if I just listened – if I just let her talk, let her blather – things
would come out, and that this was what would help her, not my
pedantic, didactic interpretations. If I could only have learned to
shut up! When I finally did learn, I began to see things that Freud
had described – to actually see for myself symptoms disappearing
as the unconscious became conscious. That was an incredible thing.
It was like looking through a telescope and realizing that you are
seeing what Galileo saw.

     Janet Malcolm, *Psychoanalysis: The Impossible Profession* (1982)

=

Transference

Then there was another dream, I think the same night, which I
never did understand thoroughly. I was alongside an enormous cat
whom I apparently was not afraid of, but who was unmoving and
indifferent.

    Freud said, 'Well, apparently we hit something very important
here. In the first dream, you obviously don't want me to pursue
your relationship with your father. You want the picture to remain
as you retouched it, and so, in the dream, you tell me not to go
digging up the past, I will not find anything important.'

    'But why,' I asked, 'did I retouch the picture of my father?'

'To make it possible for you to live with him at all. You evidently were terrified of him in your very early childhood. However, when your stepmother came, your father's character changed, and it is this revised character you wished to keep and thereby to forget the angry father of your earliest years. But you remained submissive and obedient to him in order not to arouse the sleeping dragon, the angry father.' My immediate reaction was to accept Freud's interpretation. It was not until many years later that I understood the basic error committed here by Freud.

The man who had invented the concept of transference did not recognize it when it occurred here. He overlooked one thing. *Yes, I was afraid of my father in childhood, but the one whom I feared now was Freud himself.*

A. Kardiner, *My Analysis with Freud* (1977)

=

Psychoanalysis Viennese-style and American-style

Maybe the popular American view of the psychoanalyst as a 'head-shrinker' highlights best the difference between how things are done today in America and how they were done then in Vienna. The reason this headshrinker image is so widely accepted in America (although it is always recognized as a funny and ironic image that puts the psychoanalyst down a few pegs) is, I believe, that it represents the patient's reaction to the psychoanalyst's belief that he is superior to the patient. The very notion of a headshrinker clearly implies that the therapist does to the patient what he decided needs to be done in the patient's best interest (that is, once again, the medical model).

I am not suggesting that today's analysts approach their patients differently than mine did me because they lack human decency. I believe, rather, that their attitudes largely reflect the institutionaliz-ation of psychoanalysis as a highly skilled therapeutic specialty, and by certain rigidities resulting from the long, demanding, and com-plex training psychoanalytic institutes require of candidates.

In Vienna, it should be noted, while a majority of the psychoana-lysts were physicians, a number of prominent ones were not. In the beginning days of psychoanalysis, analysts treated patients in their homes and not in offices, six sessions a week at exactly the same time each day. Freud did this, and so did nearly all the other Viennese physicians. Characteristically, Freud's treatment room, in its furnishings, especially the collection of archaeological artifacts which filled it, was testimony to his dominant interests and also a clear and definite expression of his personality. Thus the original setting in which psychoanalysis took place was a very personal one, reflecting the individuality and interest of the therapist. This contrasts strongly with the impersonal and rather sterile settings which most present-day American psychoanalysts prefer for their work.

Bruno Bettelheim, *Recollections and Reflections* (1990)

=

The allure of analysis

During those years both Claire and I were perhaps too ready to accept anything presented to us in the guise of science. For Claire, this was especially so in the area of psychology. She needed to make common cause with something bigger and, as she deeply believed, truer than what she had grown up with. In the case of Miss Baruch, the relationship was a good one. Claire was and remained an excellent teacher and a much-loved mother. If there was anything unfortunate about the attachment it was this: the apparent existence of 'psychological' solutions to life's problems prevented her, and then me, from looking elsewhere for those solutions.

What I heard about Miss Baruch's group and its work served in time to soften my own cynical attitude toward the theories of psychiatry; and a book we picked up, Robert Lindner's *Fifty-Minute Hour*, captured my imagination hitherto unexposed to the areas that it covered. I read some of Theodor Reik, Jones's biography of Freud, Freud's *Psychopathology of Everyday Life*, and *Interpretation of Dreams*. And one other book, which, as it turned out, had special consequences, A. A. Brill's *Lectures on Psychoanalytic Psychiatry*. I had seen Dr Brill once in person years before when, as a very old man, he had begun a lecture at New York University with the words 'Kiss my arse!' The idea, as it was meant to be, was thoroughly revolting; the book unfortunately was not. It was very readable.

John Balt, *By Reason of Insanity* (1972)

=

Anybody who goes to see a psychiatrist ought to have his head examined.

Samuel Goldwyn

=

Never apologize

'Let me illustrate with an incident from my practice. I once arrived fifteen minutes late for an appointment with a patient. I was appalled by my oversight and apologized profusely to the patient. Now, the analysts of the lenient sort would say, "You did the right thing. It's good to admit it when you've made a mistake; it's good to show the patient you're only human. It's an empathetic response. It strengthens the therapeutic alliance. It makes him feel you're on his side." And so on. But I knew I should *not* have apologized. I knew I should have waited to learn what the patient's response to my lateness was, instead of rushing in with my apology. In my self-analysis of the lapse, a rather vicious analyst joke came to mind, which goes like this: A new woman patient comes to a male analyst's office, and he says, "Take off your clothes and get on the couch." The woman gets undressed and lies down on the couch, and the analyst gets on top of her. Then he says, "You can get dressed now and sit in the chair." She does so, and the analyst says, "OK. We've taken care of my problem, what's yours?" It's a silly joke, and a vicious one, but it gets at something fundamental. In that situation of being late, I acted like the analyst in the joke. I put my own interests before those of the patient. I felt guilty about my lateness, and by apologizing I was seeking forgiveness from the patient. I was saying to him, "Let's take care of my problem – never mind about yours."'

Janet Malcolm, *Psychoanalysis: The Impossible Profession* (1982)

=

Free associations

'Talk, say whatever comes into your head; try not to choose or reflect, or in any way compose your sentences. Everything is important, every word.'

It was the only remedy he gave me and I gorged myself on it. Perhaps it was my weapon against the Thing: that flood of words, that maelstrom, that mass of words, that hurricane! Words swept away distrust, fear, lack of understanding, severity, will, order, law, discipline as well as tenderness, sweetness, love, warmth and freedom.

Vocabulary was like a word game, thanks to which I reconstituted the image of a little girl sitting very properly at a big table, hands on either side of her plate, sitting up straight, not touching the back of the chair, by herself, across from a man with a moustache who offers her a piece of fruit, smiling. Crystal salt cellars with silver tops, Sèvres china, the bell that hung from the chandelier and on which Columbine and Pierrot waited to sound the buzzer back in the pantry when they were made to kiss. The words made the scene come alive. Once again I was a little girl. Then, when the image became obliterated and I again became a thirty-year-old woman, I asked myself, Why the rigid posture, hands folded on the table-cloth, the back of the chair forbidden to touch? Why the boredom and embarrassment while facing my father? Who forced it upon me? Why? There I am on the couch, keeping my eyes shut tight in order to retain my hold on the little girl. I was really her and me. Then everything was easy to understand. I began to see clearly the outline of my mother's grip on me.

To find myself, I must find my mother and strip away the mask and penetrate the secrets of family and class.

> Marie Cardinal, *The Words to Say It: An Autobiographical Novel*
> (1984)

=

Loving your therapist

Jan 23

Dear Wanda,

A few days after you left me, I went into the hospital library and checked out some books on therapeutic technique. Since my own therapy had turned out so badly – it was, if you can stand the truth, the most humiliating experience of my life – I wanted to find out how the damned thing might have ended if we had been able to finish it. So I read up on such things as the therapeutic alliance, working through the transference, and finally termination. The more I read, the better I felt. We could have done that, I kept telling myself. We'd have by God made it. Under the spell of those books, and in a blaze of good feeling, I constructed a vision of what our parting should have been like. The vision was this:

Our last complete session completed, we walk back on the ward together. You're stunning in a soft gray suit, white blouse, and little black tie; I'm slicked up too, in a fresh tee shirt and brand-new khakis. We chat amiably till we reach the nurses' station. We stop there, turn to face each other, shake hands solemnly. Overcome by mutual admiration and affection, we embrace. We hold each other at arms' length for a last good look. Those kindly folk in the nurses' station beam their approval. I give you a chaste kiss on the cheek. You turn and walk slowly but purposefully down the hall, headed for new patients and new triumphs, enriched by your encounter with a tough old nut like me. At the end of the hall you look back and give a wave farewell, then disappear. I stand there, completely cured, grinning modestly as the nursing staff shower me with congratulations. Soon, maybe next week, I too will walk down that hall, a reborn man with a bright future, ready at long last to accept his share of the goods of life. That's how the books made it sound.

The vision sustained me for about a week. Then one night I found myself casually burning my legs. We hadn't, after all, really done those things, all that working through, and nothing had changed except for the worse. Instead of being something different, you had revealed yourself as an extra big helping of the same old shit. Another woman who walked away. Still, it was a nice vision while it lasted. I tried to recreate it today and got the following:

Our last session completed, we walk back on the ward together. You're wearing nothing but a pair of white underpants; I'm completely naked. You're scowling, I look defeated. We turn to face each other. Suddenly you embrace me, nuzzle my ear. My prick stirs; I'm going to get something out of this after all. You step back, leer, and give the nursing staff a wink. They produce a piano, trombone, and two B-flat tenor saxes, and break into a barrelhouse version of 'Moon River.' You reach down and tweak my swollen cock as you might tweak a small boy's chin. You give a cruel laugh and walk down the hall, pausing at the door for a lewd little number with your behind. Old-time burlesque, Wanda, performed with a flourish. The music blares, the nurses sing. The only words I can make out are 'cock teaser,' which appears in place of the words of the title. The nurses point at me, whooping and hollering. I stand there, a shit-eating grin on my face, my cock in my hand . . .

. . . Even as I sit here now, my cock in my hand. I don't know why you have to drag sex into everything, but obviously you do.

To get back to you and me. The horrible thing is that I understand, from things you said and from my reading, the explanation for my feelings for you – that they're transference feelings, a way of reliving the past, etc. I understand fully; I'm even, in some sense, willing to accept the explanation. I tell myself everyday, in a half-humorous, civilized tone: 'Be sensible there, fellow – it isn't *her* you have these feelings for,' and I quote old Freud to myself, and old whoever-else-it-was I read, and I pat myself on the back for being superior to those pathetic housewives you hear about who, not understanding a thing about transference, imagine themselves to be in love with their doctors. Doesn't do a bit of good, Wanda. In my heart I am those housewives.

And who's to say we aren't right, we housewives? Who's to say I don't, or don't 'really,' love that sympathetic, quietly attentive young woman with the soulful eyes and the dandy legs. However you try to account for it, it's you I love. No reason I couldn't, no reason I shouldn't. Except that maybe you don't love me – but what kind of reason is that? And if you don't, why won't you come right out and say so? Then I'd know where I stood. Then I'd know what I was up against. Then I could go about making myself absolutely irresistible. All I want is the same chance you'd give any one of a hundred other men.

So fuck transference. Transference is the story you tell yourself to make a dirty business sound clean. Transference is your way of distorting my feelings. It's your way of avoiding me. Of pretending I don't exist. Worse yet, of pretending *you* don't exist. It's your way of living with what you do in case something goes wrong. Let me tell you what happened.

Somewhere in the middle of that elaborate pas de deux called therapy – in response to a hundred invitations and a thousand signals that it was safe to do so – I handed you my fucking heart. I didn't hand it to the ghost of my God damned mother or my God damned female sibling or one of my God damned spouses or some other significant other in my insignificant past. Nor did I hand it to an anonymous, readily exchangeable therapeutic presence. I handed it to you, to the little bit of you that was palpably and blessedly *there*, in person, day after day. Don't you understand anything? Despite all the distortions I brought to that little room – desperate fellow that I am, I brought a lot – I didn't mistake the nature or meaning of that particular gift. You did the mistaking. Fuck transference.

I'll tell you one thing Freud was definitely right about. He said that when a patient felt rejected by a therapist, all the gains he had made would be blown away like chaff in the wind. I guess you never read that part, huh? You miserable fucking piece of asshole shit.

Sincerely,
Tim

James Twiggs, *Transferences* (1987)

=

A psychiatrist accuses psychoanalysts of cruelty towards patients.

When at one conference I pointed out that a patient had not slept for the past several nights, a famous Viennese refugee psychoanalyst working there, named Dr Helena Deutsch, whose husband I believe had been one of Freud's personal physicians, explained to me that if, as I suggested, we helped the patient by sedation and so made her feel too comfortable, she would not give us the sort of talk-material required for her psychoanalytically orientated treatment. This seemed to me very suggestive of brainwashing. But what a scaring experience it also was to participate in a conference where practically everybody present, except the junior staff, was either in the process of being psychoanalysed or had been psychoanalysed, or were going to be, and where some of the doctors were actually psychoanalysing others present! 'Transferences' were whipping backwards and forwards, and if someone ventured an independent opinion, someone else in the room might look sharply at him. He would immediately crumple up, because a transference situation was being set up and he had dared to express a viewpoint in contradiction of his analyst. This was by no means always the scientific atmosphere of detached judgment which is so necessary for assessing the whole range of new treatments becoming available for the mentally ill.

We have read accounts of the devastating effects on the morale of a member who has been drummed out of the Communist party. They remind me of another conference, when I again protested that an agitated and depressed patient had not been allowed to sleep properly for a week. She had lost over 20 lbs in weight during her illness, and was experiencing severe mental torture, with horrifying illusions of her husband being carried past her in a coffin. I dared to suggest again that it would be a sensible treatment to give her a few good nights' sleep. Moreover she might then talk intelligently at her subsequent psychoanalytically orientated interviews. For they were vainly trying to analyse out her supposed death wishes towards her husband. This suggestion mobilized enormous feelings of aggression, and the whole group turned on me for suggesting what they thought to be so wrong. Dr Cobb, Head of the Department, trying to keep the peace, remarked that the trouble with sedatives was that they often made you feel bad the morning after.

William Sargant, *The Unquiet Mind: The Autobiography of a Physician in Psychological Medicine* (1967)

=

A psychoanalyst accuses psychiatrists of not listening to their patients.

During my clinical years it became clear to me that most psychiatrists are not only not experts in communication but are not at all interested in what their patients have to tell them. The concept of 'unintelligibility' is therefore a clever ploy for masking the true nature of their operations. Quite simply many psychiatrists attribute *their own non-attempts at communication* to someone else, usually a patient or prospective patient, while, at the same time, denying that this is what they are doing. *This disturbance in communication* is then seen as a sign of the patient's 'illness' for which he must be 'treated'. Should the patient still try to comment on what he thinks is going on, his 'productions' are passed off as 'unintelligible'.

R. D. Laing gives a blow by blow description of this common practice as applied by the 'Father' of modern psychiatry, Emil Kraepelin, to an eighteen-year-old boy, in the first chapter of *The Divided Self*. Dr Laing's unusually perceptive discussion of this teenager's predicament as well as his keen understanding of the life experience of people diagnosed as 'schizoid' or 'schizophrenic' further verified the possibility of coming to terms with the language of people whom our culture would consider 'mad'.

Students of psychology no longer need remain linguistic philistines, beholden to a 'science' which treats any language but its own as an unintelligible bastardization of its own, and worse yet, a grave sign of mental derangement in anyone who speaks it. The words and movements of the 'madman' are not a bastardization of any tongue, rather they are a unique event to which one can learn to respond.

I discovered *The Divided Self* in the Bronx shop of an obnoxious purveyor of medical texts. It was the fall of 1962 and I had gone prowling for a book, any book, to rouse me out of the doldrums of surgery at a VA (Veterans Administration) hospital. The title attracted me, and also the pretty picture of the author on the back cover, another Scotsman, and from Glasgow of all places. What a mind blower when I opened the pages and found that amid the key phrases of 'existential phenomenology', 'ontological insecurity', 'false self' and 'true self', Ronald Laing had explained my own experience to me better than anyone I had ever read, and far better than I could then interpret it myself. More important, his characterizations did not remain literary cadavers, but came to life, jumped out of the book, reminded me of oh so many people I had known as friends and teachers and patients.

Mary Barnes and Joseph Berke, *Mary Barnes: Two Accounts of a Journey Through Madness* (1973)

=

Going into analysis

'How often does this psychologist want to see you?'

'Once or twice a week.'

It took me a few moments to sort everything out in my mind. The whole thing had come unexpectedly. I didn't like the idea of this strange woman insinuating herself into our problems and telling us what to do with our dog for starters, especially since I had been unable to make a decision on that very matter. I was also very well aware that a psychologist, in contrast to a psychiatrist, didn't have a medical degree.

'Maybe you ought to talk to a doctor first.'

'But I like this lady.'

'Claire, let me call Bill Connery and see what he has to say. Okay?'

She thought about it. 'Okay, John, if you think so.'

Bill was by this time a resident at a hospital in Los Angeles. When I explained the situation to him, he said he would set up an appointment with a Wilshire Boulevard psychiatrist, who would see Claire, diagnose her case, and then refer her to an appropriate colleague.

'It's getting pretty complicated, don't you think?' I asked him. 'I mean, you know Claire. As far as I'm concerned, she's all right.'

'Let her see the doctor,' he said.

Three days later Claire consulted the man on Wilshire Boulevard, and having been told that she did need treatment, she came home quite shaken. A week afterward she saw the psychiatrist to whom she had been referred. She returned late in the afternoon. Since it was Friday we were due for an exercise class in Hollywood, and she didn't have time to tell me about her interview until we were in the car on the way to town.

'These fellows are all Freudians. Strictly. They don't believe in anything but psychoanalysis. All the way. Four times a week on your back on a couch.'

'For how long?'

'Two to five years.'

'And he thinks you need all that?'

'He said so.'

'But what's wrong with you?'

'They don't just give it a name. It's what I've told you. I'm not functioning the way I should. I'm not the kind of wife and mother I want to be. I can't handle my mother or yours. I need help.'

I had thought about this since our discussion in the study. I recalled Claire's recent moodiness. There were tensions about the parents and, since Stan's birth, tensions about sex. Did all this add up to sickness? I didn't know.

'I need help,' she repeated.

I realized that I had done nothing to help her over what I saw now had been a difficult time for her. Like her, I had seen the older generation struggle ineffectually with their problems all their lives. Unlike her, however, I had sought to deny the existence of any problems of our own. I was suspicious of involvement with outsiders, afraid, perhaps of the consequences of such involvement.

'You've been busy,' she said. 'And anyway, I can't take these problems to you. They're not really yours.'

'Do you think this fellow knows what he's talking about?'

'He's a member of the institute.'

'How old is he?'

'About forty. Very serious and horn-rimmed.'

'How much does all this cost?'

'Twenty-five dollars a session.'

'That's a hundred dollars a week. Four hundred and fifty dollars a month, for maybe five years. We can't afford that.'

'Are you sure?'

'I'm sure. Four hundred and fifty a month on top of everything else.'

John Balt, By Reason of Insanity (1972)

=

Death wishes

One day, I was reminiscing about my childhood, and I remembered some of the then popular songs, one of which was 'Sweet Isaac Ben Bolt.' To which Frink remarked, 'You mean "Sweet Alice, Ben Bolt."' I had substituted my father's name for the ballad's dead Alice. 'It's obvious that you wanted your father to die,' said Frink.

The next hour, I continued to tell the story of my analysis with Frink and how I had begun to dread my visits with him.

His statement about my wishing my father dead had an immediate and devastating effect on me. My impression was that my father was my rock of ages, my dependence on him inordinately strong, and yet I wanted him to die? 'Why?' I asked Frink. The answer came at once. 'It was that you envied him the possession of your stepmother.' This revelation, that I wanted this man whom I consciously adored dead, devastated me. I did not dispute this interpretation because I felt that I had no authority to do so, but I left the hour in a state of anxiety. What frightened me most was that I could entertain ideas of which I had no awareness. For many sessions thereafter, my discomfort continued, and I had only one clear objective. I wanted out of this analysis as quickly as I possibly could. I was certain that as soon as it stopped, so would my discomfort.

In this atmosphere of resistance, guilt, and general feeling of 'How did I get into this mess?' I had a very dramatic dream, which puzzled both Frink and me – Freud, however, made some sense out of it, although I am not sure, even now, that I fully understand it.

A. Kardiner, *My Analysis with Freud* (1977)

=

The end of the analysis

The analyst had urged me frequently to bring him written reports of my dreams. I had explained when he first made this request that I never dreamed, or if I did, that the dreams vanished completely before I awoke. The analyst always looked at me suspiciously when I told him this and implied, not too subtly, that I was holding back on my dreams for fear that they would disclose an interest in the sufficiently full sex life. The night before I paid my last visit to the analyst was a memorable one for I had the first dream of my life. After having been asleep for a short time, I awoke with the dream flashing through my head. I arose, turned on a light, found some paper and hastily wrote an account of the dream, after which I went back to bed and dreamless sleep. The next day I brought the written report to the analyst's office and showed it to him.

'I was sitting in a restaurant,' I had written, 'talking to my dinner companion, a man whom I had just discovered to be a racketeer. I was very annoyed, not because he was a racketeer, but because I had also discovered that he was a third-rate racketeer.'

I was quite elated at having had a dream of any kind, even such a nondescript one as this, and I waited enthusiastically for the interpretation. None came. The analyst rolled his head as if he were going to charge, and then abruptly tightened his lips and started talking about something else.

I had read Freud in my early youth but had forgotten, consciously at least, most of what I had read. It was months after I had left the analyst before I got around to reading Freud again, whereupon I realized the significance of the dream. The interpretation staggered me, for it would appear that unconsciously I had classified all Freudians as racketeers and the analyst as a third-rate racketeer. It occurred to me as being surprisingly coincidental that I should have had my only dream just prior to my last visit to the analyst's office and it occurred to me, also, to wonder if Something had gotten in a last low smack at its sparring partner before parting company.

Barbara O'Brien, *Operators and Things:*
The Inner Life of a Schizophrenic (1958)

17

Sex

From the orgiastic release of the Dionysian dance, the associations between madness and sexuality have never been far from the surface (though, as Freud insisted, they have also been systematically repressed). But they have always been complex.

Love madness, the lunacy of young passion, Romeo and Juliet, the star-crossed lovers, the doomed sweethearts, the suicide pact, *amour fou*, Ophelia – this has always won respect in our values, and fascinated artists and poets. But if there is something noble about romantic love and its associated crazy extremes of passion, the raging infernos of *sex* have usually been depicted as disgusting, disruptive and destructive. Loathing himself (temporarily) for succumbing to a whore in St James's, Boswell entered but one word in his journal: 'madness'.

Entertaining and yielding to illicit or excessive sexual urges were long thought to precipitate insanity. Masturbation would lead to uncontrollable fantasizing and a world of delusions. Gratification of lust would produce satyriasis or nymphomania, bringing on premature senile debility; it would also risk syphilis, the long-term consequence of which – general paresis of the insane – was popularly known as the softening of the brain. The attitudes we now, only partially accurately, call 'Victorian' inculcated sexual abstinence and moderation with a view to avoiding these dangers.

Yet it was, at the same time, recognized that excessive sexual denial also spelt mental unbalance. Virginal males grew hypochondriacal; spinsters, and widows denied their accustomed pleasures, succumbed to hysteria. Medical folklore traditionally recommended marriage as the remedy for hysteria or for 'chlorosis', the mysterious wasting disorder of teenage girls –

thereby long anticipating Freud's 'discovery' of the sexual origins of the neuroses, or Charcot's observation, *à propos* of hysteria, 'c'est toujours la chose génitale'. Under the influence of Freudian ideas, several of the authors quoted below believed their own sexual inhibitions to be responsible in part for their nervous disorders.

Yet such well-meaning benevolence was ever accompanied by potent misogynistic associations linking passion, femininity and evil. Originally embodied in the figure of the sexually rampant witch, riding to her sabbat, these assumptions evolved into the *femme fatale* or the prostitute figure so prominent in nineteenth-century novels and art. There was a powerful tendency to see the feminine as an unstable amalgam of virgin, mother and whore, provoking Freud's leading question: 'what do women want?' By the close of the *belle époque*, the relations between sexuality and mental disorder had become part of the 'woman question'.

But not only women were problematic. Nineteenth-century psychiatry problematized all manner of sexual 'abnormalities'. It turned a traditional practice such as sodomy into the 'perversion' of homosexuality, and, in the name of enlightenment, sought to decriminalize other 'unnatural acts' by medicalizing or psychiatrizing them – thereby reformulating the old chestnut as to whether it was preferable to be bad or mad.

In short, the relations within our culture between sex and insanity have been deeply charged, and extremely confused and confusing. Too much sex might overexcite the system, or be seen as itself symptomatic of madness, or be regarded as the expression of an inherited degeneracy. But too little sex was clearly unhealthy repression.

—

A vision

It began in the autumn of 1938, when I was just 38 years of age. For some years I had suffered from bouts of nervous depression, and I had had one attack of elation. None of these had been really serious, however; at any rate I had not had to be confined in a Mental Hospital or Asylum. I had been free of trouble for rather more than a year and had settled down in a congenial job.

The first symptoms appeared on Armistice Sunday. I had attended the service which commemorates the gallant dead of the 'War to end Wars'. It always has an emotional effect upon me, partly because my work has had a good deal to do with the tragic aftermath of that war in Europe. Suddenly I seemed to see like a flash that the sacrifice of those millions of lives had not been in vain, that it was part of a great pattern, the pattern of Divine Purpose. I felt, too, an inner conviction that I had something to do with that purpose; it seemed that some sort of revelation was being made to me, though at the time I had no clear ideas about what it was. The whole aspect of the world about me began to change, and I had the excited shivers in the spinal column and tingling of the nerves that always herald my manic phases.

That night I had a vision. It was the only pure hallucination I have ever experienced; though I have had many other visions, they have always taken the form of what are technically known as 'illusions'. I woke up about five o'clock to find a strange, rather unearthly light in the room. As my natural drowsiness wore off, the excited feelings of the day before returned and grew more intense. The light grew brighter; I began, I remember, to inhale deep gulps of air, which eased the tension in some way. Then suddenly the vision burst upon me.

How shall I describe it? It was perfectly simple. The great male and female organs of love hung there in mid-air; they seemed infinitely far away from me and infinitely near at the same time. I can see them now, pulsing rhythmically in a circular clockwise motion, each revolution taking approximately the time of a human pulse or heartbeat, as though the vision was associated in some way with the circulation of the blood. I was not sexually excited; from the first the experience seemed to me to be holy. What I saw was the Power of Love – the name came to me at once – the Power that I knew somehow to have made all universes, past, present and to come, to be utterly infinite, an infinity of infinities, to have conquered the Power of Hate, its opposite, and thus created the sun, the stars, the moon, the planets, the earth, light, life, joy and peace, never-ending.

John Custance, Wisdom, Madness and Folly:
The Philosophy of a Lunatic (1951)

=

The courtier Fulke Greville reports how George III, sinking into delirium in 1788, became sexually uninhibited and recalled his earlier desires for Lady Elizabeth Pembroke.

In his more disturbed hours He has for some time past, spoke much of Lady Pembroke – This Evening He recollected, what He had at times said of Her, & a sense of shame accompanied his transient & deliberate moments – He very feelingly said to one of his Pages He hoped nobody knew what wrong ideas He had had, & what wrong things He had said respecting Her – This sense of his improprieties which now flashed with a gleam of returning reason, reminded Me of a similar Instance which occurr'd at Windsor on one of those days in which there had been symptoms more favourable than had yet appeared since his Attack – He observed at this time, that in his Delirium He must have said many very improper things, & that much must have scaped Him then which ought not, & that he must try & find out what had slipped from Him.

Fulke Greville, diary entry (27 December 1788), in Ida Macalpine and Richard A. Hunter, *George III and the Mad Business* (1969)

=

Fanny Burney chased by the madly amorous George III

Kew Palace, Monday, February 2. – What an adventure had I this morning! one that has occasioned me the severest personal terror I ever experienced in my life.

Sir Lucas Pepys still persisting that exercise and air were absolutely necessary to save me from illness, I have continued my walks, varying my gardens from Richmond to Kew, according to the accounts I received of the movements of the King. For this I had Her Majesty's permission, on the representation of Sir Lucas.

This morning, when I received my intelligence of the King from Dr John Willis, I begged to know where I might walk in safety. 'In Kew Gardens,' he said, 'as the King would be in Richmond.'

'Should any unfortunate circumstance,' I cried, 'at any time, occasion my being seen by His Majesty, do not mention my name, but let me run off without call or notice.'

This he promised. Everybody, indeed, is ordered to keep out of sight.

Taking, therefore, the time I had most at command, I strolled
into the gardens. I had proceeded, in my quick way, nearly half
the round, when I suddenly perceived, through some trees, two or
three figures. Relying on the instructions of Dr John, I concluded
them to be workmen and gardeners; yet tried to look sharp, and
in so doing, as they were less shaded, I thought I saw the person of
His Majesty!

Alarmed past all possible expression, I waited not to know
more, but turning back, ran off with all my might. But what was
my terror to hear myself pursued! – to hear the voice of the King
himself loudly and hoarsely calling after me, 'Miss Burney! Miss
Burney!'

I protest I was ready to die. I knew not in what state he might
be at the time; I only knew the orders to keep out of his way were
universal; that the Queen would highly disapprove any unauth-
orized meeting, and that the very action of my running away
might deeply, in his present irritable state, offend him. Nevertheless, on I ran, too terrified to stop, and in search of some short
passage, for the garden is full of little labyrinths, by which I might
escape.

The steps still pursued me, and still the poor hoarse and altered
voice rang in my ears: – more and more footsteps resounded
frightfully behind me, – the attendants all running, to catch their
eager master, and the voices of the two Dr Willises loudly exhor-
ting him not to heat himself so unmercifully.

Heavens, how I ran! I do not think I should have felt the hot
lava from Vesuvius – at least not the hot cinders – had I so run
during its eruption. My feet were not sensible that they even
touched the ground.

Soon after, I heard other voices, shriller, though less nervous,
call out, 'Stop! stop! stop!'

I could by no means consent: I knew not what was purposed,
but I recollected fully my agreement with Dr John that very morning, that I should decamp if surprised, and not be named.

My own fears and repugnance, also, after a flight and disobedience like this, were doubled in the thought of not escaping; I
knew not to what I might be exposed, should the malady be then
high, and take the turn of resentment. Still, therefore, on I flew;

and such was my speed, so almost incredible to relate or recollect, that I fairly believe no one of the whole party could have overtaken me, if these words, from one of the attendants, had not reached me, 'Dr Willis begs you to stop!'

'I cannot! I cannot!' I answered, still flying on, when he called out, 'You must, ma'am; it hurts the King to run.'

Then, indeed, I stopped – in a state of fear really amounting to agony. I turned round, I saw the two Doctors had got the King between them, and three attendants of Dr Willis's were hovering about. They all slackened their pace, as they saw me stand still; but such was the excess of my alarm, that I was wholly insensible to the effects of a race which, at any other time, would have required an hour's recruit.

As they approached, some little presence of mind happily came to my command: it occurred to me that, to appease the wrath of my flight, I must now show some confidence: I therefore faced them as undauntedly as I was able, only charging the nearest of the attendants to stand by my side.

When they were within a few yards of me, the King called out, 'Why did you run away?'

Shocked at a question impossible to answer, yet a little assured by the mild tone of his voice, I instantly forced myself forward, to meet him, though the internal sensation which satisfied me this was a step the most proper, to appease his suspicions and displeasure, was so violently combated by the tremor of my nerves, that I fairly think I may reckon it the greatest effort of personal courage I have ever made.

The effort answered: I looked up, and met all his wonted benignity of countenance, though something still of wildness in his eyes. Think, however, of my surprise, to feel him put both his hands round my shoulders, and then kiss my cheek!

I wonder I did not really sink, so exquisite was my affright when I saw him spread out his arms! Involuntarily, I concluded he meant to crush me: but the Willises, who have never seen him till this fatal illness, not knowing how very extraordinary an action this was from him, simply smiled and looked pleased, supposing, perhaps, it was his customary salutation!

I believe, however, it was but the joy of a heart unbridled, now, by the forms and proprieties of established custom and sober reason. To see any of his household thus by accident, seemed such a near approach to liberty and recovery, that who can wonder it should serve rather to elate than lessen what yet remains of his disorder!

He now spoke in such terms of his pleasure in seeing me, that I soon lost the whole of my terror; astonishment to find him so nearly well, and gratification to see him so pleased, removed every uneasy feeling, and the joy that succeeded, in my conviction of his recovery, made me ready to throw myself at his feet to express it.

What a conversation followed! When he saw me fearless, he grew more and more alive, and made me walk close by his side, away from the attendants, and even the Willises themselves, who, to indulge him, retreated. I own myself not completely composed, but alarm I could entertain no more.

Everything that came uppermost in his mind he mentioned; he seemed to have just such remains of his flightiness as heated his imagination without deranging his reason, and robbed him of all control over his speech, though nearly in his perfect state of mind as to his opinions.

What did he not say! – He opened his whole heart to me, – expounded all his sentiments, and acquainted me with all his intentions.

                          Fanny Burney, diary entry (2 February 1789)

                                    =

Eros and melancholy

Concerning desire, which is the efficient cause of erotic melancholy, I will recount to you a pleasant fable drawn from Plato's *Symposium* where Diotima relates to Socrates how, when Venus was born, all the gods came to a banquet, among them Porus, god of plenty and son of Good Counsel. After they had all dined, there arrived also, though quite late, Penia or Poverty, who remained at the gate begging a few scraps of the meat remaining from the abundant feast. Porus, drunk on nectar, went into Jupiter's garden where he was overtaken by a profound sleep. Penia lay down beside him and by this ruse conceived Love who, in keeping with his mother's nature, is always poor, lean, dirty, barefoot, wandering the earth without bed, house or blanket, sleeping in doorways and in the streets. But taking also after his father, he pursues good and beautiful objects, he is manly, courageous, impetuous, and wily, ever contriving new tricks, a huntsman, prudent, ingenious, a philosopher and subtle enchanter, a sorcerer and sophist. I will pass over in silence the allegorical interpretations of this fable by Plutarch, Marsilio Ficino, Plotinus, Pico della Mirandola, and several other academic philosophers and say that Penia or poverty represents the lover (love is desire, and desire is a kind of beggary or poverty according to Aristotle). Porus is he who is worthy to be loved, being naturally perfect; but for all that, he is indifferent to love. Notwithstanding, while he is asleep – the eyelids of his soul heavy with the poppy of carelessness, and without any regard to the imperfections of his partner – he takes his pleasure.

Jacques Ferrand, *A Treatise on Lovesickness* (1623)

=

A case at the York Retreat

CASE 651: LUCY F.

Lucy F., aged 17, single, daughter of a banker's clerk at Southampton, born at Newington Green, W. London, was admitted into the Retreat, July 14th 1842. Her father has been married twice, but has had no other offspring; her mother was not a Friend, consequently she was not born in membership; but was received into the Society in her infancy. Soon after her birth (a few weeks), her mother began to be troubled with symptoms of cancer of the womb, and died of that disease within nine months. (The disease had therefore been probably in existence during the pregnancy.) Her father married again within two or three years.

L. F. did not evince any peculiarity bodily or mental – unless some obstinacy of temper be so regarded – up to about three years of age when she had a very severe attack of whooping cough, and this was followed by water on the head; for which leeches, blistering, etc. were used, but, as appeared to the parents with prejudicial effect. The disorder was followed by squinting and defective vision, which have continued up to the present time.

There was no hereditary tendency to insanity and the friends are no doubt correct in attributing the strange perversity of the moral feelings, which had more or less been ever since noticed to the defective development arising from this disease. The parents state that the disposition and character of the patient have always been marked by the following characteristics and peculiarities. Her perception is very quick, and when a stranger would suppose from the defect in her sight, that she was almost unconscious of what was going on, she is really noticing everything very closely. She is gifted with a good memory, and an ability to acquire knowledge of some kinds, she is nevertheless defective in those mental qualities which would enable her to attain to proficiency in any eventual pursuit; for no description of which has her mind ever indicated any predilection. The moral feelings have always been marked by remarkable want of power; and though abstractedly she knows right from wrong; yet she never appeared able to follow the former, like other children, from the motive of the love of approbation, and similar motives. On the contrary there appeared to be an innate love of mischief, theft and falsehood, and great artfulness, which could never be counteracted by any ordinary methods of education. She was sent to a boarding school for three years, and would have continued much longer, but for the foregoing peculiarities of her disposition. Her parents then procured her admission into Croydon School, but the managers would not keep her on these accounts and recommended her being placed under proper care. Whilst there, she exhibited her artfulness and ingenuity by feigning blindness, and requiring to be led about, with the view of exciting commiseration, and to be discharged [from] the school.

After leaving Croydon she was placed out to board under the care of an elderly female, in a village near Southampton, with whom she has since continued. As a child she was always observed to prefer boys as her companions, but this did not attract any particular attention, until the period of puberty, which took place very early, the catamenia appearing at 13½ years. Ever since this the sexual appetite has been very prominent and has led her into numerous improprieties, and has given her parents great anxiety.

For about 7 years past, she has resided with an elderly female in the neighbourhood of Southampton, and whilst under her care, has several times eluded her vigilance and got into the company of men of low habits and with whom she has been found in the fields and lanes: — indeed the premature and excessive 'desire for the male sex' is regarded by her friends as the peculiar feature of her disorder. It was determined to place her under care in consequence of her having escaped a considerable distance about a month ago, being found in a field by the roadside in the company of a man; and being only taken by the guard of the coach and another person, after considerable resistance. Upon her return she stated that her design had been to get a situation as a laundry maid, that she might earn some money, to buy clothes, when she would get married, and go to Australia.

The disorder is considered to be gradually increasing. Her bodily health is stated to be good. She has shown no disposition to refuse food or to injure herself, nor to acts of destruction or violence of any kind; but she is stated to require 'a little care' as regards habits of cleanliness.

State on admission
Is of short stature but stout to corpulency; shoulders broad, bosoms large, arms short, lower extremities imperfectly developed; has a singular waddling walk, and altogether a very peculiar appearance, her whole manner, etc. exhibiting a decided preponderance of the physical and animal over the intellectual and moral. The bulk of the body resembles that of a stout woman but the head and limbs are those of a girl, a little girl. The head is of a round, flattened form, wide in the centre and full behind; the neck very short and thick, the forehead is low and shallow, but wide and above the eyes is moderately full.

The axes of the eyes do not correspond and the lid of the right is almost constantly dropped from loss of power over the levator palpebrae muscle; the left pupil is dilated, but it is difficult to ascertain the exact state of either eye from her unwillingness to submit to any close examination. The cheeks are plump, the expression when pleased childish but cunning and amorous, and she will often hide herself behind the door-post and pass out in a half-laughing playful mood, with the eyes but half-opened and [?] in a peculiar way. When displeased by anything which passes around her, which she is very readily and on the most trifling occasions, the impress of anger, disdain and of the other angry passions on the countenance is very marked, and the change from one to the other is as sudden as it is marked.

In bodily health there does not appear to be anything requiring notice, except that she is subject to great constipation of the bowels, and has been often two weeks without an evacuation. The catamenia are regular. The circulation in the hands is feeble and they are often blue and cold.

Mental state

L. F. is characterized by a shrewdness of observation and rapidity of perception which are exquisitely feminine. The memory too is strong and ready, so that she readily commits to memory considerable portions both of poetry and prose composition. In solidarity of judgement however she appears entirely wanting. She manifests strong attachments and aversions and her love to her father appears particularly strong. She is however very wayward, her will obstinate and capricious; and the faults of temper coupled with the early development and force of the amative propensity perhaps justify the conclusion that there is a degree of 'moral insanity' as certified by Dr Williams of Southampton, who was consulted previous to her being sent here. The case would perhaps better be regarded as one of congenital moral imbecility, the 'brutality' of Dr Mayo.

She writes a poor crabbed hand, without regard to capital letters or punctuation, but spells and reads tolerably. For a copy of one of her letters see Dec. 2nd 1842.

She was placed under the watchful care of her nurse, and as strict separation of the opposite sex, as the construction of the Retreat permits, was enjoined. Employment in domestic affairs and in needlework, with frequent exercise in the open air were also enjoined.

[From July to November of 1842 Lucy F.'s case-notes deal entirely with the treatment of various physical complaints that culminated in a serious illness in November in which the patient became delirious.]

Dec. 2nd appears quite well and looks better and stouter than I have before seen her. She only complains of a little pain occasionally in the right side (hypochondriacal). The enema last ordered was not required and the bowels and kidneys perform their functions healthily. She takes the electuary daily or on alternate days. She may now omit the quinine.

The following letter to her parents was written today:

Dear Father and Mother,

I hope these few lines will find you quite well. I am sorry to inform you I have been very ill but I am now quite well. John Thurnam was very kind to me during my illness, he was like a father to me. I think father you have certainly forgotten me, the only child you have but father I don't forget you. I think it unkind as you did not answer my letter but out of sight out of mind. I often think of what you said before I left home. I do not forget if you do, dear father. Give my love to [?] and [?] and tell them I have signed the pledge to teetotalism. Give my love to Albert and to Aunt and Uncle Hodges. Give my respects to young Mr Cray. Give my kind love to Mother, accept some for yourself. I remain your affectionate daughter,

                                                                      L. F.

[Left the Retreat on 5 May 1846 and was stated to have 'recovered': no case-notes were apparently made between 2 December 1842 and her discharge.]

> Anne Digby, *Madness, Morality and Medicine: A Study of the York Retreat, 1796–1914* (1985)

=

In the second half of the nineteenth century in particular, European psychiatry emphasized the coterminousness of mental disorder with sexual aberrations or excesses. Krafft-Ebing's Psychopathologia Sexualis *systematized these perceptions.*

Case 188

A gentleman of high social position, aged forty-five; generally respected and beloved; heredity good; very moral; married fifteen years. Previously sexually normal, the father of several healthy

children, and living in happy matrimony. Eight years ago he had a
sudden fright. For some weeks thereafter he had a feeling of
apprehension of cardiac attacks. Then came attacks, at intervals of
several months or a year, of what the patient called his 'moral
catarrh'. He became sleepless. After three days, loss of appetite,
increasing irritability, strange appearance; fixed stare, staring into
space; paleness, changing with redness; tremor of the fingers; red,
shining eyes, with peculiar glassy expression; and violent, quick
manner of speech. There was a desire for girls of from five to ten
years, even for his own daughters. He would beg his wife to guard
the children. For days at a time, while in this state, he would shut
himself in his room. Previously he was compelled to pass school-
girls on the street, and he found a peculiar pleasure in exposing his
genitals before them, by acting as if about to urinate.

For fear of exposure, he shut himself in his room, morose,
incapable of movement, and torn by feelings of fear. Consciousness
seemed to be undisturbed. The attacks lasted from eight to fourteen
days. The cause of their return was not clear. Improvement was
sudden; there was great desire for sleep, and, after this was satisfied, he was well again. In the interval there was nothing abnormal.
Anjél assumed an epileptic foundation, and considered the attacks
to be the physical equivalents of epileptic convulsions.

MANIA

With the general excitation that here exists in the psychical organ,
the sexual sphere is likewise often implicated. In maniacal individuals of the female sex, this is the rule. In certain cases, it may be
questionable whether the instinct, which, in itself, is not intensified,
is simply recklessly manifested, or whether it is present in actual
abnormal intensity. For the most part, the latter is the true assumption – certainly so where sexual delusions and their religious
equivalents are constantly expressed. In accordance with the
degrees of intensity of the disease, the intensified instinct is
expressed in different forms.

Case 189

Mrs V., from earliest youth mania for men. Of good ancestors,
highly cultured, good-natured, very modest, blushed easily, but

always the terror of the family. Quando quidem sola erat cum homine sexus alterium, negligens, utrum infans sit an vir, an senex, utrum pulcher an teter, statim corpus nudavit et vehementer libidines suas satiari rogavit vel vim vel manus ei injecit [When she found herself alone with a member of the opposite sex, be he child or adult, elderly, handsome or ugly, she would immediately remove all her clothing and urgently require him to satisfy her desires, either by coitus or onanism]. Marriage was resorted to as a cure. Maritum quam maxime amavit, neque tamen sibi temperare potuit quin a quolibet viro, si solum apprehenderat, seu verso, seu mercenario, seu discipulo coitum exposceret [Yet although she loved her husband dearly, if she found herself alone with a man, she could not refrain from making sexual demands of him].

Nothing could cure her of this failing. Even when she was a grandmother, she still remained a Messalina. Puerum quondam duodecim annos natum in cubiculum allectum stuprare voluit [Once she attempted to make love with a boy of twelve]. He tore himself away and fled, and his brother gave her a severe punishment. But it was all in vain. When sent to a convent she was a model of good conduct and committed not the slightest act of indiscretion. But the moment she returned home, she resumed her perverse practices. The family sent her away, giving her a small allowance. She worked hard to earn the money she needed for 'buying her lovers'. In looking at the trim, neat matron of sixty-five years of age, with her modest manners and a most amiable disposition, no one could ever suspect how shamelessly needy in her sexual life she was even then.

At last she was sent to an insane asylum, where she lived till May, 1858, when in her seventy-third year, she succumbed to a stroke of cerebral apoplexy. Her behaviour at the asylum when under surveillance, was beyond reproach; but if left to herself she utilized every opportunity in the same old fashion even to within a few days before her death. No other signs of mental anomaly could be detected in her. (*Trelat*, 'folie lucide.')

In simple maniacal exaltation in men, courting, frivolity, and lasciviousness in speech, and frequenting of brothels, are observed; in women, inclination for the society of men, personal adornment, perfumes, talk of marriage and scandals, suspicion of the virtue of other women; or there is manifested the religious equivalent – pilgrimages, missionary work, desire to become a monk or the servant of a priest; and in this case there is much talk about innocence and virginity.

At the height of mania there may be seen invitations to coitus, exhibition, obscenity, great excitation at sight of women, tendency to smear the person with saliva, urine, and even fæces; religio-sexual delusions, – to be under the protection of the Holy Ghost, to have given birth to Christ, etc.; open onanism and pelvic movements of coitus.

In maniacal men care must be taken to prevent shameless masturbation and sexual attacks on women.

NYMPHOMANIA AND SATYRIASIS

The description of these conditions is simply an annex to the attempt made ... to explain *hyperæsthesia sexualis*, in so far as we take into consideration temporary sexual affects emanating therefrom, no matter whether they are occasioned by abstinence or are of a permanent character. They may become so predominant that they completely sway the field of imagination and desire, and imperatively demand the relief of the affect in the corresponding sexual act. In acute and severe cases, ethics and will-power lose their controlling influence entirely, while in chronic and milder cases restraint is still possible to a certain degree. At the acme of paroxysm hallucinations, delirium and benumbed consciousness make their appearance, and often continue during a prolonged period. Irresistible impulses are forced to sacrifice feminine honour and dignity, for they are fully conscious of their painful situation, they are a toy in the grip of a morbid imagination which revolves solely around sexual ideas and grasps even the most distant points in the sense of an aphrodisiac. Even in their sleep they are pursued by lascivious dreams. In the daytime the slightest cause will produce a crisis in which a veritable *erithismus cerebralis sexualis*, coupled with painful sensations (pressure, vibration, pulsation, etc.,) in the genitals torments them. Temporary relief comes in time in the shape of *neurasthenia genitalis*, which reacts promptly on the centre of ejaculation and readily causes pollutions in lascivious dreams, or some erotic crisis when awake. Full gratification, however, they cannot find any more than those of their unfortunate fellow-sufferers who abandon themselves to men. This *anaphrodisia* explains to a large extent the persistence of the sexual affect, *i.e.*, that nymphomania which heaps crisis upon crisis.

Neurasthenia sexualis, which inhibits orgasm and sensual gratification, no doubt, fully explains this anaphrodisia which restrains the beneficent assuagement of sexual emotions, yet maintaining an incessant craving (*libido insatiata*), forces the woman, morally devoid of all power of resistance, to auto-masturbation or psychical onanism, and eventually as a Messalina to prostitution in which to find satisfaction and relief with one man after another.

This neurasthenia is often caused by an abnormally early and powerful sexual instinct, which prescribes onanism; or it may be reduced to enforced continence with strong coexisting sexual appetite.

R. von Krafft-Ebing, *Psychopathia Sexualis* (1886)

=

From the early eighteenth century, Europe underwent a great masturbation scare. Over the next two centuries, medical opinion argued that masturbation caused physical diseases, such as consumption, and mental disorder as well – above all, pathological self-absorption and fantasy-systems.

The development of puberty may indirectly lead to insanity by becoming the occasion of a vicious habit of self-abuse in men; and it is not always easy to say in such cases how much of the evil is due to pubescence and how much to the vice. But the form of mental derangement directly traceable to it has certainly characteristic features. There are no acute symptoms, the onset of the disease being most gradual. The patient becomes offensively egotistic and impracticable; he is full of self-feeling and self-conceit; insensible to the claims of others upon him and of his duties to them: interested only in hypochondriacally watching his morbid sensations and attending to his morbid feelings. His mental energy is sapped; and though he has extravagant pretensions, and often speaks of great projects engendered by his conceit, he never works systematically for any aim, but exhibits an incredible vacillation of conduct, and spends his days in indolent and suspicious self-brooding. His relatives he thinks hostile to him because they do not take the interest in his sufferings which he craves, nor yield sufficiently to his pretensions, but perhaps urge him to some kind of work; he is utterly incapable of conceiving that he has duties to them. As matters get worse, the general suspicion of the hostility of people takes more definite form, and delusions spring up that persons speak offensively of him, or watch him in the street, or comment on what passes in his mind, or play tricks upon him by electricity or mesmerism, or in some other mysterious way. His delusions are the objective explanation, by wrong imagination, of the perverted feelings. Messages may be received from heaven by peculiar telegraphic signals; and there are occasionally quasi-cataleptic trances. It is strange what exalted feelings and high moral and religious aims these patients will often declare they have, who, incapable of reforming themselves, are ready to reform the world. A later and worse stage is one of moody or vacant self-absorption, and of extreme loss of mental power. They are silent, or, if they converse, they discover delusions of a suspicious or obscene character, the perverted sexual passion still giving the colour to their thoughts. They die miserable wrecks at the last. This is a form of insanity which certainly has its special exciting cause and its characteristic features; nevertheless, I think that the vicious habit seldom, if ever, produces it without the cooperation of the insane neurosis.

Henry Maudsley, *Body and Mind: An Inquiry into their Connection and Mutual Influence, Specially in Reference to Mental Diseases* (1873)

=

Fears of sex and of venereal disease were at the root of much mental disorder.

William B. Carpenter, a patient at Ticehurst House: 'His mouth, he says, is becoming like the interior of a woman's vagina – when asked how he could account for it, he told me he thought it was a visitation from God, for a horrible, animal-like action he had committed with a female, and that he was now suffering from a disease.'

Ticehurst records (c. 1840)

—

Those driven mad by unhappy or unrequited love have commanded sympathy.

It must be said that lovesickness is a disease of the estimative faculty, since a disease is a suffering of that faculty which it harms first and in itself and directly. But lovesickness harms the estimative faculty first and directly, since there is, in lovesickness, a failure of judgment about non-sensed forms or things, such as friendship and enmity and similarly other things. And it is the estimative faculty's [task] to apprehend a non-sensed form, which is understood thus: in lovesickness, the estimative faculty judges some woman or some other thing to be better or more beautiful than all the rest, even though it might not be so, and then it orders the cogitative faculty to plunge itself in the form of that thing. And thus in lovesickness there is depressed thought. And then the imaginative faculty imagines that thing, and [sends] it to the irascible and concupiscible faculties, which are faculties located in the heart that control movement. And then these controlling faculties order the faculty of movement, which is in the nerves, to move the limbs in pursuit of that thing. And thus it is obvious that lovesickness first and in itself and directly [harms the estimative faculty, and then] the estimative faculty harms the other faculties. In this the answer to the arguments is evident, since we readily concede that lovesickness harms the imaginative and cogitative faculties and the fantasy, not, however, directly but rather indirectly, as is evident from what has been said. And therefore lovesickness ought to be called a disease of the estimative faculty, and not of the cogitative, or of the imaginative, or of the fantasy.

Peter of Spain, quoted in Mary Frances Wack,
Lovesickness in the Middle Ages (1990)

Through Moor - fields and to Bed-lam I went; I
heard a young dam-sel _ to sigh and _ la-ment. She was
wring-ing of her hands and a-tear-ing of her hair, cry-ing:
'Oh, cru - el pa-rents, you've been too se-vere'.
Var. (a)   (b)   (c)

2 'You have banished my true love away to the seas,
   Which causes me in Bedlam to sigh and to say
   That your cruel base actions cause me to complain,
   For the loss of my dear has distracted my brain'.

3 When the silk mercer first came on shore,
   As he was passing by Bedlam door
   He heard his true love lamenting full sore,
   Saying: 'Oh, I shall never see him any more'.

4 The mercer hearing that, he was struck with surprise.
   When he saw through the window her beautiful eyes
   He ran to the porter the truth for to tell,
   Saying: 'Show me the way to the joy of my soul'.

5 The porter on the mercer began for to stare,
   To see how he was for the love of his dear.
   He gave to the porter a broad piece of gold,
   Saying: 'Show me the way to the joy of my soul'.

6 And when that his darling jewel he did see
   He took her and sat her all on his knee.
   Says she: 'Are you the young man my father sent to sea,
   My own dearest jewel, for loving of me?'

7 'Oh, yes, I am the man that your father sent to sea,

Your own dearest jewel, for loving of thee'.
'Then adieu to my sorrows for they now are all fled.
Adieu to these chains and likewise a straw bed'.

8 They sent for their parents who came then with speed;
They went to the church and were married indeed.
Now come all you wealthy parents, and due warning take,
And never strive true lovers their promises to break.

'Through Moorfields and to Bedlam I went' (c. 1700)

=

*Melancholy? Take a husband. A long tradition has associated
female hysteria or melancholy with sexual frustration, and has
urged its release in marriage.*

Many other maladies there are incident to young women, out of
that one and only cause above specified, many feral diseases. I will
not so much as mention their names, melancholy alone is the
subject of my present discourse, from which I will not swerve. The
several cures of this infirmity, concerning diet, which must be very
sparing, phlebotomy, physick, internal, external remedies, are at
large in great variety in Rodericus à Castro, Sennertus, and Mer-
catus, which whoso will, as occasion serves, may make use of. But
the best and surest remedy of all is to see them well placed, &
married to good husbands in due time; hence these tears, that's the
primary cause, and this the ready cure, to give them content to their
desires. I write not this to patronize any wanton, idle flirt, lascivious
or light housewives, which are too forward many times, unruly,
and apt to cast away themselves on him that comes next, without
all care, counsel, circumspection, and judgement. If religion, good
discipline, honest education, wholesome exhortation, fair promises,
fame, and loss of good name, cannot inhibit and deter such, (which
to chaste and sober maids cannot choose but avail much), labour
and exercise, strict diet, rigour, and threats, may more opportunely
be used, and are able of themselves to qualify & divert an ill-
disposed temperament. For seldom shall you see an hired servant, a
poor hand-maid, though ancient, that is kept hard to her work and
bodily labour, a coarse country wench, troubled in this kind.

Robert Burton (see page 13), *The Anatomy of Melancholy* (1621)

Mr *Hollyer* ... told me, that among many Patients sent to be cured
in a great Hospital [St Thomas's] (of which he is one of the
Chirurgions) there was a Maid of about eighteen Years of age, who,
without the loss of motion, had so lost the sense of feeling in the
external parts of her Body, that when he had, for tryal sake, pinn'd
her Handkerchief to her bare Neck, she went up and down with it
so pinn'd, without having any sense of what he had done to her. He
added, That this Maid having remained a great while in the Hospital without being cured, Dr *Harvey*, out of Curiosity, visited her
sometimes; and suspecting her strange Distemper to be chiefly
Uterine, and curable onely by *Hymeneal* Exercises, he advised her
Parents (who sent her not thither out of poverty) to take her home,
and provide her a Husband, by whom, in effect, she was according
to his Prognostick, and to many Mens wonder, cur'd of that strange
Disease.

Robert Boyle, *Some Considerations Touching the Usefulnesse
of Experimental Naturall Philosophy* (1663)

==

But things are more complex than that.

If my sex life had been normal, none of my so-called spiritual
experiences would have happened; so I concluded when I first
started to write this book. There is just enough truth there to
confuse the issue; it is the kind of easy over-simplification that tidies
away a problem without resolving it. One thing is certain. The first
'illumination' and its after-effects gave me the basis for my adult
belief in God. All the rest, both the inspiring, vitalizing experiences
and the delusional, damaging illnesses, followed on from that. It
was the point to which, in case of doubt, I always returned. It was
the stimulus which urged me on again and again to validate my new
beliefs. Without it, none of the unusual experiences recorded here
would have happened. Without it I might possibly at some time or
another have developed a psychotic illness, for it is arguable that I
have a constitutional tendency that way; but in that case my illness
would have taken a different form and my reaction to it would have
been different too. The initial breakthrough was like a leaven in my
life that continued acting even when no physiological disturbance

was present. Until it had been worked out, no lasting stability was possible. What really happened? And what did it mean? That is a question I must attempt with care and honesty to answer now.

Morag Coate, *Beyond All Reason* (1964)

=

Mental disorder is a matter not just of sexual drives but of the intricacies of love itself.

If falling in love were not such a common experience, and if doctors in their private lives were not also subject to it, it might already have become a text-book subject for psychiatrists to study. For it is the one universally prevalent form that delusional disturbance takes. This is not meant as a flippant or cynical comment. Falling in love is a wonderful experience. But some psychotic experiences are indescribably wonderful too. I have at different times experienced both, and I have returned to full, normal enjoyment of ordinary life, and I can say with assurance that the delusional content of the state known as falling in love rises and falls in the same way as it does in an acute psychotic episode. Anyone who has tried to reason with a person who is in love can confirm that one of the most obvious features of the condition is lack of insight. Sometimes the effects of falling in love may linger on for years. The effects of a psychotic illness may do so too.

This perhaps at first sight seems disturbing, but it need not be so if the process is clearly understood. Falling in love is a healthy, normal process, and it has a vital and constructive purpose in human life. That it is highly irrational does not detract from its real and realistic purpose. It is not always wise or healthy for people to be too sane. This is not the only violently irrational condition that is rightly taken for granted as a part of normal life. Parental love of all sorts, and maternal love especially, is in its first awakening highly delusional too. What we need is to understand the meaning and purpose of the delusions, and to learn how and why these should be adjusted to the realities of external life.

Morag Coate, *Beyond All Reason* (1964)

=

An ex-patient blames much mental illness on prudery.

When I leave here, I shall take wisdom with me; for a year in a madhouse is a wonderful experience, and one I would not have missed; for with so much time on my hands, with books to read and subjects to experiment upon, the main causes of lunacy appear to be as follows:

Lack of teachers.

By telling the boy that his penis is 'private,' instead of teaching him the exact purpose his penis is meant to serve.

Lack of education in the upbringing of children.

Ill-treatment of children.

Lack of psychological knowledge.

The hiding and/or withholding of truth.

False modesty.

Bad living.

Excessive alcohol.

Intermarriage.

Intercourse by men over fifty years of age.

These being the causes, the obvious remedy lies in the removal of the cause, which can be effected by educating the people concerning sex; for of all the paths of life, this is the darkest. It is overshadowed by mystery, secrecy, social custom on the one hand, and by desire, pleasure and necessity on the other. Educate the people with regard to the far-reaching effects of venereal disease by establishing psychological clinics for mothers and children throughout our land. Tell the children what the sex organs are provided for; and make medical examination compulsory before sanctioning marriage.

Why, we remain so Victorian that when an individual receives head injury, we say he has received injury to his head; but when he receives injury to his penis, we say that he has injured his 'privates'; so that even lunatics cry out, 'Why not call a spade a spade, and a penis a penis?'

H. G. Woodley, *Certified* (1947)

=

Successful sex therapy

It is with almost unspeakable gratitude that I write of the medical treatment which I myself received. It is difficult to write adequately of this part of my life. The medicines, drugs and injections no doubt contributed to my recovery, but the thing to which I looked forward with eagerness was the analytical interview with the doctor which took place every two or three days. For the first time in my life I felt that I was in the presence of someone who completely understood. Furthermore, while I was with the psychiatrist I had the strange feeling that my individual welfare was the only thing that mattered to him. These interviews, together with the medical treatment, continued for about two months. Then the doctor told me that he was going to try hypnotic treatment, after which I was to go home for thirty-six hours only. Despite the confidence of the psychiatrist, and the trust which I placed in him, I may perhaps be forgiven for having my doubts as to whether, after six years of sexual impotence, any treatment would be successful.

The week-end when I was to go home was arranged, and an hour before my wife was due to fetch me I was taken into a room where everything had been arranged for my comfort, even to a warmed and scented pillow on the bed upon which I was to lie. The doctor gave me an injection in each arm and warned me that they would make me drowsy. He then assured me of my ability to have sexual intercourse. He did not induce a state of deep hypnosis which he said was unnecessary. All this seemed so simple that I could hardly believe in its efficacy. My wife came for me and escorted me to the bus. I gradually became more drowsy and had difficulty in walking. We had to transfer to a train, and in the carriage my chin kept drooping forward on to my chest. When we arrived at our own station we were faced with a two-mile walk. I felt quite incapable of the effort but I stumbled along, from time to time leaning against the stone wall to rest.

At last I was home, and the house seemed to wear a new and brighter aspect than when I had seen it last. In accordance with the doctor's instructions my wife and I went at once to bed. I was still drowsy. My wife was not looking forward to what was to come, and six years of enforced abstinence were not the best preparation.

But the attempt was successful. The ecstasy of that hour cannot be
described. Again and again, during that week-end, my wife and I
were in each other's arms. My honeymoon had at last arrived. I
went back to the hospital with a new song in my heart. The terrible
look of strained anxiety had for the time left the face of my wife,
and once more we kissed each other farewell at the hospital doors,
this time in a spirit that was full of hope. A week or so later the
doctor told me that he could do little more and, almost reluctantly,
I left the building where my life had been reshaped.

                              John Vincent, *Inside the Asylum* (1948)

=

No sex please: you're in analysis.

As soon as Professor Freud had returned to Vienna, Dr D. started
back to Odessa, so I was now completely alone in Vienna. Naturally this had an unfavorable effect on my spirits. I was occupied all
the time with thoughts of when Professor Freud would agree to my
seeing Therese again. I was always raising this question anew, and I
remember that once – evidently Professor Freud was in a specially
good humor that day – he raised his hands above his head and cried
out pathetically: 'For twenty-four hours now I have not heard the
sacred name Therese!'

My urging was of no avail, as Professor Freud was of the opinion
that it was not yet the right time and that I should still wait a few
months. This delay put me in bad mood, and after a while my
analysis with Professor Freud began to seem at a standstill also. It
was only at the end of February or the beginning of March 1911
that Professor Freud told me he agreed to my seeing Therese in
Munich...

I would have married Therese then and there, had this not been
contrary to the rule Professor Freud had made that a patient should
not make any decision which would irreversibly influence his later
life. If I wished to complete my treatment with Freud successfully, it
was necessary for me to follow his rule whether I wanted to or not.

In this connection, I remember how once during this time I
received an invitation from the Russian Consul in Vienna to visit
him. I have no idea how he learned my address. When I saw him, he

asked me why I did not attend the parties of the Russian diplomatic representatives and why I did not attach myself to the Russian colony in Vienna. Of course I could not accept these invitations of the Russian Consul so long as Therese and I were not married, and I made my excuses on the grounds of my illness and my treatment with Professor Freud. Apart from this insignificant matter which I mention only because it just occurred to me, it was very hard for Therese to submit to Professor Freud's rule that our marriage should be postponed until the end of my treatment. Nevertheless she never held this against him.

Muriel Gardner (ed.), *The Wolf-man and Sigmund Freud* (1972)

=

Sex will help your analysis.

I returned to the analyst's office for my next appointment with more enthusiasm than I usually felt at such times. This was the day when the analyst would attempt to determine what had brought about my schizophrenia. And even though no one knew what did cause schizophrenia, the analyst appeared to have a knowing glint in his eye, the air of a man who knew a secret or two.

The waves, usually so quiet in the analyst's office, started cascading on the beach as soon as I entered his office. I reminded him immediately that he had promised to explore the cause of my mental collapse and the analyst nodded and plunged right in.

It was simple. Psychoses, in the analyst's opinion, were the result of an inadequate sex life, particularly in America. The analyst was a Frenchman. I asked him what caused schizophrenia in France and the analyst gave me the dirty look he usually gave me when a wave prompted me to ask a question. The only thing he could not understand, the analyst told me, was why, with a full six months at its disposal, my unconscious had not gotten itself into a few thousand discussions about sex.

If Something knew the answer, it kept the answer to itself. No wave helped me. The dry beach considered the question and at that moment was as surprised as the analyst was. True, there had been also a great many other subjects with which my unconscious had not shown any particular concern. It hadn't discussed my friends or my family, or money or marriage, or politics or parents, or death or taxes. It had been concerned only with explaining the workings of the world of Operators.

'It probably has a one-track mind,' I said. The analyst blinked at me and I explained. My unconscious was probably an unconscious with a one-track mind. The comment irritated the analyst. That, it appeared, was exactly the point. All unconscious minds were one-tracked. They were singularly one-tracked. They were one-tracked about sex. There was no reason in the world why my unconscious mind should have spent six months talking about Operators and Things when it could have, just as easily, spent six months talking about sex.

The analyst, besides being a Frenchman, was a Freudian. Freudians, I decided later, had much in common with small religious cults, possessed with tight little worlds of ideas, which built little matchstick kingdoms on a wide plateau of truth before claiming the plateau. To the analyst, any breakdown in mental or emotional machinery could be traced only to one cause. A sex life that was not sufficiently full.

We discussed my sex life. It was not sufficiently full. I asked the analyst how full a sufficiently full sex life would have to be, and the analyst waved a hand airily. 'You should have had a hundred and twenty-five affairs by this time.' The number seemed staggering and I tried to calculate one hundred and twenty-five on a yearly basis but the dry beach was unable to cope with arithmetic.

'Even so,' the analyst told me, 'you might still find yourself now with emotional problems. American men are very poor lovers.' It occurred to me vaguely that with a hundred and twenty-five of them in my past, poor lovers or otherwise, I might well have emotional problems.

No. No. I wasn't looking at the problem in the right way. 'A multitude of affairs is the only solution for the career woman. You had an excellent job and a career worth following. With career women, marriage rarely mixes. The solution is a varied and full sex life.'

A wave broke on the beach. I said timidly, 'Don't you think that becoming emotionally involved with so many men might in itself cause considerable frustration?' I was pleased with my question. I was in Mars, talking the Martian language knowingly, discussing without shock the Martian point of view. But I had retained, I discovered, the Earth accent.

'There's no need for becoming involved emotionally with any one,' the analyst said irritably. 'What you mean by emotion is of no concern whatever to your unconscious. Men are more realistic about sex than are women.'

A wave rolled in and I suddenly remembered something. 'I adopted a foster child in Europe.' We discussed this for a few seconds. The analyst thought it nice of me to provide for the care of a child, but the subject was not important. I mustn't detour to side roads. Keep on the highway.

Another wave cascaded. Was I on the highway? 'I have a feeling that the maternal instinct is stronger in women than any other instinct. It seems very sensible for nature to have provided women with such a strong instinct for nest building and to have provided men with equally strong sex initiative.'

The analyst looked at me bleakly, like a sea gull.

The waves were toppling all over the shore. 'I can see where sex for the sake of sexual gratification might supply emotional security for a man. But I doubt that it would with most women. Nature seems to have arranged things differently.'

The analyst slapped his desk in irritation. 'A typical woman's point of view. And it's nonsense, do you hear, nonsense! Women don't understand themselves.'

When I left his office I was still trying to divide one hundred and twenty-five men over the years from my physical maturity. I succeeded finally.

Barbara O'Brien, *Operators and Things: The Inner Life of a Schizophrenic* (1958)

18

Madness and Genius

The mad are 'different'. So are artists and writers, scientists and other so-called 'pointy-headed' intellectuals. The result has been that, over the centuries, they have often been yoked together. Both, it has been suggested, have been kindled, consumed even, by some divine fire, or driven by some common bodily agent, such as, according to Aristotle's speculation, 'black bile', the humour of melancholy. This association has had varying implications. In Renaissance times, it served to enhance the status of the artist or poet, through the implication that they were uniquely inspired by some divine *furor*.

The accent had shifted by the late nineteenth century. Leading psychiatrists in the 'degenerationist' school, such as Cesare Lombroso, were by then arguing that the 'madness' of artists and writers (in other words, their Bohemian disregard for conventional respectabilities) revealed them as sociopaths, moral cripples and, generally, undesirables. Yet, in a more positive movement, it was about this time that enlightened asylum psychiatrists began to discover and cherish the art of the insane.

Thus the relations between the arts and insanity have always been many-faceted and contested. Certain writers – William Cowper, for instance – have clearly resorted to authorship to maintain their sanity; others, such as William Blake, have luxuriated in the aura of divine madness. Still others, Antonin Artaud perhaps, have flirted with the notion of a consuming madness firing the artistic temperament, but have ended up as the victims of their own extravagant conceits – which perhaps explains why Charles Lamb, who lived all his adult life surrounded by domestic madness, insisted so forcibly upon the 'sanity of true genius'.

Poetic madness

I stept into Bedlam, where I saw several poor miserable creatures in chains; one of them was mad with making verses.

John Evelyn, *Diary* (21 April 1657)

=

Contemplation of eternity: Van Gogh in October 1888

I am not ill, but without the slightest doubt I'd get ill if I did not eat plenty of food and if I did not stop painting for a few days. As a matter of fact, I am again pretty nearly reduced to the madness of Hugo van der Goes in Emile Wauters' picture. And if it were not that I have almost double nature, that of a monk and that of a painter, as it were, I should have been reduced, and that long ago, completely and utterly, to the aforesaid condition.

Yet even then I do not think that my madness could take the form of persecution mania, since when in a state of excitement my feelings lead me rather to the contemplation of eternity, and eternal life.

But in any case I must beware of my nerves, etc.

A. M. and Renilde Hammacher, *Van Gogh: A Documentary Biography* (1982)

=

My genius

For many years I was deeply impressed with the belief that I was possessed of talents of a high order for a particularly exciting department in science; and for the development of the fancied gift I threw my whole soul into the study. I nursed it till it became a mania. Working, eating, or sleeping, it was ever there. The ever-lasting reflection of its fiery form inflamed my brain – every thought became agony, and I went mad. My spirit was impaled upon the instrument on which it had so sinfully leant – hope fled, and in her place reigned that sleep-hating demon despair. Agony-driven, I hurried ceaselessly on through the room till every footmark of my bruised and blistered feet could be traced in blood and water upon the floor. Sleep, that oil, that priceless balm for the weary soul, had entirely departed; and my parched brain glowed like a furnace. Were anyone to ask me how long I travelled upon these bruised and bleeding feet – how long my glaring eyeballs refused protection from lids that felt like fire, my answer would break his faith in my veracity for ever.

'A Late Inmate of the Glasgow Royal Asylum for Lunatics at Gartnavel',
The Philosophy of Insanity (1947)

=

A mad clown

Everybody will say that Nijinsky has become insane. I do not care, I have already behaved like a madman at home. Everybody will think so, but I will not be put in an asylum, because I dance very well and give money to all those who ask me. People like an odd and peculiar man and they will leave me alone, calling me a 'mad clown.' I like insane people, I know how to talk to them. My brother was in the lunatic asylum.

I was fond of him and he understood me. His friends there liked me too. I was then eighteen years old. I know the life of lunatics and understand the psychology of an insane man. I never contradict them, therefore madmen like me. My brother died in an asylum.

Romola Nijinsky (ed.), *The Diary of Vaslav Nijinsky* (1937)

=

A long tradition saw connections between genius and mental abnormality. The Italian psychiatrist Cesare Lombroso gave this perception a new twist, by stressing the psychopathological features of so-called geniuses, and thereby condemning much of the literary and artistic world of the fin-de-siècle *as a crowd of degenerates.*

The paradox that confounds genius with neurosis, however cruel and sad it may seem, is found to be not devoid of solid foundation when examined from various points of view which have escaped even recent observers.

A theory, which has for some years flourished in the psychiatric world, admits that a large proportion of mental and physical affections are the result of degeneration, of the action, that is, of heredity in the children of the inebriate, the syphilitic, the insane, the consumptive, etc.; or of accidental causes, such as lesions of the head or the action of mercury, which profoundly change the tissues, perpetuate neuroses or other diseases in the patient, and, which is worse, aggravate them in his descendants, until the march of degeneration, constantly growing more rapid and fatal, is only stopped by complete idiocy or sterility.

Alienists have noted certain characters which very frequently, though not constantly, accompany these fatal degenerations. Such are, on the moral side, apathy, loss of moral sense, frequent tendencies to impulsiveness or doubt, psychical inequalities owing to the excess of some faculty (memory, aesthetic taste, etc.) or defect of other qualities (calculation, for example) exaggerated mutism or verbosity, morbid vanity, excessive originality, and excessive pre-occupation with self, the tendency to put mystical interpretations on the simplest facts, the abuse of symbolism and of special words which are used as an almost exclusive mode of expression. Such, on the physical side, are prominent ears, deficiency of beard, irregularity of teeth, excessive asymmetry of face and head, which may be very large or very small, sexual precocity, smallness or disproportion of the body, lefthandedness, stammering, rickets, phthisis, excessive sterility, with constant aggravation of abnormalities in the children.

Without doubt many alienists have here fallen into exaggerations especially when they have sought to deduce degeneration from a single fact. But, taken on the whole, the theory is irrefutable; every day brings fresh applications and confirmations. Among the most curious are those supplied by recent studies on genius. The signs of degeneration in men of genius they show are sometimes more numerous than in the insane. Let us examine them.

Height – First of all it is necessary to remark the frequency of physical signs of degeneration, only masqued by the vivacity of the countenance and the prestige of reputation, which distracts us from giving them due importance.

The simplest of these, which struck our ancestors and has passed into a proverb, is the smallness of the body.

Famous for short stature as well as for genius were: Horace

(*lepidissimum* homunculum *dicebat Augustus*), Philopœmen, Narses, Alexander (*Magnus Alexander corpore parvus erat*), Aristotle, Plato, Epicurus, Chrysippus, Laertes, Archimedes, Diogenes, Attila, Epictetus, who was accustomed to say 'Who am I? A little man.' Among moderns one may name, Erasmus, Socinus, Linnæus, Lipsius, Gibbon, Spinoza, Haüy, Montaigne, Mezeray, Lalande, Gray, John Hunter (5 ft 2 in), Mozart, Beethoven, Goldsmith, Hogarth, Thomas Moore, Thomas Campbell, Wilberforce, Heine, Meissonnier, Charles Lamb, Beccaria, Maria Edgeworth, Balzac, Quincey, William Blake (who was scarcely five feet in height), Browning, Ibsen, George Eliot, Thiers, Mrs Browning, Louis Blanc, Mendelssohn, Swinburne, Van Does (called the Drum, because he was not any taller than a drum), Peter van Laer (called the Puppet). Lulli, Pompanazzi, Baldini, were very short; so also were Nicholas Piccinni, the philosopher Dati, and Baldo, who replied to the sarcasm of Bartholo, '*Minuit præsentia fama*,' with the words, '*Augebit cætera virtus*;' and again, Marsilio Ficino, of whom it was said, '*Vir ad lumbos viri stabat*.' Albertus Magnus was of such small-size that the Pope, having allowed him to kiss his foot, commanded him to stand up, under the impression that he was still kneeling. When the coffin of St Francis Xavier was opened in Goa in 1890, the body was found to be only four and a half feet in length.

Cesare Lombroso, *The Man of Genius* (1891)

=

Modern writers play down these traditional associations between the madman and the artist, and stress the unromantic reality of madness.

There is an aspect of madness which is seldom mentioned in fiction because it would damage the romantic popular idea of the insane as a person whose speech appeals as immediately poetic; but it is seldom the easy Opheliana recited like the pages of a seed catalog or the outpourings of Crazy Janes who provide, in fiction, an outlet for poetic abandon. Few of the people who roamed the dayroom would have qualified as acceptable heroines, in popular taste; few were charmingly uninhibited eccentrics. The mass provoked mostly irritation hostility and impatience. Their behavior affronted, caused uneasiness; they wept and moaned; they quarreled and complained. They were a nuisance and were treated as such. It was forgotten that they too possessed a prized humanity which needed care and love, that a tiny poetic essence could be distilled from their over-flowing squalid truth.

Janet Frame, *Faces in the Water* (1961)

=

The genius of madness? Cold water poured on a romantic myth.

I conceive, at the same time, that there is much popular error entertained concerning the connexion of talent with madness. Every county presents one or more specimens of individuals who are reputed scientific by those more ignorant of science than themselves; eccentric men, whose wandering attention has travelled over every subject, resting nowhere long enough to gather exact information; but who, encouraged by the applause of sounder, but slower minds, indulge in bold and free declamation concerning all parts of human knowledge; confound the ignorant, amaze the vulgar, and even impose upon the mere scholar; so that in the opinion of their neighbours, they become accounted 'wonderfully clever men, but certainly a little mad'. The learned and benevolent Dr Parr used to say of such men, that they were certainly *cracked*; but that the crack *let in light*; – and even then, it is to be feared, he estimated them too highly. Such men adopt, as true, the most improbable assertions, and believe it possible to achieve impossibilities; they are full of discoveries, and secrets, and novel methods in art and science, in mechanics, in medicine, and in government. They torment the village apothecary and locksmith with specifics and perpetual motion, and fatigue the Chancellor of the Exchequer with schemes for relieving the nation from debt. The explanation is, that they can attend, but not continuously; they can remember, but not always accurately; and they can compare, but resemblances only; – differences escape them; objections are hidden from them; and their conclusions are almost invariably incorrect. They follow every loose and deceptious analogy, mistake the order of phenomena, and apply the terms of one series to a collection differing from it, except in one or two parts alone. Assuredly, when such

unsettled minds become altogether crazy, it is not just to lay the
fault upon their learning or their genius.

John Conolly, *An Inquiry Concerning the Indications of Insanity, with*
Suggestions for the Better Protection and Care of the Insane (1830)

=

The furies

CHORUS: Hounds of Madness, fly to the mountain, fly
Where Cadmus' daughters are dancing in ecstasy!
Madden them like a frenzied herd stampeding,
Against the madman hiding in woman's clothes
To spy on the Maenads' rapture!
First his mother shall see him craning his neck
Down from a rounded rock or a sharp crag,
And shout to the Maenads, 'Who is the man, you Bacchae,
Who has come to the mountain, come to the mountain spying

On the swift wild mountain-dances of Cadmus' daughters?
Which of you is his mother?
No, that lad never lay in a woman's womb;
A lioness gave him suck, or a Libyan Gorgon!'

Justice, now be revealed! Now let your sword
Thrust – through and through – to sever the throat
Of the godless, lawless, shameless son of Echion,
Who sprang from the womb of Earth!

Euripides, *The Bacchae* (5th century BC)

=

Dionysian frenzy

CHORUS: Blest is the happy man
Who knows the mysteries the gods ordain,
And sanctifies his life,
Joins soul with soul in mystic unity,
And, by due ritual made pure,
Enters the ecstasy of mountain solitudes;

Who observes the mystic rites
Made lawful by Cybele the Great Mother;
Who crowns his head with ivy,
And shakes aloft his wand in worship of Dionysus.

On, on! Run, dance, delirious, possessed!
Dionysus comes to his own;
Bring from the Phrygian hills to the broad streets of Hellas
The god, child of a god,
Spirit of revel and rapture, Dionysus!

DIONYSUS: The reason why I have chosen Thebes as the first place
To raise my Bacchic shout, and clothe all who respond
In fawnskin habits, and put my thyrsus in their hands –
The weapon wreathed with ivy-shoots – my reason is this:
My mother's sisters said – what they should have been the last
To say – that I, Dionysus, was not Zeus's son;
That Semele, being with child – they said – by some mortal,
Obeyed her father's prompting, and ascribed to Zeus
The loss of her virginity; and they loudly claimed
That this lie was the sin for which Zeus took her life.
    Therefore I have driven those same sisters mad, turned them
All frantic out of doors; their home now is the mountain;
Their wits are gone. I have made them bear the emblem of
My mysteries; the whole female population of Thebes,
To the last woman, I have sent raving from their homes.
Now, side by side with Cadmus' daughters, one and all
Sit roofless on the rocks under the silver pines.

                                 Euripides, *The Bacchae* (5th century BC)

=

And what, then, is the significance, physiologically speaking, of that
madness out of which tragic and comic art developed – the
Dionysian madness? ... Is madness perhaps not necessarily the
symptom of degeneration, decline, and the final stage of culture?
Are there perhaps – a question for psychiatrists – neuroses of
health? of the youth and youthfulness of a people? Where does that
synthesis of god and billy goat in the satyr point? What experience

of himself, what urge compelled the Greek to conceive the Dionysian enthusiast and primeval man as a satyr? And regarding the origin of the tragic chorus: did those centuries when the Greek body flourished and the Greek soul foamed over with health perhaps know endemic ecstasies? Visions and hallucinations shared by entire communities or assemblies as a cult?

Friedrich Nietzsche, *The Birth of Tragedy* (1872)

=

Art as intoxication

Towards a psychology of the artist. – For art to exist, for any sort of aesthetic activity or perception to exist, a certain physiological precondition is indispensable: *intoxication*. Intoxication must first have heightened the excitability of the entire machine: no art results before that happens. All kinds of intoxication, however different their origin, have the power to do this: above all, the intoxication of sexual excitement, the oldest and most primitive form of intoxication.

Friedrich Nietzsche, *Twilight of the Idols* (1889)

=

The healthy creativity of madness

Madness (contrary to most interpretations of 'schizophrenia') is a movement out of familialism (including family-modelled institutions) *towards autonomy*. This is the real 'danger' of madness and the reason for its violent repression. Society should be one big happy family with hordes of obedient children. One must be mad not to want such an enviable state of affairs. And one is punished for madness (the teutonic origin of 'mad' is 'maimed'). If you go mad, by normal social definition, in psychoanalysis your likely fate is the usual psychiatric incarceration with all the violent trimmings – at least until your language – words and acts – becomes normally 'grammatical' – and normally banal once again.

Mad discourse, as opening to the world, moves in the opposite direction to psychoanalytical discourse. I shall return to the theme that *all delusion is political statement* (and that all madmen are political dissidents) later but would here simply add some pertinent observations on psychoanalysis more generally.

David Cooper, *The Language of Madness* (1978)

=

At least my neurosis is creative. It could have been writer's block.

Woody Allen

=

Hamlet: unstable in mind and weak in character

HAMLET

No character in any of Shakespeare's Plays has secured such profound and world-wide attention as that of Hamlet, and no point in Hamlet's character has provoked more learned, subtle, and interminable discussion than that of his madness. Was he mad or merely feigning madness? The perplexity still attached to that question is wittily summed up by Gilbert in his *Rosencrantz and Guildenstern*:

GUILDENSTERN: 'Oh, he is surely mad!'
OPHELIA: 'Well, there again
   Opinions differ, some men hold
   That he's the sanest of all sane men,
   Some that he's really sane but shamming mad.
   Some that he will be mad, some that he was –
   Some that he couldn't be. But on the whole
   (As far as I can make out what they mean)
   The favourite theory's something like this;
   Hamlet is idiotically sane,
   With lucid intervals of lunacy.'

Few men have entered my department of medical practice, none has risen to eminence in it who have not written something about Hamlet's madness. They seem, the moment they have devoted themselves to the study of mental disease, like the Ancient Mariner, to be under an irresistible impulsion to buttonhole you and confide to you their diagnosis of the case of the Danish Prince. Of course, the specialists have differed amongst themselves, as specialists always do, but the weight of opinion amongst them is that Hamlet was mad and, at times, certifiable. Hundreds of essays, pamphlets, leaflets, and books have been published to prove that Hamlet was mad or not mad, but not one, as far as I am aware, to support the conclusion that he was both. Is it not possible that, having put 'an antic disposition on,' as he undoubtedly did in the first instance, it got the better of his very susceptible disposition?

It is a dangerous game to feign madness, and he who begins by being mad 'North-North-West' may ultimately find himself mad at all points of the compass. To those who are of fine intellectual fibre and endowed with intense emotional sensibility, mimic imperso-nations put on for an hour or two are sometimes not easily shaken off. The village mummer has no difficulty in casting aside his loose ill-fitting mask, but the great actor who has found a part that fits him like a glove, or shall I say like skin-tights, cannot always divest himself of it in a hurry. It is told of Mrs Siddons that on the nights following some of her greatest triumphs she was strangely agitated, and when unrobed, walked about for hours in the silence and solitude of her bedroom, unable to dissociate herself altogether from the feelings of the Volumnia or Mrs Haller she had repre-sented. Rachel had similar experiences, and in the affecting story of Coralie Walton, Vandenhoff tells that the fragile girl could not at the end of *Hamlet* doff the hysterical mania of Ophelia, and was actually insane.

But if a mere temporary trifling with personal identity, the assumption for a little of a character other than one's own – it may be a character strongly swayed by passion, but still within the bounds of normality – if this has its risks how much more hazard-ous must be any sustained effort to counterfeit madness.

The late Sir Francis Galton – and no more level-headed man has lived – tried experimentally to gain some idea of the commoner feelings of insanity. He determined to invest everything he met, whether human, animal, or inanimate, with the imaginary attri-butes of a spy. Having arranged his plans, he started on his ordinary morning walk from Rutland Gate and found the experi-ment only too successful. By the time he had walked one and a half miles and reached the cab-stand at Piccadilly at the east end of the Green Park, every horse on the stand seemed watching either with pricked ears or disguising its espionage. 'Hours passed,' he said, 'before this uncanny sensation wore off, and I feel that I could only too easily re-establish it.'

Now, I would suggest that Hamlet, having feigned insanity, fell under its power. Shakespeare was not bound by Saxo Grammaticus, and took his own way in dealing with legends. He made Hamlet a man of great nobility of mind, but of highly sensitive temperament, and he introduces him to us, before his knowledge of his father's ghost, reeling under the shock of a great calamity. That a man of Hamlet's intellectual capacity and moral rectitude should, even in the pursuit of what he regarded as righteous vengeance, stoop to malingering, is in itself an indication of nervous instability. But that he did malinger to begin with there can be no doubt, and that he did it badly is clear, for in the scene with Ophelia he overdid it as most malingerers do, having taken as his model some chronic maniac. After that the transition to an overpowering obsession and then to gusts of manic depressive insanity may be traced out. One such gust of some violence occurred in the interview with his mother when he had a hallucination, for the ghost was not seen by his mother, as it was by Horatio and Marcellus in the platform scene, and when he gave way to homicidal impulse as he made his pass through the arras, for he could not believe it was the King he was thrusting at, as he had just left him at his prayers in the ante-room. In this closet scene his mother, with her affectionate solicitude and maternal insight, recognized his disordered state of mind, for she asked him: 'Have you forgot me?' and later exclaimed, 'Alas, he's mad.' Without believing that Hamlet was really irresponsible by reason of mental disease, it is impossible to understand how a man of his naturally fine moral tissue and amiability should have had no sense of self-reproach for the deaths of Polonius, Rosencrantz, and Guildenstern, for his ill-usage of Ophelia, for his refined cruelty in refraining from killing Claudius while he prayed, lest he should thus give him a chance of heaven, for his constant suspicions, his hesitancy, his suddenness of mood, and for his violent behaviour at Ophelia's grave. It would seem as if the fell spirit he had called up to do his bidding had overpowered him and made him a madman outright.

In *Hamlet* as in *Lear* we have insanity under its real and its assumed aspects, and in both they are accurately delineated. The play should be a textbook of medical psychology.

Sir James Crichton-Browne, *The Doctor's After Thoughts* (1932)

=

Another view of Shakespeare's treatment of madness

'Hasn't anybody got it right?' asked Susan when we had ordered. 'Describing madness.'

'Shakespeare got it right. Lear, of course. Cerebral athero-sclerosis, a senile organic disease of the brain. Quite common in old age. Periods of mania followed by amnesia. Rational episodes marked by great fear of what he might have done while manic and great dread of the onset or renewed onset of mania. That way madness lies – let me shun that – no more of that. Perhaps even more striking – Ophelia. A particular form of acute schizophrenia, very thoroughly set up – young girl of a timid, meek disposition, no mother, no sister, the brother she depends on not available, lover apparently gone mad, mad enough anyway to kill her father. Entirely characteristic that a girl with her sort of upbringing should go round spouting little giggling harmless obscenities when mad. In fact it's such a good description that this ... subdivision of schizo-phrenia is known as the Ophelia Syndrome even to those many psychiatrists who have never seen or read the play. He was content just to describe it, you see. No theories or interpretations. Oh, she says and does plenty of things that mean a great deal to the other characters and to the audience, but she doesn't know what she's saying or doing or who anyone is, because she's mad.'

Our starters came then and I thought we might have heard the last of the topic, but not a bleeding bit of it. I had no great objection to Shakespeare as an author – it was just that I thought he was rather far back as something to talk about over lunch. Also I reckoned I had learnt enough about schizophrenia for one day. Anyhow, in less than a minute and without waiting to be asked Nash was off again.

'The play's full of interesting remarks about madness, among other things, yes. Polonius. A rather underrated fellow in my opinion. To define true madness, what is it but to be nothing else but mad? Not bad. Not bad at all. Not a complete definition, but an essential part, excluding north-north-west madness. Later in the same scene, you remember, he has a chat with Hamlet, the fish-monger conversation, and is made a fool of – the very model of a dialogue between stupid questioner and clever madman as seen by that, er, that, er, that unusual person R. D. Laing – you know, *The Divided Self* and all that.

'But actually Hamlet's only *pretending* to be mad, isn't he? No problem scoring off the other chap if that's what you're up to. Polonius gets halfway to the point. How pregnant sometimes his replies are, he says, a happiness that often madness hits on, which reason and sanity could not so prosperously be delivered of – a remarkably twentieth-century view. If he'd paused to think he might have found it just a bit suspect. But Hamlet in general very cleverly behaves in a way that lay people who've never seen a madman expect a madman to behave. Ophelia doesn't go mad till Act IV.'

The two of them went on having the time of their lives, working their way through Gothic novels and then Dickens, who either left mad people out altogether or was no good at them, though evidently terrific on neurosis. There was something about King Charles's head.

Kingsley Amis, *Stanley and the Women* (1984)

=

The lunatic, the lover and the poet

THESEUS: The poet's eye in a fine phrensy rolling
Doth glance from heav'n to earth, from earth to heav'n
And, as imagination bodies forth
The forms of things unknown, the poet's pen
Turns them to shape, and gives to aiery nothing
A local habitation and a name.

William Shakespeare, *A Midsummer Night's Dream* (1600)

=

The poet no madman

Byron was greatly irritated by current reports that he was suffering
from mental aberration, and one day said to Nathan, who set the
'Hebrew Melodies' to music, that he would try for once to write
like a madman. He seized his pen and gazed wildly into vacancy,
but he couldn't do it, for the result was that he wrote down at once
and without crossing a word, the beautiful verses beginning:

> My soul is dark – oh! quickly string
>   The harp I yet can brook to hear;
> And let thy gentle fingers fling
>   The melting murmurs o'er mine ear.

Sir James Crichton-Browne, *The Doctor's Second Thoughts* (1931)

=

*The madness of noise: the mad poet is in reality just a Grub Street
hack.*

> Now turn to diff'rent sports (the Goddess cries)
> And learn, my sons, the wond'rous pow'r of Noise.
> With Shakespear's nature, or with Johnson's art,
> Let others aim: 'Tis yours to shake the soul
> With Thunder rumbling from the mustard bowl,
> With horns and trumpets now to madness swell,
> Now sink in sorrows with a tolling bell:
> Such happy arts attention can command,
> When fancy flags, and sense is at a stand.
> Improve we these. Three Cat-calls be the bribe
> Of him, whose chatt'ring shames the Monkey tribe:
> And his this Drum, whose hoarse heroic base
> Drowns the loud clarion of the braying Ass.
> Now thousand tongues are heard in one loud din:
> The Monkey-mimics rush discordant in;
> 'Twas chatt'ring, grinning, mouthing, jabb'ring all,
> And Noise and Norton, Brangling and Breval,
> Dennis and Dissonance, and captious Art,
> And Snip-snap short, and Interruption smart,

And Demonstration thin, and Theses thick,
And Major, Minor, and Conclusion quick.
'Hold (cry'd the Queen) A Cat-call each shall win:
Equal your merits! equal is your din!
But that this well-disputed game may end,
Sound forth my Brayers, and the welkin rend.'

Alexander Pope, *The Dunciad* (1743)

＝

Was Swift mentally ill?

Insanity is generally considered to have effected a signal triumph,
when it appeared in the powerful and most prolific mind of Dean
Swift. But the mind of Swift, though powerful and prolific, was
ardently exerted, during a great part of his life, either upon works
permitting an almost unlicensed exercise of the imagination, and in
which nothing, if it proved witty, could be deemed absurd; or
wasted, according to the whim of the moment, upon mere trifles: it
was never devoted, for any length of time, to a great work which
called for a regular and persevering exercise of the reasoning and
judging faculties; and many hours and days seem to have been
yielded up to what Johnson has called, 'debauchery of the mind;' an
indulgence of the pleasure arising from the creation of fantastic
images, or the devising of extravagant incidents. Thus his attention
ran wild and unrestrained, and his strong imagination gained by
degrees entire possession of him, exercising, almost unresisted, all
the power which that faculty has been stated to possess: his judgment became habitually foiled, and eventually weakened, by his
morbid sensations, by his prejudices, by his ungoverned passions,
and by a peculiar and hateful misanthropy; and it is charitable to
say, that some of his inhuman eccentricities were the beginning of
his madness.

John Conolly, *An Inquiry Concerning the Indications of Insanity, with
Suggestions for the Better Protection and Care of the Insane* (1830)

＝

A roll-call of mad writers

Among English men of letters and poets who have become actually insane, or who have had hallucinations and idiosyncrasies characteristic of insanity, may be mentioned Swift, Johnson, Cowper, Southey, Shelley, Byron, Campbell, Goldsmith, Charles Lamb, Walter Savage Landor, and Edgar Allan Poe, with whom may be coupled, among foreign writers, Rousseau, Pascal, Chateaubriand, Tasso, Silvio Pellico, and Alfieri.

J. F. Nisbet, *The Insanity of Genius* (1891)

=

Great abnormals

Gérard de Nerval (born 1808) held conversations with Moses, Adam, and Joshua, who spoke to him through chairs and tables. He had long fits of exaltation and depression. Sometimes he danced Babylonian dances and performed cabalistic exorcisms. With honey drawn from flowers, he traced signs which encircled the form of a giantess who represented Diana, Saint Rosalie, and an actress named Jenny Colon with whom de Nerval fancied himself in love. He sent her huge bouquets and bought opera glasses of abnormal size so that he might see her more clearly. He bought a beautiful mediæval bed with a view to its being a resting place for him and his *inamorata*, hired a suitable apartment and bought superb furniture. Time passed, de Nerval fell on evil days and soon had to sell the furniture. The bed he kept as long as possible, even after it stood alone in the room; then he had it moved to a barn. But at last even the bed had to go, and he himself spent his nights in common lodging houses and low taverns. Often he wrote under trees or in doorways. He declared that she was one of the incarnations of Saint Teresa. One day when walking along a balcony, he saw a phantom figure and heard a voice which called him by name. He ran forward and fell over the balcony, but escaped with his life. Later on, ideas of personal grandeur grew in his mind, he discoursed largely about his chateaux at Ermenonville, and of his personal perfection of face and form, of which he was convinced. He bought all the coins of Nerva, saying that he did not wish his ancestral name to circulate as money, and yet Nerval was not his own name at all, merely a *nom de plume*. He quoted the Lapps, who, he said, enjoyed superb health, as his excuse for adhering to his summer clothes throughout a severe winter. He ultimately hanged himself.

Theo B. Hyslop, *The Great Abnormals* (1925)

=

Madness is the poet's mission thwarted.

> I thought of Chatterton, the marvellous Boy,
> The sleepless Soul that perished in his pride;
> Of Him who walked in glory and in joy
> Following his plough, along the mountain-side:
> By our own spirits are we deified:
> We Poets in our youth begin in gladness;
> But thereof come in the end despondency and madness.

William Wordsworth, *Resolution and Independence* (1802)

=

The necessity of madness

I therefore believe that the fear and even the actual living through of much that used to be called 'insanity' is almost an emotional necessity for every truly feeling, reacting, totally human person in America at this time – *until* he or she passes through the soul-crippling (not healing) judgment of such language and comes out of the fire at the point where other words and hence different conceptions are created from the wounds. The psychiatric vocabulary and definitions, which once seemed such a liberating instrument for modern man, have unwittingly woven a tight and ironically strangling noose around the neck of the brain; contemporary men and women – especially intellectuals – tremblingly judge themselves and others in the black light of psychopathology and shrink human nature to the size of their own fears instead of giving it the liberty of their greatest dreams. But we can be grateful that the human soul is so constructed that it ultimately bursts concepts once held as true out of its terrible need to live and creates the world anew just in order to breathe in it. One final thought: should any readers see this article as an effort at self-justification they are right, as far as they go; but they should remember that it is only out of the self and its experience (even if I have failed here) that new light has ever been cast on the perpetual burden of making life ever more *possible* at its most crucial level.

                    Seymour Krim, *Views of a Nearsighted Cannoneer* (1968)

=

Can I be divinely mad too?

Cowper came to me and said: 'O that I were insane always. I will never rest. Can you not make me truly insane? I will never rest till I am so. O that in the bosom of God I was hid. You retain health and yet are as mad as any of us all – over us all – mad as a refuge from unbelief – from Bacon, Newton and Locke.'

William Blake, Marginalia to Spurzheim, *Observations on the Deranged Manifestations of the Mind, or Insanity* (c. 1819)

=

Blake mad

Madness may overtake the dull commonplace man, and may attack the man of transcendent genius, and it did the latter in the case of Blake. Sir Edmund Gosse thought that the supposition that Blake was technically and medically mad has now been abandoned. The testimony of friends on this point was, he said, collected and summarized by Gilchrist with convincing thoroughness.

But notwithstanding all this, I venture to affirm that no physician, accustomed to observe and analyse the movements of the morbid mind, can peruse Blake's works as a whole, without concluding that he was veritably mad, whatever lucid intervals he may have had. Sir Edmund Gosse admitted that his mind was not normal, but the abnormality sometimes amounted to madness, not only in the technical, but in the popular sense of the term. He was capable of sublime beauty of conception and exquisite execution, but he was also at times absolutely incoherent and subject to hallucinations, and much of his writing is pure rhapsody. He brooded on certain ideas and churned them up into a froth of fancy.

He took orders from Ezekiel. Sir Edmund Gosse thought that his
extraordinary obstinacy accounted for much, but obstinacy is one of
the characteristics of mental disorder. He is vulgar at times and
indulges in sheer foolery. His majestic imagination often grovelled in
the dust, as in his theories of sexual indulgence, and resistance to
superstition. He was infected by Swedenborg, who in a less glorious
degree laboured under the same kind of madness. His brain functions were apt to become turgescent and disorderly. I would not put
Blake's works, with all their beauties, in the hands of anyone
neurotically inclined.

Sir James Crichton-Browne, *The Doctor's Second Thoughts* (1931)

=

Of Kit Marlowe

For that fine madness still he did retain,
Which rightly should possess a poet's brain.

Michael Drayton, *To Henry Reynolds, of Poets and Poesy* (1627)

=

The creative moment

When I was mad briefly, but for enough weeks to begin to know a
little, in Argentina five years ago in a place on the Atlantic coast
south of Buenos Aires, I found it possible to experience in total
solitude a 'philosophical problem' in all the concreteness of *embodiment*. Stopping all drugs like normal eating habits, normal ways of
being with other people, tobacco, alcohol, I lived materially on water
and nourishment that flowed and roots and rhizomes from the
ground. Rushing naked as always into the sea I nearly got drowned
by the famous undertow of that bit of the coast, in the heart of a
tempest that transformed miraculously the sand dunes into amiable
and terrifying other humps, dinosauric monsters that put the inor-
ganic finally on the march. Stopping normal habits, however, was
entirely secondary to the fact that it was the right moment in my life
to destructure and then painfully to restructure an altered existence.

I began to experience the world across a whole range of trans-
formations. First, words lost all abstract structure and became

physical objects flattened, spread out, angular or conic, founding a mathematical beyond in all that 'should be' articulated, piecing together, possible. The language stretched and new words ('neologisms') were planted in my mind by alien good or evil powers. In this autonomous cosmos there emerged the 'omnipotent delusion' of being extra-terrestrial and that there were among us other extra-terrestrial beings, allocated a function for good or for evil in their being in the world but appointed from another region, widely remote, in the cosmos that is not 'our' astronomic cosmos.

There were experiences of howling, hurling myself around even with a faintly disguised joy to find a true solitary way of experiencing one special death fully enough, in life, before the other human ones took even that away, like acting a word when the word conventionally should be said, for trying to make a circus in a 'space' where small dogs are not allowed. I underwent many metamorphoses of shame that finally proved irrelevant. What a job this disculpabilization is – getting rid of ancient and irrelevant guilt, seeing the final absurdity of all the aggression that exists on a personal, anti-political level.

After the descent from all that, I found all the cosmic extra-terrestrial things, transformed, here on earth in an animal banality, but I felt inscribed on my body the realization that there is no human subject (which is different from working this out theoretically); 'human nature' is fictive because, however hard we try we can never repeat ourselves – every return is to a new place.

David Cooper, *The Language of Madness* (1978)

=

A riddle

> Doctor, this Pusling *Riddle* pray explain;
> Others your *Physick* cures, but I complain
> It works with me the clean contrary way,
> And makes me *Poet*, who are *Mad* they say.
> The truth on't is, my *Brains* well fixt *condition*
> *Apollo* better knows, than his *Physitian*:
> 'Tis *Quacks* disease, not mine, my *Poetry*
> By the blind *Moon-Calf*, took for *Lunacy*.

James Carkesse, *Lucida Intervalla* (1671)

Tourette's syndrome

When I first saw Ray he was 24 years old, and almost incapacitated by multiple tics of extreme violence coming in volleys every few seconds. He had been subject to these since the age of four and severely stigmatized by the attention they aroused, though his high intelligence, his wit, his strength of character and sense of reality, enabled him to pass successfully through school and college, and to be valued and loved by a few friends and his wife. Since leaving college, however, he had been fired from a dozen jobs – always because of tics, never for incompetence – was continually in crises of one sort and another, usually caused by his impatience, his pugnacity, and his coarse, brilliant 'chutzpah', and had found his marriage threatened by involuntary cries of 'Fuck!' 'Shit!', and so on, which would burst from him at times of sexual excitement. He was (like many Touretters) remarkably musical, and could scarcely have survived – emotionally or economically – had he not been a weekend jazz drummer of real virtuosity, famous for his sudden and wild extemporizations, which would arise from a tic or a compulsive hitting of a drum and would instantly be made the nucleus of a wild and wonderful improvisation, so that the 'sudden intruder' would be turned to brilliant advantage. His Tourette's was also of advantage in various games, especially ping-pong, at which he excelled, partly in consequence of his abnormal quickness of reflex and reaction, but especially, again, because of 'improvisations', 'very sudden, nervous, *frivolous* shots' (in his own words), which were so unexpected and startling as to be virtually unanswerable. The only time he was free from tics was in post-coital quiescence or in sleep; or when he swam or sang or worked, evenly and rhythmically, and found 'a kinetic melody', a play, which was tension-free, tic-free and free.

Under an ebullient, eruptive, clownish surface, he was a deeply serious man – and a man in despair. He had never heard of the TSA (which, indeed, scarcely existed at the time), nor had he heard of haldol. He had diagnosed himself as having Tourette's after reading the article on 'Tics' in the *Washington Post*. When I confirmed the diagnosis, and spoke of using haldol, he was excited but cautious. I made a test of haldol by injection, and he proved extraordinarily sensitive to it, becoming virtually tic-free for a period of two hours after I had administered no more than one-eighth of a milligram. After the auspicious trial, I started him on haldol, prescribing a dose of a quarter of a milligram three times a day.

He came back, the following week, with a black eye and a broken nose and said: 'So much for your fucking haldol.' Even this minute dose, he said, had thrown him off balance, interfered with his speed, his timing, his preternaturally quick reflexes. Like many Touretters, he was attracted to spinning things, and to revolving doors in particular, which he would dodge in and out of like lightning: he had lost this knack on the haldol, had mistimed his movements, and had been bashed on the nose. Further, many of his tics, far from disappearing, had simply become slow, and enormously extended: he might get 'transfixed in mid-tic', as he put it, and find himself in almost catatonic postures (Ferenczi once called catatonia the opposite of tics – and suggested these be called 'cataclonia'). He presented a picture, even on this minute dose, of marked Parkinsonism, dystonia, catatonia and psychomotor 'block': a reaction which seemed inauspicious in the extreme, suggesting, not insensitivity, but such over-sensitivity, such pathological sensitivity, that perhaps he could only be thrown from one extreme to another – from acceleration and Tourettism to catatonia and Parkinsonism, with no possibility of any happy medium.

Oliver Sacks, *The Man Who Mistook His Wife for a Hat* (1985)

=

Prophetic madness

> Some call'd it madness – such indeed it was . . .
> If prophesy be madness; if things viewed
> By poets of old time, and higher up
> By the first men, earth's first inhabitants,
> May in these tutored days no more be seen
> With undisorder'd sight.

William Wordsworth, *The Prelude* (1805)

=

Madness and genius

> Great wits are sure to madness near allied,
> And thin partitions do their bounds divide.
>> John Dryden, *Absalom and Achitophel* (1681)

==

Degenerates become artists.

Degenerates often turn their unhealthy impulses toward art, and not only do they sometimes attain to an extraordinary degree of prominence but they may also be followed by enthusiastic admirers who herald them as creators of new eras in art. The insane depict in line and colour their interpretations of nature, and portray the reflections of their minds, as best they are able. Their efforts are usually not only genuine but there is also no wilful suppression of technique, which, were it otherwise, would brand them as impostors. They do not themselves pose as prophets of new eras, and, so long as they are in asylums and recognized as insane, both they and their works are harmless, inasmuch as they do not make any impression on the unprotected borderland dwellers from whose ranks they might otherwise enroll a large following.
>> Theo Hyslop, 'Post-Illusionism and Art in the Insane' (1911)

==

The Romantic vision of the noble madman, destroyed by the cares of the world

> 'But what is he,
> Whom we seek here?'
> 'Of his sad history
> I know but this,' said Maddalo: 'he came
> To Venice a dejected man, and fame
> Said he was wealthy, or he had been so.
> Some thought the loss of fortune wrought him woe;
> But he was ever talking in such sort
> As you do – but more sadly; he seemed hurt,
> Even as a man with his peculiar wrong,

To hear but of the oppression of the strong,
Or those absurd deceits (I think with you
In some respects, you know) which carry through
The excellent impostors of this earth
When they outface detection. He had worth,
Poor fellow! but a humorist in his way.'

'Alas, what drove him mad!'
                                        'I cannot say:
A lady came with him from France, and when
She left him and returned, he wandered then
About yon lonely isles of desert sand,
Till he grew wild. He had no cash or land
Remaining – the police had brought him here –
Some fancy took him, and he would not bear
Removal, so I fitted up for him
Those rooms beside the sea, to please his whim;
And sent him busts, and books, and urns for flowers,
Which had adorned his life in happier hours,
And instruments of music. You may guess
A stranger could do little more or less
For one so gentle and unfortunate –
And those are his sweet strains which charm the weight
From madmen's chains, and make this hell appear
A heaven of sacred silence, hushed to hear.'

'Nay, this was kind of you – he had no claim,
As the world says.'
                              'None but the very same
While I on all mankind, were I, as he,
Fallen to such deep reverse. His melody
Is interrupted now; we hear the din
Of madmen, shriek on shriek, again begin:
Let us now visit him: after this strain,
He ever communes with himself again,
And sees and hears not any.'
                                        Having said
These words, we called the keeper, and he led
To an apartment opening on the sea.

There the poor wretch was sitting mournfully
Near a piano, his pale fingers twined
One with the other; and the ooze and wind
Rushed through an open casement, and did sway
His hair, and starred it with the brackish spray;
His head was leaning on a music-book,
And he was muttering; and his lean limbs shook;
His lips were pressed against a folded leaf
In hue too beautiful for health, and grief
Smiled in their motions as they lay apart,
As one who wrought from his own fervid heart
The eloquence of passion: soon he raised
His sad meek face and eyes lustrous and glazed,
And spoke – sometimes as one who wrote, and thought
His words might move some heart that heeded not,
If sent to distant lands; – and then as one
Reproaching deeds never to be undone,
With wondering self-compassion; – then his speech
Was lost in grief, and then his words came each
Unmodulated and expressionless, –
But that from one jarred accent you might guess
It was despair made them so uniform:
And all the while the loud and gusty storm
Hissed through the window, and we stood behind.
Stealing his accents from the envious wind,
Unseen. I yet remember what he said
Distinctly, such impression his words made.

'Month after month,' he cried, 'to bear this load,
And, as a jade urged by the whip and goad,
To drag life on – which like a heavy chain
Lengthens behind with many a link of pain, –
And not to speak my grief – O, not to dare
To give a human voice to my despair;
But live, and move, and, wretched thing! smile on,
As if I never went aside to groan,
And wear this mask of falsehood even to those –
Who are most dear – not for my own repose –

Alas! no scorn, or pain, or hate, could be
So heavy as that falsehood is to me –
But that I cannot bear more altered faces
Than needs must be, more changed and cold embraces,
More misery, disappointment, and mistrust
To own me for their father. Would the dust
Were covered in upon my body now!
That the life ceased to toil within my brow!
And then these thoughts would at the last be fled:
Let us not fear such pain can vex the dead.

'What Power delights to torture us? I know
That to myself I do not wholly owe
What now I suffer, though in part I may.
Alas! none strewed fresh flowers upon the way
Where, wandering heedlessly, I met pale pain,
My shadow, which will leave me not again.
If I have erred, there was no joy in error,
But pain, and insult, and unrest, and terror;
I have not, as some do, bought penitence
With pleasure, and a dark yet sweet offence . . .

                Percy Bysshe Shelley, *Julian and Maddalo* (1818)

                            =

We are all vulnerable.

I was as wrong as you can be and still live to tell about it. In the
summer of 1955, when I was 33, the thousand unacknowledged
human (not literary) pressures in my being exploded. I ran bare-
footed in the streets, spat at members of my family, exposed myself,
was almost bodily thrown out of the house of a Nobel Prize-
winning author, and believed God had ordained me to act out every
conceivable human impulse without an ounce of hypocritical caution. I know today that my instinct was sound, but my reasoning
was self-deceptive. It was not God who ordained me, but I who
ordained God for my own understandable human purposes. I
needed an excuse to force some sort of balance between my bulging
inner life and my timid outer behaviour, and I chose the greatest

and most comforting symbol of them all. He was my lance and my shield as I tore through the New York streets acting out the bitter rot of a world-full of frustrations that my human nature could no longer lock up. I was finally cornered on the 14th floor of the St Regis Hotel by two frightened friends and another brother; and with the aid of handcuffs seriously-humorously clipped on by a couple of bobbies I was led off to Bellevue, convinced all along that I was right. I tolerated those who took me away with the kindly condescension of a fake Jesus.

From Bellevue I was soon transferred to a private laughing academy in Westchester and given insulin-shock treatments. No deep attempt was made to diagnose my 'case' – except the superficial and inaccurate judgment that I had 'hallucinated.' Factually, this was not true; I did not have visual images of people or objects which were not there; I merely believed, with the beautiful relief of absolute justice which the soul of man finds when life becomes unbearable, that God had given me the right and the duty to do everything openly that I had secretly fantasied for years. But this distinction was not gone into by my judges and indifferent captors. They did not have the time, the patience, or even the interest because work in a flip-factory is determined by mathematics: you must find a common denominator of categorization and treatment in order to handle the battalions of miscellaneous humanity that are marched past your desk with high trumpets blowing in their minds.

Like all the other patients, I was considered beyond reasoning with and was treated like a child; not brutally, but efficiently, firmly and patronizingly. In the eyes of this enclosed world I had relinquished my rights as an adult human being. The causes for my explosion were not even superficially examined, nor was the cheek-pinching house psychiatrist – with a fresh flower in the button hole of his fresh daily suit – truly equipped to cope with it even if he had tried, which he did not. Private sanitariums and state institutions, I realized much later, were isolation chambers rather than hospitals in the usual sense; mechanical 'cures' such as the one I underwent in a setup of unchallenged authority, like the Army or a humanitarian prison, slowly brought 75 per cent of the inmates down to a more temporarily modest view of reality. Within nine or ten weeks I too came down, humbled, ashamed, willing to stand up before the class and repeat the middle-class credo of limited expressiveness and the meaning of a dollar in order to get my discharge.

In three months' time I was out, shaken, completely alone, living in a cheap Broadway hotel-room (having been ashamed to go back to Greenwich Village) and going to a conventional Ph.D psychologist (I had been to three medically-trained therapists in the preceding decade) as a sop to both my conscience and family. I had broken beyond the bounds of 'reality' – a shorthand word which is used by the average psychiatrist for want of the more truthfully complex approach that must eventually accommodate our beings' increasing flights into higher altitudes – and come back to the position I was in before. But once again the causes that had flung me into my own sky continued to eat me up.

         Seymour Krim, *View of a Nearsighted Cannoneer* (1968)

=

Ezra Pound: the mad as victims of the sane

It has been your habit for long to do away with good writers,
You either drive them mad, or else blink at their suicides,
Or else you condone their drugs, and talk of insanity and genius,
But I will not go mad to please you
        Ezra Pound 'Salutation the Third', Poems from *Blast* (1914)

=

Artaud's glossolalic verse

o dedi
a dada orzoura
o dou zoura
a dada skizi

o kaya
o kaya pontoura
o ponoura
a pena
poni
        Ronald Hayman, *Artaud and After* (1977)

19

Recovery

'Mad people's writings' – always, in some sense, the outpourings of the strong and the survivors – often track towards a 'happy ending'. They focus upon the process of the gradual growth of self-awareness, self-control, autonomy and recuperation. Eventually, as Marie Cardinal acknowledges in the title of her autobiographical novel, one acquires 'the words to say it'. The recognition of sickness, the seeking of help, the capacity to distinguish illusion from reality – all these are the beginning of wisdom.

The ending of 'insanity' may also spell loss. Blake fantasized that his fellow poet, Cowper, came to him to solicit his aid to be permanently insane – in other words, bathed in visionary transports. Oliver Sacks' Tourette's syndrome patient, 'Witty Ticky Ray', resented the drugs Sacks gave him to quieten his explosive energies, since they took the lightning from his life. Various authors have at least suggested that, while insanity is no place to hide or rest, it has been a rather special phase in their lives, and a far from negative experience. Since compulsory confinement has loomed so large in the history of madness, recovery has been attended with a dramatic act: release. Often this process has been heartbreakingly tardy. The patient who claims to be cured invites rebuff; he who demands release thereby betrays (in the eyes of some authorities) his continuingly tenuous grasp upon reality; he who continues to insist on leaving – and, above all, on his rights! – shows himself to be an unstable trouble-maker. Small wonder the only recourse that has seemed open to captives like Alexander Cruden has been escape itself, carrying ball and chain as a proof to the world of the evils of the asylum. Mental illness is captivity enough: it has been a sorry state that so many patients have felt the need to escape the treatments that supposedly have been there to help them.

Looking back, some have seen madness as an enhancing experience. John Perceval continued to look upon it as a prolonged divine
test. Others have regarded it as essentially negative, a period of
isolation, pain, and fear, exacerbated by neglect and misunderstanding from the outside world. If the copious writings of the mad
are about one thing, it is above all the desire to cease to be
misunderstood.

═══════════

*John Home on the life of a madman in Morningside Asylum, under
the physician Dr Thomas Clouston.*

SHORTER CATECHISM FOR MADMEN

1 What is the chief end of a Madman
   To eat, drink, sleep and make a beast of himself
2 What does life in a Madhouse principally teach
   Madhouse life principally teaches us to do everything that we
   ought not to do, and also to do everything in our power to
   annoy the Dr and attendants
3 What is Effectual Calling
   Effectual calling is a most laborious work a Madman sometimes undertakes with a view to effect his release from a Madhouse, but as medical men are, as a rule, most obtuse and it is as
   difficult to make them understand the meaning of an Act of
   Parliament as it is to drive a joke into the head of a Scotchman,
   it is often a most futile work.
4 What is the first Commandment
   The first Commandment is thou shalt take the name of the Lord
   thy God in vain on all occasions
5 What is the second Commandment
   Thou shalt make unto thee a caricature of the hideous phiz of
   Clouston but instead of worshipping it thou shalt curse it
6 What is the third Commandment
   Thou shalt on all occasions take the name of Clouston in vain
   and blackguard him to everyone

7 What is the fourth Commandment
   Forget the sabbath day, and on it behave, if possible, even
   worse than you do on other days
8 What is the fifth Commandment
   Dishonor in every possible way every relative who has had
   anything to do with putting you into a Madhouse
9 What is the sixth Commandment
   Steal everything you can lay your hands on
10 What is the seventh Commandment
   Commit adultery whenever you get the chance, women are not
   very accessable [sic] in Madhouses
11 What is the eighth Commandment
   Kill Clouston and you will be conferring a benefit on Society
   and will be certain to inherit the Kingdom of heaven
12 What is the ninth Commandment
   Bear false witness against Clouston at all times. He is the
   biggest liar that ever lived
13 What is the tenth Commandment
   There is no chance of your coveting Clouston's Wife she is so
   hideous but covet any other nice looking married woman you meet

   John Home Letters, Medical Archive Centre MSS
   (Edinburgh University Library)

=

Does nature heal?

I have had a variety of different treatments for my own acute
illnesses. One fact stands out. No matter what treatment was given,
I recovered in the end. I cannot help wondering if I would not have
recovered equally well if I had been given custodial care and no
physical treatment at all. The treatment which upset me most was
the long course of deep insulin comas in my first illness. There is no
need for me to comment on this in detail now; suffice it to say that
it gave me a lasting phobia about mental hospital treatments which
added greatly to the stress of later illnesses. The one treatment
which was obviously effective in clearing my mind and restoring
rational insight was ECT. When given without pre-medication I
found it exceedingly frightening, and the subsequent loss of

memory was disturbing at the time, but it certainly did, on a short term view, have good results. I incline to think, though, that the enforced loss of memory removed immediate symptoms without having any effect on possible underlying causes, so that, by itself, it could do nothing to prevent a later relapse. As to the drug treatments I have had, I do not feel in a position to make any well informed comment. My personal feeling is that if I had been given a less heavy dose of drugs and had been allowed more peace and quiet, I should have recovered much more easily. I feel sure that drugs need to be adjusted to the person, and not prescribed solely on the basis of the diagnosis. I feel equally sure that if persuasion and discussion is used, rather than force, any treatment is likely to have better results. I was myself so frightened by coercion during my last illness that I fought back with trickery, and the doctors often did not know what dosage I was actually having.

Drugs doubtless have their place in the treatment of mental illness, and psychotherapy certainly must have too, but the whole person needs to be treated, and any form of therapy which regards spiritual problems as outside the doctor's province is likely to touch no more than a fringe of the problem. I have seen enough of acutely disturbed patients to know how often religious delusions and disturbances are present in psychotic illness, and I have not been in any hospital where these appeared to receive much direct attention.

Morag Coate, *Beyond All Reason* (1964)

=

The therapeutic course which Mary Barnes and Joseph Berke worked out between them allowed her to 'go down' back into replaying infancy. This proved healing. Now she 'comes up'.

Coming more out and up, I yet seemed to remain, to contain within, this time of going down. The spirit was willing but the flesh was still weak. Sickness with too much food, then beautiful writings. Then still a hard heart. My heart would physically feel like a bubble that has set hard and was wanting to be pricked. If I cried it didn't melt.

My life took on a certain structure. Painting, writing, reading the Mass of the day. My growth seemed more secure. I looked to the future as a time wherein I would grow strong enough to physically, outwardly do more, yet retaining the inner state of being I had come to know.

Joe reminded me that Ronnie says, 'Life is therapy and therapy is life.'

Moving free, I came to know the healing that is within all that happens.

In a particular way, Joe recreated, reformed me. I was able to let him because I trusted him. This trust has been rewarded. Since the spring of '67, I have grown up. To an increasing extent I have become much more involved with people both at Kingsley Hall and in the outside world. Also I have had two successful exhibitions of my paintings.

Sometimes I have felt like going down again, but never so strongly as before.

Mary Barnes and Joseph Berke, *Mary Barnes: Two Accounts
of a Journey Through Madness* (1973)

=

Seeking release

I was always hopeful about this change, as I had been told many times that a very careful survey of my case would be done for the Board of Control at the end of the year; and now that I had come under the care of a new doctor, with whom I had never had to argue about my income, my hopes were high. Surely at last the doctors must see that I was neither a danger to myself nor to any other person, a quiet and amenable patient, reading a lot, tidy, clean, ready to help in every emergency, on my toes all the time, active but not argumentative, with no queer ideas, now that the money affair was settled. Now was my big chance. I welcomed the day. The doctor was on temporary duty, and new to the hospital, and he had never seen me before. I therefore felt assured that he must take especial care in this important examination which must decide whether I ought to continue for another whole year as a certified patient.

I waited, in bed, for the physical examination. The doctor had several other patients. As I watched him with them, for there were no screens used, I decided to time my own examination. He had been an Army doctor. As he put on his stethoscope to examine my chest, he began to discuss the Tank Corps. He used the stethoscope while he talked. He never ceased to talk, not to me but to the staff nurse who stood beside the bed. The whole examination was over in two and a half minutes. The mental part of the examination was on the following Wednesday, and I was seen in the doctor's office.

'What did you have for breakfast?'

'Wheat flakes and bread and margarine.'

'When did your next of kin last visit you?'

'They have never visited me at any time.'

'What is the name of your tailor?'

'I am in a mental hospital and it is impossible for me to have a tailor.'

'That will do.'

'I should like to discuss with you the question of changing my status to that of a voluntary patient.'

To the ward sister, 'Take her away.'

I hesitated at the door.

'TAKE HER AWAY!'

D. McI. Johnson and Norman Dodds (eds), *The Plea for the Silent*
(1957)

=

Get me out: an appeal from a husband in Morningside Asylum to his wife

A POETIC APPEAL

My dearest love, upon my word,
Your conduct is at least absurd,
Leaving your husband here so long,
Is hardly subject for a song.
Now, why the devil don't you get
Me out of this madhouse, my pet?
Surely you are not so dismayed,
Or of your husband so afraid?
Even if he were a little mad,

You know he is not awful bad;
His madness is of that common kind,
Which, in a word, may be defined
As weakness for alcoholic drinks –
You used to sell them too, you minx;
And just another, I may say,
He likes, as you do, his own way.
You know I never interfered
With you, my duck, when you got drunk.
O! do not snuffle up and funk;
You know I've seen you sometimes beered,
And always treated you as a lady,
Altho' your conduct was a little shady –
Remember the Pentland Hills, my wife,
When you, so careless, lost my knife:
You were not, that is, you were not very
Overcome with Willie Gilbey's sherry,
O no, I know you hate all lies,
The sun had got into your eyes.
Now, did I make a row and fuss,
And tear my hair, or even cuss,
Although I felt my loss a loss indeed;
It almost put me off my feed.
Do you desire with me to quarrel?
If so, I admit that I'm immoral,
Hate churches as I hate ginger beer,
Aud won't again in one appear.
I flirt with other women too, you know,
Not to do so would be reckoned slow.
Now, when so much I have admitted,
The world will say you're to be pitied,
Tied to such a graceless, idle man;
You'd better go for a 'domestic can' –
A nurse's place would exactly suit,
You like kids in arm, in hand, and foot.
Allow me my paternal feelings smother,
I think I see you as a Mother.
Why, you humbug, if I'm a knave,

Then you would be a hopeless slave;
Your time would be wholly taken up
With either a male or female pup;
And as for me, if I was once a lodger,
I would become a tiresome codger,
Be routed out of every room,
In fact, you'd grudge me too a tomb;
Perhaps a toom for rubbish you might give.
But, O my darling, as I live,
Give up this horrid hide and seek,
It's last now here for forty week;
And weak am I, and awful done,
Give up, I say, take back your son.

                              Morningside Mirror (1887)

=

Restoration. William Cowper recovers during his second year in Dr Cotton's asylum. In the manner of the cure of a spiritual crisis, a providential religious event triggers the healing process.

I went to bed and slept well. In the morning I dreamed that the sweetest boy I ever saw came dancing up to my bed-side; he seemed just out of leading-strings, yet I took particular notice of the firmness and steadiness of his tread. The sight affected me with pleasure, and served at least to harmonize my spirits; so that I awoke for the first time with a sensation of delight on my mind. Still, however, I knew not where to look for the establishment of the comfort I felt; my joy was as much a mystery to myself as to those about me. The blessed God was preparing me for the clearer light of his countenance by this first dawning of that light upon me.

Within a few days of my first arrival at St Alban's, I had thrown aside the word of God, as a book in which I had no longer any interest or portion. The only instance, in which I can recollect reading a single chapter, was about two months before my recovery. Having found a Bible on the bench in the garden, I opened it upon the 11th of St John, where Lazarus is raised from the dead; and saw so much benevolence, mercy, goodness, and sympathy with miserable man, in our Saviour's conduct, that I almost shed tears even after the relation; little thinking that it was an exact type of the mercy which Jesus was on the point of extending towards myself. I sighed, and said, 'Oh, that I had not rejected so good a Redeemer, that I had not forfeited all his favours!' Thus was my heart softened, though not yet enlightened. I closed the book, without intending to open it again.

Having risen with somewhat of a more cheerful feeling, I repaired to my room, where breakfast waited for me. While I sat at table, I found the cloud of horror, which had so long hung over me, was every moment passing away; and every moment came fraught with hope. I was continually more and more persuaded, that I was not utterly doomed to destruction. The way of salvation was still, however, hid from my eyes; not did I see it at all clearer than before my illness. I only thought, that if it pleased God to spare me, I would lead a better life; and that I would yet escape hell, if a religious observance of my duty would secure me from it. Thus may the terror of the Lord make a Pharasee; but only the sweet voice of mercy in the gospel, can make a Christian.

But the happy period which was to shake off my fetters and afford me a clear opening of the free mercy of God in Christ Jesus was now arrived. I flung myself in a chair near the window, and seeing a Bible there, ventured once more to apply to it for comfort and instruction. The first verse I saw, was the 25th of the 3d of Romans: 'Whom God hath set forth to be a propitiation through faith in his blood, to declare his righteousness for the remission of sins that are past, through the forebearance of God.' Immediately I received strength to believe, and the full beams of the Sun of Righteousness shone upon me. I saw the sufficiency of the atonement he had made, my pardon sealed in his blood, and all the fulness and completeness of his justification. In a moment I believed, and received the gospel. Whatever my friend Madan had said to me, so long before, revived in all its clearness, with demonstration of the Spirit and with power.

Unless the Almighty arm had been under me, I think I should have died with gratitude and joy. My eyes filled with tears, and my voice choked with transport. I could only look up to heaven in silent fear, overwhelmed with love and wonder. But the work of the Holy Spirit is best described in his own words, it is 'joy unspeakable, and full of glory.' Thus was my heavenly Father in Christ Jesus pleased to give me the full assurance of faith; and, out of a strong, unbelieving heart, to 'raise up a child unto Abraham.' How glad should I now have been to have spent every moment in prayer and thanksgiving! I lost no opportunity of repairing to a throne of grace; but flew to it with an earnestness irresistible and never to be satisfied. Could I help it? Could I do otherwise than love and rejoice in my reconciled Father in Christ Jesus? The Lord had enlarged my heart, and 'I ran in the way of his commandments.'

For many succeeding weeks, tears were ready to flow, if I did but speak of the gospel, or mention the name of Jesus. To rejoice day and night was all my employment. Too happy to sleep much, I thought it was but lost time that was spent in slumber. Oh that the ardour of my first love had continued! But I have known many a lifeless and unhallowed hour since; long intervals of darkness, interrupted by short returns of peace and joy in believing.

My physician, ever watchful and apprehensive for my welfare, was now alarmed, lest the sudden transition from despair to joy, should terminate in a fatal frenzy. But 'the Lord was my strength and my song, and was become my salvation.' I said, 'I shall not die, but live, and declare the works of the Lord; he has chastened me sore, but not given me over unto death. O give thanks unto the Lord, for his mercy endureth for ever.'

In a short time, Dr C. became satisfied, and acquiesced in the soundness of my cure; and much sweet communion I had with him concerning the things of our salvation. He visited me every morning while I stayed with him, which was near twelve months after my recovery, and the gospel was the delightful theme of our conversation.

No trial has befallen me since, but what might be expected in a state of welfare. Satan, indeed, has changed his battery. Before my conversion, *sensual gratification* was the weapon with which he sought to destroy me. Being naturally of an easy quiet disposition, I was seldom tempted to anger; yet, that passion it is which *now* gives me the most disturbance, and occasions the sharpest conflicts. But Jesus being my strength, I fight against it; and if I am not conqueror, yet I am not overcome.

William Cowper, *Memoir of the Early Life of William Cowper, Esq*
(1816)

Daniel Schreber writes his memoirs to prove he is recovered and ready for his release.

I have decided to apply for my release from the Asylum in the near future in order to live once again among civilized people and at home with my wife. It is therefore necessary to give those persons who will then constitute the circle of my acquaintances, an approximate idea at least of my religious conceptions, so that they may have some understanding of the necessity which forces me to various oddities of behaviour, even if they do not fully understand these apparent oddities.

This is the purpose of this manuscript; in it I shall try to give an at least partly comprehensible exposition of supernatural matters, knowledge of which has been revealed to me for almost six years. I cannot of course count upon being *fully* understood because things are dealt with which cannot be expressed in human language; they exceed human understanding. Nor can I maintain that *everything* is irrefutably certain even for me: much remains only presumption and probability. After all I too am only a human being and therefore limited by the confines of human understanding; but one thing I am certain of, namely that I have come infinitely closer to the truth than human beings who have not received divine revelation.

To make myself at least somewhat comprehensible I shall have to speak much in images and similes, which may at times perhaps be only *approximately* correct; for the only way a human being can make supernatural matters, which in their essence must always remain incomprehensible, understandable to a certain degree is by comparing them with known facts of human experience. Where intellectual understanding ends, the domain of belief begins; man must reconcile himself to the fact that things exist which are true although he cannot understand them.

An obvious example is that the concept of *eternity* is beyond man's grasp. Man cannot really understand that something can exist which has neither beginning nor end, that there can be a cause which cannot itself be traced to a previous cause. And yet eternity is one of God's attributes, which with all religiously-minded people I feel I must accept. Man will always be inclined to ask: 'If God created the world, how then did God Himself come to be?' This question will for ever remain unanswered. The same applies to the concept of divine

creation. Man can always only imagine that new matter is created
through the influence of forces on matter already in existence, and
yet I believe – and I hope to prove in what follows by means of
definite examples – that divine creation is a creation out of the void.
Even in the dogmas of our positive religion there are certain matters
which escape full understanding by the intellect. The Christian
teaching that Jesus Christ was the Son of God can be meant only in a
mystical sense which but approximates the human sense of these
words, because nobody would maintain that God, as a Being
endowed with human sexual organs, had intercourse with the
woman from whose womb Jesus Christ came forth. The same applies
to the doctrine of the Trinity, the Resurrection of the Flesh, and other
Christian dogmas. By this I do not in any way wish to imply that I
acknowledge as true *all* Christian dogmas in the sense of our
orthodox theology. On the contrary, I have good reason to think that
some of them are definitely untrue or true only to a very limited
extent. This applies, for instance, to the Resurrection of the Flesh,
which could only lay claim to being relatively and temporarily true in
the form of transmigration of souls (not representing the ultimate
goal of the process), and also to eternal damnation to which some
people are supposed to have succumbed. The concept of eternal
damnation – which will always remain abhorrent to human feeling
notwithstanding the exposition, based on what I consider sophisms
by which Luthardt, for instance, tried to make it acceptable in his
Apologies – does not correspond to the truth, as indeed the whole
(human) notion of *punishment* – as an expeditious weapon for
attaining certain purposes *within human society* – must in the main
be eliminated from our ideas of the life beyond. This, however, can
only be examined more closely later.

Before I proceed with the account of how, owing to my illness, I
entered into peculiar relations with God – which I hasten to add were
in themselves contrary to the Order of the World – I must begin with
a few remarks about the nature of God and of the human soul; these
can for the time being only be put up as axioms – tenets not requiring
proof – and their proof as far as is at all possible can only be
attempted later in the book.

Daniel Paul Schreber, Memoirs of My Nervous Illness (1903)

Others found more dramatic means of emancipation.

SATURDAY, MAY 27. The Prisoner being still chained night and day to his bedstead in this hot season, and being alarmed with being sent to *Bethlehem*, happily projected to cut the bedstead thro' with a knife with which he eat his victuals. He made some progress in it this day. In the afternoon Mr *Willock* the Bookseller came in *Wightman*'s name, desiring to know the state of Mr *Conon*'s account with the Prisoner, for *Wightman* was ready to settle it with him. The Prisoner answered that he had nothing to do with *Wightman*, and would settle no accounts in concert with him, who had no power to meddle in his Affairs, and that therefore he hoped that Mr *Conon* would wait a little longer.

THE LORD'S DAY, MAY 28. The Prisoner being still chained night and day, made his own bed himself very early to conceal his design, but used not his knife this day upon the bedstead. *Thomas Lindon* Apothecary, with a Friend, came to see him, who declared that he found him in the full exercise of his reason and judgment.

MONDAY, MAY 29. The Prisoner being still chained night and day, took Physick by *Monro's* order in the morning; and in the afternoon he again used his knife upon the bedstead.

TUESDAY, MAY 30. The Prisoner being still chained wrote a Letter to Serjeant *Cruden* to send him a hand-saw, doubting of the strength of the Knife, but providentially did not deliver this Letter to his woman-keeper; for if he had, it had certainly fallen into *Wright's* Wife's hands, and been sent to *Wightman*, as other Letters were by that unfaithful woman's means, and so his Escape had been prevented, and he had been most severely used. Therefore he went to work again, prayed hard and wrought hard, till his Shirt was almost as wet as if dipt in water; and as if he had received more than common Vigour and Strength, he finished the great Operation about four o'clock in the afternoon: Upon which he kneeled down and returned God thanks. Then he sent for *Hollowel* to shave him, and began to prepare for his Escape. He prayed at night that he might awake seasonably for his Escape, and he slept some hours that night as sound as ever he did in his life, chearfully and believingly committing this affair to God *who had never left him nor forsaken him.*

WEDNESDAY, MAY 31. The Prisoner's birth-day, he awoke early, performed his Devotions, held his chain in his hand full fastened to his leg, and deliberately got out at the Window into the Garden, mounted the Garden-wall with much difficulty, lost one of his slippers, and jumped down into the back-way, just before the clock struck two. He went towards *Mile-End*, and his left-foot that wanted a slipper was sorely hurt by the gravel-stones, which greatly afflicted him, and obliged him to put the slipper on his left-foot. From thence he went towards *White-Chapel*, and in his way met with a kind Soldier, who, upon hearing his Case, endeavoured to get him a Coach, but in vain; therefore he and the Soldier walked undiscovered til they came to *Aldgate*, where the Watchman perceiving a chain, and suspecting him to be a person broke out of Gaol, several Watchmen and the Constable Mr *Wardly* followed him to *Leadenhall-Street*, and brought him back to *Aldgate* watch-house. He acquainted the two Constables Mr *Ward* and Mr *Wardly* with his Case, which did much affect them. They allowed him some refreshment, and promised to carry him before my Lord Mayor, but sent a Watchman privately to *Bethnal-Green*, to know the certainly of the Account; upon which *Davis* and two more of their bull-dogs came to the Watch-house with handcuffs to carry back the Prisoner; but the Constable perceiving his meek and sedate Conversation, would not allow it, but desired *Wright* their master to come before my Lord Mayor, at *Grocers Hall*, about 11 o'clock, where he would see his Prisoner.

The Prisoner after five o'clock desired the Constable to carry him in a coach to *North's Coffee-House* near *Guild-Hall*, where he was much refreshed and heartened about five hours. A Printer at *Aberdeen* in *Scotland* came this morning to the Coffee-house, and artfully insinuated to the Constable, that it would be the best way to deliver up the Prisoner to be confined some time longer. This Printer lodged at *Grant's* in *White's-Alley*, and it is supposed that he was sent thither by *Wightman* and *Oswald*, with whom he became suddenly much acquainted; and it's certain that he falsely said to the Prisoner, that he came to the Coffee-house accidently without knowing of his being there. He was received kindly by the Prisoner, he being lately come from *Scotland*; but this false man, as the Constable rightly-judged, proved very treacherous in several respects; and particularly upon his going to *Scotland* he greatly injured the Prisoner by poisoning his relations with false reports; and his falshood is attended with great ingratitude, he being some years ago greatly obliged to the Prisoner, upon his first coming as a Journeyman to *London*, but now *Oswald* is become his Correspondent, and the Printer appears to be a selfish, ungrateful man.

The Prisoner went to *Grocers-hall* about eleven o'clock, with his chains on, for he would not have them taken off till the Lord Mayor should see them. Before he appeared, *Wightman* with some of his friends had been with his Lordship, in order to fill him with Prejudices against the Prisoner: And *Wightman* hearing the Constable speak very favourably of the Prisoner, and of his rational Behaviour, gave him half-a-crown, which the Constable looked upon as a bribe to be silent; and *Wightman* was so base as afterwards to charge it to the Prisoner. The Constable told his Lordship the situation of the Prisoner when he seiz'd him; and the Prisoner gave his Lordship a just and full account of his illegal and barbarous Imprisonment, and demanded that *Wightman* might be immediately sent to *Newgate*, or held to bail. To which his Lordship made no reply.

Alexander Cruden, *The London Citizen Exceedingly Injured* (1739)

=

Sometimes deviousness worked: how to get out of Broadmoor.

Many years ago a wife was visiting a husband for whose release she had made frequent but ineffectual appeals. The attendant, called away for a few minutes by some urgent duty, left the couple temporarily alone. Two months had elapsed when the wife returned and asked for an interview with the Medical Superintendent. At this interview she produced a medical certificate declaring her to be *enceinte*, and stated that her husband was responsible for her condition. After an exhaustive enquiry during which both the husband and the attendant were cross-examined the truth of the woman's story was established. Whether from fear of scandal or from admiration of this example of feminine initiative, the authorities shortly afterwards restored the husband to the bosom of his family.

'Warmark', *'Guilty but Insane': A Broadmoor Autobiography* (1931)

=

About to be released, Jim Curran received some coaching on role models.

He spoke of General Grant, who was never a good student at West Point, who had been a drinker, and who was running a second-rate store when the Civil War began. But when called to duty how brilliant his career! Many men, said Dr Curtis, did not come to the fore till after they were sixty.

And then he referred to Lincoln, as Dr Carlsen had done some months before. And he reminded me that for many years Lincoln's life had been unsuccessful, that he had had thirteen or fourteen distinct failures before he arose to fame in his famous debates with Douglas.

Lincoln was a depressive, he said, slovenly in dress, and suffering from inertia. 'He would sit for hours doing nothing, just brooding,' said the doctor. 'Had he lived today, he might have been treated for mental trouble. Yet see how much he accomplished eventually.'

Dr Curtis said all this in a quiet voice, in an introspective way, and the words seemed to sink in more deeply as a result. I have not forgotten them.

Elsa Kraugh, *A Mind Restored: The Story of Jim Curran* (1937)

=

Others did not recover, until they were free of the asylum.

My wife saw that recovery was getting more hopeless – that I was getting absent and stupid; in plain terms, that I was sinking into idiocy, and she at once determined to try to save me, let the consequences be what they would. In the face of the earnest remonstrance of the physician belonging at that time to the Establishment – who had a bad opinion of my case from the first – who assured her that I was dangerous, and the advice, almost the threatenings of relations, she took me home, not in ignorance nor recklessness, for she knew that there was danger and was prepared calmly to meet it. She told me since that she never expected that I would be of much use in providing for the family; but that she intended me, when I was a little more settled, to take care of the house and children while she wrought at a business which she followed before marriage for our support.

Although very unsettled for some weeks, so much so that any one possessed of less love or less firmness than her would assuredly have sent me back to the Asylum, the change and the society of my family saved me; and although for a considerable time not quite fitted for the duties of the situation, a true friend, a cousin of my own, gave me employment, and instead of finding fault with my shortcomings encouraged me to persevere; and thus although I have always been very willing to act as nurse to her babies, she never yet has been required to work for their support; nor has she ever rued the day on which she took her poor insane husband by the hand and walked off with him from among the doctors who, I have no doubt, thought her own sanity a little doubtful.

'A Late Inmate of the Glasgow Royal Asylum for Lunatics at Gartnavel',
The Philosophy of Insanity (1947)

=

Was psychosis enriching?

On such occasions and many other times as well I have confronted myself with the question: 'Why the hell did you ever get involved with a woman like Mary?'

The answers vary with my mood and retrospective awareness of events at Kingsley Hall. When I was living there, I might have replied to such a query: 'Because I'm a damn masochist.' Nowadays, I would say that it had a lot to do with Mary's embodiment of the thesis that psychosis is a potentially enriching experience if it is allowed to proceed full cycle, through disintegration and reintegration, or death and rebirth, as Ronnie was fond of calling it. Mary had elected herself to the position of head guinea pig, although the nature of the experiment had been determined *by her*. That Mary had her 'trip' all worked out years before she had ever heard of Laing or Berke or the rest of us tends to mitigate the criticism that she was simply acting out our fantasies for us. Anyway, Mary is too strong-willed (pigheaded), to do what anyone else would want her to do for their sake, and not her own.

Mary Barnes and Joseph Berke, *Mary Barnes: Two Accounts of a
Journey Through Madness* (1973)

=

Did psychiatry help?

This is January, 1955. It is the beginning of a new year for me – a new full year of freedom from imprisonment, from treatments that knock me cold, from life among the mad and the supposedly insane.

For it has been five months now that I have been a free man. I think that statistics show that some eighty to ninety per cent of mental patients eventually are locked up again. Their minds vary from 'here today and gone tomorrow' to 'gone today and here tomorrow,' and back again. But this fact does not really bother me. I know – as well as any man in his 'right' mind can know – that I am out for good.

I have visited the State Hospital a number of times since my release. Somehow I think that the place looks different when viewed from the outside. My mind varies from thoughts like, 'Why are so many of my friends still here?' to, 'Why is it that so many of my other friends never improve except to get worse again?' to, 'How could it be that this was my home for a year and a half?' . . . Just what *did* happen, anyway?

I once read a book which tried to show how the great dictators were mentally ill – Hitler, Napoleon ('I am the state!'), etc. In *The Exploration of the Inner World*, Anton Boisen raises the question as to whether or not John Bunyan (author of *Pilgrim's Progress*), *Saint Paul* ('Christ is within me'), and even Jesus were mental cases. Certainly they and almost all of the biblical characters, plus such seers as Joan of Arc, would be classified as mentally ill in very short order if they lived today and ran into a psychiatrist. I would like to see any of them try to get out of any of our present-day State Hospitals! Without outside influence, that is.

Almost two thousand years ago Jesus was nailed to the cross because He dared to speak and act 'contrary to normalcy.' People today deplore the wickedness of this great crime, and rightly so. If Jesus appeared among us today, we would not slay Him! No, we would lock Him up 'for His own good,' and call Him 'a very sick man.' That is, we would do this if He did not have a large following like Father Divine.

I do not mean to sound bitter. I cannot deny the necessity for having mental institutions, and the need for 'sane' men to pass judgment on their fellow men, declaring some insane and locking them up. I cannot even regret my own hospital experience, for unfair and senseless as I think it was, yet it was well intended and enlightening. It broadened my understanding of life and of people so that I cannot say that the price I paid for this was not worth it.

But at the same time I want to cry out for the world to make a greater effort to save my friends. One way is to have free mental clinics for the mentally disturbed, in order to prevent the necessity of eventually committing them. Another way is to provide more doctors in State Hospitals so that they can talk with each patient more often than once in six months.

William L. Moore, *The Mind in Chains: The Autobiography of a Schizophrenic* (1955)

=

On even keel

Thus, thus I steer my bark, and sail
On even keel with gentle gale.
At helm I make my reason sit,
My crew of passions all submit.
If dark and blustring prove some nights,
Philosophy puts forth her lights;
Experience holds the cautious glass,
To shun the breakers, as I pass,
And frequent throws the wary lead,
To see what dangers may be hid;
And once in seven years I'm seen
At Bath or Tunbridge to careen.
Tho' pleas'd to see the dolphins play,
I mind my compass and my way,
With store sufficient for relief,
And wisely still prepar'd to reef,
Nor wanting the dispersive bowl
Of cloudy weather in the soul,
I make (may heav'n propitious send

Such wind and weather to the end)
Neither becalm'd, nor over-blown,
Life's voyage to the world unknown.

>   Matthew Green, *The Spleen* (1737)

Bibliography of Works Cited

Details of the edition used are preceded where relevant by those of the first or other early edition.

Kingsley Amis, *Stanley and the Women* (London: Hutchinson, 1984)

Bartholomaeus Anglicus, *De Proprietatibus Rerum* (London: Berthelet, 1535)

John Thomas Arlidge, *On the State of Lunacy, and the Legal Provision for the Insane* (London: Churchill, 1859)

W. H. Auden, *Collected Poems* (London: Faber and Faber, 1976)

M. Bailey (ed.), *Boswell's Column* (London: William Kimber, 1951)

J. D. Baird and C. Ryskamp (eds), *The Poems of William Cowper, I, 1748–1782* (Oxford: Clarendon Press, 1980)

Thomas Bakewell, *A Letter Addressed to the Chairman of the Select Committee of the House of Commons, Appointed to Enquire into the State of Madhouses* (Stafford: for the author, 1815)

John Balt, *By Reason of Insanity* (London: Panther, 1972)

Mary Barnes and Joseph Berke, *Mary Barnes: Two Accounts of a Journey Through Madness* (Harmondsworth: Penguin, 1973)

C. F. Barrett (ed.), *The Diary and Letters of Madame d'Arblay, Author of Evelina, Cecilia, etc. 1778–1840*, 7 vols (London: H. Colburn, 1842–6)

William Battie, *A Treatise on Madness*, and John Monro, *Remarks on Dr Battie's Treatise on Madness*, with an introduction by Richard A. Hunter and Ida Macalpine (1758; reprint, London: Dawsons, 1962)

Robert Bayfield, *A Treatise De Morborum Capitis* (London: Tomlins, 1663)

George Beard, *Practical Treatise on Nervous Exhaustion* (New York: Wood, 1890)

Clifford Beers, *A Mind that Found Itself: An Autobiography* (New York: Doubleday, Page and Co., 1923)

Bruno Bettelheim, *Recollections and Reflections* (London: Thames and Hudson, 1990)

Sandra Billington, *A Social History of the Fool* (Brighton: Harvester Press, 1984)

Patrick Blair, *Some Observations on the Cure of Mad Persons* (1725)

William Blake, *Complete Writings*, see under G. Keynes (ed.)

Andrew Boorde, *The Breviary of Healthe* (London: Powell, 1547)

Robert Boyle, *Some Considerations Touching the Usefulnesse of Experimental Naturall Philosophy* (Oxford: Davis, 1663)

Richard Brocklesby, *Reflections on Antient and Modern Musick* (London: Cooper, 1749)

Charlotte Brontë, *Jane Eyre* (London: Smith, Elder and Co., 1847)

W. A. F. Browne, *What Asylums Were, Are, And Ought to Be* (Edinburgh: Black, 1837)

George Man Burrows, *Commentaries on the Causes, Forms, Symptoms and Treatment, Moral and Medical, of Insanity* (London: Underwood, 1828)

R. Burton, *The Anatomy of Melancholy* (1621; ed. D. Floyd and P. Jordan-Smith, New York: Tudor Publishing Company, 1948)

L. H. Butterfield (ed.), *The Letters of Benjamin Rush*, 2 vols (Princeton: Princeton University Press, 1951)

Marie Cardinal, *The Words to Say It: An Autobiographical Novel*, trans. Pat Goodheart (London: Picador, 1984)

James Carkesse, *Lucida Intervalla* (1671; ed. Michael V. DePorte, Los Angeles: University of California Press, 1979)

Ugo Cerletti, 'Electroshock Therapy', in A. M. Sackler, M. D. Sackler, R. R. Sackler, and F. Marti-Ibanez (eds), *The Great Physiodynamic Therapies in Psychiatry: An Historical Reappraisal* (New York: Hoeber-Harper, 1956)

Jean-Martin Charcot, *Charcot the Clinician: The Tuesday Lessons – Excerpts from Nine Case Presentations on General Neurology Delivered at the Salpêtrière Hospital in 1887–88*, trans. and ed. Christopher G. Goetz (New York: Raven Press, 1987)

G. Cheyne, *The English Malady; or, A Treatise of Nervous Diseases of all Kinds, with the Author's Own Case* (London: G. Strahan, 1733; reprint, ed. Roy Porter, Routledge, 1990)

Lady Susan Chitty, *Now to My Mother* (London: Weidenfeld and Nicolson, 1985)

Morag Coate, *Beyond All Reason*, with an introduction by R. D. Laing, MB, ChB., DPM (London: Constable, 1964)

John Conolly, *The Treatment of the Insane Without Mechanical Restraint* (London: Smith and Elder, 1856; facsimile, ed. Richard A. Hunter and Ida Macalpine, Folkestone: Dawsons, 1973)

– *An Inquiry Concerning the Indications of Insanity, with Suggestions for the Better Protection and Care of the Insane* (London: Taylor, 1830; facsimile, ed. Richard A. Hunter and Ida Macalpine, London: Dawsons, 1964)

David Cooper, *The Language of Madness* (London: Allen Lane, 1978)

W. Cowper, *Memoir of the Early Life of William Cowper, Esq.* (2nd edn, London: R. Edwards, 1816)

Joseph Mason Cox, *Practical Observations on Insanity: In Which Some Suggestions Are Offered Towards an Improved Mode of Treating Diseases of the Mind ... to Which are Subjoined, Remarks on Medical Jurisprudence as Connected with Diseased Intellect* (London: Baldwin and Murray, 1806)

Sir James Crichton-Browne, *The Doctor's Second Thoughts* (London: Ernest Benn, 1931)

– *The Doctor's After Thoughts* (London: Ernest Benn, 1932)

Alexander Cruden, *The London Citizen Exceedingly Injured* (London: printed for T. Cooper and Mrs Dodd, 1739)

John Custance, *Wisdom, Madness and Folly: The Philosophy of a Lunatic* (London: Victor Gollancz, 1951)

Erasmus Darwin, *Zoonomia; or, The Laws of Organic Life*, 2 vols (London: J. Johnson, 1794 and 1796)

D. Davidson, *Remembrances of a Religio-Maniac: An Autobiography* (Stratford-on-Avon: Shakespeare Press, 1912)

Jennifer Dawson, *The Ha-Ha* (London: Anthony Blond, 1961)

A. Ross Defendorf, *Clinical Psychiatry. A Text-book for Students and Physicians, Abstracted and Adapted from the Sixth German Edition of Kraepelin's Lehrbuch der Psychiatrie* (New York: Macmillan, 1902)

Daniel Defoe, *Augusta Triumphans* (London: Roberts, 1728)

Joyce Delaney, *It's My Nerves, Doctor* (Bath: Chivers Press, 1980)

K. Dewhurst (ed.), *Willis's Oxford Casebook (1650–1652)* (Oxford: Sandford Publications, 1981)

Anne Digby, *Madness, Morality and Medicine: A Study of the York Retreat, 1796–1914* (Cambridge: Cambridge University Press, 1985)

Dorothea Dix, *Memorial of D. L. Dix Praying a Grant of Land for the Relief and Support of the Indigent and Incurable Insane in the United States, June 23, 1848* (US Thirtieth Congress, 1st Session, 'Senate Miscellaneous Document No. 150')

HD [Hilda Doolittle], *Tribute to Freud* (Boston: David R. Godine, 1974)

Michael Drayton, *To Henry Reynolds, of Poets and Poesy* (London: printed for William Lee, at the Turkes Head in Fleet Street, 1627)

Pliny Earle, 'Bloodletting in Mental Disorders', *American Journal of Insanity*, 10 (1854)

Desiderius Erasmus, *The Praise of Folly*, trans. Betty Radice (Harmondsworth: Penguin, 1971)

J.-E.-D. Esquirol, *Mental Maladies: A Treatise on Insanity* (facsimile of English edn, 1845, Library of the New York Academy of Medicine, New York: Hafner Publishing Company, 1965)

Euripides, *The Bacchae, and Other Plays*, trans. Philip Vellacott (Harmondsworth: Penguin, 1973)

Jacques Ferrand, *A Treatise on Lovesickness*, trans. and ed. Donald A. Beecher and Massimo Ciauolella (Syracuse, NY: Syracuse University Press, 1990)

Harold Kenneth Fink, *Long Journey: A Verbatim Report of a Case of Severe Psychosexual Infantilism* (New York: Julian Press, 1954)

Thomas Fitzgerald, 'Bedlam', in *Poems on Several Occasions* (London: Watts, 1733)

Paul Flechsig, 'On the Gynaecological Treatment of Hysteria' (1884), trans. in Jeffrey M. Masson, *A Dark Science: Women, Sexuality and Psychiatry in the Nineteenth Century* (New York: Farrar, Straus and Giroux, 1986)

Janet Frame, *Faces in the Water* (1961; London: The Women's Press, 1980)

Sigmund Freud, *On the Interpretation of Dreams* (1900; Harmondsworth: Penguin, 1976)

– *An Autobiographical Study* (1925; London: Hogarth Press, 1959)

Muriel Gardner (ed.), *The Wolf-man and Sigmund Freud* (London: Hogarth Press, 1972)

Robert Gittings and Jo Manton, *Dorothy Wordsworth* (Oxford: Clarendon Press, 1985)

Nikolai Gogol, *Diary of a Madman* (1834) in *Diary of a Madman and Other Stories*, trans. and ed. Ronald Wilks (Harmondsworth: Penguin, 1972)

Barbara Gordon, *I'm Dancing as Fast as I Can* (London: Bantam, 1981)

Hannah Green [pseud. for Joanne Greenberg], *I Never Promised You a Rose Garden* (London: Pan, 1964)

Matthew Green, *The Spleen* (London: A. Dodd 1737)

J. Y. T. Greig (ed.), *The Letters of David Hume*, 2 vols (Oxford: Clarendon Press, 1969)

A. M. and Renilde Hammacher, *Van Gogh: A Documentary Biography* (London: Thames and Hudson, 1982)

Ebenezer Haskell, *The Trial of Ebenezer Haskell, in Lunacy* (Philadelphia: for the author, 1869)

John Haslam, *Illustrations of Madness* (1810; ed. Roy Porter, London: Routledge, 1988)

– *Considerations on the Moral Management of Insane Persons* (London: R. Hunter, 1817)

Ronald Hayman, *Artaud and After* (Oxford: Oxford University Press, 1977)

Malcolm L. Hayward and J. Edward Taylor, 'A Schizophrenic Patient Describes the Action of Intensive Psychotherapy', *The Psychiatric Quarterly*, 30 (1956)

William Hazlitt, *Liber Amoris: The New Pygmalion* (1823; ed. Michael Neve, London: Hogarth Press, 1985)

Henry Head, 'Observations on the Elements of the Psycho-Neuroses', *British Medical Journal*, 1 (1920)

Johann Christian August Heinroth, *Textbook of Disturbances of Mental Life, or Disturbances of the Soul and their Treatment*, 2 vols, trans. J. Schmorak with an introduction by George Mora (Baltimore: The Johns Hopkins University Press, 1975)

Joseph Heller, *Catch-22* (New York: Simon and Schuster, 1961)

Robert Gardiner Hill, *Total Abolition of Personal Restraint in the Treatment of the Insane* (London: Simpkin, Marshall, 1839)

Jack Hirschman (ed.), *Artaud Anthology* (San Francisco: City Lights Books, 1965)

James Hogg, *The Private Memoirs and Confessions of a Justified Sinner* (Harmondsworth: Penguin, 1983)

Ted Hughes (ed.), *The Journals of Sylvia Plath* (New York: The Dial Press, 1982)

Theo Hyslop, 'Post-Illusionism and Art in the Insane', *The Nineteenth Century*, 69 (1911)

Theo B. Hyslop, *The Great Abnormals* (London: Philip Allan and Co., 1925)

David Irish, *Levamen Infirmi; or, Cordial Counsel to the Sick and Diseased* (London: for the author, 1700)

D. McI. Johnson and Norman Dodds (eds), *The Plea for the Silent* (London: Christopher Johnson, 1957)

Samuel Johnson, *The History of Rasselas, Prince of Abyssinia* (1759; ed. J. P. Hardy, Oxford University Press, 1988)

T. H. Johnson (ed.), *Emily Dickinson* (Cambridge, Mass.: Belknap Press, 1955)

Ernest Jones, *Free Associations: Memories of a Psycho-Analyst* (New York: Basic Books, 1959)

John Jones, *The Mysteries of Opium Reveal'd* (London: R. Smith, 1700)

Edward Jorden, *A Briefe Discourse of a Disease called the Suffocation of the Mother* (London: Windet, 1603)

C. G. Jung, *Memories, Dreams, Reflections* (1963; London: Fontana, 1977)

A. Kardiner, *My Analysis with Freud* (New York: Norton, 1977)

Margery Kempe, *The Book of Margery Kempe* (c. 1420; Harmondsworth: Penguin, 1985)

Ken Kesey, *One Flew Over the Cuckoo's Nest* (London: Calder and Boyers, 1962)

R. W. Ketton-Cremer, *Thomas Gray: A Biography* (Cambridge: Cambridge University Press, 1955)

G. Keynes (ed.), *Blake. Complete Writings* (Oxford: Oxford University Press, 1969)

Marian King, *The Recovery of Myself: A Patient's Experience in a Hospital for Mental Illness* (New Haven: Yale University Press, 1931)

Emil Kraepelin, *Lectures on Clinical Psychiatry* (1894), quoted in Charles E. Goshen, *Documentary History of Psychiatry. A Source Book on Historical Principles* (London: Vision, 1967)

R. von Krafft-Ebing, *Psychopathia Sexualis* (London: Heinemann, 1924)

Elsa Kraugh, *A Mind Restored: The Story of Jim Curran* (New York: Putnam's, 1937)

Seymour Krim, *Views of a Nearsighted Cannoneer* (New York: E. P. Dutton and Co., 1968)

Jimmy Laing and Dermot McQuarrie, *Fifty Years in the System* (Edinburgh: Mainstream Publishing, 1989)

R. D. Laing, *Knots* (Harmondsworth: Penguin, 1969)

– *The Politics of the Family* (Harmondsworth: Penguin, 1971)

'A Late Inmate of the Glasgow Royal Asylum for Lunatics at Gartnavel', *The Philosophy of Insanity* (London: The Fireside Press, 1947)

Doris Lessing, *Briefing for a Descent into Hell* (London: Cape, 1971)

André du Laurens, *A Discourse of the Preservation of the Sight* (London: Jacson, 1599)

D. H. Lawrence, *Fantasia of the Unconscious and Psychoanalysis and the Unconscious* (1922; Harmondsworth: Penguin, 1971)

Joseph Sheridan Lefanu, *The Rose and the Key* (London: Chapman and Hall, 1871)

Susan Dworking Levering, 'She Must be Some Kind of Nut', *The Radical Therapist*, 3 (1972)

John Locke, *An Essay Concerning Human Understanding*, 4th edn (London: Churchill, 1700)

Montagu Lomax, *The Experiences of an Asylum Doctor, with Suggestions for Asylum and Lunacy Law Reform* (London: George Allen and Unwin, 1921)

Cesare Lombroso, *The Man of Genius* (London: Walter Scott, 1891)

J. S. Lustig and F. A. Pottle (eds), *Boswell: The Applause of the Jury, 1782–5* (London: Heinemann, 1982)

Ida Macalpine and Richard A. Hunter, *George III and the Mad Business* (London: Allen Lane, 1969)

H. F. Mackenzie, *The Man of Feeling* (1771; Oxford: Oxford University Press, 1970)

Janet Malcolm, *Psychoanalysis: The Impossible Profession* (London: Picador, 1982)

B. Mandeville, *A Treatise of the Hypochondriack and Hysterick Diseases* (2nd edn, London: Tonson, 1730; reprint, George Olms Verlag, Hildesheim, 1981)

Jeffrey M. Masson (ed.), *The Complete Letters of Sigmund Freud to Wilhelm Fliess, 1887–1904* (Cambridge, Mass.: Harvard University Press, 1986)

Henry Maudsley, *Body and Mind: An Inquiry into their Connection and Mutual Influence, Specially in Reference to Mental Disorders* (London: Macmillan, 1873)

Perry Meisel and Walter Kendrick (eds), *Bloomsbury Freud. The Letters of James and Alix Strachey, 1924–1925* (New York: Basic Books, 1985)

Urbane Metcalf, *The Interior of Bethlehem Hospital* (London: for the author, 1818)

William L. Moore, *The Mind in Chains. The Autobiography of a Schizophrenic* (New York: Exposition Press, 1955)

Thomas More, *The Apologye of Syr T. More, Knyght* (London: Rastell, 1533)

Morningside Mirror, 39 (15 November 1884)

Morningside Mirror, 42 (15 July 1887)

A. D. Morris, *James Parkinson, His Life and Times* (Boston: Birkhauser, 1989)

William Willis Moseley, *Eleven Chapters on Nervous and Mental Conditions* (London: Simpkin, Marshall, 1838)

Friedrich Nietzsche, *The Birth of Tragedy*, in *The Basic Writings of Nietzsche*, trans. and ed. W. Kaufmann (New York: The Modern Library, 1968)

– *Twilight of the Idols*, trans. R. J. Hollingdale (Harmondsworth: Penguin, 1974)

Romola Nijinsky (ed.) *The Diary of Vaslav Nijinsky* (London: Gollancz, 1937)

J. F. Nisbet, *The Insanity of Genius* (London: Ward and Downey, 1891)

Max Nordau, *Degeneration* (London: Appleton, 1895; 4th edn, New York: Howard Fertig, 1968)

Karin Obholzer, *The Wolf-Man Sixty Years After* (London: Routledge & Kegan Paul, 1982)

Barbara O'Brien, *Operators and Things: The Inner Life of a Schizophrenic* (South Brunswick and New York: A. S. Barnes and Co., 1958)

Iona and Peter Opie (eds), *The Oxford Dictionary of Nursery Rhymes* (Oxford: Oxford University Press, 1951)

Daniel Oxenbridge, *General Observations and Prescriptions of the Practice of Physick* (London: Mears, 1715)

Elizabeth Parsons Ware Packard, *The Prisoner's Hidden Life: Or Insane Asylums Unveiled* (Chicago: for the author, 1868)

Roy Palmer (ed.), *Folk Songs Collected by Ralph Vaughan Williams* (London: Dent, 1983)

William Pargeter, *Observations on Maniacal Disorders* (Reading: for the author, 1792)

John Perceval, *A Narrative of the Treatment Received by a Gentleman, During a State of Mental Derangement*, 2 vols (London: Effingham Wilson, 1838/40); reprinted as *Perceval's Narrative: A Patient's Account of His Psychosis* ed. G. Bateson, New York: Morrow Paperback Editions, 1974)

Thomas Percy, *Reliques of Ancient English Poetry* (London: Routledge, 1857)

William Perfect, *Select Cases in the Different Species of Insanity* (Rochester: Gillman, 1787)

Philippe Pinel, *A Treatise on Insanity* (London: Cadell and Davies, 1806)

Sylvia Plath, *The Bell Jar* (1963; London: Faber and Faber, 1986)
- *Journals*, see under Ted Hughes (ed.)

Edgar Allan Poe, 'The System of Dr Tarr and Prof. Fether', in Thomas Ollive Mabbott (ed.), *Collected Works of Edgar Allan Poe*, 3, *Tales and Sketches, 1843–1849* (Cambridge, Mass.: Belknap Press, 1978)

Alexander Pope, *The Dunciad*, in J. Butt (ed.), *The Poems of Alexander Pope* (London: Methuen, 1963)

Ezra Pound, *Collected Shorter Poems* (London: Faber and Faber, 1952)

Morton Prince, *The Dissociation of Personality: The Hunt for the Real Miss Beauchamp* (Oxford: Oxford University Press, 1978)

Bryan Waller Proctor, *Dramatic Scenes and Other Poems* (London: Chapman and Hall, 1857)

Peter Quennell (ed.), *The Private Letters of Princess Lieven to Prince Metternich, 1820–1826* (London: John Murray, 1937)

Charles Reade, *Hard Cash: A Matter-of-fact Romance* (London: Sampson, Low and Marston, 1864)

Jean Rhys, *Wide Sargasso Sea* (London: Deutsch, 1966)

Nicholas Robinson, *A New System of the Spleen* (London: A. Bettesworth 1729)

John M. Robson and Jack Stillinger (eds), *Autobiography and Literary Essays by John Stuart Mill* (Toronto: University of Toronto Press, 1981): *Collected Works of John Stuart Mill*, 1.

G. Ross Roy (ed.), *The Letters of Robert Burns* (2nd edn, Oxford: Clarendon Press, 1985)

Benjamin Rush, *Medical Inquiries and Observations upon the Diseases of the Mind* (1812; reprint, New York: Hafner Reprint, 1962)

– 'On the Different Species of Phobia', *The Weekly Magazine of Original Essays*, 1 (Philadelphia, 1798)

Oliver Sacks, *The Man Who Mistook His Wife for a Hat* (London: Duckworth, 1985)

'A Sane Patient', *My Experiences in a Lunatic Asylum* (London: Chatto and Windus, 1879)

William Sargant, *Battle for the Mind: A Physiology of Conversion and Brain-washing* (London : Heinemann, 1957)

– *The Unquiet Mind: The Autobiography of a Physician in Psychological Medicine* (London: Heinemann, 1967)

Morton Schatzman, *The Story of Ruth: One Woman's Haunting Psychiatric Odyssey* (London: Duckworth, 1980)

Nancy Scheper-Hughes and Anne M. Lovell (eds), *Psychiatry Inside Out: Selected Writings of Franco Basaglia* (New York: Columbia University Press, 1987)

Daniel Paul Schreber, *Memoirs of My Nervous Illness*, ed. Ida Macalpine and Richard Hunter (London: Dawsons, 1955)

Reginald Scot, *The Discoverie of Witchcraft* (London: Brome, 1584)

William Seabrook, *Asylum* (New York: Harcourt, Brace and Co., 1935)

Marguerite Sechehaye, *Reality Lost and Regained: Autobiography of a Schizophrenic Girl, with Analytic Interpretation* (New York: Grune and Stratton, 1951)

Anne Sexton, *To Bedlam and Part Way Back* (Boston: Houghton Mifflin Co., 1960)

– *The Awful Roaring Toward God* (London: Chatto and Windus, 1977)

Lord Shaftesbury, *Diaries* (unpublished), National Register of Archives

Percy Bysshe Shelley, *Julian and Maddalo* (1818)

Richard Sibbes, *The Soules Conflict with It Selfe* (London: Dawlman, 1635)

Robert Southey, *Letters from England*, ed. J. Simmons (Gloucester: Alan Sutton, 1984)

H. Sprenger and J. Institoris, *Malleus Maleficiarum. 1486*, trans. and ed. Rev. M. Summers (London: J. Rodker, 1928; New York: Dover, 1971)

James Strachey et al. (eds), *The Standard Edition of the Complete Works of Sigmund Freud*, 5, *The Interpretation of Dreams* (London: Hogarth Press, 1958)

– *The Standard Edition of the Complete Works of Sigmund Freud*, 20, *An Autobiographical Study* (London: Hogarth Press, 1959)

William Styron, 'Darkness Visible', *Vanity Fair*, 52 (December 1989)

Jonathan Swift, *A Tale of a Tub and Other Satires* (1704; ed. K. Williams, London: Everyman, 1975)

Valeriy Tarsis, *Ward 7: An Autobiographical Novel,* trans. Katya Brown (New York: E. P. Dutton, 1965)

H. Temple Phillips, 'The History of the Old Private Lunatic Asylum at Fishponds, Bristol, 1740–1859' (M.Sc. diss., University of Bristol, 1973)

[E. Thelmar], *The Maniac: A Realistic Study of Madness from the Maniac's Point of View* (London: Rebman, 1909)

John Timbs, *Doctors and Patients* (London: Bentley, 1876)

George Trosse, *The Life of the Reverend Mr George Trosse*, ed.
A. W. Brink (Montreal and London: McGill-Queen's University
Press, 1974)

Thomas Trotter, *An Essay on Drunkenness* (1804; ed. Roy Porter,
London: Routledge Reprint, 1989)

Thomas Tryon, *A Discourse of the Causes, Natures and Cure of
Phrensie, Madness or Distraction* (1689; ed. M. DePorte, Los
Angeles: Augustan Reprint Society, 1973)

Samuel Tuke, *Description of the Retreat, an Institution near York
for Insane Persons of the Society of Friends* (facsimile of the
1813 edn, ed. Richard A. Hunter and Ida Macalpine, London:
Dawsons, 1964)

Daniel Turner, *Syphilis: A Practical Dissertation on the Venereal
Disease* (London: Bonwicke, 1724)

James Twiggs, *Transferences* (Fayetteville: University of Arkansas
Press, 1987)

John Vincent, *Inside the Asylum* (London: Allen and Unwin,
1948)

Voltaire, *Philosophical Dictionary* (1764; trans. Theodore Bester-
man, Harmondsworth: Penguin, 1971)

Mary Frances Wack, *Lovesickness in the Middle Ages: The
Viaticum and its Commentaries* (Philadelphia: University of
Pennsylvania Press, 1990)

Mary Jane Ward, *The Snake Pit* (New York: Signet, 1947)

Ned Ward, *The London Spy*, ed. Kenneth Fenwick (London: The
Folio Society, 1955)

John Wardroper, *Jest Upon Jest* (London: Routledge & Kegan
Paul, 1970)

'Warmark', *'Guilty but Insane': A Broadmoor Autobiography*
(London: Chapman and Hall, 1931)

B. and H. Wedgwood, *The Wedgwood Circle* (London: Studio
Vista, 1980)

John Wesley, *Primitive Physick: Or, an Easy and Natural Method
of Curing Most Diseases* (London: T. Trye, 1747)

Antonia White, *Beyond the Glass* (London: Eyre and Spot-
tiswoode, 1954)

Gilbert White, *The Natural History and Antiquities of Selborne*,
(1789; ed. Richard Mabey, London: Century, 1988)

Richard Whitmore, *Mad Lucas: The Strange Story of England's Most Famous Hermit* (Hitchin: North Hertfordshire District Council, 1983)

Thomas Willis, *Two Discourses Concerning the Soul of Brutes* (London: Dring, 1683)

H. G. Woodley, *Certified* (London: Gollancz, 1947)

Virginia Woolf, *Mrs Dalloway* (1925; London: Hogarth Press, 1976)

William Wordsworth, *The Prelude* (1805)

— *Resolution and Independence* (1807)

George Young, *A Treatise on Opium, Founded upon Practical Observation* (London: Millar, 1753)

Acknowledgments

The author and publishers wish to thank the following who have kindly given permission to reprint extracts and copyright material in this book.

Aitken & Stone Ltd. on behalf of Antonia White for an extract from *Beyond the Glass* (1952). Published by Eyre & Spottiswood.

The Borthwick Institute of Historical Research, University of York, for an extract from the Retreat archives reproduced in *Madness, Morality and Medicine: A Study of the York Retreat, 1796–1914* by Dr Anne Digby, published by Cambridge University Press.

Marion Boyars Publishers Ltd for an extract from *One Flew Over the Cuckoo's Nest* by Ken Kesey.

British Medical Journal for an extract from the article 'Observations on the Elements of the Psycho-Neuroses' by Henry Head, published in the *Journal*, 1 (1920).

Chapman and Hall Ltd for extracts from *Guilty but Insane: A Broadmoor Autobiography* by 'Warmark'.

City Lights Books for an extract from *Artaud Anthology*, edited by Jack Hirschman.

Constable and Company Ltd for extracts from *Beyond All Reason* by Morag Coate.

Andre Deutsch Ltd for an extract from *Wide Sargasso Sea* by Jean Rhys.

Doubleday, a Division of Bantam Doubleday Dell Publishing Group Inc., for extracts from *A Mind that Found Itself* by Clifford Beers: copyright © 1907 to 1953 by American Foundation for Mental Hygiene Inc.

Duckworth and Company Ltd for extracts from *The Man Who Mistook His Wife for a Hat* by Oliver Sacks.

Exposition–Phoenix Press for extracts from *The Mind in Chains: The Autobiography of a Schizophrenic* by William L. Moore.

Faber and Faber Ltd and HarperCollins Publishers Inc. for extracts from *The Bell Jar* by Sylvia Plath; with Dial Press for an extract from *The Journals of Sylvia Plath*, edited by Ted Hughes; with Random House Inc. for the poem 'In Memory of Sigmund Freud' from *W. H. Auden: Collected Poems*, edited by E. Mendelson: copyright © 1940 renewed 1968 by W. H. Auden; and with New Directions Publishing Corporation for the poem 'Salutation the Third' by Ezra Pound.

The Folio Society for an extract from *Ned Ward: The London Spy*, edited by Kenneth Fenwick.

Eric Glass Ltd on behalf of the Nijinsky Estate for an extract from *The Diary of Vaslav Nijinksy*, edited by Romola Nijinsky.

David R. Godine, Publisher, Inc. for an extract from *Tribute to Freud* by H.D: copyright © 1974 by H.D.

Grune and Stratton Inc. for extracts from *Reality Lost and Regained: Autobiography of a Schizophrenic Girl* by Marguerite Sechehaye.

Harcourt Brace Jovanovich Inc. for extracts from *Asylum* by William Seabrook: copyright © 1935 by the Publishers and renewed 1963 by Constance Seabrook.

HarperCollins Publishers Ltd and Pantheon Books, and Division of Random House Inc. for an extract from *Memories, Dreams, Reflections* by C. G. Jung, recorded and edited by Aniela Jaffe, translated by Richard & Clara Winston. Translation © 1961–63 by Random House Inc.; and with E. P. Dutton, an imprint of New American Library, a division of Penguin Books USA Inc., for extracts from *Ward 7: An Autobiographical Novel* by Valeriy Tarsis.

Harvard University Press for extracts from *The Complete Letters of Sigmund Freud to Wilhelm Fliess, 1887–1904*, edited by Jeffrey M. Masson: copyright © 1985 by the Publishers and under the Bern Convention, Sigmund Freud Copyrights Ltd, translation and editorial matter copyright © 1985 by J. M. Masson.

Houghton Mifflin Company for the poems 'Noon Walk on the

Asylum Lawn' and 'Said the Poet to the Analyst', from *To Bedlam and Part Way Back* by Anne Sexton, and with Sterling Lord Literistic Inc. for the poem 'The Sickness Unto Death', from *The Awful Roaring Toward God* by Anne Sexton.

The Johns Hopkins University Press for an extract from *Textbook of Disturbances of Mental Life, or Disturbances of the Soul and their Treatment* by Johann Christian Heinroth.

Lucy Kroll Agency on behalf of A. Kardiner for extracts from *My Analysis With Freud*.

Mainstream Publishing Company for extracts from *Fifty Years in the System* by Jimmy Laing and Dermot McQuarrie.

John Murray (Publishers) Ltd for an extract from *The Private Letters of Princess Lieven to Prince Metternich, 1820–1826*, edited by Peter Quennell.

Oxford University Press for extracts from *Dorothy Wordsworth* by Robert Gittings and Jo Manton, and from *The Oxford Dictionary of Nursery Rhymes*, edited by Iona and Peter Opie.

Pan–Macmillan Books Ltd for extracts from *The Words to Say It: An Autobiographical Novel* by Marie Cardinal; from *Psychoanalysis: The Impossible Profession* by Janet Malcolm, and from *I Never Promised you a Rose Garden* by Hannah Green.

Penguin Books Ltd for extracts from *The Book of Margery Kempe* translated by B. A. Windeatt (Penguin Classics 1985): copyright © 1985 by B. A. Windeatt; from *The Praise of Folly* by Erasmus, translated by Betty Radice (Penguin Classics 1971): translation copyright © 1971 by Betty Radice, and from *Twilight of the Idols* by Nietzsche, translated by R. J. Hollingdale (Penguin Classics 1968): translation copyright © 1968 by R. J. Hollingdale.

The Putnam Publishing Group for extracts from *A Mind Restored: The Story of Jim Curran* by Elsa Kraugh.

Random Century Group and Random House Inc., for an extract from *Darkness Visible* by William Styron, published by Jonathan Cape Ltd: copyright © by William Styron 1990. With Basic Books Inc. (a division of HarperCollins Publishers) for extracts from *The Wolfman and Sigmund Freud* by Muriel Gardner, published by Chatto and Windus Ltd; an extract from 'On the Interpretation of Dreams', from *The Standard Edition of the*

Complete Psychological Works of Sigmund Freud, translated and edited by James Strachey, reproduced by permission of Sigmund Freud Copyrights Ltd, The Institute of Psycho-Analysis and The Hogarth Press; an extract from *Free Associations: Memories of a Psychoanalyst* by Ernest Jones: copyright © 1959 by Kathryn Jones; for an extract from *Bloomsbury/Freud: The Letters of James and Alix Strachey, 1924–1925*, edited by Perry Meisel and Walter Kendrick: text of Letters copyright © 1985 The Strachey Trust, Introduction, Epilogue, selections and critical apparatus copyright © 1985 Perry Meisel and Walter Kendrick. With Harcourt Brace Jovanovich Inc. for an extract from *Mrs Dalloway* by Virginia Woolf. With W. W. Norton Inc. for an extract from 'An Autobiographical Study', from *The Standard Edition of the Complete Psychological Works of Sigmund Freud* translated and edited by James Strachey, reproduced by permission of Sigmund Freud Copyrights Ltd., The Institute of Psycho-Analysis and The Hogarth Press. For an extract from *Stanley and the Women* by Kingsley Amis, published by Hutchinson Publishing; and an extract from *Briefing for a Descent into Hell* by Doris Lessing, published by Jonathan Cape Ltd.; for an extract from *The Snake Pit* by Mary Jane Ward.

Raven Press for extracts from *Jean-Martin Charcot the Clinician: The Tuesday Lessons – Excerpts from Nine Case Representations on General Neurology Delivered at the Salpetriere Hospital in 1887–88*, translated with commentary by Christopher G. Goetz.

Rogers, Coleridge and White Ltd. on behalf of the Estate of David Cooper for extracts from *The Language of Madness*, and on behalf of Joseph Berke for extracts from *Mary Barnes: Two Accounts of a Journey Through Madness*.

Routledge and Continuum Publishing Company for extracts from *The Wolfman: Sixty Years After* by Karin Obholzer.

Sandford Publications for an extract from *Willis's Oxford Casebook 1650–52*, edited by K. Dewhurst.

Mrs Margaret Sargant for extracts from *Battle for the Mind* and *The Unquiet Mind: The Autobiography of a Physician in Psychological Medicine* by Dr William Sargant.

Simon and Schuster Inc. for an extract from *Catch-22* by Joseph Heller.

Alan Sutton Publishing for an extract from *Letters from England* by Robert Southey, edited by J. Simmons.

Syracuse University Press for an extract from *A Treatise on Lovesickness* by Jacques Ferrand, translated and edited by Donald A. Beecher and Massimo Ciavolella.

Tavistock Publications Ltd for an extract from *The Politics of the Family* by R. D. Laing; and for 'there is something the matter with him' from *Knots* by R. D. Laing.

Thames and Hudson Ltd. for extracts from *Recollections and Reflections* by Bruno Bettelheim.

University of Arkansas Press for an extract from *Transferences* (1987) by James Twiggs.

Unwin Hyman, part of HarperCollins Publishers, for extracts from *Inside the Asylum* by John Vincent.

John Wardroper for an extract from *Jest Upon Jest*.

Weidenfeld Publishers Ltd. and the Curtis Brown Group on behalf of Susan Chitty, for an extract from *Now to My Mother*.

Richard Whitmore for an extract from *Mad Lucas* published by North Hertfordshire District Council.

The Women's Press Ltd for extracts from *Faces in the Water* by Janet Frame.

Every effort has been made to trace all the copyright holders, but if any have been inadvertently overlooked the publishers will be pleased to make the necessary arrangement at the first opportunity.

Index

Oct 9   9:45
Oct 10   9:45
Oct 12   9:45

Oct 2,3,4
   9:45

Back off

Oct 31, 2007

Oct 17 11:00
Oct 18 11:00
Oct 20 9:45